The tangled rainforests of Belize, Guatemala and Southern Mexico are the setting for the other-worldly ruined cityscapes of the ancient Maya: hidden palaces snarled with roots and jungle vines, skyward temples inscribed with cryptic hieroglyphs, dark statuary sentinel among the trees, and sculpted friezes depicting the jade-encrusted pageantry of royal coronations, ritual warfare and human sacrifice.

Poised at the tectonic juncture between North America and the Caribbean, the cultures which emerged from the tropical hothouse of Mesoamerica revered the land in all its diversity. The pyramids of Mayan evolution were not only symbols of royal authority, but of the mountains themselves, where dwelled the gods of creation as they conversed endlessly on the subject of Time. This was the land of the mythical plumed serpent, a deity symbolic of the regenerative forces of nature, mystic vision, the union of earth and sky, and civilization itself.

Centuries later, the modern-day nation states that replaced the Mayan polities continue to thrive as vibrant cultural hubs. Replete with high-blown grandeur, Spanish-built colonial cities play host to world-class art and music scenes. Fringed by white-sand beaches and incandescent coral reefs, African-descendant fishing villages languish along the shores of the Caribbean coast. Echoing ancient lore and traditions, indigenous communities subsist in secluded mountain enclaves, barely touched by modernity or colonialism. To travel in Belize, Guatemala and Southern Mexico is to encounter a land of staggering ethnic and ecological diversity, as vivid, mystical and worthy of reverence as it was to the ancients.

Richard Arghiris

Best of
Belize, Guatemala & Southern Mexico

top things to do and see

❶ Oaxaca City

A dazzling kaleidoscope of colours, flavours, rhythms and textures, the breezy capital of Oaxaca state – a UNESCO World Heritage Site thanks to its fine colonial architecture – is a creative and artistic powerhouse, home to abundant workshops, galleries, topnotch restaurants, markets and *mezcalerías*. Page 61.

❷ Oaxaca's Pacific coast

Punctuated with languid lagoons and golden-sand beaches, Oaxaca's rugged Pacific coast has something for everyone: epic waves at the world-class surf spot of Puerto Escondido; authentic hippy communes at the brazen party haunt of Zipolite; low-key beach culture at San Agustinillo and Mazunte; and resort-style convenience at Bahías de Huatulco. Page 91.

❸ San Cristóbal de las Casas

The twin themes of indigenous mysticism and revolutionary struggle rarely fail to inspire. A favourite with anthropologists, activists and bohemian travellers, the colonial stronghold of San Cristóbal de las Casas is an administrative hub for the Chiapas highlands, fabled homeland of the Tzotzil Maya and the Zapatista Liberation Army. Page 124.

❹ Palenque

If you only visit one Mayan ruin in Mexico, make it Palenque. The rainforest setting of this urban masterpiece, constructed at the height of Mayan civilization, only adds to its mystique: beyond the vast temples of its ceremonial centre lies a rambling sprawl of ancient edifices half-consumed by the jungle. Page 152.

❺ Tulum

The Mayans knew what they were doing when they built the cliff-top city of Tulum, perfectly poised to greet the sunrise. Boasting miles of white-sand beaches and eternally calm, warm, translucent waters, this is Mexico's most alluring Caribbean coast destination, the perfect place to sling a hammock. Page 198.

❻ Mérida

Mérida, the so-called 'White City', is the heart and soul of the Yucatán, a lively university city with busy colonial plazas and Parisian-style boulevards, the cultural and intellectual capital of the state. Don't miss the weekly extravaganza of traditional Yucatec dances, music and street food. Page 213.

❼ Belize's northern cayes

Celebrated for their indolent beaches and off-shore coral reefs, Belize's northern cayes are a portrait of ramshackle Caribbean easiness with their wealth of colourful characters and vibrant clapboard houses. Swim, sunbathe, snorkel or simply sip rum and watch the sunset. Page 270.

❽ Blue Hole

Recommended by Jacques Cousteau as one of the world's top 10 dive sites, the Blue Hole is a giant, cavernous, perfectly circular underwater sinkhole, 1000 ft across and 400 ft deep; a true abyss habouring everything from delicate reef species to giant pelagics. Page 283.

❾ Placencia

Scarlet macaws, manatees and schools of migrating whale sharks are among the tropical fauna you might spot around the ecotourism hub of Placencia, formerly a Creole fishing village perched at the tip of a remote coastal peninsula. Off-shore cayes, rainforests and coral reefs lie within striking distance. Page 314.

❿ Antigua

Backed by a simmering panorama of jagged volcanic peaks, the outstandingly baroque, partially ruined and unrepentantly hedonistic city of Antigua was the de facto capital of Central America for two centuries, resulting in an unrivalled architectural legacy that has earned it UNESCO World Heritage Site status. Page 347.

⓫ Lago Atitlán

Described by Alexander Von Humboldt as "the most beautiful lake in the world" and by Aldous Huxley as "too much of a good thing", Lake Atitlán is an entrancingly serene body of water fringed by Mayan villages and hazy blue volcanoes. Laze in a hammock or explore the local communities; it's up to you. Page 365.

⓬ Semuc Champey

The numinous spectacle of Semuc Champey consists of multiple turquoise pools fed by a series of low waterfalls. Set in the remote karst landscape of Guatemala's Alta Verapaz, you'll have to travel off the beaten track to reach this natural wonder, one of the most enchanting in all Central America. Page 452.

⓭ Tikal

The ruined city of Tikal earned its place in sci-fi history as the location for a rebel moon in George Lucas's *Star Wars*. Once one of the most powerful polities in the Mayan world, it has astoundingly tall pyramids that reach high above the rainforest canopy: the 'New York of Mesoamerica'. Page 466.

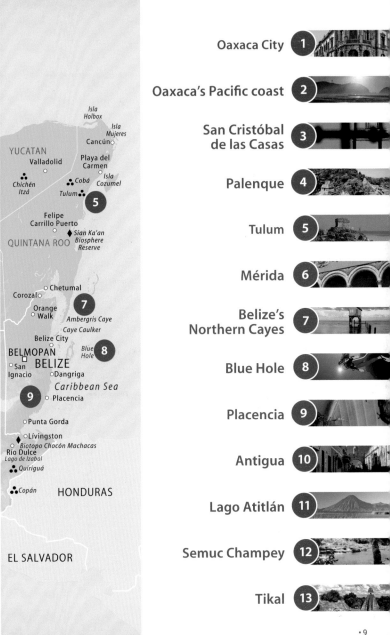

Isla
Holbox
Isla
Mujeres
Cancún

YUCATAN
Valladolid
Playa del
Carmen
Chichén
Itzá
Isla
Cozumel
Cobá
Tulum
5

Felipe
Carrillo Puerto
QUINTANA ROO
Sian Ka'an
Biosphere
Reserve

Chetumal
Corozal
Orange
Walk
7
Ambergris Caye
Caye Caulker
Belize City
Blue
Hole
BELMOPAN
8
San
Ignacio
BELIZE
Dangriga
Caribbean Sea
9
Placencia

Punta Gorda
Lívingston
Biotopo Chocón Machacas
Río Dulce
Lago de Izabal
Quiriguá

Copán
HONDURAS

EL SALVADOR

Route planner

Belize, Guatemala and Southern Mexico are so culturally and geographically diverse, that with enough imagination, the potential for adventure is limitless – your only likely restraint is time. The classic backpacker itinerary begins in Mexico City, heads south into Oaxaca, Chiapas and the Yucatán Peninsula, crosses into Belize and ends in Guatemala, where you can circle west back into Mexico. The distances involved in this trip are reasonably long and we do not recommend it with anything less than a month to spare (two months is better). However, the following itineraries are suitable for trips of two to three weeks.

The Yucatán, the Petén and Belize

Star gods and pyramids

Ever since the intrepid 19th-century explorer, John Lloyd Stephens, stumbled upon the long lost cities of the ancient Maya, travellers have been drawn to Mesoamerica's haunting, jungle-shrouded ruins. This intensive archaeological itinerary follows a circular route from Cancún through the Yucatán, the Petén and Belize. Starting from the gateway of Cancún, head inland to the colonial town of Valladolid, where you can marvel at the ruins of Ek-Balam and wash away your jet lag in the local *cenotes*. Chichén Itzá, 30 minutes' drive west, is the largest and most-visited site in the Yucatán. Next stop is Mérida, with the Gran Museo del Mundo Maya and the nearby Puuc ruins. In Chiapas, eight to ten hours south, the rainforest city of Palenque is the epitome of Mesoamerican beauty. From there, travel east to the remote Lacandón rainforest and visit the riverside city of Yaxchilán and Bonampak with its bloodthirsty murals.

Cross the Usumacinta river to Guatemala where the metropolis of Tikal beckons with its massive temples. The final leg of your Mayan pilgrimage takes you into Belize and onto Mexico, with options for Xunantunich near the Guatemalan border, and Altun Ha and Lamanai north of Belize City. Before returning to Cancún, pause at Tulum, perfectly placed above the Caribbean Sea.

Right: Ek-Balam
Opposite page: Sumidero Canyon, Chiapas

• 11

Travelling between the capitals of Mexico and Guatemala, this rewarding cultural itinerary takes you on a vivid journey to indigenous communities. Starting in Mexico City, take a day or two to acclimatize. The outstanding Museo Nacional de Antropología and the Museo de Arte Popular are recommended as primers. From the capital, the colonial stronghold of Oaxaca City is six hours south, an ideal base for exploring the Valles Centrales and their Zapotec and Mixtec villages. Kick back for a few days on the Oaxaca coast then head east and base yourself in San Cristóbal de las Casas for trips to Tzotzil Mayan communities, such as San Juan Chamula, where traditional healers practice their arts.

From here, the bus journey into western Guatemala, homeland of the Mam Maya, requires six to eight hours. Huehuetenango is the transport hub for exploring remote highland villages such as the fascinating Todos Santos Cuchumatán. Further south again, Lake Atitlán and its environs are also filled with interesting Mayan communities: in Santiago, you can visit a hard-drinking, cigar-smoking god called Maximón. In Chichicastenango, you can shop for textiles at the famous twice-weekly market. Santa Cruz del Quiché and the deeply indigenous Ixil Triangle are other options here. Conclude your cultural odyssey in the colonial masterpiece of Antigua, or in Guatemala City, one hour away.

A vibrant patchwork of Mayan, Creole and Garífuna cultures, the Caribbean coast has a special allure beyond the obvious appeal of sweltering tropical beaches. This itinerary skirts the coast from Cancún to Belize to Puerto Barrios in Guatemala, before concluding at Guatemala City.

We recommend you exit Cancún as fast as possible and forgo the big tourist hubs for the more intimate island destinations of Isla Mujeres or Isla Holbox. Heading south on the mainland, the village of Tulum is a definite highlight. From here, you can explore the eerie underwater world of the Yucatán's *cenotes* (sinkholes) or organize kayak trips to observe wildlife in Sian Ka'an Biosphere Reserve.

Above: Lívingston community
Below: Isla Mujeres
Opposite page top: San Juan Chamula
Opposite page bottom: Sololá women

Continuing south to Chetumal, six hours away on the Belizean border, you can take a bus to shambolic Belize City – recommended for lovers of sketchy Caribbean port towns – or skip it by taking a high-speed *panga* directly to the northern cayes. Ambergris Caye has the best beaches and expeditions to the Blue Hole, but Caye Caulker is more relaxed, authentic and better value. Continuing south on the mainland is the Garífuna town of Dangriga and the southern cayes. However, an essential stop is Placencia, where you can organize fishing, diving, hiking and snorkelling trips.

The southernmost town in Belize is the ethnically diverse Punta Gorda. From here, take a water taxi to Lívingston in Guatemala, an idyllic Garífuna town flanked by dense rainforest. Before

heading overland to Guatemala City, conclude your Caribbean adventure by exploring the Biotopo Chocón Machacas and the Mayan ruin of Quiriguá, where the famous calendar depicting the Mayan long count was discovered.

Best
festivals & traditions

Day of the Dead

Commemorated on 1 and 2 November, the Día de los Muertos is an occasion when families and friends get together to remember friends and relatives who have died. A national holiday in Mexico and throughout Central America, you can respectfully join in at any cemetery; for example, the Panteón General (main cemetery) in Oaxaca City. Traditions and activities vary greatly between towns and countries; Oaxaca state has a particularly strong reputation. See page 76.

Guelaguetza

Also known as Lunes del Cerro, this impressive annual celebration in Oaxaca city on the last two Mondays in July is where all the colour and variety of the state's many different cultural groups come together in one place. For those with an interest in native costumes, music and dance, it should not be missed. The main event is a grand folk dance show held at the Guelaguetza stadium on the slopes of Cerro del Fortín. See box, page 77.

Garífuna Settlement Day
One of the most popular festivals in Belize celebrates the settlement of the Garífuna people in the country, on 19 November. There's a re-enactment of the 1832 landing of the Black Caribs, who had fled from a failed rebellion in Honduras. Centred on Dangriga in southern Belize, there's dancing all night to the Garífuna beat: *punta*. See box, page 313.

Semana Santa
The week-long Easter event in Antigua, Guatemala, is a spectacular display of religious ritual and floral design. Through billowing clouds of incense, processions of floats carried by men robed in purple make their way through town, accompanied by music. The largest processions with some of the finest floral carpets are on Palm Sunday and Good Friday. The whole occasion is one of the biggest Easter events in Latin America, so plan your trip well in advance. See box, page 357.

Todos Santos Cuchumatán
The horse festival of Todos Santos Cuchumatán, Guatemala, is one of the most celebrated and spectacular in Central America. On All Saints' Day on 2 November riders race between two points, having a drink at each turn until they fall off. It's a frenzied day that usually degenerates into a drunken mass. The origin dates back to the arrival of the *conquistadores* who came on horseback, draped in flowing scarves. Page 404.

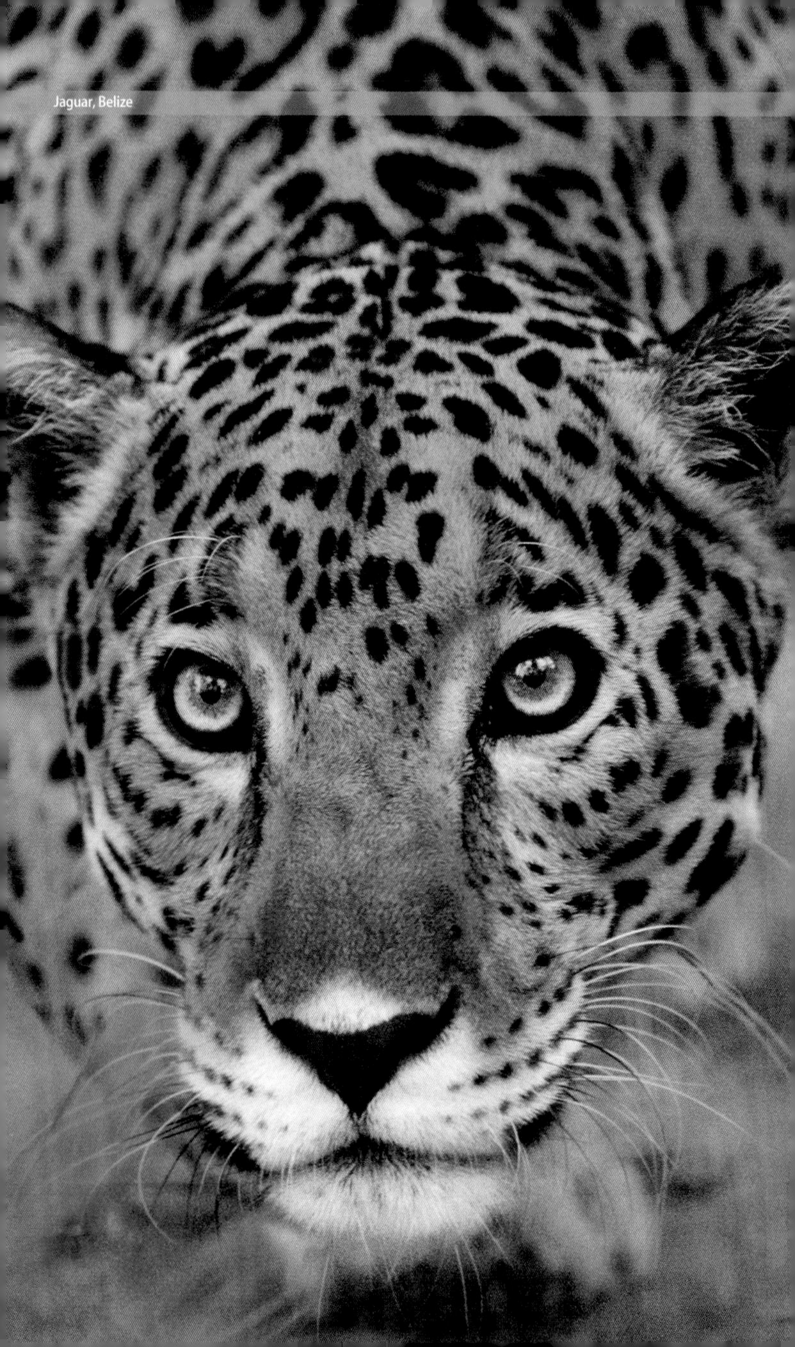
Jaguar, Belize

When
to go

Climate

The best time to go is between November and April, when there is virtually no rain, although there are slight regional variations and a handful of microclimates that do not obey the rule. The rainy season works its way up from southern Central America in May and runs through until October. At the start of the season, rain falls for a just couple of hours a day, usually in the afternoon, but towards the end, it is more torrential and disruptive. However, don't be put off by the term 'rainy season'; most years, the rains only affect travellers for an hour or two a day. This period is also hurricane season in the Caribbean. Despite the high-profile storm of Hurricane Wilma and a few lesser known local hurricanes and tropical storms, landfall is relatively rare. If a hurricane does arrive while you're in the area you can get details at www.nhc.noaa.gov.

Southern Mexico

There is a wide variety of climates in southern Mexico. Broadly speaking, the highlands tend to be warm and bright during the day, cool or chilly after dark. The lowlands tend to be blazing hot and, depending on the season, sweaty and humid. Dry season runs from November to April, when it becomes bone dry in Oaxaca and parts of the Yucatán, but less so in the evergreen rainforests of lowland Chiapas. Wet season is a few degrees warmer than dry season. It runs May-October with the downpours increasing in frequency and intensity as the season progresses. The best months for travel are the interim periods of March and April, and November, when there is a bloom of greenery but the weather is not excessively hot, dry or rainy.

Belize

The high season runs from mid-December to March and pushes into May with clear skies and warm temperatures (25-30°C). Inland, in the west, day temperatures can reach 38°C, but the nights are cooler and usually pleasant.

Between November and January there are cold spells. Humidity is normally high, making it 'sticky' most of the time in the lowlands.

There are sharp annual variations in rainfall. From 1270 mm in the north, there is a huge increase up to 4310 mm down in the south. The driest months are April and May; in June and July there are heavy showers followed by blue skies. Around August the *mauger* occurs in some areas, a mini dry season of about six weeks. September to November tend to be overcast and there are more insects during these months.

Hurricanes threaten the country from June to November along the coast. An efficient warning system was put in place after Hurricane Mitch and most towns and large villages have hurricane shelters. 'Hurricane Preparedness' instructions are issued annually. Do not ignore local instructions about what to do following a forecast.

Guatemala

Climate is dependent upon altitude and varies greatly. Most of the population lives at between 900 m and 2500 m, where the climate features warm days and cool nights, so you'll need warm clothes at night. The majority of visitors spend most of their time in the highlands, where the dry season lasts from November to April. The central region around Cobán has an occasional drizzle-like rain called *chipi chipi* in February and March. Some places enjoy a respite from the rains (the *canícula*) in July and August. On the Pacific and Caribbean coasts you can expect rain all year round, heaviest on the Pacific in June and September with a dry spell in between, but with no dry season on the Caribbean. In the lowlands of El Petén, the wet season is roughly May to October, when the mosquitoes are most active. December to February are cooler months, while March and April are hot and dry. In terms of festivals, the key events are Semana Santa at Easter in Antigua, see box, page 357, and All Saints' Day in Todos Santos, see box, page 404.

If the time and mood is right, there is little to beat a Latin American festival. Fine costumes, loud music, the sounds of firecrackers tipped off with the gentle wafting of specially prepared foods all (normally) with a drink or two. Whether you're seeking the carnival or happen to stumble across a celebration, the events – big or small – are memorable. If you want to hit the carnivals there are a few broad dates generally significant throughout the region. Carnival is normally the week before the start of Lent. It's more important in Mexico but you'll probably find regional celebrations in most places. Semana Santa (Easter Week) is an understandably more spiritual affair. On 2 November is Día de los Muertos (Day of the Dead), again most popular in Mexico but significant throughout the region when families visit cemeteries to honour the dead. Christmas and New Year result in celebrations of some kind, but not always public.

Beyond that each country celebrates wildly on Independence Day: 16 September in Mexico, 21 September in Belize and 15 September in Guatemala. Other important local fiestas are also busy times; book ahead. August is holiday time for Mexicans and Central Americans so accommodation can be scarce, especially in the smaller resorts.

Public holidays throughout the region lead to a complete shut-down in services. There are no banks, government offices and usually no shops open, and often far fewer restaurants and bars. It is worth keeping an eye on the calendar to avoid changing money or trying to make travel arrangements on public holidays.

Mexico

Feb/Mar Carnival/Mardi Gras. Traditionally throughout Latin America, this week is a time for celebration before the hardships of Lent; in Mexico it is particularly popular in Mérida.

15 Sep Cry for Independence. Celebrations which are particularly impressive in Mexico City.

16 Sep Independence Day. Regional festivities and parades.

2 Nov Day of the Dead. The souls of the deceased return to earth and family and friends turn out in costume and to meet them.

12 Dec Guadalupe Day. Pilgrimage of thousands to the Basílica de Guadalupe, in northeast Mexico City, the most venerated shrine in Mexico. Well worth a visit. Also celebrated in places in southern Mexico, such as San Cristóbal de las Casas.

Belize

10 Sep St George's Caye Day.
With celebrations in Belize City that start with river races in San Ignacio.

Guatemala

Mar/Apr Semana Santa. Particularly colourful in Antigua with floats carrying Christ over wonderfully coloured and carefully placed carpets of flowers (see box, page 357); also spectacular in Santiago Atitlán.

19 Nov Settlement Day. Celebrating the liberation (or arrival) of the Garífuna from distant shores. Also celebrated in Guatemala.

Nov Todos Santos Cuchumatán. All Saints' Day in the small town of Todos Santos, a colourful and drunken horse race with lots of dancing and antics. See page 403.

What to do

Archaeology

Archaeological sites run the gamut from a handful of unexcavated mounds to heavily restored citadels with vast pyramids and palatial complexes. The sheer scale of metropolizes such as Chichén Itzá is mind-boggling, but it is often the smaller, quieter, less popular sites, such as Yaxchilán and Toniná, which leave the deepest impressions.

Along with a quiet, contemplative attitude, solitude is key to experiencing the ruins and their subtle atmosphere. Set out as early as possible in the day, especially if the site lies within striking distance of Cancún and its hordes of package tourists; opening time is best. If the site is shrouded in forests, you have a better chance of seeing wildlife in the early morning too, and there may be photogenic mists. A route-based run-down of the more popular ruins is given on page 11, but you will find many more described in the text. To comprehend the richness and complexity of Mayan civilization, it is worth reading in-depth before setting out. We recommend anything and everything by Linda Schele.

Birdwatching and wildlife observation

In typical tropical exuberance, Belize, Guatemala and southern Mexico are brimming with wildlife and you won't have to venture far out of urban settings to encounter it. Casual strolling at any of the larger archaeological sites is often rewarded with the sight of iguanas sunning themselves on rocks, scampering agoutis, coatis and other rodents, mot-mots, hawks and occasional monkeys in the trees.

In southern Mexico, the best places for birdwatching are the Río Largartos Biosphere Reserve and the Celestún Biosphere Reserve, both home to spectacular colonies of flamingos. Also good for aquatic birds is the Sian Ka'an Biosphere Reserve. Slow-moving manatees can sometimes be seen coastal lagoons of the Caribbean, while crocodiles are relatively common in the mangroves; a few have even begun lurking on golf courses in Cancún (with unpleasant consequences for one or two golfers). The region's lowland rainforests conceal the most impressive wildlife of all, including jaguars and tapirs, but these are extremely difficult to spot. Palenque is the best place to organize forays into the jungle.

Across the border in Guatemala, the Maya Biosphere Reserve is the big natural attraction, encompassing more than 57,000 ha of teeming rainforest and dry forest and numerous archaeological sites, including Tikal; the wildlife observation is superb.

In Belize, conservation is a high national priority with tourism vying for the top spot as foreign currency earner. Among the private organizations managing the country's protected areas is the Belize Audubon Society; see box, page 284. Its seven nature reserves include the outstanding Cockscomb Basin Wildlife Sanctuary (41,800 ha), the world's only jaguar reserve; and Crooked Tree Wildlife Sanctuary (6480 ha), with its swamp forests and lagoons filled with wildfowl. There are many, many other natural highlights.

Caves and cenotes

Caving, or speleology, in Mexico is more than just going down into deep dark holes. Sometimes it is a sport more closely related to canyoning as there some excellent underground river scrambles. The biggest cave systems in the country are in Chiapas with excursions best organized from San Cristóbal de las Casas. The Yucatán Peninsula has a very extensive system of subterranean caves too. The largest and most famous are the Loltún caves, extensively studied for their ancient human and animal remains, and their prehistoric frescoes. The Calchetok caves are similarly large with a labyrinth of passages and impressive carbonate sculptures. Near Chichén Itzá, the Balankanché caves played an important ceremonial role in the life of the city; its eerie stalactites and stalagmites resemble thrones and ceiba trees. Near Tecoh, outside Mérida, Tzabnah has a cathedral-like chamber. *Cenotes* are sinkholes; caves with collapsed roofs. Some of these serve as popular local swimming holes, including Dzitnup and Zaci in Valladolid, but some of the more visually impressive wells are now snorkelling and dive sites. Note some underground cavern diving is quite technical and requires special training beyond PADI certification.

Belize also has some of the longest caving systems in the world. The main attractions in caves are crystal formations, but most caves in Belize were also used by the Maya, and in some Maya artefacts have been found. While government permission is required to enter unexplored systems, simple cave exploration is easy. From San Ignacio, tours go to Chechem Ha, Barton Creek and Actun Tunichil Muknal Cave, known for their Maya artefacts. The best one-stop shop for all levels is the **Caves Branch Jungle Lodge** (see page 309) on the Hummingbird Highway, close to the entrance to the Blue Hole National Park.

Diving

The Yucatán is a world-class diving destination. The astonishing Mesoamerican Barrier Reef, the second largest reef system in the world, lies off the coast of Quintana Roo, a scintillating expanse of coral skirting the shore south from Isla Contoy. Most serious divers head to Isla Cozumel, but there are dive centres

at all the major resorts on the Riviera Maya. As elsewhere in the world, the reefs in this region are under threat from mass tourism, climate change and hurricanes. Near Cancún and Isla Mujeres, don't miss the superb Museo Subacuático de Arte, an underwater sculpture park.

South into Belize, the Mesoamerican Barrier Reef continues to skirt the shore with its beautiful coral formations, canyons, coves, overhangs, ledges, walls and endless possibilities for underwater photography. Lighthouse Reef, the outermost of the 3 north–south reef systems, offers pristine dive sites in addition to the incredible Blue Hole. Massive stalagmites and stalactites are found along overhangs down the sheer vertical walls of the Blue Hole. This outer reef lies beyond the access of most land-based diving resorts and even beyond most fishermen, so the marine life is undisturbed. An ideal way to visit is on a liveaboard boat. An exciting marine phenomenon takes place during the full moon every Jan in the waters around Belize when thousands of the Nassau groupers gather to spawn at Glory Caye on Turneffe Reef.

Note There are decreasing numbers of small fish – an essential part of the coral lifecycle – in the more easily accessible reefs, including the underwater parks. The coral reefs around the northerly, most touristy cayes are dying, probably as a result of tourism pressures, so do your bit to avoid further damage.

Fishing

Belize is a very popular destination for sport fishing, which is normally quite pricey but definitely worth it if you want to splash out. The rivers offer increasingly few opportunities for good fishing, and tilapia, escaped from regional fish farms, now compete with the catfish, tarpon and snook for the food supply. The sea still provides game fish such as sailfish, marlin, wahoo, barracuda and tuna. On the flats, the most exciting fish for light tackle – the bonefish – is found in great abundance.

Note In addition to the restrictions in Belize on turtle and coral extraction, the following regulations apply: no person may take, buy or sell crawfish (lobster) between 15 Feb and 14 Jun, shrimp between 15 Mar and 14 Jul, or conch between 1 Jul and 30 Sep.

Hiking

A network of paths and tracks covers much of the region. In southern Mexico, the sierras of Oaxaca are popular with hikers; you can find guides and professional tour operators in Oaxaca City. In Chiapas, there are also good opportunities for hiking in the hills, as well as in the lowland Lacandón jungle, but seek current advice regarding Zapatista activity and narco-trafficking. The Yucatán is almost entirely flat and the hiking is monotonous. It is possible to trek between ruins and *cenotes*, but many of the forests shed their leaves in the dry season and thus offer little respite from the heat. Some of the larger archaeological zones, notably Cobá and Calakmul, have easy and mostly circuitous trails snaking into the

undergrowth, a convenient experience of the jungle with reasonable opportunities for glimpsing fauna.

In Guatemala, the Petén is the most popular trekking destination with a variety of routes connecting jungle-shrouded ruins, some of them very remote. You will need to be physically fit to complete the 5- to 7-day odyssey to El Mirador, but lighter day treks to other interesting sites are possible too; Flores is the usual jumping-off point. In the west of the country, the Cuchumatanes mountains are a very mysterious and beautiful locale with a network of highland villages and the highest non-volcanic peak in the country (3837 m). The Sierra de las Minas in eastern Guatemala is relatively unexplored while the countryside around Quetzaltenango, Antigua and Lake Atitlán offers many opportunities for casual walking and volcano climbing. Always check on the security situation before setting out.

Even if you only plan to be out a couple of hours you should have comfortable, safe waterproof footwear and a daypack to carry your sweater and waterproof. At high altitudes the difference in temperature between sun and shade is remarkable. The longer trips mentioned in this book require basic backpacking equipment. Essential items are: a good backpack, sleeping bag, foam mat, stove, tent or tarpaulin, dried food (not tins), water bottle, compass and trowel for burying human waste. Hikers have little to fear from the animal kingdom apart from insects; robbery and assault are rare. You are much more of a threat to the environment than vice versa. Leave no evidence of your passing; don't litter and don't give gratuitous presents of sweets or money to rural villagers. Respect their system of reciprocity; if they give you hospitality or food, then is the time to reciprocate with presents.

Most Central American countries have an Instituto Geográfico, which sells topographical maps of a scale 1:100,000 or 1:50,000. The physical features shown on these are usually accurate; the trails and place names less so. National parks offices also sell maps.

Kayaking

The coasts of the Yucatán are filled with mangroves and wetlands rich in wildlife where you might spot crocodiles, manatees and scores of elegant waterbirds. One of the most popular areas to kayak is the Sian Ka'an Biosphere Reserve, where tours can be easily extended to include a visit to *cenotes* and ruins. Inland, the Laguna de Bacalar is another fun place for paddling about.

Casual sea kayaking is possible at numerous beach destinations throughout the region with many hotels renting equipment to their guests.

Surfing

On Mexico's Pacific coast, Oaxaca lays claim to some legendary stretches with a string of laid-back beach towns, the surf mecca of Puerto Escondido and the family resort of Huatulco. The Soconusco in Chiapas is pleasant enough, though less beautiful. Similarly, in Guatemala the beaches of the Costa Sur are black sand and sweltering, but also buffeted by refreshing sea breezes and waves, some of them fit for surfing.

Whitewater rafting

The variety of Mexico's rivers opens the activity up to all levels of experience. The attraction is not just the run but the trek or rappel to the start and the moments between rapids, drifting in deep canyons beneath hanging tropical forests, some of which contain lesser known and inaccessible ruins. Rafting in Chiapas covers the spectrum from sedate floats on rivers such as the Lacan-Há through the Lacandón jungle to Grade IV/V rapids on the Río Jataté, which gathers force where the Lacan Tum enters it and gradually diminishes in strength as it nears the Río Usumacinta. Jan-Feb are the preferred months because the climate is cooler.

Rafting is possible on a number of rivers in Guatemala across a range of grades. However, trips have to be arranged in advance. In general, the larger the group, the cheaper the cost. **Maya Expeditions**, www.mayaexpeditions.com, is the country's best outfitter. It rafts the Río Cahabón in Alta Verapaz (Grade III-V), the Río Naranjo close to Coatepeque (Grade III), the Río Motagua close to Guatemala City (Grade III-IV), the Río Esclavos, near Barbarena (Grade III-IV), the Río Coyolate close to Santa Lucía Cotzumalguapa (Grade II-III) and the Río Chiquibul in the Petén (Grade II-III). It also runs a rafting and caving tour in the Petén and a combined archaeology and rafting tour where you would raft through a canyon on the Río Usumacinta (Grade II). For a little extra excitement, Maya Expeditions also arrange bungee jumping in Guatemala City.

Where to stay

from homestays to hammocks

Hotels and guesthouses

Hotels are widespread in all major towns and cities, but less prevalent in villages and small communities. Most rooms come with their own bathroom, running hot and/or cold water, cable TV, a fan, writing desk and Wi-Fi. Air conditioning will ratchet up the price, sometimes by an extra US$10-20. The very cheapest rooms have a shared bathroom (note that in the text the term 'with bath' usually means 'with shower and toilet', not 'with bathtub'). Couples should ask for a room with a *cama matrimonial* (double bed), which is cheaper than a room with two beds.

Rates vary seasonally, especially on the coast. In Mexico and Guatemala, you may also be charged 'gringo rates' based on your appearance and command of Spanish. Many hotels have a few cheap and very basic rooms set aside from their standards; politely ask if they have something *más económico*. A cheap but decent hotel might be US$20-25 a night upwards in Mexico and Belize (US$35 or more on the beach), around US$15 in Guatemala. In many popular destinations there is often an established preferred choice budget option.

Making reservations is a good idea, particularly at times you know are going to be busy or if you are travelling a long distance and won't have the energy to look around for a room. At the lower end of the market, having reservations honoured can be difficult. Ask the hotel if there is anything you can do to secure

Price codes

Where to stay	
$$$$	over US$150
$$$	US$66-150
$$	US$30-65
$	under US$30

Price of a double room in high season, including taxes.

Restaurants	
$$$	over US$12
$$	US$7-12
$	US$6 and under

Prices for a two-course meal for one person, excluding drinks or service charge.

the room. If arriving late, make sure the hotel knows what time you plan to arrive. Beware 'helpers' who try to find you a hotel, as rates increase to pay their commission. Try www.airbnb.co.uk for stays with local hosts in apartments or houses. Although owners are not

Tip...
Used toilet paper should be placed in the receptacle provided and not flushed down the pan, even in quite expensive hotels. Failing to do this blocks the pan or drain.

always necessarily present in the property while you're there, they will answer any questions before you get there and welcome you on arrival.

All-inclusive resorts tend to be concentrated on the Pacific and Caribbean coasts, and on the islands, especially in Yucatán and Belize. Most resorts have beach access, pools, restaurants and a small army of staff to cater to your needs.

For those on a really tight budget, look for a boarding house, called a *casa de huéspedes, hospedaje, pensión, casa familial* or *residencial*; they are normally found in abundance near bus stations and markets. They are usually quite basic and family-run and may or may not have television, running hot water, windows or sunlight. 'Love motels' can be found on highways, designed with discretion in mind. Although comfortable if occasionally seedy, their rates tend to be hourly.

Youth hostels

Hostels have sprung up in all the big destinations across the region. They remain a cheap and sociable option for international backpackers, and useful for those who want to get together groups for tours. No two hostels are the same, as the cleanliness, quality and clientele vary greatly, but most offer a reliable range of amenities including free coffee, lockers, shared kitchen, Wi-Fi, tourist information and tours. Although you can save money by cooking your own meals, private rooms in hostels are not usually a good deal compared to hotels. Dorm accommodation, around US$7-15 per night, is the best bet for solo travellers on a budget. The **International Youth Hostel Association** ⓘ *www. hihostels.com*, has a growing presence in the region, especially in Mexico. With other affiliated hostels joining it is worth considering getting membership if you are staying in the country for a while.

B&Bs

Throughout the region, the extent and popularity of B&Bs has taken off in recent years and most of them imply a level of quality, comfort and personal service above and beyond your bog-standard hotel. Some of the converted townhouses in the big colonial cities are especially beautiful. On the beach,

luxury 'rustic chic' *cabañas* have become de rigueur. Most B&Bs cost upwards of US$50 per night and it's worth shopping around as style, comfort, intimacy and overall value vary greatly between establishments. Also check what kind of breakfast is included, as some do not extend to a full cooked spread. It's worth checking out www.airbnb.co.uk too, which has plenty of great value places listed to stay in the region.

The web has spawned some great communities and independent travellers should take a look at www.couchsurfing.com. It's a way of making friends by kipping on their sofa. It's grown rapidly in the last few years and appears to be a great concept that works.

Nature lodges

Nature lodges are famed for their romantic settings and access to areas of outstanding natural beauty, including rainforests, cloud forests, mountains and beaches. They are among the world's best places for wildlife observation, especially for birds. Although nature lodges are comparatively expensive – most fall in our $$$ and $$$$ range – they promise a unique and intimate experience of the wilderness that is sure to leave lasting impressions. Everyone should consider splashing out at least once.

Homestays

Homestays are a great way to learn about local culture and are best arranged through Spanish schools or community tourism projects. Reasonably comfortable options are available in big towns and cities, but in more remote places, expect rustic conditions, including an outdoor toilet, little or no electricity, and cold running water (or just a bucket and wash bowl). Simple meals are usually included in rates. For homestays in Belize, see box, page 326. See also **Experiment in International Living**, page 535, which organizes homestays in Mexico and Central America.

Camping

There are few official campsites in the region but camping is generally tolerated. Obey the following rules for wild camping: arrive in daylight and pitch your tent as it gets dark; ask permission to camp from a person in authority; never ask a group of people – especially young people; avoid camping on a beach (because of sandflies and thieves). If you can't get information, camp in a spot where you can't be seen from the nearest inhabited place and make sure no one saw you go there. Camping supplies are usually only available in the larger cities, so stock

up on them when possible. In some national parks, simple rangers' station offer rustic lodging in cots. Bring your own food and water and some warm bedding; the rainforest can get quite chilly in the early hours.

Hammocks

A hammock can be an invaluable piece of equipment, especially if travelling on the cheap. It will be of more use than a tent because many places have hammock hooks, or you can sling a hammock between trees or posts. A good tip is to carry a length of rope and some plastic sheeting. The rope gives a good choice of tree distances and the excess provides a hanging frame for the plastic sheeting to keep the rain off. Metal S-hooks or a couple of climbing karabiners can also be very useful, as can strong cord for tying out the sheeting. Don't forget a mosquito net if travelling in insect-infected areas.

Food
& drink

An excellent general rule when looking for somewhere to eat is to ask locally. Most restaurants serve a daily special meal, usually at lunchtime called a *comida corrida* or *comida corriente*, which works out much cheaper and is usually filling and nutritious. Vegetarians should list all the foods they cannot eat; saying '*Soy vegetariano/a*' (I'm a vegetarian) or '*No como carne*' (I don't eat meat) is often not enough. Universally the cheapest place to eat is the local market.

Safety The golden rule is boil it, cook it, peel it or forget it, but if you did that every day, every meal, you'd never eat anywhere. A more practicable rule is that if large numbers of people are eating in a regularly popular place, it's more than likely going to be OK.

Mexico

Food for most Mexicans represents an integral part of their national identity and much has been written since the 1960s about the evolution of Mexican cooking. Experts suggest that there have been three important developmental stages: first, the combination of the indigenous and the Spanish traditions; later, the influence of other European cuisines, notably the French in the 19th century; and finally the adoption of exotic oriental dishes and fast food from the USA in the 20th century. In 2010, the importance of Mexican food was recognized by its inclusion on the UNESCO Intangible Cultural Heritage List.

Mexican cooking is usually perceived as spicy or hot due to the prolific use of chilli peppers, but equally, maize is a very typical ingredient and has been a staple crop since ancient times. It is mainly consumed in *antojitos* (snacks) and some of the most common are tacos, *quesadillas, flautas, sopes, tostadas, tlacoyos* and *gorditas*, which consist of various shapes and sizes of *tortillas*, with a variety of fillings and usually garnished with a hot sauce. Historically influenced by trade contact with the Caribbean, Europe and the southern US, Yucatec cuisine is distinctive, and you should not leave without sampling some of its classic dishes. *Poc chuc* is grilled pork in a sour orange marinade. *Pollo pibil* is chicken marinated in sour orange and *achiote*, wrapped and banana leaves and baked; the same dish made with pork is called *cochinita pibil*. A *panucho* is a cooked tortilla with shredded chicken and a salad garnish; *salbutes* are *panuchos* with refried beans

ON THE ROAD
Oaxacan cooking

The food of the state of Oaxaca is a fine representation of the complexity and variety of its cultures.

A stroll through any of Oaxaca's markets will quickly bring you into contact with vendors selling *chapulines*. These small grasshopper-like creatures, turn bright red when fried, are then served with lime and chillies. Another interesting ingredient in the diet is *gusanito*, a small red caterpillar from the agave plant, that is used to make a special sauce with pasilla chillies. This is also the worm found in some mescals.

There are local delicacies for vegetarians as well. *Flor de calabaza*, pumpkin flowers, are used in soups, *empanadas*, *quesadillas* or simply as garnish. Soup is prepared from *nopales*, young leaves of prickly-pear cactus.

The most typical regional snacks are *tlayudas*, huge crispy tortillas, covered with a variety of toppings (beef, sausage, beans or cheese) and grilled over coals. Oaxacan white string cheese, known as *quesillo*, is also famous, as is the area's excellent chocolate, best enjoyed as a hot beverage. Also popular is a slightly fermented drink made from corn flour known as *atole*.

Barbacoa is barbequed meat, often lamb or goat. Although there many veggie options with corn, cheese and mushroom dishes, Oaxacans love their meat. *Tasajo*, skirt steak of salted beef, and *cecina*, salted pork, are popular, as is *salchicha Oaxaqueña*, beef sausages from Ejutla.

The essence of Oaxacan cooking, however, and the recipes for which the state is most famous, are its many *moles*, which come in a variety of colours. They are served as sauces accompanying turkey, chicken or even pork and fish dishes.

inside. *Huevos motuleños* is a breakfast dish consisting of fried eggs on a bed of tortilla and refried beans, all doused in tomato sauce, chopped ham, peas and cheese. Oaxaqueña cuisine is also unique and very intriguing (see box, above).

Meals in Mexico consist of breakfast, a heavy lunch between 1400 and 1500 and a light supper between 1800 and 2000. Costs in modest establishments are US$3-4 for breakfast, US$4-6 for a set lunch, sometimes called *comida corrida*, *menú del día*, or *menú ejecutivo*. Dinner costs are higher, US$7-10 (and there's generally no set menu). À la carte meals at modest establishments cost about US$8-12. A very good meal costs US$15-20 at a middle-level establishment, but choose wisely. Street stalls are by far the cheapest – although not always the safest – option. The best value is undoubtedly in small, family-run places. If self-catering, markets are cheaper than supermarkets.

There are always plenty of non-alcoholic *refrescos* (soft drinks) and mineral water. *Agua fresca* – fresh fruit juices mixed with water or mineral water – and *licuados* (milk shakes) are good and usually safe. Herbal teas – for example chamomile (*manzanilla*) and mint (*hierba buena*) – are readily available. The native alcoholic drinks are *pulque*, made from the fermented juice of the agave plant, tequila and mescal, both made from distilled agave. *Mezcal* usually has a *gusano de maguey* (worm) in the bottle, considered to be a particular delicacy but, contrary to popular myth, is not hallucinogenic. National **beer** is also good with a wide range of light and dark varieties.

Belize

Dishes suffer a wonderful preponderance of rice'n'beans – a cheap staple to which you add chicken, fish, beef and so on. For the cheapest meals, order rice which will come with beans and (as often as not) banana or plantain, or chicken, vegetables or even a blending of beef with coconut milk. Belize has some of the best burritos in Central America but you have to seek them out, normally in hidden-away stalls in the markets.

Along the coastal region and on the cayes seafood is abundant, fresh and reasonably cheap, but avoid buying lobster between 15 February and 14 June (when it's out of season) as stocks are worryingly low. (Conch is out of season between 1 July and 30 September; Nassau grouper, between 1 December and 31 March.)

Better restaurants offer a greater variety and a break from the standards, often including a selection of Mexican dishes; there are also many Chinese restaurants, which are not always good and are sometimes overpriced.

Belikin beer is the local brew, average cost US$3 a bottle. Many brands of local rum are available too. Several local wines and liqueurs are made from available fruit. One favourite, called *nanche*, is made from *crabou* fruit and is very sweet, as is the cashew wine, made from the cashew fruit rather than the nut. All imported food and drink is expensive.

Guatemala

Traditional Central American/Mexican food such as tortillas, *tamales*, *tostadas*, etc, are found everywhere. Tacos are less spicy than in Mexico. *Chiles rellenos* (chillies stuffed with meat and vegetables) are a speciality in Guatemala and may be *picante* (spicy) or *no picante*. *Churrasco*, charcoal-grilled steak, is often accompanied by *chirmol*, a sauce of tomato, onion and mint. Guacamole is also excellent. Local dishes include *pepián* (thick meat stew with vegetables) in Antigua, *patín* (small lake fish wrapped in leaves and served in a tomato-based sauce) from Lake Atitlán and *cecina* (beef marinated in lemon and bitter orange) from the same region. *Fiambre* is widely prepared for families and friends who

gather on All Souls' Day (1 November). It consists of all kinds of meat, fish, chicken, vegetables, eggs or cheese served as a salad with rice, beans and other side dishes. Desserts include *mole* (plantain and chocolate), *torrejas* (sweet bread soaked in egg and *panela* or honey) and *buñuelos* (similar to profiteroles) served with hot cinnamon syrup. For breakfast try *mosh* (oats cooked with milk and cinnamon), fried plantain with cream and black beans in various forms. *Pan dulce* (sweet bread), in fact bread in general, and local cheese are recommended. Try *borracho* (cake soaked in rum).

Local beers are good (Monte Carlo, Cabra, Gallo and Moza, a dark beer); bottled, carbonated soft drinks (*gaseosas*) are safest. Milk should be pasteurized. Freshly made *refrescos* and ice creams are delicious and made of many varieties of local fruits; *licuados* are fruit juices with milk or water, but hygiene varies, so take care. Water should be filtered or bottled. By law alcohol cannot be consumed after 2000 on Sundays.

This is
Southern
Mexico

Forged in the flames of conquest, the deeply indigenous southern states of Mexico embody a vivid synthesis of European and Mesoamerican traditions: the merging of disparate worlds has spawned unique forms of art, cooking, song, dance, religion and philosophy.

A procession of vibrant colonial towns and cities echo the faded glory of imperial Spain, but beneath and behind them, at the foundations of lavish government palaces and grandiloquent baroque cathedrals, lie the hidden remnants of a much older and stranger reality. Millennia before Cortés and his conquistadors clambered ashore, southern Mexico was a crucible for competing civilizations: the Olmec, Zapotec, Mixtec and Maya chief among them. Today, their descendants breathe life into ancient traditions, for as much as the old gods are clothed in the respectable robes of Catholic saints, shamanism continues to thrive.

Perhaps no single indigenous symbol has become more firmly embedded in Mexican national identity than that of Lord Death. Encapsulating the ancient Mesoamerican concept of duality, death in Mexico is not a place of gloom or rest, but the source of spirited, irrepressible activity. Charged with colour, music, spectacle and celebration, Lord Death is an honoured guest at the feast, a garish skeleton festooned with flowers, drunk on mescal, delightfully raucous and dancing in the village square as church bells ring and fireworks explode. Death is a provocation to seize the moment for all it's worth. Death is Life, and by extension, so is Mexico.

Essential Mexico City

Finding your feet

Mexico City is vast, but many of the interesting sites are within a relatively small area. The heart of the city is the Zócalo, the main square in the Centro Histórico, surrounded by colonial streets. Just west of the Zócalo are the gardens of the Alameda. From here, the grand boulevard of Paseo de la Reforma heads southwest to Chapultepec Park, 'the lungs of the city'. The city's main thoroughfare, Avenida Insurgentes, bisects Reforma about halfway between the Alameda and Chapultepec Park, sweeping past the Basílica de Guadalupe in the north, and heading south towards the beautiful bohemian suburbs of San Angel and Coyoacán.

Best places to stay

Hostel Catedral, Zócalo, page 48
San Diego, La Alameda, page 49
Casa de los Amigos, Plaza de la República, page 49
Casa González, Paseo de la Reforma, page 49
La Casona, Roma, page 49

Getting around

A handy smartcard called Tarjeta DF is valid on Mexico City's various mass transit systems, including the Metro and Metrobús, both straightforward, cheap and easy to navigate; you can purchase cards and top up credit at machines, shops or ticket booths.

The Centro Histórico is best explored on foot. If this is your first visit to Mexico City, it is recommended you get a hotel here; you'll be at the heart of the action and a short walk from many sights.

Taxis are widespread, but for safety reasons, you should only use official *sitio* stands.

For the athletic and environmentally conscious, there are numerous cycle lanes and a commuter bike-sharing scheme, **Ecobici**. See also Transport, page 53.

Best restaurants

El Cardenal, Zócalo, page 50
Pujol, Polanco, page 51
Azul Condesa, Condesa, page 51
Contramar, Roma, page 51

Safety and pollution

The vast majority of visitors have a trouble-free experience, but big city rules do apply. Take care in Bosque de Chapultepec, Mercado Merced, the Zona Rosa and major touristy areas, where robberies have occurred. Be vigilant at night and at quiet times, when you are advised to travel by *sitio* taxi. As always, crowded buses and metro trains are a favourite haunt of pickpockets.

Pollution is a real issue in the city with chronic industrial smog trapped in the Valley of Mexico (worst December to February). Common ailments are a burning sensation in the eyes (contact lens wearers take note) and nose, and a sore throat.

When to go

The cheapest months are also the coldest months, January-February, which are usually comfortable during the day and occasionally icy after dark. March-May are the warmest months; June-September are warm and rainy. The city dries out October-December as temperatures start to fall and prices rise for the high season.

Time required

Four to five days is enough time for a quick jaunt around some of the main sights. A more complete exploration might take two to three weeks, or longer.

Mexico City

A vast, swarming, unrepentant chaos of humanity, Mexico City, known locally as the Distrito Federal, or DF for short, is the fabled capital of the nation. Few cities are so behemoth in spirit and scope – or so thrilling.

Periodically destroyed and reborn through conquest, revolution, earthquakes and war, Mexico City's historical incarnations are many: the Aztec capital of Tenochtitlán, the administrative heart of colonial New Spain, and later, federal capital of an independent, post-revolutionary Mexico. Today, as a teeming 21st-century megapolis, it is a home to an intricate mosaic of 22 million lives.

Unsurprisingly, it has harboured generations of world-class writers and artists, from William Burroughs to Frida Kahlo. Among its attractions are a wealth of architectural wonders, outstanding museums, cultural centres, art galleries, night clubs and restaurants. This is a city of insatiable energy, and like all great imperial capitals, Mexico City possesses style and intrigue in abundance.

The Zócalo is a good starting point, home to Latin America's oldest cathedral, the Palacio Nacional and the Templo Mayor, the ancient centre of the Aztecs. A few blocks away are handsome colonial buildings clustered around Plaza Santa Domingo, while in the gardens of nearby La Alameda is the impressive Palacio de Bellas Artes. In the Mexico City's largest park, the Bosque de Chapultepec, is the capital's unmissable sight: the Museo Nacional de Antropología.

★ Zócalo

The Zócalo (also known as Plaza Mayor or Plaza de la Constitución) is the second largest public square in the world after Moscow's Red Square. In Aztec times, it was a central meeting point for the causeways that joined the island city of Tenochtitlán to the mainland. Today, it acts as a vast staging ground for festivals, concerts, military parades, and political rallies. The large national flag in the centre of the square, symbol of Mexico City's political authority, is ceremonially raised at 0600 (0500 in winter) and solemnly lowered at 1800 (1700 in winter).

On the Zócalo's north side stands the **Metropolitan Cathedral** ① *daily 0800-2000, free, with a US$1 donation to visit the sacristy, dress appropriately and be discreet during Mass*. The largest and oldest cathedral in Latin America, construction began in 1573 under the direction of Spanish architect Claudio de Arciniega, but did not finish until 1813, some 240 years later. Stylistically, the cathedral combines elements of Gothic, baroque, Churrigueresque, neoclassic and Herrerian. It is singularly harmonious considering the many architects who have contributed to it. The cathedral is built directly over the ruins of Tenochtitlán's holiest precinct, where the soft soil has been causing the structure to sink, somewhat unevenly, for centuries. Next to the cathedral is the **Sagrario Metropolitano** (1769) with a fine Churrigueresque façade. Unlike the cathedral, it was built on the remains of an Aztec pyramid and, whilst sinking, is more stable than the former. Occupying the eastern side of Zócalo where the Aztec Palace of Moctezuma once stood is the **Palacio Nacional** ① *daily 0800-1800, free, but bring ID to enter, knowledgeable English-speaking guides available*. Initially a fortress-like structure with heavy armaments, it was destroyed by angry mobs and rebuilt in colonial baroque in 1692. Over the central door hangs the Liberty Bell, rung every year at 2300 on 15 September by the president, who commemorates independence from Spain with the spirited *grito* (cry): *¡Viva México!* Inside the palace, don't miss the rousing frescoes by Diego Rivera that flank the staircase and two walls of the first floor.

★ Templo Mayor (Great Temple)

Seminario 8, entrance in the northeast corner of the Zócalo, T55-4040 5600, www.templomayor.inah.gob.mx, Tue-Sun 0900-1700, last tickets 1630, museum and temple US$4.50, guided tours in Spanish, audio guides in English and other languages.

Located at the heart of Tenochtitlán's sacred precinct, this was the spiritual, social and political centre of the Aztec universe, where the earth, sky and underworld met. On a mundane level, it marked the axis about which the four major quarters of the city were orientated. Partly, the temple is believed to be a symbolic representation of the sacred hill, Coatepec. Its construction began in 1325 on the supposed spot where the legendary omen of an eagle perched on a cactus and devouring a snake was beheld, indicating to the wandering Aztec tribe where to settle and build their empire. First as a simple shrine and later, with six subsequent builds, as a grand pyramid, the temple was dedicated to two principal gods: Huitzilopochtli, the beloved god of war and tribute; and Tlaloc, god of rain and agriculture. After the Spanish conquest of Tenochtitlán in 1521, the temple was dismantled and covered with earth. It lay hidden until 1978 when electrical workers uncovered a great stone monolith depicting the dismembered moon goddess, Coyolxauqui. For the next four years, a team of archaeologists conducted a thorough excavation of the area. Levelling four city blocks and some 13 historic buildings, they resurrected the temple and uncovered over 7000 artefacts, now housed in the excellent Templo Mayor museum.

Plaza Santo Domingo and around

Plaza Santo Domingo, four blocks north of the Zócalo's northwest corner, is an intimate little plaza surrounded by fine colonial buildings. There is the **Antigua Aduana** (former customs house) ① *daily 1000-1730, US$2, Sun US$1.30*, on the east side, and the **Portales de Santo Domingo** on the west side, where public scribes and owners of antiquated hand-operated printing presses are still in business. One block east of the plaza, don't miss the **Antiguo Secretaría de Educación** ① *Argentina 28, Mon-Fri 0900-1800, free*, where there are more than 200 murals by a number of different artists, including some of Diego Rivera's masterpieces. Painted between 1923 and 1928, they depict the lives and sufferings of the common people, as well as satirize the bourgeoisie, as in *El banquete de Wall Street* (The Wall Street Banquet) and the *La cena del capitalista* (The Capitalist's Supper).

★Antiguo Colegio de San Ildefonso

Justo Sierra 16, T5702-2991, www.sanildefonso.org.mx, Tue 1000-2000, Wed-Sun 1000-1800, US$3.50.

One block south and half a block east of the Antiguo Secretaría de Educación, you can admire more murals at the Antiguo Colegio de San Ildefonso, built in splendid baroque style in 1749 and originally a Jesuit school. It contains important frescoes by Orozco, Rivera, and Leal, all in excellent condition.

La Alameda and around

The gardens of La Alameda, six blocks west of the Zócalo, were formerly an Aztec market and later the place of execution for the Spanish Inquisition. Today, it's a public park, with wide paths linking fountains and marble statues beneath the broken shade of eucalyptus, cypress and palms. On its east side stands Mexico's most important cultural centre and one of the capital's finest buildings, the sumptuous **Palacio de Bellas Artes** ① *T55-5512 2593, www.palacio.bellasartes.gob.mx, Tue-Sun 1000-1800, free when no performances are showing.* Beyond its harmonious Art Nouveau exterior, the interior features stylish art deco flourishes, a fabulous stained-glass skylight, works of art and sculpture including spirited murals by Rivera, Orozco, Tamayo and Siqueiros, and a glass curtain designed by Tiffany that is solemnly raised and lowered before each performance of the Ballet Folklórico de México. The palace's website has an up-to-date schedule of upcoming music, opera, theatre, and ballet productions.

On Calle Tacuba, east off the Alameda, is the **Museo Nacional de Arte** ① *Tacuba 8, T55 8647-5430, www.munal.com.mx, Tue-Sun 1000-1730, US$3*, one of the country's finest museums. The building has magnificent Italian staircases and houses a large collection of Mexican paintings, drawings, sculptures, and ceramics dating from the 16th century to 1950, including a large number of paintings (more than 100) by José María Velasco, as well as works by Miguel Cabrera, Gerardo Murillo, Rivera, Orozco, Siqueiros, Tamayo and Anguiano.

On the northern side of the Alameda stands the **Museo Franz Mayer** ① *Hidalgo 45, T55-5518 2266, www.franzmayer.org.mx, Tue-Fri 1000-1700, Sat-Sun 1100-1800, US$3.50*, housed in the former 17th-century Hospital de San Juan de Dios. It houses a library and an important decorative arts collection of ceramics, glass, silver, timepieces, furniture and textiles, as well as Mexican and European paintings from the 16th to the 20th centuries. Its cloister is an oasis of peace in the heart of the city. At the west end of the Alameda, Diego Rivera's huge (15 m by 4.8 m) and fascinating mural, the *Sueño de una Tarde Dominical en la Alameda Central*, is housed by the **Museo Mural Diego Rivera** ⓘ *Balderas y Colón, T55-5512 0754, www.museomuraldiegorivera.mx, Tue-Sun 1000-1800, US$1.50.* One of Rivera's finest works, it presents a pageant of Mexican history from the Conquest up to the 1940s with vivid portraits of national and foreign figures, heroes and villains as well as his wife, Frida Kahlo.

Centro Histórico: Zócalo & Alameda

Where to stay 😴
Catedral **1** *B5*
Gran Hotel de México **2** *C4*
Hostel Catedral **3** *B4*

Marlowe **4** *C3*
Mexico City Hostel **5** *B4*
San Diego **6** *D2*

Restaurants 🍴
Café El Popular **3** *B4*
Café Tacuba **5** *B4*
Dulcería de Celaya **6** *B4*

Along the south side of La Alameda runs Avenida Juárez, a broad street with a mixture of old and new buildings, including the sobering but highly acclaimed **Museo Memoria y Tolerancia** ⓘ *Av Juárez, T55-5130 5555, www.myt.org.mx, Tue-Fri 0900-1800, Sat-Sun 0900-1900, US$5.50, displays in Spanish with English audio guide available, US$6.50, note the museum is not suitable for children*. Using an array of modern displays, this thought-provoking museum explores the difficult theme of genocide. There is a particular focus on the Jewish Holocaust, but the atrocities in Guatemala, Yugoslavia, Armenia, Cambodia and Rwanda are also featured. A block south of Juárez at the corner of Avenida

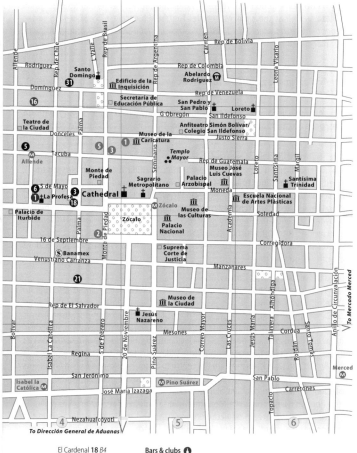

El Cardenal **18** *B4*
Hostería Santo
  Domingo **31** *A4*
Pastelería Ideal **21** *C4*

Bars & clubs 🎵
Bar la Opera **2** *B3*
La Perla **16** *A4*
Zinco Jazz Club **1** *B4*

Independencia and Revillagigedo, you'll find the **Museo de Arte Popular** ⓘ *Revillagigedo 11, a block south of the Alameda, Tue, Thu-Sun 1000-1800, Wed 1000-2100, US$3.10*, which exhibits wonderfully outlandish *artesanías* from all the country – a great introduction to Mexican craft traditions, particularly if you're aiming to explore some of the interesting markets outside of the capital.

About four blocks north of Bellas Artes off Eje Central Lázaro Cárdenas is Plaza Garibaldi, best visited on Friday or Saturday evening when up to 200 mariachis descend in their traditional costume of huge sombrero, tight silver-embroidered trousers, pistol and *sarape*. They will play your favourite Mexican serenade for between US$5 (for a bad one) and US$10 (for a good one). There is a gigantic and very entertaining eating hall on the plaza as well as the small **Museo del Tequila y Mezcal** ⓘ *T55-5529-1238, www. mutemegaribaldi.co.mx, Mon-Wed 1300-2200, Thu-Sun 1300-0000, US$4*, complete with samples and *cantina*.

★Torre Latinoamericana
Corner of Av Madero and Eje Central Lázaro Cárdenas, www.torrelatino.com, daily 0900-2200, US$4.65.

East of the Alameda, is the modern Torre Latinoamericana which has a viewing platform with telescopes on the 42nd floor, some 139 m up. The vista is exceptional, if sometimes smoggy, so try to come on a clear day if possible.

Plaza de la República and around
Plaza de la República lies west of the Alameda on Avenida Juárez, a major landmark dominated by the **Monumento a la Revolución,** its large copper dome and supporting columns set on the largest triumphal arches in the world. It was originally commissioned by Porfirio Díaz as a legislative chamber, but ended up as a kind of mausoleum for heroes of the revolution, with the remains of Madero, Villa, Carranza, Calles and Cardenas contained inside. The neighbourhoods around the plaza, including **Tabacalera**, are quiet, leafy and residential, and the high concentration of cheap hotels makes this area a long-time favourite of budget travellers.

Paseo de la Reforma and Zona Rosa
Paseo de la Reforma is Mexico City's most elegant thoroughfare. Named after Benito Juárez's reform laws of 1861, it was previously known as Carlotta's promenade, after Empress Carlotta, who designed it during the reign of her husband Emperor Maximilian as a European-style boulevard connecting the Centro Histórico with their castle residence in Chapultepec. It flourished as a bourgeois enclave until the 1957 earthquake drove out its wealthy residents and big business took over, building the high-rise towers of glass that line it today. You can walk Reforma from the centre to Chapultepec (one to two hours, lots of traffic) and admire the buildings and statues stationed at the *glorietas* (roundabouts), variously dedicated to Christopher Columbus, **Cuauhtémoc** (the last Aztec emperor) and Diana the huntress. Don't miss the **Monumento a la Independencia**, also known as 'El Angel', who grasps the wreath of victory in one hand and the chains of tyranny in the other, said to be an elegant symbol of Mexico City itself – or of its soaring spirit, at least.

The famous **Zona Rosa** (pink zone) lies to the south of Reforma, roughly contained by Reforma, Sevilla, Avenida Chapultepec and Insurgentes Sur. This was once the setting for Mexico City's most fashionable stores, restaurants and nightclubs, with roads bearing the names of European cities. It suffered considerable damage in the 1985 earthquake and subsequently lost ground to Polanco. In recent times it has seen a revival and is once again a pleasant area in which to stroll, shop (or window-shop) and dine. Don't expect too much authenticity, however, as the majority of the Zona Rosa's establishments cater to tourist clientele.

Bosque de Chapultepec and Polanco
Mexico City's largest and most verdant public park

Formerly an Aztec imperial resort and hunting ground, Bosque de Chapultepec (meaning 'Hill of Crickets' in Nahuatl) is particularly popular on Sundays, when families arrive to partake in picnics, stroll around, visit the numerous free museums, or otherwise enjoy the refreshing shade of the thousands of *ahuehuete* (Montezuma cypress) trees. The park is divided into three sections.

The lion's share of attractions, including the phenomenal **Museo Nacional de Antropología** (see below) and the imposing **Castillo de Chapultepec**, are contained by the first section. Commissioned in 1785, the *castillo* was built as a replacement for another fortress which was destroyed in an accidental gunpowder explosion. The present structure took several decades to complete and remained empty until 1841 when it found purpose as a military academy. It was here that the famous *niños* heroes (the brave child cadets immortalized in a white marble monument at the base of the hill) staved off an attack by US marines in 1847. Rather than surrender to the gringos, the last survivors committed suicide by jumping to their deaths. In 1864, Emperor Maximilian and his wife, Empress Carlotta, converted the castle into their personal residence, sculpting the park to their tastes and importing all manner of sumptuous furnishings. The **Museo Nacional de Historia** ⓘ *inside the castle, www.mnh.inah.gob.mx, Tue-Sun 0900-1700, US$4.50*, displays the personal effects of the doomed couple, including luxurious carriages and lavish salons, along with antique furniture, paintings, murals and exhibitions chronicling Mexican history.

In the northeast corner of the park, the **Museo de Arte Moderno** ⓘ *Paseo de la Reforma, T55-5553 6233, www.mam.org.mx, Tue-Sun 1000-1800, US$1.70*, has a superb permanent collection of Mexican art. Memorable works include Orozco's *El Prometo*, several oil paintings by Rivera and O'Gorman, and Siqueros' legendary *Nuestra Imagen*. The real jewel in the crown is Frida Kahlo's *Las Dos Fridas*, but the entire exhibition is a venerable tour de force and a sweeping portfolio of Mexico's masters. Nearby, on the other side of Reforma, you'll find the **Museo Rufino Tamayo** ⓘ *www.museotamayo.org, Tue-Sun 1000-1800, US$1.50, free Sun*, home to a fine collection of works by national and international painters, including Oaxacan artist Rufino Tamayo. The building of glass and concrete was designed by González de León and Zabludovsky and won the National Architecture award.

★Museo Nacional de Antropología
Paseo de la Reforma, T55-4040 5300, www.mna.inah.gob.mx. Tue-Sun 0900-1900. US$4.50. Nearest metro Auditorio or Chapultepec, or take a colectivo down Reforma marked 'Auditorio'. Written explanations in Spanish and English, audio guide in English, US$5.75. Guided tours in English or Spanish free with a minimum of 5 people. If you want to see everything in detail, you need at least 2 days. Permission to photograph (no tripod or flash allowed) US$3.50.

The crowning glory of Chapultepec park was designed by architect Pedro Ramírez Vásquez to house a staggeringly vast archaeological collection of pre-Conquest Mexican culture. The largest exhibit (8.5 m high, weighing 167 tonnes) is the image of Tlaloc, the rain god, removed (accompanied by protesting cloudbursts) from near the town of Texcoco. Inside, the museum is very well organized; each major culture of Mesoamerican civilization is represented in its own room.

Introduction to Anthropology and Mesoamerica The museum's two orientation rooms explore the major concepts, techniques and fields of research that serves as the foundation of our existing knowledge of ancient Mexico. Introduction to Anthropology examines the four main pillars of anthropological inquiry: physical anthropology, archaeology, linguistics and ethnography. The next room explores the cultural and geographical concept of Mesoamerica itself.

Origins The origins room focuses on early settlers: the first migratory waves of hunter-gatherers across the Bering strait through to the early farming cultures which flourished after the thaw of the ice age. Particularly interesting are the remains of a mammoth found in Santa Isabel Ixtapan in 1954.

Pre-Classic Dating from 2500-100 BC, the artefacts exhibited in the pre-Classic room, illustrate the formative practices, social structures, and philosophical concepts that became the foundation for Mesoamerican culture in its entirety. During the pre-Classic era, rudimentary civic-religious structures began evolving into grand ceremonial centres. Vital to the success of these early agricultural people was fertility, a preoccupancy reflected by an abundance of 'pretty lady' sculptures, complete with large hips and thighs. The concept of duality, also central to the pre-Columbian thought, is illustrated by two-headed clay statues and masks.

Teotihuacán Teotihuacán, Mesoamerica's first great city, rose to dominance during the Classic era, 100 BC-AD 750. In this room, the exhibited artefacts demonstrate a new mastery of artistic form, with a well-developed pantheon of gods depicted variously, from simple clay statues to exuberant carved reliefs to monumental sculptures fashioned from boulders of volcanic rock. Intricate clay braziers and tripod vessels reveal the rich ceremonial aspect to their society, but it is the abundance of striking masks for which this city's artisans are particularly famous.

Toltec The Toltecs of central Mexico (AD 700-1300), were largely concerned with military supremacy, evidenced by a range of artefacts from Cacaxtla, Xochitécal, Xochicalco and, in the later part of this period, Tula. Particularly noteworthy are the large columns representing upright warriors. These warriors supported the roofs of important buildings and can be interpreted, quite literally, as the pillars of Toltec civilization.

The Mexica The room devoted to the Aztecs, or Mexica, is the most dramatic room in the museum. Filled with dark slumbering idols, you might detect a slightly electric edge to the atmosphere. The most fabulous display is the mighty sun stone, or Aztec calendar, discovered in the Zócalo in 1790. It represents a complete depiction of the Aztec cosmos with primary gods, astrological symbols and numerous feathered serpents. Elsewhere, there are statues relating to the earth and death, including many rattlesnakes and several unsettling renditions of Mictlantecuhtli (Lord of the Underworld).

Oaxaca Cultures The Oaxaca room follows the development of the region's major cultures, the Zapotecs and Mixtecs, from the pre-Classic era through to the Conquest. There is particular emphasis on Monte Albán and Mitla, the region's main conurbations and power centres. Particularly interesting are the various funerary relics, uncovered at places such as Monte Alban's tomb 104, reproduced here with colourful murals and offerings. Clay was utilized widely with productions including magnificent urns, usually depicting gods, often very naturalistic and adorned with complex headdresses.

Gulf Coast Cultures The Olmec, Huastec and central Veracruz civilizations are the focus of the Gulf Coast room. Giant stone heads, uncovered at pre-Classic sites throughout southern Veracruz and Tabasco, are the most impressive display in the Olmec section. Also noteworthy are the chubby childlike 'baby face' figurines. Many Olmec designs feature a mysterious hybrid of human and animal characteristics – the elongated foreheads in some productions probably relate to the practice of cranial deformation. El Tajín is the most famous of the Central Veracruz sites and an idealized reproduction of the pyramid of the niches is presented here.

The Maya The vast and inspirational Maya collection was drawn from two main areas: the lowlands, including the Yucatán Peninsula and rainforests of present-day Chiapas, and the highlands. It charts the epic development of these enigmatic peoples from the pre-Classic to the post-Classic. Many of these artefacts are the most skilfully designed of all pre-Columbian art. Those belonging to the Classic Maya, particularly, are the epitome of elegance, often adorned with sumptuous hieroglyphics. Spirituality and religion are central concerns of many pieces, such as the stelae from Yaxchilán, which show ritual scenes of blood-letting.

Northern cultures The Northern cultures comprised three broad groups. The first room is dedicated to Arid American culture – hunters and gatherers that forged an existence from the desert. The second room focuses on Marginal Mesoamerica, which shared features of its more developed neighbours to the south and was based on a mixed, but most agricultural economy. The third room deals with Oasis America, an extension of the southwest cultures of the United States.

Western cultures West Mexico is a vast and culturally complex area that includes the present-day states of Guanajuato, Michoacán, and the Pacific coast from Sinaloa to Guerrero. Principal among these cultures are the Tarascans, or Purépechas, a warrior tribe whose relics include weapons, tools, precious jewellery and a wealth of innovate and rather strange pottery, some with unique globular feet. They often sculpted geometric structures into human or animal form, evidenced by a throne in the shape of a coyote.

Ethnography The ethnography rooms on the first floor are less dramatic than the archaeological rooms, but fascinating nonetheless, and obligatory if you wish to explore indigenous communities beyond the capital. Various rooms supply an overview of languages, settlement patterns, economy and culture, before exploring Mexico's major indigenous groups in turn, including the Huicholes and Coras, Purépechas, Otomi-Pame, Sierra de Puebla peoples, Oaxaca peoples, Maya, Northwest cultures and Nahuas.

Polanco

Upscale Polanco lies directly northwest of the Museo de Antropología. It is home to exclusive private residences, commercial art galleries, fashion stores, upmarket restaurants, and some of the most modern (and conspicuous) hotels in the city. Many of its older houses have carved stone façades, tiled roofs and gardens, especially on **Calle Horacio**, a pretty street lined with trees and parks. Polanco is the setting for a few recent cultural developments, including the controversial **Museo Jumex** ⓘ *Miguel de Cervantes Saavedra 303, Colonia Ampliación Granada, T55-5395 2615, www.fundacionjumex.org, Tue-San 1100-2000, Sun 1100-2100, US$3.85, free on Fri.* Critics have generally hailed this new gallery, designed by British architect David Chipperfield, as an important and dynamic addition to Latin America's contemporary art scene; others have dismissed it as inscrutable. Nearby – and even more controversial – is the shimmering hour glass-shaped **Museo Soumaya** ⓘ *Miguel de Cervantes Saavedra 303, T55-1103 9800, www.soumaya. com.mx, daily 1030-1830, free.* Bankrolled by Mexican billionaire Carlos Slim, it hosts some outstanding works by European and Latin American masters, but has attracted criticisms for its overall lack of coherence.

South of the city centre

attractive middle-class areas with elegant buildings and fine restaurants

Insurgentes Sur: Roma and Condesa

Celebrated as the city's most hip quarters, Roma and Condesa are filled with bohemian loft spaces, minimalist apartments, leafy parks, galleries, bookshops and restaurants. Easily reached on foot from the Zona Rosa, Roma is the less gentrified and hipper of the two, with Avenida Obregón as its principal boulevard, which crosses Insurgentes Sur east to west. At its intersection with Orizaba you'll find the **Casa Lamm** ⓘ *Obregón 99, www. casalamm.com.mx*, a historic mansion built in 1910 by Lewis Lamm, a key figure in Roma's development. It contains an interesting cultural centre with galleries, library, bookshop and a fine restaurant. A few blocks north on Orizaba lies **Plaza de Río de Janerio**, one of the district's oldest public squares. Condesa, to the south and west of Roma, is built on the site of an old race track at **Parque México**, a great spot for a stroll. Throughout the neighbourhood there's a wealth of sumptuous art deco architecture and most of Condesa's famed restaurants are concentrated around the junction of Michoacán, Atlixo and Suárez.

San Angel

To get to San Angel, take the Metrobús to La Bombilla and walk 300 m west on La Paz. Alternatively, take a bus from Chapultepec park or metro Line 3 to Miguel Angel de Quevado.

Filled with cobblestone streets and opulent mansions, ancient trees and exuberant flowers, the well-heeled suburb of San Angel, 13 km southwest of the city centre, exudes the charm of an era now largely past. It derives its name from a 17th-century Carmelite convent, but owes its most distinguished architecture to the wealthy *chilangos* (inhabitants of Mexico City) who built summer residences here in the 19th century, when San Angel was still a separate town. The house where Diego Rivera and his wife, Frida Kahlo, lived and worked between 1934 and 1940 – which was undoubtedly witness to some interesting domestic scenes – is today the **Museo Casa Estudio Diego**

Rivera ⓘ *Av Altavista y Calle Diego Rivera, www.estudiodiegorivera.bellasartes.gob.mx, Tue-Sun 1000-1800, US$1, free Sun.* It displays several of Rivera's works, reproductions, memorabilia and belongings, including the bed where he died in 1957. Many people come to San Angel on a Saturday to visit the **Bazar del Sábado** ⓘ *0900-1400*, a splendid folk art and curiosity market that takes place on its main square, Plaza San Jacinto.

Coyoacán and around

To get to Coyoacán from the city centre, it is easiest to take the metro to Coyoacán, Viveros, Miguel Angel de Quevedo or General Anaya and walk the remaining 2-3 km. The colectivo from Metro General Anaya to the centre of Coyoacán is marked 'Santo Domingo'; get off at Abasolo or at the Jardín Centenario. From San Angel, you can get to Coyoacán via a delightful walk through Chimalistac, across Avenida Universidad and down Avenida Francisco Sosa; or you can take a bus or pesero marked 'Taxqueña' as far as Calle Caballocalco.

Coyoacán, 3 km east of San Angel, is the place from which Cortés launched his attack on the Aztec capital of Tenochtitlán (the name means 'place of the coyotes' in Nahuatl). It is one of the most beautiful and best-preserved parts of the city with elegant tree-lined avenues, hundreds of fine buildings from the 16th to 19th centuries, and carefully tended parks. Of the many historic houses in Coyoacán, the most visited is the **Museo Frida Kahlo** ⓘ *Allende y Londres 247, www.museofridakahlo.org.mx, Tue-Sun 1000-1800, US$6.15 (US$7.70 at weekends), no photographs,* also known as the **Casa Azul**, where the legendary artist lived, worked and died, as her art attests, in the considerable suffering of her broken body. The collections are not particularly vast, but the museum does offer an intimate glimpse into the daily life of the national heroine. Two rooms are preserved as lived in by Frida and her husband Diego Rivera, and the rest contain drawings and paintings by both, including interesting sketches of archaeological sites.

Another important historic home is **Casa de Trotsky** ⓘ *Río Churubusco 410, between Gómez Farías and Morelos, www.museocasadeleontrotsky.blogspot.mx, Tue-Sun 1000-1700, US$3,* where the exiled Russian revolutionary (who famously had an affair with Kahlo) lived and worked before he was murdered by the Stalinist agent Ramón Mercader in 1940. It is a rather dark and sombre place, and includes the study where – in the colourful manner of Russian assassinations – he was bludgeoned to death with an ice pick. Outside there is a tomb where his ashes were laid and a red flag keeps the faith.

Tourist information

Secretaría de Turismo
Nuevo León 56, 9th floor, Condesa, T55-5553 1260, www.mexicocity.gob.mx.
They have a detailed website and can supply maps, flyers, and general information. They also manage several information booths at various locations around the city, including at the airport, bus terminals, Museo de Antropología, Alameda Central, Catedral, Templo Mayor and others.

For general enquiries, you can also call **tourist assistance**, toll-free T01800-008 9090. Any complaints should be referred to tourist information centres or **tourist police**, in blue uniforms. For up-to-date cultural listings, track down the Spanish-language *Tiempo Libre*, www.tiempolibre.com.mx, on sale all over the city every Thu.

Zócalo and around

$$$$-$$$ Gran Hotel de México
16 de Septiembre 82, Metro Zócalo, T55-1083 7700, www.granhotel ciudaddemexico.com.mx.
One of the city's finest hotels with an incredible 1930s-style foyer, wrought-iron furnishings, antique elevators, and a superb Tiffany-designed stained glass ceiling. The 5th-floor restaurant and balcony are great for people-watching on the Zócalo, especially on Sun morning when brunch is served. Classically sophisticated and the epitome of Old World elegance.

$$$-$$ Catedral
Donceles 95, Metro Zócalo, T55-5518 5232, www.hotelcatedral.com.
A professionally managed and fairly priced mid-range option with an excellent central location and stylish interior design. Rooms are clean, comfortable, carpeted, modern, and well-attired; ask for one with views and a balcony. All the usual amenities

including concierge service, city tours, restaurant, terrace bar, business centre, taxi, laundry and Wi-Fi. Affordable and attentive. Recommended.

$$-$ Hostel Catedral
Guatemala 4, Metro Zócalo, T55-5518 1726, www.mundojovenhostels.com.
A thriving backpacker hostel in a convenient central location, just behind the cathedral. Lodgings span more than 200 beds in private rooms ($$-$) and dorms ($). Amenities include restaurant, kitchen, bar, laundry, internet, secure storage, Wi-Fi, travel agency and more. The rooftop bar is popular in the evenings with regular live music and dance classes. Cheaper for YHI members or when booked online. On the noisy side, but fun and sociable. Breakfast included.

$$-$ Mexico City Hostel
República de Brasil 8, Metro Zócalo, T55-5512 3666, www.mexicocityhostel.com.
Housed in a beautiful colonial building and quieter than **Hostel Catedral**, Mexico City Hostel is a well-established budget lodging with a range of 8 and 12-bed dorms ($), and large private rooms ($$) with shared bath. Interesting tours available, including a visit to a *lucha libre* wrestling match. Breakfast and Wi-Fi included. They also run **Mexico City Hostel Suites**, with 4, 6, and 8-bed dorms and private rooms. Neat, tidy, orderly and quiet.

La Alameda and around

$$ Marlowe
Independencia 17, Metro San Juan de Letrán, T55-5521 9540, www.hotelmarlowe.com.mx.
A clean and modern hotel, finished to a high standard. Rooms are comfortable, carpeted, and kitted with TVs. Suites have jacuzzi, sofa, and balcony. Amenities include secure parking, gym and a restaurant. Generally good value, but ask to see the room before accepting.

$$ San Diego

Luis Moya 98, Metro Banderas, T55-5512 2653, www.hotelsandiego.com.mx.
A modern 3-star option, well-maintained and good value. Rooms are clean, carpeted and comfortable, if generic. Those overlooking the courtyard may be a bit noisy. Poor Wi-Fi connection, but otherwise decent and recommended. A good deal.

Plaza de la República and around

$$-$ Casa de los Amigos

Ignacio Mariscal 132, Metro Revolución, T55-5705 0521, www.casadelosamigos.org.
An excellent guesthouse run by Quakers for Quakers, or development-work travellers; other travellers are taken only if space is available. Accommodation includes single-sex dorms ($) and doubles ($$), 2 nights must be paid in advance, maximum 15-day stay. Good information on volunteer work, travel and language schools, breakfast and laundry on roof, use of kitchen, safe luggage store, English library. Advance booking necessary. Recommended.

Paseo de la Reforma and Zona Rosa

$$$ Suites Amberes

Amberes 64, Metro Insurgentes, T55-5533 1306, www.suitesamberes.com.mx.
Attractive, comfortable, fully equipped suites with own kitchen, dining room, bedroom and all conveniences including cooker, microwave, safe, coffee maker, Wi-Fi, and satellite TV. The building also has a gym and business centre. Rates include American breakfast and airport shuttle.

$$$-$$ Casa González

Lerma y Sena 69, Metro Insurgentes, T55-5514 3302, www.hotelcasagonzalez.com.
A very quiet and secluded hotel with 33 homely rooms and peaceful, flower-filled gardens. Breakfast and other meals available in the 24-hr café. Laundry, Wi-Fi and TV. Interior rooms are more attractive and

expensive ($$$). Very helpful, hospitable and friendly. Highly recommended.

$$$-$$ María Cristina

Lerma 31, Metro Insurgentes, T55-5566 9688, www.hotelmariacristina.com.mx.
A handsome colonial-style hotel with a fine lobby and superb spiral staircase, lots of antique furnishings, pleasant green lawns and an internal patio. Accommodation spans 150 comfortable rooms with bar, restaurant, laundry, Wi-Fi, business centre and secure parking among the amenities. Helpful staff, solid and reliable. Recommended.

Polanco

$$$$ Las Alcobus

Presidente Masaryk 390, T55-3300 3900, www.lasalcobas.com.
This impeccable boutique hotel boasts a superb contemporary design with bespoke rosewood furnishings. Rooms are lavish and tastefully attired with Italian bed linens by Rivolta Carmigiani. Excellent restaurant and luxury spa facilities available. Great service, one of the best, extravagant and recommended.

Insurgentes Sur: Roma and Condesa

$$$$ La Casona

Durango 280, Col Roma, Metro Sevilla, T55-5286 3001, www.hotel lacasona.com.mx.
This converted early 20th-century mansion has spacious rooms and plenty of amenities for business travellers, including gym, business centre, restaurant, Wi-Fi, spa and valet parking. Rooms are individually decorated and follow an artistic or musical theme.

$$ Milán

Obregón 94, Col Roma, T55-5584 0222, Metro Insurgentes, www.hotel milan.com.mx.
A good, clean, efficient and well-maintained hotel, professional managed with lots of staff. Rooms are fresh and modern with marble sinks, fan, telephone and cable TV. Some have good views of the street below. A good mid-range option, recommended.

Restaurants

Cheap, filling street food is ubiquitous in Mexico City, from mobile kitchens to holes-in-the-wall. Frequented by crowds of office workers at breakfast and lunch time, the streets around the Monumento Revolución are particularly rich pickings. Offerings include fresh fruit, juice, tacos, burritos, *tortas*, *tamales* and more. Pick a place that looks clean, busy and popular; strictly avoid anything that looks or smells unsanitary. For more ideas, try the blog of Nicholas Gilman, www. goodfoodmexicocity.com, or his book, *Good Food in Mexico City*.

Zócalo and around

$$$ Café Tacuba
Tacuba 28, Metro Allende,
www.cafedetacuba.com.mx.
Founded in 1912, a Mexico City institution with lots of history and character. The interior features superb art work and traditional tile decor, a sweeping staircase and wood panelled dining halls. They specialize in Mexican cuisine, including very good *enchiladas*, excellent meat dishes, *tamales* and fruit desserts, although portions are a little small and service a bit slow. Live music and mariachis. A popular family restaurant, not touristy.

$$$ El Cardenal
Palma 23, Metro Allende,
www.restauranteelcardenal.com.
Excellent Mexican food impeccably served in an elegant mansion. Aside from the usual staples, you can also sample regional specialities like enchiladas Michoacanas or *chile en nogada*. The bravest gourmands might try the highly nutritious Aztec inspired *tortilla de huevo con escamoles* (egg tortilla with ant larvae). **El Cardenal** is particularly recommended for brunch or breakfast, when a traditional feast of hot chocolate and sweet rolls is served.

$$$ Hostería Santo Domingo
70 and 72 Belisario Domínguez,
2 blocks west of Plaza Santo Domingo,
Metro Allende, T55-5510 1434,
www.hosteriadesantodomingo.mx.
A witness to more than 150 years of history, the oldest restaurant in town with former diners creating a who's who of Mexican history. Good service, warm family ambience and Mexican specialities, including often-recommended *chile en nogada* (chicken in a sweet pomegranate sauce). Excellent live music.

$$-$ Café El Popular
5 de Mayo 52, on corner of alley to Hotel Juárez, Metro Allende. Open 24 hrs.
Economical and unpretentious, and as the name might suggest, quite popular, mainly with Mexicans. Offerings include a plethora of breakfasts and Mexican staples, Oaxacan omelettes, tacos, enchiladas and freshly baked pastries. Bustling and buzzing, a well-established and reliable city diner.

Bakeries and sweet shops

Dulcería de Celaya
5 de Mayo 39, Metro Allende,
www.dulceriadecelaya.com.
Famous traditional (and expensive), handmade candy and cake store in lovely premises. Established in the 19th century, a city institution.

Pastelería Ideal
Uruguay 74, Metro San Juan de Letrán.
A long-running and highly popular bakery with a huge array of delicious sweet cakes, breads, sweet rolls and pastries. Also a branch at 16 de Septiembre 18.

Paseo de la Reforma and Zona Rosa

$$$ Les Moustaches
Río Sena 88, Metro Insurgentes, T55-5533 3390, www.lesmoustaches.com.mx.
Mon-Sat 1300-2330.
This award-winning French restaurant is one of Mexico City's finest, a long-standing

favourite for romantic dinners and business lunches. They serve classic French dishes like foie gras, onion soup and Gruyère prawns along with more exotic fare such as crocodile with kiwi and walnuts. Romantic, high calibre and suitably pricey.

$$$ Quebracho
Río Lerma 175, Metro Insurgentes, www.quebracho.com.mx.
Succulent Argentine steaks for all your carnivorous needs. Smart but unfussy, casual, laid-back, with chequered floors and terraced seating outside for people-watching. Good evening atmosphere, popular with business people and middle-class Mexicans. They have branches in other parts of the city, including Condesa and the Centro Histórico (see their website for more).

Polanco

$$$ Pujol
Francisco Petrarca 254, Metro Polanco, T55-55453507, www.pujol.com.mx.
Pujol was named best restaurant in the city by the *Wall Street Journal* and is widely considered one of the best restaurants in the world. Chef Enrique Olvera, who trained in the Culinary Institute of America, brings personal, creative and contemporary innovations to ancient Mexican recipes. A beautiful and intimate restaurant, not to be missed.

Insurgentes Sur: Roma and Condesa

$$$ Azul Condesa
Nuevo León 68, T55-5286 6380, www.azul.rest.
Superb gourmet Mexican cuisine from award-winning Chef Ricardo Muñoz Zurita, who has been described as 'the anthropologist' for his intrepid exploration of the country's regional output. His kitchen presents delicious dishes from Yucatán, Oaxaca, Veracruz, Michoacán and more. Every month there is a festival focused on a selected ingredient. Recommended.

$$$ Contramar
Durango 200, T5514 9217, www.contramar.com.mx.
Exceptional seafood, fresh, simple, exquisitely prepared and full of flavour. The grilled fillets are good and everyone raves about the *tostadas de atún* (tuna tostadas). Terraced seating and attentive service. Not cheap, but one of the best. It gets busy at lunchtime, so arrive early or make reservations. Recommended.

$$$ Specia
Amsterdam 241, T5564-1367.
This renowned restaurant serves hearty plates of tasty Polish cooking, the best in Mexico. Their highly recommended signature dish is *pato tin* (roast duck), wonderfully succulent, just enough for 2, and served with sweet blueberry sauce and apple stuffing. If you have any room left, the desserts are great too, as is the Polish vodka. Good service, reservations recommended.

$$ Origenes Organicos
México y Cacahuamilpa, Condesa, Metrobús Sonora, www.origenesorganicos.com.
This small, busy café-restaurant and health food store, overlooking Plaza Popacatapetl, serves wholesome organic meals including soups, salads, smoothies and snacks. On the pricey side, but good ambience. Some tables outside and free Wi-Fi for customers.

$ El Tizoncito
Tamaulipas y Campeche, Condesa, Metro Patriotismo; also at Campeche y Cholula.
This well-established and popular eatery enjoys kudos as the inventor of *tacos al pastor* (meat tacos carved from a Lebanese-style spit). They now have several branches across the city. Good, cheap street food.

Bars and clubs

The most popular districts for nightlife are Condesa, Roma, Zona Rosa, Polanco, San Angel and Coyoacán. You can go for a drink at any time; clubbing starts late with most just getting going by 2400. Remember that, because of the high altitude, one alcoholic drink in Mexico City can have the effect of two at lower altitudes. Many bars and nightclubs are closed on Sun.

La Alameda and around

Bar La Opera
5 de Mayo 10, Metro Allende.
Fantastic old bar-restaurant with a range of national drinks and a bullet hole in the ceiling left by Pancho Villa. Dark, cosy and possessing great ambience.

La Perla
República de Cuba 44, Metro Allende. Thu-Sat 2000-0400.
US$4 cover charge. Seedy but popular little club in the centre. Everything from dance to freaky cabaret has been reported.

Zinco Jazz Club
Motolinia 20, Metro Allende, www.zinco jazz.com. Wed-Sat 2100-0330.
Atmospheric jazz hall located in the basement of an art deco building. Great ambience and captivating live performances. Popular, so book ahead.

Insurgentes Sur: Roma and Condesa

La Bodeguita del Medio
Cozumel 37, Roma, Metro Sevilla, T55-5553 0246, www.labodeguitadelmedio. com.mx.
Extremely popular Cuban bar-restaurant where drinks like *mojitos* became famous, and graffiti is an art form.

Mamá Rumba
Querétaro 230 y Medellín, Roma, Metrobús Sonora, T55-5564 6920, www.mamarumba. com.mx.
Live music Thu-Sat from 2300. One of the first places in Mexico City with Cuban rhythms, famous for its *rumba*, now with a couple of floors. Also a new branch opened in San Angel (T55-5550 8099)

with live music Wed-Sat from 2100. Get there early, it gets packed.

Entertainment

Listings for all cultural events can be found in the publication *Tiempo Libre*, available every Thu from newsstands (US$1). Monthly programmes are available from the bookshop at the Palacio de Bellas Artes (see page 39).

Cinema
A number of cinemas show non-Hollywood films in the original language (with Spanish subtitles); check *Tiempo Libre* magazine for details. Most cinemas, except **Cineteca Nacional**, offer reduced prices on Wed. Cinemex is the main cinema. For arthouse films, courses in film appreciation or an otherwise more involved look at the cinematic form, try:

Cinemex Casa de Arte
France 120, Metro Polanco, T55-5280 9156, www.cinemex.com.
Alternative, independent and art-house films.

Ciudad Universitaria
Insurgentes Sur 3000, T55-5665 0709, www.filmoteca.unam.mx.
The university's cultural centre has 2 good cinemas that regularly screen art-house films.

Shopping

Art and handicrafts

Fondo Nacional para el Fomento de las Artesanías (FONART)
Av Patriotismo 691, Metro Mixcoac, T55-5598 1666, www.fonart.gob.mx; branches at Av Juárez 89, Metro Hidalgo, and Paseo de Reforma 116, Metro Cuauhtémoc.
A state organization founded in 1974 in order to rescue, promote and diffuse the traditional crafts of Mexico. Competitive prices and superb quality.

Markets

La Ciudadela
Mercado Central de Artesanías, beside Balderas 95, between Ayuntamiento y Plaza Morelos, Metro Balderas, Mon-Sat 1100-1800, Sun 1100-1400.

Government-sponsored market with fixed prices and good selection. Reasonable and uncrowded, and generally cheaper than San Juan, but not for leather. Craftworkers from all Mexico have set up workshops here (best for papier mâché, lacquer, pottery and Guatemalan goods), but prices are still cheaper in places of origin.

Mercado Merced
Metro Merced.

The gargantuan **Mercado Merced** is said to be the largest market in all the Americas, dates back over 400 years. A riot of commercial activity, its stalls and stores are spread over several blocks. Take care, as robberies have been reported (this is not a good place to flash a camera). Be sure to check out the **Mercado Sonora**, opposite **La Merced** on Av Fray Servando Teresa de Mier. This is a **witches' market**, where you'll find all manner of curious trinkets from love potions to giant toads embalmed in glass jars. The safest way to get the market is by Metro (Merced).

Tianguis del Chopo
Aldama 211, between Sol and Luna, Metro Buenavista. Sat 1000-1600.

Clothes, records, etc, frequented by hippies, punks, rockers and police.

Transport

Air
From Benito Juárez International Airport, 13 km east of the city centre, official fixed-price taxis to the centre cost around US$16. Tickets are available at kiosks.

Airport information

Benito Juárez International Airport, T55-5571 3214, www.aicm.com.mx, has 2 terminals divided into sections, each designated by a letter, and modern facilities. Retail units in each section provide currency exchange and ATMs. There are airport information kiosks at Salas A and E1 (international arrivals). A shuttle train connects the terminals for ticketed passengers, for the rest there is a bus. For more information on domestic flights, see page 507.

Transport to/from the airport
Fixed-price *taxis autorizados* charge by zone; buy tickets from booths, around US$16 to the Centre/Zócalo (per vehicle, not per person). Several operators compete for your custom; a good one is Sitio 300, T55-5571 9344, www.sitio300.com. Present your ticket to a driver once outside. Do not use unauthorized taxis as scams and rip-offs abound. A cheap, smart alternative is the Metrobús (see below), which connects the airport with Centro Histórico via Line 4. You will need to buy a smart card, US$0.75, and ensure it has sufficient credit for the journey, US$2.30 (30 pesos). Pick up points are door 7 in terminal 1 and door 3 in terminal 2. Long-distance buses also depart from the airport bound for **Cuernavaca**, **Puebla**, **Querétaro**, **Toluca**, **Pachuca** and **Cordoba**. The Metro (Aérea) also has connections to the city, but this should be avoided if you're carrying heavy luggage or travelling at rush hour. Metro Terminal Aérea, Line 5, is located 200m from Terminal 1. Buses connect Terminal 2 with Metro Hangares, Line 5 (see below).

Bus
Local
Metrobús, www.metrobus.df.gob.mx, is a modern and efficient bus network that uses pre-paid Tarjeta DF or Metrobús smartcards only, US$0.75 for the card plus US$0.50 for 1 journey, top-up available at machines

Mexico City metro

on Metrobús platforms, exact money only. Particularly useful is Line 1, running 24 hrs between Indios Verdes and Tlalpan via Insurgentes Sur, Roma and Condesa, San Angel, and Ciudad Universitaria. Other lines run 0500-0000, including: Line 2, Tacubaya–Tepalcates via Condesa and Central de Abastos; Line 3 Tenayuca–Ethopia via Reforma, Roma, and Alameda Central; and Line 4 Buenavista–San Lázaro via the airport (US$2.30) and Centro Histórico; and Line 5 Río de los Remedios–San Lázaro.

Additionally, the city's trolley buses, www.ste.df.gob.mx, traverse the city's main thoroughfares along 9 colour-coded lines. One of the more useful is Autobuses del Sur and Autobuses Norte, which connects north and south bus terminals via the Centro Histórico. For complete information on their network, see their website. *Peseros* are privately operated microbuses which display routes on the windscreen. They connect Metro stations with major landmarks and stop whenever required; most fares don't exceed US$0.40. Beware thieves and pickpockets.

Long distance
Advance booking is recommended for all trips over 6 hrs, especially during national holidays. Southern Mexico is served by **ADO**, www.ado.com.mx, and its subsidiaries: **AU**, **OCC**, **ADO GL** and **ADO Platino**. You can book seats through their website, as well as through **Boletotal**, www.boletotal.mx (commission attached). Luggage must be checked in 30 mins before departure. Most buses bound for southern Mexico depart from **Terminal Oriente** (**TAPO**), Calzada Ignacio Zaragoza, Metro San Lázaro, Line 1, but a handful also leave from the northern and southern terminals (see below).

To **Bahías de Huatulco**, 6 daily with **AU**, **OCC** and **GL**, 15 hrs, US$63-US$88; to **Campeche**, 8 daily with **ADO** and **GL**, 17 hrs, US$109-129; to **Cancún**, 7 daily with **ADO** and **GL**, 24 hrs, US$140-165; to **Chetumal**, 2 daily with **ADO**, 1045

(Terminal Norte), 1700 (TAPO), 19 hrs, US$117; to **Mérida**, 8 daily with **ADO** and **GL**, 20 hrs, US$122-144; to **Oaxaca**, hourly with **OCC**, **ADO**, **GL** and **Platino**, 6 hrs, US$45-72; to **Palenque**, 2 daily with **ADO**, 1720 (Terminal Norte), 1755 (TAPO), 14 hrs, US$86; to **Puerto Escondido**, 3 daily with **OCC**, 1640 (Terminal Norte), 1730 (TAPO), 1930 (Terminal del Sur), 14 hrs, US$75; to **San Cristóbal de las Casas**, 12 daily with **OCC**, **ADO** and **GL**, 13 hrs, US$95-113; to **Tapachula**, hourly with **OCC**, **GL** and **Platino**, 18 hrs, US$102-141; to **Tuxtla Gutiérrez**, hourly with **OCC**, **ADO**, **GL** and **Platino**, 12 hrs, US$88-128; to **Villahermosa**, hourly with **AU**, **ADO**, **GL** and **Platino**, 11 hrs, US$63-122.

For other parts of the country, **Terminal Norte**, Av Cien Metros 4907, T55-5587 1552, www.centraldelnorte.com.mx, serves northern Mexico; **Terminal Sur**, corner of Tlalpan 2205, Metro Taxqueña, Line 2, serves **Cuernavaca**, **Acapulco** and **Zihuatanejo** areas; **Terminal Poniente**, Metro Observatorio, Line 1, serves western Mexico. All bus terminals operate taxis with voucher systems and there are long queues (check change carefully at the taxi office). The terminals are connected by metro, but this is not a good option at rush hour, or if carrying too much luggage.

Car
Driving in the capital is highly challenging. If you have a car, it is best to park it in a hotel and explore the city by bus, metro or on foot. To reduce pollution, cars are required to stay off the road for 1 working day (0500-2200) per week. You must check which '*hoy no circula*' applies to your vehicle. The last digit of your number plate indicates the day: **Mon** 5 and 6; **Tue** 7 and 8; **Wed** 3 and 4; **Thu** 1 and 2; **Fri** 9 and 0. Occasionally, when contamination levels are even worse than usual, the programme runs at weekends too: **Sat**, all even numbers and 0; **Sun**, all odd numbers. Normally, you can drive freely in 'greater' Mexico City weekdays 2200-0500.

A controversial new rule states that only the most recent models are allowed to circulate in Mexico City on Sat.

Car hire
Cars can be hired at the airport. Inside the city, most firms have branches in the Zona Rosa, particularly along Reforma. Established international companies include: **Avis**, Reforma 308 (across from US embassy), T55-5511 2228; **Budget**, Calle Dakota 95, T55-5488 8580; and **National**, Reforma 107, T55-5703 2222.

Cycling
Cycle lanes have been added to the city as part of the municipal government's greening programme, including along sections of Paseo de la Reforma, Av Chapultepec, Nuevo León, 20 de Noviembre and Pino Suárez. One of the best ways to explore them is using the commuter bike share scheme, **Ecobici**, Nuevo León 78, T55-5005-2424, www.ecobici.df.gob.mx. It has 275 docking stations around the city where you can pick up and park using a smart card. Take your passport and credit card to the **Ecobici** office to register and receive your map; 1, 3, and 7 day plans are available, but you are only permitted 45 mins cycle time before re-docking. For casual peddling, Bosque de Chapultepec is a popular area and you can hire bikes for free (3 hrs) from a stand outside the **Museo de Antropología**; bring your passport as a deposit. The *ciclovía* is a classic route that follows the old Cuernavaca railroad; ask the tourist office for a map.

Metro
The metro, www.metro.df.gob.mx, is an efficient system and the best method of getting around the city. Trains are fast and frequent, if overcrowded during rush hours (0730-1000 and 1500-2000). Between 1800 and 2100, men are separated from women and children at Pino Suárez and certain other central stations. 2 pieces of medium-sized luggage are permitted. Beware of pickpocketing on the metro. It's not especially dangerous, more a natural aspect of large numbers of people. **Pino Suárez**, **Hidalgo** and **Autobuses del Norte** are particularly infamous for thieves. The fare for 1 journey is US$0.25. Purchase tickets from station booths (exact money only), or top up your Tarjeta DF or Metro smart card at a machine. There are 12 colour-coded lines and every station has a unique symbol, eg the grasshopper signifies Chapultepec. Check the train direction before entering the turnstile or you may have to pay again. The service operates Mon-Fri 0500-2400, Sat 0600-2400, Sun and holidays 0700-2400.

Taxi
Tourist taxis operate from first-class hotels, the **Museo Nacional de Antropología**, etc, and are the most expensive. **Sitio taxis** (fixed ranks) operate from bus terminals and other landmarks; no meters. They are about 2-3 times the price of cruising cabs but highly recommended for safety reasons, especially for lone women at night. You pay in advance at a booth (check your change); they charge on a zone basis. You or your hotel can also phone for a *sitio* taxi. Try **Servitaxis**, T55-3626 9800, www.servitaxis. com.mx or **Taximex**, T55-9181-8888, www. taximex.com.mx. Taxis on unfixed routes can be flagged down anywhere, but should be avoided due to the risk of robbery or assault. If you must use one, check the driver's ID and that the license plate matches the number painted on the vehicle; it should begin with an A or B. They have meters (check they are working properly and set at zero).

Oaxaca state

From prehistoric hunter-gatherers to the earliest known agricultural settlements in the Americas, from warring kingdoms to the 15 indigenous groups comprising the complex modern Oaxequeño identity, Oaxaca has always been a cradle of Mesoamerican civilization.

The first blooms of progress in Oaxaca state flourished around 500 BC at the mountain top city of Monte Albán. Two millennia later, the twin upheavals of genocide and colonialism wrought massive social change.

The region's rich variety of cultivable land – spanning high altitude cloud forests, bountiful valleys and sweltering coastal lowlands – was acquired and administered by Cortés personally. Since then Oaxaca has been sown with scores of lucrative crops, including coffee, sesame, mangos, tobacco, vanilla, and sugar.

In the conquest of souls, the Dominican Order were given monopoly and their grandiose monasteries and convents still pepper the landscape. The colonial project reached its apex in the sunny state capital of Oaxaca City, a UNESCO World Heritage Site impeccably framed by fine historical edifices.

Indigenous society is remains the lifeblood of Oaxaca, where artisan villages specialize in weaving or pottery, barely changed for millennia, and hold frenetic rural *tianguis* (open-air markets).

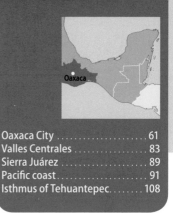

Footprint
picks

★ **Oaxaca city markets**, page 66
All of Oaxaca city's colourful markets are worth a wander.

★ **Templo y Ex-Convento de Santo Domingo**, page 67
Behind a dazzling façade, this complex houses the state's most comprehensive history museum and a garden filled with rarities.

★ **Monte Albán and Mitla**, pages 68 and 85
These pre-Columbian power centres are the most significant archaeological sites in Oaxaca state.

★ **Craft villages in the Valles Centrales**, pages 83, 86 and 88
These villages produce Mexico's most beautiful *artesanías*.

★ **Sierra Juárez**, page 89
A highland region of great biodiversity.

★ **Zipolite, San Agustinillo and Mazunte**, page 94
Zipolite draws an alternative crowd, while down the beach is the diminutive San Agustinillo and ramshackle Mazunte.

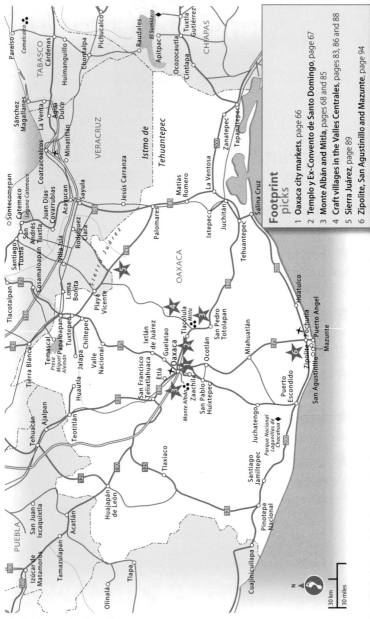

Footprint picks

1 **Oaxaca city markets**, page 66
2 **Templo y Ex-Convento de Santo Domingo**, page 67
3 **Monte Albán and Mitla**, pages 68 and 85
4 **Craft villages in the Valles Centrales**, pages 83, 86 and 88
5 **Sierra Juárez**, page 89
6 **Zipolite, San Agustinillo and Mazunte**, page 94

Oaxaca City

Bright, bold, breezy and bohemian Oaxaca City is the forward-looking capital of Oaxaca state. It was, at its foundation in 1522, the region's seat of colonial and evangelical power, a hub of trade and transport, and later, as its lofty assembly of churches and convents expanded, a singularly aesthetic monument to the unashamedly florid Churrigueresque style of architecture.

Today, thanks to its universities and tireless creative spirit, it is also a youthful destination renowned for its thriving arts scene. From priceless canvases by Mexican masters to hand-woven silk tapestries that fetch thousands of dollars on the international market, scores of galleries, community co-operatives and graphic arts institutes display the finest popular and contemporary work in the country.

Oaxaqueña cuisine, not to be missed, is something of an art form too. Wholesome kitchens and traditional markets serve home-cooked fare in generous and inexpensive portions, including dishes incorporating Oaxaca's seven feisty *moles* (sauces), but there's no shortage of sophisticated culinary establishments either; for years, world-class chefs have been experimenting with local ingredients and redefining the state's famous, flavourful cuisine. Don't miss the chance to sample Oaxaca's many varieties of *mezcal*, a long-revered and increasingly prestigious local firewater that is now finding its way into hip New York watering holes. *Colour map 1, A1.*

Essential Oaxaca City

When to go

The climate in Oaxaca City is generally dry. November to January are the driest, coolest months (with fresh evenings); April and May are the hottest and wettest. You may wish to time your visit with one of the city's many lively festivals, such as Day of the Dead in early November or the Guelaguetza in the last two weeks of July.

Best places to stay

Casa Oaxaca, page 71
Casa Cid de León, page 72
Casa de Las Bugambilias, page 72
Casa Angel Youth Hostel, page 73
Posada del Centro, page 73

Time required

Three days are sufficient to see Oaxaca City.

Best restaurants

Casa Oaxaca, page 73
Luvina, page 74
Origen Oaxaca, page 74
Zincanda, page 74
Mercado Pochote, page 75

Centro Histórico and around
shaded plazas and colourful colonial houses

Eminently strollable, Oaxaca City's compact historic centre is marked by the lively Zócalo (properly known as the Plaza de la Constitución), the city's largest and most thriving public square. Surrounded by arches and arcades, it plays host to a restless throng of itinerant street vendors, musicians, performers, pedestrians, tourists, and local families. This Oaxaca institution is busiest and best attended on Saturday and Sunday evenings when temporary markets stalls peddle everything from tasty hot *tamales* to colourful woven textiles. If it all gets too hectic, several terraced cafés and restaurants invite weary travellers to put up their feet and enjoy a dram of locally sourced coffee, hot chocolate or *mezcal*.

On the south side of the Zócalo stands the 19th-century **Palacio de Gobierno**, home to high charged murals by Arturo García Bustos which depict the political evolution of the state. The palace is often a rallying point for protesters and political groups and they can overtake the Zócalo for weeks or months with banners, signs, and encampments. On the Zócalo's north side stands the **cathedral**, which has suffered several episodes of earthquake damage. It was consecrated in 1733 after 160 years

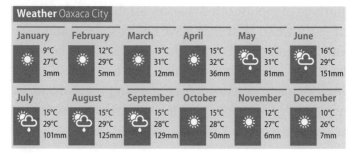

Weather Oaxaca City					
January ☀️ 9°C 27°C 3mm	**February** ☀️ 12°C 29°C 5mm	**March** ☀️ 13°C 31°C 12mm	**April** ☀️ 15°C 32°C 36mm	**May** 🌦️ 15°C 31°C 81mm	**June** 🌦️ 16°C 29°C 151mm
July 🌦️ 15°C 29°C 101mm	**August** 🌦️ 15°C 29°C 125mm	**September** 🌦️ 15°C 28°C 129mm	**October** ☀️ 15°C 28°C 50mm	**November** ☀️ 12°C 27°C 6mm	**December** ☀️ 10°C 26°C 7mm

The Zapotecs

The Zapotec language is used by more than 300,000 people in the state as a first or second language (about 20% of the Oaxaca State population speaks only an indigenous language).

The Zapotec people weave fantastic toys of grass. Their dance, the Jarabe Tlacolula Zandunga, is performed by barefoot girls splendid in becoming coifs, wearing short, brightly coloured skirts, ribbons and long lace petticoats. The men, all in white with colourful handkerchiefs, dance opposite them with their hands behind their backs.

Only women, from Tehuantepec or Juchitán, dance the slow and stately Zandunga. Their costumes involve embroidered velvet blouses, full skirts with white pleated and starched lace ruffles and *huipiles*.

of construction and reconstruction. In typical Churrigueresque exuberance, the west-facing façade features carved stone pillars with overflowing vines and niched saints. It overlooks a second plaza, **La Alameda**, much like the adjoining Zócalo, filled with scenes of mercantile zeal. The cathedral's neoclassical interior hosts an Italian statute by Tadoini depicting Nuestra Señora de Asunción, to whom the structure is dedicated.

On the northern edge of the Alameda, **Avenida Independencia** is an important east–west avenue. Here, you'll find the **Museo de los Pintores Oaxaqueños** ① *Independencia 607 y Vigil, T516-5645, www.museodelospintores.blogspot.mx, Tue-Sat 1000-2000, Sun 1000-1800, US$1.50*, one of the city's most influential galleries, showcasing local artists, past and present. A few blocks east, the **Teatro Macedonio Alcalá** ① *Armenta y López y Independencia*, is a Versaille-style theatre from Porfirio Díaz's times, boasting a Louis XV-style entrance and a white marble staircase; regular performances are held here. One block south and one block east of the theatre, you'll find the **Museo Textil de Oaxaca** ① *Hidalgo 917, T951-501 1104, www.museotextildeoaxaca.org.mx, Mon-Sat 1000-2000, Sun 1000-1800, free; guided tours in English or Spanish on Wed 1700-1800*. It houses six private collections of several hundred pieces of fine hand-woven Oaxaqueña textiles. One block south and one block west, on Guerrero, the sand-coloured Templo de San Agustín has a fine façade with a bas relief depicting St Augustine holding the City of God above adoring monks. It is apparently modelled on that of San Agustín in Mexico City, now the National Library.

Parallel to Independencia, you'll find several sites of interest on and around **Avenida Morelos**. Established in 1974 with donations from the Oaxacan painter Rufino Tamayo, the **Museo de Arte Prehispánico Rufino Tamayo** ① *Morelos 503, T951-516 7617, Mon, Wed-Sat 1000-1400, 1600-1900, Sun 1000-1500, US$3*, boasts an outstanding and well-presented private collection of pre-Columbian artefacts dating from 1250 BC to AD 1100, including numerous ghoulish urns from the Gulf coast region; information is in Spanish only. Near here is the **Casa de la Ciudad** ① *Porfirio Díaz 115, esq Morelos, T951-516 9648, www.casadelaciudad.org*, an education and cultural centre offering courses, talks, conferences, film screenings and temporary exhibitions relating to the life and function of the city. Several blocks further west on Morelos, the massive 17th-century **Basílica de La Soledad** has a complex façade, one of the finest works of masonry in the city. Building of the church began in 1682 and was completed in 1690; note the characteristically low bell towers designed to withstand earthquakes. Inside, you can see the Virgen de la Soledad, the revered patron saint of Oaxaca. At the back of the church, the **Museo Religioso de la Soledad** ① *Independencia 107, daily 0900-1400 and 1600-1900, US$0.35 donation requested*, has a display of religious artefacts. Refreshments and ice cream are sold in the small plaza beyond the encircling wall.

South of the Zócalo and Avenida Independencia, the city is increasingly gritty and down-to-earth, its lightly crumbling working-class neighbourhoods peppered with unpretentious family-run eateries, budget hotels, and men-only *cantinas*. The busy street of 20 de Noviembre is one of the city's main southbound thoroughfares and is close to several of the city's famous markets; see below. At the corner of 20 de Noviembre and Aldama stands the **Iglesia de San Juan de Dios**, originally dedicated to Santa Catalina Mártir and today painted red. Inside, there is an indigenous mural of the conquistadors' arrival in the

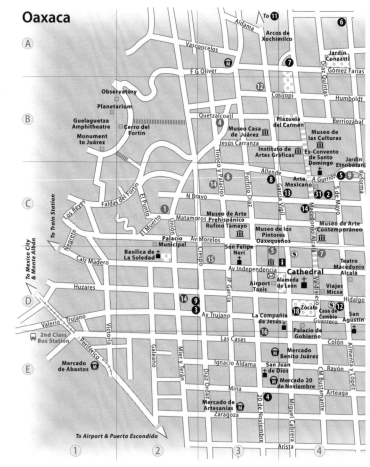

Oaxaca

region and an anti-Catholic uprising in 1700. At the junction of 20 de Noviembre and Mina, you'll catch the rich aroma of freshly milled cacao mixed with almond and cinnamon. Here, several stores serve cups of delicious hot and cold chocolate, as well as pre-packaged beans and powder. Brands include **Mayordomo**, **Guelaguetza** and **La Soledad**, and these same outlets sell Oaxacan *mole* – a thick paste used for preparing sauces.

By contrast, the neighbourhoods north of the Zócalo and Avenida Independencia are clean, ordered, aesthetic, and almost entirely gentrified. Between brightly painted townhouses and immaculately restored colonial churches, you'll find middle-class residences and thriving local businesses, including the lion's share of upscale hotels, restaurants, bars, and coffee houses. Running north from the Zócalo's west side, Calle García Vigil leads to the former home of the Zapotec president and Liberal reformer Benito

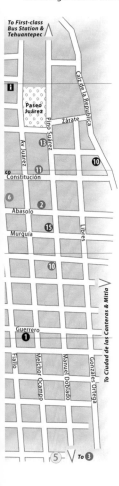

N

200 metres
200 yards

Where to stay 🛏
Azucenas 1 *C2*
Azul 2 *C5*
Azul Cielo 3 *E5*
Casa Angel
  Youth Hostel 4 *B3*
Casa Cid de León 5 *D3*
Casa de las
  Bugambilias 6 *C5*
Casa de Siete Balcones 7 *D4*
Casa del Sótano 8 *C3*
Casa Oaxaca 9 *C4*
El Diablo y La Sandía 10 *D5*
Hostal Casa del
  Sol Oaxaca 11 *C5*
La Casona de Tita 12 *B2*
Las Mariposas 13 *B5*
Los Golondrinas 14 *C3*
Posada del Centro 15 *D3*

El Morocco 6 *A4*
El Quinque 7 *A4*
Hostería de Alcalá 14 *C4*
La Coronita 9 *D2*
Los Danzantes 31 *C4*
Luvina 10 *B5*
Mercado Pochote 11 *A3*
Origen Oaxaca 12 *D4*
Zincanda 13 *C4*

Bars & clubs 🍸
Café Central 14 *D2*
La Candela 15 *C5*
La Farola 16 *D3*

Restaurants 🍴
Asador Vasco 18 *D4*
Café Alex 3 *D2*
Café Bistrot Epicuro 1 *D5*
Café Brújala 8 *C3*
Café Los Cuiles 2 *C4*
Café Mayordomo 4 *E3*
Casa Oaxaca 5 *C4*

ON THE ROAD

Art galleries and photography studios

In addition to the state-managed art museums, the **Museo de Arte Contemporáneo** and the **Museo de los Pintores Oaxaqueños** (see page 63), there are a number of small private galleries and graphic institutes, many more than can be listed here.

Arte de Oaxaca, Murguía 105, T951-514 1532, www.artedeoaxaca.com. Partly founded by Rudolfo Morales, a famous artist from Ocotlán (see page 87), this long-running commercial gallery has good exhibits by local talents.

Centro Fotográfico Alvarez Bravo, Bravo y García Vigil, T951-516 9800, www.cfmab.org. Excellent and changing exhibitions by national and international photographers. They have a library and host regular workshops too.

Galería Quetzalli, Constitución 104-1, T951-514 2606, www.galeriasquetzalli.com. Established in 1986, this renowned art gallery features fine contemporary work by an impressive stable of gifted locals, including Fransisco Toledo.

Instituto de Artes Gráficas de Oaxaca, Alcalá 507, www.institutodeartesgraficas deoaxaca.blogspot.mx, Wednesday-Monday 0900-2000, donation requested. This is housed in a grand old 18th-century building. It has interesting exhibitions of national artists, a good reference library and beautiful courtyards.

La Mano Mágica, Alcalá 203, www.lamanomagica.com.mx. Founded in 1987, La Mano Mágica represents some of the finest of Oaxaca's creative community with superb galleries of popular and contemporary art, including the highest quality textile collection in Oaxaca. In addition to selling *artesanía*, original art and prints, they host graphics and ceramics workshops, and can organize weaving demonstrations.

Juárez, now the pleasant but relatively modest **Museo Casa de Juárez** ⓘ *García Vigil 609, daily 1000-1800, US$3*. It contains some of his possessions, historical documents and some bookbinding tools. At the northern end of the street you'll find the **Arcos de Xochimilco**, the remains of an old aqueduct complete with arches and cobbled passageways. Here, it's worth perusing the fine crafts for sale at the **Instituto Oaxaqueño de las Artesanías (ARIPO)** (see Shopping, below).

One block east of García Vigil, Calle Macedonio Alcalá is the city's most important north–south thoroughfare, joining the Zócalo with the church of Santo Domingo (see below). This entirely pedestrianized cobblestone street has a procession of fine restaurants, coffee shops, craft shops, museums and art galleries, including the excellent **Museo de Arte Contemporáneo** ⓘ *Alcalá 202, www.museomaco.com, Wed-Mon 1030-2000, US$1.50, free Sun*, which exhibits modern art in a range of media. For more information on the city's many artistic establishments, see box, above.

★Markets

Both Oaxaca state and the city itself are famed for their arts and crafts, which can be seen at many of the central markets, including the **Mercado de Artesanías** in JP García and Zaragoza and Mercado Benito Juárez in 20 de Noviembre. They sell excellent handicrafts from the nearby villages or made in workshops in the city itself. The bustling 20 de

Noviembre offers pedestrian access to several pungent markets where you can observe the frenetic comings and goings of daily Oaxaqueña life, starting with **Mercado Benito Juárez** and ending with the labyrinthine sprawl of **Mercado de Abastos**, west of the Perférico near the second class bus station (see Shopping, below). Oaxacan markets are also great for cheap and tasty food, such as the oversized tortillas known as *tlayudas* with all manner of fillings, and they are a good place to pick up Oaxacan specialities, such as coffee, chocolate, mole sauce and mescal. See also Shopping, below.

Templo y Ex-Convento de Santo Domingo

★Dedicated to Santo Domingo de Guzmán, the founder and spiritual father of the Spanish Dominican order, this lavish church and its adjoining monastic complex are among the most aesthetic Baroque structures in Mexico. Located at the northern end of Calle Alcalá, opposite a busy plaza planted with rows of spikey maguey plants, work on their construction began in 1570 and lasted two centuries. They were occupied by Dominican friars from 1608 to 1857, later serving as a military barracks during Mexico's revolutionary conflicts. From 1902, the church reverted to religious use. The former monastery, now under the control of the Universidad Benito Juárez, was converted into a cultural complex and museum in 1972 (see below). In 1993, the church underwent a six-year restoration programme, which included the decoration of its interior with some 60,000 sheets of 23.5 karat gold leaf. The result is stunning and must be to seen to be believed (no flash photography please).

Museo de las Culturas
Tue-Sun 1000-1815, US$4.50, video US$3, no flash photography. Displays are in Spanish. A very good but antiquated English language audio guide is available and recommended, US$3.85.

The colonial courtyards and arcades of the ex-Convento de Santo Domingo supply an appropriately theatrical backdrop to the city's big history and culture museum, established in 1972 and sometimes referred to as 'the Louvre of Oaxaca'. Fourteen galleries cover the development of the state from Pre-Hispanic times to the contemporary period, exploring themes such as 'Millenary Cultures', 'Order and Progress' and 'Cultural Plurality'. The colonial-era art and antiques are interesting enough, but the museum's real treasures are the artefacts recovered from Tomb 7 in Monte Albán, including dazzling jewellery and funerary decorations fashioned from gold, pearls and jade. Look out of the human skull adorned in turquoise, thought to have been a receptacle of sorts. Other archaeological artefacts include an astonishing array of Mixtec urns in the form of cross-legged figures representing gods, calendar signs and alter-egos.

Jardín Etnobótanico
Reforma s/n esq. Constitución, T951-516 5325, www.jardinoaxaca.org.mx, guided tours in Spanish daily, 1000-1100, 1200-1300, 1700-1800, US$3.85; in English, Tue, Thu and Sat 1100-1300, 1 hr, US$7.70.

Established in 1994 with the help of local artist Francisco Toledo, the city's ethnobotanical garden protects a superb regional plant collection of mostly wild natives arranged by ecological and cultural themes. Illustrating the role of different species in the daily lives of Oaxaca's various ethnic groups, local gardeners and shamans contributed to the garden's design. Specimens includes robust barrel, prickly pear and candelabra cacti, grand balsa and ceiba trees, cacao, vanilla, achiote, and many, many other flora used in everything from *mezcal* production to textile dyes to herbal medicine. Bridge, fountains, walkways and other landscaped details complement the collection. Sadly, bio-pirates pilfered some of the rarer species and now the only way to see the garden is on a guided tour.

Beyond the Centro Histórico

There is a grand view from **Cerro de Fortín**, the hill to the northwest of the centre. Here, you will find the famous **Guelaguetza amphitheatre** (see box, page 77), an **observatory**, a **planetarium**, and a **monument to Juárez** on a hillside below. Take care, as muggings have been reported on the trails that go through the woods, as well as on the dirt road. If you don't have your own vehicle, it is best to take a taxi up the hill and ask them to wait until you're ready to return.

On Calzada Niños Héroes de Chapultepec, at the east end of Calzada Eduardo Vasconcelos, you'll find **Ciudad de las Canteras**, where stone was extracted from quarries for the city's monumental churches and public buildings. The site has been converted into a beautifully landscaped park with a small stadium. It also stages the Expo Feria Oaxaca, a seasonal fair with rides, craft exhibits and live performances (check with the tourist information office for dates).

Monte Albán → *Colour map 1, A1.*

hilltop ruined Zapotec stronghold

★Monte Albán is situated about 10 km (20 minutes) west of Oaxaca, on a hilltop dominating the surrounding valley. It features pyramids, walls, terraces, tombs, staircases and sculptures of the ancient capital of the Zapotec culture, and the ruins were declared a UNESCO World Heritage Site in 1987.

Site information Daily 0800-1800. US$4.40; US$3 to use video cameras; optional guided tour costs around US$20 per group, ask several and beware of overcharging. To get there, buses and shuttles depart every 30-60 minutes, US$4 return with **Autobuses Turísticos** ⓘ *Mina 501, T951-516 6175, and from the opposite side of the street with Lescas Co, Mina 518, inside Hotel Rivera Angel, T951-516 0666. Last return bus at 1700.*

Although the city of Monte Albán extended far beyond the confines of the **Main Plaza**, it is this particular place that archaeologists, art historians, historians and tourists have looked to, when assessing and interpreting the raison d'être of this fascinating site. Constructed 400 m up a steep mountain, without immediate access to water or cultivable land, the Main Plaza has at times been considered the site of a regional marketplace or ceremonial centre. The marketplace theory becomes less convincing when access to the site is considered: not only would the visitor have had to haul merchandise up the back-breaking hill, but entrance to the plaza was severely restricted. In ancient times the only way into the site was through three narrow passageways, which could easily have been guarded to restrict entry. The modern ramp cuts across what was the ball court to the southeast of the **North Platform**. The space at the centre of the Main Plaza would seem ideal for religious ceremonies and rituals but the absence of religious iconography contradicts this interpretation. The imagery at Monte Albán is almost exclusively militaristic, with allusions to tortured prisoners and captured settlements.

Monte Albán

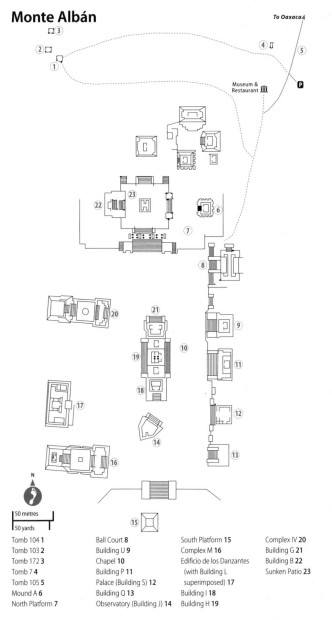

To Oaxaca

Museum & Restaurant

Tomb 104 **1**	Ball Court **8**	South Platform **15**	Complex IV **20**
Tomb 103 **2**	Building U **9**	Complex M **16**	Building G **21**
Tomb 172 **3**	Chapel **10**	Edificio de los Danzantes	Building B **22**
Tomb 7 **4**	Building P **11**	(with Building L	Sunken Patio **23**
Tomb 105 **5**	Palace (Building S) **12**	superimposed) **17**	
Mound A **6**	Building Q **13**	Building I **18**	
North Platform **7**	Observatory (Building J) **14**	Building H **19**	

To the right, before getting to the ruins, is **Tomb 7**, where a fabulous treasure trove was found in 1932. Most items are now in the Museo de las Culturas de Oaxaca (see page 67) and the entrance is closed off by a locked gate. **Tomb 172** has been left exactly as it was found, with skeleton and urns still in place, but these are not visible. Tombs 7 and 172 are permanently closed.

There are trilingual (Spanish, English and Zapotec) signs throughout the site, as well as a good **museum** (explanations in Spanish only), exhibiting stone glyphs and sculptures as well as smaller artefacts. Note that flash photography is prohibited. Informative literature and videos in several languages are sold in the visitor centre bookshop, which also houses a small restaurant. From the ruins at Monte Albán there are paths leading to the valleys below. If you're in reasonable shape, consider hiring a bike for the day.

Main Plaza

The Main Plaza at Monte Albán is delineated north and south by the two largest structures in the city, which have been interpreted as palace and/or public building (North Platform) and temple (South Platform). Apart from these two impressive structures, the ball court and the arrow-shaped building in front of the South Platform, the Main Plaza has 14 other structures, six along the west side, three in the middle and five along the east side. One structure, known as **Edificio de los Danzantes** (Dancers), has bas-reliefs, glyphs and calendar signs. During the period AD 450-600, Monte Albán had 14 districts beyond the confines of the Main Plaza: it has been proposed that each of the 14 structures located within the Main Plaza corresponded with one of the 14 districts outside. Each pertained to a distinct ethnic group or polity, brought together to create a pan-regional confederacy or league. The arrow-shaped structure functioned as a military showcase; it also has astronomical connotations.

Confederacy

The presence of a number of structures in, or bordering, the Main Plaza that housed representatives of distinct ethnic groups supports the theory that Monte Albán came into being as the site of a confederacy or league. Its neutral position, unrelated to any single polity, lends credence to this suggestion. The absence of religious iconography, which might have favoured one group over the others, emphasizes the secular role of the area, while the presence of the Danzantes sculptures suggests a trophy-gathering group. However, although Monte Albán may have served defensive purposes, the presence of the Danzantes and the captured town glyphs argues for an offensive and expansionist role. In all, about 310 stone slabs depicting captives, some of whom are sexually mutilated with streams of blood (flowers) flowing from the mutilated parts, have been found. Some of these woeful captives are identified by name glyphs, which imply hostilities against a settlement and the capture of its warriors. The fact that most of them are nude denotes the disdain and contempt with which they were treated by their captors: nudity was considered shameful and undignified by the peoples of Mesoamerica. It is very likely that the rulers of Monte Albán were determined to bring into the confederacy as many polities as possible in order to extract tribute, which would permit the expansion of the capital. The growth of Monte Albán was a direct response to events in the Valley of Mexico, where Teotihuacán was exercising dominion over most of the area. Although Monte Albán had been developing a policy of offence and capture as early as 200 BC, the growth of the city really gained impetus with the growth of Teotihuacán, whose administrators must have cast an avaricious eye on the rich soil of the Valley of Oaxaca. From the ceramics and architecture analysed at Monte Albán, it is clear that Teotihuacán never realized its ambitions in that area; the confederacy functioned well.

Collapse

Monte Albán reached its maximum size around AD 600, with a population estimated at between 15,000 and 30,000. Shortly after, the city changed dramatically in form and function. There was an 80% decrease in population, the Main Plaza was abandoned and the majority of the people moved nearer to the valley floor, but behind protective walls. They were much closer to major roads, implying that Monte Albán was now becoming more commercially minded and aspired to be self-sufficient, which it had never been in its long history.

The abandonment of the Main Plaza was a direct result of the collapse of the political institution centred there. This collapse has been seen as a consequence of the fact that, beginning early in the seventh century AD, Teotihuacán was already showing signs of decadence. Gaining momentum, the decadence led to the massive abandonment of that great centre. It is unlikely to have been coincidental that the Main Plaza at Monte Albán was abandoned around this time. The removal of the Teotihuacán threat made redundant the Confederacy that was so costly to maintain: the collapse was complete.

Listings Oaxaca City *map p64*

Tourist information

Sectur tourist office
Av Juárez 703, T951-502 1200,
www.oaxaca.travel. Daily 0800-2000.
This office has maps, brochures, flyers and information about both city and state; additional Sectur modules can be found in the Museo de los Pintores, the Teatro Alcalá, and the 1st class **ADO** bus terminal.

There is also a helpful **municipal tourist office** (Matamoros 102, T951-516 8299) with an additional location opposite the Cathedral. For topographical maps, visit the **Instituto Nacional de Estadística** (Geografía e Informática (INEGI), Emiliano Zapata 316, corner of Escuela Naval Militar, T951-512 4823). Useful websites include *Oaxaca Times,* www.oaxacatimes.com; *Oaxaca Nuestro,* www.oaxacanuestro.com; and Ron Mader's excellent ecotourism portal, Planeta, www.planeta.com.

Where to stay

For budget hotels and *posadas*, try the block formed by the streets Mina, Zaragoza, Díaz Ordaz and JP García; also on Trujano (4 blocks from the Zócalo).

$$$$ Casa Oaxaca
Garcia Vigil 407, T951-514 4173,
www.casaooaxaca.com.mx.
A beautifully renovated colonial townhouse with a variety of boutique rooms and suites, all stylish, modern and impeccably presented. The property features a shady patio, pool, garden terrace, and library. Spa treatments are offered, including massage, *temazcal* (steam bath), and manicures. Romantic and aesthetic. Recommended.

$$$$ Hotel Azul
Abasolo 313, T951-501 0016,
www.hotelazuloaxaca.com.
Tastefully decorated with crisp contemporary furnishings, this modern boutique hotel has swish suites and tidy standards, all overlooking a sunny central courtyard with cacti and shady trees. On the roof, there's a breezy bar and terrace overlooking the city, perfect for an evening tipple of mescal. Creative restaurant, worth a look.

$$$$ La Casona de Tita
Garcia Virgil 805, T951-516 1400,
www.hotelcasonadetita.com.
Stylish, tranquil and secluded, **La Casona de Tita** is a renovated 19th-century mansion with 6 spacious boutique rooms overlooking

a terracotta courtyard; they feature great art work by local talent. Tasteful and eco-friendly with all the mod cons. Recommended.

$$$$-$$$ Casa Cid de León
Av Morelos 602, 2 blocks from the Zócalo, T951-516 0414, www.casaciddeleon.com.
This intimate and interesting boutique hotel offers 4 different suites, all luxurious and lavishly decorated. The service is first rate and personal, overseen by the gracious and hospitable Leticia Ricárdez. The hotel also organizes tours and offers massage. Low season and longer stay discounts. Highly recommended.

$$$$-$$$ Casa de Las Bugambilias
Calle de la Reforma 522, T951-514 9536, www.lasbugambilias.com.
Adorned with antiques and local folk art, **Casa de Las Bugambilias** is a fabulous B&B managed by the Cabrera family. They offer 8 comfortable, modern, minimalist rooms and a 2-bedroom suite. Additionally, the family manages 2 other quality establishments: **Casa de Los Milagros**, a restored colonial house with just 3 rooms; and **El Secreto** with 4 rooms and rooftop deck. Rates include a gourmet breakfast. Recommended.

$$$ Casa del Sótano
Tinoco y Palacios 414, T951-516 2494, www.hoteldelsotano.com.mx.
Casa del Sótano is a 3 storey house dating to the late 18th century. Rooms overlook a central courtyard and feature lots of traditional colonial finishes: wood beams, terracotta tiled floors, handsome stonework and locally sourced antique furniture. The roof terrace has panoramic views over the city.

$$$ Casa de Siete Balcones
Morelos 800, T951-516 0133, www.casadesietebalcones.com.
Dating from the 16th century, a very historic and centrally located house with lots of attractive architectural details. They have 7 unique rooms, simple, bright, tasteful and adorned with good, solid, handmade furniture. Helpful and friendly staff.

$$$ El Diablo y La Sandía
Libres 205, T951-514 4095, www.eldiabloylasandia.com.
Managed by a friendly mother and daughter team, **El Diablo y La Sandía** is a homely bed and breakfast set inside a colonial house. They offer 5 beautifully attired rooms with rustic furniture, naïve art, and folkloric flourishes. They can also organize paragliding flights and have their own brand of mescal.

$$ Azucenas
Aranda 203, T951-514 7918, www.hotelazucenas.com.
A Canadian-owned colonial house with simple, cheery rooms overlooking a central patio. Upstairs, there's a lovely rooftop terrace with a self-service bar and views. Donna, the owner, studied anthropology and provides information about local communities. Located in a pleasant neighbourhood about 6 blocks from the main square.

$$ Las Mariposas
Pino Suárez 517, T951-515 5854, www.hotellasmariposas.com.
A quiet, friendly hotel with a pleasant garden patio and sun roof upstairs. They have a range of rooms and self-catering studio apartments; those downstairs are cool and shady. Staff are thoughtful and helpful. Breakfast included, bike rental available. Recommended.

$$ Los Golondrinas
Tinoco y Palacios 411, T951-514 3298, www.lasgolondrinasoaxaca.com.
This family-run hotel has simple, pleasant rooms set around 3 leafy patios. Lots of potted plants and trees that provide shade, oxygen and a sense of well-being. Friendly, lush, quiet and tranquil.

$$ Posada del Centro
Independencia 403, T951-516 1874,
www.hotelposadadelcentro.com.
This pretty, colourful, locally owned *posada*
has 22 spacious rooms set around courtyard;
6 of them have shared bath. A long-standing
favourite with travellers, very friendly, good
value and at the heart of the historic centre.
Organizes tours. Recommended.

$$-$ Azul Cielo
*Arteaga 608, Entre Gonzales Ortega y
Manuel Doblado, T951-205 3564,*
www.azulcielohostel.mex.tl.
Chilled out and homely hostel 10 mins
from the Zócalo. Accommodation includes
mixed and single-sex dorms with 8 beds ($),
and private rooms ($$). Lots of amenities
including garden, Wi-Fi, DVD library, bike
rental, cinema club and free salsa classes
on Sat. Simple breakfast included.

$$-$ Casa Angel Youth Hostel
Tinoco y Palacios 610, T951-514 2224,
www.casaangelhostel.com.
An immaculately clean and tidy hostel
with small mixed and single-sex dorms
($) and comfortable private rooms ($$).
Amenities include an excellent rooftop
terrace (very popular in the evenings), a
well-equipped kitchen, and a chilled-out
common area. Good tourist info, Wi-Fi
and breakfast included. Great place, lots
of attention to detail, a cut above the rest
and recommended.

$$-$ Hostal Casa del Sol Oaxaca
Constitución 301, T951-514 4110,
www.hostalcasadelsol.com.mx.
A very relaxed, hospitable and intimate
hostel, well presented and calm. Rooms are
individually themed, simple, tasteful and
attractive. Dorms are spacious and contain
only a few beds. No televisions, just good
books and a tranquil inner patio. Simple,
healthy breakfast is included. Good reports,
recommended, especially for couples.

The most popular place to eat *tlayudas*
(oversized tortillas) and other local snacks
in the evening is from stalls and restaurants
along Aldama, between Cabrera and 20
de Noviembre.

$$$ Asador Vasco
*Above Bar Jardín, Portal de Flores 10-A,
T951-514 4755, www.asadorvasco.com.*
Something of a Oaxaca institution, located
at the heart of the action on the Zócalo.
They serve good regional drinks and dishes,
including mescal and grasshoppers with
guacamole, as well as international fare and
Basque food. Good service and atmosphere
with live Mexican music in the evening.
At busy times, you should book ahead for
balcony views.

$$$ Café Bistrot Epicuro
T951-514 9750, Guerrero 319.
A refined Italian restaurant serving flavourful
handmade pastas, raviolis, seafood,
lasagne, lamb chop and authentic pizzas
baked in wood-fired ovens. Don't miss the
sumptuous desserts or the stock of wine.
Stylish, modern, classy and romantic.

$$$ Casa Oaxaca
*Calle Constitución 104-A, T951-516 8531,
www.casaoaxacaelrestaurante.com.*
Casa Oaxaca, where food is art. This
award-winning establishment specializes in
Oaxaqueña regional delicacies, often with a
contemporary twist. Main courses include
organic rabbit with yellow *mole* sauce from
Pinotepa and lamb chops with garlic and
guajillo chile sauce from the Mixteca region.
Superb courtyard setting, excellent service
and food, earning this place the reputation
as one of the best in town. Reservations very
necessary, popular with artists and writers.

$$$ Hostería de Alcalá
*Macedonio Alcalá 307, T951-516 2093,
www.hosteriadealcala.com.*
Another Oaxaca institution, established
decades ago and patronized more by

Mexicans than foreigners. They serve excellent Mexican and Oaxaqueña cuisine in a beautiful colonial courtyard. Popular dishes include *tlayudas* with *mole*, *chiles rellenos* and grasshoppers. Attentive service, impeccable setting and quiet atmosphere. Not cheap.

$$$ Luvina
Martires de Tacubaya 517, T951-132 5912, www.luvinaoaxaca.wix.com/luvina. Closed Mon.
Creative fusion cuisine served in a delightful aesthetic space. Chef Carlos García draws inspiration from local and international sources to create intriguing courses like snook confit with fennel oil and braised quinoa and *xoconostle*. Ideal for a special or romantic evening meal. Off the beaten track a few blocks, but well worth tracking down.

$$$ Origen Oaxaca
Hidalgo 820, www.origenoaxaca.com.
Fresh, creative and contemporary gastronomy from chef Rodolfo Castellanos. Beautifully presented dishes include delicious ceviche, roast octopus salad, duck and lentil stew, goat confit, pork loin, quail, organic chicken and catch of the day. A handsome colonial setting and good reports.

$$$-$$ Los Danzantes
Macedonio Alcalá 403, www.los danzantes.com. Open 1430-2330.
Los Danzantes belongs to a group of companies dedicated to 'heightening Mexico's gastronomic and cultural riches', including 3 restaurants and an artisan mescal distillery. Their Oaxaca City restaurant serves fine Mexican fusion cuisine in a stylish colonial courtyard. The well-stocked bar is particularly good.

$$$-$$ Zincanda
García Vigil 409A.
A young, fun, dynamic restaurant serving interesting contemporary Oaxaqueña cuisine, some of it quite innovative and experimental. Directing the kitchen is chef Yiannis Rojas, a Oaxaca local who

trained and worked in the US and Mexico City. His offerings include chicken stuffed with cheese and grasshoppers, plantain dumplings in black *mole*, succulent pork belly, and grilled octopus with basil pesto. Reflecting its creative ethos, the restaurant boasts a bold mural and modern decor. Often buzzing, a good one for foodies.

$$ El Morocco
Reforma 905, www.elmoroccocafe.com. Tue-Sun 0800-2300.
As the name might suggest, authentic Moroccan and Mediterranean dishes, including couscous, falafel, kefta, humus and baklava. For a casual bite, there's also some European and American staples, including bagels, burgers, and sandwiches. A good clean place, and a pleasant change from Mexican food.

$$ El Quinque
Macedonio Alcalá 901, esq Gómez Farías.
This family-run, slightly quirky and chilled out little restaurant on the corner serves really good home-cooked food in generous portions. Mum works the kitchen, sons work the front of house. Fare is international, including excellent burgers and fish and chips. Great place, very friendly. Recommended.

$$-$ Café Alex
Díaz Ordaz 218 y Trujano.
A good option for budget travellers seeking simple, local food at low prices. Over 20 different breakfasts are offered at this long-standing eatery, including pancakes with fruit and various Oaxacan specialities. There's also a good *comida corrida* at lunchtime with 4 different menus to choose from. Modest, cheap and unpretentious, but the parrots in the cages want to be free.

$$-$ La Coronita
Díaz Ordaz 208, below Hotel Valle de Oaxaca.
Much more popular with locals than tourists, especially on Sun, this long-established, homely and affordable restaurant serves an array of tasty Oaxacan specialities, including

various *mole*-based recipes. One of the oldest restaurants in town, the place to sample home-cooked regional cuisine in the company of Mexicans.

$ Mercado 20 de Noviembre
Calle 20 de Noviembre, between Aldama and Las Casas.
This indoor market is the place for ultra-economical grub, lovingly dished up by *señoras* at an array of informal comedores. Pick a stall that looks clean and popular and pull up a stool; Comedor Típico La Abuelita is a good one.

$ Mercado Pochote
Outside the Templo de Santo Tomás, Barrio Xochimilco. Fri and Sat, breakfast and lunch only.
Staged in the aesthetic locale of a tranquil neighbourhood churchyard, **Mercado Pochote** is a superb weekly farmers' market that showcases delicious local produce, including honey, sweets, fresh fruit and veg, juices, preserves and coffee. Don't miss the home-cooked regional cuisine, including Mixtec tacos and other wholesome fare. Very relaxed, pleasant, and highly recommended, especially for foodies.

Cafés

Café Brújula
García Vigil 409D, www.cafebrujula.com.
The place for really excellent, carefully sourced Oaxacan coffee, as well as smoothies, sandwiches, and other freshly prepared, home-made snacks. American-owned, friendly and popular with local artists, they are passionate about coffee. There are several branches, the one at Alcalá 104 has a colonial courtyard. Recommended.

Café Los Cuiles
Labastida 115, www.cuiles.com.
A breezy little café with Oaxacan art work on the wall. A good place to tap away on your laptop. Very friendly and popular with gringos.

Café Mayordomo
Alcalá 302, www.casamayordomo.com.mx.
Don't leave Oaxaca without trying its sumptuous hot chocolate. Mayordomo is one of the big local producers and their swish café on Alcalá serves cups of it with sweet bread or dessert, if you desire. Their adjoining restaurant serves decent regional cuisine too. For something lower key, there is another café on Calle 20 de Noviembre, bustling with locals.

Bars and clubs

You can drink *mezcal* in some form at any bar in the city. For specialist outlets that deal in artisan varieties, you'll want a *mezcalería* (see What to do, below).

Café Central
Hidalgo 302, www.colectivocentral.com. Wed-Sat from 2100.
Café Central is a hub for local artists and bohemians, an alternative social space that hosts live music, theatre, exhibitions and art house films. Great bar and kitsch decor, including a wall-mounted swordfish and French horns. Recommended.

La Candela
Murguía 413 y Pino Suárez.
The candlelit courtyard of a handsome colonial house is the stage for this swinging Latin dance club. Salsa, merengue and live music from 2200. Popular with visitors and locals, cover US$5. Dance classes available during the week.

La Casa de Mezcal
Flores Magón 209, in front of the market.
This hugely popular and often crowded traditional *cantina* features ornate carved wood furnishings and hammy murals of the Aztec empire. Naturally, they serve the liquor of their namesake, but a lot of the locals just drink beer. Occasional karaoke.

La Farola
20 de Noviembre 3C. Daily 1000-0200.
Fans of the English novelist Malcolm Lowry

should look out for the heavy wooden doors of **La Farola**, a dark and spirited *cantina* that was (according to unverified local lore) the inspiration for his grotesque alcoholic masterpiece, *Under the Volcano*. It is a very atmospheric old building with a good stock of mescal, lots of ghosts and a relaxed crowd. Occasional live music.

Entertainment

Folkloric dancing

Several hotels regularly host Guelaguetza-style shows, the most convenient way to observe Oaxaca's wide variety of folkloric dances:

Casa de Cantera, *Murguía 102, T951-514 9522, www.casadecantera.com*. Live dance and music performances every evening at 2030 with a minimum of 20 reservations. The show costs US14, with dinner US$27.

Hotel Monte Albán, *Alameda de León 1, T951-516 2777*. Nightly performances to recorded music in the hotel's handsome colonial courtyard at 2030, 90 mins, US$7, photography permitted. Book if you can. Special group prices.

Quinta Real Oaxaca, *5 de Mayo 300, T951-501 6100, www.quintareal.com*. Every Fri at 1900, the **Quinta Real** hosts a 3-hr dance extravaganza with live music, a range of crafts, 20 performers on a stage, and a dinner buffet with typical Oaxaqueña cuisine, US$30 per person, the best.

Festivals

Jul Guelaguetza, also called **Los Lunes del Cerro**, is the city's most important festival. A festive atmosphere permeates the city for more than 2 weeks, particularly the last 2 Mon of the month (see box, opposite).

Oct El Señor del Rayo, a 9-day event in the 3rd week of Oct, including excellent fireworks.

2 Nov Day of the Dead, a mixture of festivity and solemn commemoration, best appreciated at the Panteón General (main cemetery). Always ask before photographing. In recent years Oaxaca has hosted a rugby 'tournament of death' in conjunction with the festival; for information, www.planeta.com.

8-18 Dec Fiesta de la Soledad, patroness of Oaxaca, with fine processions centred around the Basílica and throughout the city.

Dec During the 9 days before Christmas, the **Novenas** are held. Groups of people go asking for shelter, *posada*, as Joseph and Mary did, and are invited into different homes. This is done in the centre as well as other neighbourhoods like San Felipe (5 km north) and at Xoxo, to the south. The *posadas* culminate on the night of 24 Dec with what is known as **Calendas**, a parade of floats representing allegories from the birth of Christ; every church in town prepares a float honouring its patron saint, the groups from all the parishes converging at the cathedral at 2300 (best seen from balcony of the restaurants around the Zócalo; go for supper and get a window table).

23 Dec Noche de Rábanos, outside the Palacio de Gobierno, is a unique contest of figures carved out of radishes. Stands made of flowers and corn stalks have been added in recent years to this old tradition.

Shopping

Artesanía and produce

In addition to the co-operatives below, crafts can be purchased in souvenir shops on Alcalá, directly from village workshops or in the city's big markets (listed below).

Casa de las Artesanías, *Matamoros 105, Esq García Vigil, T951-516 5062, www.casa delasartesanias.com.mx*. This large, successful co-op displays the craftwork of 27 communities and 70 families. Offerings include fine *alebrijes*, weavings and pottery.

Instituto Oaxaqueño de las Artesanías, *García Vigil 809, T951-516 9211, www.artesaniasaripo.com*. Representing over 30,000 artisans across the state, this government-run shop is cheaper and

ON THE ROAD

Guelaguetza (Lunes del Cerro)

A well-organized large-scale folklore festival celebrating native traditions in Oaxaca state, held at the end of July, Guelaguetza is not to be missed. The word Guelaguetza originally means something like 'reciprocity' in Zapotec, the interchange of gifts or favours. Some elements of the celebration may well date from pre-Hispanic times.

The main event is a grand folk dance show held at the Guelaguetza stadium on the slopes of Cerro del Fortín, on Monday morning. The performance is lively and very colourful, with the city below serving as a spectacular backdrop.

Among the favourite presentations are always Flor de Piña, danced by women from the Tuxtepec area with a pineapple on their shoulder, and Danza de la Pluma, performed by men from the Central Valleys using enormous feather headdresses. The most elaborate costumes are those of the women from the Isthmus of Tehuantepec, including stiffly starched lace *resplandores* (halos) on their heads. At the end of each performance, gifts are thrown from the stage to the audience; watch out for the pineapples!

Los Lunes del Cerro are usually the last two Mondays in July. The performance begins at 0900 and ends around 1300. Tickets for seats in the lower galleries (A and B) are sold in advance through Sedetur and cost US$35. Details from the Oaxaca State Tourism Department, Murguía 206, Centro Histórico, Oaxaca, T(951) 514-8501. Advance tickets go on sale from early May. The upper galleries (C and D) are free, line up before 0600, gates open around 0700, the performance begins at 1000 and finishes around 1400. Take a sweater as it is chilly in the morning, but the sun is very strong later on. A sun hat and sunscreen are essential, a pair of binoculars is also helpful in the upper galleries. Drinks and snacks are sold.

In addition to the main event, there are scores of other happenings in Oaxaca at this time of year, ranging from professional cycling races to classical music concerts, a Feria del Mezcal, and several smaller celebrations in nearby villages. Many events are free and a complete programme is available from Sedetur. On the Saturday before Lunes del Cerro, at around 1800, participating groups parade down the pedestrian mall on Macedonio Alcalá, from Santo Domingo to the Zócalo. This is a good opportunity to see their splendid costumes close up and to meet the participants. On Sunday is the election of the Diosa Centeotl (goddess of the new corn), who presides over the following week's festivities. Candidates are chosen based on their knowledge of native traditions.

On Monday night, following the Guelaguetza, the Donají legend is presented in an elaborate torchlight performance at the same stadium starting around 2000. Donají was a Zapotec princess who fell in love with a Mixtec prince, Nucano, and eventually gave her life for her people. Some claim that the two lovers are buried in the same grave in Cuilapan de Guerrero.

better than most. It displays its products beautifully and service is good.

Mujeres Artesanas de las Regiones de Oaxaca (MARO), *5 de Mayo 204, T951-516 0670, www.mujeresartesanas.mex.tl. Daily 0900-2000*. A well-established regional association of Oaxacan craftswomen. Products include textiles, pottery and hammocks.

Unión de Palenqueros de Oaxaca, *Abasolo 510, T951-513 0485*. This modest co-operative represents a handful of local *mezcal* distillers with a decent variety of product on sale. You can also purchase bottles from some of the *mezcalerías* (below).

Bookshops

Amate, *Alcalá 307*. **Amate** is a form of paper bark produced in Mexico since pre-Columbian times for writing and record-keeping. This long-running store offers a great selection of English-language books about Mexican history and Oaxaqueña culture. Recommended.

Jewellery

Oro de Monte Albán, *Porfirio Díaz 311, T951-516 4528, www.orodemontealban.com*. In 1985, the National Institute of Anthropology and History granted permission to these jewellers to reproduce some of the gold pieces recovered from Tomb 7 at Monte Albán. Today, their output consists of specialist gold charms, brooches and bracelets made using the 'lost wax' technique. They offer tours of their workshop.

Markets

The city has several main markets, all of which are worth a visit, and several smaller ones; polite bargaining is the rule everywhere.

Mercado 20 de Noviembre, *Aldama on the corner of 20 de Noviembre, in the centre of town*. Clean stalls selling home-cooked meals, prepared foods, cheeses and baked goods. Try the *quesadillas de flor de calabaza* – pumpkin flower quesadillas, an excellent, filling snack.

Mercado Artesanal, *Zaragoza y JP García*. An indoor craft market with an array of hand-woven textiles.

Mercado Benito Juárez, *next door to Mercado 20 de Noviembre*. Household goods, fruits, vegetables, crafts and regional produce, such as *quesillo* (string cheese), bread and chocolate.

Mercado de Abastos, *also known as the Central de Abastos, near the 2nd-class bus station*. The largest market. A cacophony of sights, sounds and aromas, busiest on Sat and not to be missed. Prices here tend to be lower than in the smaller markets, and it's a good place to find cheap crafts.

What to do

Adventure and ecotourism

Expediciones Sierra Norte, *Manuel Bravo 210, T951-514 8271, www.sierranorte.org.mx*. This reputable ecotourism agency organizes expeditions to the mountains and Los Pueblos Mancomunados, 1-5 days in length. Activities include hiking, biking, zip-lining, traditional healing, community tourism and volunteering. Tours depart daily; call in advance for information and reservations.

Tierraventura, *Callejón del Carmen 108, T951-516 4644, www.tierraventura.com*. German and Swiss run, this long-standing and highly reputable ecotourism agency runs a range of tours all over the state, from the sierras to the coast. Wildlife, indigenous medicine, birds, botany and ecology are some of their environmentally aware themes. It's best to book at least a week in advance.

Cooking classes

Many language schools and restaurants offer cooking classes. We particularly recommend: **Seasons of my Heart**, *T951-508 0469, www. seasonsofmyheart.com*. Susana Trilling, the famous TV host, chef, teacher and writer, offers wide-ranging instruction in the sublime art of Oaxacan cooking with culinary

ON THE ROAD
Mescal

Mescal derives from the Nahuatl word for the agave plant, *metl*, more commonly known in Mexico as *maguey*. The drink dates from 16th-century Mexico. The natives were brewing a lightly alcoholic drink called *pulque* from agave juice, used in rituals and ceremonies. But the Spaniards were used to wine or beer with their meals, and it wasn't long before they started making mescal 'wine', using the distillation process brought over to Spain by the Moors several hundred years earlier. Despite this early start, mescal took some 400 years to develop into more than just small-scale distilling for local consumption and it wasn't until after the 1910 Mexican Revolution that production really took off. The main mescal-making territories are Oaxaca, Guerrero, Zacatecas, San Luis Potosí and Durango, with a few brands from Tamaulipas and Guanajuato. Two-thirds of mescal hails from Oaxacan soil and although up to 28 different varieties of agave can be used in the making, the *espadín* agave is by far the most popular, used in 90% of brands.

While tequila, from nearby Jalisco, is big business, mescal has remained low-key in comparison. Many producers, particularly in Oaxaca, are indigenous and keep production small scale and family-run, making mescal the traditional way. Due to the industrialization and production methods of tequila, quality and taste have become consistent, but with mescal this isn't always the case. Although larger scale production and regulations do exist, mescal from smaller producers – the home-made kind – is totally different.

To make mescal, traditionally, the thick stem-like leaves are chopped off, with a type of machete known as *coa*, leaving the heart of the plant, the *piña*, thus named for its resemblance to a pineapple. The *piñas* are baked or roasted in *palenques*, conical pits buried in the ground and lined with rocks. Wood is placed at the bottom of the pit, turning the rocks red hot when set alight. The *piñas* are added on top, covered with agave or palm leaves and finally a layer of earth. They are then left to cook for several days, absorbing the earthy and smoky flavours unique to mescal. After resting for up to a week, the *piñas* are mashed by a stone grinding wheel, drawn by a burro or horse. The resulting mash has pure water added to it and is left to ferment naturally, in wooden vats. At this stage sugars and other additives can be included in the mash, but by law it has to contain at least 80% agave. The alcohol content is similar to tequila, but some mescals are up to 50% proof or stronger. Once fermented, the pulp (*tepache*) yields a low-alcohol drink similar to *pulque*, which is double-, or even triple-distilled, to produce mescal. The finished product is divided into *abocado* (also known as *blanco* or *jóven*) bottled straight after distillation, *resposado* aged for up to 11 months, and finally *añejo* aged for at least 12 months.

tours and week-long courses. Half-day classes, including a trip to the market, every Wed, US$60.

Cycling

Bicicletas Pedro Martínez, *Aldama 418, T951-514 5935, www.bicicletaspedromartinez. com*. In addition to running personalized biking and hiking tours, this award-winning operator sells cycle supplies.

Zona Bici, *García Vigil 406, T951-516 0953, www.zonabici.com.mx. Mon-Sat 1000-1430 and 1630-2030*. Bike rental, including new aluminium frame bikes with good front suspension. They also sell bikes, along with general supplies. Tours are available, make reservations.

Mezcalerías

Sampling Oaxaca's many delicious varieties of high quality *mezcal* is a rewarding cultural experience best savoured at a leisurely pace. The city boasts scores of increasingly sophisticated *mezcalerías* that pride themselves on their collections; they will be happy to share their knowledge, enthusiasm and advice during your tasting session. The average cost is US$10-15 for 3 or 4 samples. For more information on *mezcal*, see box, page 79. Note: the evil moonshine informally available on the street in red gas tanks, although technically *mezcal*, is quite rough on the palate (not to mention the liver) and not recommended.

Cuish, *Díaz Ordaz 712, www.mezcalcuish. blogspot.com*. **Cuish** is dedicated to revitalizing local culture and communities through the manufacture, marketing and distribution of *mezcal*, including their own 9 varieties made from 9 species of maguey. They work with 39 palenqueros around the state and have a small bar where you can sample their offerings, or buy a bottle to take away.

In Situ, *Av Morelos 511, www.insitumezcaleria. com*. Founded by Ulises Torrentera, an author who has written about ancient *mezcal* cults, and Sandra Ortíz Brena, an editor, **In Situ** contains a collection of over 180 varieties of traditional and artisanal *mezcal*, some of them very obscure and hard to obtain, which together comprise the largest collection in the world. Recommended.

Language schools

There are many schools in the city which offer homestays to enhance learning. The following have been recommended:

Becari, *M Bravo 210, Plaza San Cristóbal, T951-514 6076, www.becari.com.mx, 4 blocks north of the Zócalo*. US$150 for a 15-hr week with fully qualified teachers. Courses including culture, history, literature and politics, with workshops on dancing, cooking or art, flexible programmes.

Instituto Cultural Oaxaca, *Av Juárez 909, T951-515 3404, www.icomexico.com*. In addition to Spanish classes, local crafts and culture (including dance, cooking, weaving and pottery) are taught. 4 hrs of formal Spanish teaching, 2 hrs spent in cultural workshops and 1 hr of informal conversation with a native speaker; US$178 per week.

Instituto de Comunicación y Cultura, *Escaleras del Fortín 105, T951-501 2359, www.iccoax.com*. Cultural workshops and field trips included in the programme, US$150 per week, 3 hrs per day. Also teaches specialized Spanish courses (eg medical and business Spanish) and indigenous languages.

Soléxico Language and Cultural Center, *Abasolo 217 y Juárez, T951-516 5680, www.solexico.com*. Programme with options for homestay, excursions and volunteering. Has branches in Playa del Carmen and Puerto Vallarta.

Los Amantes, *Allende 107, www.losamantes. com*. Using techniques that have not changed for 300 years, **Los Amantes** own brand of *mezcal* is produced in Tlacolula from a maguey species called *espadín*. Their bar stocks a wide variety of handmade *mezcal* and seeks to promote knowledge and admiration for the maguey plant and its derivatives. A successful brand.
Mezcaloteca, *Reforma 506, www. mezcaloteca.com. Open 1630-2200.*
Mezcaloteca offers a formal and educational tasting experience where you will be served 3 types of traditional *mezcal* and taught how to discern and appreciate their aromas and flavour. The production process will also be explained. Advance reservations recommended.

Tour operators

There are many in town, most running the same tours, daily to Monte Albán, El Tule, Mitla and city tours; Fri to Coyotepec, Jalietza and Ocotlán; Thu to Cuilapan and Zaachila; Sun to Tlacolula, Mitla and El Tule (for local markets). If visiting archaeological sites, check if entry is included.
Eugenio Cruz Castaneda, *T951-513 4790.* Offers excellent guided trips to Monte Albán, other archaeological sites and can arrange custom itineraries throughout Oaxaca state.
Viajes Xochitlán, *Garcia Vigil 617, T951-514 3271, www.xochitlan-tours.com.mx.* This reputable, well-established agency runs tours to the Central Valleys, visiting all the sights including Mitla and Hierve el Agua.

Transport

Air

Xoxocotlán (OAX) international airport is 8 km south of the city on the highway to Puerto Angel, T 951-511 5088, www.asur. com.mx. **Transporte Terrestre** *colectivos* from the airport to downtown cost US$4.60 per person; US$20 per vehicle. For collection to go to the airport, book

at Alameda de León No 1-G, opposite the cathedral, T951-511 5453.

Flights to **Mexico City** with **Aeroméxico, Interjet,** and **Volaris**; to **Huatulco, Puerto Escondido** and **Tuxtla Gutiérrez** with **Aerotucán**; to Monterrey with **VivaAerobus** and **Volaris**; to **Tijuana** with **Volaris**; to **Houston** with **United**. For more information on domestic flights, see page 507.

Bus

Local town minibuses mostly charge US$0.30. For the 1st-class bus terminal, buses marked 'VW' leave from Av Juárez; for the 2nd-class terminal, buses are marked 'Central'.

The **1st-class ADO terminal** is northeast of the Zócalo on Calzada Niños Héroes de Chapultepec (Highway 190) with left luggage facilities. **ADO, ADO GL, ADO Platino, OCC,** and **Cuenca** operate from here; taxi to/from centre US$2-3. Bus tickets can be purchased in advance from **Boletotal** at Valdivieso 2 and 20 de Noviembre 103. For journeys longer than 8 hrs, including **San Cristóbal de las Casas**, book 48 hrs in advance. **Note**: 1st class services to the Pacific coast go via the Isthmus of Tehuantepec, taking a long detour. 2nd-class services (see below) are more direct, 7-8 hrs, but involve a tortuous winding descent to sea level; pack Dramamine and a sick bag. *Colectivos* (see below) are the best and fastest option, 5-6 hrs, but also cramped and nauseating.

Services from the ADO terminal to **Bahías de Huatulco**, 5 daily, 8 hrs, US$28; **Mexico City**, hourly, 6 hrs, from US$43; **Pochutla**, 4 daily, 9-10 hrs, US$30; **Puerto Escondido**, 4 daily, 10-11 hrs, US$32; **San Cristóbal de las Casas**, 4 daily, 11 hrs, from US$46; **Tapachula**, 2 daily, 1910, 2100, 12 hrs, from US$41; **Tehuantepec**, hourly, 4½ hrs, US$20; **Villahermosa**, 3 daily, 1700, 1900, 2130, 12-13 hrs, US$57.

The **2nd-class terminal** is west of Zócalo on Calzada Valerio Trujano, just west of the Periférico, across from the Central de

Abastos market. It is referred to as the 'Central Camionera' (has left-luggage office, open until 2100) and serves destinations across Oaxaca state, including the **Pacific coast**, the Sierras, the **Isthmus de Tehuantepec**, and the **Valles Centrales**. Buses to **Mitla** depart every 30 mins with **Fletes y Pasajes**, 1½ hrs, US$1.10, with access to all sights in the **Tlacolula Valley** except Hierve de Agua; *colectivos* (shuttles and taxis) are also available nearby (see below). **Autobuses Unidos** (**AU**) has its own terminal (2nd class) northwest of the Zócalo at Prolongación Madero, on the Periférico, serving major destinations in Oaxaca.

Colectivos

For the **Valles Centrales**, destinations in the north are served by *colectivo taxis* departing from Trujano, north of the Mercado de Abastos and west of the Peréférico; *colectivos* for the south and east leave from between Mercaderes and Galeana, south of the Mercado de Abastos and west of the Peréférico. Most fares US$1-3 per person.

Several companies offer shuttle services to the coast. To **Puerto Escondido**, hourly, 0430-2130, 5-6 hrs, around US$13 with **Villa Escondida**, Galeana 420, T951-226 7419, and **Villa del Pacífico**, Galeana 322A; **Pochutla**, hourly, 0500-2100, 5-6 hrs, around US$12 with **Atlántida**, Armenta y Lopez 621 esq. **La Noria**, T951-514 7077, and **Eclipse 70**, Armenta y López 504, T951-516 1068; **Huatulco**, 8 daily, 6-7 hrs, US$14 with **Huatulcos 2000**, Hidalgo 208, T951-516 3154.

Car hire

Phone ahead to book, a week before if possible. **Alamo Rent a Car**, 5 de Mayo 203, T951-514 8534, www.alamomexico. com.mx (airport, T951-511 6220); **Europcar**, Matamoros 101, T951-516 9305, www. europcar.com.mx (airport, T951-143 8340).

Valles
Centrales

Oaxaca City is a great base for exploring the surrounding Valle Centrales (Central Valleys). These dusty valleys are a land of crumbling, pre-Columbian ruins, indigenous villages and other-worldly natural wonders. The villages scattered throughout the valleys also conceal several interesting attractions including El Tule, one of the world's oldest trees, and countless markets. The state's finest crafts are produced in the valleys, including sleek black pottery, dazzling tapestries and psychedelic animal sculptures, *alebrijes*.

Valle de Tlacolula → *Colour map 1, A2.*

colourful villages and pre-Hispanic archaeological sites

★The fascinating Tlacolula valley, which runs east from Oaxaca City, has many worthwhile sights including petrified waterfalls and one of the world's largest trees. Exploring the valley is easy if you have your own vehicle, but independent travel is quite straightforward with second-class buses and *colectivo* taxis travelling Highway 190 at far as Mitla; nearly all sights lie within a walking distance of the main road, or a short taxi ride away. See also Transport, page 81.

El Tule
El Arbol del Tule, US$0.75, guided tour around US$3.50 (Spanish); US$7 (English).

The diminutive village of Santa María del Tule, 9 km east of Oaxaca City, is famed for its enormous, ancient and incredibly gnarled *ahuehuete* (Montezuma cypress or *Sabino* tree), which was, according to local lore, planted by a Zapotec priest around the time of the birth of Christ; the sacred site it occupies has long since been appropriated by the Catholic church. Estimated to be 1500-2000 years old, **El Arbol del Tule** has a height of 40 m, circumference of 42 m, diameter of 11.6 m, and an estimated mass of 550 tonnes. It is not quite the world's largest tree, but it is certainly the stoutest. Sadly, despite an elaborate irrigation system, it is slowly dying from thirst and air pollution.

Teotitlán del Valle

Nestled in the foothills of the Sierra de Juárez, the extremely ancient (and increasingly touristy) Zapotec town of Teotitlán del Valle is famous for its sublime weaving, practiced there since 500 BC. In pre-Columbian times, cloth was woven from cotton and *ixtle* (maguey fibres) using laborious back strap looms, but these were replaced with treadle looms and wool in the early colonial era. Today, some 150 families continue to be involved in textile production with the town specialized in intricate rugs and wall hangings. Designs run the gamut from traditional Mixtec geometric patterns to recreations of works of Picasso. Big shops line the town's 5-km-long access road, located 25 km east of Oaxaca City on Highway 190, but they tend to cater to tour groups and will typically inflate their prices to pay the guide's commission. You will find much better deals by buying directly from the weavers in their workshops, where you will also be able to observe the production process and ask any questions related to it. Make sure you know whether you are getting all wool or a mixture. Natural dyes – such as those made from indigo, moss, wild tarragon or cochineal beetles – are more expensive to procure and far less vibrant than synthetic colours. A well-made rug will not ripple when unfolded on the floor.

Whilst in town, don't miss the **Templo de la Preciosa Sangre de Cristo**, located on the main plaza and built 1581-1758 with stones from a dismantled Zapotec temple. Examine the façade and you'll see remnants of it with carved pre-Columbian motifs. On the same plaza, there is an artisan market and the **Museo Comunitario Balaa Xtee Guech Gulal** ① *daily 1000-1800, US$0.75*, which contains archaeological finds and exhibitions on local culture, history, and traditions.

Tlacolula and around

Located 30 km from Oaxaca City, Tlacolula is the valley's main commercial and administrative hub, highly recommended for its labyrinthine Sunday *tiangui* (market), an event that draws more than 1000 indigenous and *campesino* tradespeople from across the region. True to the town's Nahautl name, Tlacolullan, which means 'place of abundance', it is one of the oldest, busiest and best stocked markets in Mesoamerica, with everything imaginable on sale from hand-crafted *artesanías* to squawking livestock. Items are grouped by zones, but half the pleasure is wandering aimlessly in the profusion of sights, sounds, and smells. Aside from its market, Tlacolula is known for *mezcal* production, and for its **Capilla del Santo Cristo**, attached to the 16th-century Dominican church. The chapel is similar in style to Santo Domingo in Oaxaca City, with intricate white and gold stucco, lots of mirrors, silver altar rails and sculptures of martyrs in gruesome detail: two beheaded saints guard the door to the main nave. The town's bus station is just off Highway 190, several blocks from the centre; pickpockets are common here, be especially careful at the Sunday market and in the scrum to board the bus.

Approximately 4 km north of Tlacolula, **Santa Ana del Valle** is known for its quality weavings and for its small museum showing ancient textile techniques; ask any villager for the keyholder.

Yagul

Daily 0800-1800, US$2.60. Tours in English on Tue, US$18, from Oaxaca agencies. The turning for Yagul is 5 mins from Tlacolula on Highway 190, site is 1.5 km north of Highway 190.

Yagul is an outstandingly aesthetic archaeological site where the ball courts and priests' quarters are set in a wiry landscape of candelabra cactus and agave. Home to more than 6000 inhabitants at the time of the Spanish conquest, the settlement was founded by the

Zapotecs around 500 BC and reached its zenith only after the fall of Monte Albán, when it was abandoned and resettled by the Mixtecas. During the Spanish conquest, Yagul's population was forcibly relocated to Tlacolula, where their descendants live on.

Yagul's ball court is said to be the second largest in Mesoamerica and is one of the most perfect. Other notable structures include several tombs and the Palacio de los Seis Patios, a complex of corridors, tunnels and rooms said to be the former residence of Yagul's leader. The hilltop ruins of the Fortaleza are worth the stiff climb for the commanding views over the valley. The all-encompassing vistas suggest the site was founded for strategic military purposes. Beyond Yagul, in the mountains to the north, a complex of 147 prehistoric caves and shelters recently yielded the oldest evidence of plant domestication in the Americas. Seed gourds discovered inside the Guilá Naquitz cave contained 10,000-year-old Cucurbitaceae (squash) seeds and fragments of *teosinte*, the ancient precursor to modern maize. Sadly, due to vandalism, the caves are closed to the public.

★Mitla
42 km southeast of Oaxaca, turn left off Ruta 190, 5 km after Yagul and continue for 4 km. La Cuchilla is the turn-off. Daily 0800-1800, US$2.60, video US$3.50, literature sold at entrance.

The deeply mystical pre-Columbian city of Mitla served as the symbolic and ritual gateway to the afterlife – a sacred burial ground for Zapotec nobles and kings. Its name is derived from 'Mictlán', a Nahuatl word for 'underworld' (in Zapotec, it was known as 'Lyobaa', meaning 'Place of Rest'). The city was established in the late pre-classic and early classic era, 100-650 AD, but did not peak until much later, 750-1521 AD. By the time of the Spanish conquest, it was the most important religious centre in the Tlacolula valley, and although lacking scale and grandeur, it is considered the most important archaeological site in Oaxaca after Monte Albán.

The city's structures exhibit both Zapotec and Mixtec influence with stunning geometric mosaics arranged in bands on their exteriors, a completely unique innovation in Mesoamerica. Designs are said to depict feathered serpents and other spiritual motifs. The many thousands of cut and polished stones are not held in place with mortar, but by the weight of other stones around them. Mitla was sadly sacked and vandalized during the Spanish conquest, but a handful of its finer buildings survived. Next to the Catholic church, which is built upon one of the site's main temples, you can observe patios, mosaics and the remains of a frieze with murals. To the south, the Group of Columns is the site's most important excavated area, encompassing several patios, underground tombs and the Palace of Columns, thought to have been the residence of an oracle. Beneath the Patio of the Crosses, inside a burial chamber, you'll find the so-called Columna de la Muerte (Column of Death). Legend holds if you embrace the column and then measure the distance you can't reach, this indicates how many years you have left to live (which is rather hard on long-armed people).

Hierve el Agua
The phenomenon of pale white stone cascading down the mountainside – the so-called petrified waterfalls of Hierve el Agua – was formed over thousands of years by seeping groundwater saturated with calcium carbonate (limestone). The site features sublime cliff-top pools where you can bathe in cool, refreshing, mineral-rich spring water and breathe in expansive highland vistas. To get to Hierve el Agua, take a bus to Mitla and ask to be let out at La Cuchilla, where *colectivo* trucks make the uphill haul on a bumpy,

unpaved track, 45 minutes, US$3; a private taxi costs US$15. Before making the journey, check with the Oaxaca City tourist board that the site is open, as it often closes in the wet season (and sometimes the early dry season). There are changing rooms, cabins and a place to eat at the pools.

Listings Valle de Tlacolula

Where to stay

In 13 towns, throughout the Central Valleys around Oaxaca, including Tlacolula, there is tourist accommodation run by local communities (**$** per person, US$5 to camp). Each house has a room with 6 beds, equipped kitchen, bathroom with hot water. For details contact the Sectur office in Oaxaca, see page 71.

Mitla

$$ Hotel Don Cenobio
Av Juárez 3 y Morelos, T951-568 0050, www.hoteldoncenobio.com.
Don Cenobio's is the best place in town, conveniently located on the central

plaza. Rooms are bright, comfortable and adequate, and they feature cheery hand-painted furniture. Grounds include a pool and restaurant. There are cheaper and more basic *posadas* in town too.

Festivals

Teotitlán del Valle
3 May **Fiesta de las Cruces**, when people climb to a cross on a beautiful summit above town (across river); good hiking at any time of year.
Jul **Fiesta Antigua Zapoteca** is celebrated here to coincide with the Guelaguetza in Oaxaca.
8 Sep **Feast of Virgen de la Natividad**.

Valle de Zimatlán → Colour map 1, A1.

pre-Columbian remains and craft towns

★The Zimatlán Valley opens up south of Oaxaca City. On Highway 147, pre-Columbian and Dominican heritage can be explored at Zaachila and Culiapan. On Highway 175 to Pochutla, there are several towns that specialize in the production of crafts, including sleek black pottery and brilliantly painted *alebrijes*.

San Bartolo Coyotepec

The Zapotec community of San Bartolo Coyotepec, 12 km southeast of Oaxaca, has been producing pottery for at least 2000 years. Until relatively recently, production techniques remained largely unchanged with most output consisting of unglazed grey utilitarian vessels. In the 1950s, the community's fortunes transformed when Doña Rosa Real Mateo de Nieto accidentally discovered the technique for making shiny *barro negro* (black pottery). Her family continues the tradition, as do many other potters in town. The technique involves drying the clay almost completely before firing and polishing its surface with a curved quartz stone. You can shop for ceramics and learn more about the process at her family's workshop, **Doña Rosa Alfarería** ⓘ *Juárez 24, T941-551 0011, open 0830-1930*. It is also worth checking out the **Museo Estatal de Arte Popular (MEAPO)** ⓘ *Independencia s/n, 1a Sección Barrio La Calera, Tue-Sun 1000-1800, US$1.50*, which exhibits hundreds of works of popular art, including fine black pottery, vivid masks and *alebrijes*. Don't miss the pieces by Carlomagno Pedro Martínez, the museum's director, who is celebrated for his ghoulish, fantastical and darkly humorous black clay sculptures.

San Martín Tilcajete

The Zapotec village of San Martín Tilcajete, 21 km from Oaxaca and 1 km west of the main road, is known for its outlandish *alebrijes*: wood-carved animal figurines painted in vibrant colours. The concept of *alebijes* was originally spawned in the 1930s by a Mixe artist, Pedro Linares. After falling ill with a fever in Mexico City, he had a hallucination of a multi-coloured menagerie of mythical beasts, all shouting the word: *'alebrijes!'*. His subsequent creations were made of papier mâché and had an appropriately delirious quality, but families of artisans in his home state of Oaxaca had been carving animals as totems and children's toys for generations, and so using their preferred material of copal wood, adapted his concept to their traditional forms. Today, there are workshops all over San Martín. The most beautiful and inventive *alebrijes* of all are produced by the incredibly talented **Jacobo and María Angeles** ① *C Olvido 9, T951-524 9047, www. jacoboymariatilcajete.org*.

Ocotlán

The Zapotec town of Ocotlán is best known for its gifted son, the painter Rodolfo Morales (1925-2001), who is regarded as one of Mexico's finest 20th-century artists. His dreamlike canvases did much to promote the beauty and tranquility of rural Oaxaqueña communities, but more than this, he made considerable contributions to the fields of education, culture and restoration. He renovated part of Ocotlán's former Dominican monastery, the **Templo y Ex-Convento de Santo Domingo de Guzmán**, for use as an **art museum** ① *0900-1800, US$1.10*, and his former home, an 18th-century mansion located north of the main plaza, is a theatre and gallery operated by the **Fundación Cultural Rodolfo Morales** ① *www.fcrom.org.mx*. The town hosts a big market on Fridays.

Culiapan de Guerrero

In the aftermath of the Spanish conquest Culiapan, 12 km southwest of Oaxaca City, a permanent settlement since 500 BC, required a suitably imposing Christian edifice for the purpose of converting its native population. Ignoring the viceroy's mandate that the construction ought to be 'modest', architectural plans for the town's Dominican monastery incorporated an extravagant blend of Gothic, Renaissance, Plateresque and Moorish styles. By the turn of the 17th century, however, the native population had plummeted from 40,000 to 7000 and work on the building was halted. Today, ruined and unfinished, the **Templo y Ex-Convento de Santiago** ① *US$2.20*, features a gothic cloister and an open chapel with a collapsed roof. The town's namesake, Vicente Guerrero, a hero of the Mexican Independence movement, was notoriously imprisoned and executed here; a monument outside commemorates the tragic event. Also buried in Culiapan was Princess Donají, daughter of Cosijoeza, the last Zapotec ruler of Zaachila, and her husband, a Mixtec prince. On their grave is an inscription with their Christian names: Mariana Cortez and Diego Aguilar.

Zaachila and beyond

Zaachila, 5 km beyond Culiapan, was the last capital of the Zapotec empire. The town maintains some of its ancestral traditions in its local cooking, and there is also black pottery production. Market day is Thursday. Most visitors come to view the modest, partially excavated **archaeological site** ① *daily 0800-1800, US$2.20*, which features two Mixtec tombs. The outer chamber depicts owls in stucco work and there are carved human figures with skulls for heads inside. Some 80 km south of Zaachila on Route 131 is a system of caves at **San Sebastián de las Grutas** ① *10 km northwest of El Vado, off the main road; guide obligatory, US$2*. One 400-m-long cave, with five chambers up to 70 m high, has been explored and is open to visitors. Public transport to and from the caves is nonexistent after 1200, so it is recommended you visit with an ecotour operator from Oaxaca City.

Valle de Etla

archaeological sites and artisan crafts

★The Etla Valley extends 40 km northwest of Oaxaca City, followed by Highway 190. In pre-Hispanic times, the region played host to several important settlements.

San José el Mogote, 17 km from the city and 2 km west of the highway, was a centre of power before the rise of Monte Albán, and **Huijazoo** sits atop a hill at **Santiago Suchilquitongo**, 27 km from Oaxaca City, which once controlled the trade between the Central Valleys and the Cañada region. The local museum has a reproduction of a Huijazoo polychromatic mural, which has been compared to those at Bonampak. **San Pedro y San Pablo Etla**, 19 km from Oaxaca, has an important Wednesday market specializing in Oaxacan foods such as *quesillo* (string cheese), *tasajo* (dried meat) and different types of bread; the town has a 17th-century church and convent.

Santa María Atzompa

Green glazed and terracotta ceramics are produced at Santa María Atzompa, 8 km northwest of Oaxaca at the foot of Monte Albán. You can see the artisans at work; their wares are sold at **Mercado de Artesanías**, Avenida Libertad 303. Around 2 km from the village is **Cerro El Bonete archaeological site** ① *0800-1700, free*, which has only been recently uncovered, revealing a ball court and several ceremonial plazas. On the way up, you'll pass a small community museum with examples of ancient pottery from the ruins, providing an interesting comparison with contemporary productions. *Colectivos* to Atzompa leave from Trujano near the second-class terminal.

San Agustín Etla

The town of San Agustín Etla (turn-off east from Route 190 at Guadalupe Etla) was once an important industrial centre. In the 19th century, it had two large cotton mills, but the introduction of synthetic fibres signalled the area's decline. Since 1998, however, the town has found a new use for the cotton and other natural fibres in the region, with the production of handmade paper for artists. The old cotton mills themselves have been transformed into the excellent **Centro de las Artes de San Agustín** ① *Independencia s/n, T951-521 3042, www.casa.oaxaca.gob.mx*, a cutting-edge arts institute founded by artist Francisco Toledo complete with galleries, workshops, libraries and studios; see the website for details on current events and exhibitions.

Sierra
Juárez

★With pristine landscapes and great biological diversity, Sierra Juárez north of Oaxaca City is filled with 400 species of bird, along with seven of the nine types of vegetation that exist in Mexico. Several distinct regions make up the range, which grows increasingly high and occasionally icy before gradually dropping to the Papaloapan valley to the north. The Sierra is starting to develop ecotourism with community participation; permits are required to camp on community land.

Pueblos Mancomunados → *Colour map 1, A2.*

Zapotec communities

The tourist office in Oaxaca City can advise on visiting the Pueblos Mancomunados, a network of eight Zapotec villages with trained guides, rudimentary overnight facilities, and access to many kilometres of highland hiking trails. Alternatively, talk to Expediciones Sierra Norte in Oaxaca City (www.sierranorte.org.mx), who are very experienced in organizing trips to the region.

There are two access roads, Highway 175 from Oaxaca to Tuxtepec, and the small roads that go north from Highway 190, past Teotitlán and Santa Ana del Valle (see page 84). The Oaxaca–Tuxtepec road has been recommended as exhilarating for cyclists.

Huautla de Jiménez → *Colour map 1, A2.*

mountain town famed for hallucinogenic mushroom ceremonies

Famous for its unique candlelit rite of the Eucharist where hallucinogenic mushrooms are substituted for the body of Christ, the indigenous town of Huautla de Jiménez is nestled high among the clouds in the Sierra Mazateca.

The consumption of psilocybin is a very old Shamanic practice that until recently had much more to do with healing than with union with God. In 1957, an unlikely Wall Street banker, Gordon Wasson, changed all that when he visited Huautla, tripped his head off and reported his experiences to *Life* magazine. The end result was a cavalcade of hippies and spiritual seekers – Timothy Leary among them – who inundated the town for many years until the army was forced to install a roadblock (now removed). During that time, the Mazatec healer, María Sabina, became a counter-culture icon as the chief minister of mushroom rituals; it is her wizened face that today adorns T-shirts in the tourist shops in Oaxaca City.

Many healers continue to work in the town and if you are interested in participating in a *velada* it is best to acquaint yourself with the local culture, the law and the general pitfalls of seeking spiritual experiences via hallucinogenic drugs. The best authority is the anthropologist Ben Feinberg, author of *The Devil's Book of Culture*. If driving to Huautla, do not stop for people on the road, they may be bandits.

Pacific coast

Oaxaca's fabled Costa Pacífica is blessed with a string
of some of Mexico's most gorgeous beaches. From laid-
back San Agustinillo to the sprawling surf town of Puerto
Escondido, the emphasis is firmly on the feel-good factor.
Options include all-night partying, skinny dipping, chilling
out in an oceanfront hammock, or being pampered with
five-star spa treatments. Construction has been rather
rustic and low-key, with the exception of Puerto Escondido
and, further south, Bahías de Huatulco, a favourite stop-off
point for cruise ships.

Puerto Escondido and around → *Colour map 1, B1.*

fine beaches and world-class waves

Once faithful to its name, as recently as the 1970s Puerto Escondido was little
more than a sleepy shipment point for coffee exports: a 'hidden port' with a
smattering of hotels and restaurants catering to intrepid surfers. Today, it is a
bustling and commercial seaside resort. For better or worse, grandiose plans
for an Acapulco-style development didn't quite pan out and tourism instead
developed over decades in a low-rise, haphazard manner without much concern
for environmental and social impact. Parts of Puerto have now become ramshackle
and downtrodden and, like Acapulco, risks becoming a case study in unsustainable
tourism development. But despite its flaws, the 'hidden port' manages to maintain
a mostly friendly and laid-back atmosphere, boasting just enough off-beat style
and seediness to claim status as a legend among Mexican surf and party towns.

Broadly dividing local residences from tourist outlets, the Carretera Costera strikes through
the heart of Puerto to connect with **Playa Zicatela**, home to the fabled Mexican Pipeline,
where surfers and international travellers like to hang out. The real town, where prices are
lower and there is less of a hard-sell atmosphere, is located north of the highway up the
hill. **El Adoquín** (Avenida Pérez Gasga), in the tourist sector, is a pedestrian mall teeming
with Mexican families, sunburnt foreigners and hardcore wave-seekers, especially in high
season, December to January (May to June are the quietest and hottest months). You'll
find an excellent **tourist information kiosk** ⓘ *at the west end of El Adoquín, T954-582
1186, ginainpuerto@yahoo.com*, run by the fabulous Gina Machorro, who speaks English,
Spanish and French, and possesses an unrivalled knowledge of the town and region (see
What to do, below, for her walking tours of the area.)

Many fast-talking *amigos* around town offer an impressive array of goods and services; be polite and friendly, but also wary, as there is no shortage of overpricing and trickery. Security has improved in Puerto in recent years, but you should stay alert and not walk on the beaches after dark. For swimming and surfing, there are several options. Abutting El Adoquín, **Playa Principal** has the calmest water, but it is not very clean. A few fishermen still bring in the catch of the day here. On the east side of the same bay is **Playa Marinero**, which is a bit cleaner and washed with slightly stronger surf (reportedly a good place for beginners). Further south and east, past a rocky outcrop called Rocas del Morro, lies the wide expanse of **Playa Zicatela**, which claims to be Mexico's best surfing beach. Here, the **Mexican Pipeline** produces the world's fastest-breaking waves which can be more than 3.5 m high. The surf is at its most epic from May to July, early morning and late afternoon. Note the pipeline is suitable only for experienced surfers, who should watch out for treacherous currents and rip tides. The beach is far too dangerous for swimming. Most of the surf action is concentrated at the north end of the beach, but **Punta Zicatela** in the south is also viable.

To the west of Playa Principal are a series of picturesque bays and beaches, all accessible by road or boat from town. The closest (an easy 15-minute walk) are **Playa Manzanillo** and **Playa Angelito**, which share the Bahía Puerto Angelito. They are reasonably safe for

Puerto Escondido

Where to stay		Vivo Escondido **6**	Pascale **5**
Aldea del Bazar **3**			Vivaldi **1**
Mayflower **12**		**Restaurants**	
Paraíso Escondido **1**		El Nene **2**	
Quinta Lili **5**		El Sultan **3**	
Villa Mozart y Macondo **2**		Los Crotos **4**	

swimming but very commercial. Every square millimetre of shade is proprietary here, so prepare to fry or fork out for a parasol. Further west is **Playa Carrizalillo**, good for swimming and gentle surfing, accessed by a steep path of 170 steps, or by boat. **Playa Bacocho** is next, a long beautiful stretch of less-developed beach, where the ocean, alas, is too dangerous for swimming but makes for great sunset viewing.

Laguna de Manialtepec

Laguna de Manialtepec, 16 km west of Puerto Escondido, is a quiet, pretty and secluded spot, great for birdwatching and worth a visit. Rich in red and white mangroves, water lilies and marine flora, the 6-km-long *laguna* is home to several salt and freshwater species of fish, plentiful crustaceans, reptiles, amphibians and some 320 bird species, most of them aquatic. In the rainy season (June-October) it connects with the sea at Barra Grande, and nearby, at Puerto Suelo, the Río Manialtepec provides a complete contrast of flowers and vegetation (it is possible to swim in the river, but the sea itself is too rough). The unforgettable night time spectacle of bioluminescent plankton, which light up when disturbed in the water, can also be observed June to December.

Exploring the lagoon independently is possible, but taking a tour gives great insights into the local bird conservation initiatives (see **Lalo Ecotours** in Tour operators, below). To reach Manialtepec under your own steam, take a *colectivo* (US$1) or taxi (around US$10) towards the village of Las Negras and asked to be dropped at the Flor del Pacífico restaurant. Here, it is possible to rent a kayak or canoe (US$10 per hour) or charter a motorboat with a guide and driver (two to three hours, US$70-90 per group). The restaurant itself is one of few women's cooperatives in the area and good for a nice meal after seeing the lagoon.

Parque Nacional Lagunas de Chacahua

Seventy-four kilometres west of Puerto Escondido is the 140,000-ha Parque Nacional Lagunas de Chacahua, a wildlife refuge punctuated by sand dunes, interconnected lagoons, mangroves and forest. **La Pastoría** is the largest lagoon, connected to the sea by an estuary. It has nine islets that harbour thousands of birds, both resident and migratory. On the shores of the lagoon is the village of **Chacahua**, home to some of the area's small Afro-Mexican population. There is a crocodile hatchery nearby, aimed at preserving this native species. The easiest way to see the park and learn about its wildlife is with a tour. To go independently, start early or plan to spend the night in one of the beach's rustic *cabañas* ($). First take a minibus to Río Grande (from 2a Norte and 3a Poniente, every 20 minutes), then another one to Zapotalito from where there are boats (US$12 per person if there are enough passengers, or US$50 for the whole boat) to the village of Chacahua. If you plan to stay, take a mosquito net.

Pochutla and around → *Colour map 1, B2.*

San Pedro Pochutla, 66 km east of Puerto Escondido and 240 km south of Oaxaca, is a hot, busy, grubby town with an imposing church set on a small hill. There is a prison here, and inmates carve crafts out of coconut husks for their families to sell at local shops. For most travellers, Pochutla is not a final destination but a transport hub connecting the extremely winding northbound Highway 175 with coastal Highway 200. Puerto Angel, Zipolite, San Agustinillo and Mazunte are all accessible via Pochutla; bus terminals are concentrated on the downhill side of Cárdenas. There is a new ATM at Mazunte, but it is best to stock up on cash before setting out in case of malfunctions or shortages. The **Fiesta de San Pedro** takes place on 29-30 June.

Puerto Angel → *Colour map 1, B2.*

Puerto Angel lies 13 km south of Pochutla at the end of a pretty road that winds through hilly forest. Tourism and fishing are the main economic activities, although the former has dwindled in recent years. Once upon a time, this was a prime destination, but it has now been eclipsed by hipper places further west. The town lies above a beautiful flask-shaped bay, but unfortunately the turquoise water is polluted. A short walk from the dock, either along the road or on a concrete path built on the rocks (not safe at night), is **Playa del Panteón**, a small beach with a lovely setting, but crowded with poor-value restaurants (touts await visitors on arrival) and many bathers in high season. There are cleaner and more tranquil beaches east of town, including **Playa La Boquilla** (taxi from Puerto Angel, US$11). **Estacahuite**, with simple *cabañas*, 1 km from town, about a 20-minute walk, has good snorkelling (gear rental from hut selling drinks and snacks), but beware of the strong waves, currents and sharp coral.

★ Zipolite → *Colour map 1, B2.*

Located 4 km west of Puerto Angel, the village overlooks a stretch of ocean so ferocious and fraught with wildly shifting rip tides, it appears to be possessed by a raging, discarnate spirit. According to legend, the name Zipolite is derived from a Zapotec word meaning 'beach of the dead'; take heed, swimmers drown here every year. In truth, no one comes to Zipolite to bathe, but to kick back and relax. In high season, hordes of sprightly young gringos, straggly backpackers and bongo-toting hippies descend en masse to fill the lively beach bars, which provide nightly entertainment in the form of live music, fire-juggling and dance. Illicit drugs are readily available and the usual penalties for possession apply. As a display of force, the Mexican military make a point of visiting the beach, guns at the ready, every now and again, although this all seems to be just for show. The west side of the beach is the more racy and hedonistic side, with the lion's share of bars and restaurants, internet cafés and paved roads. There is also a small nudist beach here, mostly frequented by older Western men and nothing much to get excited about. There is a quieter, family atmosphere at the less-developed eastern side. Low season can be eerily quiet everywhere, although there is an expat community living here year round.

★ San Agustinillo → *Colour map 1, B2.*

Another 3 km west is San Agustinillo, a long, pretty beach with an extraordinary cave in the cliffs. The western end is quite built up with private homes and the rest of this small resort is also expanding rapidly with new hotels, *cabañas* and beach bars. The beach is smaller than nearby Zipolite and Mazunte (see below), but there are nice coves and cliffs to explore and the vibe is laid back and relaxing. Swimming is safest at the west end of the beach, surfing best near the centre. Nude bathing is prohibited.

★ Mazunte → *Colour map 1, B2.*

One kilometre further west is Mazunte, which is developing rather haphazardly on the edge of a beautiful curved bay. The beach is on federal land and drug laws are strictly enforced; nude bathing is prohibited. At the east end of Mazunte is the **Centro Mexicano de la Tortuga** ⓘ *T958-584 3376, www.centromexicanodelatortuga.org, guided tours in Spanish and English, Wed-Sat 1000-1630, Sun 1000-1430, US$2, crowded with tour buses from Huatulco 1100-1300 during high season.* This government institute studies and conserves endangered sea turtles, and maintains several interesting viewing tanks. It aims to educate visitors about turtle biology and their life cycle, along with the local population, who were until quite recently economically dependent on hunting turtles and pilfering their eggs. For swimming, head to **El Rinconcito** at the west end of the beach. From here, a trail leads to **Punta Cometa**, a headland with lovely views of the thundering breakers below. This is a popular spot to view the sunset and well worth the 30-minute walk. Hand-painted signs for yoga, massage and vegetarian and vegan food abound in Mazunte, thanks in part to its proximity to Zipolite. It's a good place to try local therapies; by the cemetery there's a spiritual healer offering to treat everything from stress to insomnia.

La Ventanilla

Two kilometres west of Mazunte is a signed turn-off for La Ventanilla and its teeming lagoon; from here it is 1.5 km to the village and visitor centre. Wildlife tours are run by local residents, who have been working on a mangrove reforestation project after the damage inflicted by Hurricane Pauline in 1997. They combine a rowing boat ride through the mangroves, where you will observe numerous birds and reptiles, a visit to their crocodile farm and a walk on the beach, US$8 per person, maximum 10 people (the guides speak Spanish only). Horse riding tours are also available for US$40 per hour, along with nocturnal turtle tours, US$8 per person. There are two competing co-operatives offering largely identical services: **Servicios Ecoturísticos La Ventanilla** ⓘ *T958-108 7288, www.laventanilla.com.mx*; and **Lagarto Real** ⓘ *T958-589 8419*; both with offices by the roadside. Those wishing to spend the night can stay in *cabañas* (**$$**) or with a family. Simple meals are available in the village.

Bahías de Huatulco → *Colour map 1, B2.*

Surrounded by 34,000 ha of protected deciduous forests, Huatulco, 50 km east of Pochutla on the coastal highway, is a meticulously engineered international resort overlooking nine splendid bays with 36 beaches. After the environmental calamities of Acapulco and Cancún, the architects of Huatulco wanted to move away from 'traditional' high-rise models of mass tourism. The final product is a safe, clean, efficient, and somewhat sanitized holiday destination with gold standard certification in sustainability from EarthCheck (one of the world's leading sustainable tourism organizations). However, despite its green ethos and lovely setting, the resort hasn't entirely taken off. The bays are lined with unfinished roads and grand schemes left mid-building, adding a few eyesores to the otherwise stunning landscape.

The Huatulco complex encompasses several interconnected towns and development areas immersed in forest. **La Crucecita**, 2 km inland, is the resort's service town. Here you'll find bus stations, banks, a small market, shops, bars, plus cheaper hotels and restaurants. There's a useful **tourist information booth** on the Plaza Principal, as well as signs indicating taxi prices for destinations up and down the coast. **Tangolunda** (meaning 'beautiful woman' in Zapotec), on the bay of the same name (and also known as the Zona Hotelera), is set aside for large luxury hotels and resorts; it also has the golf course and the most expensive restaurants, souvenir shops and nightlife. Here you'll find the **Sedetur tourist office** ⓘ *Blv Benito Juárez, T958-581 0176, sedetur6@oaxaca.gob.mx*. **Chahué**, on the next bay west, where development only began in 1999, has a town park with spa and beach club, a marina and a few hotels. Further west (6 km from Tangolunda) is **Santa Cruz Huatulco**, once an ancient Zapotec settlement and Mexico's most important Pacific port during the 16th century. It has the marina where tour boats leave for excursions, as well as facilities for visiting yachts and cruise ships, several upscale hotels, restaurants, shops and a few luxury homes. An attractive open-air chapel, the Capilla de la Santa Cruz, is by the beach.

Where to stay

Puerto Escondido
Downtown

$$$ Quinta Lili
Cangrejos 104, Playa Carrizalillo,
T55-5406 4759, www.quintalili.mx.
An award-winning boutique B&B with
tranquil ambience and whimsical
architecture. Accommodation includes
4 individually styled rooms and 1 suite,
all bright and airy. Amenities include a
pool with sun loungers, luxurious hot tub
spa, Wi-Fi in common areas, barbeque
grill, and complimentary airport pickup.
Intimate and romantic. Good reports.

$$$-$$ Aldea del Bazar
Benito Juárez 7, T954-582 0508,
www.aldeadelbazar.com.mx.
A veritable sultan's palace, reminiscent of
Persia or India with its Mughal-style arches
and domes. Rooms are spacious, airy and
clean with a crisp, whitewashed simplicity.
Rambling grounds include a garden, pool
and spa facilities. Good value, ocean views,
a short taxi ride from downtown.

$$$-$$ Paraíso Escondido
Unión 10, Centro, T954-582 0444,
www.hotelpe.com.
Built in the style of a grand old colonial
hacienda, this hotel has fine landscaped
grounds and lots of character.
Accommodation includes simple rooms
and suites (**$$$**), some with ocean views,
as well as reasonable economy quarters
with fan (**$$**). There's a large pool and the
restaurant opens in high season. Hospitable
management, good reports.

$$$-$$ Villa Mozart y Macondo
Av Tortugas 77, Carrizalillo, T954-104 2295,
www.hotelmozartymacondo.com.
Simple, relaxing, villa-style hotel in a
beautiful location close to Carrizalillo beach.
They offer comfortable rooms, apartments,
and bungalows, all with good artwork and
attention to detail. Grounds include a rustic
patio-garden filled with leafy plants where
a fine local breakfast is served. German run
and bohemian. Recommended.

$$-$ Mayflower
Andador Libertad, on pedestrian walkway
perpendicular to El Adoquín, T954-582 0367,
www.mayflowerhostel.com.
An established presence on the scene, this
hip backpacker hostel has 9 dorms and
14 rooms. Amenities include Wi-Fi, free
internet, lockers, safety deposit box, kitchen
facilities and pool table. There's a great
terrace and upstairs sitting area with a grand
piano and views over the bay. The owner,
Minne Dahlberg, is an attentive hostess.
Recommended.

$$-$ Vivo Escondido Hostel
Barriletes 2, Rinconada, T954-582 3926,
www.vivoescondido.com.
Owned by a traveller from New Hampshire,
this brand spanking new hostel features
funky artwork, a refreshing pool and
is only a 6-min walk from the beach.
Accommodation includes 5, 6, and 8-bed
dorms (**$**), and private rooms with (**$$**)
or without (**$**) private bath. Table tennis,
Wi-Fi, lockers, kitchen, and breakfast
included. Friendly and relaxed.

Playa Zicatela

$$$ Santa Fe
Calle del Morro, T954-582 0170,
www.hotelsantafe.com.mx.
A colonial-style 4-star resort overlooking
the beach, well-established and reliable.
Grounds are lush and rambling, punctuated
by pleasant patios, courtyards and pools.
Accommodation includes 50 comfortable
and understated standards, 10 suites and
8 bungalows. The restaurant serves good,
if pricey, seafood.

$$$ Zicatela Suites
Calle del Morro, T954-582 1673,
www.zicatelasuites.com.
3 lovely 1-bedroom suites that recall
both Mexico and Bali with *talavera* tile
work, hand-carved furniture and *palapa*
overhangs. There's a lush tropical garden,
elevated terrace with ocean views, pool
and hammocks. Owner Vicki Cole has lived
in Puerto Escondido for 23 years, can offer
lots of tips and is generally a great hostess.
Recommended.

$$$-$$ Inés
Calle del Morro, T954-582 0792,
www.hotelines.com.
A cheerful, friendly, family-run hotel with
colourful, comfortable, pleasant rooms
($$), and a chilled-out garden slung with
hammocks. If you require more space and
comfort, they also have *cabañas*, apartments
and suites with jacuzzi ($$$-$$). Facilities
include a bar, pool and travel agency.
Popular, good reports.

$$ Bungalows Zicatela
Calle del Morro s/n, T954-582 0798,
www.bungalowszicatela.com.
This popular and well-established haven
for gringos and surfers offers simple and
reasonable oceanfront rooms with terraces.
The cheapest have the basics of a fan
and bed. Much more comfortable are the
bungalows, with a/c and kitchenette. There's
a restaurant and several interesting pools
surrounded by wood decking. Low season
prices are much cheaper.

$$ Hotelito Swiss Oasis
Calle del Morro s/n, T954-582 1496,
www.swissoasis.com.
A relaxed little guesthouse managed by
seasoned Swiss travellers Manuela and
René, who found their home in Puerto
after travelling the world. They offer simple
lodging in spotless rooms and homely
duplexes. Not quite on the beach, but very
close. The garden has a pool and hammocks.
Friendly, helpful, good reports.

$$-$ Aqua Luna
Vista Hermosa s/n, T954-582 1505,
www.hotelaqualuna.com.
This hospitable surf hotel has a crisp and
contemporary design with a range of
tasteful, good value accommodation from
simple standards ($) to well-kitted suites
that might suit self-caterers. There's an
excellent rooftop terrace with a hot tub,
pool, laundry, internet room. Managed by
Clive and Adriana, a friendly Australian-
Mexican couple. Recommended.

Pochutla
There are several economical hotels
in Pochutla, but with all those miles of
beautiful coast a short ride away, why
would you want to stay?

$$-$ Izala
Lázaro Cárdenas 59, T958-584 0115.
This 2-star cheapie has slightly tired rooms
with a/c, cheaper with fan ($), TV, hot water,
nice patio. Clean and comfortable enough
for a night.

Puerto Angel

$$$ Bahía de la Luna
Playa La Boquilla, T958-589 5020,
www.bahiadelaluna.com.
Romantic and secluded, **Bahía de la Luna**
has 12 simple but comfortable thatched
roof *cabañas* on the edge of the beach. In
this tranquil enclave, you might spot turtles
clambering ashore. Operated with a socially
and environmentally aware ethos, the best
place in Puerto Angel. Rustic chic, but not
scruffy. Recommended.

$$ La Cabaña
Pedro Sáenz de Baranda s/n,
Playa del Panteón, T958-584 3105,
www.lacabanapuertoangel.com.
Steeped in green plants and leafy foliage,
La Cabaña is a clean, comfortable, cosy
option with a small pool, restaurant and
terrace. The hosts are attentive and the
rooms are reasonably priced, all have

fridge, cable TV and hot water, a/c and/or fan (cheaper).

$$ Puesta del Sol
On road to Playa del Panteón, T958-584 3315, www.puerto angel.net.

Lovely rambling hotel with lots of enclaves, vegetation, and a rooftop terrace with hammocks. Comfortable rooms, movies and internet available, as well as light breakfast and snacks. The friendly German management has a wealth of information on the area. Recommended.

Zipolite
The shore is lined with *palapas* offering cheap meals, accommodation and informal discos. The western end of the beach is more lively and popular than the quieter eastern end.

$$$ Casa Sol
6 Calle Arcos Iris, T958-100 0462, www.casasolzipolite.com.

Overlooking Playa Camarón around 300 m from Playa Ziplote, this tranquil guesthouse on a cliff has fabulous views of the ocean from its upper terrace. They offer 4 comfortable and well-kitted rooms with private terraces, Wi-Fi, kitchenettes, and hammocks. There's also a pool deck and you're welcome to use the boogie boards and snorkel equipment. Romantic and secluded.

$$$ Nude Bungalows and Sky Lounge
On the western end of beach, T958-584 3062, www.nudezipolite.com.

This upmarket option is not a naturalist establishment, but it is located near the nudist beach, hence the name. It boasts excellent views (of the sea, that is), an international restaurant and über-cool bar, perfect for sundowners. Its comfortable *cabañas* have TV, private bathrooms and kitchen, beach chairs, and there's also a nice pool and holistic therapies.

$$ Posada México
T958-584 3194, www.playazipoliteposada mexico.com, western end of beach.

Nice, spacious, comfortable *cabañas* in gorgeous colours, all kitted out with nets and hammocks. There's an attractive cactus garden and an Italian restaurant that serves authentic stone-baked pizzas in high season.

$$-$ Shambhala
T958-584 3152, www.shambhalavision. tripod.com, western end of beach near the rocks.

'Where the 60s never end' – and they mean it. There's an unrepentant hippy ethos at this long-standing bohemian colony. It has rustic dorms ($) and rooms ($$), a meditation point, ceremonial site, fire pit, various social spaces and inspiring views over the Pacific. Their restaurant serves good fish and Mexican dishes. No alcohol or recreational drugs permitted.

$ Lo Cósmico
www.locosmico.com, western end of beach.

Lovely rustic *cabañas* built with all natural materials like clay, wood, mud and palm thatch. Each unit is unique and some are much larger than others. Prices vary with distance from the hill to the beach; the best (and most expensive) cabins have excellent views. There are also hammocks ($) if you're very impoverished (or just enjoy sleeping outdoors). Very economical, would suit thrifty travellers.

$ Lola's Lino
Along the quieter eastern end of the beach, T958-584 3201, www.lolaslino. wix.com/lolas-lino.

A brightly painted pinky-purple building with solid brick walls, for those who don't want to stay in a hut. Rooms are colourful, spacious and cheap. There's also a bar and restaurant with reasonably priced meals ($$-$). A quiet setting, friendly, good value.

$ Posada Brisa Marina
T958-584 3193, www.brisamarina.org, western end of beach.

A fairly large hotel (for Zipolite), wood built with 3 floors and balconies overlooking the ocean. Rooms are large, rustic and spartan;

the best have private bath, sea views and hammocks. Daniel, the owner, is very friendly and helpful and can assist with bus tickets and information. Free Wi-Fi. A good option for backpackers.

San Agustinillo

$$$$ Casa Aamori
Calle Principal, T555-436 2538,
www.aamoriboutiquehotel.com.
Crisp, comfortable and beautiful boutique suites and *cabañas* with spacious high-thatched roofs, rustic-chic decor and interesting ethnic touches from around the world. Pool, beach club area with lounge chairs and swinging beds, spa treatments, yoga, restaurant and bar.

$$$ Punta Placer
On main beach, T958-100 7539,
www.punta placer.com.
Lovely, colourful, artfully designed *cabañas*, all rounded and without corners. One of the best in town, popular, well kept, and clean. Owner also runs **Coco Loco** surf club (www.cocolocosurfclub.com) with surf board rental, lessons in English, Spanish and French, surfing tours (also in 3 languages), and mountain hikes. Restaurant attached. Recommended.

$$$ Un Sueño
Calle Principal, T958-113 8749,
www.unsueno.com.
Whitewashed stone bungalows with thatched rooftops and terraced decking on the sand. Each unit has its own bathroom, mosquito net, table, chairs, and fan. The double doors open fully so you can admire the ocean sunset from the comfort of your bed. Facilities include Wi-Fi, laundry service, restaurant and a hammock area. Rustic chic.

$$$-$$ Bambú
Calle Principal, www.bambuecocabanas.com.
Overlooking the beach, **Bambú** is a sociable travellers' hub with 6 aesthetic and individually styled *cabañas*, all whitewashed and comfortable; 4 are located on the beach,

2 have sea views. No restaurant but a shared kitchen and Wi-Fi are available. Relaxed, friendly place, casual and easy-going. The owner, Guillermo (Memo), is a friendly and very helpful host. Recommended.

$$$-$$ La Mora Posada
Calle Principal, T958-584 6422,
www.lamoraposada.com.
This lovely little guesthouse on the beach has 3 simple, well-kept rooms with Wi-Fi, fridge, fan, hot water, and a shared oceanfront terrace ($$); one of them has a kitchenette. On the top floor there's a good spacious apartment ($$$) with well-equipped living spaces and a private terrace. Downstairs, there's a casual café serving Mexican and Italian food. Clean, reasonable and friendly.

Mazunte
Several *palapas* offer simple accommodation along the middle of the beach.

$$$$ Zoa Hotel
Cerrada del Museo de la Tortuga,
T55-5290 2288, www.zoahotel.com.
A chic and exquisitely designed hotel nestled in a secluded section of the cliff. Lodging is in 5 luxury *cabañas* with ocean views, services include yoga and massage. Stylish and romantic, very exclusive with rates to match.

$$$$-$$$ Casa Pan de Miel
300 m down 1st road on the right past the Turtle Museum, T958-584 3509,
www.casapandemiel.com.
This immaculate small hotel has 8 spacious rooms and 1 suite with a kitchen, all opening on to private terraces. The fabulous infinity pool has commanding views of the ocean below. Relaxed and romantic with great service and lots of attention to detail.

$$$ Celeste del Mar
Camino a Playa Mermejita s/n, T958-107 5296, www.celestedelmar.com.
Tasteful whitewashed *cabañas* constructed from natural materials including adobe clay,

wood and bamboo. Standard quarters are simple and comfortable with some units enjoying garden space and ocean views; all have a porch and hammock. Superior cabins feature panoramic lofts with terraces and one has a private pool. Friendly and tranquil.

$$ Ziga
At the eastern end near Centro Mexicano de la Tortuga, www.posadaziga.com.
Perched on a ledge very close to the beach, a comfortable and reasonably priced option for Mazunte, but rooms are cheapest without bath or views. There's a good terrace with hammocks overlooking the Pacific. Friendly and family run.

$$-$ Balamjuyuc
Camino a la Punta Cometa, next to Posada Alta Mira, T958-583 7667, www.balamjuyuc.blogspot.mx.
Friendly owners Emiliano and Gaby run this tranquil ecotourism venture with gorgeous views from its cliff-top vantage. They offer a range of lodging, from rooms to rustic *cabañas*, and various holistic therapies, including massage and *temazcal*. The restaurant **Pacha Mama** does home-made veggie food with everything from the bread to the pasta made on location. Tent space or hammocks available. English, German and Italian spoken. Highly recommended.

Huatulco
Discounts of up to 50% in the low season. You won't find budget options at the beaches, only downtown in La Crucecita.

$$$$ Quinta Real
Blv Benito Juárez 2, Tangolunda, T958-581 0428, www.quinta real.com.
Part of a chain with properties all over Mexico, this exclusive and secluded resort boasts superb views over the bay. Facilities include golf club, beach club, pool, bar and restaurant. Romantic and luxurious.

$$$ Meigas Binniguenda
Blv Sta Cruz 201, Santa Cruz, T958-587 0077, www.binniguendahuatulco.com.mx.

A modern, tidy, medium-sized hotel with gardens, pool, restaurant and beach club. Accommodation includes 80 deluxe rooms, all comfortable, tasteful and generic. Lots of services, good reports and reasonable value. Recommended.

$$$-$$ Misión de los Arcos
Gardenia 902 and Tamarindo, La Crucecita, T958-587 0165, www.misiondelosarcos.com.
A colonial-style boutique hotel with bright standards and well-equipped suites, all adorned in contemporary and popular art. Guests have use of **Chahué** beach club and there is a decent restaurant attached. The best downtown option, good value for the area. Recommended.

$$ Hotel María Mixteca
Guamuchil 204, La Crucecita, T958-587 2338.
A good-value option for those on a budget, but street-facing rooms may be noisy. Rooms are comfortable and have a/c, cable TV, and hot water; some have balconies. Very helpful, clean, and tidy, and perfectly adequate if your needs are modest.

Restaurants

Puerto Escondido

Downtown

$$$-$$ Pascale
Playa Principal s/n, T954-582 1093, www.pascale.mx.
Probably the best oceanfront restaurant in Puerto Escondido, stylish, attentive, and professionally managed by a French-Mexican couple. The menu includes seafood, local specialities and Mediterranean dishes. An impeccable romantic setting with candle-lit tables and occasional live music. Ideal for a special evening meal.

$$ El Nene
Blv Benito Juárez 9, Rinconada.
For wholesome comfort food prepared with fresh, simple, and locally sourced ingredients, head to **El Nene**. Offerings

include an eclectic mix of Mexican and international cuisine, Cajun and Creole specials among them. The meat and fish dishes are perfectly grilled, including tuna steaks, mahi mahi, burgers, and shrimp. Casual, friendly and often recommended as one of the best. Try the margaritas.

$$ Los Crotos
Av Pérez Gasga (Adoquín).
This open-air restaurant serves fresh seafood and traditional Mexican dishes. Offerings include fish tacos, shrimps, lobster, whole fish and fillet, best washed down with a cold beer. Lovely ocean views with easy access to and from the beach. Casual and friendly.

$ El Sultan
Blv Benito Juárez, Rinconada,
www.el-sultan.com.
A casual downtown food shack serving great value Middle Eastern and Mediterranean snacks, including shawarma and falafel sandwiches on Arabic bread with a side of salad, tahini and hot sauce. Healthy, fresh and tasty. Recommended.

Cafés

Vivaldi
Av Pérez Gasga.
A pleasant downtown café serving proper cappuccinos and lattes, frappes, home-made cakes and other sweet treats and caffeinated fare. More filling snacks are available too, including crepes and sandwiches, as well as light meals. Outdoor seating and Wi-Fi.

Playa Zicatela

$$$ Hotel Santa Fe
Blv Zicatela y Calle del Morro,
www.hotelsantafe.com.mx.
Overlooking the ocean under an open-air *palapa*, the restaurant at **Hotel Santa Fe** is a good spot for a romantic evening meal. Their menu sports a range of Mexican staples, fresh seafood, salads and other international fare prepared by Chef Rojas,

but their vegetarian dishes are their stand out offerings. Expensive, but worth it for the views at sunset.

$$$-$$ Portus
Calle del Morro.
Overlooking the beach with shaded sun loungers and terraced seating, **Portus** is laid back beach club and restaurant serving fresh seafood and international fare, including shrimp burritos, grilled octopus, burgers and steaks. Chef Rafael is friendly and hospitable. Good for beer and snacks.

$$-$ Dan's Café Deluxe
Hotel Casa de Dan, Calle Jacarandas 14.
This popular breakfast and brunch joint serves up an eclectic range of international fare including plentiful vegetarian and vegan options, French toast, fish tacos, chilaquiles, and pancakes. For drinks, there's refreshing fruit smoothies, ice cold beer and good strong coffee with free refills. A local institution, 20 years in business, casual and fun with table tennis, sports TV and surf videos.

Cafés and ice cream parlours

El Cafecito
Calle del Morro.
A great place for a little coffee and something sweet, as well as for excellent breakfasts and wholesome, home-cooked Mexican fare. Tasty and popular. Recommended.

Kühl Frozen Yoghurt
Calle del Morro.
The perfect summer refreshment, tasty frozen yoghurt with a range of toppings, including fresh fruit and chocolate.

Zipolite
The majority of hotels strung along the beach have a restaurant or bar attached. They mostly serve breakfasts, pizzas, seafood and good, cold beer.

$$$ La Providencia
Shambala s/n, Col. Roca Blanca,
www.laprovidenciazipolite.com.
Open for dinner only.

Quirky and creative, **La Providencia**
serves contemporary fusion, international
and Mexican cuisine, including regional
specialities and outstanding seafood like
tuna steak and coconut shrimp. Colourful,
kitsch, bohemian decor and an enchanting
setting on the edge of the jungle. The best
restaurant in town, don't miss it.

$$$-$$ El Alquimista
Western end of the beach near the rocks,
www.hotelelalquimista.com. Open for
breakfast, lunch and dinner.

Overlooking the nudist beach and
violently crashing waves, **El Alquimista**
has a wonderful evening ambience with
tables and chairs on the sand. They serve
international food, cold beer and cocktails.
They also maintain highly rated *cabañas* for
rent, right on the beach and definitely worth
checking out. Magical and romantic.

$$ Pacha Mama
Mangle s/n, Col. Roca Blanca.

A cosy little Italian restaurant serving simple,
tasty and authentic home-cooked food from
the motherland, including gnocchi, ravioli,
spaghetti and bruschetta, well-established
and one of the best places on the coast.
They also do fine wine, good grilled meats
and some seafood. Intimate and romantic
ambience after dark. Recommended.

$$-$ Piedra de Fuego
Mangle s/n, Col. Roca Blanca.

A low-key, friendly, family-run place, popular
with locals and tourists. They serve tasty
home-cooked seafood in hearty portions,
including ceviche, fillets, and shrimp. Good
value and economical.

$$-$ Sal y Pimienta
On the beach.

This rustic seafood joint serves good, cheap
grilled fish at a superb location right on the
sand. Lovely candlelit ambience after dark,

tasty cocktails and friendly service. Fresh,
simple food in generous servings.

San Agustinillo

$$$-$$ La Termita
Calle Principal, attached to the hotel.

A highly popular evening haunt dishing up
excellent and fully authentic Italian pizzas
stone-baked in a wood-fired oven. Chilled-
out place, right on the beach, great for a
dinner date. Recommended.

$$-$ El Sueño de Frida
Calle Principal, San Agustinillo. Closed Mon
and 1300-1600 daily, open breakfast and
dinner only.

Casual little Frida Kahlo-themed café and
ice cream parlour with a terrace.

$$-$ Luz del Sol
Calle Principal, above El Sueño de Frida.

Cheery hippy café-restaurant serving tasty,
health-conscious vegetarian and vegan
food, including veggie burgers, quinoa
salads, smoothies and raw vegan desserts.
They also sell organic produce, have restful
hammocks and spiritual literature, and offer
yoga and meditation classes, massage and
other holistic therapies.

Mazunte

$$$-$$ Estrella Fugaz
Playa Rinconcito.

A good breakfast spot where you can
enjoy views of the sea whilst sipping
fresh fruit juices and organic coffee.
Lunch and dinner offerings include
seafood, Italian and Mexican fare.
There's also cocktails and happy hour
after dusk, fast Wi-Fi, and live music.

$$ Siddharta
Playa Rinconcito.

A relaxed beachfront restaurant with a
breezy outdoor terrace, colourful New Age
murals and occasional live bands. They serve
mostly Italian cuisine, fresh, tasty and simple,
with a smattering of seafood and other

international options. 2 for 1 happy hour 1500-1900; try the mojitos.

Huatulco

Restaurants on the beach out of town tend to be the cheapest. There are luxury restaurants at the Tangolunda hotels. In La Crucecita, prices get cheaper as you get away from the plaza

$$$-$$ El Sabor de Oaxaca
Guamúchil 206, La Crucecita, www.el-sabordeoaxaca.com.
As the name suggests, the place to sample the flavours of Oaxaca with wholesome *tlayudas*, *moles*, grasshoppers and other regional specialities. There are burgers, breakfasts, seafood and regular Mexican fare too.

$ Frida's Fish Tacos
218 Monte Alban, La Crucecita, www.fridasfishtacos.com.
Baja-style fish, shrimp and nopal tacos sold truck side. Great street food, clean, tasty and healthy.

Cafés

Café Huatulco
Kiosko de Santa Cruz, near the marina, www.cafehuatulco.com.mx.
Tranquil spot in the kiosk where you can enjoy excellent coffee from their own farm, breakfasts, light meals and snacks.

Bars and clubs

Puerto Escondido

Playa Zicatela
It's not advisable to stay at bars and discos past 0300.

Barfly
Calle del Moro, above the popular Banana's restaurant.
This breezy rooftop terrace plays good, lively music and regularly screens films. A good dance spot.

Casa Babylon
Calle del Moro.
A long-standing Puerto favourite. This funky little bar draws an alternative, bohemian crowd with its shelves of books and assortment of other-worldly masks. Great mojitos and regular live music including blues, funk and rock. Recommended.

Festivals

Puerto Escondido
Jan-Feb blues festival at various venues.
Feb Marlin fishing tournament. Bajos de Chila, 15 mins from Puerto Escondido, has an annual festival, with games and firework displays. Best to go with a local if possible, as it can get quite drunken and rowdy.
Mar Long board tournament.
Aug Master World Surf Championship.
Nov The **city's festivities** are held throughout the month, along with a **surfing tournament** and a fishing tournament. The **Festival Costeño de la Danza**, with colourful, lively folk dances, is held mid-month.
Dec Large-scale *posada*, visitors welcome to participate.

Puerto Angel
1 Jun **Día de la Marina.**
1 Oct **Fiesta de San Angel.**

Huatulco
1st week Apr **Fiesta del Mar**
3 May **Fiesta de la Santa Cruz.**
1st week May **International sail-fishing tournament.**
8-12 Dec **Fiesta de la Virgen de Guadalupe.**

Shopping

Mazunte
Cosméticos Naturales de Mazunte, *on main road out of Mazunte, www.cosmeticosmazunte.com.* Women's cosmetics collective, at one time affiliated to the **Body Shop**. Good-value cosmetics and toiletries.

Huatulco

Mercado de Artesanías de Santa Cruz,
Blv Santa Cruz, corner Mitla. Regional crafts.
Museo de Artesanías Oaxaqueñas,
Flamboyán 216, Plaza Principal, La Crucecita.
Exhibits and sells Mexican crafts.
Good display of regional dresses
from the Guelaguetza.

What to do

Puerto Escondido

Adventure and ecotourism

For marine wild-life observation, including
dolphin- and whale-watching, contact
Omar Sportfishing (see Fishing, below).
Hidden Voyages Ecotours, *Pérez Gasga
905B, T954-582 2305, www.hiddenvoyages
ecotours.com, inside Turismo Dimar Travel
Agency*. Superb kayaking and boating tours
on the lagoons with Canadian ornithologist
Michael Malone, formerly employed by the
Canadian Wildlife Service; Dec-Mar only.
Recommended.
Lalo Ecotours, *T954-588 9164, www.lalo-
ecotours.com*. This ecotour operator is
managed by knowledgeable locals who
know the region's lagoons, such as nearby
Laguna de Manialtepec, intimately. They
also offer turtle observation, birdwatching
expeditions, kayak trips and tours to bioluminescent waters. Highly recommended.

Diving

The coastline offers good opportunities for
snorkelling and scuba diving; snorkelling
from the beach is easiest at Puerto Angelito.
May-Nov has best visibility but strong swells.
Sep-Oct are considered the worst months.
Deep Blue Dive, *Calle del Morro, Playa
Zicatela, T954-100 3071, www.deepblue
divemexico.com*. PADI certification up to Dive
Master, snorkelling tours, boat tours and
sports fishing. Professional and experienced
outfit managed by an Italian-French team.
Puerto Dive Center, *T01954-102 7767,
www.puertodivecenter.com*. NAUI and PADI

certification up to Dive Master, equipment
rental and tours. 1 tank US$50, 2 tanks
US$60, 2-hr snorkelling tour with gear
US$25, open water diving lessons, US$320
for a 4-day course.

Fishing

Boats can be hired for fishing at Playa
Principal through the **Sociedad Cooperativa
Turística Nueva Punta Escondida,** for
US$30-40 per boat per hr, maximum
4 passengers. Alternatively, try:
Omar Sportfishing, *T954-559 4406, www.
tomzap.com/omar.html*. Professional fishing
charters with Captain Omar Ramírez. Boats
include all safety equipment, and on full
day charters, lunch. Captain Omar also runs
dolphin- and whale-watching tours.

Pelota Mixteca

A modern version of an ancient Mixtec ball
game is played on Sat or Sun in Bajos de
Chila, 15 mins from Puerto Escondido, on the
road to Acapulco. Check dates with tourist
information kiosk in Bajos de Chila. In a 9 m
by 35 m court, teams of 5-7 players propel
a rubber ball weighing almost 1 kg, using
elaborately decorated leather mitts that
weigh between 3.5 kg and 6 kg. A game
can take up to 4 hrs.

Surfing

Playa Zicatela is a surfer's haven, but
dangerous for the novice. Beginners
should instead practice their skills at
Playa Carrizalillo. Board rental is typically
US$8-10 per day with many surf shops
and suppliers. Recommended schools
and teachers include:
Oasis Surf Academy, *Blv Juárez 6, T954-
582 1445, www.spanishandsurflessons
mexico.com*. Founded by a famous local
surfer and board-maker, Roger Ramírez,
this small but professional surf school
near Playa Carrizalillo offers Spanish
classes and accommodation along with
surfing instruction.

Puerto Escondido Surf Lessons, *Guerrero 4, Punta Zicatela, T954-109 9520, www.puerto surflessons.com*. Managed by Celestino Rodríguez, who grew up on the coast and learned to surf at a young age, this family-run outfit offers patient, professional and recommended one-to-one surfing instruction.

Tour operators

Gina Machorro, *tourist information kiosk, Av Pérez Gasga, T954-582 1186, ginainpuerto@ yahoo.com*. Gina offers a variety of interesting local tours, including a 2-hr gastro walking tour of Puerto Escondido on Sat, visiting the house of *tamales* and the house of chocolate. Sun is an archaeology tour. Highly knowledgeable and personable. The best source of information on the region. Recommended.

Puerto Angel

Diving and snorkelling

Azul Profundo, *next door to Cordelia's on Playa del Panteón, T958-584 3109, www. hotelcordelias.com*. Scuba diving with experienced instructors, up-to-date equipment, PADI service available. Also runs snorkelling trips to beaches along coast.

San Agustinillo
Surfing

Coco Loco Surf Club, *Calle Principal, T958-115 7737, www.cocolocosurfclub.com*. 1-hr surf lessons in English, Spanish or French, around US$27 for one-to-one, cheaper for groups of 4. Also board rentals, wax, leashes, lycras and other paraphernalia for sale or rental, and surf trips across the state.

Mazunte
Whitewater rafting

Ola Verde Expediciones, *Calle Rinconcito, T958-109 6751, www.olaverdeexpediciones. com.mx*. **Ola Verde** offers whitewater rafting trips on the Copalita and San Francisco rivers with sections Class II-IV. They also do river hikes, kayaking trips, expeditions and coffee plantation tours.

Yoga

Hridaya Yoga, *at the top of the hill past the turtle centre, T958-100 8958, www.hridaya-yoga.com*. Yoga classes, meditation retreats, workshops and teaching training. **Hridaya Yoga** was developed by meditation master Sahajananda and draws diverse influence from classical yoga, Sufism, Buddhism, Christianity and Taoism.

Huatulco

Huatulco is a popular tourist hub with scores of activities on offer. A mountain bike is a good way to get around this area and to reach the high points with many views of the bays. Full-day boat tours to see the different bays are offered by numerous agencies for US$15 per person, with stops for swimming, snorkelling and a meal on a catamaran. Good snorkelling can be enjoyed on reefs by the beach at La Entrega (Bahía Santa Cruz), Riscalillo (Bahía Cachacual) and San Agustín (Bahía San Agustín). The islands of Cacaluta (Bahía Cacaluta) and La Montosa (Bahía Tangolunda) are also surrounded by reefs. Launches and yachts for deep-sea fishing charge US$100 per hour, minimum rental 3 hrs. Spa treatments are available at numerous resorts. Hiking, whitewater rafting, rock climbing and watersports are also possibilities. Speak to the tourist office or your hotel reception for recommended operators.

Transport

Puerto Escondido
Air

The international airport (PXM) is 10 mins' drive west of town, Ctra Costera Km 6.5, T954-582 0977, www.flyto.mx. Flights to **Mexico City** with **Aeromar, Aeroméxico, Interjet, Volaris** and **VivaAerobus**; **Oaxaca City** with **Aerotucán**. *Colectivo* taxis to downtown US$2.70 per person.

Bus

Colectivos (see below) are the best way to get to **Pochutla** for onward connections to **Puerto Angel**, **Zipolite**, **San Agustinillo** and **Mazunte**. For destinations further afield, the ADO terminal is on the Ctra Costera (Highway 200) near Av Oaxaca. It is used by **ADO**, **OCC** and **SUR**. Departures to **Bahías de Huatulco**, 12 daily, mostly after 1300, 2½ hrs, US$11; **Mexico City**, 3 daily, 1530, 1800, 1800, 17-19 hrs, US$80, also departures from the Terminal Turística (see below); **Pochutla**, hourly with **Sur**, 1½ hrs, US$5.20, also *colectivos* (see below); **Salina Cruz**, 10 daily, mostly after 1300, 5-6 hrs, US$21; **San Cristóbal de las Casas**, 2 daily, 1830, 2130, 12½ hrs, US$51. There is a 2nd bus terminal in the north of town, **Terminal Turística**, Av Oaxaca and 4 Pte. It is used by **Altamar** and **Turistar** bus lines which offer transit to Mexico City (Tasqueña) via **Acapulco**, just 12 hrs.

Colectivos

To **Oaxaca**, hourly, 5-6 hrs, around US$13 with **Villa Escondida**, Av Hidalgo 209, behind **Super Che**, and **Villa del Pacífico**, Av Hidalgo 5, next to **Minisuper El Manguito**; **Pochutla**, from corner Ctra Costera and Av Oaxaca, every 15 mins, 0530-2000, 1 hr, US$2.20; alternatively, get off at the crossroads at San Antonio and take a *colectivo* (US$0.50, every 30 mins) or taxi (US$3-4, usually waiting at the bus stop) to your desired beach, avoiding Pochutla altogether.

Pochutla

Bus

Pochutla is a transport hub for the region, with **OCC** and **Estrella Blanca** as the main 1st-class operators departing from the Terminal San Pedro Pochutla, Av Cárdenas and Constitución. There are also several 2nd-class lines including **Estrella del Valle** and Sur. To **Bahías de Huatulco** (La Crucecita), hourly, 1 hr, US$4.60 (also with **Transportes Rápidos de Pochutla**,

see below); **Mexico City**, 2 daily, 1650 and 1930, 17 hrs, US$78; **Puerto Escondido**, hourly with Sur, 1½ hrs, US$5.20, also *colectivos* (see below); **Salina Cruz**, hourly after 1430, 4 hrs, US$16; **San Cristóbal de las Casas**, 2 daily, 2000, 2250, 11 hrs, US$45; **Tapachula**, 1 daily, 1840, 12-13 hrs, US$51. The 2nd-class **Transportes Rápidos de Pochutla** is just north of the main terminal with departures to **Bahías de Huatulco**, every ½ hr, 1 hr, US$3.50.

Colectivos

For **Puerto Angel**, **Zipolite** and other beaches, pick-up trucks with benches and *colectivo* taxis do round trips on the coastal road in both directions; these taxis also offer private service (*carreras*). In Pochutla, services depart from the Capilla del Niño Jesus, Calle Jamaica, 250 m north and 150 m west of the **ADO** terminal; or wait at marked bus stops along the main road. *Colectivo* fares are US$1-2 per person; US$6-10 for the vehicle. Overcharging is common.

Colectivo shuttles to **Oaxaca** roughly hourly, 6 hrs, US$12 with **Atlántida**, from **Hotel Santa Cruz**, Lázaro Cárdenas 88, T958-572 0380, and **Eclipse 70** from Lázaro Cárdenas 85, T958-516 0840. To **Puerto Escondido**, with departures from side street near church, every 15 mins 0530-2000, 1½ hrs, US$3.50.

Huatulco
Air

Aeropuerto Bahías de Huatulco is 17 km northwest of Huatulco, Ctra Costera Km 237, T958-581 9004. Flights to **Mexico City** with **Aeromar**, **Aeroméxico** (and **Connect**), **Interjet**, **Magni** and **Volaris**; **Oaxaca** with **Aerotucán**; **Tuxtla Gutiérrez** with **Aerotucán**; **Toronto** (and other Canadian cities) with **Air Canada**, **Air Transat** and **Sunwing**; **Chicago** with **Frontier Airlines**; **Houston** with **United**.

Transporte Terrestre from the airport to **La Crucecita**, **Santa Cruz**, **Chahué** or **Tangolunda** costs US$7.70 per person;

US$28-45 for the vehicle. Fares are 50% cheaper from the highway intersection 300 m south of the terminal. Buses to **La Crucecita** and **Pochutla** can also be caught from the highway, US$0.50-1.

Bus

There are 2 main bus terminals. The **ADO** terminal, Blv Chahué, 500 m north of the Plaza Principal, La Crucecita, is used by **ADO**, **ADO GL**, **OCC**, **SUR** and **AU**. To **Mexico City**, 11 daily, 15 hrs, around US$77; **Oaxaca City**, 5 daily, 8 hrs, from US$28; **Pochutla**, every 30-60 mins, 0525-1215, 1 hr, US$4.60; **Puerto Escondido**, hourly with **Sur**, 2 hrs, US$10.60; **Salina Cruz**, hourly with most departures after 1540, 2-3 hrs, US$12.40; **San Cristóbal de las Casas**, 3 daily, 2110, 2240, 2355, 10 hrs, US$42. The Central Camionera (also known as the Estrella Blanca station), Capinteros s/n, is located 1.2 km northwest of La Crucecita. It is used by **Turistar**, **AltaMar**, and **Transportes Rápidos de Pochutla** and it serves **Mexico City**, **Puerto Escondido** and **Pochutla** with frequent 1st- and 2nd-class services.

Autotransportes Istmeños, Carrizal and Blv Chahué, have frequent 2nd-class departures to **Salina Cruz**, **Juchitán** and **Tehuantepec**. **Note**: the village of Santa María Huatulco is some distance north of the airport, far from the beach and not to be confused with the resort of Huatulco.

Colectivos

Colectivos and private taxis to the **Huatulco beaches** run from the main plaza in La Crucecita (prices posted on signs). *Colectivos* to **Pochutla**, 1 hr, US$2, depart from Blv Chahué and Bugambilia, 500 m north of the Plaza Principal in La Crucecita. Make connections at the crossroads at Pochutla for *colectivos*, minibuses and taxis for **Puerto Angel**, **Mazunte**, **Puerto Escondido** and **Zipolite**. Shuttles to **Oaxaca**, roughly hourly, 6 hrs, US$14 with **Huatulco 2000**, Av Huamuchil, T958-587 2910.

Isthmus
of Tehuantepec

Only a 210-km-wide strip of jungly, hot and humid land separates the Atlantic and the Pacific oceans, at the narrowest point in Mexico and the geographic boundary between North and Central America. Heavily influenced by its Zapotec population, the Isthmus has a strong cultural character which can be seen its prolific art, traditions and local fiestas. Echoing their matriarchal heritage, Zapotec women continue to play a very important role in local affairs. Their traditional dress is intricate and beautiful, and they are renowned as high-pressure saleswomen. The men generally work in the fields, as potters or weavers, or at the Salina Cruz oil refinery.

The climate throughout the area can be hot, humid, and oppressive, hence cultural events usually take place late in the evening. Winds are very strong due to the intermingling of Pacific and Caribbean weather systems, and ocean currents can be dangerously powerful. There is a Trans-Isthmian Highway between Salina Cruz and Coatzacoalcos, the terminal cities on the two oceans. *Colour map 1, A5.*

An industrial city with broad avenues and a large central plaza, Salina Cruz is surrounded by hills and many poor neighbourhoods. Some of the nearby beaches are quite scenic but oil pollution, high winds, dangerous surf and sharks all conspire against would-be bathers. Do not park close to the beach, as your vehicle may be sandblasted.

Ten kilometres to the southeast is a picturesque fishing village with **La Ventosa** beach, which, as the name says, is windy. In 1528 the Spanish conquerors established a shipyard here; the old lighthouse, **El Faro de Cortés**, can still be seen. The coast west of Salina Cruz is quite scenic, with several high sand dunes and lagoons; shrimp farms have been set up in this area. Just west of the city is the village of **Salinas del Marquez**; the beach of **Las Escolleras** in Salinas is popular with locals.

Listings Salina Cruz

Transport

Bus

Regional service to **Tehuantepec** (US$1) and **Juchitán** (US$2.50) every 10 mins with **Autotransportes Istmeños**, 0500-2400, from Progreso west of Tampico, by railway. To **La Ventosa** beach, buses leave every 30 mins from main square. To **Salinas del Marquez**, buses from the park every 30 mins. Frequent 2nd-class service to **Huatulco**, 3 hrs. There is a joint bus station for **OCC**, **ADO**, **AU** and **Sur** at the north end of town, by the Ctra Transístmica. The **Estrella Blanca** station is at Frontera 25. From the **ADO** terminal, departures to **Bahías de Huatulco**, hourly, most before 0930, 2-3 hrs, US$12.50; **Juchitán**, hourly, 1 hr, US$5; **Oaxaca City**, 7 daily, 5-6 hrs, US$22; **Pochutla**, hourly, most before 0930, 3-4 hrs, US$16; **Puerto Escondido**, hourly, most before 0930, 5 hrs, US$21; **San Cristóbal de las Casas**, 1 daily, 0135, 7-8hrs, US$31; **Tapachula**, 1 daily, 2230, 8-9 hrs, US$33; **Tehuantepec**, hourly, 20 mins, US$3.50.

Tehuantepec and around → *Colour map 1, B4.*

culturally rich Zapotec settlements

Santo Domingo Tehuantepec (altitude 150 m), 257 km from Oaxaca, is a colourful town that conserves the region's indigenous flavour. Robust Zapotec matrons in bright dresses ride standing in the back of motorized tricycles known as *moto-carros*. Life moves slowly here, centred on the plaza, which has arcades on one side, and an adjacent market. In the plaza is a statue of Máximo Ramón Ortiz (1816-1855) composer of the *zandunga*, the legendary music of the Isthmus, which is still very popular. The meandering Río Tehuantepec is two blocks from the plaza, by the highway. Due to the importance of Tehuantepec during the early colonial period, many churches were built here.

The **Casa de la Cultura** is housed in the run-down 16th-century Dominican ex-convent Rey Cosijopi, which has some original frescoes. There is a library and some simple exhibits of regional archaeology, history and costumes. The **Museo Casa de la Señora Juana C Romero** is a chalet built entirely with materials brought from France. Señora Romero's great-granddaughter lives there today, ask for permission to visit the house. The two tourist offices are **SEDETUR** ① *Ctra Transístmica, next to the bridge into town*, the regional office for the Isthmus, and the **Regiduría de Turismo** ① *Palacio de Gobierno*.

To the northwest of town, off the road to Oaxaca, are the unrestored ruins of **Guiengola**, 'the Mexican Machu Picchu', so called because of its lonely location on a mountain. It has walls up to 3 m high, running, it is said, for 40 km; there are the remains of two pyramids and a ball court. This last fortress of the Zapotecs was never conquered (*guiengola* is the Zapotec word for fortress); Alvarado and his forces marched past it in 1522. Take the 0500 bus from Tehuantepec towards Oaxaca and get off at the Puente las Tejas bridge (8 km from Tehuantepec); this is the last place to buy water on the way to the ruins. Take the turning at the signpost 'Ruinas Guiengola 7 km'. Walk 5 km then turn left, uphill, to the car park. From here it takes 1½ hours to walk to the ruins, there are no facilities or entry fees. Try to return before 0900 because it gets very hot; take plenty of water. Alternatively, take a taxi to the car park and ask the driver to return for you three hours later (US$5.50 each trip).

Juchitán

Twenty-seven kilometres from Tehuantepec is the larger and more modern city of Juchitán de Zaragoza, an important commercial and cultural centre on the Isthmus. It has a nice plaza next to impressive colonial municipal buildings and many churches including that of **San Vicente Ferrer**, the city's patron saint. Many Zapotec women here still wear traditional costumes as everyday dress. The **tourist office** is at the Palacio de Gobierno. The **Mercado Central 5 de Septiembre** is the largest market on the Isthmus; traditional barter still takes place here. The crafts section on the second floor is worth a visit; this is the best place to see the elaborate embroidered Zapotec dresses, which sell for up to US$600.

Listings Tehuantepec and around

Transport

Tehuantepec
Bus

Regional **Istmeños** buses leave from the highway (Ctra Cristóbal Colón), at the end of 5 de Mayo. To **Salina Cruz**, every 10 mins, 0500-2400, US$1, 45 mins. To **Juchitán**, every 10 mins, 0500-2400, US$1.50, 1 hr. There is a joint bus station for **OCC**, **ADO**, **AU** and **Sur** on the outskirts of town with comparable schedules to Salina Cruz; taxi to Zócalo US$1, *moto-carro* US$0.50 or 15 mins' walk (walking not recommended at night). For **Chiapas** destinations, it is not always possible to get a 1st-class reservation; you have a better chance from Salina Cruz or Juchitán, where more buses stop.

Taxis

3-wheeled motorized rickshaws (*moto-carros*) take locals around town; you have to stand and hold on to the railing.

Juchitán
Bus

Regional bus service to **Tehuantepec** (US$1) and **Salina Cruz** (US$1.50). Every 15 mins with **Istmeños**, 0500-2400, from Prolongación 16 de Septiembre, by the highway to Tehuantepec. Joint bus station for **OCC**, **ADO**, **Sur** and **AU** at Prolongación 16 de Septiembre, just south of highway to Tehuantepec with comparable schedules to Salina Cruz.

Chiapas & Tabasco

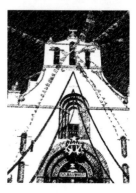

Encompassing jungles and mangrove swamps, the hot, humid, infrequently visited Gulf coast state of Tabasco holds special status as the forebear of all Mesoamerican societies. Out of this region came the Olmec with their shape-shifting jaguar shamans and their stone heads.

This was Mexico's first great culture, the mother culture. In the neighbouring state of Chiapas, lowland rainforests were home to the dazzling royal metropolises of Palenque, Bonampak, Yaxchilán, and Toniná. Today, many of their indigenous descendants still speak their native tongue, follow ancestral rites and observe the arcane procession of the Tzolk'in, an ancient Mayan calendar.

Isolated by convoluted highlands, western Chiapas is a remote landscape framed by desolate peaks, patchwork fields, wild flowers and clear clean mountain light. Daily life revolves around the cultivation of maize. So attuned to the symbols and lifestyles of its ancestors, it is no wonder that Chiapas has become a bastion for political movements focused on land rights, indigenous resistance, cultural preservation and food sovereignty.

Footprint
picks

⭐ **Sumidero Canyon**, page 123

Take a boat trip on the reservoir that fills this stunning steep-sided chasm, with sheer walls up to 1 km high.

⭐ **San Cristóbal de las Casas**, page 124

Stay in the capital of Mexico's Mayan highlands, a fascinating stronghold of indigenous culture.

⭐ **San Juan Chamula**, page 139

Visit the atmospheric village church in this highland Mayan village where shamanism is practised.

⭐ **Lagunas de Montebello**, page 142

Swim in the crystal-clear magically multi-coloured lakes set in pine forest.

⭐ **Palenque, Bonampak and Yaxchilán**, pages 152, 156 and 158

Explore these eerily atmospheric Mayan ruins buried deep in the rainforest.

⭐ **Parque Nacional La Venta**, page 161

Marvel at the huge Olmec stone heads that dominate this interesting outdoor museum.

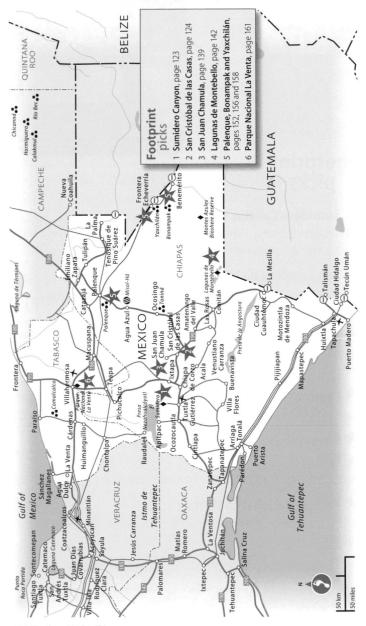

Footprint picks

1 **Sumidero Canyon**, page 123
2 **San Cristóbal de las Casas**, page 124
3 **San Juan Chamula**, page 139
4 **Lagunas de Montebello**, page 142
5 **Palenque, Bonampak and Yaxchilán**, pages 152, 156 and 158
6 **Parque Nacional La Venta**, page 161

Chiapas State

In Chiapas, the land of the Classic Maya (whose descendants still inhabit the highland villages today), the attractions are well known; San Cristóbal de las Casas is the end of the line for many travellers who base themselves in this delightful colonial and indigenous town while they soak up the atmosphere and explore the surrounding area. Around San Cristóbal are jungle waterfalls, the dramatic Sumidero Canyon; the multi-coloured lakes, and – the highlight of any trip to Mexico – the ruins at Palenque, with a jungle setting that is arguably the most atmospheric and beautiful of all the Maya sites.

Chiapas is also a good entry point for Guatemala. You can head straight for northern Guatemala and the ruins of Tikal or take a more genteel entry through the western highlands and idyllic Lake Atitlán.

Chiapas seems largely impervious to the intrusion of outsiders. The Lost World feeling is created by indigenous inhabitants and their villages which make everything seem timeless. The appalling treatment the inhabitants have suffered over centuries was the fundamental cause of the rebellion on 1 January 1994, which led to the occupation of San Cristóbal by the revolutionaries of the EZLN (Zapatista Army of National Liberation) and their continuing struggle in and beyond the boundaries of Chiapas.

The state capital since 1892, Tuxtla Gutiérrez is an expanding business and transport hub. It is relatively modern and lacking in personality, but generally safe, clean and on the up. First settled by the Zoque and later incorporated into the Aztec empire, the city's name is derived from the Nahautl 'Tuchtlan', or Land of Rabbits ('Gutiérrez' refers to Joaquín Gutiérrez, a 19th-century politician). Today, you won't find many rabbits in Tuxtla, but like any capital, it has its share of decent museums, restaurants, shops and nightclubs. The downtown area can be walked but you may need a taxi to reach some outlying attractions. Streets follow a grid system with *avenidas* running east–west and *calles* running north–south around a central axis.

Sights

At the intersection of Avenida and Calle Central, the **Plaza Cívica** is surrounded by government offices and historical buildings, including the **Catedral de San Marcos**, founded in the 16th century and renovated in modernist style. Its tower contains 48 bells and features an hourly parade of clockwork Apostles. One block east of the plaza, you'll find the **Museo del Café** ① *2a Oriente Norte 236, T961-611 1478, www.museodelcafe.chiapas. gob.mx, Mon-Sat 0900-1700, US$0.75*, with exhibitions on the economy, history and culture of coffee production in Chiapas.

Tuxtla Gutiérrez

N

200 metres
200 yards

Where to stay 🛏
Hilton Garden Inn **1**

Hostal San Miguel **2**
Hostel Tres Central **3**

Restaurants 🍴
Bonampak **1**
Las Pichanchas **2**
Los Molcajetes **3**

Marimba music is an integral part of Chiapaneco identity and its history, traditions and heroes are explored at the **Museo de la Marimba** ① *9a Poniente Norte and Av Central, T961-616 0012, Tue-Sun 1000-2200, US$2.30*. Opposite the museum, the **Jardín de la Marimba** is the place to hear rousing live performances in the evening.

Approximately 1.2 km northeast of the Plaza Cívica (15 minutes' walk), **Parque Madero** is a parched park space with several museums strung along the **Calzada de los Hombres Ilustres**. The best and most important is the **Museo Regional de Antropología e Historia** ① *T961-613 4375, Tue-Sun 0900-1800, US$3.50*, which charts the cultural and historical evolution of Chiapas with important exhibits of local archaeology and colonial antiques. Next door, you can observe a collection of 200 prehistoric fossils, including a reconstructed skeleton of a fearsome *megatherium* (giant sloth) inside the **Museo de Paleontología** ① *Mon-Fri 1000-1700*,

Sat-Sun 1100-1700, US$1.25. The **Jardín Botánico Faustino Miranda** ① *Mon-Fri 0900-1500, Sat 0900-1300, free,* covers 4.4 ha with hundreds of botanical specimens but the space is now neglected.

Zoológico Miguel Alvarez del Toro (Zoomat)

Calzada Cerro Hueco s/n, T961-639 2856, www.zoomat.chiapas.gob.mx, Tue-Sun 0830-1630, US$4. Colectivos to 'Zoológico' and 'Cerro Hueco' depart every 20 mins from Mercado, Calle 1a Oriente Sur y 7 Sur Oriente, US$0.; taxis charge around US$3 from centre or town buses charge US$0.20.

Animal enclosures don't appeal to everyone, but Zoomat, Tuxtla's premier attraction, is a decent facility and internationally renowned for its efforts in conservation, outreach, environmental education and research. From highlands to lowlands, the zoo exclusively features fauna from Chiapas, Mexico's most biodiverse state. Here, you can observe a staggering cornucopia of magnificent neo-tropical beasts: tapirs, jaguars, ocelots, monkeys, coyotes, deer, snakes, lizards, insects, as well as scores of dazzling avian species, including raptors, macaws and quetzals. Originally founded in 1942, the zoo has changed locations twice and now enjoys verdant landscaped grounds inside the El Zapotal nature reserve. The enclosures are generally spacious.

Listings Tuxtla Gutiérrez *map p116*

Tourist information

There are municipal tourist information kiosks on the Plaza Cívica and inside the Museo de Marimba, 9a Calle Poniente Norte, www.turismo.tuxtla.gob.mx.

SECTUR office
Blv Andrés Serra Rojas 1090, Edif Torre Chiapas, 5th floor, T961-617 0550, www. turismo chiapas.gob.mx. Daily 0800-1900.
Inconveniently located, has information on Chiapas state.

Where to stay

$$$ Hilton Garden Inn
Blv Belisario Domínguez 1641, T961-617 1800, www.hiltongardeninn3.hilton.com.
Although not central, this is probably the best business-class hotel in the city, and there are many to choose from. The building is fairly new and it offers high quality, well-equipped standards and suites. A pool, gym, business centre, bar and restaurant

are among the amenities. A good deal for the price.

$$-$ Hostal San Miguel
3ra Sur Pte 510, T961-611 4459, www.hostalsanmiguel.com.mx.
Hostal San Miguel offers 2 classes of lodging. The 'gold' rooms (**$$**) consist of smart, modern, above average mid-range quarters fully kitted with desk, cable TV and Wi-Fi. The 'hostal' rooms (**$**) are economical 6-bed dorms with lockers, a cooking area, shared bathroom, and a TV room.

$ Hostal Tres Central
Calle Central Norte 393, T961-611 3674, hostaltrescentral@gmail.com.
This socially and ecologically aware outfit has an excellent sustainable ethos, good value lodgings, great contemporary design and lots of attention to detail. Both private rooms and dorms are available: all crisp, clean, comfortable and well maintained. Upstairs there's a great rooftop terrace where you can sip mojitos or swing in a hammock. Relaxed and intimate. Highly recommended.

Restaurants

$$$-$$ Bonampak
Blv Belisario Domínguez 180, T961-602 5916.
Formerly an upmarket hotel, now only the
restaurant remains. Decent Mexican and
North American dishes, but quite pricey.

$$-$ Las Pichanchas
*Av Central Ote 857, T961-612 5351, www.
laspichanchas.com.mx. Daily 1200-2400.*
Pretty courtyard, typical food, live marimba
music 1430-1730 and 2030-2330 and
folkloric ballet 2100-2200 daily. Its sister
restaurant **Mirador Copoya** overlooks
Sumidero Canyon.

$ Los Molcajetes
In the arches behind the cathedral.
Cheap all-day meal deals including tacos,
enchiladas suizas, chilaquiles and other
staples. Several other restaurants lining
the arches offer similar good value.

Transport

Air
Tuxtla's international airport, **Aeropuerto
Angel Albino Corzo (TGZ)**, is located 27 km
south of the city. Fixed prices taxis into town
cost US$16; to **San Cristóbal**, US$46. **OCC**
minibuses also run from the airport to **San
Cristóbal**, 4 daily, US$12.50.

Flights to **Mexcio City** with Interjet,
Aeroméxico (Connect), TAR Aerolineas, and
Volaris; **Oaxaca** with Aerotucán; **Cancún**
with VivaAerobus; **Guadalajara** with
Volaris and VivaAerobus; **Monterrey**
with Volaris and VivaAerobus; **Tijuana**
with Volaris; and **Houston** with United.

Bus
The 1st class **ADO** bus station is on 5a Norte
Poniente at the corner of Angel Albino
Corzo, next to the large Plaza del Sol mall on
the northwestern outskirts of the city; buses
to the centre pass outside, US$0.50.

Departures to **Cancún**, 7 daily, 18-20 hrs,
US$85-139; **Comitán**, every 45 mins, 3 hrs,
US$7.50; **Mérida**, 8 daily, 13-15 hrs, US$66-92;
Mexico City, hourly, 12-13 hrs, US$89-112;
Oaxaca City, 5 daily, 10-11 hrs, US$41-62;
Palenque, 6 daily, 6-7 hrs, US$20-25; **Puerto
Escondido**, 3 daily, 2030, 2200, 2315, 11-
12 hrs, US$45; **San Cristóbal de las Casas**,
hourly, 1½ hrs, US$4-5; **Tapachula**, hourly,
4-6 hrs, US$30-51; **Tonalá**, hourly, 2 hrs,
US$14-16; **Villahermosa**, 11 daily, 4-5 hrs,
US$26-38. There's a 2nd-class terminal at
9a Av Sur Ote and 13a Calle Oriente Sur,
about 1 km southeast of the centre, serving
destinations in Chiapas.

Colectivos
Shuttles to **Chiapa de Corzo** depart
frequently from 1 Av Sur Ote and Calle 5a
Ote Sur; and from the **Transportes Chiapa–
Tuxtla** station, 2a Ote Sur and 1a Av Sur
Ote, 20 mins, US$0.85. To **San Cristóbal de
las Casas** (recommended, faster and more
frequent than **ADO**), from 15a Calle Ote Sur
and 4a Av Sur Ote; and from 13a Calle Ote
Sur near Av Central Ote, 1 hr, US$3.50.

El Soconusco

low-lying coastal shoreline with extensive sandy beaches

Backed by the peaks of the Sierra Madre de Chiapas, El Soconusco is a 200-km-long
strip of fertile coastal lowlands fringed by brackish mangrove swamps, teeming
estuarine outlets, rustic fishing villages, verdant fruit plantations, and miles of
desolate, wave-swept beaches.

Settled in 2000 BC by the Mokoya, one of the oldest of Mesoamerican cultures, the region
has always enjoyed a distinctive identity rooted in agriculture and trade, serving as a
tribute province for various powers including the Aztecs. Its name is derived from the

Nahuatl 'Xoconochco' (land of sour cactus fruit) and modern crops of bananas, coffee, cacao, mangos, maize, papaya, African palm and sesame seeds thrive in its rich volcano soil, staples of the local economy which are now complimented by tourism.

The beaches of the Soconusco are popular with weekenders from Tuxtla, but deserted during the week. The sands are grey and the currents can be strong (watch out for riptides, a definite danger), but the water is clear, clean and inviting, and the sunsets immense. If your final destination is Quetzaltenango or the Pacific coast of Guatemala, the crossing at Tapachula is the most convenient point of entry. Note the region is subject to high humidity, bloodthirsty bugs and torrential downpours during the wet season, May to October.

Tonalá and around → *Colour map 2, B2.*

Around 20 km east of the Oaxaca state border, the town of **Arriaga** marks an intersection of highways connecting Tehuantepec and Tuxtla Gutiérrez to the Soconusco. From here, Route 200 winds 24 km east to Tonalá, a small, sweltering agricultural city steeped in cattle pastures and farmlands. This is the gateway to more alluring destinations on the coast and you should stock up on supplies of cash as ATMs are nonexistent beyond here. Around 14 km west of Tonalá, perched on Laguna del Mar Muerto, the village of **Paredón** is good for fresh seafood, but there is no beach.

The region's main tourist hub is the sleepy village of **Puerto Arista**, 19 km south of Tonalá, home to a 30-km-long grey sand beach partly fronted by *palapas*, bars, restaurants, simple hotels and guesthouses. Turtles nest here from July to October and you'll find a sanctuary, the **Santuario Tortuguero Puerto Arista**, roughly 3 km northwest of town, which releases hatchlings and offers night tours. Around 14 km east of Puerto Arista, there are tranquil, low-key lodgings at the rustic fishing village of **Boca del Cielo**. A few kilometres further, **El Madresal** ⓘ *T966-666 6147, www.elmadresal.com*, is a conservation and ecotourism operator with *cabañas*, restaurant, and knowledgeable guides for wildlife and birding excursions. From Tonolá, the best way to get to the beaches is by *colectivo*; they run from dawn till dusk from Matamoros, between 20 de Marzo and Belisario Domínguez, 20-45 minutes, US$1.50-3. Private taxis cost US$10-15.

Reserva de la Biósfera La Encrucijada → *Colour map 2, C3.*

A federally protected biosphere reserve since 1995, La Encrucijada encompasses 144,868 ha of mangroves and semi-deciduous forest, permanently flooded wetlands and seasonal canals. It is home to caiman, monkeys, raccoons, boa constrictors, abundant amphibians and at least 90 species of bird, including waders, waterfowl and seabirds, and the only bird species endemic to Chiapas, the giant wren. Tours of the park are offered by the **La Red de Ecoturismo la Encrucijada** ⓘ *www.ecoturismolaencrucijada.com*, who can guide you through the mangroves by *lancha* or kayak, connect you with local communities, or set you up with rustic accommodation on the beach; they offer various all-inclusive packages starting at around US$190 per person, contact in advance of travel. To get to the reserve, first travel to **Escuintla**, 150 km east of Tonalá on Route 200. From there, *colectivos* go to **Acapetahua**, 6 km south, US$0.50. Combis ply the last 18 km to the **Embarcadero Las Garzas**, US$1.50, where you can hire onward *lanchas*. Take plenty of cash and plan carefully to avoid getting stranded.

Tapachula and around → *Colour map 2, C4.*

Optimistically dubbed 'Pearl of the Soconusco', Tapachula is a busy border town and flood-prone regional capital. In pre-Columbian times, it belonged to a rural province controlled by the Mam Maya, until it was assimilated and urbanized by the Aztecs in the 13th century. Its Nahautl name is Tapachollan (appropriately 'Between the Waters' of 'Place of Floods'). Today, it is a small city built on coffee exports and cross-border trade. Its economy is heavily supplemented by its cargo port, **Puerto Chiapas**, which was upgraded in 2005 to accommodate cruise ships. Downtown, the action is focused on **Parque Miguel Hidalgo**, a large plaza flanked by historical buildings, including the **Casa de Cultura**, an art deco edifice constructed in 1929 and embellished with Mexican motifs. The plaza is home to the city's only recommended attraction, the **Museo Arqueológico del Soconusco** ① *8a Av Norte, T962-626 4173, Tue-Sun 0900-1800, US$2.70 (plus US$3.50 to take photos)*, which houses a collection of artefacts from the site of Izapa (see below), including numerous stelae and a dazzling jade-encrusted human skull.

Around Tapachula If you have the time or inclination, there are several interesting diversions around Tapachula; for more details, including recommend guides, talk to the Sectur tourist office ① *6a Av Sur s/n, entre 2a y Central Poniente, T962-625 5409*. Options include **La Ruta Café**, an agro-tourism development that includes more than a dozen coffee fincas, many of German origin. Some of them are stunningly located with luxury mountain-top accommodation and spas; others have facilities for adventure sports like biking and zip-lining. Hardcore adventurists should consider a guided hike up **Volcán Tacaná** (4150 m), Mexico's fourth largest mountain, which takes two to three days from the town of Unión Juárez. There are waterfalls on the lower slopes and some *cabañas* at the top; a sleeping bag is essential.

Izapa → *Colour map 2, C4.*
Tapachula–Talismán highway Km10-12, 0900-1700, pay a donation to the caretaker. To get there, take any bus or a combi towards Talismán, US$0.80.

Founded in 1500 BC, the ceremonial centre of Izapa is one of the oldest urban sites in Mesoamerica. Probably of Mixe-Zoque origin, it reached its zenith 600 BC-AD 100 and remained inhabited until AD 1200. Its main axis is aligned with Volcán Tacaná and its urban core of 161 buildings includes pyramids, platforms, and ball courts. Izapa is most notable for its 283 monuments, including 89 stelae and 61 altars depicting mythological entities such as frogs symbolizing rain gods.

Pointing to the site's distinctive artwork, the archaeologist Michael Coe argued that Izapa acted as a 'bridge culture' between the pre-Classic Olmec and Maya. Olmec motifs like downturned human mouths and scrolling skies are evident at Izapa, whilst distinctive Izapa motifs have also been discerned at Mayan sites in Guatemala. It has also been argued that Izapa is the birthplace of the 260-day Mesoamerican calendar. Although the site is historically important, it is visually underwhelming with around 100 mounds and restored platforms divided between three sections: F in the north, A and B in the south. A good guide will bring it to life; contact the archaeological museum in Tapachula for recommendations.

Mexico to Guatemala: Tapachula–El Carmen/Ciudad Tecún → *Colour map 2, C4.*
The Talismán bridge lies 20 km from Tapachula and connects the towns of **Talismán** in Mexico and **El Carmen** in Guatemala. It provides good onward connections to the Pacific coast and the western highlands, but it's also a fairly grubby crossing with sneaky and aggressive moneychangers who you should avoid doing business with.

Further south, 37 km from Tapachula, **Ciudad Hidalgo** connects with **Ciudad Tecún Umán** in Guatemala. Perched on the Pan-American Highway, this is a much busier border town and the preferred route of international buses. Start as early as possible to avoid travelling in Guatemala during the hours of darkness. See also box, page 512.

Where to stay

Tonalá and around

$$$-$$ Awa Hotel
Blv Mariano Matamoros, Puerto Arista, T994-600 9187, awahotelboutiquespa@gmail.com.
Situated on the coast road next to the beach, this small boutique hotel is one of the more upscale options in Puerto Arista. It is a modern, Mediterranean-style building with contemporary furnishings and clean comfortable rooms overlooking a pool and sunbeds. Spa facilities are available.

$$-$ Hotel Galilea
Hidalgo 138, Tonalá, T966-663 0239.
If you get stuck in Tonalá, or just need to make an early start, there are a few budget hotels and *posadas*. **Hotel Galilea** is one of the better ones, complete with adequate a/c and balconies overlooking the main plaza.

$$-$ José's Cabañas
Niño Perdido 100, 1 block north of the beach, Puerto Arista, T994-600 9048, www.josescampingcabanas.com.
This Canadian-owned camping park offers basic brick-built bungalows with own bath, rustic *cabañas* with shared bath, dorm accommodation, RV hook-up and campground. No frills, but quiet and restful.

$$-$ La Luna
Boca del Cielo, T966-106 4893, www.lunachiapas.com.mx.
This tranquil and remote place has rustic, wood-built *cabañas* on the sand, solar powered and complete with hammocks and mosquito nets. There's a restaurant serving good seafood and a fun evening bar called the 'Loco Mosquito'. To get there take a taxi to the dock at Rancho Don Lupe, then call the hotel for boat transit.

Tapachula

$$$$-$$$ Argovia Finca Resort
Carretera Nueva Alemania Km 39+2, T962-692 3051, www.argovia.com.mx.
Founded by a Swiss family in 1880, this handsome highland coffee finca holds numerous awards and certificates for its quality organic produce, sustainable practices and high standard of hospitality. They offer coffee tours, gourmet cuisine, nature walks, adventure sports and spa facilities. Lodging is in cosy rooms, wood cabins, houses and bungalows. Secluded and restful. Recommended.

$$$$-$$$ Finca Hamburgo
Carretera Nueva Alemania Km 54, T962-626 7578, www.fincahamburgo.com.
Established in 1888 by Arthur Edelmann from Germany, **Finca Hamburgo** has also been recognized for its quality and distinction and has fabulous views of the countryside. Lodging includes tastefully decorated wood-panelled double rooms ($$$) and suites ($$$$). Restaurant, spa, coffee tours, nature tours, rappelling and zip-lining are among the services and amenities on offer.

$$$ Hotel Boutique Casa Mexicana
8a Av Sur 19, T962-626 6605, www.casamexicanachiapas.com.
There are scores of business hotels in Tapachula offering generic comfort for your pesos, but for something with style and personality head to this fabulous historic townhouse. It's strikingly adorned with folk art, antiques, paintings and statues. The superb atmosphere, quality rooms, intriguing decor, lush garden, pool, bar and restaurant combine to make this one of the best in town.

$ Hotel Cervantino
1a Calle Ote 6, T962-620 0008, www.hotelcervantino.com.mx.

Most of Tapachula's budget hotels are a bit insalubrious, but this place is a definite exception. They offer clean, simple rooms with Wi-Fi, parking, common areas and complimentary coffee. Friendly, helpful, good value and a good central location.

Restaurants

Tapachula

$$ La Jefa
1 Av Nte 16 esq.
1 Calle Ote, This friendly little joint serves up hearty tacos and other Mexican fare, best washed down with a cold beer. Wi-Fi is available and there are free snacks when you order booze.

Transport

Tapachula
Air
Tapachula airport (TAP) is 25 mins from town centre, at Km 18.5 Carretera a Puerto Madero. Flights to **Mexico City** with **Aeroméxico** and **Volaris**; **Tuxtla Gutiérrez** with **Ka'an Air**. *Colectivos* to downtown, US$6.50; US$13 for the whole vehicle.

Bus
The 1st class **ADO** terminal is 1 km northeast of the Parque Central, Calle 17a Ote, between Av 3a and 5a Nte. There is a 2nd-class terminal at Calle 9a Pte 62; *colectivos* depart from Calle 5a Pte. From the **ADO** terminal, departures to **Comitán**, 11 daily, 4-5 hrs, US$26-38; **Escuintla**, 7 daily, 1½ hrs, US$7.70; **Mexico City**, 5 daily, 17-19 hrs, US$104; **Oaxaca City**, 2 daily, 1915, 2000, 12-13 hrs, US$41-54; **San Cristóbal de las Casas**, 8 daily, 8 hrs, US$26-33; **Tonalá**, hourly, 3½ hrs, US$18; **Tuxtla Gutiérrez**, hourly, 5-6 hrs, US$30-34.

International buses Several bus lines offer services from Tapachula's 1st-class bus station to **Guatemala City**, including **Ticabus**, www.ticabus.com, 0700, US$22, 6 hrs; **Línea Dorada**, www.lineadorada.com.gt, 0600, US$17; and **Trans Galgos Inter**, www.transgalgosinter.com.gt, 0600, 1215, 2345, US$22-32. For more information on crossing the border see page 120 and box, page 512.

Colectivos

From Tapachula to **Ciudad Hidalgo** with onward connections to **Ciudad Tecún Umán**, combis depart from Calle 7a Pte, between Av 2 Norte and Av Central Norte, every 15 mins, US$1.90. Stamp out in Ciudad Hidalgo and cross the bridge into Guatemala to submit to formalities there. It is another 20-min walk from the border to Tecún Umán, or take a bici-taxi, US$1.50, where you can catch numerous onward connections.

From Tapachula to **Talismán** with onward connections to **El Carmen** in Guatemala, combis leave from near the Unión y Progreso bus station and from the *colectivo* terminal, Calle 5 Pte between Av 12 y Av 14 Norte, every 15 mins, 30 mins, US$1.15. Taxi **Tapachula–Talismán**, negotiate fare to about US$4. You may have to walk 5 mins to the border. A taxi between Guatemalan and Mexican Immigration offices will cost US$2, but it may be worth it if you are in a hurry to catch an onward bus. If travelling to Quetzaltenango, you will need to change in Coatepeque or Retalhuleu, or take a *colectivo* taxi to Malacatán. Hitchhikers should note that there is little through international traffic at the Talismán bridge. As a rule, hitchhiking is not advisable in Chiapas.

a thriving colonial town best known for its vertiginous canyon

Situated on a bluff overlooking the Grijalva River, Chiapa de Corzo, 15 km east of Tuxtla, is famous for its Parachico dancers, who descend on the streets in great numbers during the Great Feast, January 4-22 (see Festivals, below). Their striking attire includes colourful *sarapes* (blanket-type shawls), massive blond wigs, and lacquered wooden masks reminiscent of pale-faced Europeans.

Originally settled around 1400 BC by Mixe-Zoque speakers with close ties to the Olmec, the site evolved into an important city until its decline around 400 AD. By the time of the Spanish conquest, the war-like Chiapa tribe had established their capital less than 2 km away, which was subjugated by Diego de Mazariegos in 1528 only after fierce resistance. The administrative centre of Chiapa de los Indios was founded in the shade of La Pochota, an ancient and venerated ceiba tree, but soon abandoned for the cooler and more hospitable climes of San Cristóbal de las Casas. In the 19th century, the suffix of 'de Los Indios' was replaced to honour Liberal politician, Angel Albino Corzo.

Sights

The town is laid out in a classic colonial grid with a plaza at the centre, municipal buildings, commercial *portales*, and a particularly handsome 16th-century Moorish fountain, **La Pila**, boasting numerous arches and a brick-built watchtower in the shape of a crown. By the river, the **Iglesia de Santo Domingo** is perched on a small hill. Built in Moorish style by Pedro de Barrientos and Juan Alonso, it boasts one of the largest bells in the country, said to weigh more than four tonnes. The adjoining *ex-convento* houses a cultural centre and the **Museo de la Laca** ⓘ *Tue-Sun 1000-1700, free*, with fine examples of local lacquer work dating back to the 17th century. Remnants of the region's distant Zoque heritage can be encountered at the town's small but important **archaeological site** ⓘ *Av Hidalgo, 0800-1630, free, 1.5 km from the plaza behind the Nestlé plant*. It includes some restored temple complexes, many unexcavated mounds, and the oldest known pyramid tomb in Mesoamerica. Around 10 km beyond Chiapa de Corzo is the **Cueva del Chorreadero**, with refreshing waterfalls and swimming pools. The underground cave system here should not be explored without a professional guide and safety equipment; there are several adventure and ecotourism operators in San Cristóbal de las Casas (see What to do, page 136).

★Sumidero Canyon

Engulfing the Río Grijalva with its vast and precipitous walls, the Sumidero Canyon, as deep as 1 km in some sections, is a truly sheer natural spectacle that rarely fails to impress. According to local legend, Chiapaneco warriors hurled themselves into this hungry chasm rather than submit to the Spanish conquistadors. In recent times, the construction of the Chicoasén Dam created a 25 km-long reservoir, allowing visitors to experience the canyon by motorboat. The journey takes around two hours. You'll see intriguing rock formations and prolific wildlife, such as crocodiles, monkeys, pelicans and vultures, but remember to pack a sweater, as it gets chilly when you're speeding along.

Boats depart from the riverside in **Chiapa de Corzo** when full, but you shouldn't have to wait long for other passengers. Tickets are available at the **Turística de Grijalva office** ⓘ *west side of the plaza, 0800-1700, US$12.50*. If you have your own vehicle, you may wish to forgo Chiapa de Corzo (parking can be tricky) and use the *embarcadero* beneath

Cahuaré bridge, 5 km north of town. It is also possible to view the canyon from on high at a sublime series of miradors. **Transporte Panorámico Cañón del Sumidero** ⓘ *T961-166 3740*, visits the main ones, departing from Jardín de la Marimba in Tuxtla at 0930 and 1300, US$11.50, if there is sufficient demand (five people); call ahead to confirm.

Listings Chiapa de Corzo

Where to stay

$$ Hotel La Ceiba
Av Domingo Ruíz 300, T961-616 0389,
www.laceibahotel.com.
You'll find a handful of adequate *posadas* in Chiapa de Corzo, but La Ceiba is the only lodging of any decent standard. This handsome 3-storey colonial house boasts a rambling, leafy garden, pool, restaurant and spa facilities. Rooms are reasonable, but sometimes noisy due to tour groups.

Festivals

The fiestas here are outstanding.
Jan Daylight fiestas, **Los Parachicos**, on 15, 17 and 20 Jan to commemorate the miraculous healing of a young boy some 300 years ago, and the **Chunta Fiestas**, at night, 8-23 Jan. There are parades with men dressed up as women in the evenings of the 8, 12, 17 and 19 Jan. All lead to the climax, 20-23 Jan, in honour of **San Sebastián**, with a pageant on the river.
25 Feb **El Santo Niño de Atocha**.
25 Apr **Festival de San Marcos**, with various *espectáculos*.

Transport

Colectivos
Frequent *colectivos* to **Tuxtla** depart from Av 21 de Octubre on the plaza. Buses to **San Cristóbal** now bypass Chiapa de Corzo, meaning you'll have to pick one up on the highway or go via Tuxtla.

San Cristóbal de las Casas → *Colour map 2, A3.*
a rambling colonial city with cobblestone streets and adobe houses

★Nestled on the floor of a high green valley is the cool, bright, mysterious mountain enclave of San Cristóbal de las Casas, sometimes known by its Tzotzil name, 'Jovel'. It is the largest urban settlement in the Chiapas highlands and a vital hub of trade for Mayan communities dispersed in the surrounding hills and pine forests. Despite serving as the capital of Chiapas until its relocation to Tuxtla in 1892, it has always been an insular place, characterized by its many poor indigenous barrios, and during the colonial era, its devout monastic institutions and its somewhat over-privileged Spanish elite.

In recent years, for better or worse, the outside world has intruded in the form of tourism: scores of international restaurants, youth hostels, boutique hotels, rowdy bars, art house cinemas, yoga schools, and meditation centres give the city a vibrant, bohemian, New Age feel that may ultimately dissipate as gentrification intensifies. During the busiest tourist months, the atmosphere can verge on carnivalesque, sadly masking the city's essential character: beyond its fetching exterior and sociable vibe, a deeply political current here has long accented social divisions, inequalities and inequities.

Essential San Cristóbal de las Casas

Getting around

Most places are within walking distance of each other although taxis are available in town and to the nearby villages; the cheaper *colectivos* run on fixed routes only.

Best places to stay

Don Quijote, page 131
Na Bolom, page 131
Sol y Luna, page 131
Posada del Abuelito, page 132

When to go

Day time temperatures in the highlands are consistently warm throughout the year at around 20°C. However, evening temperatures can drop to 5°C or less from December to February, requiring a light jacket or sweater. December to February are the driest months; August to October can be extremely wet and buggy.

Best restaurants

Tierra y Cielo, page 132
Cocoliche, page 133
El Punto Pizzería, page 133
Te Quiero Verde, page 133
Oh La La, page 134

Sights

Plaza 31 de Marzo, named after the date of San Cristóbal's foundation in 1528, is the social heart of the city, informally known as the Zócalo or the Parque Central. Pleasantly landscaped with evergreens, tallipot palm trees, ornamentals, pathways, and benches, it is a hub for wandering pedestrians, shoe-shiners, and vendors, including traditionally attired Tzotzil and Tzeltal women who sell everything from hand-woven textiles to lovable Zapatista dolls, sweet organic strawberries and corn on the cob. At the centre of the plaza stands a Porfirato kiosk where jaunty marimba performances are staged on Sundays – there are terraced cafes on the south and east sides where you can enjoy hot Chiapaneco coffee, relax to the melodies and watch the world go by.

The **Casa de la Sirena**, a late 16th-century mansion commissioned by the conquistador Diego de Mazariegos, stands on the southeast corner of the plaza. It is a rare but crude example of colonial residential architecture in the plateresque style (an ornate decorative style suggestive of silverware; literally 'in the manner of a silversmith'); the portals on Avenida Insurgentes feature stucco coats of arms and the wide-eyed mermaids of its namesake. Built in 1885, the relatively modern **Palacio Municipal** (City Hall) stands on the west side of the plaza with rows of arches on Tuscan columns. It is the focal point of regular protests by students, *campesinos*, Zapatistas and other local activists.

Weather San Cristóbal de las Casas

January	February	March	April	May	June
4°C	4°C	6°C	8°C	9°C	11°C
21°C	22°C	24°C	24°C	24°C	23°C
9mm	8mm	12mm	45mm	94mm	229mm

July	August	September	October	November	December
10°C	10°C	11°C	9°C	7°C	4°C
23°C	23°C	22°C	22°C	21°C	21°C
174mm	191mm	226mm	116mm	35mm	11mm

San Cristóbal's mustard-coloured **cathedral** stands on the north side of the Zócalo. Construction of it probably began in the late 17th century to replace the modest brick and adobe structure that served as the principle house of worship from its foundation in 1528, the first public building in the city. The main façade was completed in the 18th century

San Cristóbal de las Casas

Where to stay 🛌
Axkan Arte 1 *D2*
Balam 2 *B3*
Bela's 3 *B2*
B¨o 4 *B1*
Don Quijote 5 *B3*
Guayaba Inn 6 *A4*
Iguana Hostel 7 *A2*
La Joya 8 *C3*
Los Camellos 9 *C4*
Na Bolom 10 *A4*

Posada del Abuelito 11 *A4*
Posada San Cristóbal 12 *C2*
Puerta Vieja 13 *C1*
Santo Tomás 14 *A4*
Sol y Luna 15 *A3*

Restaurants 🍴
Belil 1 *B3*
Cocoliche 2 *C3*
El Caldero 3 *D2*
El Cau 4 *C3*

El Mercadito 5 *B4*
El Punto Pizzeria 6 *C3*
Juguería Ana Banana 14 *D2*
La Casa del
Pan Paplotl 33 *C3*
La Tertulia 7 *C2*
Madre Tierra 18 *D2*
Miura 9 *C2*
Oh La La 10 *C2*
Te Quiero Verde 11 *D2*
TierrAdentro 12 *C2*

Tierra y Cielo 23 *C2*

Bars & clubs 🍸
Dada Club 13 *B2*
El Cocodrilo 8 *C2*
Entropia 15 *B3*
Revolución 30 *B2*

BACKGROUND
San Cristóbal de las Casas

Throughout much of its colonial life, San Cristóbal was known as Ciudad Real, in reference to the birthplace of the Spanish conquistador, Diego de Mazariegos, who violently subjugated the region. It was later renamed in honour of the patron Saint Christopher, but the suffix referencing the 16th-century Dominican friar, Bartolomé de las Casas, the first Bishop of Chiapas, 'Protector of the Indians', who famously preached in the city and petitioned King Ferdinand over abuses committed against the indigenous peoples, was only added in the 19th century.

As a focal point for human rights activism, San Cristóbal hit global headlines on 1 January 1994 when the Zapatista Liberation Army (EZLN), driven by centuries of abuse and feudal injustice, came down from the hills and seized the city by force.

and numerous changes to the overall structure were made after the 1901 earthquake, including a complete remodeling of the cavernous interior. Today, it features rows of neoclassical Corinthian columns, three altars, and a gilded 16th-century wood pulpit. The cathedral's main west-facing façade overlooks a large open square, the **Plaza Catedral**, also known as the Plaza de la Paz, where concerts and other events are sometimes staged. Mayan women often gather on the steps here. The large cross in front of the church is not a Catholic crucifix, but a Mayan cross symbolizing the World Tree. Behind the cathedral, the much smaller, simpler **Templo San Nicolás** was built for the indigenous population by the Augustinian order in 1621.

Half a block north of Plaza Catedral you'll find the **Museo Mesoamericano de Jade** ① *Av 16 de Septiembre 16, T967-678 1121, www.eljade.com, Mon-Sat 1200-2000, Sun 1200-1800, US$2.30*, home to an extensive private collection of reproduction jade artefacts. This is more of a commercial jewellery shop than a true museum, but their exhibition does include a faithful recreation of the death mask of Lord Pakal of Palenque. Three blocks west of Plaza 31 de Marzo you'll find the modest **Museo de Cultura Popular** ① *Diego de Mazariegos 34 esq. 12 de Octubre*, which hosts small temporary exhibitions with ethnic or folkloric themes. On the opposite side of the street, the Iglesia Merced houses the **Museo de Ambar** ① *Diego de Mazariegos, T967-678 9716, www.museo delambar.com.mx, Tue-Sun 1000-2000, US$1.50*, not to be confused with jewellery shops bearing the same name. This one-room museum has a display of raw and cut amber, including some beautiful sculptures, and videos in Spanish explaining how jade is crafted. One block north of the Merced, it is well worth checking out the **Museo de Trajes Regionales** ① *Guadalupe Victoria 38, T967-678 4289, www.yokchij.org, guided visits by appointment only, various languages, at 1930, 1½ hrs, US$2.70*. This small but fascinating museum houses an array of traditional Mayan costumes, masks, musical instruments, textiles and more, comprising the personal collection of humanitarian Sergio Castro (who also offers interesting tours of the region).

Three important pedestrian streets lead off the two central plazas, all with an array of touristy restaurants, terraced cafés, bars, craft stores, and jade and amber workshops. Heading south off the southwest corner of Plaza 31 de Marzo, Manuel Hidalgo leads to the L-shaped **Templo El Carmen**, the only surviving part of the La Encarnación convent, founded in 1597. At its east side stands a superb Mudéjar-style tower, squat, square and striking red. This unique architectural contribution was added to the convent in the

ON THE ROAD

Subcomandante Marcos and the Zapatistas

On New Year's Day 1994, at the moment when NAFTA came into force, the Ejército Zapatista de Liberación Nacional (EZLN) briefly took control of several towns in the southern state of Chiapas. Demanding social justice, indigenous people's rights, democracy at all levels of Mexican politics, an end to government corruption and land reform for the peasantry, the EZLN attracted international attention, helped by their use of modern communications technology. The government was forced to open peace talks.

President Zedillo later suspended the controversial PRI governor of Chiapas, but then allowed the army to launch a brief, but unsuccessful, campaign to capture the EZLN's leader, Subcomandante Marcos. Resumed talks between the government and the EZLN led to the first peace accord being signed in February 1996. The pace of change was slow, however, and in 1997 the EZLN renewed its protests, accusing the government of trying to change the terms of the agreed legal framework for indigenous rights. Physical conflict continued with 60,000 troops heavily outnumbering the Zapatista guerrillas.

In December 1997 45 civilians, mainly women and children, were massacred in Acteal near San Cristóbal de las Casas by paramilitaries linked to the PRI. Although the local mayor was implicated in the atrocity and arrested along with 39 others, there were calls for more senior government officials to be removed and in 1998 the Minister of the Interior and State Governor were forced to resign.

Tensions remained after Vicente Fox was elected in 2000 when the constitutional reforms long promised to the EZLN once again failed to materialize. Talks broke down and in 2003 the Zapatistas turned their attention inwards, consolidating support and developing self-governing committees – Juntas de Buen Gobierno (Committees of Good Government) – in those villages where approval was strongest. These, however, were criticized as unaccountable and bureaucratic.

In 2005, Subcomandante Marcos restyled himself Subdelegado Cero and attempted to broaden the Zapatista agenda by appealing to the whole country, not just the indigenous peasantry. He toured Mexico drumming up support for his broad leftist movement, although did not gain the same momentum as the mainstream parties, who were running their 2006 presidential election campaigns at the same time. In 2014, Marcos stepped down as an EZLN spokesman to make way for entirely indigenous leadership although he still writes for them from time to time. Today, the situation in Chiapas remains relatively stable, if tense.

17th century to replace a belfry destroyed in a tornado. In the surrounding buildings, you'll find **El Carmen Cultural Centre** ⓘ *Tue-Sun, 0900-1700, free*, with chess tournaments and other events. Just north of the tower, a road, Hermanos Domínguez, heads west to Cerrito San Cristóbal – a small, isolated, tree-covered hill with a church and views over the city. Heading east off the northeast corner of Plaza 31 de Marzo, the pedestrianized street of **Real de Guadalupe** concludes at the **Templo de Guadalupe**, another small church perched on a hill. The surrounding indigenous barrio of Guadalupe was historically populated by candle-makers, saddle-makers and wooden toy makers. The third pedestrian street is Avenida 20 de Noviembre, which leads north off the northeast corner of Plaza Catedral past the **Teatro Daniel Zebadúa** (1931) and on to the sumptuous **Iglesia and ex-Convento de Santo Domingo**, arguably the finest building in the city (see below).

Running along the east side of Santo Domingo church, Avenida General Utrilla becomes Salomón González Blanco, home to the **Centro de Desarollo de la Medicina Maya** ⓘ *Salomón González Blanco 10, T967-678 5438, Mon-Fri 0900-1800, Sat-Sun 1000-1600, US$2*. This humble community museum maintains a working prayer room where healings are performed, a small garden filled with medicinal herbs, a *temazcal* (indigenous sauna) and several exhibitions relating to traditional Mayan medicine and bio-piracy (ask for the information cards). It is a very modest place that makes the best of its scant resources, but an excellent primer if you plan on visiting Tzotzil communities. Continuing north on Salomón González Blanco for 400 m, you'll meet the Periférico Norte. Turn right (east) and head straight for another 600 m and you'll arrive at the **Orquideas Moxviquil Botanical Garden** ⓘ *Periférico Norte 4, T967-678 5727, www.orchidsmexico.com, Mon-Sat 0900-1700, Sun 1000-1600, US$1.50*. Their gardens and greenhouses are home to a stunning collection of 3000 rescued and endangered plants, including specimens of roughly half the orchid species in Chiapas state.

Iglesia and Ex-Convento de Santo Domingo

The west-facing Churriguersque façade of the church of Santo Domingo boasts the finest stonework in San Cristóbal: an incredibly extravagant tableau reminiscent of Oaxaca City's high-blown Dominican structures. Its sculpted surface features numerous Solomonic columns, niched saints and florid decorative details, best observed in the warm textured hues of the afternoon sun. Both the church and its adjoining monastery were originally constructed in the mid-16th century to house the first Dominican order in Chiapas, but little remains of those early adobe buildings. The current structures, which have been in constant use for four centuries, date to the late 17th century at the earliest.

Inside the ex-convent complex, on the ground floor, is the **Museo de los Altos de Chiapas** ⓘ *Calzada Lázaro Cárdenas, T967-678 1609, Tue-Sun 0900-1800, US$3.70*. This small regional museum charts the history of the Chiapas highlands from pre-Columbian times through the conquest to the colonial era. Its exhibitions comprise colonial antiques, religious art and archaeological finds: arrow heads, ceramics, stelae, implements, and ancient textiles. The ex-convent is also home to the highly recommended **Centro del Textiles Mundo Maya** ⓘ *upstairs on the first floor, T967-631 3094, www.fomentoculturalbanamex.org/ctmm, entrance included with the Museo de los Altos*. Opened in 2012, it documents the vast and extremely ancient heritage of Mayan textiles with examples of brilliantly woven pieces from Chiapas to El Salvador; hundreds of samples are exhibited in pull-out drawers. There are also interesting several videos that demonstrate the traditional methods of dyeing and weaving. Locally produced textiles can be purchased in the cooperatively managed store downstairs, or in the markets sprawled outside the church.

Na Bolom Museum and Cultural Center

Vicente Guerrero 33, T967-678 1418, www.nabolom.org. Guided tours daily, 1130 in Spanish, 1630 in English, US$4.50, US$3.50 without tour; library Mon-Fri 0930-1330 and 1630-1900.

Founded in 1951 by the Danish archaeologist Frans Blom and his wife, the Swiss photographer Gertrudis Duby, both of them ardent Mayanists, Na Bolom ('Jaguar House' in Tzotzil) began life as a study centre for the universities of Harvard and Stanford. After the death of Frans Blom in 1963, Gertrudis Duby continued campaigning for the conservation of the Lacandón area. She died in 1993, aged 92, after which the centre continued to function as a non-profit-making organization dedicated to conserving the Chiapan environment and helping the Lacandón people.

Situated in a 19th-century neoclassical mansion, the museum and its photographic archives are fascinating and contain a detailed visual history of 50 years of daily life of the Maya people with beautifully displayed artefacts, pictures of Lacandones, and information about their present way of life. There are five galleries with collections of pre-Columbian Maya art and colonial religious paintings. There is also a great anthropological library. A shop sells products made by the indigenous people helped by the centre.

Na Bolom runs various projects, staffed by volunteers. Prospective volunteers spend a minimum of three months, maximum six, at the centre. They must have skills that can be useful to the projects, such as anthropology, organic gardening, or be multi-linguists. Volunteers are given help with accommodation and a daily food allowance. Na Bolom also has 12 rooms to rent (see Where to stay, below).

Listings San Cristóbal de las Casas *map p126*

Tourist information

Municipal Office
Palacio Municipal on the main plaza,
T967-678 0665.
Has a good free map of the area. There is also a kiosk on the plaza with irregular opening hours.

Where to stay

$$$$ Guayaba Inn
Calle Comitan 55, T967-674 7699,
www.guayabainn.com.
This tranquil, beautiful and tasteful boutique B&B is the creation of Kiki and Gabriel Suárez, who have 40 years' experience in the hospitality industry. Set in a traditional converted home with koi ponds and orchid gardens, the inn has tranquil suites with fine wooden floors, original artwork, 4-poster beds and cosy fire places. Romantic and sublime.

$$$$ Hotel B¨o
5 de Mayo 38, Barrio de Mexicanos,
T967-678 1515, www.hotelbo.mx.

The word 'B¨o' means 'water' and this luxury boutique hotel embodies a highly evolved contemporary design that will delight trendy young things and those with a discerning sense of aesthetics. Rooms and suites are the epitome of good taste.

$$$$ La Joya
Francisco Madero 43A, T967-631 4832,
www.lajoyahotelsancristobal.com.
An impeccable upscale option built and managed by former Peace Corp volunteers, Ann and John. Secluded behind heavy wooden doors, there are 5 stylish boutique suites with names like 'The White Duchess' and 'The Black Orchid', all very unique, chic, extravagant and smart.

$$$ Axkan Arte Hotel
Álvaro Obregón 2, T967-116 0293,
www.axkanhotel.com.
This modern new downtown hotel has its own art gallery with works by Chiapaneco artists. Set on 3 floors around a central courtyard, it has 18 functional, well-equipped, impeccably clean rooms. Services include parking, travel agency, and restaurant serving traditional food. Breakfast included. Safe and reliable.

$$$ Bela's
Calle Dr Navarro 2, T967-678 9292, www. belasbandb.com. 3-night minimum stay.
Managed by the hospitable **Bela**, this perfectly tranquil B&B features a verdant, flowery and impeccably well-kept garden complete with hummingbirds. Lodging is in cosy rooms, with or without private bath, including a suite and a top-floor quarter with views. There are 4 friendly resident dogs too.

$$$ Na Bolom
Vicente Guerrero 33, T967-678 1418, www.nabolom.org.
Set in a 19th-century mansion that now functions as the **Na Bolom** cultural centre and museum (see above), this beautiful 17-room guesthouse was the former home of Mayanists Franz Blom and Gertrude Duby. Rooms are very cosy and feature popular art and interesting photography. A traditional Mexican meal is served every night at 1900 in the courtyard restaurant. A special place, lots of atmosphere. Recommended.

$$$ Sol y Luna
Tonalá 27, T967-678 5727, www.solylunainn.com.
Centred around a patio with cacti, potted plants, and orchids, this lovely little family-run B&B has just 2 rooms, 'Sol' and 'Luna', both wonderfully decorated with popular art, rustic furnishings, fine antiques and books. There's a shared kitchen and communal area with a chimney. Hospitable, intimate, and bohemian. Book in advance. Recommended.

$$ Don Quijote
Av Cristóbal Colón 7, T967-678 0346, www.hoteldonquijote.com.mx.
Popular with tour groups, this reliable option has an ultra-convenient downtown location just off Real de Guadalupe. Rooms are simple, comfortable, affordable and down-to-earth, and come complete with the usual amenities like cable TV and Wi-Fi. The same owners manage a much larger and more

upscale property, **Rincón del Arco ($$$)**, www.rincondelarco.com, recommended for its fine lawns and gardens.

$$ Hotel Balam
Calle Ejército Nacional 34, between Cristóbal Colón and Diego Dugelay, T967-674 7771, www.hotelbalam.mx.
A small, friendly hotel with 16 impeccably clean and comfortable quarters. Some rooms are on the small side, but all are well-appointed with modern facilities and solid wood furniture. The hotel has been maintained with care since its opening a few years ago and it remains a good deal for your pesos. Reliable.

$$ Hotel Posada San Cristóbal
Insurgentes 3, T967-678 6881.
Complete with a leafy patio and creaky floorboards, this *posada* is housed in one of the city's most historic buildings, the Casa de la Sirena (see Sights, above) in an unbeatable central location. It is an atmospheric place, although the service is more functional than fabulously hospitable. Unfussy travellers who can tolerate flaws like musty aromas and chipped paintwork will find good value here; most rooms are massive for the price.

$$ Hotel Santo Tomás
Calle Franz Blom 1, T967-674 5227, hotel_santothomas@hotmail.com.
Off-the-beaten track around 15 mins from the centre, this large colonial-style hotel encloses a massive lawn and courtyard like a rambling monastic complex. Rooms are large, cosy and kitted with chimneys, perfect for those chilly winter nights. Secluded and good value.

$ Iguana Hostel
Chiapa de Corzo 16, T967-631 7731, www.iguanahostel.com.
A good, clean, well-managed hostel overlooking a pleasant neighbourhood plaza near the Santo Domingo church. The hosts and staff are exceptionally friendly and helpful with lots of good reports from former guests. Lodging is in dorms and

rooms. There's a garden, hammocks, table tennis and travel agency. Sociable, relaxed and fun.

$ Los Camellos
Real de Guadalupe 110, T967-116 0097, www.loscamellos.over-blog.com.
This highly likeable French/Mexican-owned hostel is one of the oldest backpacker places in town. It's a quiet and chilled out place, very friendly, colourful, down-to-earth and bohemian. They have dorms and private rooms, free coffee and drinking water, book exchange, communal areas, a well-equipped kitchen and hammocks.

$ Posada del Abuelito
Tapachula 18, T967-678 1741, www.posadadelabuelito.com.
A homely little *posada* and one the city's best budget options. It has a handful of snug private rooms and dorm beds in a low-key colonial setting, with or without private bath. Facilities include chill-out patios and a common room with a toasty chimney. Laid-back, friendly and sociable, but not a party place. Recommended.

$ Puerta Vieja
Diego de Mazariegos 23, T967-631 4335, www.puertaviejahostel.com.
Set in a handsome colonial townhouse, Puerta Vieja is a very popular and sociable backpackers' hostel with an emphasis on shared activities like cinema and pizza, yoga, live music, parties and evening cocktails. Accommodation is in private rooms and dorms (mixed and female-only). Facilities include a garden, hammocks, lounge, kitchen and *temazcal* steam bath.

Restaurants

As one of Mexico's busiest tourist hubs, there is an extensive and competitive restaurant scene in San Cristóbal, including lots of vegetarian places. Note many businesses close at 1700 on Sun.

$$$ Miura
Real de Guadalupe 26.
Vegetarians are certainly at home in San Cristóbal, but carnivores need not despair. For mouth-watering cuts of certified Angus beef, including delectable fillet and rib-eye hand-picked from a selection and grilled to taste, head to **Miura**. Their burgers aren't bad either and there's a buffet option too. Good service.

$$$ Tierra y Cielo
Juárez 1, T967-678 1053, www.tierraycielo. com.mx.
With an award-winning chef, **Tierra y Cielo** is celebrated for its traditional Chiapaneco cuisine with an intriguing contemporary twist. Well-presented recipes use good, fresh, local ingredients and wholesome produce to creative effect. One of the best dining experiences in the city, the place for a special evening out. Recommended.

$$$-$$ El Cau
Real de Guadalupe 57A.
Almost as if you've stepped into Barcelona, this cheery tapas joint serves authentic dishes from the motherland, including cod croquettes, Spanish tortilla and *escalivada* (grilled eggplant and red peppers). They have a fine stock of Spanish wine too and regular live jazz or acoustic guitar in the evenings. Trendy, friendly, warm and cosy, with a great atmosphere.

$$ Belil
María Adelina Flores 20B.
'Belil' is a Tzotzil word that broadly translates as 'sustenance'. In that spirit, Belil is much more than a restaurant serving good coffee and tasty, organic Chiapaneco specialities, but a place of cultural nourishment. The manager, Ricardo, has spent years working in Chiapas in the field of human rights and can connect you with interesting guides and organizations for exploring the surrounding countryside.

$$ Cocoliche
Cristóbal Colón 3.
Authentically bohemian with kitsch art house decor, this charismatic bar-restaurant has a fantastic international menu that includes flavourful curries from Thailand, Indonesia and Cambodia, enormous heart-warming bowls of pasta, generous salads, sandwiches and wraps. Evenings are an occasion for cabaret and live music. Great atmosphere, good food, lovely hosts, friendly service. Highly recommended.

$$ El Punto Pizzería
Real de Guadalupe 47.
El Punto cooks up the best pizzas in town, no question. Authentically Italian and stone-baked in a wood-fired oven, they're close to perfect and large enough to satisfy 2 people. Seating is indoors or out and they have another branch on Calle Comitán, Barrio El Cerillo. Highly recommended.

$$ La Casa del Pan Papalotl
Inside the Centro Cultural El Puente, Real de Guadalupe 55, www.casadelpan.com.
Using organic ingredients in many recipes, this is one of the city's first and oldest vegetarian restaurants with ties to many local farming cooperatives. They serve excellent bread, soups, salads, sandwiches, quesadillas, cooked breakfasts, juices and coffee. It's in a pleasant setting.

$$ La Tertulia
Cuauhtémoc 2. Closed Mon.
This friendly, low-key little café is a great breakfast spot. They serve delicious *huevos rancheritos* with nopal cactus, spicy *chilaquiles*, sweet and savoury crêpes, pastas, thick fruity smoothies and a range of good, strong locally sourced coffee. There's Wi-Fi too. If you were wondering about the name, a *tertulia* is a type of Spanish literary salon, or an informal meeting to discuss art, politics, or culture.

$$ Te Quiero Verde
Niños Héroes 5. Wed-Mon 0900-1100 and 1330-2100.
This cosy, casual, chilled-out café with just a handful of tables serves excellent healthy fare such as veggie burgers made with love, including Moroccan and Indian options. They come complete with hand-cut fries and a side of hummus and nachos. Good fruit smoothies and *licuados* too. Friendly management. Recommended.

$$-$ El Caldero
Insurgentes 5A, www.elcaldero.com.mx.
The perfect antidote to those chilly winter evenings: a bowl of piping hot stew. As the name might suggest, the popular locals' haunt of El Caldero (the Cauldron) serves nothing else. A range of flavourful meat-based and vegetarian broths are on offer, with or without an addition of local white cheese. Massive portions.

$$-$ Madre Tierra
Insurgentes 19, opposite Franciscan church, T967-678 4297.
This long-established Anglo-Mexican café-bakery is recommended for its breakfasts, wholemeal breads, pies, brownies, cakes, and other sweet treats. There's cosy seating indoors or outdoors in an enclosed courtyard. Popular with travellers, Wi-Fi available.

$$-$ TierrAdentro
Real de Guadalupe 24.
This cavernous cultural centre with Zapatista affiliation has an extensive menu of economical Mexican staples and international snacks, coffee, juices, breakfasts and lunches. Items can be a bit a hit and miss, but servings are reasonably generous and most people come for the EZLN connection and to meet other travellers.

$ El Mercadito
Diego Dugelay 11.
Short on charm but rich in flavor, El Mercadito is a very low-key and unassuming locals' joint, and it serves great home-cooked grub at economical prices. They cook up a fresh buffet every day with an array of Mexican staples and regional specialities. A good casual lunch place.

Coffee shops and bakeries

Oh La La
Miguel Hidalgo esq Cuauhtémoc.
This exquisite French patisserie bakes an array of delicious treats every day: croissants, *pain au chocolate*, and a sumptuous variety of desserts. Friendly service and great coffee too. There's a smaller branch on Real de Guadalupe, just off Parque 31 de Marzo. Recommended.

Bars and clubs

Dada Club
1 de Marzo 6, www.dadajazzclub.net.
Thu-Sun, performances commence at 2200;
hours vary with the seasons, see their
website or Facebook page for more details.
This intimate little club is the place to enjoy local jazz music performed live before Twin Peaks-style red curtains. In addition to beer, mescal and cocktails, they serve international cuisine.

El Cocodrilo
Insurgentes 1, opposite Parque 31 de Marzo.
Adjoining **Hotel Santa Clara** in the historic premises of the Casa de la Sirena, **El Cocodrilo** is a popular and well-to-do lounge bar that's usually busy with tourists most evenings in high season. They host an eclectic range of talented local musicians for live performances.

Entropia
Maria Adelina flores 22, esq Cristóbal Colón.
The preferred bohemian option, set inside a colonial townhouse with kitsch-style details, toasty fireplace and a handsome inner courtyard. They serve good grub and host live music most nights. One of the town's best watering holes. Good crowd, with a fun vibe. Highly recommended.

Revolución
20 de Noviembre and 1 de Marzo,
www.elrevo.com. Open 1300-0200,
live music daily 2000 and 2230.

A San Cristóbal institution, lots of fun, but definitely touristy, with a grungy, alternative and bohemian vibe. They host good local bands and DJs with a buzzing crowd and a raucous atmosphere most nights. Skip the cocktails and food, stick to bottled beer.

Entertainment

Cinema and theatre

Cinema El Puente
Real de Guadalupe 55,
www.elpuenteweb.com.
Part of **El Puente** language school, this small cinema screens documentaries, art house films and classics at 1800, with later showings Fri-Sat at 2000.

Foro Cultural Kinoki
Belisario Domínguez 5A esq Real de Guadalupe, www.forokinoki.blogspot.com.
This excellent cultural centre shows thought-provoking documentaries and alternative, Latin American and art house films. They have 3 screening rooms, a bar, restaurant and a tea room with an upstairs terrace where you can sip herbal infusions and watch the bustle below. Recommended.

Festivals

Jan/Feb Carnival is held during the 4 days before Lent, dates vary.
Mar/Apr There is a popular **spring festival** on **Easter Sun** and the week after.
Early Nov Festival Maya-Zoque, which lasts 4 days, promoting the 12 different Maya and Zoque cultures in the Chiapas region, with dancing and celebrations in the main plaza.
12 Dec La Fiesta de Guadalupe.

Shopping

Artesanías and produce
Colourful textiles, clay sculptures and other *artesanías* are sold on the streets by Mayan women at very low prices, mostly in the tourist hubs and plazas. Additionally, there

are craft markets and cooperatives (see below). The following retail outlets are recommended:

Casa Chiapas, *Niños Héroes and Hidalgo, www.casachiapas.gob.mx*. This state-run shop sells high quality crafts from across Chiapas, including large furniture items you won't find at the market. Other offerings include textiles, lacquer boxes, baskets, costumed figurines.

Poshería, *Real de Guadalupe 46A, www. poxceremonial.com*. Consumed widely in Chiapas, for religious reasons as much as for pleasure, *pox* (pronounced 'posh') is a distilled alcoholic drink made from maize. This colourful little store sells artisanal varieties, some of them are not quite as strong as the crazy fire water the locals guzzle, but much more palatable.

Bookshops

La Abuelita, *Cristóbal Colón 2, www.abuelita books.com*. A good stock of classics, non-fiction, guidebooks, Spanish language, politics, history and spirituality titles. As well hosting regular events, including movie screenings, they serve good local coffee and supply complimentary Wi-Fi. A good place to hang out.

La Pared, *Av Miguel Hidalgo 13B, near the Arco del Carmen, T967-678 6367, www.lapared bookstore.com*. A very good selection of Mexico books in English and a few in other European languages, and many travel books including Footprint guides. American owner Dana Burton is very helpful.

Cooperatives

El Camino de los Altos, *Insurgentes 19, www.el-camino.fr*. A very successful association of 9 French designers and 130 Mayan weavers, **El Camino de los Altos** produces some lovely textiles that feature in many of Chiapas's upmarket hotels. Designs are contemporary, bold and beautiful.

Sna Jolobil, *Av 20 de Noviembre, next to the Museo de Textiles*. Meaning 'House of Weavers' in Tzotzil, this is the best

cooperative and is comprised of 800 highland artisans producing some stunning traditional and contemporary textiles. Their very finest work can fetch thousands of dollars on international markets. Recommended.

Taller Leñateros, *Flavio A Paniagua 54, www.tallerlenateros.com*. Founded in 1975 by Mexican poet Ambar Past, this Mayan-operated paper-making workshop produces attractive paper and prints from natural materials. Their profits help support around 30 Maya families.

Jewellery

Handmade jade and amber jewellery is widely available in San Cristóbal de las Casas. The quality of workmanship varies greatly. The finest pieces can be found in luxury boutiques and stores attached to the jade and amber museums (see above). More affordable productions – including some fine original work and a few hidden bargains – can be found in a multitude of small stores and workshops clustered in the streets around Parque 31 de Marzo, and on Real de Guadalupe. The very cheapest jewellery is available from market vendors (beware fakes, including glass that's peddled as amber). If you've never bought jade or amber before, it's best to shop around and ask lots of questions. Both stones come in a variety of hues (red amber is especially beautiful) and are often set in Taxco silver (look for the hallmark '.925').

Markets

Mercado de Artesanías, *Av General Utrilla, outside the Iglesia y Convento de Santo Domingo*. This sprawling open-air market outside the church sells an array of textiles, woodwork, ceramics, basketry, and FZLN mementos. Lots of colour and bargains. Recommended.

Mercado de Dulces y Artesanías, *Av Insurgentes, next to the Templo de San Francisco*. A large indoor market purveying all the usual crafts as well as an assortment of local sweets, such as *cocada* (caramelized shredded coconut).

Mercado Municipal, *Av General Utrilla, a few blocks north of the Iglesia y Convento de Santo Domingo*. The bustling and pungent main city market where you can chow on street food or pick up some fruit and veg. Get some fresh organic strawberries if they're in season; you won't find any sweeter.

What to do

Adventure tourism

Petra Vertical, *Isabel La Católica 9b, T967-631 5173, www.petravertical.com*. The operator of choice for the hardcore adventurists. Their intensive packages include canyoning, abseiling, caving and hiking trips. Professional and knowledgeable. Recommended.

Xaman Expediciones, *1 de Marzo 45, T967-631 5376, www.xaman.com.mx*. **Xaman** offers a range of adrenalin-charged activities including explorations of the subterranean Río El Chorreadero (1 May-15 Nov), rappelling, whitewater kayaking on the Río Tzaconeja, zip-lining, and personalized expeditions. Rafting, birdwatching and trekking packages are planned for the near future.

Body and soul

San Cristóbal is an alternative lifestyle hub and home to numerous New Age practitioners, yoga schools and Buddhist meditation centres.

Ananda Healing Centre, *Real de Guadalupe 55, T967-672 7477*. This healing centre offers a range of classes and private therapies including yoga, meditation, acupuncture, herbalism and reiki.

Casa Plena, *Diego Dugelay 22A, T967-678 7072, www.casaplena.org*. **Casa Plena** offers workshops and diplomas in dance, meditation, Tai Chi, Bach flower remedies and more. Healing therapies include a range of massage techniques, such as Mayan and Ayurvedic.

Shaktipat Yoga, *Niños Héroes 2, inside Casa Luz, 3rd floor, T967-130 3366, www.shaktipat yoga.com.mx*. Daily yoga and body work classes, including Kundalini, Vinyasa, Hatha and Shanti styles, as well as pilates. Cost per class is US$3.85 with reductions for 5- or 10-class packages.

Community tourism

Na Bolom, *Vicente Guerrero 33, T967-678 1418, www.nabolom.org*. Any tour operator can take you for a spin around the Mayan villages, but as a trusted organization with well-established links to local communities, **Na Bolom** is uniquely placed to provide one of the most intimate, authentic and interesting community tours possible; their trips to Chamula and Zinacantán depart daily at 1000, US$23 per person. Na Bolom is also renowned for its tailor-made expeditions to the Selva Lacandona, where you can visit any or all of the 3 Lacandón communities, stay overnight in a jungle camp (or in more solid lodgings if you desire), costs are approximately US$250 per person per day, 4 person minimum. Highly recommended.

Cultural centres

See also Na Bolom and Kinoki above and El Puente Spanish school in the Language schools box, opposite.

Centro Cultural El Carmen, *Hidalgo and Hermanos Domínguez*. Part of the colonial complex adjoining the Iglesia el Carmen, this cultural centre has a range of activities on offer: concerts, films, lectures, art exhibitions, chess games and conferences.

El Paliacate, *5 de Mayo 20, T967-125 3739, www.elpaliakate.blogspot.com*. A socially and ecologically aware cultural centre that promotes artistic and cultural events such as theatre, live music and independent film screenings.

Wapaní, *Flavio Paniagua 10*. This low-key cultural centre hosts live music events, theatre, art exhibitions and film screenings. They also organize workshops in yoga, dance, and lay on a gastronomic market on Sun.

Cycling tours
Marcospata O En Bici, *General Utrilla 18, T967-141 7216, www.marcosapata1.wordpress. com.* Guided cycling tours in the countryside around San Cristóbal, including trips to Chamula and Zinacantán. The length of trips varies, from 15 km to 80 km, or 3 hrs to a day.

Horse riding
Horse-riding tours are popular and widely available in San Cristóbal. Most go to Chamula and cost US$15 for 4-5 hrs. Hotels, tourist offices and travel agencies can easily organize them, or look for advertising flyers in tourist cafés and restaurants. Also, Señor Ismael rents out horses and organizes treks, T961-678 1511.

Kayaking and rafting
Explora, *1 de Marzo 30, T967-631 7498, www.ecochiapas.com.* This eco-sensitive company with a sustainable ethos offers whitewater rafting, sea kayaking, river trips and multi-day camping expeditions on a variety of rivers, in addition to caving in El Chorreadero and conventional nature tours. Recommended.

Tour operators
The lion's share of San Cristóbal's tour operators are clustered on Real de Guadalupe. There are many to choose from and their prices and services are broadly similar.
Nichim Tours, *Hermanos Domínguez 15, T678-3520, www.nichimtours.com.mx.* Daily tours of the city and surrounding villages, including Chamula and Zinacantán, 1-day tours to Palenque and Agua Azul, Sumidero, Montebello, rafting and kayaking, and multi-day packages to attractions across the state.
Otisa Travel, *Real de Guadalupe 3, T967-678 1933, otisatravel.com.* This smart, professional company runs daily tours to Sumidero Canyon, San Juan Chamula and Zinacantán, Lagunas de Montebello, Yaxchilán, Bonampak and the Yucatán, among other places.

Transport

Air
San Cristóbal has a small airport about 15 km from town, but at present does not serve passenger planes. Tuxtla Gutiérrez is now the principal airport.

Bus
The 1st-class **ADO** bus terminal is at the junction of Insurgentes and Blv Sabines Gutiérrez, several blocks south of the Zócalo. 2nd-class lines, including **AEXA** and **Rodolfo Figueroa**, also have nearby terminals

Language schools

El Puente, Real de Guadalupe 55, T967-678 3723. This long-established Spanish school offers 1-to-1 lessons at hourly or weekly rates, and homestays with local families. It also maintains a cultural centre with a small cinema; see their noticeboard for upcoming events. A good place to meet other travellers.
Instituto Jovel, Madero 45, T967-678 4069, www.institutojovel.com. Group or 1-to-1 classes, homestays arranged, said to be the best school in San Cristóbal as their teachers undergo an obligatory 6-week training course. Very good reports from students; all teachers are bilingual to some extent.
La Casa en El Arbol, Madero 29, T967-674 5272, www.lacasaenelarbol.org. This culturally aware school offers individual or group classes, medical Spanish, CME credits, DIE Exam and University credits. They also arrange homestays and apartments, and stage adventure activities and workshops in Tzotzil, weaving and cooking.

on Gutiérrez, which soon becomes the Pan-American Highway. *Colectivo* shuttles (combis) are more efficient for many regional destinations (see below). If you want to book tickets in advance without venturing to the terminal, there is a **Boletotal office**, Guadalupe 16, www.boletotal.mx, 0730-2000.

From the ADO terminal to **Campeche**, 1820, 10 hrs, US$42; **Cancún**, 1215, 1545, 1630, 17 hrs, US$91-95; **Chetumal**, 1215, 1545, 1630, 12 hrs, US$56-65; **Ciudad Cuauhtémoc**, 1140, 1530, 1730, 3 hrs, US$10; **Comitán**, frequent services, 1½ hrs, US$5; **Mérida**, 1820, 13 hrs, US$60; **Mexico City**, 12 daily most after 1550, 14 hrs, US$96-101; **Oaxaca City**, 1805, 2000, 2245, 10 hrs, US$46-55; **Palenque**, 7 daily, 5 hrs, US$16; **Pochutla**, 1915, 2200, 12 hrs, US$45; **Puerto Escondido**, 1915, 2200, 13 hrs, US$51; **Tapachula**, 7 daily, 8 hrs, US$27-33; **Tuxtla Gutiérrez**, many daily, 1 hr, US$4; **Tulum**, 1215, 1545, 1630, 14½ hrs, US$74-85; **Villahermosa**, 1000, 7 hrs, US$31.

Colectivos

Colectivo shuttles (combis) are recommended for journeys of less than 4 hrs, including trips to the border. The terminals are clustered on Gutiérrez near the **ADO** terminal. To **Comitán**, with onward connections to **Ciudad Cuauhtémoc** and the **Guatemala border** (1½ hrs), every 20 mins, 1½ hrs, US$4-5; **Ocosingo**, with onward connections to **Palenque** and **Agua Azul**, every 20 mins, 2-3 hrs, US$4-5; **Tuxtla Gutiérrez**, every 15 mins, 1 hr, around US$3.50. For those heading into Guatemala, numerous tour operators run direct shuttles to the border and beyond, including

Travesía Maya. Destinations include **La Mesilla**, **Quetzaltenango**, **Antigua**, **Flores** and **Panajachel**, US$30-60. It's a convenient and comfortable option if you can afford it. There are also regular departures to **Guatemala** from the **ADO** terminal itself, all departing at 0745 daily.

For reasons of cultural sensitivity, it is recommended that you visit Mayan villages as part of a tour. If you go independently, be prepared for culture shock and possibly some suspicious treatment. Crowded microbuses to **Chamula**, **Zinacantán**, **San Andrés Larráinzar**, **Tenejapa** and other villages from around the market, north of the centre on Utrilla. Don't get stranded, as there isn't any tourist infrastructure.

Car

Those travelling to Palenque by car will have fine views but should avoid travelling at night because of armed robberies.

Car hire **Optima**, Diego de Mazariegos 39, T967-674 5409; and **Hertz**, Villas Mercedes, Panagua 32, T967-678 1886. Rental is for within Chiapas only; do not attempt to go beyond.

Scooters

Croozy Scooters, Belisario Domínguez 7. Tue-Sun 0900, closing times vary. Swiss/British-run, rents out bikes and small scooters. Minimum payment US$20, 3 hrs, US$31 per day. They provide maps and suggested routes. Deposit and ID required. Friendly. Recommended.

Taxi

US$1.75 anywhere in town, *colectivo* US$0.70.

Travellers are strongly advised not to wander around in the hills surrounding San Cristóbal, as they could risk assault. Warnings can be seen in some places frequented by tourists. Remember that locals are particularly sensitive to proper dress (that is neither men nor women should wear shorts or revealing clothes) and manners; persistent begging should be countered with courteous, firm replies.

The communities of San Juan Chamula and Zinacantán (see below) are near to the city, but several visitors have felt ashamed at going to look at the villagers as if they were in a zoo; there were many children begging, especially at Chamula. You are recommended to call at Na Bolom (see page 129) before setting out, to get cultural information and to seek advice on the reception you are likely to get. Good guides will introduce you to close contacts in the communities, personalizing the experience. **Note** Photography is strictly resisted by some of the indigenous people because they believe the camera steals their souls. Either leave your camera behind or ask your guide to let you know when you can and cannot take pictures. Cameras may be confiscated by villagers (and not returned) when photography is deemed inappropriate.

★San Juan Chamula

For reasons of cultural understanding and safety, it is strongly recommended that you visit Chamula on a tour (see What to do, below). If you wish to go independently, you can catch a VW bus from the market in San Cristóbal every 20 mins, last at 1700, last one back at 1900, US$1 per person (or taxi, US$4). It is an interesting walk from San Cristóbal to Chamula, and onwards from Chamula to Zinacantán (see below), but these journeys may be currently unsafe, especially for solo travellers. Consult the tourist office for up-to-date information and for detailed instruction on the routes.

In the Tzotzil village of San Juan Chamula, 10 km northwest of San Cristóbal, the men wear grey, black or light pink tunics, while the women wear black wool skirts, bright blouses with colourful braid and navy or bright blue shawls. It is a very conservative community and its religious leaders have expressed hostility to the missionary work of intrusive Protestant churches. Many of the street vendors in San Cristóbal, who live in shanty towns on the outskirts of the city, are religious exiles from Chamula.

The community's main house of worship, the Catholic **Templo de San Juan**, is a fascinating esoteric experience. To enter, a permit (US$1.50) is needed from the village tourist office. **Note** Photography is absolutely forbidden. There are no pews but family groups sit or kneel on the floor, chanting in clouds of incense smoke, rows of candles lit in front of them, each representing a member of the family, a certain significance attached to their colours. The religion is centred on the 'talking stones' and three idols, as well as certain Christian saints. If you're lucky, you may witness shamans participating in the ritual consumption of *pox*, curing patients with eggs or even sacrificing chickens.

At the end of August, Pagan rituals are held in small huts. The pre-Lent festival ends with celebrants running through blazing harvest chaff. This happens just after Easter prayers are held, before the sowing season starts. Festivals in Chamula should not be photographed; if you wish to take other shots ask permission, people are not unpleasant, even if they refuse (although children may pester you to take their picture for a small fee).

There are many handicraft stalls on the way up the small hill southwest of the village. This has a good viewpoint of the village and valley. Take the road from the southwest corner of the square, turn left towards the ruined church then up a flight of steps on the left.

Zinacantán
It is best to visit on a tour. To go independently, VW buses leave from San Cristóbal's market when full, 30 mins, US$0.75, sometimes with frequent stops while the conductor lights rockets at roadside shrines; taxi US$4.

The community of Zinacantán is roughly 12 km northwest of San Cristóbal. The men of the village typically wear pink/red jackets with embroidery and tassels, the women vivid blue-purple shawls and navy skirts. Annual festival days here are 6 January, 19-22 January, 8-10 August; visitors are welcome. At midday every day the women prepare a communal meal, which the men eat in shifts. The main gathering place is around the roofless fire-damaged church, US$1.50 for entering, official ticket from tourist office next door. Photography inside is strictly prohibited. There were two museums, but both appear to have closed; check on their status before planning a visit.

Above the municipal building on the right, the creative, resourceful Antonia has opened **Antonia's House** ① *Isabel la Católica 7*. There is a small crafts shop and she and her family will demonstrate back-strap weaving, the making of tortillas and many other aspects of life in the village. She usually has some *pox* (pronounced 'posh', a liquor made of sugar cane and corn) on the go; it's strong stuff, and the red variant will set your throat on fire – be ready with a couple of litres of water! Antonia is very easy going and she may not charge for a sample of *pox*; however, bear in mind that she makes her living from the shop, so buy something or leave a contribution.

Tenejapa
Few tourists visit Tenejapa, 30 km northeast of San Cristóbal. The village is very friendly and many men wear local costume. Ask permission to take pictures and expect to pay. The Thursday market is traditionally for fruit and vegetables, but there are a growing number of stalls. The market thins out by noon. Excellent woven items can be purchased from the weavers' cooperative near the church. They also have a fine collection of old textiles in their regional ethnographic museum adjoining the handicraft shop. The cooperative can also arrange weaving classes.

Other Mayan villages
Two other excursions can be made, by car or local bus, from San Cristóbal. The first goes south on the Pan-American Highway (30 minutes by car) to Amatenango del Valle, a Tzeltal village where the women make and fire pottery in their yards – their creations include fearsome and beautiful jaguar sculptures – and then southeast (15 minutes by car) to Aguacatenango, a picturesque village at the foot of a mountain. Continue one hour along this road past Villa Las Rosas (which has a hotel) to Venustiano Carranza, where the women wear fine costumes, and there is an extremely good view of the entire valley. There is a good road from Las Rosas to Comitán as an alternative to the Pan-American Highway and there are frequent buses.

Las Grutas de San Cristóbal
Daily 0900-1700, US$1.50. To get there, take a combi towards Teopisca from the Pan-American highway and ask the driver to drop you at Km 94 for the 'grutas'. The caves are a 5-min walk south from the highway.

Las Grutas (caves), 10 km southeast of the city, contain huge stalagmites and reach a depth of 2445 m. Only the first 350 m are lit, however, and there is a concrete walkway for admiring the carbonate sculptures. Snacks and refreshments are available. Horse can be hired for US$15-20 for a five-hour ride (guide extra) on lovely trails in the surrounding forest. Some of these are best followed on foot. Yellow diamonds on trees and stones mark the way to beautiful meadows. Stay on the trail to minimize erosion. The land next to the caves is taken up by an army football pitch, but once past this, it is possible to walk most of the way back to San Cristóbal through woods and fields.

Comitán and around → *Colour map 2, B4.*

friendly, tranquil highland city near the Guatemalan border

Popular with Mexican tourists but largely overlooked by foreign visitors, Comitán de Domínguez is a small colonial city located south of San Cristóbal and close to the Guatemala border. It is an easy-going and elevated place, offering cool respite from the stifling lowlands, and a welcome pause before or after the frenetic environs of Guatemala. Flanked by handsome traditional edifices with overhanging eaves and clay-tile roofs, a large shady Zócalo marks the heart of the Centro Histórico with a host of modern art sculptures. Modest diversions lie within the city limits, but the best attractions are further afield in the surrounding countryside.

Sights

Far from the madding crowd, Comitán is a pleasant place to simply hang out and unwind, but if you do need cultural stimulation, there are a few small museums worth checking out. **The Museo de Arte Hermila Domínguez de Castellanos** ⓘ *Av Central Sur and 3a Sur Pte, Tue-Sat, 1000-1730, Sun 1000-1400, US$0.50*, maintains a collection of modern art and sculptures, including work by Rufino Tamayo, José Luis Cuevas, José Guadalupe Posadas and Francisco Toledo. The **Casa Museo Dr Belisario Domínguez** ⓘ *Av Dr Belisario Domínguez Sur 35, Mon-Sat 1000-1845, Sun 0900-1245, US$0.40*, is the former home and birthplace of the good doctor Belisario, who was assassinated after speaking out against President Huerta. The museum includes memorabilia and historical exhibits dedicated to his professional and political life. For a dose of Mayan relics, head to the **Museo Arqueológico de Comitán** ⓘ *1 Calle Sur Ote, Tue-Sun 0900-1800, free.*

Around Comitán

The waterfalls of **El Chiflón** lie 41 km southwest of Comitán off Highway 226. Amenities and activities include wildlife tours (specialized in iguana observation), a zip-line, swimming areas and *cabañas*, all managed by the **Centro Ecoturístico de Cascadas El Chiflón** ⓘ *T963-596 9709, www.chiflon.com.mx.* Hourly vans run to the turn-off (where taxis continue to the site) with **Autotransportes Cuxtepeques** ⓘ *Blv Belisario Domínguez, between 1a and 2a Calles Nte Pte, from 0400 to 2000, 45 mins, US$2.*

South of Comitán, you'll find the archaeological site of **Tenam Puente** ⓘ *5 km off Highway 190, 0900-1600, US$2.50, the turn-off for the ruins is 10 km south of Comitán on Highway 190; vans to the ruins depart from 3a Av Pte Sur 8, every 40 mins, 0800-1800 (last return at 1600), US$1.10*, situated in a forest. Thought to have been a minor Mayan commercial centre, its construction dates back to the Classic era (AD 300-600) and includes three ball courts, a pyramid and some temple complexes. South of the turn-off, the tiny settlement of **La Trinitaria** marks the turn-off for Highway 307 and the Lagunas de Montebello (see below), frequently plied by *colectivo* vans. At Km 22, you'll pass the **Parador-Museo Santa María** ① *T963-632 5116, www.paradorsantamaria.com.mx*, a handsome 19th-century hacienda with a decent restaurant, eight fine guest rooms ($$$$), and a religious museum in its chapel. At Km 30, you'll pass the turn-off for the aesthetically situated ruins of **Chinkultic** ① *0900-1700, US$3*, with temples, ball court, and carved stone stelae; from the signpost the ruins are about 3 km along a dirt road. The structures are divided into two groups with striking views from the Acrópolis, a temple overlooking a massive *cenote* (deep round lake).

★Parque Nacional Lagunas de Montebello → *Colour map 2, B5.*

Highway 307, entrance to the park is around Km 37, US$2. From Comitán, combi vans or buses marked 'Tziscao' or 'Lagos' go to the lakes, every 20-40 mins, 1 hr, US$1.50, via the Lagunas de Siete Colores, departing from Av 2 Pte Sur y Calle 3 Sur Pte, four blocks from the plaza. The last bus and colectivo back from the lakes connecting with the 1900 bus to San Cristóbal is at 1600. For those with their own transport there are several dirt roads from Comitán to the Lagunas; a recommended route is the one via La Independencia, Buena Vista, La Patria and El Triunfo (beautiful views), eventually joining the road west of the Chinkultic ruins.

The state's first national park and a designated UNESCO Biosphere Reserve since 2009, the Parque Nacional Lagunas de Montebello encompasses 6400 ha of rambling pine forests and no less than 59 multi-coloured highland lakes, which due to their rich and varied mineral content, span multiple shades of blue and green from bright sapphire to turquoise. A trip to the lakes from Comitán can be easily done in a day and is also possible from San Cristóbal, but it's a bit tiring; bring your passport and tourist card for immigration checks.

From the ticket booth on Highway 307, the road forks north to the **Lagunas de Siete Colores**, a cluster of five tranquil lakes, including **Bosque Azul**, 3 km away. The area is noted for its orchids and birdlife, including the famous *quetzal*, but it gets very busy at weekends and holidays. There is a group of caves nearby called Grutas San Rafael del Arco, and several *cenotes*. Guides can be hired in the Bosque Azul cark park at the end of the road for horse tours, US$12 per person, two to three hours. East of the ticket booth, Highway 307 passes turn-offs for **Laguna de Montebello**, the **Cinco Lagunas**, and **Laguna Pojoj**, before arriving at the large **Laguna Tziscao** near the Guatemala border, and its village of the same name, 9 km from the entrance.

Mexico to Guatemala: Ciudad Cuauhtémoc–La Mesilla → *Colour map 2, B5.*

From Comitán the road winds down to the Guatemalan border at Ciudad Cuauhtémoc via La Trinitaria; see Transport, below. Despite its name, Ciudad Cuauhtémoc is not a city, but a very small hamlet. Before proceeding to the border, surrender your tourist card and get your exit stamp. Opposite the immigration office is the **Cristóbal Colón** bus station, with an overpriced restaurant and a hotel. *Colectivo* taxis run from here to Guatemalan immigration at La Mesilla a few kilometres away; they charge around US$0.60 per person, or US$2.50 for the whole vehicle. At La Mesilla, once you've stamped in, grab a mototaxi to the second-class bus station, where services depart for Huehuetenango, two hours, and onwards to Quetzaltenango (Xela), four hours. The journey into the Guatemalan western highlands winds through remote villages and stunning canyons and is far more interesting than the crossing at Tapachula. See also box, page 512.

Tourist information

Municipal tourist office, in the green building on the north side of the Parque Central. Mon-Fri 0800-1800, Sat 0800-1600.

Where to stay

$$$ Hotel Casa Delina
1a Calle Sur Pte 6, T963-101 4793,
www.hotelcasadelina.com.
Set in a traditional 19th-century mansion, this stylish and aesthetic 'art hotel' show-cases work from emerging contemporary artists in its 8 boutique rooms. There's parking, a courtyard garden, café and a screening room where movies are shown in the evenings. Hip, interesting, and creative. Recommended.

$$$-$$ Los Lagos de Montello
Belisario Domínguez 144, corner of 3 Av,
T963-632 0657, www.hotelloslagosde
montebello.com.
Often overlooked by foreign tourists but popular with Mexicans, this excellent business hotel has 56 well-appointed rooms, restaurant, garden and a large indoor pool. Located 10 mins' walk from the Centro Histórico. A good deal, recommended for families.

$$ Hotel Real Junchavin
2a Calle Norte, Oriente 8, T963-101 4337,
www.realjunchavin.com.
Located on a quiet street, this good, clean, budget option, recently renovated with crisp, simple rooms, modern decor, comfortable mattresses, cable TV and Wi-Fi. Good value.

Around Comitán

$$ Centro Ecoturístico El Chiflón
Tzilmol, T963-596 9709, www.chiflon.com.mx.
Cooperatively managed by the population of the San Cristobalito *ejido*, this place maintains 12 single and duplex *cabañas*

complete with private bath, double beds, hot water, and lots of nice touches like attractive stone-work and clay sculptures from Amatenango. For more information on the park's attractions, including how to get there, see above.

$$ Villas Tziscao
Carretera Fronteriza del Sur Km 61,
T502-5780-2775, www.centro
ecoturisticotziscao.com.mx.
Overlooking the largest of Montebello's lakes, these wood-built cabins with high slanted roofs (ask to see a few before accepting) belong to the **Centro Ecoturístico Tziscao**, which is operated as part of a communally owned 300-ha *ejido*. Lots of activities are available from kayaking to hiking, and there's Wi-Fi in the common area. Conventional rooms inside the main building. It's a good place for families who like the outdoors.

Restaurants

There are lots of terraced cafés and restaurants on the Zócalo.

$$$-$$ Pasta di Roma
1 Av Pte Sur 1, www.pastadiroma.com.
As the name might suggest, wholesome Italian fare including lasagna and spaghetti is served here. Simple and authentic, good reports.

Transport

Bus

The **ADO** terminal is at Blv Belisario Domínguez Sur 43. Daily departures to **Cancún**, 1420, 21 hrs, US$88; **Mexico City**, 8 daily, all after 1400, 15½ hrs, US$107-124; **Palenque**, 1420, 6½ hrs, US$25; **San Cristóbal de las Casas**, frequent services, 1½ hrs, US$5; **Tapachula**, 5 daily, 5½ hrs, US$14; **Tuxtla Gutiérrez**, many daily, 3 hrs, US$7.50.

Colectivos

Shuttle terminals are clustered on Belisario Domínguez, a few blocks north from the **ADO** terminal and a 10- to 15-min walk to the Zócalo. To **Ciudad Cuauhtémoc** (Guatemala border), every 15 mins, 1½ hrs, US$4. To **San Cristóbal de las Casas**, 1½ hrs, US$4-5. To **Ocosingo** via an interesting back route, go to Altamirano and change, terminal on east side of town, take a taxi.

Mexico to Guatemala: Ciudad Cuauhtémoc–La Mesilla

Bus

The **ADO** terminal is inside the hotel opposite the Mexican Migración with infrequent services to **Palenque**, **San Cristóbal de las Casas**, **Tuxtla** and **Tapachula**. More national connections are available in Comitán, including services to **San Cristóbal** and **Tuxtla** (see *colectivos*, below).

Colectivos

Colectivo taxis to **La Mesilla** and **Guatemala immigration**, around 6 km away, depart from opposite the **Mexican Migración**, US$0.75. *Colectivo* shuttles to **Comitán** depart from a small terminal around the corner from the Migración, 1½ hrs, US$4.

Ocosingo → *Colour map 2, A4.*

unpretentious town off the tourist track with an authentic market

The friendly, if roughly hewn, provincial city of Ocosingo lies half-way between San Cristóbal de las Casas and Palenque on Highway 199. The ride each way is astounding with wending mountain vistas and a patchwork of rolling maize fields and wood-built villages, many of them belonging to the Ejército Zapatista de Liberación Nacional (EZLN). If driving, you may be stopped occasionally to pay unofficial tolls of a few dollars, but it is worth it for this intriguing backdoor glimpse of highland Mayan communities. Ocosingo itself saw some of the fiercest fighting of all during the 1994 Zapatista uprising: pitched gun battles in the market and main plaza left dozens dead on both sides. There's a frenetic market but the big attraction is the Mayan ruin of Toniná, 12 km away (see below).

Toniná → *Colour map 1, B1.*

Daily 0800-1700, US$3.50, drinks are available at the site; also toilets and parking. The museum is closed Mon. Colectivos to the site depart from behind the market, every 30 mins, US$1.

Toniná was one of the last Classic Maya sites and a powerful militaristic stronghold which terrorized and dominated lowland Chiapas before its final collapse. The site's history, only recently and partially deciphered, includes numerous bloodthirsty conflicts with surrounding regional powers, especially Palenque, that lasted several generations until its ultimate ascent. Much of the city's art and sculptures depict prisoners of war bound and poised for ritual decapitation, such as the ball court, which features torsos of captured Palenque vassals as markers.

The site's buildings – which include palaces and ritual labyrinths – are in the Palenque-style with internal sanctuaries in the back room. Architectural influences from many other different Maya styles have also been identified, suggesting that captured artists were incorporated into Toniná society, or else forced to work. The most important structure is the south-facing Acropolis, which fills seven terraces with temple-pyramids and climbs to 71 m over the plaza.

The fifth terrace contains an outstanding example of stucco work, for which Toniná is uniquely renowned, along with its famous sculptures in the round. Uncovered in 1992, the 'Frieze of the Four Suns' (sometimes called the Frieze of the Dream Lords) is a complex mystical representation featuring a sacrificial scaffold covered with feathers, four decapitated human heads – symbolic of four suns, four ages, and four races of man – and prominent Lords of the Underworld.

Listings Ocosingo

Where to stay

$$-$ Hotel Central
Av Central 5, opposite the Parque Central,
T919-673 0024.
Conveniently located on the main square, reasonably priced and with friendly staff, this is the best place in town. Beyond the shabby lobby, it has several clean, comfortable, modest and perfectly adequate rooms with hot water, Wi-Fi and cable TV. There's a so-so restaurant downstairs and a communal balcony upstairs, ideal for watching life on the plaza.

Transport

Bus and colectivo
Many buses and *colectivos* to **Palenque**, 2½ hrs, US$4-5, **Agua Azul** and **San Cristóbal de Las Casas**, terminals clustered outside the centre. For **Comitán**, go to Altamirano and change, *colectivos* leave from the market.

Agua Azul and around → *Colour map 2, A4.*

an entrancingly beautiful series of jungle waterfalls and rapids

The main swimming area has many restaurants and indigenous children selling fruit. In good weather, the water is clear and blue; after the rains, it is muddy brown (but still very refreshing).

Site information Entry US$2.90, US$4 for cars. Entry price is not always included in day trips from Palenque, which typically allow up to three hours at the site. Due to the risk of theft, do not bring valuables. For information on getting there, see Transport, below.

Swimmers should strictly stick to the roped areas where they can be seen by others; the various graves on the steep path up the hill alongside the rapids are testament to the risks of drowning. One of the falls is called 'The Liquidizer', an extremely dangerous area of white water which you must not enter. Even in the designated areas, the currents can be ferocious. Beware of hidden tree trunks and other obstacles if the water is murky.

The path on the left of the rapids can be followed for 7 km with superb views and secluded areas for picnics. There are also several *palapas* for hammocks, plenty of space for free camping and some rooms to rent (see Where to stay, below).

Misol-Há → *Colour map 2, A5.*
Entry US$2.

At Misol-Há there is a stunning waterfall usually visited for 20 minutes or so before Agua Azul on day trips from Palenque. A narrow path winds around behind the falls, allowing you to stand behind the immense curtain of water. Swimming is possible in the large pool at the bottom of the tumbling cascade of water, but it is usually better to wait until you get to Agua Azul for a good swim. That said, during the rainy season, swimming is reported to be better at Misol-Há. Organized tours usually include only a brief stop at Misol-Há, so confirm with your operator or go by bus if you would like to spend longer there.

Listings Agua Azul and around

Where to stay

Misol-Ha

$$ Cabañas Misol-Ha
Misol-Ha, T55-5151 3377, www.misol-ha.com.
Part of the tourist complex at Misol-Ha waterfall, these *cabañas* include 8 rustic units with hot and cold water, fan, mosquito net and simple furniture, and 4 bungalow-style units complete with kitchen appliances. All are nestled in lovely landscaped grounds on the edge of the jungle.

Transport

Public buses travelling between Palenque and Ocosingo can drop you at the Agua Azul turn-off, US$1. There are some 2nd-class buses between San Cristóbal de las Casas and Palenque which will stop at the turn-off, but check before purchasing tickets. A tour or *colectivo* shuttle from Palenque is definitely the best option, as this includes a trip to Misol-Ha, see Palenque Transport, below.

From the Agua Azul turn-off, walk the 4 km downhill to the falls on a beautiful jungle-lined road (or hitch a ride in a taxi or minibus for US$1). If, after a long day at the falls, you have no desire to walk the steep 4 km back to the main road you may be able to catch a ride back to Palenque on tour buses that have extra space. They leave from the Agua Azul car park between 1500 and 1800. Tour companies can also arrange bus tickets with **AEXA** from the turn-off to San Cristóbal and other places if you don't wish to return all the way to Palenque to catch an onward bus.

Palenque Town → *Colour map 3, C4.*

a hot, humdrum town and gateway to the famous ruins

Palenque's inhabitants are very friendly and helpful, but the streets can be stifling and airless, especially in the months of June, July and August.

The **tourist office** ① *daily 0900-2100*, is on Juárez, a block west of the plaza. They are fairly useless but provide a good free map of the town and the ruins. The **Fiesta de Santo Domingo** is held on the first week of August.

Many travellers avoid downtown altogether, preferring to stay in the cool, quiet and leafy tourist barrio of **La Cañada**, a 10-minute walk northwest of the Parque Central. Flanked by alternating patches of rainforest and cattle pasture, the most appealing and isolated lodgings of all are strung along the **road to the ruins**. It is about 10°C cooler here than Palenque town thanks to the dense foliage cover (although it is also wetter, buggier, and much more humid). The highway begins near the western entrance to town, just south of the Mayan head near the **ADO** terminal. For details of travel along the highway to the ruins, see Transport, below. If walking on the highway during the rainy months, you may be approached by shifty-looking local entrepreneurs peddling bags of interesting Mayan *hongos* (mushrooms), which flourish in the fields thanks to the prodigious quantity of cow dung. These are hallucinogenic and their psilocybin content is astronomically high: consume at your own risk.

Mexico to Guatemala: Tenosique–El Ceibo → *Colour map 3, C5/C6.*

Approximately 80 km east of Palenque on Highway 203, Tenosique is a small, friendly town, and the starting point for a classic cross-border adventure that takes you by road to La Palma, by boat to El Naranjo in Guatemala, and finally, by road to Flores. However, since the completion of a new paved highway, this slow if somewhat scenic route is no longer used by the locals and thus impractical (for a price, a tourist operator in Palenque can probably arrange it for you).

The new road from Tenosique to Flores can be crossed in six to eight hours, but it is best to start at dawn and travel in daylight only. *Colectivos* to Tenosique with 'Transportes Palenque' leave from Allende Sur and 20 de Noviembre in Palenque, hourly, two hours, US$4. You may be dropped on the outskirts of Tenosique, in which case take a tuk-tuk to the market. From here, *colectivo* taxis travel to El Ceibo and the Guatemala border, one hour, US$3. After completing border formalities, you can catch onward connections to Flores, US$6, a straightforward four- to five-hour trip, but you may have to wait up to two hours for the bus to leave. See also box, page 512.

Listings Palenque town

Where to stay

There is a plethora of cheap lodgings here, but the town is generally a hot, dirty and unappealing place to stay.

$$ Maya Rue
*2a Av Pte, between Av Central
and 1a Av Sur, T916-345 0743.*
Maya Rue wins the downtown style prize for its contemporary interior design that outshines the dated decor you'll find most

other places. Rooms are spotlessly clean and have large, comfortable beds, Wi-Fi, hot water and cable TV. Good central location with a café downstairs. Recommended.

$$-$ Quinta Avenida
Av Juárez 173, T916-345 0098.
Quinta Avenida is chiefly recommended for its tranquil garden decking fringed by tropical foliage, and for its pool. The rooms are economical, modest and functional,

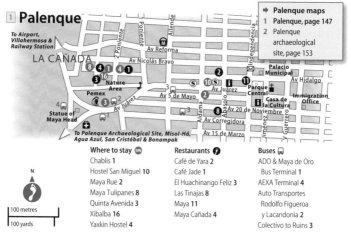

1 Palenque

To Airport,
Villahermosa &
Railway Station

LA CAÑADA

Nature Area

Pemex

Statue of
Maya Head

To Palenque Archaeological Site, Misol-Há,
Agua Azul, San Cristóbal & Bonampak

Av Reforma
Av Nicolás Bravo
Av 5 de Mayo
Av Juárez
Av 20 de Noviembre
Av Corregidora
Av 15 de Marzo

Palacio Municipal
Av Hidalgo
Parque Central
Casa de la Cultura
Immigration Office

→ Palenque maps
1 Palenque, page 147
2 Palenque archaeological site, page 153

100 metres
100 yards

Where to stay	Restaurants	Buses
Chablis 1	Café de Yara 2	ADO & Maya de Oro
Hostel San Miguel 10	Café Jade 1	Bus Terminal 1
Maya Rue 2	El Huachinango Feliz 3	AEXA Terminal 4
Maya Tulipanes 8	Las Tinajas 8	Auto Transportes
Quinta Avenida 3	Maya 11	Rodolfo Figueroa
Xibalba 16	Maya Cañada 4	y Lacandonia 2
Yaxkin Hostel 4		Colectivo to Ruins 3

but ask for one in the garden out back (the main building suffers street noise). It's not amazing, but for the money it's one of the best budget options in town. On the west side, within easy walking distance of the **ADO** terminal.

$ Hostel San Miguel
Hidalgo and Aldama, above Unión Pharmacy, T916-345 0152.
More of a budget hotel than a hostel, although they do have dorm space. The no-frills private rooms are spacious; some have balconies, TV and a/c. Good value for groups.

La Cañada

$$$ Chablis
Merle Green 7, T916-345 0870, www.hotelchablis.com.mx.
Painted sunny yellow, this small resort-style hotel has 51 tidy if unadventurous rooms with king-size beds, a/c, 32-inch TVs, Wi-Fi and solar-heated hot water. The real draw is the leafy patio with a pool and jacuzzi, perfect for chilling out after a day at the ruins. Popular, helpful and well-maintained. Recommended for families.

$$$ Maya Tulipanes
Cañada 6, T916-345 0201, www.mayatulipanes.com.mx.
Another resort-style lodging with the same owners as Chablis down the road. The 78 slightly generic rooms vary in price, size and quality, but all are spotless and most have a/c, large TVs and Wi-Fi. Amenities include a garage, pool, karaoke bar, garden and restaurant. Check out the colourful murals inside the entrance.

$$ Xibalba
Merle Green 9, T916-345 0411, www.hotelxibalba.com.
A decent, popular, hospitable hotel with 2 wings (1 older, 1 newer). They offer clean, comfortable, simple, bug-free rooms with a/c. Fun archaeological decor, including an impressive and authentically proportioned

Mayan arch and a reproduction lid of Pacal's tomb, somewhat larger than the original. The owner is friendly and knowledgeable.

$ Yaxkin Hostel
Av Hidalgo corner with 5a Pte, T916-345 0102, www.hostalyaxkin.com.
Popular with backpackers, this is La Cañada's best economical alternative, and reasonably smart for a hostel. It has tidy if small private rooms, which are simple, clean and comfortable, and cheap mixed and women-only dorms. Facilities include a *temazcal* and massage, Wi-Fi, movie lounge, free use of bikes, kitchen, lovely garden and a good bar and restaurant.

Road to the ruins
The most alluring and atmospheric place to stay is along the road to the ruins. Lodgings are nestled inside the exuberant rainforest, but be aware that humidity is high and there are abundant creepy-crawlies, so bring repellent, especially in the wet season. Tropical decay is rampant too, meaning poorly maintained lodgings go downhill fast. Before accepting your room or *cabaña*, thoroughly check its security (thefts have been reported), screens and netting. Shop around and don't be pressured by touts. Note the highway to the ruins has opened up significantly in recent years and there is now plenty of robust competition to the long-established El Panchán.

$$$$ Quinta Cha Nab Nal
Carretera a las Ruinas Km 2.2, T916-345 5320, www.quintachanabnal.com.
The owner of **Quinta Cha Nab Nal** is an enthusiastic Mayanist who set out to carefully create a hotel in the architectural style of a Classic-era Mayan palace complex. Surprisingly, it worked out quite tastefully, even if some of us prefer the aesthetic of ruin to reconstruction. Most guests leave this place enchanted and you won't find a higher standard of accommodation in Palenque. Recommended.

$$$ La Aldea del Halach Huinic
Carretera a las Ruinas Km 2.8, T916-345 1693,
www.hotellaaldea.net.
Rooms at the **Aldea** have been designed
according to principles of classic
Mayan architecture with curved edges,
numerological proportions, solar and
astronomical alignments. In effect, they're
very tranquil and well-presented. The
grounds are lush and include a good
restaurant, *temazcal*, and a fabulous pool
with wavy sides. Recommended.

$$$ Piedra de Agua
Carretera a las Ruinas Km 2.5, T999-924 2300,
www.palenque.piedradeagua.com.
A new boutique option with an aesthetic
minimalist design and an emphasis on
immersion in the environment. Thatched
cabañas are crisp and simple and feature
private terraces fully equipped with hot tub
and hammocks where breakfast is served
in the morning (at an extra cost). General
services include spa, pool, tours and a
welcome cocktail. There's no dinner, so it
helps to have your own transport. Rustic
chic, secluded and romantic.

$$-$ Margarita and Ed's
Carretera a las Ruinas Km 4.5, El Panchán,
margaritaandedcabanas.blogspot.com.
Margarita and Ed are very gracious and
hospitable hosts and they offer a range of
decent accommodation in simple, spacious
rooms or economical *cabañas*, some with
a/c and views of the forest. All of them all
kept rigorously clean and fresh with floors
scrubbed daily and mattresses regularly
aired. An oasis of cleanliness in the jungle
and easily the best lodgings in El Panchán.
Recommended.

$ El Panchán
Carretera a las Ruinas Km 4.5,
www.elpanchan.com.
The classic travellers' haunt, a sprawling
jungle resort that has long drawn
backpackers, adventurers and hippies to
its fabled enclaves. Its founder, Don Moisés,

first came to Palenque as an archaeologist
and was one of the first guides to the ruins.

Restaurants

The options below are adequate,
but don't expect fine dining.

$$$-$$ Restaurante Maya
Hidalgo and Independencia.
Overlooking the main square, this popular
and reliable downtown option was
established in 1958. It offers set menu
lunches and à la carte breakfasts and
dinners. Fare includes regional dishes,
typical Mexican and international. Efficient
service and free Wi-Fi.

$$-$ Café de Yara
Hidalgo 66.
This sunny café on the corner serves good
strong Chiapaneco coffee (recommended,
try an Americano) and fair light meals
including breakfasts, a *menu del día* and
international and Mexican fare. Whole beans
are sold in the shop next door if you want
to take some of their coffee home. There's
occasional live music in the evenings.

$$-$ Las Tinajas
20 de Noviembre 41 and Abasolo.
This long-established family-run restaurant
has seating indoors and out. They serve the
usual Mexican fare and reasonable home-
cooked grub in massive portions; the *pollo
frito* is half a chicken on a bed of chunky
chips. Good value, one of the better places
to eat.

La Cañada

$$ El Huachinango Feliz
Av Merle Green.
A decent seafood joint and one of the better
places for an evening meal in La Cañada.
They serve ample plates of shrimp, grilled
octopus, whole fish and more. Popular with
locals and tourists and occasionally host to
lively crowds. Slow service, but good value.

$$ Maya Cañada
Av Merle Green.

Catering to a moneyed tourist crowd, the Maya Cañada has pleasant evening atmosphere and an appealing open-air setting. Offerings on the menu include Chiapaneco specialities and *comida típica*. Many rate the food highly, but we found the chicken in *mole* quite average. Hit and miss perhaps.

$$-$ Café Jade
Prolongación Av Hidalgo 1.

Attached to Hostel Yaxchin, the best coffee shop in La Cañada. They serve decent light meals, including fruit breakfasts, soups, pastas, salads, stuffed peppers, tasty tacos, nachos and more. Also an array of indulgent desserts and refreshing fruit juices. Very mellow and popular with travellers. Recommended.

Road to the ruins

$$ Don Mucho
El Panchán.

This long-running outdoor restaurant is hugely popular in the high season and usually thronging with travellers and backpackers. It serves average international and Mexican fare and a good breakfast. Beyond the food, it's a place to sip beer and enjoy the spectacle of evening entertainment which may include travelling musicians, jugglers or fire-dancers. Quite exotic and a great atmosphere.

$$ Monteverde Pizzeria
Turn-off on the Carretera a las Ruinas, 1.5 km.

Authentic Italian cuisine in a secluded jungle setting, including pastas and thin-crust pizzas. Occasional live music adds to the great atmosphere. One of the best in Palenque, but inconveniently located at the end of a dirt road; take a taxi, especially at night.

What to do

Tour operators

Palenque is the best place to arrange guided tours of Bonampak and Yaxchilán. To see both sites, it is recommended you take at least 2 days and stay overnight in Lacanjá or Frontera Corozal, otherwise expect a very long, tough day of at least 14 hrs. Note that some tours to Agua Azul include onward connections to San Cristóbal. This should be clarified before agreement as some travellers have reported being bundled onto a public bus after the waterfalls. There are many reasonable tour operators around town offering broadly similar services, we particularly recommend the following:

Alonso Méndez, *ask at Don Mucho's in El Panchán.* Available in high season only. Alonso is a well-versed guide with extensive knowledge of flora and fauna, medicinal uses of plants, and an intimate knowledge of Palenque ruins. A respected authority on ethnobotany in Chiapas, Alonso has the gift of academic and spiritual understanding of the rainforest. He speaks English, Spanish and Tzeltzal fluently.

Center of Mayan Exploration, *www.maya exploration.org.* Continuing the good work of Linda Schele and other key Mayanists, this excellent NGO has made significant research contributions to Mayan archaeology by mapping Palenque and uncovering hidden aspects of its astronomical alignments. They offer superb custom-made tours of the entire Mayan world, as far afield as Honduras and Guatemala. Contact well in advance of your trip.

Transportadora Turística Scheerrer and Barb, *Av Juárez 1, opposite the Burger King, T916-103 3649.* Managed by Fernando Mérida, a Lacandón guide with some interesting views on Mayan prophecy, this long-running tour operator offers solid excursions to Bonampak and Yaxchilán, as well as some more off-beat tours not offered by anyone else. Options include multi-day trips to Metzabok and Na-Ha ecological reserves, Mitziha jungle treks, including options for zip-lining and kayaking, trips to Chinikiha Archaeological zone and Xibalba caves, kayaking on Sun Lagoon, and many others. Custom-made tours are also an option.

Transport

Air
Palenque Airport (PQM) recently opened to commercial flights with **ADO** minibuses shuttling arrivals into town. Flights to **Mexico City** with **Interjet** and **Tuxtla Gutiérrez** with **Ka'an Air**. Speak to a tour agent if you would like to organize chartered flights within Chiapas (including **Yaxchilán** and **Bonampak**), **Yucatán** or **Guatemala**.

Bus
The new 1st-class **ADO** terminal is at the western end of Juárez near the Mayan head. The Rodolfo Figueroa y Lacandonia terminal is further east on Juárez with a few 2nd-class departures to San Cristóbal. An **AEXA** terminal is also on Juárez, serving a handful of destinations in Chiapas, as is **Autotransportes Tuxtla**, with 2nd-class departures to **Quintana Roo**.

From the **ADO** terminal to **Cancún**, 1740, 2230, 2300, 13 hrs, US$67-80; **Campeche**, 4 daily, 5 hrs, US$29; **Mérida**, 4 daily, 8 hrs, US$44; **Mexico City**, 1830, 14 hrs, US$91; **Oaxaca City**, 1730, 15 hrs, US$66; **San Cristóbal de las Casas**, 5 daily, mostly 5 hrs (some are 9 hrs), US$16; **Tulum**, 1740, 2230, 2300, 10-11 hrs, US$58-68; **Tuxtla Gutiérrez**, 6 daily, 6 hrs, US$20; **Villahermosa**, many daily, 2-3 hrs, US$11.50.

Colectivos
For **Palenque ruins**, microbuses run back and forth along Av Juárez, turning onto the highway at the Mayan head, every 10 mins, US$1.50 (taxi US$8). Catch one of these for **El Panchán** and other nearby accommodation. For destinations in Chiapas state, there are numerous *colectivo* shuttles leaving from many terminals. To **Agua Azul** and **Misol-ha**, **Transportes Chambalú**, Allende and Juárez, 0900, 1200, US$11.50 excluding entrance fees. They stop for 30 mins at Misol-Há and 3 hrs at Agua Azul. To **Frontera Corozal** (for **San Javier**, **Bonampak**, **Lacanjá** and **Yaxchilán**), **Transportes Chamoan**, Hidalgo 141, roughly hourly from 0500-1700, 2-3 hrs, US$9.20. To **Tenosique**, **Transportes Palenque**, Allende and 20 de Noviembre, hourly, 2 hrs, US$4. To **Playas de Catazajá** (for Escárcega and Campeche) **Transportes Pakal**, Allende between 20 de Noviembre and Corregidora, every 15 mins, US$3.

Taxi
Taxis charge a flat rate of US$1.50 within the town, US$5 to **El Panchán**.

Mexico to Guatemala: Tenosique–El Ceibo
Bus
ADO services to **Emiliano Zapata**, hourly, 1 hr, US$5.50; **Mexico City**, 1700, 15 hrs, US$94; **Villahermosa**, 5 daily, 3½ hrs, US$16.

Colectivos
Shuttles to **Palenque**, hourly with **Transportes Palenque**, US$4. Or catch a Villahermosa bus to **El Crucero de la Playa** and pick up a frequent *colectivo* from there. *Colectivo* taxis to El Ceibo and the border depart from the market in Tenosique, 1 hr, US$3; see also page 147.

★Enveloped in thick canopies of foliage, the ruined metropolis of Palenque is one of Mexico's most striking and enigmatic archaeological sites. It's this lush rainforest setting as much as its cultural and artistic achievements that conspire to make it one of Mexico's most vivid destinations.

Site information Daily 0800-1700, US$4.50; entrance to national park US$2.15, payable at the toll by El Panchán. Water at the site is expensive, so bring your own. The cheapest food is the tacos from the stalls. *Colectivos* back to the town leave from outside the main entrance, US$1.50, every 6-18 minutes. Guides of varying quality can be hired for around US$70 per group, two hours.

Built at the height of the Classic period on a series of artificial terraces surrounded by jungle, Palenque was constructed for strategic purposes, with evidence of defensive apertures in some of the retaining walls. In the centre of the site is the Palace, a massive warren of buildings with an asymmetrical tower rising above them, and fine views to the north. The tower was probably used as an astronomical observatory and a watchtower. The outer buildings of the palace have an unusual series of galleries, offering shade from the jungle heat of the site.

From about the fourth century AD, Palenque grew from a small agricultural village to one of the most important cities in the pre-Hispanic world, although it really achieved greatness between AD 600 and 800. During the long and illustrious reign of Lord Pacal, the city rapidly rose to the first rank of Maya states. The duration of Pacal's reign is still a bone of contention among Mayanists because the remains found in his sarcophagus do not appear to be those of an 81-year-old man, the age implied by the texts in the Temple of the Inscriptions.

Since its discovery, choked by the encroaching jungle that pushed against its walls and scaled the stairs of its temples once climbed by rulers, priests and acolytes, the architecture of Palenque has elicited praise and admiration and begged to be reconstructed. The corbelled vaults, the arrangement of its groupings of buildings, the impression of lightness created by walls broken by pillars and open spaces make Palenque-style architecture unique. It was only later that archaeologists and art historians realized that the architecture of Palenque was created mainly to accommodate the extraordinary sculptures and texts that referred not only to historical individuals and the important events in their lives, but also to mythological beings who endorsed the claims of dynastic continuity or 'divine right' of the rulers of this great city. The structures most illustrative of this function are the Palace, a group of buildings arranged around four patios to which a tower was later added, the Temple of the Inscriptions that rises above the tomb of Lord Pacal, and the temples of the Group of the Cross, used by Chan Bahlum, Pacal's successor, who made claims in the inscriptions carved on the tablets, pillars and balustrades of these exceptional buildings, claims which, in their audacity, are awe inspiring.

Warning The ruins are surrounded by thick, mosquito-infested jungle so wear insect repellent and make sure you're up to date with your tablets (May to November is the worst time for mosquitoes). It is extremely hot and humid at the ruins, especially in the afternoon, so it is best to visit early. Unfortunately, as well as mosquitoes, there have also been reports of criminals hiding in the jungle. Try and leave valuables at your hotel to minimize any loss.

The Palace

The Palace and Temple XI are located in the centre of the site. The Palace stands on an artificial platform over 100 m long and 9 m high. Chan Bahlum's younger brother, Kan Xul, was 57 when he became king. He devoted himself to enlarging the palace, and apparently built the four-storey tower in honour of his dead father. The top of the tower is almost at the level of Pacal's mortuary temple, and on the winter solstice the sun, viewed from here, sets directly above his crypt. Large windows where Maya astronomers could observe and chart the movement of the planets, ancestors of the royal lineage of Palenque, pierce the walls of the tower. Kan-Xul reigned for 18 years before being captured and probably

② Palenque archaeological site

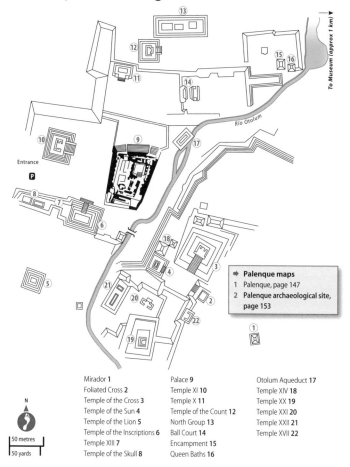

To Museum (approx 1 km)

Río Otolum

Entrance

➡ **Palenque maps**
1 Palenque, page 147
2 Palenque archaeological site, page 153

N

50 metres
50 yards

Mirador **1**	Palace **9**	Otolum Aqueduct **17**
Foliated Cross **2**	Temple XI **10**	Temple XIV **18**
Temple of the Cross **3**	Temple X **11**	Temple XX **19**
Temple of the Sun **4**	Temple of the Count **12**	Temple XXI **20**
Temple of the Lion **5**	North Group **13**	Temple XXI **21**
Temple of the Inscriptions **6**	Ball Court **14**	Temple XVII **22**
Temple XIII **7**	Encampment **15**	
Temple of the Skull **8**	Queen Baths **16**	

Sarcophogus

Pacal's sarcophagus, or coffin, is carved out of a solid piece of rock, with a carved slab covering it. Every element in the imagery of the sarcophagus lid is consistent with Maya iconography. It is exquisitely beautiful. The central image is that of Lord Pacal falling back into the fleshless jaws of the earth monster who will transport him to Xibalba, the realm of the dead. A cruciform world-tree rises above the underworld maw. The same world-tree appears on the tablets in the sanctuaries at the backs of the buildings known as the Group of the Cross. A long inscription runs around the edge of the lid, which includes a number of dates and personal names that records a dynastic sequence covering almost the whole of the seventh and eight centuries.

Four plugs in the corners of the lid filled the holes used with ropes to lower the lid into place; the plug in the southeast corner had a notch cut in it so that the channel, built into the stairway leading to the upper world, would allow spiritual communion between the dead king and his descendants above. Although the imagery of the sarcophagus lid refers to Pacal's fall into Xibalba, the location of the tower of the palace ensures that he will not remain there. The sun, setting over the crypt on the winter solstice, will have to do battle with the Nine Lords of the Night before re-emerging triumphantly in the east; the nine tiers of the pyramid represent the nine battles to be fought during his downward journey. Pacal, who awaits the sun at the point where the final battle had been fought, will accompany the sun as he re-emerges from Xibalba in the east. Palenque, the westernmost city of the Classic Maya, was in the 'dead zone', which placed it in the perfect position to accommodate the descent of the sun and Lord Pacal into the underworld.

sacrificed by the rulers of Toniná. During his reign Palenque reached its greatest degree of expansion, although recent excavations at the site may prove differently.

Temple of the Inscriptions

The Temple of the Inscriptions, along with Temple XII and Temple XIII, lies to the south of the Palace group of buildings and is one of the rare Maya pyramids to have a burial chamber incorporated at the time of its construction. This building was erected to cover the crypt in which Lord Pacal, the founder of the first ruling dynasty of Palenque, was buried. Discovered in 1952 by Alberto Ruz-Lhuillier, the burial chamber measured 7 m long, 7 m high and 3.75 m across, an incredible achievement considering the weight of the huge pyramid pressing down upon it. According to the inscriptions, Lord Pacal was born in AD 603 and died in AD 684. Inside, Ruz-Lhuillier discovered his bones adorned with jade jewellery. Around the burial chamber were various figures carved in stucco, depicting the Bolontikú, the Nine Lords of the Night of Maya mythology. There was a narrow tube alongside the stairs, presumably to give Pacal spiritual access to the outside world. Pacal also left a record of his forebears in the inscriptions. These three great tablets contain one of the longest texts of any Maya monument. There are 620 glyph blocks; they tell of Pacal's ancestors, astronomical events and an astonishing projection into the distant future (AD 4772). One of the last inscriptions reveals that, 132 days after Pacal's death, his son, Chan Bahlum, ascended to power as the new ruler of Palenque.

While finishing his father's funerary monument, Chan Bahlum had himself depicted as a child being presented as heir by his father. The portraits of Chan Bahlum, on the outer pillars of the Temple of the Inscriptions, display features that are both human and divine. He took and assumed attributes that rightly belong to the gods, thus ensuring that the heir to the throne was perceived as a divine human.

Group of the Cross

To the extreme southeast of the centre of the site lie Temple XIV and the buildings known as the *Grupo de la Cruz*. These include the Temple of the Sun, with beautiful relief carvings, which would probably have been painted in their day. The three temples in this group all have dramatic roof-combs, originally believed to have a religious significance, although traces of roof-combs have been found on buildings now known to have been purely residential. In all of the temples there was discovered a huge stone tablet with bas-relief, now removed to the museum, from whose images the name of each temple was taken.

Human and mythological time come together in the inscriptions of these temples. In each tableau carved on the tablets at the back of the temples, Chan Bahlum, the new ruler, receives the regalia of office from his father, Pacal, now in the underworld and shown much smaller than his living son. The shrines in the three temples are dedicated to the Palenque Triad, a sacred trinity linked to the ruling dynasty of the city, whose genealogy is explained in the inscriptions. They were certainly long lived: the parents of the triad were born in 3122 or 3121 BC and the children arrived on 19 October, 23 October and 6 November, 2360 BC. It has been shown that these were dates of extraordinary astronomical phenomena: the gods were intimately related to heavenly bodies and events. They also provided a mythological origin for the dynasty which is detailed on the three main tablets from the Group of the Cross. Rulers died and gods were born in an impressive merging of historical and mythological events. At their completion, the three temples of the Group of the Cross housed the divine sanction for the dynasty as a whole and gave the rationale for its descent through females and males.

On each set of balustrades, Chan Bahlum began his text with the birth of the patron god of each temple. On the left side of the stairs, he recorded the time elapsed between the birth of the god and the dedication of the temple. Thus, mythological time and contemporary time were fused. Each temple was named for the central image on its inner tablet. When Chan Bahlum died in 702 after ruling for 18 years, his younger brother and heir erected a fourth shrine to record the apotheosis of the departed king (Temple XIV). On these reliefs, Chan Bahlum emerges triumphantly from the underworld and dances towards his mother, Lady Ahpo-Hel.

The lengths to which the rulers of Palenque went to establish legitimacy for their claims of divine right could not guarantee the survival of Palenque after the collapse felt throughout the Classic Maya region, when the building of elite religious structures stopped and stelae were no longer engraved with the details of dynastic events. Toniná, the city that captured and probably sacrificed the Palenque ruler Kan-Xul, outlived the great centre made glorious by Pacal and Chan Bahlum. The last-known dated monument from the Maya region registers AD 909 at the lesser site; it is to be supposed that soon afterwards, Toniná went the way of the other centres of the Classic Maya world.

The **museum** ① *Tue-Sun 0900-1630, free with ruins ticket*, is on the way back to the town, with an expensive restaurant and gift shop. Many of the stucco carvings retrieved from the site are here, as well as jade pieces of jewellery, funerary urns and ceramics. If you want to learn more about the iconography and writing system of the Classic Maya see *A Forest of Kings*, by L Schele and D Freidel (William Morrow and Company, NY 1992).

East of Palenque: the Carretera Fronteriza
jungle-clad remote border region with Mayan villages and archaeological sites

From Palenque, Highway 307, also known as the Carretera Fronteriza, follows the eastern outskirts of Chiapas state where it meets the frontier with Guatemala, eventually joining the Pan-American Highway at La Trinitaria, south of Comitán. This area encompasses tracts of pristine rainforests, isolated Lacandón Maya communities, endless enchanting waterfalls, lakes, and the lesser visited archaeological sites of Bonampak and Yaxchilán. The region is heavily militarized due to cross-border narco-trafficking and you may be stopped at a number of checkpoints during your journey. For safety, you should not travel on the highway after dark. The international crossings in this part of Chiapas provide an adventurous backdoor route into Guatemala's Petén.

Lacanjá Chansayab

Lacanjá Chansayab, 6 km from the tiny hamlet of San Javier on the Carretera, is one of only three permanent Lacandón communities in Mexico. Forest-dwelling nomads until the late 20th century, the Lacandón settlers in this little village continue to speak their native language, but have otherwise abandoned their traditions and converted to Protestant Christianity. The experience of staying in the community is nonetheless fascinating, and the setting, on the edge of the rainforest, is certainly magical with its vast starry skies and swarms of twinkling fireflies. Accommodation consists of 'campamentos' with simple wood-built *cabañas* ($$-$) and shared dorms. Please contribute to the community by buying some artesanías from your hosts and/or by hiring the services of a guide: there are several jungle hikes, waterfalls and hidden ruins to check out, and it is also possible to hike to Bonampak, 12 km away (see below); expect to pay US$30-40 per group for a three- to four-hour tour. For more information on the community and Lacandón culture, drop into the **Na-Bolom** cultural centre in San Cristóbal de las Casas. In Lacanjá, Lucas Chambor at the **Casa de Cultura** is a good source of advice.

★Bonampak → *Colour map 2, A6.*
Open 0800-1645, US$3.50. To get there on public transport, ask the driver to drop you at 'Crucero Bonampak', 4 km from the site. If the bus only stops at San Javier, taxis can shuttle you 12 km to the entrance.

Bonampak, originally under the political domination of Yaxchilán, was built in the late-Classic period on the Río Lacanjá, a tributary of the Usumacinta. It is famous for its murals, dated at AD 800. Painted on the walls, vault rises and benches of three adjoining but not interconnecting rooms, they depict the rituals surrounding the presentation at court of the future ruler. Some of the rituals were separated by considerable intervals which added to the solemnity of the ceremony. It is very likely that the rituals illustrated were only a small selection of a far greater series of events. The people participating were mainly elite, including the royal family, and a strict hierarchy was observed in which eminent lords were attended by minor nobility.

Structure 1 The rituals portrayed on the walls of Structure 1 at Bonampak are thought to have been performed between 790 and 792, a time when the collapse of the Classic Maya was beginning to be felt. The extravagant use of enormous amounts of fine cloth, expensive jaguar pelts, jade beads and pectorals, elegant costumes, headdresses made from rare feathers, and spondylus shells was not enough to reverse the decadence of the civilization that had produced magnificent works in art, architecture, jewellery, mathematics, astronomy and glyphic writing: within a hundred years, the jungle was to claim it for its own.

Room 1 In the first room of Structure 1, the celebration opens with the presentation of the young prince, in which a porter introduces the child to an assembly of lords, dressed for the occasion in white robes. The king watches from his throne. Also present are two representatives from Yaxchilán, one male and one female. It is probable that the female is the wife or consort of Chaan-Muan, the ruler of Bonampak. After this simple opening, the spectacle begins. Lords are represented dressed in sumptuous clothing and jewellery, musicians appear playing drums, turtle carapaces, rattles and trumpets and they all line up for a procession, which will bemuse the peasantry, labourers and artisans waiting outside. We never see the lower orders but, open-mouthed, we can stand with them to observe the spectacle. The headdresses alone are enough to bedazzle us and the great diversity in the attire of the participants illustrates the wide spectrum of social functions fulfilled by those attending the ceremony.

Room 2 The imagery and text of the sculptured lintels and stelae at nearby Yaxchilán proclaim the right of the heir to accede to the throne while emphasizing the need to take captives to be sacrificed in honour of the king-to-be. This need is echoed in the paintings of Room 2, Structure 1, at Bonampak. A ferocious battle is in progress in which the ruler, Chaan-Muan, proves his right to the throne. In the midst of battle, he shines out heroically. The local warriors pull the hair of those of the opposite side, whose identity is not known. Many captives were taken. In the ensuing scene, the full horror of the fate of those captured by the Maya is illustrated.

On a stepped structure, the ruler Chaan-Muan oversees the torture and mutilation of the captives taken in the recent battle. This event is clearly in the open air and surely witnessed by the inhabitants of Bonampak, whose loyalty is rewarded by admission to the bloody circus. The torture of the captives consisted of mutilation of the hands; some disconsolate individuals hold up their hands dripping blood, while one has clearly been decapitated, his head resting on a bed of leaves. It is to be supposed that the torture of the captives would be followed by death, probably by decapitation. The gods demanded sacrifice, which was provided by the rulers in an extravaganza of bloodletting. It must be understood that what appears to be outright bloodthirstiness was a necessary part of Maya ritual and probably accepted by all the polities throughout the Classic Maya region. It is very probable that the heir would not have been acceptable without this gory ritual.

Room 3 The murals of the third room at Bonampak express the events that were meant to close the series of rituals designed to consolidate the claim to the throne by the son of the ruler. At first sight, the paintings that cover the walls of room three of Structure 1 appear to celebrate the sacrifices of the previous depictions in an exuberant public display of music, dance and perhaps song. The background is a pyramid, and 10 elegantly dressed lords dance on different levels, colourful 'dance-wings' sprouting from their hips. The dominant dancer on the uppermost level is believed to be the ruler, Chaan-Muan. However, it has been noted that a very strong element of sacrifice accompanies the extrovert display. In a more private corner, the royal family is portrayed preparing to engage in blood sacrifice; a servant proffers them a container that the sacred bloodletting instruments. There are also indications that the male dancers had already drawn blood by means of penis perforation. As at Yaxchilán, blood endorsed the dynastic claims of the royal family.

Frontera Corozal → *Colour map 2, A6.*

Formerly known as Frontera Echeverria, the town of Frontera Corozal is perched on the banks of the Río Usumacinta, the cradle of Classic Mayan civilization, and today the physical border between Mexico and Guatemala. The town serves as a small but important river port with connections by *lancha* downstream to the ruins of Yaxchilán, or across the frontier to Guatemala. There is an immigration office, a few adequate hotels, restaurants, a regional museum and a military presence. *Colectivos* travel directly from Palenque to Corozal, otherwise you can get a taxi from the highway turn-off (Crucero Corozal), US$1.50; or from San Javier, 16 km away, US$2 per person, plus a toll US$1 (retain your ticket until exiting). See also Mexico to Guatemala: Frontera Corozal–Bethel/ La Técnica, below, and box, page 512.

★ Yaxchilán → *Colour map 2, A6.*

Yaxchilán 0800-1600, US$4.50. Lanchas to the site depart from Frontera Corozal on demand, 40-60 mins each way, costing from US$60 for 1-3 people up to US$120 for 8-10, with a 2- to 3-hr wait at the site. Prices are hard to negotiate so it's best to join a group to keep down costs.

Yaxchilán was a powerful Maya city-state built on terraces and hills above a bend in the Río Usumacinta. Founded in the Pre-Classic era, it reached its apogee in the late Classic, dominating Bonampak and other regional population centres to become the most important city on the river. Now ruined and rather remote, the site is very haunting and tranquil, except for the troupes of occasionally vociferous howler monkeys who live in the surrounding forests.

Entering Yaxchilán on the west side, the Labyrinth is a three-level structure with numerous rooms and stairways, and a population of squeaking bats, which leads onto the Gran Plaza. Structures flank the plaza on all sides and climb the hills to the south. The finest building in Yaxchilán is Structure 33, dedicated in the 8th century and boasting an impressive roof-comb. A staircase leads to it from Stela 1 and the final step is engraved with hieroglyphs and a pictorial representation of the sacred ball game.

The site is generally renowned for its stelae and stone inscriptions, which include two hieroglyphic stairways, visual depictions of ceremonies and descriptions of the city's dynastic history. Sadly, some lintels have been removed from the site and taken out of Mexico, such as the famous Lintel 24, now on display in the British Museum in London. It depicts a blood-letting ritual performed by King Balam II and his wife Lady Kabal Xook. Lintel 15, also in the British Museum, depicts a similar scene Lady Wak Tuun, a wife of King Bird Jaguar IV, conjuring Vision Serpents from a bowl of blood-stained scrolls.

Mexico to Guatemala: Frontera Corozal–Bethel/La Técnica → *Colour map 2, A6.*
Adventurers will enjoy the remote Frontera Corozal crossing. The first leg includes a 40-minute *lancha* ride upstream to Bethel in Guatemala (see Transport, below). You must stamp out in Corozal and surrender your tourist card before proceeding. Once in Bethel, there is an immigration office for stamping into the country and buses run to Flores at least four times daily, four to five hours, US$3. A slightly cheaper alternative is to cross the river to La Técnica on the opposite bank (see Transport, below). From there, infrequent buses run to Bethel 12 km away (where you must submit to formalities) and onwards to Flores. The first hour or two of the trip to Flores is on a bumpy unpaved dirt road. Due to the unreliability of onward connections, some travellers like to have the whole journey booked on private transport. Tour operators in Palenque can organize this. See also box, page 512.

Listings East of Palenque: the Carretera Fronteriza

Transport

Frontera Corozal
Boat
From Frontera Corozal to **Yaxchilán** it costs from US$60 for 1-3 passengers; prices rise with additional people. You can try to bargain the boatmen down (be warned, they're stubborn), or hitch a ride with a tour group. If you are travelling from Frontera Corozal to **Guatemala**, ensure your papers are in order before crossing the border. Visit immigration offices on both sides for exit and entry stamps, and keep a photocopy of your passport handy for possible military inspection.

River crossings to La Técnica US$3.50, 5 mins. To Bethel in **Guatemala**, US$30 for 1-3 passengers, up to US$60 for 8-10.

Bus
A few different companies run hourly *colectivo* services to **Palenque**, including **Transportes Chamoan**, 0400-1600, 2-3 hrs, US$9.20 (see Palenque *Colectivos*, page 151). For Lacanjá or Bonampak, catch one of these and exit at the junction and military checkpoint at San Javier. From there, you will need to hike or take a taxi, if you can find one. Bear in mind this is a remote destination, so pack water, travel light and plan your time accordingly.

Tabasco State

Until recently, low-lying, hot, steamy, swampy Tabasco was considered an oil state with little appeal for tourists. But oil wealth has brought Villahermosa, the state capital, a certain self-assurance and vibrancy, and the parks, nature reserves and huge meandering rivers in the eastern and southern regions of the state are beginning to attract visitors. Be sure to pack insect repellent, especially in the wet season.

Villahermosa → *Colour map 3, C3.*

a busy, prosperous city, attracting mainly business travellers

Capital of Tabasco state, Villahermosa is on the Río Grijalva, which is navigable to the sea. The cathedral, ruined in 1973, has been rebuilt, its twin steeples beautifully lit at night; it is not in the centre. There is a warren of modern colonial-style pedestrian malls throughout the central area.

The **Centro de Investigaciones de las Culturas Olmecas** (CICOM) is set in a modern complex with a large public library, expensive restaurant, airline offices and souvenir shops, a few minutes' walk south, out of town along the river bank. The **Museo Regional de Antropología Carlos Pellicer** ⓘ *Pereférico Carlos Pellicer, www.iec.tabasco.gob. mx, Tue-Sun 0900-1700, US$3.80,* on three floors, has well laid-out displays of Maya and Olmec artefacts. Two other museums worth visiting are the **Museo de Cultura Popular** ⓘ *Zaragoza 810, Tue-Sun 0900-2000, free,* and the **Museo de Historia de Tabasco** ⓘ *Av 27 de Febrero corner of Juárez, Tue-Sun 0900-1900, US$1.50.* The **Mercado Pino Suárez** at Pino Suárez and Bastar Zozaya offers a sensory overload as every nook and cranny is taken up with a variety of goods; everything from barbecued *pejelagarto* (gar, a type of fish) to cowboy hats, colourful handmade fabrics, spices and dangling naked chickens en route to the kettle. The local drink, *pozol*, is believed to cure a hangover. You can watch it being made here as the *pozoleros* grind the hominy into a thick dough to then mix it with cacao and water; its grainy starchiness is somewhat of an acquired taste. Nonetheless it is popular, and the *pozoleros* will serve you the drink *al gusto*, that is, with as much or as little sugar as you want.

★Parque Nacional La Venta → *Colour map 3, C3.*

Adolfo Ruiz Cortines, T993-314 1652, Tue-Sun 0800-1600, US$4; it takes up to 2 hrs to do the park justice; excellent guides speak Spanish and English, recommended. Taxis charge US$2 to the Parque. Bus Circuito No 1 from outside 2nd-class bus terminal goes past Parque La Venta. From Parque Juárez in the city, take a 'Fraccionamiento Carrizal' bus and ask to be let off at Parque Tomás Garrido, of which La Venta is a part.

In 1925, an expedition of archaeologists discovered huge sculptured human and animal figures, urns and altars at La Venta, the centre of the ancient Olmec culture, buried in near imprenetrable forest, 120 km west of Villahermosa. In the 1950s, the monuments were threatened with destruction by the discovery of oil nearby. The poet Carlos Pellicer got them hauled all the way to a woodland area near Villahermosa, now the Parque Nacional de La Venta, also called the Museo Nacional de la Venta. There is nothing to see now at the original site of La Venta.

The park, with scattered lakes, next to a children's playground, is almost opposite the old airport entrance (west of downtown). There, the 33 exhibits are dispersed in various small clearings. The huge heads, one of them weighing 20 tonnes, are Olmec, a culture that flourished about 1150-150 BC. The figures have suffered a certain amount of damage through being exposed to the elements (those in the Xalapa Anthropological Museum are in far better condition) but to see them here, in natural surroundings, is an experience not to be missed.

There is also a zoo with creatures from the Tabasco jungle, including monkeys, alligators, deer, wild pigs and birds. Outside the park, on the lakeside, is an observation tower, **Mirador de las Aguilas** ⓘ *free*, with excellent views, but only for the fit as there are lots of stairs.

Listings Villahermosa

Tourist information

Institute of Tourism
Av Paseo Tabasco 1504, T993-316 8271, www.vistetabasco.com. Daily 0800-1800.
English spoken, good for maps and advice on Tabasco state. There is also a tourist information kiosk at the ADO terminal.

Where to stay

$$$-$$ One Villahermosa Centro
Carranza 101 esq Zaragoza, T993-131 7100, www.onehotels.com.
Unlike many other chain hotels, this reliable business class lodging is conveniently located downtown. Its rooms are crisp, minimalist and somewhat generic, but

they are all well equipped with the usual comforts and amenities.

$$ Hotel Santo Domingo Express
Madero 802, T993-131 2674, www.santodomingohotel.com.mx.
Immaculately clean, modern and stylish, this small business hotel has 27 well-attired rooms with Wi-Fi and plasma TVs. Good comfort to value ratio. Recommended.

$$-$ Hotel Oriente
Madero 425, T993-312 0121, hotel-oriente@hotmail.com.
A reliable budget option; nothing special, charming or fancy, but fair and adequate. Rooms are clean and modest, and those with fan and no a/c are slightly cheaper.

Restaurants

In the high season a number of eateries, bars and discos open up along the riverfront. Good for sunset drinks and dining, but take mosquito repellent. For good tacos head to Calle Aldama, Nos 611, 613 and 615, where there are 3 decent places. These are cheap and cheerful, but excellent value, with great selections.

$$$-$$ Los Manglares
Madero 418, inside Hotel Olmeca Plaza.
Attractive restaurant serving seafood, meat, chicken and breakfast. Excellent 4-course lunch buffet.

$$$-$$ Rodizio do Brasil
Parque la Choca, Stand Grandero, T993-316 2895, informacion@ restauranterodizio.com.
Speciality *espadas*, good Brazilian food.

$$ El Matador
Av César Sandino No 101a, www.elmatador. com.mx. Daily 24 hrs.
Local meat dishes, *tacos al pastor*, good value.

Cafés

Café La Cabaña
Juárez 303-A, across the way from the Museo de Historia de Tabasco.
Has outdoor tables where town elders congregate to debate the day's issues over cappuccinos. Very entertaining to watch. No meals.

Festivals

Feb Ash Wednesday is celebrated from 1500 to dusk by the throwing of water bombs and buckets of water at anyone who happens to be on the street!

Transport

Air
Airport Carlos R Pérez (VSA), 18 km from town, has international flights to **Havana** and **Houston**, and has good national connections. VW bus to town US$5 each, taxi US$11.

Bus
Reserve your seat as soon as you can; buses to Mexico City can sometimes be booked up well in advance. 1st-class **ADO** bus terminal is on Javier Mina and Lino Merino, 12 blocks north of centre, computerized booking system. The **Central Camionera** 2nd-class bus station is on Av Ruiz Cortines, near the roundabout with the fisherman statue, 1 block east of Javier Mina, opposite Castillo, 4 blocks north of **ADO**.

1st-class **ADO** services to **Cancún**, many daily, 13-14 hrs, US$61-113; **Chetumal**, 6 daily, 8½ hrs, US$44; **Campeche**, many daily, 6 hrs, US$36; **Emiliano Zapata**, many daily, 2½ hrs, US$12; **Mérida**, many daily, 8 hrs, US$49-86; **Mexico City**, many daily, 10-12 hrs, US$77-97; **Palenque**, **many daily**, 2½ hrs, US$11.50; **San Cristóbal de las Casas**, 2340, 7 hrs, US$31; **Tenosique**, many daily 3½ hrs, US$16.

Taxi
City taxis charge US$1 for journeys in the centre.

Yucatán Peninsula

Once a vast coral reef in a prehistoric ocean, the Yucatán Peninsula now divides the Gulf of Mexico from the Caribbean. Relentlessly flat, its inhospitable interior is consumed by arid scrubland, swamps lagoons and impenetrable jungle.

Yet the Yucatán thrived as a hub of civilization long before the Spanish arrived. Its horizon is broken by the ruins of skyward-reaching pyramids, overgrown temples, fallen palaces and astronomical observatories: sprawling Mayan metropolises where great dynasties once reigned.

None of it would have been possible without the peninsula's network of *cenotes* (sink holes), a subterranean labyrinth of submerged caverns and canyons. The ancient Maya venerated their sacred wells as sources of life and as portals to another dimension.

The Yucatán is a fiercely independent place and can often seem more like an island. It took three brutal campaigns by Francisco de Montejo to 'pacify' the region, and today, scores of rambling old haciendas, sumptuous mansions and religious buildings are testament to the grandeur of the colonial era. But beyond them, in remote rural enclaves, determined Mayan communities stage rituals to honour the ancestral gods of thunder and rain.

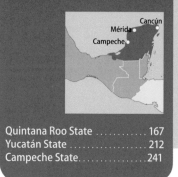

Footprint
picks

★ **Playa Norte on Isla Mujeres**, page 178
A white-sand beach on the Campeche Gulf Coast.

★ **Palancar Reef off Isla Cozumel**, page 195
This section of the Mesoamerican Barrier Reef has some spectacular coral and great diving opportunities.

★ **El Gran Museo del Mundo Maya**, Mérida, page 215
An impressive contemporary museum with lots of interactive exhibits on the Maya.

★ **Chichén Itzá**, page 232
The Toltec-influenced El Castillo pyramid looms over these Mayan ruins, the peninsula's most visited archaeological site.

★ **Cenote Dzitnup near Valladolid**, page 237
A beautiful underground lake with limestone features and tunnels leading off it.

★ **Calakmul**, page 252
The highlight of this archaeological site, one of the ancient Maya's most important capitals, is the huge pyramid of Structure II.

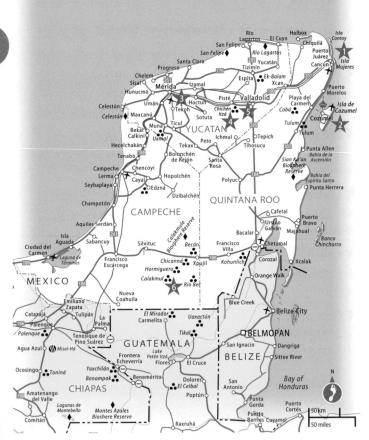

Quintana Roo
State

With its Caribbean shoreline and coral reefs, Quintana Roo is marketed to tourists as the exotic land of the Maya. Amply serviced by the international resorts of Cancún and Playa del Carmen, it is the most visited place in Mexico and, given its natural assets, it's easy to see why: soft white-sand beaches, sapphire blue waters and reclining palms… images of paradise so heavily traded they have become an oversold travel brochure cliché.

Is Quintana Roo a paradise? As a traveller, that depends on you. Some will delight in the region's well-oiled tourist infrastructure; others will want to run away. If so, forgo the resorts and head out to the islands, bastions of low-key tranquility where you can swim, dive, snorkel or eat delicious fresh seafood right on the beach. Or instead, explore the region's intriguing Mayan heritage: the many remnants of ancient Mayan ports and city states, including Tulum.

For some, paradise means getting as far from the crowds as possible, and fortunately Quintana Roo still has many unspoiled pockets: remote wetlands where you might glimpse grazing manatees, tropical rainforests with birds and vociferous howler monkeys, and forgotten Mayan villages where Yucatec is still spoken. If you look beneath the surface, Quintana Roo is far from a travel brochure cliché.

Essential Yucatán Peninsula

Getting around

Most destinations on the peninsula are well connected and easy to reach. The exceptions are Isla Holbox, Calakmul and some other ruins in the south, which require extra time and planning. Zipping up and down the coast of Quintana Roo on ADO buses is very easy. Ferries and high-speed *pangas* travel between the mainland and the islands of Holbox, Mujeres and Cozumel, as well as south from Chetumal to the Cayes of Belize.

When to go

The Caribbean coast is inundated with tourists during the summer and winter holiday period. Spring break is notorious for its unfettered hedonism, especially in Cancún. The region is very hot year round and positively sweltering April to September. Hurricane season corresponds to the wet season, May to October, with a mini-dry season July and August.

Time required

Seven to 10 days is enough for some chill-out time on one of the islands, a trip to Tulúm, a few days in Mérida, and day trips to a ruin or two. Two to three weeks is necessary to see Campeche, rural Yucatán and the lesser visited ruins.

Cancún → *Colour map 1, A6.*
a bold, brassy pleasure resort

Love or hate Cancún, its presence on the world tourism market is indisputable. From spring breakers to honeymooners to conference goers to cruise ship passengers, more than three million visitors flock to the city annually. When the Mexican tourist board 'discovered' the place in 1967, it was little more than a tiny fishing village, barren and inaccessible, but blessed with miles of white-sand beaches.

Two decades later, meticulous planning and massive international investment saw Cancún transformed into a city of more than 600,000 inhabitants. Clambering skyward from a sinuous spit of land that flanks the Caribbean Sea on one side, mangrove-fringed lagoons on the other, its high-density Zona Hotelera has become a potent symbol of mass tourism – and all the convenience, sterility and cynicism it brings. For those seeking cloistered protection and 24-hour creature comforts, the amenities are many: high-class shopping malls, international restaurants, gaudy theme parks, rambling golf courses, hedonistic night clubs and a procession of grandiose resort complexes that recall everything from Disney's Cinderella Castle to Nicolae Ceausescu's Palace of the People. By contrast, the city outside is a gritty urban sprawl, down-to-earth and unapologetically real.

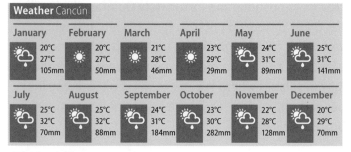

Weather Cancún					
January	**February**	**March**	**April**	**May**	**June**
20°C 27°C 105mm	20°C 27°C 50mm	21°C 28°C 46mm	23°C 29°C 29mm	24°C 31°C 89mm	25°C 31°C 141mm
July	**August**	**September**	**October**	**November**	**December**
25°C 32°C 70mm	25°C 32°C 88mm	24°C 31°C 184mm	23°C 30°C 282mm	22°C 28°C 128mm	20°C 29°C 70mm

The city centre is laid out in street blocks called *manzanas* (M), grouped between major avenues as *supermanzanas* (SM). The precise building is a *lote* (L). Thus a typical address might read, for example, SM24, M6, L3. Streets also have names, often not mentioned in addresses, which can lead to confusion. If lost, look closely at the street signs for the SM/M number. Taxi drivers generally respond better to addresses based on the *manzana* system.

Sights

Cancún Centro, or downtown Cancún, is a world apart from the Zona Hotelera. It evolved from a collection of temporary workers' shacks and is today a massive city with very little character. The main avenue is Tulum, formerly the highway running through the settlement when it was first conceived.

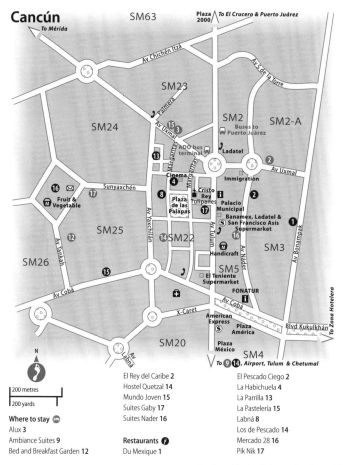

Cancún

Where to stay
Alux **3**
Ambiance Suites **9**
Bed and Breakfast Garden **12**
El Rey del Caribe **2**
Hostel Quetzal **14**
Mundo Joven **15**
Suites Gaby **17**
Suites Nader **16**

Restaurants
Du Mexique **1**
El Pescado Ciego **2**
La Habichuela **4**
La Parrilla **13**
La Pastelería **15**
Labná **8**
Los de Pescado **14**
Mercado 28 **16**
Pik Nik **17**

ON THE ROAD

A brief history of the Caste War

Throughout the colonial era, the Yucatán enjoyed considerable independence from Mexico City, thanks to its geographic distance and its international trade. In the 19th century, as the capital relented to instability, the Yucatán enjoyed a prodigious economic boom fuelled by its expanding sugar and henequen (sisal) plantations.

But beyond the façade of urban gentrification, ethnic tensions festered in the countryside, especially when the sprawl of Yucatec haciendas began encroaching on communal Mayan lands. Against a backdrop of high taxes and shifting political transformations – independence from Spain, the emergence of a short-lived independent Yucatán, and its eventual incorporation into a federal Mexico – the Caste War broke out in 1847. Marred by atrocities on both sides, the conflict claimed 200,000 lives and very nearly resulted in an autonomous Mayan state.

The roots of the conflict lay far back in the Spanish conquest. In 1526, Francisco de Montejo and Alonso de Dávila were sent to conquer the Yucatán, but it was not until 1560 that the region fell decisively under the jurisdiction of the *audencia* of Mexico. Like other parts of New Spain, a strict racial hierarchy pervaded the colonial way of life: government was made up of Spanish-born upper classes only and based on the subordination of the *indígenas* and *mestizos*. In the same spirit, the prevailing *encomienda* system was tantamount to slavery, but it was soon replaced by the hacienda system with its feudal airs and absolute title to land. Christianization of the Yucatán intensified in 1571, the year of the Inquisition.

But despite the best efforts of the church to suppress Mayan culture – including those of Bishop Diego de Landa, who destroyed scores of Mayan

A good place for people-watching and soaking up the local atmosphere is **Parque de las Palapas**, a large plaza with cheap restaurants and wandering street vendors. It comes to life on Sunday evenings, an occasion for live music and dancing, ambling couples, families and children. Nearby, a mildly enthralling 'Zona Rosa' (entertainment district) can be found on **Avenida Yaxchilán**. The city's largest and most visited *artesanía* market is **Mercado 28** ① *0900-1800*, but many prefer the laid-back locals' market, **Mercado 23** (see Shopping, below).

If you're based in Cancún Centro, a trip to **Playa Delfines**, the white-sand beach on the eastern flank of the Zona Hotelera, is somewhat obligatory, if not to bathe in the calm Caribbean waters then to behold the panorama of high-rise hotels. On the other side of the spit, **Laguna Nichupté** separates the Zona from the mainland; it is fringed by mangroves, inhabited by crocodiles, a bit smelly and unfit for swimming.

Archaeological sites

There are several very modest archaeological sites in Cancún, recommended only for Maya enthusiasts and those unable to visit any of the larger sites. **El Rey** ① *Blv Kukulcán Km 18, 0800-1700, US$3.25*, inhabited from 1200 AD, was a minor fishing and trade centre and a contemporary of Tulum. The site includes the foundations of two palaces and a idols and ancient manuscripts in a single day of religious zeal – the *indígenas* managed to preserve their customs and spiritual beliefs. Rebellions and armed uprisings against the Spanish Yucatecos were frequent, but none were as bloody and protracted as the Caste War.

During the conflict, the Maya received considerable military support from the British, who smuggled weapons into the region from their own colony in British Honduras. By 1848, having taken the entire peninsula except the cities of Campeche and Mérida, the Maya seemed poised for victory. What happened next is a matter of academic debate. Some historians claim that the Maya ran out of supplies and were forced to retreat. Another more poetic version recounts how the annual emergence of swarms of flying ants, a phenomenon traditionally signaling the onset of planting season, prompted the Maya to return to their beloved crops of maize.

Seizing the moment, the Yucatecos mounted a formidable counter-offensive with the help of the Mexican government and US mercenaries, driving the rebels into the southeastern corner of the peninsula. But the Maya, undaunted by their defeats and unfettered from Spanish oppression, soon declared their own independent state at the newly forged settlement of Noh Cah Santa Cruz Xbalam Nah, better known as Chan Santa Cruz (today, Felipe Carrillo Puerto), where a fervent religious revival had culminated in the 'cult of the talking cross' (the cross predated Christianity as a symbol of the Mayan World Tree).

Their military theocracy enjoyed some years of stability and autonomy, but sporadic skirmishes with the Yucatecos continued. The war officially ended when President Porfirio Díaz negotiated the border of British Honduras and the British agreed to stop supplying arms to the Maya. Soon after, General Ignacio Bravo was sent to stamp out any remaining dissent in the region. In 1901, he occupied Chan Santa Cruz, ending the experiment in Mayan autonomy.

pyramidal platform where an extravagant burial chamber was discovered. **El Meco** ⓘ *Carretera Puerto Juárez–Punta Sam, 0800-1700, US$3.25*, was formerly occupied by the Itzas of Chichén Itzá. It features a palace with structural columns and a pyramidal temple with vestiges of serpent iconography; to get there, take a Punta Sam bus from Avenida Tulum (US$0.90) or a taxi (US$3-4).

Museo Maya de Cancún

Blv Kukulcán Km 16.5, T998-885 3842, www.inah.gob.mx, Tue-Sun 0900-1800, US$4.50, expository text in Spanish and English, labels mostly Spanish.

Opened in 2012, the Museo Maya showcases a small but compelling collection of archaeological pieces from across southern Mexico. Ceramic gourds, incense burners, carved stone stelae and statuary depicting feathered serpents and shamans are on display, fine examples of Mayan art and its other-worldly motifs. The first exhibition room is dedicated to the state of Quintana Roo and its historical development from early settlement to the Spanish conquest. The second room explores Mayan civilization by theme: culture, agriculture, commerce, science and religious ritual. The third room features temporary exhibits. Outside, the excavated site of San Miguelito is underwhelming, but offers a shady stroll through mangrove forest where you might see an iguana or two.

Museo Subacuático de Arte (MUSA)

www.musacancun.org; costs vary, consult a local tour operator. A typical 2-tank dive from Cancún (4 hrs), US$70-80; snorkel tour (2 hrs), US$50.

One of the world's largest and most thought-provoking underwater art attractions, the MUSA contains more than 500 life-size sculptures, all fixed to the seabed and crafted from material that promotes rapid coral growth. Installations include crowds of people modelled on real persons, a sleeping dog, a piano and a Volkswagen beetle. Inaugurated in 2010, the sculptures are now 'in bloom' and the overall effect is stunning. There are two galleries: **Salón Manchones**, 8 m deep, lies just off the southern tip of Isla Mujeres and should be dived. Off the southern edge of the Zona Hotelera, **Salón Nizuc**, 4 m deep, is suitable only for snorkelling. The stated aim of MUSA is to promote recovery of local reefs and offset the damages caused by climate change, hurricanes and 800,000 tourists to the region annually.

Listings Cancún *map p169*

Tourist information

See also the official Cancún tourism portal, www.cancun.travel, which is a good source of information.

FONATUR tourist office
Av Nader and Cobá, SM5, T998-884 1426, www.fonatur.gob.mx. Mon-Fri 0800-1500.
Flyers, maps, brochures and general information about Cancún and the surrounding attractions.

SEDETUR office
Av Yaxchilán, SM17, T998-881 9000, www.caribemexicano.gob.mx.
Not well located and deals with tourism in the state of Quintana Roo.

Where to stay

By law, beaches in Mexico are public, so you don't have to stay in a pricey seafront resort to enjoy them. Nonetheless, meandering along the strand is not encouraged by some of the larger hotels. Cancún Centro or downtown area has many economical no-frills options, but prices are still higher than other parts of the Yucatán Peninsula. Rates everywhere in Cancún can fall by 25-50% in low season (and double or triple during Christmas and New Year).

Zona Hotelera

Almost all accommodation in the Zona Hotelera – decent or otherwise – starts at around US$100, rises quickly and is best arranged as part of a package holiday. The increased costs, already the highest in Mexico, are partly the result of a government-mandated rebuilding drive after 2 devastating hurricanes, which required all existing hotels to upgrade structures for safety. Just 2 reputable options are:

$$$$ Le Blanc Spa Resort
Blv Kukulcán Km 10, T1800-712-4236, www.leblancspa resort.com.
Sublime, all-inclusive luxury accommodation, complete with first-rate service and spa treatments that promise to take pampering, just like their nightly rates, to a 'transcendent level'.

$$$$ Sun Palace
Blv Kukulcán Km 20, T1-888-414-5538, www.cancunpalaceresorts.com.
A romantic and highly luxurious couples-only resort that's sure to ignite passions. From the same chain as **Le Blanc**.

Cancún Centro

Many downtown hotels, especially the budget ones, tend to be full during Semana

Santa, in Jul and over the Dec-Jan holidays. It is best to get a room as early as possible in the morning, or make a reservation if you are returning to Cancún after an overnight trip. Outside the ADO bus terminal, beware 'friendly' and persistent touts looking to make a commission.

$$$ Ambiance Suites
Av Tulum 227, SM20, T998-892 0392, www.ambiancecancun.com.
Immaculately clean, professionally managed business hotel with helpful English-speaking staff, located close to Plaza de las Américas. Rooms and suites are crisply attired with modern furnishings, all in great condition. Amenities include small pool and business centre. Toast and coffee in the morning, welcome cocktail on arrival.

$$$ El Rey del Caribe
Av Uxmal 24 and Nader, SM2, T998-884 2028, www.reycaribe.com.
El Rey del Caribe is an ecologically aware B&B with solar hot water and other green technologies. Its leafy courtyard, complete with small pool and jacuzzi, is tranquil and shady, a quiet place to unwind. Rooms are clean, comfortable and include kitchenettes. Spa treatments are available, including massage. Good for couples and families. An oasis of the calm in the chaos of downtown Cancún.

$$$-$$ Suites Gaby
Av Sunyaxche 46-47, SM25, T998-887 8037, www.suitesgaby.com.
The exterior of **Suites Gaby** is utilitarian and uninspired, but inside you'll find simple, comfortable, recently remodelled rooms with a modern touch. Hot-water showers are strong and the rooms are generally quiet, although the walls are thin. Convenient for Mercado 28 and the restaurants on Yaxchilán.

$$$ Suites Nader
Av Nader 5, SM5, T998-884 1584, www.suitesnadercancun.com.
The rooms at this downtown lodging are just adequate, but the suites are definitely

worth a look – all are very comfortable, clean, spacious and quite good value. Each has a fully equipped kitchen and living area, and 2 beds, good for small families with young children. The adjoining restaurant is an excellent breakfast spot and always buzzing with customers.

$$ Alux
Av Uxmal 21, T998-884 0556, www.hotelalux.com.
Conveniently located a block from the ADO bus terminal and a stone's throw from the action on Yaxchilán, **Hotel Alux** has clean, safe, simple, comfortable rooms with a/c, TV, Wi-Fi and hot-water showers; rates include coffee and toast in the morning. Recommended for budget travellers, good rates off season ($). An *alux*, if you were wondering, is a kind of mythical Mayan elf.

$$-$ Bed and Breakfast Garden
Jícama 7, SM25, T998-267 7777, www.bedand breakfastcancun.com.mx.
A cross between a hostel and B&B, this homely, cosy lodging has small dorms ($) and simple rooms ($$), shared kitchen and a comfortable living room with TV and reading material. Located in a quiet, residential part of town, 5 mins from Mercado 28. Surf and yoga lessons available. Breakfast included.

$$-$ Hostel Quetzal
Orquídeas 10, SM22, T998-883 9821, www.quetzal-hostel.com.
Lots of good reports about **Hostel Quetzal**, a fun, sociable place that will suit outgoing backpackers and whippersnappers. Amenities include single- and mixed-sex dorms ($), private rooms ($$), rooftop terrace, bar and garden. Daytime excursions to the local sights are available, as well as legendary nights out to the clubs in the Zona.

$$-$ Mundo Joven
Av Uxmal 25, SM23, T998-271 4740, www.mundojoven.com.
Conveniently located 1 block from the ADO bus terminal, this clean and professionally

managed hostel is part of an international franchise. This one has functional dorms ($) and rooms ($$), and a great rooftop terrace complete with bar, barbecue and hedonistic hot tub. Rock on.

Restaurants

The Hotel Zone is lined with expensive restaurants, with every type of international cuisine imaginable, but with a predominance of Tex-Mex and Italian. Restaurants are cheaper in the centre, where the emphasis is on local food.

Cancún Centro

$$$ Du Mexique
Bonampak 109, SM3, T998-884-5919.
Intimate and extravagant fine dining with superb French/Mexican fusion cuisine by Chef Alain Grimond; try the delicious rack of lamb. Courses are served in 3 different areas: sala, dining room and garden. Smart-casual attire and just 7 tables; advance reservations a must.

$$$ La Habichuela
Margaritas 25, SM22, www.lahabichuela. com; a new branch is now open in the Zona Hotelera, Blv Kukulcán Km 12.6 Hotel Zone.
Award-winning restaurant serving delicious Caribbean seafood in a tropical garden setting. Good ambience, attentive service, Mayan-themed decor and jazz music. Recommended.

$$$ Labná
Margaritas 29, SM22, www.labnaonline.com.
The best in Yucatecan cooking, serving dishes like *poc chuc* and *pollo pibil*. Try the platter and sample a wide range of this fascinating regional cuisine. Good lunchtime buffet ($$). Highly recommended.

$$$ La Parrilla
Yaxchilán 51, SM22, www.laparrilla.com.mx.
A buzzing, lively joint, always busy and popular, especially with Mexican families.

They serve mouth-watering grill platters, ribs, steaks and other carnivorous fare. Try the enormous margaritas in exotic flavours – hibiscus flower and tamarind.

$$$-$$ El Pescado Ciego
Av Nader esquina Rubia, SM3.
Closed Thu and Sun.
Low-key and relaxed, a good place for friends and lovers, **El Pescado Ciego** serves flavourful contemporary seafood dishes with a Mexican twist. Offerings include tasty shrimp tacos, lobster quesadillas, tuna steaks and filleted catch of the day.

$$ Pik Nik
Calle Tulipanes, SM22.
A fun, local, friendly place to kick back and gorge on hearty Mexican food and drink. Expect the usual staples, including tacos, burritos and quesadillas, as well as Mexican beers and cocktails. Good service, a great place for groups, with terraced seating on a pedestrian street near Plaza del las Palapas.

$ Los de Pescado
Av Tulum 32, SM20, www.losdepescado.com.
Lunch and early supper only.
Excellent Baja California-style fish burritos and tacos, prawn ceviche, beer, soda and absolutely nothing else. Charmless setting and service, but great fast food. Recommended.

$ Mercado 28
SM28. Open for lunch and early supper.
The half dozen or so kitchens nestled inside in the *artesanía* market serve the best budget meals in the city; **Mi Rancho** is one of the better ones. Set meals include generous Mexican staples and specialities, such as *pollo con mole poblano* (chicken in chocolate and chilli sauce). Most come with a soup starter, tortillas, nachos, salsa and a drink, all for US$5. If the waiter hands you the more expensive à la carte menu, insist on *comida del día*. Wandering mariachis may serenade you. Recommended.

Know your hammock

Different materials are available for hammocks. Some you might find include sisal, which is very strong, light, hard-wearing but rather scratchy and uncomfortable, and is identified by its distinctive smell; cotton, which is soft, flexible, comfortable, not as hard-wearing but, with care, is good for four or five years of everyday use. It is not possible to weave cotton and sisal together, although you may be told otherwise, so mixtures are unavailable. Cotton/silk mixtures are offered, but will probably be an artificial silk. Nylon is very strong and light but it's hot in hot weather and cold in cold weather.

Never buy your first hammock from a street vendor and never accept a packaged hammock without checking the size and quality. The surest way to judge a good hammock is by weight: 1.5 kg (3.3 lb) is a fine item, under 1 kg (2.2 lb) is junk (advises Alan Handleman, a US expert). Also, the finer and thinner the strands of material, the more strands there will be, and the more comfortable the hammock. The best hammocks are the so-called 3-ply, but they are difficult to find. There are three sizes: single (sometimes called *doble*), *matrimonial* and family (buy a *matrimonial* at least for comfort). If judging by end-strings, 50 would be sufficient for a child, 150 would suit a medium-sized adult, 250 a couple. Prices vary considerably so shop around and bargain hard.

Cafés

La Pastelería
Av Cobá and Guanábana, SM25.
La Pastelería, formerly known as La Crepería, is a European-style café-patisserie serving aromatic coffee and a host of elegant desserts, including sumptuous cakes and pastries adorned with lashings of rich, dark Mexican chocolate.

Bars and clubs

Cancún is famous for its debauched nightlife. Clubs are mostly concentrated at Blv Kukulcán Km 9 in the Zona Hotelera. All tastes are catered to, but most of the action gravitates to chic lounge bars and enormous discos, invariably packed to the rafters with revellers during spring break. Establishments come and go with the seasons, but one that has withstood the test of time is **Coco Bongo**, www.cocobongo. com.mx, famous for its vivid dance and acrobatic displays. Some tour agencies offer 'club crawl' excursions, allowing you to sample a few different places in one evening, a good option for groups; try **Party Rockers Cancún**, T998-883-0981, www.partyrockerscancun.com. Downtown, you'll find comparatively low-key bars and pubs in the Zona Rosa on Av Yaxchilán.

Shopping

There are several shopping malls in the Zona Hotelera. The main one is **Kukulcán Plaza**, Blv Kukulcán Km 13, www.kukulcanplaza. com, with more than 170 retail outlets. There are others, including **La Isla**, Blv Kukulcán Km 12.5, mostly catering to the luxury shopper. Downtown, the big *artesanía* market is **Mercado 28**, where you'll find a plethora of handmade items including silver jewellery from Taxco, hammocks from Mérida, ceramic Mayan figurines, cowboy boots, sombreros, masks, sarapes, t-shirts and more; the quality of production varies. Note prices are hiked to the limit and the salesmen are mean and aggressive.

ON THE ROAD
Cenote diving

There are more than 50 *cenotes* in this area – accessible from Ruta 307 and often well signposted – and cave diving has become very popular. However, it is a specialized sport and, unless you have a cave diving qualification, you must be accompanied by a qualified Dive Master.

A cave diving course involves over 12 hours of lectures and a minimum of 14 cave dives using double tanks, costing around US$600. Accompanied dives start at around US$60. Specialist dive centres offering courses are: **Aquatech**, Villas de Rosa, PO Box 25, T984-875 9020, www.cenotes.com. **Aventuras Akumal** No 35, Tulum, T984-875 9030; **Aktun Dive Centre**, PO Box 119, Tulum, T984-871 2311, and **Cenote Dive Center**, Tulum, T984-876 3285, www.cenotedive.com, Norwegian owned.

Two of the best *cenotes* are 'Carwash', on the Cobá road, good even for beginners, with excellent visibility; and 'Dos Ojos', just off Ruta 307 south of Aventuras, the second largest underground cave system in the world. It has a possible link to the Nohoch Nah Chich, the most famous *cenote* and part of a subterranean system recorded as the world's largest, with over 50 km of surveyed passageways connected to the sea.

A word of warning: *cenote* diving has a higher level of risk than open-water diving – do not take risks and only dive with recognized operators.

Whatever happens, smile politely and bargain hard; most vendors expect to get at least half what they originally asked. Due to credit card rip-offs, it is safer to pay cash only. You could also try the locals' market, **Mercado 23**, at the end of Calle Cedro, off Av Tulum. It's a bit tatty and tacky, but has cheaper souvenirs and friendlier salesmen. For an American-style mall experience in Cancún Centro, your best option is **Plaza de las Américas** on Av Tulum.

What to do

From booze cruises to canopy tours, parasailing to paintballing, the array of activities on offer in Cancún is vast. The listings below highlight some of the more interesting options, but are in no way exhaustive. Consult your hotel or the tourist information office for more possibilities.

Cooking

Can Cook in Cancún, *T998-147 4827, www.cancookincancun.com*. A master of Mexican cuisine, chef Claudia has been in kitchens all her life. Classes are fun and intimate, take place in Claudia's home and include an overview of traditions and regional specialities, as well as practical instruction in ingredients and flavours.

Diving and snorkelling

See box, above, for information on cave diving.

Scuba Cancun, *Kukulcán Km 5, T998-849 7508, www.scubacancun.com.mx*. A medium-sized dive centre run by Captain Luis Hurtado who has more than 3 decades' diving experience. He offers a range of sea, cavern and *cenote* dives, including trips to the MUSA, snorkelling tours and accelerated PADI courses.

Sports cars

Exotic rides, *Carretera Cancún Airport Km 7.5, T998-882 0558, www.exoticridescancun.com.* Experience the speed, power and performance of Ferrari, Lamborghini and other 'exotic' sports cars. Training and test driving takes place at a private race track.

Surfing

360 Surf school, *Blv Kukulcán Km 9.5, opposite Señor Frog, T998-241 6443, www.360surfschoolcancun.com.* The waves in Cancún are relatively gentle, making it a great place to learn how to surf. Managed by David '360Dave' Wanamaker, **360 Surf School** has been getting beginners up onto boards for more than 14 years. You'll surf, or your money back.

Tour operators

Ecocolors, *Calle Camarón 32, SM27, T998-884 3667, www.ecotravelmexico.com.* Socially responsible and environmentally aware tours of the Yucatán Peninsula and beyond. Specialities include biking, birdwatching, hiking and wildlife photography.

Transport

Air

The airport is 16 km south of the city. Shared fixed-price shuttles to the **Zona Hotelera** or the centre depart hourly Mon-Fri 0800-2000, US$12; pay at the kiosk outside airport. Private taxis are US$45 one way, US$70 round trip. Be sure to know the name and address of your hotel, or the driver may offer to take you to a lodging of their own choice.

Cancún airport (**CUN**), Carretera Cancún–Chetumal Km 22, T998-848 7200, www.cancun-airport.com, has expensive shops, restaurants, currency exchange, car rental, hotel reservation agencies and ATMs. Terminal 1 serves domestic airlines; Terminal 2 and Terminal 3 serve international airlines. ADO buses go from the airport to **Cancún Centro**, every 30 mins, ½ hr, US$4; **Puerto Morelos**, every 30-40 mins, ½ hr, US$6,

and **Playa del Carmen**, every 30-40 mins, 1½ hrs, US$10.

Bus

Local Ruta 1 and Ruta 2 buses travel between Cancún Centro (downtown) and the Zona Hotelera, US$0.70. Ruta 1 runs 24 hrs and follows Av Tulum, the city's principal thoroughfare. Ruta 2 runs 0500-0330 and goes via Av Cobá. Shuttle buses to **Puerto Juárez** for the ferry to Isla Mujeres follow Av Tulum, US$0.65, opposite side to the bus station.

Long distance Cancún's **ADO** bus terminal, C Pino, SM23, at the junction of Av Tulum and Uxmal, is a hub for routes west to Mérida and south to Tulum and beyond to Chetumal, open 24 hrs, left luggage, rates vary depending on size, open 0600-2200. Rapid ticket booths for the airport and Playa del Carmen.

To **Cancún Airport**, every 30 mins, ½ hr, US$4. To **Chetumal**, frequent departures, 6 hrs, US$27.To **Chichén Itzá**; all 2nd-class buses to Mérida stop here, fewer 1st-class buses, 4 hrs, US$14. To **Mérida**, frequent departures, 4½ hrs, US$25. To **Palenque**, 1st class, 1545, 2030, 12½ hrs, US$62; and an **ADO GL**, 1745, 13 hrs, US$68. To **Playa del Carmen**, every 10 mins, 1½ hrs, US$4. To **Puerto Morelos**, frequent departures, 30 mins, US$2.30. To **San Cristóbal**, OCC, 1545, 2030 18 hrs, US$69, **ADO GL**, 1745, US$83. To **Tulum**, ADO, frequent departures, 2½ hrs, US$9, and many cheaper 2nd-class buses. To **Valladolid**, frequent departures, 2½ hrs, US$12.50. To **Villahermosa**, 1st class, many departures, 13 hrs, US$62. **Expreso de Oriente** also has services to the more obscure destinations of **Tizimín** (3 hrs, US$10), **Izamal**, **Cenotillo** and **Chiquilá**.

Car

Car hire There are many car hire agencies, including **Dollar**, **Hertz**, **Thrifty**, **Budget** and others, with offices on Av Tulum, in the Hotel Zone and at the airport; look out for special deals, but check vehicles carefully.

Car parking Do not leave cars parked in side streets; there is a high risk of theft. Use the car park on Av Uxmal.

Ferry

For ferries to **Isla Mujeres**, regular *combis* and buses travel along Av Tulum en route to **Puerto Juárez** (marked Pto Juárez or Punta Sam), US$0.80, where services to the island depart from the **Ultra Mar** terminal, T998-843 2011, www.granpuerto.com.mx, at Gran Puerto (recommended), every 30 mins, 0500-2330, US$5.50, children US$3.50; and from the **Magaña Express** terminal, T998 877 0618, 2 blocks north of Ultra Mar, hourly, 0800-2000. **Ultra Mar** services also depart from the Zona Hotelera (Playa Caracol, Playa Tortugas and El Embarcadero), every 1-2 hrs, US$11. Car ferries depart 4-5 times daily from **Punta Sam**, north of Puerto Juárez on the coast, US$20 for a car and driver, US$1.50 for each additional passenger.

Taxi

Taxis are abundant in Cancún. Fares are based on a zone system and most short journeys downtown cost US$2. Overcharging is common; avoid taxis waiting outside hotels or restaurants.

Isla Mujeres → *Colour map 5, A6.*

a refreshing antidote to the urban sprawl of Cancún

★Blending Caribbean and Mexican styles, and more than faintly recalling the Mediterranean too, Isla Mujeres (Women Island) is a place to unwind, unravel and forget about the hurly burly of package tourism. In pre-Hispanic times, the island served as a shrine to Ixchel, the Mayan goddess of childbirth, traditionally associated with midwifery, fertility, femininity and the moon. It received its current name after Spanish conquistadors came ashore in the 16th century and discovered scores of clay idols depicting the goddess and her daughters: Ixchebeliax, Ixhunie and Ixhunieta.

Blessed with one of the finest beaches in Mexico, kaleidoscopic coral reefs and, of course, an appropriately alluring name, Isla Mujeres has been a popular tourist destination since the 1960s. Unlike its younger sibling on the mainland, Cancún, it has endured remarkably well; even with the pressure of big dollars on its doorstep, it remains defiantly low-key, a sanctuary for travellers everywhere. The magic begins after dusk, once the day-trippers have gone.

Sights

An unkempt seasonal refuge for pirates and fishermen, Isla Mujeres was largely uninhabited in the colonial era. It saw significant settlement only in 19th century when the violence and persecution of the Caste War drove scores of refugees to its shores. Today, tourism has all but replaced fishing as the mainstay of the local economy. Fortunately, **Isla Mujeres Town** remains strictly low-rise and unobtrusive, its colourful grid of streets boasting scores of intimate little restaurants, bars, cafés and *artesanía* shops. The island is 7 km long and 650 m wide. The town, at the northern end, can be easily covered on foot. For explorations further afield, hire a golf cart, moped or bicycle, or take the bus. The best beach on the island, **Playa Norte**, is conveniently located on the fringe of the action.

Heading south from the town, the main seafront artery, **Avenida Rueda Medina**, becomes the **Carretera Garrafón** and skirts the airport, marinas and a series brackish lagoons which the ancient Maya harvested for their salt. Inland, near the southern tip of Laguna Makax, the ruined **Hacienda Mundaca** ⓘ *0900-1700, US$2.50*, was constructed in 1860 on the site of a Mayan temple. Originally called 'Vista Alegre', its owner, a notorious Spanish slave trader,

Fermín Antonio Mundaca, fell madly in love with a local girl, Martiniana (Prisca) Pantoja, but she rejected him for a younger lover. Mundaca eventually went insane, dying alone in the city of Mérida on the mainland. His tomb on Isla Mujeres remains empty, but its bitter epitaph was carved by his own hand: "As you were, so was I. As I am, so you will be."

For something a bit lighter, the **Capitán Dulché Beach Club** ① *Cra Garrafon Km 4, T998-849 7594, www.capitandulche.com, daily 1030-1930*, is a new addition to the island, complete with sun loungers, bar, restaurant and a small museum of maritime artefacts, historic photos and handsome model ships. To the northwest, the **Carretera Sac Bajo** doubles back on a narrow spit, passing between the Caribbean sea and the shores of Laguna Makax. The government-sponsored **Tortugranja** ① *Cra Sac Bajo Km 5, daily 0900-1700, US$2.50*, is a small turtle hatchery with fish-filled aquariums and young turtles at different stages of development; knowledgeable staff explain their life cycles and migratory habits.

At the southern end of the island, the **Garrafón Natural Reef Park** ① *Cra Garrafón, Km 6, T01-866-393 5158, www.garrafon.com*, is a luxury adventure resort offering snorkelling, kayaking, zip-lining and bike tours; packages from US$59. Nearby, the **Santuario a la Diosa Ixchel** ① *daily 0900-1700, US$2.50*, is a crumbling ruin of a temple dedicated to Ixchel. The structure has been sadly damaged by hurricanes, but nonetheless commands a potent position on cliffs above the crashing ocean (take care on the slippery paths). If you can get there, it is a magical place to experience the sunrise.

Isla Mujeres town

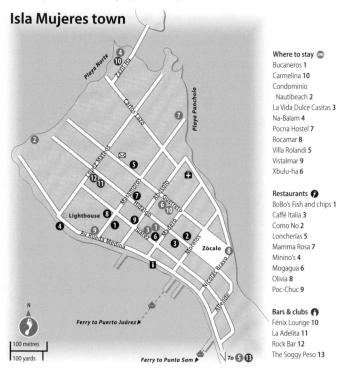

Where to stay 😊
Bucaneros **1**
Carmelina **10**
Condominio Nautibeach **2**
La Vida Dulce Casitas **3**
Na-Balam **4**
Pocna Hostel **7**
Rocamar **8**
Villa Rolandi **5**
Vistalmar **9**
Xbulu-ha **6**

Restaurants 🍴
BoBo's Fish and chips **1**
Caffé Italia **3**
Como No **2**
Loncherías **5**
Mamma Rosa **7**
Minino's **4**
Mogagua **6**
Olivia **8**
Poc-Chuc **9**

Bars & clubs 🍸
Fénix Lounge **10**
La Adelita **11**
Rock Bar **12**
The Soggy Peso **13**

Tourist information

The official online information portal is
www.isla-mujeres.com.mx.

Tourist office
Av Rueda Medina 130, T998-877 0767.
Located on the seafront opposite the
ferry terminals, the tourist office has
maps, flyers and helpful staff, some
of whom speak English.

Where to stay

$$$$ Condominio Nautibeach
Playa Los Cocos, T998-877 0606,
www.nautibeach.com.
Condominio Nautibeach boasts
an enviable setting on Playa Norte,
undoubtedly the best beach on the island.
The hotel is vast and its accommodations
include rooms, studios and apartments,
all comfortable and predictably well
appointed. Pool and restaurant are among
the amenities, perfectly placed to admire
the sunset.

$$$$ Hotel Villa Rolandi
Cra Sac-Bajo, T998-999 2000,
www.villarolandi.com.
A large, popular, award-winning 5-star
luxury beach resort with astonishing ocean
views. Suites are very comfortable, adorned
in Italian marble and boast jacuzzi terraces.
General amenities include 2 pools, 'private'
beach, spa services, bar-restaurant and,
at extra cost, a private yacht. No children
under 13.

$$$$-$$$ Na Balam
Zazil Ha 118, T998-881 4770,
www.nabalam.com.
Overlooking blissful Playa Norte, **Na Balam**
is a boutique yoga and spa resort with
35 rooms and suites, 2 restaurants, pool and
jacuzzi. Daily yoga classes include relaxation,

pranayama, asana, chanting and meditation;
retreats and packages available.

$$$ La Vida Dulce Casitas
Juárez 13, T515-974 6777, www.islatrip.com.
A lot of love has gone into this *hotelito*,
a very popular lodging that will suit couples
or small families. Managed by attentive
and hospitable hosts, Steve and Jerri, they
offer 3 comfortable, cosy apartments that
sleep 3-4. Book in advance.

$$$ Rocamar
Nicolás Bravo and Zona Marítima, T998-
877 0101, www.rocamar-hotel.com.
Crisp and minimalist, the **Rocamar** is an
island favourite, now more than 30 years
old. Its rooms and suites are clean and
unfussy; the best of them enjoy expansive
views of the Caribbean sea and sunrise.
Note the **Rocamar** is located on the quieter,
eastern side of the island, where swimming
is not recommended.

$$$-$$ Xbulu-ha
Guerrero 4, T998-877 1783, www.sites.
google.com/site/hotelxbuluha.
A very clean, cosy and unpretentious hotel
with simple but comfortable rooms, all
equipped with fridges, a/c and microwave.
The suites are best and have kitchenettes
($$$). Quiet, friendly and good value.
Recommended. The name means 'bubbling
water' in Yucatec Maya.

$$ Hotel Bucaneros
Hidalgo 11, T998-877 1228,
www.bucaneros.com.
Located right in the heart of town, **Hotel
Bucaneros** is a pleasant, well-established,
professionally managed hotel. It has a
variety of modern rooms and suites, all
with calm, neutral interiors; some have
balconies and views.

$$-$ Vistalmar
Av Rueda Medina on promenade,
T998-877 0209.

Popular with Canadian and American retirees, who stay long-term during the northern winter. The friendly **Vistalmar** has a range of reasonable rooms, some better equipped than others. Ask for one on the top floor, where you will enjoy sea breezes. Better to reserve in advance Jan-May. $ for longer stays.

$ Hotel Carmelina
Guerrero 4, T998-877 0006,
hotel_carmelina@hotmail.com.
Locally owned motel-style place with parking. The rooms are simple, sparse and clean, all with a/c, Wi-Fi and hot water, some with fridge. Good value, recommended for budget travellers.

$ pp Pocna Hostel
Top end of Matamoros on the northeast coast, T998-877 0090, www.pocna.com.
An island institution, popular with backpackers, but not beloved by all. Grounds are large and warren-like with scores of scruffy dorms and rooms, as well as a campground. There's internet access, lounge and beach bar, dive shop, bike rental, spa services, free activities like yoga and drumming, and DJs and live music in the evenings, often continuing until 0300. Book in advance in high season.

Restaurants

$$$ Olivia
Av Matamoros between Juárez and Medina, www.olivia-isla-mujeres.com. Dinner only, closed Mon except Jan-Mar.
Founded by an Israeli couple, Lior and Yaron, **Olivia** serves fabulous Mediterranean home cooking, including old family recipes, and Greek, Moroccan and Middle Eastern specialities, such as kebabs, home-baked breads and sweet baklava. A great spot for a romantic meal. Recommended.

$$$-$$ Como No
Hidalgo 7, www.isla mujeresdining.com.
A popular rooftop restaurant-bar that serves tasty Mediterranean food alongside eclectic international dishes including schnitzel, tapas and Thai curry. The mojitos are particularly delicious and highly recommended. A joint venture with **The Patio**, downstairs, also good.

$$$-$$ Mamma Rosa
Hidalgo and Matamoros.
A well-attired and authentic Italian restaurant with a relaxed, romantic ambiance. They serve good pasta, pizzas and seafood, with a fine selection of Italian wines. Personable service with dining inside or al fresco.

$$ BoBo's Fish and Chips
Av Matamoros 14A.
A casual little joint with a few seats on the street outside. They serve wholesome beer-battered fish, burgers, chicken wings, chips and cheap beer; comfort food for weary travellers. Owner Brian is friendly and talkative, tending bar as he serves.

$$ Minino's
Av Rueda Medina.
One of the best seafood restaurants in town, unpretentious, scruffy and often recommended by the locals. They offer delicious fresh fish fillets, squid, octopus, ceviche and lobster. Dining is on the sand at plastic tables. Good place, good food.

$$ Mogagua
Av Juárez and Madero.
Closely resembling a North American coffeeshop, **Mogagua** has a laid-back, arty vibe. They serve good coffee from Chiapas (try the iced frappés), Spanish tapas and other international fare, and in the evening, sangria. A sociable place for breakfast before hitting the beach. Good, friendly service. Recommended.

$$-$ Caffé Italia
Av Hidalgo between Morelos and Madero.
A cute little eatery serving breakfast, lunch and light snacks. Offerings include sweet and sour crêpes ($), fresh fruit juices, excellent strong coffee and authentic Italian

home-cooking, including pizzas and pasta. Friendly, hospitable owner.

$ Loncherías
Northwest end of Guerrero, around the municipal market. Open till 1800.
Busy and bustling, good for breakfast, snacks and lunch. All serve the same local fare at similar prices.

$ Poc-Chuc
Juárez and Abasolo.
A simple little locals' joint on the corner serving good-value Mexican staples in large portions. Good, cheap and tasty.

Bars and clubs

Fénix Lounge
Playa Norte, next to Na Balam, www.fenixisla.com.
Low-lit and laid-back, Playa Norte's premier beach club and bar often features live music in the evening. In the day time, there's shaded futon beds for chilling out. A fun, casual place and a superb location.

La Adelita
Hidalgo 12.
Adelita stocks over 200 types of tequila, the bar staff really know their stuff and are happy to make recommendations. Pull up a stool, roll up your sleeves – it's going to be a long night.

Rock Bar
Av Hidalgo 8.
As the name suggests, the haunt of spirited rock 'n rollers and other wild things. Great crowd and music at this intimate little downtown bar, not to mention killer cocktails. Cool place, recommended.

The Soggy Peso
Av Rueda Medina, www.soggypeso.com, south out of town, halfway down the airstrip. No under 21s.
This quirky little tiki bar attracts its share of castaways and raconteurs. It's a friendly place, scruffy, unpretentious and laid back. They serve good margaritas and Tex-Mex on the side.

What to do

Diving and snorkelling
There are numerous good dive shops on Isla Mujeres, more than can be mentioned here. 2 established options are:
Carey Dive Center, *Matamoros 13 and Av Rueda Medina, T877-0763, www.carey divecenter.com.* Reef, drift, deep, night and *cenote* dives, PADI certification up to Dive Master, snorkelling and fishing. 2-tank dives cost US$65-140, dependent on destination.
Sea Hawk, offers PADI certification up to Dive Master, deep-sea fishing, snorkelling, and a range of Adventure Dives (2 tanks, US$75-85) including wreck sites, night dives, sleeping shark caves and the MUSA subaquatic museum. They have simple lodging in the attached guesthouse.

Tour operators
Co-operativa Isla Mujeres, *Muelle 7, Av Rueda Medina.* The oldest tourism co-operative on the island, established 1977 and committed to sustainable practice. All their guides are qualified to take tourists to Isla Contoy (US$60 per person). Additionally, they offer sports fishing (US$200, 4 hrs) and snorkelling (US$25).
Co-operativa Isla Bonita, *Av Rueda Medina, T998-897 1095 (Adolfo), find them outside Restaurant Macambo.* This local co-operative specializes in half-day snorkel tours, including dolphin watching, shark handling, and a traditional Yucatec meal (US$25). They also offer trips to Isla Contoy (U$60), fishing (US$200, 4 hrs) and sell *artesanías*.

Transport

Air
The small airstrip in the middle of the island is mainly used for private planes, best arranged with a tourist office in Cancún.

Bicycle, golf cart and moped

Lots of people like to zip around the island in their own transport. You'll find rental places concentrated on the seafront, Av Rueda Medina and the surrounding streets. Rates vary with age and quality of vehicle: bicycles, US$15 per day; mopeds/motorbikes, US$8-11 per hr or US$25-35 per day; golf carts, US$40-50 per day; a credit card is often required as a deposit.

Bus

A public bus runs from the ferry dock to Playa Paraíso every 30 mins, US$0.80. Timings can be erratic, especially on Sun.

Ferry

Ultramar operate ferries to Isla Mujeres every 30 mins from Puerto Juárez, to the north of Cancún (and at slightly higher cost, from the Zona Hotelera); **Magaña Express** ferries depart from their own terminal 2 blocks north of Ultramar.

Taxi

Fixed-rate taxis depart from a rank on Av Rueda Medina, opposite the **HSBC**. A taxi from town to **El Garrafón** and vice versa is US$6. For the return journey, sharing a taxi will work out marginally more expensive than the bus for 4 people. Taxis charge an additional US$1 at night.

Isla Contoy → Colour map 5, A6.
an uninhabited and strictly protected wildlife refuge

Encompassing 317 ha, Isla Contoy (www.islacontoy.org), 30 km north of Isla Mujeres, is covered in mangroves, tropical forests and white-sand beaches. It is one of the most important seabird nesting sites in the Mexican Caribbean, closely studied by biologists, and home to some 150 migratory and resident avian species, including vociferous colonies of frigates, pelicans and cormorants. Additionally, four species of sea turtle (loggerhead, green, hawksbill and leatherback) nest on the island.

Visitor numbers are limited to 200 per day and only licensed guides may conduct tours (see Isla Mujeres Tour operators, above). Facilities include a visitor centre, museum, souvenir store, observation tower, interpretive trails, resting area with benches and *palapas*. You can snorkel at the Ixlachxé Reef en route to the island.

Isla Holbox → Colour map 5, A6.
an indolent island with a white-sand beach and colourful village

As yet unspoiled by mass tourism, Isla Holbox, whose name means 'Black Hole' in Yucatec Maya, is a remote and sparsely populated island off the northern coast of Quintana Roo. It has a tiny wood-built village, home to robust fishing people and a small but thriving band of expats. Enclosed by the 154,000-ha Yum Balam Ecological Reserve, Isla Holbox has opportunities for swimming, diving, snorkelling, fishing, kitesurfing and wildlife observation, along with the timeless and strongly recommended pursuit of simply lolling in a hammock.

First contact: the ill-fated journey of the Santa Lucía

Lost in a small boat in the Caribbean sea, the sight of land must have seemed like divine providence. After 13 days at the mercy of prevailing winds, the band of shipwrecked Spanish travellers were wretched, starved, thirsty and sick. They clambered ashore at Cabo Catoche in Quintana Roo, the first Europeans to set foot in Mexico. But as hordes of hungry Mayan warriors surrounded them, it became clear that their ordeal was only beginning…

The Spaniards had come from the tenuous colony of Santa María la Antigua del Darién, a tempestuous Spanish settlement forged in the wilderness of eastern Panama. In 1511, Captain Enciso y Valdivia had felt compelled to sail to the island of Santo Domingo to report on the colony's troubles – a matter of intrigue had culminated in the exile in a leaky boat of a Spanish nobleman, Diego de Nicuesa, never to be seen again. En route, Valdivia's caravel, the *Santa Lucía*, struck a sandbar and sunk. The 18 survivors were captured by a Mayan chief at Cabo Catoche and, one by one, sacrificed to the gods.

Just two survived. Gerónimo de Aguilar was a devout Franciscan friar from Ecija; Gonzalo Guerrero a sailor from Palos de la Frontera. They escaped but were soon captured and forced into slavery by the Mayan chief Xamanzana.

Months turned to years and Aguilar, who maintained his Catholic vows of celibacy, became a domestic servant for Xamanzana, watching over his wives and daughters. Guerrero ended up in the city of Chaacte'mal (Chetumal), under the dominion of Ah Nachan Kan Xiu, where he impressed the population with his skills in sailing, fishing and carpentry, eventually embraced Mayan customs, and in a historic union of indigenous and Spanish bloodlines, married the chief's daughter, the haughty Zazil Há.

In 1519, Hernán Cortés sailed from Cuba with 500 men, horses and goods for barter and, whilst exploring the island of Cozumel, heard stories about bearded men on the mainland. Following correspondence with messengers, Aguilar soon joined his campaign, becoming a vital informant and translator. But Guerrero remained in the Yucatán, writing to Aguilar: "I am married and have three children, and they look on me as a cacique here... My face is tattooed and my ears are pierced. What would the Spaniards say about me if they saw me like this?"

As the Aztec empire fell, Guerrero organized the Maya of the south, teaching them Spanish war craft and strategy. His efforts were not in vain: under the relentless onslaughts of Francisco de Montejo, it took 30 years to subjugate the Yucatán, a bastion of fierce resistance during the conquest of the New World. Guerrero himself died in battle in 1532, having brought 50 war canoes from Chetumal to aid a Honduran cacique in his fight against Pedro de Alvarado. Reviled by his 16th-century Spanish compatriots as a traitor, Guerrero is today lauded as a Mexican cultural icon. Misfortune or divine providence, the landing at Cabo Catoche was fateful in so many ways.

Sights

Many visitors and locals enjoy a dip in the **Yalahau swimming hole** ⓘ *US$0.80*, a refreshing cold-water spring that has long been an important source of fresh water for islanders; keep an eye out for crocodiles and bring bug repellent.

Offshore, there are several interesting islands and islets, many of them rich in wildlife. **Isla Pájaros** is home to some 140 avian species, mostly waterfowl and seabirds, including pelicans, flamingos, ducks and cormorants. It has two observation towers connected by a walkway designed to minimize human impact. **Isla Pasión**, 15 minutes away by boat, has a white-sand beach with facilities for day trippers. **Cabo Catoche** lies on the mainland 53 km north of Cancún, the point where European explorers are purported to have infamously first set foot on Mexican soil in 1517 (see box, opposite). The area is good for snorkelling and with some planning you can visit the ruins of the ancient church at **Boca Iglesia**, some say the oldest Catholic structure in the country.

From June to September the waters east of Holbox are visited by hundreds of gentle whale sharks, the world's largest fish, who come to feast on plankton blooms and tuna eggs. In the past, the island had a monopoly on tours, but now Cancún is in on the act, partly because the sharks have begun aggregating closer to Isla Mujeres than Isla Holbox. Despite the good intentions of many ecotourism operators, there are some concerns about lax environmental regulation and unchecked negative impacts. For the moment, whale shark tours cannot be recommended.

Listings Isla Holbox

Tourist information

Most hotels will be able to help with tourist information. Online, consult www.holbox.gob.mx.

Where to stay

$$$ La Palapa
Av Morelos 231, T984-875 2121,
www.hotellapalapa.com.
La Palapa is a very comfortable and relaxing boutique lodge on the beach, good for couples and families. They have 19 rooms, studios and bungalows, most with sea view, balconies or wooden verandas. Attentive service, spa therapies available.

$$$ Mawimbi
T984-875 2003, www.mawimbi.com.mx.
An intimate and well-kept boutique hotel with attractive decor and a good reputation. Rooms and bungalows are arty, chic and rustic; very romantic and relaxing. The

grounds are private and secluded, yet close to town. Recommended.

$$$-$ Hostel y Cabañas Ida y Vuelta
Av Paseo Kuka, between Robalo y Chacchi,
www.holboxhostel.com.
Popular with backpackers and budget travelers, Ida y Vuelta offers accommodation in a private house (**$$$**), simple *cabañas* with sand floors (**$$**), or *cabañas* with a/c and concrete floor (**$$$**). For the ultra-thrifty there are dorm beds, tents or hammocks (**$**).

$$-$ Hostel Tribu
Av Pedro Joaquín Coldwell 19, T984-875 2507,
www.tribu hostel.com.
A new hostel, brightly painted, cheerful and brilliantly done. The crowd at **Tribu** is young, fun and sociable. Lots of activities on offer from Spanish lessons to kite surfing to jam sessions in the bar. Clean, comfortable, simple rooms (**$$**) and dorms (**$**) available. Recommended.

Restaurants

$$$ La Guaya
Calle Palomino s/n, on the plaza.
Closed Mon, dinner only.
Creative and authentic Italian cuisine
professionally prepared with fresh, organic
ingredients. Dishes include seafood,
steak cuts and handmade pastas; try the
lobster ravioli. Good desserts, cocktails and
wine are also available. Gracious service.
Recommended.

$$$ Zarabanda
Palomino 249, a block from the plaza.
Long-established Holbox favourite serving
typical island cuisine with a Cuban twist.
There is an emphasis on fresh seafood and
locally sourced ingredients. **Zarabanda** also
has a bar and features occasional live music.

$$$-$$ Los Peleones
On the plaza.
An international menu with an emphasis on
seafood and Italian. **Los Peleones** offers a
laid-back, friendly ambience, quirky *lucha
libre* decor, great mojitos and excellent
hospitable service. A good spot for watching
the coming and going of the town in the
plaza below. Recommended.

$$$-$$ Pizzeria Edelyn
On the plaza.
There are certainly better Italian restaurants
in town, but **Edelyn** is casual, reliable and
local, and open late. Most people rate their
famous thin-crust lobster pizza quite highly,
but don't expect gourmet. A good place to
see local life.

$$-$ La Tortillería
*Tiburón Ballena. Open breakfast and
lunch only.*
A modest and friendly little eatery run by
a young Spanish couple. They serve great
Spanish tortillas, good salads, smoothies,
coffee, pies and vegetarian dishes.
Recommended.

Cafés and bakeries

Le Jardin
Calle Lisa.
An authentic French bakery and café serving
croissants, baguettes, sandwiches, fruit and
omelettes. Good coffee and muffins too.

Transport

Isla Holbox
Bicycle and golf cart hire
There are no cars on the island, but golf
carts and bicycle rentals are available.

Ferry
Ferries to Isla Holbox depart from the town
of **Chiquilá**, hourly, 0600-2130, US$6.25.
Public transport to Chiquilá is infrequent,
4 buses daily from **Cancún**, 3½ hrs, US$8.
If driving, there are car parks in Chiquilá,
US$2-3 daily.

South on the Riviera Maya → *Colour map 5, A6/B6.*
sandy beach resorts strung along the Caribbean coast

Formerly known as the 'Cancún–Tulum Corridor', the Mayan Riviera unfolds along
the Caribbean shore with a procession of luminous white-sand bays, fishing
villages, lively beach towns, gated resort complexes, palatial health spas and
immaculately manicured lawns, where the only sounds to disturb your meditations
are the occasional thwack of a club and the persistent hiss of water sprinklers. There
isn't much authentically Mayan about it, but a lot of businesses trade shamelessly
on the beauty and exoticism of Mayan culture.

Adventure parks

The exact boundaries of the Riviera, a marketing concept introduced in 1999, appear to be expanding too. Once limited to a stretch of the Federal Highway, some maps now show it engulfing half the state of Quintana Roo from Isla Holbox to Felipe Carrillo Puerto. Whatever its limits, the service and convenience of the Riviera between Cancún and Tulum will appeal to families, especially its ecologically themed adventure parks, which make fun use of caves, *cenotes*, lagoons and beaches.

Near Playa del Carmen, perhaps the oldest and most famous is **Xcaret** ① *www.xcaret.com.mx, US$89*, built on the ruins of a Mayan port. Its theatrical displays are iffy, but many visitors enjoy the outdoor element. **Xplor** ① *www.xplor.travel, US$109 adults, children US$55*, is a new one, offering zip-lining, amphibious vehicles and other adrenalin-charged thrills. Further south, 13 km from Tulum, **Xel-Ha** ① *www.xelha.com, US$79 adults, US40 children*, is an aquatic park with snorkelling, tubing through mangroves and other water-based activities. You can get a package for all three parks: US$197 adults, US$149 children; note certain experiences may cost extra. And there are more: **Labna Ha Ecopark Adventures** ① *Cancún–Tulum Km 240, T984-100 1362, www.labnaha.com*; and near the resort of Akumal, **Parque Natural Aktun Chen** ① *T984-806 4962, www.aktunchen.com*; both these offer a cave, *cenote* and zip-line combo.

Puerto Morelos

Despite the advent of tourism and a more than tenfold population increase in the last 10 years, Puerto Morelos, 34 km south of Cancún, has managed to retain the intimacy of its former existence as a fishing village, for now. Look out for the tilted lighthouse, an emblem of the port that has survived some of the region's worst hurricanes since 1967.

Many travellers find relief in Puerto's lazy ambience: the dusty main plaza overlooks the beach, a handful of roads skirt the mangroves. For divers and snorkellers, the **Mesoamerican Barrier Reef**, the second largest reef system in the world, lies just 500 m offshore. To get to Puerto Morelos, public transport from Cancún drops passengers on the **Carretera Cancún–Chetumal**, every 15 minutes; it's 2 km to the beach on an access road; bus US$0.70, taxi US$3; you can walk but cover up and bring insect repellent. Back on the highway, there's an interesting botanical garden by Dr Alfredo Barrera Marín, **Yaax Che** ① *Carretera Cancún–Chetmual Km 320, T998-206 9233, www.ecosur.mx/jb/YaaxChe, Mon-Sat 0900-1700*, and a zoo.

Playa del Carmen → See map, page 188.

Unlike Cancún, the entertainment hub of Playa del Carmen has not evolved into a gritty metropolitan sprawl, but it doesn't glisten either; few of its buildings exceed four storeys and most of the action is concentrated into a relatively small downtown area. And yet 'Playa', as it is affectionately known, is to the European tourist what Cancún is to the North American: a well-oiled resort where you are invited to gorge your appetites, flop about on the sand and forget about the world of toil you left behind. Fun, perhaps, but something got lost in the throng of gaudy souvenir stores, fast-food joints, jewellers, boutiques and department stores and, just like Cancún, you'll either love it or hate it.

Many travellers use Playa as a base for exploring ruins and *cenotes* in the region, otherwise there isn't much to do besides the obvious: eat, shop and drink. The town is laid out on a grid with most establishments within walking distance. Day and night, the herds ramble up and down the main commercial drag, **Quinta Avenida** (Fifth Avenue), a pedestrianized thoroughfare running from Calle 1 Norte to Calle 40. During high season, the swell of crowds and persistent attention of touts can be tiresome (just keep smiling). The **beach**, two blocks east of Quinta Avenida, is lovely and somewhat redeeming. The main plaza, next to the ADO bus terminal, has an intimate, modern church. In the afternoon, you'll see Totonac dancers – *voladores* – from Veracruz State, who spiral down a 30-m-high pole with rope around their ankles; please tip kindly if you watch the show.

Playa del Carmen

Where to stay 🛏
Alhambra **1** *B4*
Casa de Gopala **3** *C3*
Casa Tucán **5** *B3*
Cielo **7** *B3*
Hostel Playa **8** *A2*
Mom's **11** *B2*
Viceroy Riviera Maya **2** *A1*
The Yak **4** *A3*

Restaurants 🍴
Babe's **1** *A3*
Buenos Aires **6** *A4*
Carboncitos **7** *B3*
Curry Omm **2** *D2*
El Fogón **8** *A2*
Glass Bar **12** *A4*
La Famiglia **3** *A3*
La Tarraya **4** *C4*
Xulam the Mayan Fisher **5** *D2*

Bars & clubs 🍸
Dirty Martini Lounge **7** *A4*
Fusion Bar **9** *B4*

Where to stay

Puerto Morelos

$$$ Rancho Sak-Ol Libertad
Next door to Caribbean Reef Club,
T998-871 0181, www.ranchosakol.com.
Pleasant B&B accommodation in 2-storey
thatched bungalows; each unit has a
wooden terrace and hammock for chilling
out. A very tranquil, restful spot, right next to
the beach. Spa therapies, shared kitchen and
snorkelling gear available. Recommended.

$$ Posada Amor
Av Javier Rojo Gómez, opposite the beach,
T998-871 0033, www.posada-amor.wix.com/
puertom.
A small, charming *posada*, well established
and affordable, but also quite simple with no
frills. A good central location, fine restaurant-
bar and friendly Mexican owners.

Playa del Carmen

Accommodation in Playa del Carmen
is generally expensive and poor value
compared to other parts of Mexico,
particularly around the beach and Av 5.
The prices given below are for the high
season and can drop by as much as
50% at other times of the year.

$$$$ Viceroy Riviera Maya
Playa Xcalacoco, Fracc 7, 10 km north
of Playa del Carmen, T984-877 3000,
www.viceroyhotelsandresorts.com.
Secluded, exclusive, chic and tasteful, this
impeccable spa resort on the beach has 41
luxurious villas in a verdant jungle setting,
and excellent, attentive service. A host of
facilities include pool, sun deck and gym.

$$$$-$$$ Alhambra
Calle 8 Norte con playa, T984-873 0735,
www.alhambra-hotel.net.
The interior of the family-run **Alhambra** has
a light, clean, airy, palatial feel. All rooms
have balcony or sea view and general

amenities include yoga instruction, jacuzzi,
massage, spa and excellent restaurant.
Quiet and peaceful, despite its setting near
beach bars. French and English spoken.
Recommended.

$$$ Casa de Gopala
Calle 2 Norte s/n, entre Av 10 y 15 Centro,
T984-873 0054, www.casadegopala.com.
The interior of **Casa de Gopala** is
handsomely attired in traditional Mexican
style. The rooms are spacious, airy and
comfortable, but the suite has more
character. There's a dive shop, rooftop pool,
relaxing garden and jacuzzi. Helpful staff.

$$$ Hotel Cielo
Calle 4, between 5 and 10, T984-873 1227,
www.hotelcielo.com.
Appropriately named **Hotel Cielo**
boasts commanding views from its
rooftop terrace. Located just off Av 5,
accommodation includes standard rooms,
cabañas and studios, all tastefully attired
in traditional Mexican style. Rates include
a 50% breakfast discount in **Carboncitos**
restaurant, 10% off other meals. Good
service, cheaper if paying cash.

$$$-$$ Casa Tucán
Calle 4 Norte, between Av 10 and 15,
T984-873 0283, www.casa tucan.de.
German-owned hotel with simple, rustic
cabañas, studios and no-frills rooms. The
grounds are rambling and labyrinthine
with a lovely lush garden, painted murals
and a deep pool where diving instruction
takes place.

$$$-$$ Mom's Hotel
Calle 4 and Av 30, about 5 blocks from
bus station or beach, T984-873 0315,
www.momshotel.com.
Excellent value, friendly, family-run hotel
with pleasant, colourful rooms and a small
pool. There are also studios and apartments
and good rates for long-term stays. The

attached restaurant serves international food in the evening. Recommended.

$$-$ Hostel Playa
Av 25 with Calle 8, T984-803 3277, www.hostelplaya.com.
There's a comfortable, friendly atmosphere at this well-maintained and professionally run hostel. Amenities include a single- and mixed-sex dorms ($), private rooms ($$), a superb, well-equipped shared kitchen, lounge space, paddling pool and rooftop *palapa*. Shared bathrooms are clean. Recommended for backpackers and solo budget travellers.

$$-$ The Yak
Calle 10 Norte, between Av 10 and 15, T984-148 0925, www.yakhostel.com.
A bohemian new hostel, very intimate and friendly, and home to a sociable backpacker scene. They offer clean, homely rooms ($$), dorm beds ($), shared kitchen, popular bar and garden, and activities such as movie night. Good hosts, good reports.

Restaurants

Puerto Morelos

$$$ El Merkadito
Rafael Melgar lote 8-B, www.elmerkadito.mx.
Perched on the edge of the beach, **El Merkadito** is a popular seafood restaurant that serves hearty plates of octopus *tostadas*, shrimp ceviche, tuna steak, marlin tacos and more. A casual option with open-air seating under a terraced palm-thatched *palapa*.

$$-$ El Nicho
Av Tulum and Rojo Gómez, www.elnicho.com.mx. Closes 1400.
Laid-back, pleasant, low-key eatery serving great brunch and breakfasts, including most excellent eggs benedict. Good juices, waffles, coffee and iced tea. Mexican staples served at lunchtime.

Playa del Carmen
The majority of the town's restaurants line Quinta Avenida, where most tourists limit themselves and a meal costs no less (and usually a bit more) than US$10. Popular, big-name restaurants dominate the southern end of the street. Quieter, subtler settings lie north, beyond Calle 20. For budget eating, head west, away from the main drag.

$$$ Buenos Aires
5a Av and Calle 34.
Probably the best meat dishes in town, professionally prepared and authentically Argentine. Offerings include succulent cuts of fillet and mixed grill platters. Occasional displays of tango dancing.

$$$ Curry Omm
10a Av and Calle 3 Sur, www.letseat.at/Curryomm.
Great, authentic Indian cuisine, good and spicy. Offerings include old favourites like samosas, papadums and naan, a range of hearty curries, including masala, madras and vindaloo, along with tasty traditional drinks such as mango lassi and chai. Great friendly service. Recommended.

$$$ The Glass Bar
5a Av and Calle 12, www.theglassbar.com.mx.
The place for an intimate, romantic dinner, **The Glass Bar** is a sophisticated Italian restaurant serving Mediterranean cuisine and seafood. It is recommended chiefly for its stock of fine wine, however, a rarity in Playa.

$$$ Xulam the Mayan Fisher
10a Av and Calle 3 Sur, www.xulam.com.mx.
Good seafood and traditional Mayan dishes, creatively prepared and presented. The themed decor is reminiscent of a ruined Mayan temple, complete with archaeological relics, colourful chattering parrots and creeping vegetation. Touristy, but lots of fun.

$$$-$$ Babe's
Calle 10, between 5a and 10a Av,
www.babesnoodlesandbar.com.
Casual Thai noodle bar with kitsch decor and a superb menu of red, yellow and green curries, spring rolls, samosas, soups and more. Belting flavours, decent service and a fine stock of liquor at the bar. Highly recommended.

$$$-$$ Carboncitos
Calle 4, between 5a and 10a Av.
Seafood and steaks with a Mexican twist. Popular offerings include grilled jumbo shrimps, the salsa sampler and the frozen mojitos. Breakfast is very good too, try the *huevos rancheros*. Good service with al fresco dining on the pedestrian street. Recommended.

$$ La Famiglia
10a Av and Calle 10.
In a town with no shortage of Italian restaurants, **La Famiglia** is one of the better and more affordable ones. They serve wholesome traditional fare from the motherland, including handmade pastas, lasagne and stone-baked pizzas. Casual dining.

$$-$ El Fogón
Av 30 and Calle 6.
A buzzing locals' joint, hugely popular and economical. They serve grilled meat, wholesome *tortas*, tacos, quesadillas and other Mexican staples. Highly recommended.

$$-$ La Tarraya
Calle 2 and the beach.
Economical seafood on the shore, including shrimp tacos and fried whole fish. Very simple and no frills, sometimes hit and miss, but a nice place to soak up ocean views and knock back a beer or two. Check your bill.

Bars and clubs

Playa del Carmen
Playa competes with Cancún as a major entertainment hub. Overall, the scene is a little quieter and more nuanced, offering many down-to-earth alternatives alongside the usual big-name clubs like **Coco Bongo** and **Señor Frog**.

Dirty Martini Lounge
1a Av, between Calle 10 and 12.
There's a good boozy atmosphere at the **Dirty Martini Lounge**, the place to settle in for a long, hard drink. Fun crowd, seasoned bartenders and no shortage of Martini, naturally.

Fusion Bar
Calle 6 and the beach,
www.fusionhotelmexico.com.
One of the better beach lounges, **Fusion Bar** has a romantic ambience with low-lighting rustic oil lanterns, tables and *palapas* on the sand. They often feature live music in the evenings and the kitchen serves good food.

What to do

Playa del Carmen

Diving and snorkelling
The Abyss, *T984-876 3285, www.abyssdive center.com.* **The Abyss** is a professional, first-rate operation with more than 14 years' experience of local waters. Owned and

Language schools

Playalingua, Calle 20 between Av 5 and 10, T984-873 3876, www.playalingua.com. Weekend excursions, a/c, library, family stays, from US$225 per week (20 hrs).
Solexico Language and Cultural Center, Av 35 between 6 and 6 bis, T984-873 0755, www.solexico.com. Variable programme with workshops, also have schools in Oaxaca and Puerto Vallarta.

managed by Canadian Dave Tomlinson, who offers ocean and *cenote* dives, certification, and a host of specialized and technical training. No physical premises, contact in advance by email.

Tank-Ha, *T984-873 0302, tankha.com*. The only dive shop in town with a licence to go to Cozumel, cutting out the ferry trip. They offer certification up to Dive Master, speciality courses, ocean and *cenote* dives, as well as the interesting option to hunt lion fish, an invasive species that apparently makes good ceviche.

Tour operators
Alltournative, *Carretera Chetumal–Puerto Juárez Km 287, T984-803 9999, www.alltournative.com*. A well-established ecotourism 'pioneer' with a proven commitment to sustainability. They offer adventure tours to the Yucatán's *cenotes* and national parks, as well as cultural visits to archaeological sites and Mayan communities.

Transport

Puerto Morelos
Bus
ADO buses (and others) travelling between Cancún and Playa del Carmen stop on the Carretera Cancún–Chetumal outside Puerto Morelos every 15 mins. Taxi to/from the beach, US$3.

Playa del Carmen
Bus
The **ADO** bus terminal is on the corner of Av Juárez and Quinta Avenida (5a Av).

To **Cancún**, frequent departures, 1½ hrs, US$4; 2nd-class services with **Mayab**, less frequent, US$3. To **Cancún airport**, frequent between 0700 and 1915, 1 hr, US$10. To **Chetumal**, ADO, frequent departures, 4½ hrs, US$21; and many 2nd-class buses. To **Chichén Itzá**, ADO, 0800, 4 hrs, US$22;

also with 2nd-class buses bound for Mérida. To **Cobá**, ADO, 0800, 0900, 1000, 2 hrs, US$7. To **Mérida**, frequent departures, 5 hrs, US$28. To **San Cristóbal de las Casas**, OCC, 1715, 2155, 16 hrs, US$66; an ADO GL, 1900, US$78. To **Tulum**, frequent departures, 1 hr, US$6; many 2nd class. To **Valladolid**, frequent, 3 hrs, US$12.50 (most buses going to Mérida stop at Valladolid. 2nd-class buses to Valladolid go via Tulum). To **Xcaret**, frequent departures, 15 mins, US$4. To **Xel Há**, frequent departures, 1 hr, US$5.

Car
Car hire Alamo, 5a Av and Calle 6 Norte, T984-826 6893, www.alamo.com; **Fiesta**, Av 144 No 35, T984-803 3345, www.fiesta carrental.com; **Hertz**, 5a Av between Calles 10 and 12, T984-873 0703, www.hertz.com; and many others.

Ferry
Ferries to **Cozumel** depart from the main dock, just off the plaza. There are 2 competing companies, **Ultramar**, T998 843-2011, www.granpuerto.com.mx, and right next door, **Mexico Water Jets**, T987-879 3112, www.mexicowaterjets.com.mx, departures every 2-4 hrs each from 0500 until 2200, US$11.50 one way. Buy ticket 1 hr before journey. Car ferries to Cozumel, 4 daily (2 on Sun) with **Transcaribe**, www.transcaribe.net, family-sized car US$60, departing from Calica (Punta Venado) south of Playa del Carmen, but they will not transport rental vehicles.

Taxi
Cancún airport US$40 for 4 persons. Tours to **Tulum** and **Xel-Há** from kiosk by boat dock US$35-40; tours to Tulum, Xel-Há and **Xcaret**, 5-6 hrs, US$60-70; taxi to Xcaret US$10. Taxis congregate on the Av Juárez side of the square (**Sindicato Lázaro Cárdenas del Río**, T998-873 0032).

a mecca for divers

The 'discovery' and popularization of Isla Cozumel and its dazzling coral reefs is often incorrectly attributed to the French oceanographer and documentary film-maker, Jacques Cousteau. In fact, it was a Mexican director, René Cardona, who first documented Cozumel's vivid underwater world with his 1957 film *Un Mundo Nuevo* (he was, to an extent, inspired by Cousteau's 1956 explorations of the Mediterranean and Red Sea in *Un Monde du Silence*). Cousteau himself did visit the island in 1960 and famously declared, "Cozumel is one of the best places around the world for diving, thanks to its fantastic visibility and its wonderful marine life…" but by then, the word was already out.

1 Cozumel

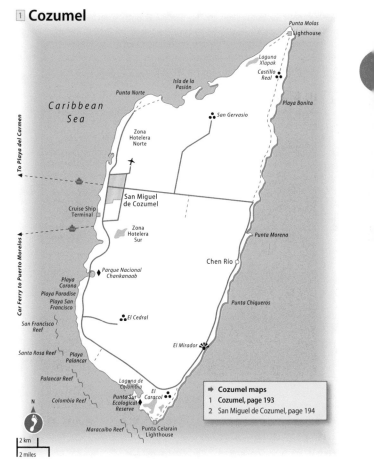

➡ Cozumel maps
1 Cozumel, page 193
2 San Miguel de Cozumel, page 194

Today, despite more than 50 years of touristic development, the controversial intrusion of cruise ships and the devastating impact of hurricanes, many of Cozumel's reefs remain healthy and vibrant, if endangered. Isla Cozumel, the largest of Mexico's Caribbean islands, continues to serve as a world-class scuba destination.

Sights

The town, **San Miguel de Cozumel**, is touristic and commercial, increasingly marketed to cruise ship passengers arriving from Miami and Cancún, and lacking much nightlife or a discernible personality, a rather uninspired and overpriced destination. There isn't much to detain you apart from the **Museo de la Isla** ① *Calle 4 and 6, Mon-Sat 0900-1600, US$2.50*, which charts the historical development of Cozumel.

Similarly, the island's beaches are pleasant enough, but not worth a special trip from the mainland. The northern and western shores are generally sandy and good for swimming (poor for snorkelling), if a bit narrow; popular stretches include **Playa San Francisco** ① *US$8*, with a beach club that caters to cruisers and, 14 km south of town, **Playa Paradise**, also resort-style. Swimming on the rugged, exposed east coast is very dangerous due to ocean underflows; the exception is the sheltered bay at **Chen Río**. Surfers could try **Punta Morena**.

② San Miguel de Cozumel

Where to stay 🛏
Amaranto **1**
Amigo's Hostel **3**
Flamingo **2**
Hostelito **6**
Pepita **5**
Posada Edem **4**

Tamarindo **10**
Villa Escondida **7**

Restaurants 🍴
Casa Denis **3**
Casa Mission **1**
La Candela **2**

La Choza **5**
Las Palmeras **4**

Bars & clubs 🍸
Kelley's **6**
Wet Wendy's **7**

➡ **Cozumel maps**
1 Cozumel, page 193
2 San Miguel de Cozumel, page 194

Like the Mayan Riviera, Cozumel now boasts adventure parks for day-trippers. Perched between a lagoon and a sandy beach, **Parque Chankanaab** ① *Carretera Costera Sur Km 9.5, www.cozumelparks.com, Mon-Sat 0800-1600, US$21, children US$14, some activities cost extra*, offers a world of fun including botanical garden, crocodile sanctuary, spa facilities, dolphinarium, snorkelling, restaurants, hammocks and *palapas*. **Punta Sur Park** ① *Carretera Costera Sur Km 30, T987-872 0914, www.cozumelparks.com, Mon-Sat 0800-1600, US$12, children US$8, some activities cost extra*, is a much wilder 1 sq km ecological park encompassing reefs, beaches and lagoons. Sights include the **Celarain lighthouse**, now converted to a nautical museum, Mayan ruins (see below) and wildlife observation towers.

★Dive sites

Cozumel's reef system is part of the **Mesoamerican Barrier Reef** with sections on the southern side of the island protected by the 120 sq km **Parque Nacional Arrecifes de Cozumel**. There are dozens of sites to suit beginners and advanced divers. Favourites include **Palancar Reef**, which has deep and shallow sections, impressive coral outcrops, troughs and canyons. **Santa Rosa Wall** is a steep vertical shelf with very impressive blooms. **Colombia Reef** has shallow sections with a pretty coral garden and gentle currents; the deep section has massive corals and swim-throughs where you are likely to glimpse pelagic species. For more experienced divers, the reefs at **Punta Sur**, **Maracaibo** and **Baracuda** should not to be missed. Almost all Cozumel diving is drift diving, so if you are not used to a current, choose an operator you feel comfortable with. Snorkelling on Isla Cozumel is possible, but many sites were badly damaged by Hurricane Wilma in 2005 and have not yet recovered.

Archaeological sites

Inhabited from 300 AD, Cozumel, whose name means 'Island of Swallows' in Yucatec Maya, was an ancient centre of worship for Ixchel. The journey to her temples involved a perilous passage by sea canoe and her pilgrims, according to the Bishop of Yucatán in the 16th century, Diego de Landa, "held Cozumel in the same veneration as we have for pilgrimages to Jerusalem and Rome". Sadly, the mysteries of Cozumel were lost forever after the Spaniards brought a devastating plague of small pox.

Today, all that remains are some 32 very modest archaeological sites, mostly single buildings thought to have been lookouts and navigational aids. The most interesting and easy to reach (and therefore often overrun with tour groups) is the post-Classic site of **San Gervasio** ① *Carretera Transversal Km 7, 0800-1545, US$8, Spanish-speaking guides are on hand, US$18*. There are *sacbés* (sacred roads) between the groups of buildings, no large or monumental structures, but an interesting plaza and an arch, and surviving pigment in places. The site is located in the north of the island, 7 km from San Miguel, then 6 km to the left up a paved road, toll US$1; taxis are expensive, US$45 with two-hour wait; consider cycling. **Castillo Real** is one of many sites on the northeastern coast, but the road to this part of the island is in bad condition and the ruins themselves are very small. **El Cedral** in the southwest (3 km from the main island road) is a two-room temple, overgrown with trees, in the centre of the village of the same name. **El Caracol**, where the sun in the form of a shell was worshipped, is 1 km from the southernmost Punta Celarain.

Tourist information

Tourist office

Plaza del Sol, Av 5 Sur, between Av Juárez and Calle 1 Sur, upstairs above the bank, T987-869 0211, www.cozumel.travel. Mon-Fri 0800-1500.

Maps, flyers and general information.

Where to stay

$$$ Flamingo

Calle 6 Norte 81, T987-872 1264, www.hotelflamingo.com.

An intimate boutique lodging with a range of rooms and a penthouse suite, all spacious, tastefully attired and equipped with modern conveniences. Spa, diving and sports fishing packages available, see website for more. Friendly and helpful staff.

$$$ Tamarindo

Calle 4 Norte 421, between Av 20 and 25, T987-872 6190, www.tamarindobedand breakfast.com.

This tranquil B&B accommodation is located in a residential street and offers restful rooms and a leafy garden complete with plunge pool. A second property near the seafront has apartments and bungalows.

$$$ Villa Escondida

Av 10 Sur 299, T987-120 1225, www.villaescondidacozumel.com.

Villa Escondida is a cosy B&B with 4 very clean, comfortable rooms and a well-tended garden with hammocks and plunge pool. Breakfasts are excellent and the Canadian/ Mexican owners, David and Magda, are great hosts. Adults only. Recommended.

$$ Amaranto

Calle 5 Sur, between Av 15 and 20, T987-872-3219, www.amaranto bedandbreakfast.com.

Attractive thatched-roof Mayan-style bungalows and suites, complete with hammocks and kitchenettes. Spanish,

English and French are spoken by the owners, Elaine and Jorge. There's a pool, and childcare is available on request. Rustic, tasteful and good value. Recommended.

$$ Pepita

Av 15 Sur 120 y Calle 1 Sur, T987-872 0098, www.hotelpepitacozumel.com.

A well-established and family-run budget hotel with simple rooms set around a plant-filled courtyard, each with fridge and a/c. Clean, quiet and inexpensive for the island. Free coffee in the morning.

$$-$ Amigos Hostel

Calle 7 Sur 571, between Av 30 and 25, T987-872 3868, www.cozumelhostel.com.

Formerly a B&B, **Amigos Hostels** features a large leafy garden with pool, various communal areas, a shady *palapa*, pool table, hammocks, simple shared kitchen, mixed dorms ($) and clean rooms ($$). The owner, Kathy, has lots of information about the island.

$$-$ Hostelito

Av 10 No 42, between Juárez and 2 Nte, T987-869 8157, www.hostelito.com.mx.

This downtown backpackers' hostel has large dorms ($) and simple whitewashed rooms ($$), suites, sun-decks and a shared kitchen. Clean and hip.

$ Posada Edém

Calle 2 Norte 124, T987-872 1166, gustarimo@hotmail.com.

Very basic, economical rooms with Wi-Fi and the usual bare necessities, including fan or a/c. A little run down these days, but friendly.

Restaurants

There are few eating options for budget travellers. The cheapest places for breakfast, lunch or an early dinner are the *loncherías* next to the market on A R Salas, between Av 20 and 25. They serve fairly good local *comida corrida*, 0800-1930.

$$$ Casa Mission
Av 55, between Juárez and Calle 1 Sur, www.missioncoz.com. Daily 1700-2300.
Established in 1973, this restaurant survived hurricanes Wilma and Gilbert and is now a Cozumel institution. Fine Mexican, international and seafood in an elegant hacienda setting. Recommended.

$$$ La Choza
Salas 198 and Av 10, www.lachoza restaurant.com.
A large, airy restaurant serving classic Mexican dishes, seafood and regional cuisine. Good service and atmosphere, colourful decor. Popular with both tourists and nationals.

$$ La Candela
Calle 5 Norte 298. Closed Sun.
Modest and affordable little restaurant serving good breakfasts and set lunches, Cuban and Mexican staples, including fish tacos. A Cozumel favourite with pleasant service.

$$ Las Palmeras
At the pier, Av Melgar, www.restaurante palmeras.com. Open 0700-1400.
Las Palmeras serves reliable and wholesome grub, a popular spot for breakfast. The restaurant overlooks the pier and is a great place for people-watching.

$$-$ Casa Denis
Calle 1 Sur 164, close to plaza, www.casadenis.com.
An charming, intimate little eatery, one of the oldest on the island, owned by Denis and Juanita Angulo. They serve excellent and affordable tacos, tortas and other Mexican fare. Former diners include Jackie Onassis. Recommended.

Bars and clubs

The big-name clubs like Señor Frog's and Carlos 'n' Charlie are clustered around the pier. They tend to draw tourists and very few locals. For something casual, try:

Kelley's
Av 10, www.kelleyscozumel.com.
A grungy Irish sports bar, recommended chiefly because it serves beer on tap, including Guinness. Bring pesos, poor exchange rate.

Wet Wendy's
Av 5, between Calle 2 and Juárez, www.wetwendys.com.
A popular place serving the most insane margaritas anywhere. Wet Wendy, the bar's namesake, is a legendary local mermaid, not an adult entertainer.

What to do

Diving
There are 2 different types of dive centre: the larger ones, where the divers are taken out to sea in big boats with many passengers; the smaller, more personalized dive shops, with a maximum of 8 people per small boat, some of which are recommended below:
Deep Blue, *A R Salas 200, corner of Av 10 Sur, T987-872 5653, www.deepbluecozumel.com.*
A PADI facility since 1995, **Deep Blue** specializes in deep dives, including trips to Punta Sur, Maracaibo and Barracuda reefs. They also offer PADI, NAUI and SSI certification up to Dive Master. All dives are computerized for maximum bottom time and increased safety. Helpful and knowledgeable.
Scuba Tony, *Av Xel Ha 151, T987-869 8268, www.scubatony.com.* Tony loves diving so much he quit an 11-year career with the Los Angeles Sheriff's department to establish a dive shop on Cozumel. He offers reef, twilight and night dives, certification up to Advanced Open water, private charters and accommodation. No physical premises, contact through the website.

Transport

Air
The airport is just north of the town with a minibus shuttle service to the hotels.

There are 10-min flights to and from the airstrip near Playa del Carmen, as well as flights linking to Mexico City, Cancún and some international destinations.

Bicycle and moped
The best way to get around the island is by hired moped or bicycle. Mopeds cost US$25-35 per day, credit card needed as deposit; bicycles are around US$15-20 per day, US$20 cash or TC deposit. Rental stalls at the ferry terminal, or try **El Aguila**, Av Melgar, between 3 and 5 Sur, T987-872 0729; and **El Dorado**, Av Juárez, between 5 and 10, T987-872 2383.

Bus
There are no buses, but Cozumel town is small enough to visit on foot, or you can hire a moped or bicycle (see above) or take a taxi (see below).

Car
Car rental There are many agencies, including **Avis**, airport, T987-872 0219; **Budget**, Av 5 between 2 and 4 Norte, T987-872 0219; **Hertz**, Av Melgar, T987-872 3955.

Ferry
The passenger ferry to and from Playa del Carmen runs every 2 hrs and the car ferry leaves 4 times daily from Calica (see page 192).

Taxi
Taxis are plentiful. Beware taxis looking for kick-backs.

Tulum and around → *Colour map 5, B5.*
clifftop compact Mayan site overlooking the turquoise Caribbean

Perched high on a sea cliff overlooking the eastern horizon, Tulum was originally named Zama, meaning 'City of the Dawn' in Yucatec Maya. Rising to prominence during the late post-Classic era (1200-1450 AD), it was an important trade hub where itinerant merchants exchanged precious commodities such as obsidian, jade and copper. Home to approximately 1500 inhabitants, the settlement was accessed by sea canoe through a gap in the offshore reef. The word 'Tulum' means wall or fence in Maya and the entire city was surrounded by walls, partially standing today.

Site information www.inah.gob.mx, 0800-1700, US$4.50, parking, US$2.50, guides US$20. Buses drop passengers 1 km from the ruins at an access road on the Carretera Cancún–Chetumal. Taxis from Tulum village, US$5.50. The site is very popular and swamped with tour groups after 0900 or 1000.

Compared with the jungle-shrouded metropolizes further inland, Tulum is a very small site, easily explored in an hour or two. Its buildings are small, squat versions of the architecture at Chichén Itzá, very typical of the east coast style. The **Temple of the Descending God** contains a well-preserved stucco sculpture of a downward diving deity, a recurring motif and the personification of the setting sun, to whom all west-facing buildings were consecrated. Nearby, the **Temple of Frescoes** was an observatory for tracking the sun. The façades of its inner temple have murals depicting deities and serpents, sadly no longer open to the public; its outer temple has stucco figures in bas-relief, including masks on the corners. The grandest building in Tulum is **El Castillo**, a fortress-like structure built in several phases on the edge of the cliff. It contains shrines and vaulted rooms, but you are not permitted to climb its steps. Bring a swimsuit if you want to scramble down from the ruins to one of the beaches for a swim. Do not attempt to swim out to the reef, 600 m to 1 km away.

Tulum town

Approximately 3 km from the ruins, Tulum town, until recently, was nothing more than a dusty strip of houses on the edge of the highway. Today it is blossoming into a minor tourist town complete with international restaurants, coffee houses, dive shops and lodgings to suit all budgets. You'll find the ADO bus terminal and taxi ranks on the Carretera Cancún–Chetumal, which changes its name to Avenida Tulum as it enters the town. A small tourist information kiosk, irregularly staffed, is on the plaza. Just outside town, on the highway to Cobá, you'll find the **Tulum Monkey Sanctuary** ① *T984-115 4296, www.tulummonkeysanctuary.com*, a private reserve with many spider monkeys and two refreshing *cenotes*; reservations essential.

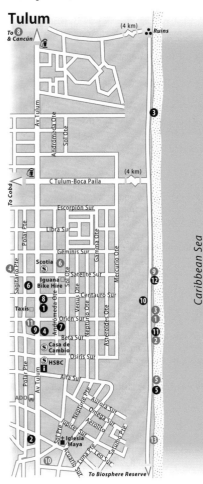

Tulum

To ⑧ & Cancún

Ruins (4 km)

To Cobá

Av Tulum
Andromeda Ote
Sol Ote
C Tulum-Boca Paila (4 km)
Escorpión Sur
Libra Sur
Géminis Sur
Scotia
Satélite Sur
Gamma Ote
Mercurio Ote
Iguana Bike Hire
Sol Ote
Venus Ote
Centauro Sur
Taxis
Orión Sur
Andromeda Ote
Neptuno Ote
Asteroides Ote
Beta Sur
Casa de Cambio
HSBC
Osiris Sur
Alfa Sur
Polar Pte
Sagitario Pte
ADO
Nutria Pte
Aurora Sur
Ortega Sur
Aerolito
Júpiter Sur
Iglesia Maya
Acuario Pte
Luna Pte
Leo Sur
To Biosphere Reserve

Caribbean Sea

Not to scale

Where to stay 🛏
Ahau Tulum **2**
Cabañas La Luna **3**
Dos Ceibas **13**
Hostel Sheck **4**
Los Arrecifes **1**
Nueva Vida de Ramiro **5**
Posada 6 **6**
Posada Los Mapaches **8**
Posada Luna del Sur **10**
Posada Margherita **9**
Suites Nadet **11**

Restaurants 🍴
Doña Tinas **2**
El Gourmet **1**
El Pequeño Buenos Aires **4**
Ginger **6**
La Gloria de Don Pepe **7**
La Malquerida **8**
La Nave **9**
La Zebra **5**
Margherita **12**
Mezzanine **3**
Restaurare **10**
Ziggy's **11**

Tulum beach

Fronted by a procession of luxury hotels, upscale boutiques, B&Bs and *cabañas*, the sublime white-sand beach running south of the ruins was 'discovered' by property speculators some years ago. The treatment has been relatively rustic and low-rise (many establishments lack electricity during daylight hours), but there are now limited economical lodging options on this fabled stretch. If determined, you may find a scruffy cabin with a sand floor and shared bathroom for around US$30, but you should bring padlocks, carefully check the security situation and consider stashing valuables elsewhere. Access to the beach is via the Carretera Tulum–Boca Paila, which branches south from a crossroad on the Carretera Cancún–Chetumal and skirts the shore as far as Punta Allen. Taxis from the town to the beach US$5.50 minimum; cycling is an option.

Around Tulum

ruined Mayan city, jungle-fringed lake and vast biosphere

Cobá → *Colour map 5, B5.*
www.inah.gob.mx, 0800-1700, US$4.50.

An important Mayan city in the eighth and ninth centuries AD, whose population is estimated to have been between 40,000 and 50,000, Cobá was abandoned for unknown reasons. The present-day village of Cobá lies on either side of Lago Cobá, surrounded by dense jungle, 47 km inland from Tulum. It is a quiet, friendly village, with few tourists staying overnight.

The entrance to the ruins of this large but little-excavated city is at the end of the lake between the two parts of the village. A second lake, **Lago Macanxoc**, is within the site. There are turtles and many fish in the lakes, and it's a good birdwatching area. Both lakes and their surrounding forest can be seen from the summit of the **Iglesia**, the tallest structure in the **Cobá Group**. There are three other groups of buildings to visit: the **Macanxoc Group**, mainly stelae, about 1.5 km from the Cobá Group; **Las Pinturas**, 1 km northeast of Macanxoc, with a temple and the remains of other buildings that had columns in their construction; the **Nohoch Mul Group**, at least another kilometre from Las Pinturas. Nohoch Mul has the tallest pyramid in the northern Yucatán, a magnificent structure, from which the views of the jungle on all sides are superb. You will not find at Cobá the great array of buildings that can be seen at Chichén Itzá or Uxmal, or the compactness of Tulum. Instead, the delight of the place is the architecture in the jungle, with birds, butterflies, spiders and lizards, and the many uncovered structures that hint at the vastness of the city in its heyday (the urban extension of Cobá is put at some 70 sq km). An unusual feature is the network of *sacbés* (sacred roads), which connect the groups in the site and are known to have extended across the entire Maya Yucatán. Over 40 *sacbés* pass through Cobá, some local, some of great length, such as the 100-km road to Yaxuná in Yucatán State.

At the lake, toucans may be seen very early; also look out for greenish-blue and brown mot-mots in the early morning. The guards at the site are very strict about opening and closing time so it is hard to get in to see the dawn or sunset from a temple.

The paved road into Cobá ends at **Lago Cobá**; to the left are the ruins, to the right **Villas Arqueológicas**. The roads around Cobá are badly potholed. Cobá is becoming more popular as a destination for tourist buses, which come in at 1030; arrive before that to avoid the crowds and the heat (ie on the 0430 bus from Valladolid, if not staying in Cobá). Take insect repellent.

Sian Ka'an Biosphere Reserve → *Colour map 5, B5.*

Daily 0900-1500, 1800-2000, US$2. For information, visit Los Amigos de Sian Ka'an in Cancún, T998-892 2958, www.amigosdesiankaan.org; they are very helpful.

Meaning 'where the sky is born', the enormous reserve of Sian Ka'an, the third largest and one of the most diverse in all Mexico, was declared a UNESCO World Heritage Site in 1987 and now covers 652,000 ha (4500 sq km) of the Quintana Roo coast. About one-third is covered in tropical forest, one-third is savannah and mangrove, and one-third coastal and marine habitats, including 110 km of barrier reef. Mammals include jaguar, puma, ocelot and other cats, monkeys, tapir, peccaries, manatee and deer; turtles nest on the beaches; there are crocodiles and a wide variety of land and aquatic birds. If you want to see wildlife, it is best to use a qualified guide or tour operator (see Tour operators, below). You can drive into the reserve from Tulum village as far as Punta Allen (58 km; the road is opposite the turning to Cobá; it is not clearly marked and the final section is badly potholed), but beyond that you need a boat. Do not try to get there independently without a car.

Muyil → *Colour map 5, B5.*

www.inah.gob.mx, 0800-1700, US$2.70.

The ruins of Muyil at **Chunyaxché** comprise three pyramids (partly overgrown) on the left-hand side of the road towards Felipe Carrillo Puerto, 18 km south of Tulum. One of the pyramids is undergoing reconstruction; the other two are relatively untouched. They are very quiet, with interesting birdlife, but also mosquito infested. Beyond the last pyramid is Laguna Azul, which is good for swimming and snorkelling in blue, clean water (you do not have to pay to visit the pool if you do not visit the pyramids).

Listings Tulum and around *map p199*

Where to stay

Tulum town

Scores of new budget hotels and restaurants are opening apace, making it a good base for backpackers and cost-conscious travellers. However, expect to offset those lower hotel rates with additional transport costs. There are no buses to the beach, only taxis and infrequent *colectivos*. For places to stay in Sian Ka'an Biosphere Reserve, see below.

$$$ Posada 6
Andrómeda Ote, between Gemini Sur and Satélite Sur, T984-116 6757, www.posada06tulum.com.
A stylish Italian-owned hotel with an interesting interior design that employs curves and enclaves to aesthetic effect. Rooms and suites are clean and comfortable, and amenities include garden, terraces, pool and jacuzzi.

$$$ Posada Luna del Sur
Luna Sur 5, T984-871 2984, www.posadalunadelsur.com.
An intimate downtown lodging with light, airy, elegantly attired rooms, all with crisp white linen. The owner, Tom, is very hospitable and attentive, with lots of useful knowledge on the area. Immaculately clean and comfortable, and breakfast is included in the price. Recommended.

$$ Suites Nadet
Orion Norte by Polar Ote and Av Tulum.
The recently remodelled rooms at Suites Nadet are clean, simple and comfortable, all with smart new furnishings, a/c, hot water and cable TV. The suites (**$$$**) are much better and have kitchen and dining room. A good overall deal for the quality, cleanliness and location.

$ Hostel Sheck
Av Satelite Norte and Sagitario, T984-133 3992, www.hostelsheck.com.

A new, clean, laid-back hostel with a sociable vibe and accommodation in mixed dorms only. The garden is lush and tranquil with inviting hammocks and seating areas, and amenities include a full-service bar and well-equipped industrial kitchen. Good cooked breakfast is included. Recommended for thrifty backpackers.

$ Posada Los Mapaches
Carretera Cancun–Chetumal, T984-871 2700, www.posadalosmapaches.com. 1.5 km north of the village, near the entrance to the ruins.

A very sweet and basic lodging bursting with colourful flowers. The rooms are clean and simple, with shared bath. Mother and son hosts, Chela and Joaquín, are helpful and hospitable. Complimentary bikes and breakfast included. Highly recommended.

Tulum beach
A plethora of lodgings run the length of the coast from Tulum ruins to the Sian Ka'an Biosphere reserve. There is little infrastructure beyond these hotels and it's best to reach them by taxi; official rates are posted on a sign at the rank in the village.

$$$$ Cabañas La Luna
Carretera Tulum–Boca Paila Km 6.5, T1-818-631 9824 (US reservations), www.cabanaslaluna.com.

Lots of love and care has gone into **La Luna**, a very popular and reputable boutique hotel with interesting and creative lodgings, including 9 themed *cabañas*, an ocean-view room, a garden suite and 2 villas. Stunning setting, great service and attention to detail.

$$$$-$$$ Nueva Vida de Ramiro
Carretera Tulum–Boca Paila Km 8.5, No 17, T984-877 8512, www.tulumnv.com.

Nueva Vida de Ramiro prides itself on attentive service and sustainable, ecologically aware practices. They offer luxury lodging in 30 wooden bungalows situated on a 7.5-ha beachfront property. Each unit boasts comfortable and tasteful furnishings, the height of rustic chic.

$$$$-$$$ Posada Margherita
T984-801 8493, www.posadamargherita.com.

There's a shabby-chic aesthetic at the **Posada Margherita**, with some furnishings made from reclaimed driftwood. The vibe is relaxed, the crowd trendy. A generally decent and hospitable lodging with 24-hr electricity and wheelchair access. Many people come for the excellent Italian food, but be warned, it's not cheap (**$$$**).

$$$ Dos Ceibas
9 km from the ruins, T984-877 6024, www.dosceibas.com.

This verdant ecolodge on the edge of the Sian Ka'an Biosphere Reserve has a range of comfortable and cheerful *cabañas*. Massage, cleansing rituals, New Age therapies and yoga instruction available. Friendly and tranquil ambience.

$$$-$$ Los Arrecifes
7 km from ruins, T984-155 2957, www.losarrecifestulum.com.

Clean, simple and affordable rooms and *cabañas*, a little tired, but with an excellent location on the beach and superb views of the ocean. The ambience is quiet and peaceful, the service adequate.

$$ Ahau Tulum
Carretera Tulum–Boca Paila Km 7.5, T984-167 1154, www.ahau tulum.com.

Named after the Mayan sun god, **Ahau Tulum** is a community-oriented resort with a New Age philosophy. They offer yoga, retreats and spa treatments. Recommended as one of the few reasonable budget beach options; rustic lodging is in the guesthouse. Asian-style *cabañas* are more expensive (**$$$-$$**), as are the luxurious suites (**$$$$**). Book in advance.

Cobá

$$ Hotelito Sac-Be
Calle Principal, 150 m from Town Hall.

Simple, clean, adequate rooms below a restaurant. Nothing outstanding, not great value, but the best available. Amenities include hot water and a/c. Friendly owner.

Sian Ka'an Biosphere Reserve

$$$$ Rancho Sol Caribe
Punta Allen, T984-139 3839,
www.solcaribe-mexico.com.
Luxurious, extravagant and exclusive, **Rancho Sol Caribe** boasts a handful of handsome suites and *cabañas*, and an enviable location on the beach. Very hospitable and deeply relaxing, but not cheap. All-inclusive packages available. Recommended.

$$$ Centro Ecológico Sian Ka'an
T984-871 2499, www.cesiak.org.
Environmentally considerate and sensitive accommodation in the heart of the Reserve, profits contribute to conservation and education programmes in the region. Tours, kayaking and fly fishing arranged.

Restaurants

Tulum Town

$$$ El Pequeño Buenos Aires
Av Tulum, www.pequenobuenosaires.com.
High-quality cuts of beef, including rib eye, tenderloin, sirloin and more, all prepared and cooked to perfection the Argentine way, as the name suggests. Cosy setting with open-air seating on the main drag. One great meat feast, the servings are large.

$$$ Ginger
Calle Polar between Av Satélite and Centauro,
www.gingertulum.com.
A very decent, creative restaurant, if not the best in town. Starters include ceviche with mango and green apple and balsamic-glazed strawberry salad with goat cheese. For the main course, try the pan-seared fish fillet in passion fruit salsa or the grilled chicken in Yucatán spices. Recommended.

$$$ La Gloria de Don Pepe
Orion Sur 57.
An intimate little Spanish restaurant with just a few tables and a welcoming host. They serve authentic tapas, including *albóndigas* (meatballs) and *chistorra* (cured sausages), Catalan salads, tasty seafood paella, sangria and crisp white wine.

$$$-$$ La Malquerida
Calle Centauro Sur and Av Tulum.
A cheery Mexican restaurant serving tacos, fajitas, nachos, quesadillas and the usual local fare, with a smattering of Caribbean and seafood. Large portions, friendly service and a laid-back, sociable ambience. A good stock of tequila.

$$ La Nave
Av Tulum.
A very popular Italian restaurant and pizzeria. Good, authentically Italian stone-baked pizzas and a lively atmosphere most evenings.

$$-$ El Gourmet
Av Tulum corner of Centauro Sur.
An Italian deli stocking good cheeses and cured hams, salami, olives and other treats. They do delicious panini and ciabatta sandwiches for picnics or food on the go.

$ Doña Tinas
Good basic and cheap, in a grass hut at southern end of town. **El Mariachito** next door also does good, cheap and cheerful grub.

Ice cream parlours

La Flor de Michoacán
Av Tulum.
This ice cream parlour on the main drag offers a wide variety of flavoured cones (try the coconut), a refreshing antidote to the searing Caribbean heat.

Tulum beach
Restaurants on the beach tend to be owned by hotels. For dinner, book in advance where possible. Strolling between establishments after dark isn't advisable.

$$$ Mezzanine
Carretera Tulum–Boca Paila Km 1.5.
Excellent authentic Thai cuisine conceived by TV personality Chef Dim Geefay, who has successfully infused old family recipes with local, Mexican flavours. Specialities include Pad Thai and a host of flavourful curries. Highly recommended.

$$$ Restaurant Margherita
Carretera Tulum–Boca Paila Km 4.5, in Posada Margherita, www.posada margherita.com. Closed Sun.
Excellent, freshly prepared Italian food in an intimate setting. Hospitable, attentive service. Book in advance. Recommended.

$$$ La Zebra
Carretera Tulum–Boca Paila Km 7.5, www.lazebratulum.com.
Fresh, tasty barbequed fish, shrimps, ceviche and Mexican fare. Lashings of Margarita at the **Tequila Bar**.

$$$-$$ Restaurare
Carretera Tulum–Boca Paila Km 6.
Excellent vegan cuisine, healthy and flavourful, all served under the trees in a verdant jungle garden (bring repellent). Offerings include avocado soup, coconut curry and delicious fresh fruit juices. No alcohol served, bring your own if desired.

$$$-$$ Ziggy's
Carretera Tulum–Boca Paila Km 7, www.ziggybeachtulum.com.
Ziggy's serves seafood and vegetarian dishes, all carefully prepared with local ingredients. Offerings include mushroom ceviche, coconut shrimp and smoked pork chop and pineapple wrap. The sun loungers and *palapas* are part of the beach club.

What to do

Cenote diving
Koox Diving, *Av Tulum, between Osiris and Beta Norte, T984-131 6543, www.kooxdiving. com.* **Koox** is a friendly, personable and professional company with a solid team

headed by Jesús 'Chucho' Guzmán. They offer reef and *cenote* dives, snorkel tours and certification up to Dive Master.
Xibalba Dive Center, *Andrómeda, between Libra and Gemini, T529-848 7129, www.xibalbahotel.com/diving.asp.* Headed by Robert Schmittner, **Xibalba** has been diving *cenotes* in the Yucatán for more than a decade. They visit around a dozen sites and offer PADI certification up to Dive Master, as well as NACD technical cave and cavern certification.

Kitesurfing
Extreme control, *El Paraíso Beach Club, T984-745 4555, www.extremecontrol.net.* Managed by Marco and Heather, **Extreme Control** is a very successful kite-boarding operation with branches across Mexico and Brazil. Basic lessons for groups start at US$60 per person. They also offer paddle-boarding and diving.

Tour operators
Community Tours Si'an Kaan, *Osiris Sur, between Sol Ote and Andrómeda Ote, T984-871 2202, www.siankaantours.org.* A socially responsible and environmentally aware tour operator entirely operated by Maya from local communities. They offer a range of professional cultural and adventure excursions, including wetland kayaking, birding and visits to *chicle* (chewing gum) farms.
Yucatán Outdoors, *T984-133 2334, www. yucatanoutdoors.com.* **Yucatán Outdoors** offers ecotourism for adventurous souls, including personalized kayaking, hiking, birding and biking tours. Committed to sustainability and passionate about the local culture and environment.

Transport

Bicycle
Bikes can be hired in the village from **Iguana Bike Shop**, Calle Satélite Sur and **Andrómeda Ote**, T984-119 0836 (mob) or T984-871 2357.

Bus

Regular buses go up and down the coastal road travelling from Cancún to Tulum en route to Chetumal, stopping at most places in between. Some buses may be full when they reach Tulum; very few buses begin their journeys here.

To **Chetumal**, frequent departures, 4 hrs, 2nd class, US$14, 1st class US$17. To **Cobá**, mostly 2nd class, 1 hr, US$4. To **Escárcega**, ADO, 1825, 2300, 7 hrs, US$35. To **Felipe Carrillo Puerto**, frequent departures, 1½ hrs, US$6; also *colectivos* from the highway. To **Mérida**, ADO, 10 daily, 4 hrs, US$20; and numerous 2nd-class departures. To **Mexico City**, ADO, 1340, 23½ hrs, US$130. To **Palenque**, OCC, 1825, 2300, 10-11 hrs, US$52; and **ADO GL**, 2015, US$58. To **San Cristóbal**, OCC, 1825, 15 hrs, US$61; and an **ADO GL**, 2015, US$74. To **Villahermosa**, ADO, 4 daily, 11 hrs, US$54.

Taxi

Tulum town to Tulum **ruins** US$5.50. To the **beach** US$5.50 minimum, check the board by the taxi stand on Av Tulum for a full list of fixed rates. **Tucan Kin** run shuttles to Cancún airport, T01-800-702-4111 for reservations, www.tucankin.com, from US$29, 1½ hrs.

Cobá

Bus

Buses into the village turn round at the road end. To **Playa del Carmen**, ADO, 1510, 1530, 2 hrs, US$9. To **Tulum**, ADO, 1510, 1530, 1 hr, US$5.

Felipe Carrillo Puerto and around → *Colour map 5, C5.*

The cult of the 'talking cross' started in Felipe Carrillo Puerto, a small town founded Chan Santa Cruz by Mayan rebels in 1850. The Santuario de la Cruz Parlante is five blocks west of the Pemex station on Highway 307. The beautiful main square is dominated by the Balam Nah Catholic church. Legend has it that the unfinished bell tower will only be completed when the descendants of those who heard the talking cross reassert control of the region.

Mahahual → *Colour map 4, B5.*

Further south on Route 307, at Cafetal, a good road heads east to Mahahual (Majahual) on the coast (56 km from Cafetal), a peaceful place with clear water and beautiful beaches. Unfortunately, the Costa Maya cruise ship dock, 3 km from the village, means occasional interruptions to the peace and calm. From Mahahual, an offshore excursion is possible to **Banco Chinchorro**, where there is a coral bank and a white-sand beach. There is an ADO bus stop in Mahahual, but services from Cancún and Chetumal are quite infrequent (see Transport, page 206).

Listings Felipe Carrillo Puerto and around

Where to stay

Felipe Carrillo Puerto

$$ Hotel Esquivel
Calle 65 No746, between 66 y 68, T983-834 0344, www.hotelesquivel.blogspot.mx.

The best in town, but simple. Rooms are clean and spacious, and include good hot water, a/c and Wi-Fi. Helpful service, close to the bus station, but perhaps not the best value.

$$-$ Chan Santa Cruz
Calle 68, 782, just off the plaza, T983-834 0021.

The 2nd best option, generally good, clean and friendly. Rooms have a/c, cable TV, fridge and disabled access.

Mahahual and around

$$$ El Hotelito
Av Mahahual, T983-834 5702,
www.elhotelitomahahual.com.
A new, comfortable, tastefully decorated boutique hotel located at the southern end of the *malecón*, just across the street from the beach. Rooms on the top floor enjoy unobstructed ocean views and refreshing breezes. Good hosts and friendly, attentive service. Recommended.

$$$ Posada Pachamama
Huachinango s/n, T983-834 5762.
A homely little *posada* with clean, cosy, smallish rooms, modern conveniences and attractive decor. Italian owners Max and Michela are helpful and hospitable. Not quite on the beach, 1 min away, but most guests don't seem to mind. Recommended.

$$ Kabah-na
Camino Costero Mahahual–Xcalak Km 8.6,
T983-838 8861, www.kabah na.com.
Simple, comfortable, relaxing beach *cabañas*, located several kilometres out of town, far from the hurly burly of the cruise-ship crowds. Neither chic nor rustic, but somewhere in between. Best accessed with own vehicle.

Mahahual

$$$-$$ Tropicante
Av Mahahual, on the Malecón, www.
sandalsandskis.com/Tropicante.html.
Mexican and American food served on the beach. They have sun loungers too, if you prefer to simply rest up with a beer or cocktail. Note **Tropicante** often caters to the cruise-ship crowd, so time your visit accordingly. Steve, the owner, is a good host.

$$ Pizza Papi
Av Paseo del Puerto.
Casual little Italian eatery serving very good, authentic, stone-baked pizzas. Good service. Recommended.

Felipe Carrillo Puerto
Bus
Bus station opposite Pemex. To **Cancun**, frequent 1st- and 2nd-class departures, 4 hrs, US$16. To **Chetumal**, frequent departures, 2½ hrs, US$10. To **Playa del Carmen**, frequent departures, 2½ hrs, US$11.50. To **Tulum**, frequent departures, 1½ hrs, US$7.50; also frequent *colectivo* minibuses.

The state capital of Quintana Roo, Chetumal, 240 km south of Tulum, is a necessary stopover for travellers en route to Mayan sites in the south of the peninsula and across the frontier to Belize and Guatemala; see box, page 511. Although attractions are thin on the ground, Chetumal does have the advantage of being not devoted to tourism unlike other towns on the Riviera Maya. The Chetumal bay has been designated a natural protected area for manatees and includes a manatee sanctuary.

Chetumal

N

200 metres
200 yards

Where to stay
Gandhi 1
Los Cocos 6
Paakal's Hostel 2

Ucum 10
Villanueva 3

Restaurants
El Emporio 2
La Casita del Chef 3
Los Milagros 4
Pasión Turca 5
Sergio's Pizza 1

Sights

The avenues are broad, busy and in the centre lined with huge shops selling cheap imported goods. The main local activity is window-shopping and the atmosphere is more like a North American city, with an impression of affluence that can be a culture shock to the visitor arriving from the much poorer country of Guatemala. The downtown area is compact and can be navigated on foot; Avenida Héroes is the main commercial thoroughfare.

The *paseo* near the waterfront on Sunday night is worth seeing. The State Congress building has a mural showing the history of Quintana Roo. The **Museo de la Cultura Maya** ⓘ *Av Héroes de Chapultepec by the market, Tue-Sun 0900-1900, US$5*, is highly recommended. It has good models of sites and touch-screen computers explaining the Mayan calendar and glyphs. Although there are few original Mayan pieces, it gives an excellent overview; some explanations are in English, guided tours are available.

Around Chetumal

Some 6 km north of Chetumal are the stony beaches of **Calderitas**, bus every 30 minutes from Colón, between Belice and Héroes, US$1.80, or taxi US$5, which has many fish restaurants. Beyond are the unexcavated archaeological sites of **Ichpaatun** (13 km), **Oxtancah** (14 km) and **Nohochmul** (20 km). Sixteen kilometres north on Route 307 to Tulum is the **Laguna de los Milagros**, a beautiful lagoon for swimming. Further on, 34 km north of Chetumal, is **Cenote Azul**, over 70 m deep, with a waterside restaurant serving inexpensive and good seafood and regional food (but awful coffee) until 1800. Both the *laguna* and the *cenote* are deserted in the week.

Bacalar

About 3 km north of Cenote Azul is the village of Bacalar on the **Laguna de Siete Colores**, good for swimming and skin-diving; *colectivos* from terminal (Suchaa) in Chetumal, corner of Miguel Hidalgo and Primo de Verdad, 0700-1900 every 30 minutes, US$3, return from the plaza when full; also buses from Chetumal bus station every two hours or so, US$3. Built 1725-1733, the Spanish fort of **San Felipe** overlooks the shallow, clear, freshwater lagoon. It is a structure designed to withstand attacks by English pirates and smugglers who regularly looted Spanish galleons laden with Peruvian gold. Today, there are many old shipwrecks on the reef and around the Banco Chinchorro, 50 km out in the Caribbean. At the fort, there is a plaque praying for protection from the British and a small **museum** ① *Tue-Sun 0900-1700, US$4*. There is a dock for swimming north of the plaza, with a restaurant and disco next to it.

Towards Campeche State → *Colour map 4, B4.*

From Chetumal you can visit the fascinating Mayan ruins that lie west on the way (Route 186) to Francisco Villa and Escárcega, if you have a car. There are few tourists in this area and few facilities. Take plenty of drinking water. About 25 km from Chetumal at **Ucum** (where fuel is available), you can turn off 5 km south to visit **Palmara**, located along the Río Hondo, which borders Belize; there are swimming holes and restaurant.

Just before Francisco Villa (61 km from Chetumal), the ruins of **Kohunlich** ① *0800-1700, US$4.25*, lie 8.5 km south of the main road, 1½ hours' walk along a sweltering, unshaded road; take plenty of water. Descriptions are in Spanish and English. Every hour or so the van passes for staff working at **Explorer Kohunlich**, a luxury resort hotel halfway to the ruins, which may give you a lift, but you'll still have 4 km to walk. There are fabulous masks (early Classic, AD 250-500) set on the side of the main pyramid, still bearing red colouring; they are unique of their kind (allow an hour for the site). About 200 m west of the turning for Kohunlich is an immigration office; wait here for buses to Chetumal or Xpujil, which have to stop, but first-class buses will not pick up passengers. *Colectivos* 'Nicolás Bravo' from Chetumal, or buses marked 'Zoh Laguna' pass the turning.

Other ruins in this area are **Dzibanché** and **Knichná** ① *0900-1700, US$3.50*. Both are recent excavations and both are accessible down a dirt road off the Chetumal–Morocoy road. In the 1990s the remains of a Mayan king were disinterred at Dzibanché, which is thought to have been the largest Mayan city in southern Quintana Roo, peaking between AD 300 and 1200. Its discoverer, Thomas Gann, named it in 1927 after the Maya glyphs he found engraved on the sapodilla wood lintels in Temple VI – *Dzibanché* means 'writing on the wood' in Maya. Later excavations revealed a tomb in Temple I, believed to have belonged to a king because of the number of offerings it contained. This temple is also known as the **Temple of the Owl** because one of the artefacts unearthed was a vase and lid carved with an owl figure. Other important structures are the **Temple of the Cormorants** and **Structure XIII**, known as 'The Captives', due to its friezes depicting prisoners. Knichná means 'House of the Sun' in Maya, christened by Thomas Gann in reference to a glyph he found there. The **Acropolis** is the largest structure. To reach these sights follow the Chetumal–Escárcega road, turn off at Km 58 towards Morocoy, 9 km further on. The road to Dzibanché is 2 km down this road, crossing the turning for Knichná.

Tourist information

Municipal tourist office
Corner of 5 de Mayo and Carmen Ochoa de Merino, T983-833 2465.
Stocks of maps and flyers, and enthusiastic staff.

Where to stay

$$$-$$ Los Cocos
Av Héroes de Chapultepec 134, T983-835 0430, www.hotelloscocos.com.mx.
A large, modern, professionally managed hotel with clean, comfortable rooms and suites, a good restaurant, decking and outdoor jacuzzi. Good value and popular, if a bit generic.

$$$-$$ Villanueva
Carmen Ochoa de Merino 166, T983-267 3370, www.hotel-villanueva.com.
A swish new business hotel with sparse contemporary furnishings and a wealth of facilities including pool, gym, business centre, restaurant and room service. Good value when promotions are available (**$$**).

$$ Hotel Gandhi
Av Gandhi 166, T983-285 3269, www.hotelgandhichetumal.com.
A step up from the bare-bones **Ucum** across the street, **Hotel Gandhi** is a reliable business hotel with clean, comfortable a/c rooms, complete with Wi-Fi, a/c and cable TV. Convenient for a night, but ultimately unremarkable.

$$-$ Paakal's Hostel
Av Juárez 364A, T983-833 3715.
Paakal's is a good, clean, friendly hostel with both private rooms (**$$**) and dorms (**$**), a well-equipped shared kitchen, lounge space, table tennis, plunge pool and relaxing

garden. A newish property in excellent condition, very quiet and chilled out. Recommended for budget travellers.

$$-$ Ucum
Gandhi 167, corner of 16 de Septiembre, T983-832 6186.
Motel-style lodging with parking, centrally located and no frills. Rooms are ultra-basic, with a bed, a/c, hot water, Wi-Fi and cable TV. Charmless, but a good deal for thrifty wanderers.

Bacalar

$$$$ Akal Ki
Carretera Federal 307, Km 12.5, Bacalar Lagoon, T983-106 1751, www.akalki.com.
A marvellously peaceful retreat with romantic thatched bungalows built right over the water. Though surrounded by jungle, this strip of the lagoon has few rocks and little vegetation, making it crystal clear and ideal for swimming.

$$$ Rancho Encantado
3 km north of Bacalar, Carretera Federal 307, Km 24, on the west shore of the lagoon, T983-839 7900, www.encantado.com.
Comfortable, clean, spacious *cabañas*, suites and rooms, all in verdant surroundings by the lagoon. Services include private dock, tour boat, paddle boat, kayaks, restaurant and spa treatments.

$$ Casita Carolina
T983-834 2334, Costera 15, between Calle 16 and 18, www.casitacarolina.com.
Colourful, comfortable, good-value rooms at this friendly guesthouse, the best budget option in the village. The garden backs directly onto the lagoon and the plaza is just 2 blocks away. There are kayaks for rent, a shared kitchen and hammocks. Recommended.

$$$-$$ El Emporio
Merino 106.
Delicious Uruguayan steaks served in a historic old house near the bay. Popular with businessmen at lunchtime.

$$$-$$ Sergio's Pizza
Av Obregón 182.
A convenient downtown location for a popular family restaurant serving pizzas, fish and steaks. Good drinks and service, and a refreshing a/c interior. Very reasonable, but not amazing.

$$ La Casita del Chef
Obregón 163.
Featuring 100-year-old photos of Chetumal, **La Casita del Chef** is a pleasant little eatery serving traditional Mexican dishes with contemporary flair. Convenient downtown location and a traditional wooden building.

$$-$ Pasión Turca
Av Héroes and Ignacio Zaragoza,
www.pasionturca.com.mx.
Chetumal is home to a large Turkish community and the **Pasión Turca** is one of the best places to sample Turkish cuisine, with a Mexican twist, naturally. A simple place with slightly tired decor, but the food makes up for it.

$ Los Milagros
Zaragoza and 5 de Mayo.
This locals' café serves economical Mexican fare, *comida corrida* and breakfasts. Busy with patrons in the morning, worth a look.

$ Mercado.
Cheap meals in the market at the top of Av Héroes, but the service is not too good and tourists are likely to be stared at. Lots of cheap *taquerías* on the streets nearby.

Bacalar

Los Hechizos
Hotel Rancho Encantado, Carretera Federal 307, www.encantado.com/restaurante.htm.
A rustic *palapa* with great views of the lagoon and refreshing breezes. Good food, the best in town, including a range of well-presented Mexican, seafood and meat dishes. Recommended.

Cafés

In Chiich
Calle 22, on the plaza.
Cute little café serving crêpes, smoothies, ice cream, snacks and good coffee.

Transport

For more information on crossing the border to Belize, see box, page 511.

Air
The airport (CTM), T983-834-5013, is 2.5 km from town. There are no local buses so take a taxi into town.
Flights to **Cancún**, **Mérida**, **Belize City**, **Mexico City**, **Monterrey** and **Tijuana**.

Boat
Boats from Belize dock at the pier on the waterfront on the south side of the city.

To Belize You can avoid a lot of the hassle of travelling overland to Belize, skipping Belize City altogether, by taking a boat from the Muelle Fiscal on the south side of the city, journey time 2 hrs (excluding immigration formalities). There are 2 companies, both with departures at 1500 to San Pedro, US$40, and on to Caye Caulker, US$45; fares rise by US$10 at weekends and holidays. Try **Water Jets International**, www.sanpedrowatertaxi.com, or **Belize Express Water Taxi**, T983-832 1648, www.belizewatertaxi.com. Buy tickets at least 24 hrs in advance.

Bus
The **ADO** bus terminal is 3 km out of town at the intersection of Insurgentes y Belice. Taxi into town US$2. There is a bus into the centre from Av Belice. 2nd-class buses from Belize arrive at the **Nuevo Mercado**

Lázaro Cárdenas, on Calle Antonio Coria s/n, near the concrete tower in the market. Shuttles from Santa Elena and the border arrive at their own terminal, Primo de Verdad, between 16 de Septiembre and Hidalgo.

Bus information, T983-832 5110. At the ADO bus terminal left-luggage lockers cost US$0.30 per hr. If buying tickets in advance, go to the ADO office on Av Belice esq Gandhi, 0800-1600. There are often more buses than those marked on the display in the bus station, always ask at the information desk. Long-distance buses are often all booked a day ahead, so avoid unbooked connections. For local destinations in southern Quintana Roo, speedy minibuses depart from the terminal at Av Hidalgo and Primo de Verdad.

To **Bacalar**, very frequent 1st- and 2nd-class departures, 1 hr, US$3.50. To **Campeche**, **ADO**, 1200, 6 hrs, US$29. To **Cancún**, many 1st-class departures, 6 hrs, US$25. To **Escárcega**, **ADO**, 11 daily, 4 hrs, US$19. To **Felipe Carrillo Puerto**, many 1st- and 2nd-class departures, 2½ hrs, US$11. To **Mérida**, **ADO**, 5 daily, 5½ hrs, US$30. To **Palenque**, OCC, 0220, 2150, 7 hrs, US$32; and **ADO GL**, 2350, US$39. To **Playa del Carmen**, frequent 1st- and 2nd-class departures, 5 hrs, US$21. To **San Cristóbal**, OCC, 0220, 2150, 12 hrs, US$47; and **ADO GL** 0005, US$56. To **Tulum**, frequent 1st- and 2nd-class departures, 4 hrs, US$17. To **Villahermosa**,

ADO, 6 daily, 8½ hrs, US$38. To **Xpujil**, **ADO**, **Sur** and **OCC**, 2 hrs, US$9.

To Belize Battered 2nd-class buses to Belize depart from a parking area in the Nuevo Mercado Lázaro Cárdenas, Calle Antonio Coria s/n, every 30-60 mins. To **Corozal**, 30-60 mins, US$1.50; to **Orange Walk**, 2 hrs, US$3.50; to **Belize City**, 3-4 hrs, US$5. Alternatively, if light on luggage, take a local bus to Santa Elena from the terminal on Primo de Verdad, between 16 de Septiembre and Hidalgo, 15 mins, US$0.80, cross the border on foot and pick up Belizean transport on the other side. Taxi from downtown Chetumal to the border, US$6. Money-changers in the bus terminal offer marginally poorer rates than those at the border. If intending to stay in Belize City, do not take a bus that arrives at night as you are advised not to look for a hotel in the dark.

To Guatemala San Juan Travel Services provide 1 daily service between Chetumal, Belize City and Flores in Guatemala, departs from **ADO** bus terminal 0700, US$31. Schedules are subject to change so always check times in advance, and be prepared to spend a night in Chetumal if necessary.

Taxi
There are no city buses; taxis run on fixed-price routes, US$1.50 on average. Cars with light-green licence plates are a form of taxi.

Yucatán State

Yucatán State is a vivid celebration of Yucatecan history and traditions: its wealth of cathedrals, convents and rambling haciendas, frequently set against a backdrop of crumbling Mayan pyramids, recall the passion and drama of another age.

The state capital of Mérida was the seat of power for the colonial administration. Today, it is a deeply cultural place filled with museums, theatres and art galleries, teeming markets and plazas, historic mansions, churches and bright townhouses. The city of Valladolid, although much smaller, is no less romantic.

Beyond its urban centres, the state is peppered with bucolic towns and villages, many rich in Mayan heritage and specializing in artesanía, while communities on the Convent Route are so called for their ancient religious architecture.

As the once-thriving heart of the Mayan world, the Yucatán State is also home to the vast city of Chichén Itzá, laden with sculpted feathered serpents and pyramids, ball courts and sacrificial slabs, a tremendous monument to an ancient culture. It is also worth exploring Uxmal, a stunning example of sumptuous Puuc-style architecture. Yucatán State has natural attractions too, including mysterious limestone cave systems and refreshing cenotes. On the coast, the wetlands Río Lagartos and Celestún are places to observe pelicans, egrets and flamingos.

bold colonial buildings in varying states of repair

Mérida, the cultural and intellectual capital of the Yucatán Peninsula, is a bustling, tightly packed city. There is continual activity in the centre, with a huge influx of tourists during the high season mingling with busy *Meridanos* going about their daily business. Although the city has been developed over many years for tourism, there is plenty of local flavour, including the pungent and warren-like city market, a throng of commotion, noise and colour. Whether sipping coffee in a leafy colonial courtyard or admiring the mansions on the regal Paseo de Montejo, much of the pleasure in Mérida comes from exploring its architecture, a rich blend of European styles that spans the centuries. In the evenings, there is usually open-air dancing, music or singing. It is perhaps no surprise that many inhabitants of Mexico City are now relocating to the infinitely more civilized and urbane destination of Mérida.

You can see most of Mérida on foot. Although the city is big, there is not much to see outside the blocks radiating from the Plaza Grande; it is bound by Calles 60, 61, 62 and 63. The city centre is laid out in a classic colonial grid with even-numbered streets running north–south, odd-numbered east–west.

Plaza Grande and around
The city revolves around the large, shady Plaza Grande, site of the **cathedral**, completed in 1559, the oldest cathedral in Latin America, which has an impressive baroque façade. It contains the Cristo de las Ampollas (Christ of the Blisters), a statue carved from a tree that burned for a whole night after being hit by lightning, without showing any damage at all. Placed in the church at Ichmul, it suffered only a slight charring (hence the name) when the church was burned to the ground. To the left of the cathedral on the adjacent side of the plaza is the **Palacio de Gobierno**, built 1892. It houses a collection of 27 enormous murals by Fernando Castro Pacheco, depicting the bloody struggle of the Maya to integrate with the Spanish. The murals can be viewed until 2100 every day. The **Casa de Montejo** ⓘ *www.casasdeculturabanamex.com, Tue-Sun 1000-1900, Sun 1000-1400, free*, is on the south side of the plaza, a 16th-century palace built by the city's founder, today a branch of Banamex and a minor art museum. It features elaborate stonework above the doorway flanked by statues of conquistadors standing victorious on the necks of their (presumably Maya) enemies.

Away from the main plaza along Calle 60 is **Parque Hidalgo**, a charming tree-filled square, which borders the 17th-century **Iglesia de Jesús.** A little further along Calle 60 is the **Teatro Peón Contreras**, built at the beginning of the 20th century by an Italian architect, with a neoclassical façade, marble staircase and Italian frescoes.

Churches
There are several 16th- and 17th-century churches dotted about the city: **La Mejorada**, behind the Museum of Peninsular Culture (Calle 59 between 48 and 50), **Tercera Orden, San Francisco** and **San Cristóbal** (beautiful, in the centre). The **Ermita**, an 18th-century chapel with beautiful grounds, is a lonely, deserted place, 10 to 15 minutes from the centre.

Paseo de Montejo
Attempts to create a sophisticated Champs Elysées-style boulevard in the north of the city at Paseo Montejo have not been quite successful; the plan almost seems to go against

Mérida

To ⑧ ⑨ ⑯ ㉔, El Gran Museo del Mundo Maya
& Progreso

Felipe Carrillo
Puerta Monument

Museo de
Antropología
e Historia

Parque
Santa Ana

Plaza
Santa
Lucía

Museo de
la Canción
Yucateca

La Mejorada

Teatro Peón
Contreras

Museo
de Arte
Popular

Museum of
Peninsular
Culture

Mercado
Municipal 2

Jesús

Casa
Catherwood

Parque
Hidalgo

Palacio de
Gobierno

Palacio
Municipal

Cathedral

Zócalo

Museo
Macay

Las
Monjas

Casa de
Montejo

Museo de
la Ciudad

Colectivos to
Plaza de Los
Americas

Combis to
Izamal

Autoprogreso

Noreste

Municipal

Colectivos
to Ticul

Parque
San Juan

San
Cristóbal

CAME

Terminal de
Autobuses

Parque San
Sebastián

La Ermita

300 metres
300 yards

To Chichén-Itzá & Cancún

To Campeche & Mexico City

N

Where to stay 🛏

Aventura Hotel **1** *C1*
Casa Alvarez **2** *B2*
Casa Ana **3** *B4*
Casa Lecanda **4** *A3*
Hacienda Mérida VIP **5** *B2*
Hacienda Xcanatún **8** *A3*
Hostal Zócalo **17** *C2*
Hotel del Pelegrino **6** *B3*
Julamis **7** *B3*
Los Arcos **9** *B2*
Luz en Yucatán **10** *B3*

Medio Mundo **19** *B2*
Nómadas Youth
  Hostal **13** *B2*
Rosas and Xocolate
  Boutique **11** *A3*
Santa María **12** *B3*
Trinidad **22** *B2*

Restaurants 🍴

Amaro **1** *B2*
Bistro Rescoldos **13** *A2*
Café Chocolate **23** *B3*

Café El Hoyo **7** *B2*
Cafetería Pop **2** *B2*
Casa de Piedra **24** *A3*
Chile Habanero **6** *B3*
El Colón Sorbetes y
  Dulces Finos **10** *C3*
El Nuevo Tucho **4** *B3*
El Trapiche **3** *C2*
La Chaya **8** *B2*
La Recova **9** *A3*
Manjar Blanco **11** *A3*
Marlín Azul **18** *B2*

Mérida **20** *C2*
Pizzeria Raffaello **12** *A3*
Rosas and Xocolate **14** *A3*
Trotter's **16** *A3*

Bars & clubs 🎵

Cantina La Negrita **21** *A2*
Hennessy's Irish Pub **17** *A3*
Mayan Pub **22** *B2*

the grain of Mérida's status as an ancient city, which has gradually evolved into a place with its own distinct identity. Nonetheless, the Paseo, which is the principal parade route during the city's fantastic carnival celebrations, features numerous impressive mansions dating to the late 19th century. You can take a casual stroll or hire a horse-drawn carriage and do it in style. For a glimpse of the *paseo* at its heyday, the **Casa Museo Montes Molina** ① *Paseo de Montejo No 469 between Calles 33 and 35, www.laquintamm.com, English tours Mon-Fri 0900, 1100, 1500, Sat 0900, 1100; Spanish tours Mon-Fri 1000, 1200, 1400, 1600, Sat 1000, 1200, US$4*, is a finely attired mansion with sumptuous antiques and art deco pieces.

Museums and art galleries

Mérida's wealth of museums is enough to keep most visitors busy for a few days. The **Museo Regional de Antropología** ① *Paseo de Montejo 485, Tue-Sun 0800-1700, US$3.70*, housed in the beautiful neoclassical Palacio Cantón, has a collection of Mayan crafts and changing anthropological exhibits. However, most of its archaeological pieces have now been relocated to the Gran Museo del Mundo Maya (see below).

The **Museo de la Ciudad** ① *Calle 56 between Calles 65 and 65-A, Tue-Fri 0900-2000, Sat 0900-1400, free*, has modest visual exhibits outlining the history of the city. The **Museo Macay** ① *Calle 60, on the main plaza, www.macay.org, daily 1000-1800, free*, has a permanent exhibition of Yucatec artists, with temporary exhibits by contemporary local artists.

The **Museo de Arte Popular** ① *Calle 50-A No 487 and Calle 57, Tue-Sat 0900-1700, Sun 1000-1500, free*, has a permanent exhibition of Mayan art, handicrafts and clothing, with a good souvenir shop attached. In the Casa de Cultura, the **Museo de la Canción Yucateca** ① *Calles 57 and 48, Tue-Fri 0900-1700, Sat-Sun 0900-1500, US$1.50*, has an exhibition of objects and instruments relating to the history of music in the region. For contemporary painting and sculpture, head to the **Pinacoteca Juan Gamboa Guzmán** ① *Calle 59, between Calles 58 and 60, Tue-Sat 0900-1700, Sun 1000-1700, US$2.40*.

Established in 2007, the **Galería de Arte Municipal** ① *Calle 56, between Calles 65 and 65-A, Tue-Fri 1000-1900, Sun 1000-1400*, exhibits and promotes work by local Meridano artists. **Galería Tataya** ① *Calle 60 No 409, between Calles 45 and 47, www.tataya.com.mx, Mon-Fri 1000-1400 and 1600-2000, Sat 1000-1400*, is a private gallery specializing in Mexican and Cuban contemporary art and high quality *artesanías*. Dedicated exclusively to local artists, **Galería Mérida** ① *Calle 59 No 452, between Calles 52 and 54, Tue-Fri 1000-1230 and 1430-1700, www.galeriamerida.com*, is a small gallery featuring a range of fine and contemporary art; exhibits change monthly.

Railway fanatics might get some joy in the **Museo de los Ferrocarriles** ① *Calle 43 between Calles 46 and 58, Col. Industrial, Wed-Sun 0900-1400, US$1.50*, but there's little for the casual visitor. Fans of John Lloyd Steven's seminal travelogue *Incidents of Travel in Central America, Chiapas and Yucatán* should check out **Casa Catherwood** ① *Calle 59 between 72 and 74, www.casa-catherwood.com, Mon-Sat 0900-1400 and 1700-2100, US$5*. Dedicated to Steven's companion and illustrator, Mr Catherwood, this museum contains stunning colour lithographs of Mayan ruins, as they were found in the 19th century.

★El Gran Museo del Mundo Maya

Paseo Montejo and Calle 60, on the outskirts of the city, www.granmuseodelmundo maya.com, Wed-Mon 0800-1700, closed Tue, US$11.50; buses to the museum depart from the corner of Plaza Grande, Calle 62 and 61, check with the driver first, US$0.70, or take a taxi, US$5.50. To return to the city centre, take a bus directly outside the museum.

BACKGROUND

Mérida

Mérida was originally a large Mayan city called Tihoo. It was conquered on 6 January 1542, by Francisco de Montejo. He dismantled the pyramids of the Maya and used the stone as the foundations for the cathedral of San Ildefonso, built 1556-1559. For the next 300 years, Mérida remained under Spanish control, unlike the rest of Mexico, which was governed from the capital. During the Caste Wars of 1847-1855, Mérida held out against the marauding forces of indigenous armies, who had defeated the Mexican army in every other city in the Yucatán Peninsula except Campeche. Reinforcements from the centre allowed the Mexicans to regain control of their city, but the price was to relinquish control of the region to Mexico City.

Mérida's Gran Museo Mundo Maya is a state-of-the-art interactive museum dedicated to Mayan history and identity. Opened in 2012, its collection of 1160 cultural and archaeological pieces are supplemented by scores of touch screens, computers, projection rooms and a full-sized cinema. The museum has one temporary exhibition wing and a permanent collection wing with four main sections. The first section deals with the geographic and social landscape of the Yucatán, its ethnic and ecological diversity, its various territories, forms of social organization and languages. The second section is a detailed exploration of the Yucatán's present-day economy and culture, including exhibitions on education, health, tradition and work. The colonial era is the theme of the third section with an array of antiques and old machines relating to the colonial industries, the conquest, the church and Mayan rebellions. The fourth and final section hosts an impressive array of archaeological pieces from statues depicting Mayan deities to examples of Mayan hieroglyphs. It explores the ancient Mayan world through the diverse themes of cosmovision, art, architecture, astronomy, time and more.

Around Mérida

birdwatching, beaches and Mayan ruins

Celestún → *Colour map 5, B1.*

A small, dusty fishing resort west of Mérida much frequented in summer by Mexicans, Celestún stands on the spit of land separating the Río Esperanza estuary from the ocean. The long beach is relatively clean except near the town proper, with clear water ideal for swimming, although rising afternoon winds usually churn up silt and there is little shade; along the beach are many fishing boats bristling with *jimbas* (cane poles), used for catching local octopus. There are beach restaurants with showers.

The immediate region is a biosphere reserve, created to protect the thousands of migratory waterfowl who inhabit the lagoons; fish, crabs and shrimp also spawn here, and kingfishers, black hawks, wood storks and crocodiles may sometimes be glimpsed in the quieter waterways. In the winter months Celestún plays host to the largest flamingo colony in North America, perhaps more than 20,000 birds – in the summer most of the flamingos leave Celestún for their nesting grounds in the Río Lagartos area. Boat trips to view the wildlife can be arranged at the beach or the **visitor centre** ① *below the river bridge 1 km back along the Mérida road, US$100 for 1-6 people, plus US$4 per person for the* *reserve entrance fees, 1½ hours*. Make sure your boatman takes you through the mangrove channel and to the Baldiosera freshwater spring in addition to visiting the flamingos. It is often possible to see flamingos from the bridge early in the morning and the road to it may be alive with egrets, herons and pelicans. January to March is the best time to see them. It's important to wear a hat and use sunscreen. There are hourly buses to Mérida's terminal at Calle 50 and 67, 0530-2000, two to three hours, US$5.

Progreso and around → *Colour map 5, A2.*
Some 36 km north of Mérida, Progreso has the nearest beach to the city. It is a port and slow-growing resort town, with the facilities improving to service the increasing number of US cruise ships that arrive every Wednesday. Progreso is famous for its industrial pier, which at 6 km is the longest in the world. It has been closed to the public since someone fell off the end on a moped. The beach is long and clean and the water is shallow and good for swimming.

A short bus journey (4 km) west from Progreso are **Puerto Yucalpetén** and **Chelem**. Balneario Yucalpetén has a beach with lovely shells, but also a large naval base with further construction in progress.

Some 5 km east of Progreso is another resort, **Chicxulub**; it has a narrow beach, quiet and peaceful, on which are many boats and much seaweed. Small restaurants sell fried fish by the *ración*, or kilogram, served with tortillas, mild chilli and *cebolla curtida* (pickled onion). Chicxulub is reputed to be the site of the crater made by a meteorite crash 65 million years ago, which caused the extinction of the dinosaurs. (The site is actually offshore on the ocean floor.) The beaches on this coast are often deserted and, between December and February, 'El Norte' wind blows in every 10 days or so, making the water turbid and bringing in cold, rainy weather.

Dzibilchaltún → *Colour map 5, A2.*
0800-1700, US$9. Combis to the ruins depart from Calle 58 between Calles 59 and 57.

Halfway between Mérida and Progreso turn right for the Mayan ruins of Dzibilchaltún. This unique city, according to carbon dating, was founded as early as 1000 BC. The site is in two halves, connected by a *sacbé* (sacred road). The most important building is the **Templo de Las Siete Muñecas** (Temple of the Seven Dolls), at the east end, which is partly restored. At the west end is the ceremonial centre with temples, houses and a large plaza in which the open chapel, simple and austere, sticks out like a sore thumb. The evangelizing friars had clearly hijacked a pre-Conquest sacred area in which to erect a symbol of the invading religion. At its edge is the **Cenote Xlaca** containing very clear water that is 44 m deep (you can swim in it, take mask and snorkel as it is full of fascinating fish); there's a very interesting nature trail starting halfway between the temple and the *cenote*; the trail rejoins the *sacbé* halfway along. The **museum** is at the entrance by the ticket office (site map available). *Combis* stop here en route to **Chablekal**, a village along the same road.

South to Campeche State → *Colour map 5, B1/B2.*
South of the city, 18 km away, the first place of any size is **Umán**, a henequen- (sisal-) processing town with a large 17th-century church and convent dedicated to St Francis of Assisi; there are many *cenotes* in the flat surrounding limestone plain. Further south, a turn-off leads to the turn-of-the-20th-century Moorish-style henequen hacienda at **San Bernardo**, one of a number in the state that can be visited; an interesting museum chronicling the old Yucatán Peninsula tramway system is located in its spacious grounds.

At **Maxcanú**, the road to Muná and Ticul branches east; a short way down it is the recently restored Mayan site of **Oxkintoc** ① US$3. The Pyramid of the Labyrinth can be entered (take a torch) and there are other ruins, some with figures. Ask for a guide at the village of Calcehtoc, which is 4 km from the ruins and from the Grutas de Oxkintoc (no bus service). These, however, cannot compare with the caves at Loltún or Balankanché (see pages 227 and 233).

Listings Mérida and around *map p214*

Tourist information

It's worth getting hold of a copy of the excellent free tourist magazine, *Yucatan Today*, www.yucatantoday.com, published monthly and packed with useful information about the state and its attractions. Online, *Yucatán Living*, www.yucatanliving.com, is an informative expat site with news, reviews and current events.

Municipal tourist office
Calle 62, between Calles 61 and 63, T999-942 0000, www.yucatan.travel.
In the Palacio Municipal on the Plaza Grande, this main municipal tourist office is helpful and well stocked with maps and flyers; additional modules are in the Museo de Ciudad, TAME Terminal and the Paseo Montejo.

State tourist office
Calles 60 and 62, T999-930 3101, www.yucatan.travel.
In the Palacio de Gobierno, also on the Plaza Grande, with additional branches in the Teatro José Peón Contreras and the airport.

Where to stay

Mérida
If booking into a central hotel, always try to get a room away from the street side, as noise on the narrow streets begins as early as 0500.

$$$$ Casa Lecanda
Calle 47 No 471, between Calle 54 and 56, T999-928 0112, www.casalecanda.com.
Recalls the beauty and elegance of a traditional Meridano home with handsome

interior patios and gardens. It has 7 rooms, all impeccably attired and luxurious.

$$$$ Hacienda Mérida VIP
Calle 62 No 441A, between Calle 51 and 53, T999-924 4363, www.hotelhaciendamerida.com.
An elegant art deco townhouse in the Centro Histórico, complete with pool, spa and parking. Boutique rooms have all modern amenities, artistic and tasteful furnishings, and luxurious touches such as Egyptian cotton sheets.

$$$$ Hacienda Xcanatún
Carretera Mérida–Progreso Km 12, 10 mins out of town, T999-930 2140, www.xcanatun.com.
A very elegant and carefully restored former henequen hacienda. They boast 18 sumptuous suites, spa facilities and one of the best restaurants in Mérida. Luxurious and romantic.

$$$$ Rosas & Xocolate Boutique Hotel & Spa
Paseo de Montejo No 480 and Calle 41, T999-924 2992, www.rosasandxocolate.com.
A stylish and romantic lodging with smart rooms in shades of pink, superb contemporary decor that echoes the traditional Yucatec style, excellent restaurant, and spa facilities. This boutique hotel would suit couples and hip young things.

$$$ Los Arcos
Calle 66 No 448-B, between Calle 53 and 49, T999-926 0145, www.losarcosmerida.com.
Classically elegant, **Los Arcos** is a 19th-century colonial house converted to an intimate B&B. It has rooms with high ceilings,

fantastic displays of folk art and antiques, swimming pool and verdant garden. Friendly, personable service.

$$$ Medio Mundo
Calle 55 No 533 between Calle 64 and 66, T999-924 5472, www.hotelmediomundo.com.
Renovated old home now a charming classically Yucatec hotel with 12 tasteful, high-ceiling rooms, lush garden patio and pool. Friendly, pleasant and quaint. Nice handicraft shop forms part of the hotel.

$$$-$$ Julamis
Calle 53 No 475B and Calle 54, T999-924 1818, www.hoteljulamis.com.
An award-winning B&B with stylish high-ceilinged rooms and a superb rooftop terrace, great for sipping tequila after dusk. Owner, Alex, is Swiss and a good host. A generous breakfast is included in the rates.

$$$-$$ Luz en Yucatán
Calle 55 No 499, between Calle 60 and 58, T999-924 0035, www.luzenyucatan.com.
A very welcoming, relaxed and slightly quirky 'urban retreat' with a range of comfortable rooms, studios and apartments. All have a contemporary look and good furnishings, including fridge. Outside, there's a pool and chilled-out garden. Interestingly, nightly rates vary according to your ability to pay, so those of modest means can stay too.

$$ Casa Alvarez
Calle 62 No 448 and Calle 53, T999-924 3060, www.casaalvarez guesthouse.com.
A pleasant, homely little guesthouse with a small pool and comfortable rooms, all well equipped with TV, a/c and other modern amenities. Family-run and friendly.

$$ Casa Ana
Calle 52 No 469, T999-924 0005, www.casaana.com.
A sweet little B&B with 5 rooms (a/c costs extra) and a family atmosphere, tropical garden and a small pool. Homely and quaint.

$$ Hotel del Pelegrino
Calle 51 No 488, between Calle 54 and 56, T999 924-3007 www.hoteldelperegrino.com.
This remodelled colonial house with its original tile work has 14 rooms, all different and very clean, and a outdoor terrace with a jacuzzi that's accessible at all hours. A small, friendly, family-run place, helpful and good value.

$$ Hotel Santa María
Calle 55 No 493, between Calle 58 and 56, T923-6512, www.hotelsantamariamerida.com.
A bit generic and uninspiring, but rooms are spacious, comfortable and fully equipped with cable TV, a/c and hot water. Pleasant lobby and a small pool. Modern and good value.

$$-$ Trinidad
Calle 62 No 464 esq 55, T999-923 2033, www.hotelestrinidad.com.
A bit dishevelled, but irresistibly bohemian. The lightly crumbling courtyard features trees, art work and signs reading 'don't feed the possum'. Friendly owners, a range of rooms, some much better (and more pricey) than others, the cheapest have shared bathroom. There's a 2nd **Hotel Trinidad** with a pool. Bring mosquito repellent.

$ Aventura Hotel
Calle 61 No 580, between Calle 74 and 76, T999-923 4801, www.aventurahotel merida.com.
Small, simple, basic rooms along a leafy outside corridor, peaceful, 5-min walk from the centre, well-kept and clean, excellent value with a/c, hot water, cable TV and Wi-Fi.

$ Hostal Zócalo
On the south of the plaza, T999-930 9562, www.hostalzocalo.com.
Popular hostel with economical rooms and clean dormitories. There's TV, DVD, kitchen, laundry, chilled-out balconies and sunny terraces, tours and Wi-Fi. Full breakfast buffet included with the private rooms. Friendly management and good location.

$ Nómadas Youth Hostal
Calle 62 No 433, end of Calle 51, 5 blocks north of the plaza, T999-924 5223, www.nomadas travel.com.

A sociable hostel with private rooms and dorms. General services include hot water, full kitchen, drinking water, hammocks, swimming pool and internet. Owner Raúl speaks English and is very helpful. Good value and a great place to meet other travellers. Lots of activities, including salsa, trova music, yoga and cooking classes. Bring mosquito repellent.

Celestún

Most lodgings are along Calle 12.

$$$$ Hotel Xixim
Km 10 off the old Sisal Hwy, T988-916 2100, www.hotelxixim.com.

Tranquil luxury bungalows and suites in a coconut grove on the edge of the beach and the reserve. They offer spa facilities, yoga, bicycles, kayaks, pool, and ecotours to surrounding area including flamingos, turtle nesting, etc.

$$ Gutiérrez
Calle 13 s/n, between Calles 12 and 14, T988-916 2609.

Modest and functional hotel on the beach. Rooms on top floor get ocean views and breezes. Amenities include Wi-Fi, patio and restaurant. Check the room and bed before accepting.

Progreso and around

$$ Hotel Quinta Progreso
Calle 23 No 64-C, between Calles 48 and 50, 600 m from the malecón, T969-934 4414, www.hotelquinta progreso.com.

A handsome colonial building with beautiful tile work and large, clean, tastefully decorated rooms. Amenities include swimming pool and tea bar. Prices include breakfast. Recommended.

$ Hostel Progreso
Calle 21 and 54, T969-103 0294, www.hostelprogreso.com.

This budget 2-storey restored mansion 2 blocks from the *malecón*. It has dorm beds and simple private rooms, shared kitchen, ocean-facing decks, hammocks, and breakfast included.

Restaurants

There are a number of taco stands, pizzerias and sandwich places in Pasaje Picheta, a small plaza off the Palacio de Gobierno.

$$$ Casa de Piedra
Hacienda Xcanatún, Calle 20 s/n, Carretera Mérida–Progreso Km12.

Live music Fri-Sat. Inside an old machine room with high ceiling, this award-winning restaurant serves French-Yucatec fusion, creative appetizers and mains, local seafood and meat. The place for a very romantic dinner or special occasion.

$$$ La Recova
Paseo de Montejo No 382, T999-944 0215, www.larecovamerida.com.

A popular Argentine steakhouse serving all certified 'Aberdeen Angus' and Kobe beef, huge cuts of meat, burgers and seafood. Modern and elegant interior, smart-casual and often busy. A good stock of wine.

$$$ Rosas and Xocalate
Paseo de Montejo No 480 and Calle 41, T999-924 2992, www.rosasandxocolate.com.

The place for a romantic candlelit dinner. They serve fusion cuisine by chef David Segovia, including courgette salad, catch of the day and chocolate tart, among other treats. Try the 6-course taster menu. Elegant, creative and interesting.

$$$ Trotter's
Circuito Colonias, between Paseo Montejo and Calle 60 Norte, www.trottersmerida.com.

Stylish steakhouse with a good wine list and a mouth-watering array of Angus steaks, fresh fish and tapas. Includes a smart wine bar and great ambience in the romantic garden. Classy place, sophisticated. Take a taxi.

$$$-$$ Bistro Rescoldos
Calle 62 No 366, between Calles 41 and 43, T999-286 1028, www.rescoldosbistro.com.
Bistro Rescoldos, meaning 'burning embers', serves flavourful Italian and Greek cuisine with love, including falafels, hummus, tzatziki, calzones and wood-fired pizzas. Lovely outdoor patio, wonderful atmosphere. Recommended.

$$$-$$ Chile Habanero
Calle 60 No 483B, www.elchilehabanero restaurante.com.
Good clean place with attentive staff, pleasant evening atmosphere and art work on the walls. Recommended for its Yucatec specialities, including *pollo pibil* and a good sample platter *delicias de Yucatán*. Pizzas look good, also does hamburgers.

$$$-$$ La Chaya
Calle 62 and 57, www.lachayamaya.com.
A famous and massively popular restaurant specializing in Yucatec dishes such as *poc chuc* and *pollo pibil*. Tortillas are prepared in front of diners and waitresses wear traditional clothes. Often busy and buzzing with locals and fun. Another branch on Calle 55, between Calles 60 and 62, is a larger and more atmospheric building with antique carriage, often serving big tour groups.

$$ Amaro
Calle 59 No 507 between Calle 60 and 62, near the plaza. Open late daily.
Good vegetarian food served in an open courtyard and covered patio. Try *chaya* drink from the leaf of the *chaya* tree; their curry, avocado pizza and home-made bread are also very good.

$$ El Nuevo Tucho
Calle 60 near University.
Local dishes, mostly meat and fish, and an extensive drinks menu. A rousing locals'

joint, good fun place in the evenings, often with live music. Give it a go.

$$ Manjar Blanco
Calle 47 between Calles 58 and 60.
A very pleasant family-run restaurant with a smart, clean interior. Friendly service, Yucatec specialities and 'grandmother's authentic recipes'.

$$ Pizzeria Raffaello
Calle 60 440A.
Italian-style thin-crust pizzas, many to choose from, stone-baked in an oven outside. There's seating in the garden or casual dining indoors. Relaxed place, friendly owner, good service and pizzas.

$ Cafetería Pop
Calle 57, between 60 and 62.
Low-key café attached to a hotel, they serve Mexican staples and international fare, breakfast, lunch and dinner. The *pollo con mole poblano* (chicken in chocolate and chilli sauce) is good. Clean and casual.

$ El Trapiche
Calle 62 half a block north of the plaza.
Sizzling spit of meat outside, hearty specials at lunchtime and economical grub à la carte. Staff are very friendly. Reasonable and cheap food, usually good. Sometimes a fun atmosphere in the evenings. Unpretentious.

$ Marlín Azul
Calle 62, between Calle 57 and 59.
Looks like a grotty hole in the wall, but there's an a/c section next door. Amazing fresh seafood, including fileted catch of the day and ceviche, very simple and delicious, completely local. Recommended for a quick, casual lunch.

$ Mérida
Calle 62 between Calle 59 and 61.
This economical restaurant has been in Mérida for at least 10 years, always cheap and reliable, and now with an attractive remodelled interior and smartly attired waiters. Breakfast and lunch specials are

popular with local office workers. They serve simple Yucatec and Mexican food, not bad.

Cafés and ice cream parlours

Café Chocolate
Calle 60 No 442 y Calle 49, T999-928 5113, www.cafe-chocolate.com.mx.
In addition to coffee, this café and art space does good *mole*, an economical breakfast buffet, a lunchtime menu and evening meals. Cosy and bohemian, free Wi-Fi, sofas indoors or outdoor courtyard seating.

Café El Hoyo
Calle 62, between Calle 57 and 59.
Chilled-out tea house serving refreshing fruit and herbal infusions, coffee too, good sandwiches. Literature, board games.

El Colón Sorbetes y Dulces Finos
Calle 61 and 60, on the plaza.
Serving ice cream since 1907, great sorbets, *meringue*, good menu with explanation of fruits in English. About 30 different flavours of delicious ice cream.

Celestún
Many beachside restaurants along Calle 12, but be careful of food in the cheaper ones; recommended is **La Playita**, for simple fried fish, seafood cocktails. Food stalls along Calle 11 beside the bus station should be approached with caution.

$ Chivirico
Across the road from La Playita.
Offers descent fish, shrimp and other seafood.

$$ El Lobo
Calle 10 and 13, on the corner of the main square.
Best spot for breakfast, with fruit salads, yoghurt, pancakes, etc. Celestún's best pizza in the evenings.

Progreso and around
The Malecón at Progreso is lined with seafood restaurants, some with tables on the beach. For cheaper restaurants, head for the centre of town, near the bus terminal.

$$ Flamingo's
Calle 69 No 144-D and Calle 72.
Overlooking the ocean, **Flamingo's** serves wholesome fresh seafood, including fillets and coconut shrimp, standard Yucatec fare and good hot sauce. Strolling musicians may serenade you.

$$-$ Las Palmas and El Cocalito
2 of several reasonable fish restaurants in Chelem.

Bars and clubs

See also the free listings magazine *Yucatán Today.*

Cantina La Negrita
Calle 62 and 49 No 415.
Neighbourhood bohemian bar with lots of history, founded 1918. Buzzing, good crowd, fun vibe. Drinking up front, hearty food available out back. Modern and young, not a *cantina* in the traditional sense. Recommended.

Hennessy's Irish Pub
Paseo Montejo No 486-A, between 41 and 43.
Remarkably authentic Irish pub in a fantastic building on the Paseo Montejo, a social hub for the city's expatriates. Good cold beer, expensive food.

Mayan Pub
Calle 62, between Calles 55 and 57, www. mayanpub.com. Wed-Sun 0700-0300.
Superb outdoor colonial patio with ambient lighting, live music, jam sessions, Banksy wall art, beer, tequila, happy hours, snacks.

Entertainment

See the free listings magazine *Yucatán Today.*

Cinema
There is a cinema showing subtitled films in English on Parque Hidalgo.

Teatro Mérida, Calle 62 between 59 and 61, shows European, Mexican and independent movies as well as live theatre productions. The 14-screen multiplex **Cinépolis** is in the huge Plaza de las Américas, north of the city; *colectivo* and buses take 20 mins and leave from Calle 65 between 58 and 60. For art house films, head to the intimate **Cairo Cinema Café**, Calle 20 No. 98A between Calles 15 and 17, Col Itzimná (take a taxi), www.cairocinemacafe.com.

Theatre
There are many fine playhouses in Mérida, including:

Teatro Peón Contreras
Calle 60 with 57.
One of the most beautiful theatres in Mexico, showing plays, ballet and orchestral performances. Shows start at 2100. For the latest programme, see www.merida.gob.mx/cultura.

Festivals

The city lays on a weekly programme of free cultural events. On Mon at 2100, there is a *vaquería*, with traditional Yucatec dancing, outside the Palacio Municipal; Tue at 2030, big band music in Parque de Santiago; Wed at 2100, a concert in the Centro Cultural Olimpio; Thu at 2100, Yucatec music, dance and song in the Parque Santa Lucía; Fri, usually an event in the University building, but not always; Sat at 2100, the 'Heart of Mérida' festival on the plaza and Calle 60; Sun, the central streets are closed to traffic, the plaza comes alive with music, performances and stalls.

6 Jan Mérida celebrates its birthday.
Feb/Mar Carnival takes place the week before Ash Wed (best on Sat). Floats, dancers in regional costume, music and dancing around the plaza and children dressed in animal suits.

Shopping

Crafts and souvenirs
You'll find an abundance of craft shops in the streets around the plaza. They sell hammocks (see box, page 175), silver jewellery, Panama hats, *guayabera* shirts, *huaraches*, baskets and Mayan figurines. The salesmen are ruthless, but they expect to receive about half their original asking price. Bargain hard, but maintain good humour, patience and face. And watch out for the many touts around the plaza, using all sorts of ingenious ploys to get you to their shops (and away from their competitors).

There are 2 main craft markets in the city: the **Mercado Municipal**, Calle 56a and 67 and the **García Rejón Bazaar**, Calle 65 and 60. The former sprawls, smells and takes over several blocks, but it's undeniably alive and undeniably Mexican. It sells everything under the sun and is also good for a cheap, tasty meal, but check the stalls for cleanliness. The latter is excellent for handicrafts and renowned for clothing, particularly leather *huaraches* and good-value cowboy boots – good, cheap Yucatecan fare. The state-sponsored **Casa de las Artesanías**, www.artesanias. yucatan.gob.mx, has several branches around the Yucatán, including **Tienda Matriz**, Calle 63 between Calle 64 and 66, and **Tienda Montejo**, Av Paseo de Montejo, opposite the Palacio Cantón; they sell everything from hammocks to *huipiles*, all made in the Yucatán, and provide social and economic programmes to support local artistic talent. For something special, **Artesanaria**, Calle 60 No 480 and Calle 55, deals in high-quality work.

If you're looking for a hammock, several places are recommended, but shop around for the best deal (also see box, page 175). **El Mayab**, Calle 58 No 553 and 71, are friendly, have a limited choice but good deals available; **La Poblana**, Calle 65 between Calle 58 and 60, will bargain, especially for sales of more than 1 – they have a huge stock. **El Aguacate**, Calle 58 No 604, corner of Calle 73, good hammocks and no hard sell. Recommended. **Casa de Artesanías Ki-Huic**, Calle 63, between Calle 62 and 64, is a friendly store with all sorts of handicrafts from silver and wooden masks, to hammocks and batik. Shop owner Julio Chay is very knowledgeable and friendly, sometimes organizes trips for visitors to his village, **Tixkokob**, which specializes in hammocks. Open daily, 0900-2100. Julio can also organize trips to other nearby villages and the shop has tequilas for sampling.

For silver, there are a handful of stores on Calle 60, just north of the plaza.

Mexican folk art, including *calaveras* (Day of the Dead skeletons), is available from **Minaturas**, Calle 59 No 507A; and **Yalat**, Calle 39 and 40.

If you're in the market for a *guayabera* shirt, you'll find stores all over the city, particularly on Calle 62, between 57 and 61.

What to do

Tour operators
Most tour operators can arrange trips to popular local destinations including Chichén Itzá, Uxmal, Celestún and nearby *cenotes*. **Carmen Travel Services**, *Calle 27 No 151, between 32 and 34, T999-927 2027, www. carmentravel.com*. 3 other branches. This well-established agency can organize flights, hotels and all the usual trips to the sights. Recommended.

Language schools

Centro de Idiomas del Sureste, Calle 52 No 455, between 49 and 51, T999-923 0954, www.cisyucatan.com.mx. A well-established Spanish school offering tried and tested language and cultural programmes.
Modern Spanish Institute, Calle 15, No 500B, between 16A and 18, T999-911 0790, www.modernspanish.com. Courses in Spanish, Mayan culture, homestays.

Ecoturismo Yucatán, *Calle 3 No 235, between Calle 32A and 34, T999-920 2772, www.ecoyuc.com.mx*. Specializes in educational and ecotourism tours including jungle trips, birding expeditions and turtle-hatching tours. Also offers adventure and archaeological packages.
Mayan Ecotours, *Calle 51 No 488 between Calles 54 and 56, T999-987 3710, www.mayan ecotours.com*. An adventure and ecotourism operator offering high-quality tailor-made tours focussed on a variety of adrenalin-charged activities including rappelling, kayaking and mountain biking. They also offer trips to haciendas, archaeological sites and little-known *cenotes*.

Transport

Air
The airport is 8 km from the city. Bus 79 takes you to the centre; taxis to the centre charge US$12.

From Calle 67, 69 and 60, bus 79 goes to the airport, **Aeropuerto Rejón (MID)**, T999-946 1530, marked 'Aviación', US$0.50, roughly every 20 mins. Taxi set price voucher system US$8; *colectivo* US$2.50. Good domestic flight connections. International flight connections with **Belize City**, **Houston**, **Miami**, San José (Costa Rica), Orlando and **Havana**. Package tours Mérida–Havana–Mérida available (be sure to have a confirmed return flight). For return to Mexico ask for details at Secretaría de Migración Av Colón and Calle 8.

Bus
All buses from outside Yucatán State arrive at the CAME terminal on Calle 70 between Calle 69 and 71, several blocks south of the centre. There is a 2nd-class bus terminal, **TAME**, around the corner on Calle 69, where buses from local destinations such as Uxmal arrive.

There are several bus terminals in Mérida, as well as various *combis* for some local destinations (often more rapid).

The 1st-class bus station, **Terminal CAME**, Calle 70, between Calles 69 and 71, serves major destinations in Mexico and Yucatán State. Bus companies include **ADO**, **ADO GL**, **UNO**, **Platino** and **OCC**. The station has lockers and is open 24 hrs; left luggage charges from around US$0.50 per bag, depending on size. The walk to the centre is about 20 mins, taxi US$2.50. Schedules change frequently.

To **Cancún**, hourly, 4 hrs, US$24. To **Campeche**, hourly, 2 hrs, US$14. To **Chichén Itzá** (ruins and Pisté), 0630, 0915, 1240, 2 hrs, US$9; more frequent services from the 2nd-class Terminal TAME. To **Palenque**, 0830, 1915, 2200, 2300, 8 hrs, US$37. To **Tulum**, 1040, 1240, 1740, 2340, 4-5 hrs, US$20. To **Valladolid**, every 1-2 hrs, 1½ hrs, US$13. To **Villahermosa**, every 1-2 hrs, 9 hrs, US$43; and several **ADO GL** services, US$52. To **Tuxtla Guitérrez**, 5 daily with **OCC** and **ADO GL**, US$57-79. To **San Cristóbal de las Casas**, 1 daily with **OCC**, 1915, 15-16 hrs, US$52.

There are also 1st-class departures from the Hotel Fiesta Americana, Calle 60 and Colón, which are mostly 'luxury' services to **Cancún**.

Around the corner from CAME, the main 2nd-class bus station, **TAME Terminal**, Calle 69 between Calles 68 and 70, mostly serves destinations in the Yucatán Peninsula, including Uxmal, Chichén Itzá and the Ruta Puuc. Bus companies include **OCC**, **Mayab**, **Sur**, **FTS**, **Oriente** and **TRT**.

To **Cancún**, frequent departures, 5 hrs, US$15. To **Chichén Itzá**, hourly, 2-3 hrs, US$5.50. To **Ruta Puuc**, 2nd-class **ATS** service, Sun 0800, US$14. To **Uxmal**, 2nd-class **SUR** services at 0600, 0905, 1040, 1205, 1705, 1½ hrs, US$3.50. To **Valladolid**, hourly, 2 hrs, US$7.50

There is another 2nd-class terminal, **Terminal del Noreste**, near the market at Calle 50 and 65. It deals with obscure local destinations, including villages on the convent route, 11 departures daily, including **Acanceh**, **Tekit**, **Tecoh**, **Mamá**, **Chumayel**, **Teabo**, **Tipikal**, **Mani** and **Oxckutzcab**,

US$1.25-3.60. To **Celestún**, frequent 2nd-class **Oriente** services, 2 hrs, US$3.50.

Buses to **Progreso** depart every 15 mins, US$1.25, from their own Autoprogreso terminal at Calle 62 No 524, between 65 and 67. For **Izamal**, it is fastest to use the *combis* that depart from Calles 65 and 54, 1 hr, US$3.50.

To Guatemala Take a bus from Mérida to San Cristóbal and change there for Comitán, or to Tenosique for the route to Flores. Another alternative would be to take the bus from Mérida direct to Tuxtla Gutiérrez (times given above), then connect to Ciudad Cuauhtémoc or to Tapachula.

To Belize Take a bus to **Chetumal**, **ADO** services at 0730 (except Wed and Sat), 1300, 1800, 2300, 6 hrs, US$30.50 and cross the border.

Car

Car hire Car reservations should be booked well in advance if possible. Hire firms charge around US$45-50 a day although bargains can be found in low season. All agencies allow vehicles to be returned to Cancún for an extra charge, and most have an office at the airport where they share the same counter and negotiating usually takes place. Agencies include: **Budget**, at the airport, T999-946 0762; **Easy Way Car Rental**, Calle 60, between 55 and 57, T999-930 9021, www.easywayrentacar-yucatan.com; **Mexico Rent a Car**, Calle 57A Depto 12, between 58 and 60, T999-923 3637, mexicorentacar@hotmail.com.

Taxi

Both fixed-priced and metered taxis are available. Metered taxis are identified by a 'Taximetro' sign on the roof; if using an unmetered taxi, always arrange the price beforehand. Most fares start at US$3.

There are various *sitio* stands, including **Sitio Santa Ana**, Calle 47 between Calle 58 and 60, T999-928 5000, www.taxiyturismo.com. Sample fares from downtown to Terminal CAME, US$4; to Gran Museo del

Mundo Maya, US$5.50; to airport, US$11.50, to Hacienda Xcanatún, US$11.50; to Dzibilchaltún, US$15.

Celestún
Bus
Buses leave every 1-2 hrs from the local bus station on Calle 65 between 50 and 52, in **Mérida**, 2-hr journey, 2nd class US$3.50.

Progreso and around
Boat
Boats can be hired to visit the reef of **Los Alacranes** where many ancient wrecks are visible in clear water.

Bus
Buses from **Mérida** leave from the terminal on Calle 62 between 67 and 65, next to Hotel La Paz, every 10 mins. US$1.25. Returns every 10 mins until 2200.

Dzibilchaltún
Bus
5 direct buses a day on weekdays, from Parque San Juan, marked 'Tour/Ruta Polígono'; returns from the site entrance on the hour, passing the junction 15 mins later, taking 45 mins from the junction to **Mérida** (US$1).

Shuttles Leave from Parque San Juan in Mérida, corner of Calle 62 y 67A, every 1 or 2 hrs between 0500 and 1900.

The Convent Route → Colour map 5, B2.
Mayan villages and ruins, colonial churches, cathedrals, convents and cenotes

For this route it's best to be on the road by 0800 with a full fuel tank. It's possible to explore the route using public transport (departures from the Noreste terminal on Calle 50), but keep an eye on the clock (few or no buses after dark) and consider overnighting in Ticul or Oxkutzcab. If driving, get on the Periférico to Ruta 18 (signs say Kanasín, not Ruta 18).

At **Kanasín**, La Susana is known especially for local delicacies like *sopa de lima*, *salbutes* and *panuchos;* it's clean, and there is excellent service and abundant helpings at reasonable prices. Follow the signs to **Acanceh**. Here you will see the unusual combination of the Grand Pyramid, a colonial church and a modern church, all on the same small plaza (similar to the Plaza de las Tres Culturas in Tlatelolco, Mexico City). About four blocks away is the Temple of the Stuccoes, with hieroglyphs. Eight kilometres further south is **Tecoh**, with an ornate church and convent dedicated to the Virgin of the Assumption. There are some impressive carved stones around the altar. The church and convent both stand at the base of a large Mayan pyramid. Nearby are the caverns of **Dzab-Náh**; you must take a guide as there are treacherous drops into *cenotes*. Next on the route is **Telchaquillo**, a small village with an austere chapel and a beautiful *cenote* in the plaza, with carved steps for easy access.

Mayapán and around
US$2.70.

A few kilometres off the main road to the right (west) you will find the Mayan ruins of Mayapán, a walled city with 4000 mounds, six of which are in varying stages of restoration. Mayapán, along with Uxmal and Chichén Itzá, once formed a triple alliance, and the site is as big as Chichén Itzá, with some buildings being replicas of those at the latter site. The restoration process is ongoing; the archaeologists can be watched as they unearth more and more buildings of this large, peaceful, late-Maya site. Mayapán is easily visited by bus from Mérida (every 30 minutes from terminal at Calle 50 y 67 behind the municipal market, one hour, US$1 to Telchaquillo). It can also be reached from Oxcutzcab.

Some 30 km along the main road is **Tekit**, a large village containing the church of San Antonio de Padua, with many ornate statues of saints. The next village, 7 km further on, is called **Mama**, with the oldest church on the route, famous for its ornate altar and bell-domed roof. Another 9 km is **Chumayel**, where the legendary Mayan document *Chilam Balam* was found. Four kilometres ahead is **Teabo**, with an impressive 17th-century church. Next comes **Tipikal**, a small village with an austere church.

Maní

Twelve kilometres further on is Maní, the most important stop on this route. Here you will find a large church, convent and museum with explanations in English, Spanish and one of the Mayan languages. It was here that Fray Diego de Landa ordered important Mayan documents and artefacts to be burned, during an intense period of Franciscan conversion of the Maya people to Christianity. When Diego realized his great error, he set about trying to write down all he could remember of the 27 scrolls and hieroglyphs he had destroyed, along with 5000 idols, 13 altars and 127 vases. The text, entitled *Relation of Things in Yucatán*, is still available today, unlike the artefacts. To return to Mérida, head for Ticul, to the west, then follow the main road via Muná.

Ticul and Oxkutzcab

Eighty kilometres south of Mérida, Ticul is a small, pleasant little village known for its *huipiles*, the embroidered white dresses worn by the older Maya women. You can buy them in the tourist shops in Mérida, but the prices and quality of the ones in Ticul will be much better. It is also a good base for visiting smaller sites in the south of Yucatán State, such as Sayil, Kabah, Xlapak and Labná (see page 229).

Sixteen kilometres southeast of Ticul is **Oxkutzcab**, a good centre for catching buses to Chetumal, Muná, Mayapán and Mérida. It's a friendly place with a market by the plaza and a church with a 'two-dimensional' façade on the other side of the square.

Grutas de Loltún and around
Tue-Sun 0930, 1100, 1230 and 1400. US$8 Guided tours are at 0930, 1100, 1230, 1400, 1500, 1600; please tip generously.

Nearby, to the south, are the caverns and pre-Columbian vestiges at Loltún (supposedly extending for 8 km). Take a pickup (US$0.30) or truck from the market going to Cooperativa (an agricultural town). For return, flag down a passing truck. Alternatively, take a taxi, US$10 (can be visited from Labná on a tour from Mérida). The area around Ticul and Oxkutzcab is intensively farmed with citrus fruits, papayas and mangoes. After Oxkutzcab on Route 184 is **Tekax** with restaurant **La Ermita** serving excellent Yucatecan dishes at reasonable prices. From Tekax a paved road leads to the ruins of **Chacmultún**. From the top you have a beautiful view. There is a caretaker. All the towns between Muná and Peto, 14 km northeast of Oxkutzcab off Route 184, have large old churches. Beyond the Peto turn-off the scenery is scrub and swamp as far as the Belizean border.

Where to stay

Ticul

$$-$ Posada El Jardín
Calle 27 No 216c, between Calles 28 and 30,
T997-972 0401, www.posadajardin.com.
Sweet little guesthouse with a handful of
simple, economical, brightly painted rooms,
a verdant garden, relaxing patios and a pool.
Charming hosts.

Oxkutzcab

$$-$ Hotel Puuc
Calle 55 No 80 and Calle 40, 997-975 0103
www.hotelpuuc.com.mx.
Convenient, functional and modest
motel-style lodgings, but very clean and
comfortable. There's a splendid pool, a
restaurant and parking. Rooms are cheaper
without a/c.

Restaurants

Ticul

$$$-$$ Tutul-Xiu
Calle 29 No 191, between Calles 20 and 22.
Good-quality Yucatec and Mexican cuisine,
including *poc chuc*, *queso relleno* and a host
of turkey dishes, served by waitresses in
traditional Yucatec dress. Also branches in
Oxkutzcab, Maní and Mérida.

$$ Pizzería La Góndola
Calle 23, Ticul.
Good, moderately priced pizzas.

Transport

Ticul and Oxkutzcab
Colectivo
There are frequent VW *colectivos* to Ticul
from Parque San Juan, **Mérida**, US$3.

The Puuc Route → *Colour map 5, B2.*

hilly Mayan route south of Mérida

Taking in the four sites of Kabah, Sayil, Xlapak and Labná, as well as Uxmal, this
journey explores the hilly (or *puuc* in Maya) region to the south of Mérida. All five sites
can be visited in a day on the 'Ruta Puuc' bus, which departs from the first-class bus
station in Mérida on Sunday at 0800, US$14, entry to sites not included, returns from
Uxmal to Mérida at 1500. This is a good whistle-stop tour, but does not give you much
time at each of the ruins, although five sites in one day is normally enough for most
enthusiasts; if you want to spend longer seeing these sites, stay overnight in Ticul.

Kabah
0800-1700, US$3.25.

On either side of the main road, 37 km south of Uxmal and often included in tours of the
latter, are the ruins of Kabah. On one side there is a fascinating **Palace of Masks** (*Codz-
Poop*), whose façade bears the image of Chac, mesmerically repeated 260 times, the
number of days in the Almanac Year. Each mask is made up of 30 units of mosaic stone.
Even the central chamber is entered via a huge Chac mask whose curling snout forms
the doorstep. On the other side of this wall, beneath the figure of the ruler, Kabal, are
impressive carvings on the door arches, which depict a man about to be killed, pleading
for mercy, and two men duelling. This side of the road is mostly reconstructed; across the
road the outstanding feature is a reconstructed arch marking the start of the *sacbé* (sacred

road), which leads all the way to Uxmal, and several stabilized but impossible to climb mounds of collapsed buildings being renovated. The style is Classic Puuc.

Sayil, Xlapak and Labná
Entrance US$3.25 at each site.

Sayil means 'The Place of the Ants'. Dating from AD 800-1000, this site has an interesting palace, which in its day included 90 bathrooms for some 350 people. The simple, elegant colonnade is reminiscent of the architecture of ancient Greece. The central motif on the upper part of the façade is a broad mask with huge fangs, flanked by two serpents surrounding the grotesque figure of a descending deity. From the upper level of the palace you can see a tiny ruin on the side of a mountain called the Nine Masks.

Some 13 km from Sayil, the ruins of **Xlapak** have not been as extensively restored as the others in this region. There are 14 mounds and three partially restored pyramids.

Labná has a feature that ranks it among the most outstanding sites of the Puuc region: a monumental arch connecting two groups of buildings (now in ruins), which displays an architectural concept unique to this region. Most Mayan arches are purely structural, but the one at Labná has been constructed for aesthetic purposes, running right through the façade and clearly meant to be seen from afar. The two façades on either side of the arch differ greatly; the one at the entrance is beautifully decorated with delicate latticework and stone carving imitating the wood or palm-frond roofs of Mayan huts.

Uxmal
Daily 0800-1700, US$14 including light and sound show; rental of translation equipment US$3. Shows are at 2000 in summer and 1900 in winter. Mixed reports. Guides available with 1½-hr tours. Tours in Spanish US$40, in English, French, German and Italian US$45. For transport to Uxmal, see Transport, below.

Built during the Classic period, Uxmal is the most famous of the ruins in the Puuc region. The characteristic features of Mayan cities in this region are the quadrangular layout of the buildings, set on raised platforms, and an artificially created underground water-storage system. The **Pyramid of the Sorcerer** is an unusual oval-shaped pyramid set on a large rectangular base; there is evidence that five stages of building were used in its construction. The pyramid is 30 m tall, with two temples at the top. The **Nunnery** is set around a large courtyard, with some fine masks of Chac, the rain god, on the corners of the buildings. The east building of the Nunnery is decorated with double-headed serpents on its cornices. There are some plumed serpents in relief, in excellent condition, on the façade of the west building.

The **House of the Governor** is 100 m long, and is considered one of the most outstanding buildings in all of Mesoamerica. Two arched passages divide the building into three distinct sections that would probably have been covered over. Above the central entrance is an elaborate trapezoidal motif, with a string of Chaac masks interwoven into a flowing, undulating serpent-like shape extending to the façade's two corners. The stately two-headed jaguar throne in front of the structure suggests a royal or administrative function.

The **House of the Turtles** is sober by comparison, its simple walls adorned with carved turtles on the upper cornice, above a short row of tightly packed columns, which resemble the Mayan *palapas*, made of sticks with a thatched roof, still used today. The **House of the Doves** is the oldest and most damaged of the buildings at Uxmal. It is still impressive: a long, low platform of wide columns topped by clusters of roof combs, whose similarity to dovecotes gave the building its name.

Where to stay

Uxmal
There is no village at Uxmal, just some high end hotels. For cheap accommodation, go to Ticul, 28 km away (see above) or to Santa Elena, 10 mins from the ruins by car.

$$$$ The Lodge at Uxmal
30 m from the entrance to ruins, T997-976 2102, www.mayaland.com/lodgeuxmal.
Luxurious Mayan-style *casitas* with tasteful wood furniture. Facilities include pool, restaurants, and spa. The same owners operate the comfortable **Hacienda Uxmal** ($$$), 400 m from the ruins (see website for more).

$$$-$$ The Fly-catcher Inn
Near the corner of Highway 261 and Calle 20, Santa Elena, T997-978 5350, www.flycatcherinn.com.
Pleasant B&B with verdant grounds and clean, comfortable rooms and *casitas* with a/c and screened windows. Prices include full breakfast.

$$ The Pickled Onion B&B
Highway 261 Uxmal–Kabah, Santa Elena, T997-111 7922, www.thepickledonion yucatan.com.
Friendly and helpful B&B with quaint Mayan-style accommodation, leafy garden and a pool. Rooms are simple, clean, comfortable and pleasant. Reiki and massage are available, there's Wi-Fi in public areas and a continental breakfast is included.

$$-$ Sacbé Bungalows
Highway 261 Km 159, Santa Elena, T997-978 5158, www.sacbebungalows.com.mx.
Set in 3 ha of verdant grounds, Sacbé Bungalows offers 8 simple, comfortable, clean, quiet and shaded bungalows. There's Wi-Fi and a pool.

Transport

Uxmal
Bus
5 buses a day from **Mérida**, from the terminal on Calle 69 between Calle 68 and 70, US$4. Return buses run every 2 hrs, or go to the entrance to the site on the main road and wait for a *colectivo*, which will take you to Muná for US$0.50. From there, many buses (US$1.70) and *colectivos* (US$1.40) go to Mérida.

Car
Parking at the site costs US$1 for the whole day. Uxmal is 74 km from **Mérida**, 177 km from **Campeche**, by a good paved road. If going by car from Mérida, there is a circular road round the city: follow the signs to Campeche, then 'Campeche via ruinas', then to 'Muná via Yaxcopoil' (long stretch of road with no signposting). Muná–Yaxcopoil is about 34 km. Parking US$1.

Some 68 km east of Mérida is Izamal. Once a major Classic Maya religious site founded by the priest Itzamná, Izamal became one of the centres of the Spanish attempt to convert the Maya to Christianity.

Fray Diego de Landa, the historian of the Spanish conquest of Mérida (of whom there is a statue in the town), founded the huge **convent** and **church**, which now face the main **Plaza de la Constitución**. This building, constructed on top of a Mayan pyramid, was begun in 1549 and has the second largest atrium in the world. If you carefully examine the walls that surround the magnificent atrium, you will notice that some of the faced stones are embellished with carvings of Mayan origin, confirming that, when they had toppled the pre-Columbian structures, the Spaniards re-used the material to create the imported architecture. There is also a throne built for the Pope's visit in 1993. The image of the Inmaculada Virgen de la Concepción in the magnificent church was made the Reina de Yucatán in 1949, and the patron saint of the state in 1970.

Just 2½ blocks away, visible from the convent across a second square and signposted, are the ruins of a great mausoleum known as the **Kinich-Kakmo pyramid** ① *0800-1700, free, entrance next to the tortilla factory.* You climb the first set of stairs to a broad, tree-covered platform, at the end of which is a further pyramid (still under reconstruction). From the top there is an excellent view of the town and surrounding henequen and citrus plantations. Kinich-Kakmo is 195 m long, 173 m wide and 36 m high, the fifth highest in Mexico.

In all, 20 Mayan structures have been identified in Izamal, several on Calle 27. Another startling feature about the town is that the entire colonial centre, including the convent, the arcaded government offices on Plaza de la Constitución and the arcaded second square, is painted a rich yellow ochre, giving it the nickname of the 'golden city'.

From Izamal you can go by bus to **Cenotillo**, where there are several fine *cenotes* within easy walking distance from the town (avoid the one in town), especially **Ucil**, excellent for swimming, and **La Unión**. Take the same bus as for Izamal from Mérida. Past Cenotillo is Espita and then a road forks left to Tizimín (see page 238).

The cemetery of **Hoctún**, on the Mérida–Chichén road, is also worth visiting; indeed it is impossible to miss, there is an 'Empire State Building' on the site. Take a bus from Mérida (last bus back 1700) to see extensive ruins at **Aké**, an unusual structure. Public transport in Mérida is difficult: from an unsigned stop on the corner of Calle 53 y 50, some buses to Tixkokob and Ekmul continue to Aké; ask the driver.

Listings Izamal

Where to stay

$$ Macan Ché
Calle 22 No 305 between Calle 33 and 35, T988-954 0287, www.macanche.com.
Intimate and friendly B&B with a lush tropical garden setting, pool, restaurant and hammocks. They offer comfortable rooms and *casitas*, all uniquely decorated. Recommended.

Restaurants

There are several restaurants on Plaza de la Constitución.

$$$-$$ Kinich

Calle 27 No 299 between Calle 28 and 30,
www.kinichizamal.com.

Kinich serves very good Mexican and
Yucatec cuisine in an open-air colonial
courtyard. Rustic ambience and good
service. It's located near the ruins of the
same name.

$$-$ Los Arcos

Calle 28, between Calles 31 and 34,
opposite Parque Zamná.

Simple and reasonably priced little eatery
on the plaza serving wholesome tacos,
quesadillas and other Mexican fare.
Wi-Fi, breakfast and coffee too.

Shopping

Hecho a mano, *Calle 31A No 308 between 36
and 38*. A fine collection of Mexican
folk art, postcards, textiles, jewellery,
papier-mâché masks.
Market, *Calle 31, on Plaza de la Constitución,
opposite convent*. Closes soon after lunch.

Transport

Bus

Bus station is on Calle 32 behind government
offices, can leave bags, but better to
take the *combi*, every 30 mins, US$4. 2nd
class to **Mérida**, every 45 mins, 1½ hrs,
US$1.50, lovely countryside. 6 a day to/from
Valladolid (96 km), about 2 hrs, US$2.30-3.

Chichén Itzá → *Colour map 5, B4.*

one of the most spectacular Mayan sites

★Chichén Itzá means 'mouth of the well of the water-sorcerer'. The Castillo, a
giant-stepped pyramid, overlooks the site, watched over by Chacmool, a Maya
fertility god who reclines on a nearby structure. The city was built by the Maya in
late Classic times (AD 600-900). By the end of the 10th century, the city was more
or less abandoned. It was re-established in the 11th to 12th centuries, but much
debate surrounds by whom. Whoever the people were, a comparison of some of
the architecture with that of Tula, north of Mexico City, indicates they were heavily
influenced by the Toltecs of Central Mexico.

The major buildings in the north half display a Toltec influence. Dominating them is
El Castillo ① *1100-1500, 1600-1700, closed if raining*, its top decorated by the symbol of
Quetzalcoatl/Kukulcán, the plumed serpent god. The balustrade of the 91 stairs up each
of the four sides is also decorated at its base by the head of a plumed, open-mouthed
serpent. The interior ascent of 61 steep and narrow steps leading to a chamber is currently
closed; the red-painted jaguar that probably served as the throne of the high priest once
burned bright, its eyes of jade, its fangs of flint.

There is a **ball court** with grandstand and towering walls, each set with a projecting
ring of stone high up; at eye-level is a relief showing the decapitation of the winning
captain (sacrifice was an honour; some theories, however, maintain that it was the
losing captain who was killed). El Castillo stands at the centre of the northern half of
the site, and almost at a right angle to its northern face runs the *sacbé* (sacred road), to
the **Cenote Sagrado** (Well of Sacrifice). Into the Cenote Sagrado were thrown valuable
propitiatory objects of all kinds, animals and human sacrifices. The well was first
dredged by Edward H Thompson, the US Consul in Mérida, between 1904 and 1907;
he accumulated a vast quantity of objects in pottery, jade, copper and gold. In 1962
the well was explored again by an expedition sponsored by the National Geographic

Essential Chichén Itzá

Entry fees

US$14 including light and sound show, free bag storage, free for Mexicans on Sun and holidays, when it is incredibly crowded; you may leave and reenter as often as you like on day of issue.

Tours

Guided tours US$40 per group of any size; it is best to try and join one, many languages available.

Opening hours

Daily 0800-1730. It's best to arrive before 1030 to beat the crowds.

Facilities

The tourist centre at the entrance to the ruins has a restaurant and small museum, bookshop and souvenir shop with exchange facilities. Drinks, snacks and toilets are available at the entrance and at the *cenote*.

What to take

Take a hat, suncream, sunglasses, shoes with good grip and drinking water.

Tip...

On the morning and afternoon of the spring and autumn equinoxes, the alignment of the sun's shadow casts a serpentine image on the side of the steps of El Castillo.

Society and some 4000 further artefacts were recovered, including beads, polished jade, lumps of *copal* resin, small bells, a statuette of rubber latex, another of wood, and a quantity of animal and human bones. Another *cenote*, the Cenote Xtoloc, was probably used as a water supply. To the east of El Castillo is the **Templo de los Guerreros** (Temple of the Warriors) with its famous reclining **Chacmool** statue. This pyramidal platform is closed off to avoid erosion.

Chichén Viejo (Old Chichén), where the Mayan buildings of the earlier city are found, lies about 500 m by path from the main clearing. The famous **El Caracol**, or Observatory, is included in this group, as is the **Casa de las Monjas** (Nunnery). A footpath to the right of the Casa de las Monjas leads to the **Templo de los Tres Dinteles** (Temple of the Three Lintels) after 30 minutes' walking. It requires at least one day to see the many pyramids, temples, ball courts and palaces, all of them adorned with astonishing sculptures. Excavation and renovation is still going on. Interesting birdlife and iguanas can also be seen around the ruins.

Grutas de Balankanché

0900-1700, US$7.50 (allow about 45 mins for the 300-m descent), closed Sat afternoons. Guided tours in English at 1100, 1300, 1500; in Spanish at 0900, 1000, 1100, 1200, 1300.

Tours run daily to the Grutas de Balankanché caves, 3 km east of Chichén Itzá just off the highway. There are archaeological objects, including offerings of pots and *metates* in an extraordinary setting, except for the unavoidable, awful *son et lumière* show (five a day in Spanish; 1100, 1300 and 1500 in English; 1000 in French; it is very damp and hot, so dress accordingly). To get there, take the Chichén Itzá or Pisté-Balankanché bus hourly at a quarter past, US$0.50, taxi US$15.

Chichén Itzá

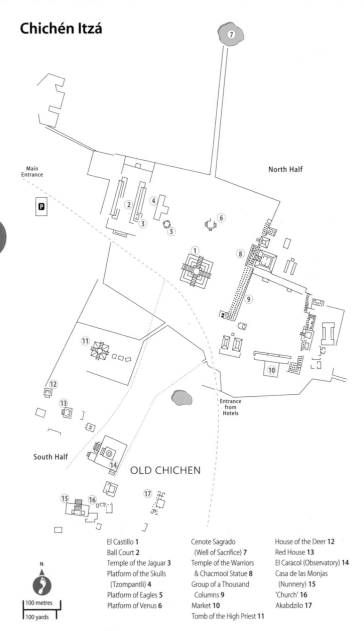

Main Entrance

North Half

South Half

OLD CHICHEN

Entrance from Hotels

El Castillo **1**
Ball Court **2**
Temple of the Jaguar **3**
Platform of the Skulls
  (Tzompantli) **4**
Platform of Eagles **5**
Platform of Venus **6**

Cenote Sagrado
  (Well of Sacrifice) **7**
Temple of the Warriors
  & Chacmool Statue **8**
Group of a Thousand
  Columns **9**
Market **10**
Tomb of the High Priest **11**

House of the Deer **12**
Red House **13**
El Caracol (Observatory) **14**
Casa de las Monjas
  (Nunnery) **15**
'Church' **16**
Akabdzilo **17**

N

100 metres
100 yards

Where to stay

$$$$ Hacienda Chichén
T999-924 8407, www.haciendachichen.com.
Luxury resort and spa, close to the ruins, with tasteful rooms, suites and bungalows. There's a garden, library and restaurant, all contained in historic colonial grounds.

$$$-$$ Hotel Chichén Itzá
Pisté, T999-851 0022, www.mayaland.com.
Large hotel with 3 types of rooms and tariffs. The best are clean, tasteful, overlook the garden and have a/c, internet, phone and fridge. Cheaper rooms overlook the street.

$$$-$$ Villas Arqueológicas
T997-974 6020, Carretera Mérida–Valladolid Km 120, Piste, www.villasarqueologicas. com.mx, 800 m from the ruins.
A large hotel with a tropical garden, small pool, book collection, and 45 clean and comfortable rooms. The restaurant is on the expensive side, beds are quite firm, but otherwise a tranquil and pleasant lodging.

$$ Dolores Alba Chichén
Km 122, T985-858 1555, www.doloresalba.com.
Small, Spanish-owned hotel, 2.5 km on the road to Puerto Juárez (bus passes it), 40 clean if old bungalows with shower, a/c and cable TV. Pool, restaurant, English is spoken, free morning shuttle to the ruins.

$$-$ Pirámide Inn Resort
1.5 km from ruins, at the Chichén end of Pisté, Km 117, T999-851 0115, www.chichen.com.
Economical and functional Pisté option with many clean, colourful rooms, a pool, hammocks and *palapas. Temazcal* available, book 24 hrs in advance. Camping costs US$5, or US$15 with a car. Friendly owner, speaks English.

Restaurants

Mostly poor and overpriced in Chichén itself (cafés inside the ruins are cheaper than the restaurant at the entrance, but still expensive). You can also try the larger hotels. Barbecued chicken is available on the streets of Pisté, sit-down restaurants close 2100-2200.

$$ Fiesta Maya
Calle 15 No 59, Pisté.
Reportedly the best restaurant in town. Serves Yucatecan food, tacos, meat and sandwiches. Lunch buffet every day at 1200, US$10.

$ Sayil
In Pisté.
Serves Yucatecan dishes like *pollo pibil*, as well as breakfast *huevos al gusto.*

Festivals

21 Mar and 21 Sep On the morning and afternoon of the spring and autumn equinoxes, the alignment of the sun's shadow casts a serpentine image on the side of the steps of El Castillo. This occasion is popular and you'll be lucky to get close enough to see the action. Note that this phenomenon can also be seen on the days before and after the equinox, 19th-23rd of the month.

Transport

ADO bus office in Pisté is between Stardust and Pirámide Inn. Budget travellers going on from Mérida to Isla Mujeres or Cozumel should visit Chichén from Valladolid (see below), although if you plan to go through in a day you can store luggage at the visitor centre.

Bus
Frequent 2nd-class buses depart from Mérida to Cancún, passing Chichén Itzá and

Pisté. Likewise, there are frequent departures to/from Valladolid. To **Mérida**, 2nd class, hourly, US$5.50; and 1st class, 1420 and 1700, US$9. To **Cancún**, 2nd class, hourly, US$9. To **Valladolid**, 2nd class, hourly, US$2.50. To

Tulum, 2nd class, 0810, 1420, 1615, US$11. The ruins are a 5-min ride from Pisté – the buses drop off and pick up passengers until 1700 at the top of the coach station opposite the entrance.

Valladolid and around → Colour map 5, B4.

handsome colonial city unspoilt by tourism

Situated roughly halfway between Mérida and Cancún, Valladolid is filled with colourful houses, cobblestone streets, historic churches and plazas. There is a slightly medieval feel to the place, some of the streets tapering off into mud tracks. The *Vallisoletanos*, as they are known, are friendlier than their *Meridano* neighbours, and Valladolid's location makes it an ideal place to settle for a few days while exploring the ruins of Chichén Itzá, the fishing village of Río Lagartos, and the three beautiful *cenotes* in the area, one of which is right in the town itself. Valladolid is still relatively untouched by tourism (aside from the cavalcade of monstrous tour buses on the plaza every afternoon), but it is now showing signs of gentrification. The town is small and easily explored on foot.

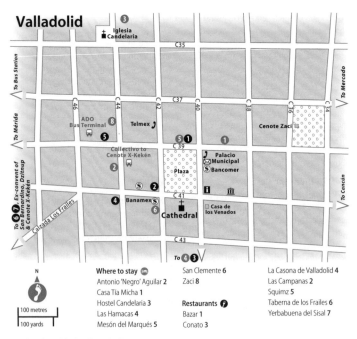

Valladolid

Where to stay
Antonio 'Negro' Aguilar **2**
Casa Tía Micha **1**
Hostel Candelaria **3**
Las Hamacas **4**
Mesón del Marqués **5**
San Clemente **6**
Zaci **8**

Restaurants
Bazar **1**
Conato **3**
La Casona de Valladolid **4**
Las Campanas **2**
Squimz **5**
Taberna de los Frailes **6**
Yerbabuena del Sisal **7**

N
100 metres
100 yards

Sights

Valladolid is set around a large plaza flanked by the imposing Franciscan **cathedral** (which is more impressive outside than in) and the **Palacio de Gobierno**, which has striking murals inside. Most of the hotels are clustered around the centre, as well as numerous restaurants catering for all budgets. Just off the plaza, **Casa de los Venados** ⓘ *Calle 40 No 204, T985-856-2289, www.casadelosvenados.com, guided tours Mon-Fri 1000, suggested donation US$3*, is a private home with a stunning collection of Mexican folk art, painstakingly acquired over a decade by enthusiasts John and Dorianne Venator.

The **Calzada de los Frailes** is a historic lane running diagonally southwest from the corner of Calles 46 and 41. Near its entrance, there is a tequila tour, **Los Tres Toños** ⓘ *Calle 41 No 222, 1000-2000*, where you can learn about production techniques and sample some local liquor; the tour is free, essentially a sales pitch for the distillery. Further down the Calzada is a little chocolate factory also offering 'free' tours with samples at the end. At the conclusion of the calzada, the 16th-century **Ex-Convento de San Bernardino** ⓘ *Mon-Sat, 0900-1800, US$2*, is one of Mexico's most important Franciscan structures, more of a fortress than a convent. It contains interesting frescoes and sacred art, as well as gardens pleasant for strolling.

Cenote Zací ⓘ *Calle 36 between Calle 37 and 39, daily 0800-1800, US$3, half price for children*, right in town, is an artificially lit *cenote* where you can swim, except when it is occasionally prohibited due to algae in the water. There is a thatched restaurant and lighted promenades. A small town **museum** ⓘ *Calle 41, free*, housed in Santa Ana church, shows the history of rural Yucatán and has some exhibits from recent excavations at the ruins of Ek-Balam.

★Cenote Dzitnup
Daily 0800-1800, US$2.50. Colectivos leave when full from in front of Hotel María Guadalupe, US$1, returning until 1800, after which you'll have to get a taxi back to Valladolid, US$6.

Seven kilometres from Valladolid is the beautiful **Cenote X-Kekén**, at **Dzitnup**, the name by which it is more commonly known. It is stunningly lit with electric lights, the only natural light source being a tiny hole in the cavernous ceiling dripping with stalactites. Swimming is excellent, the water is cool and refreshing, although reported to be a little dirty, and harmless bats zip around overhead. Exploratory walks can also be made through the many tunnels leading off the *cenote*, for which you will need a torch. There is also the easily reached *cenote* close by, called **Samulá** ⓘ *US$3*, only recently opened to the public.

Ek-Balam
Daily 0800-1700, US$7.50. To get there by car, take Route 295 north out of Valladolid. Just after the village of Temozón, turn right for Santa Rita. The ruins are 5 km further on. Colectivos to Ek Balam depart from Calle 44 between Calle 37 and 35, 4-person minimum, US$3. A round-trip taxi with a wait is around US$20.

Some 25 km north of Valladolid are the Mayan ruins of Ek-Balam, meaning 'Black Jaguar'. The ruins contain an impressive series of temples, sacrificial altars and residential buildings grouped around a large central plaza. The main temple, known as 'The Tower', is an immaculate seven-tiered staircase leading up to a flattened area with the remains of a temple. The views are stunning and, because they are not on the tourist trail, these ruins can be viewed at leisure, without the presence of hordes of tour groups from Cancún.

Río Lagartos and around → *Colour map 5, A4.*

Tizimín is a dirty, scruffy little town en route to Río Lagartos, where you will have to change buses. If stuck, there are several cheap *posadas* and restaurants, but with frequent buses to Río Lagartos, there should be no need to stay the night here.

Río Lagartos is an attractive little fishing village on the north coast of Yucatán State, whose main attraction is the massive biosphere reserve containing thousands of pink flamingos, as well as 250 other species of bird. The people of Río Lagartos are extremely friendly and very welcoming to tourists. The only route is on the paved road from Valladolid; access from Cancún is by boat only, a journey mainly made by tradesmen ferrying fish to the resort. Development in Río Lagartos, however, is on the horizon.

Boat trips to see the flamingo reserve can be easily arranged by walking down to the harbour and taking your pick from the many offers you'll receive from boatmen. You will get a longer trip with fewer people, due to the decreased weight in the boat. As well as flamingos, there are 250 other species of bird, some very rare, in the 47-sq-km reserve. Make sure your boatman takes you to the larger colony of flamingos near **Las Coloradas** (15 km), recognizable by a large salt mound on the horizon, rather than the smaller groups of birds along the river. Early morning boat trips can be arranged in Río Lagartos to see the flamingos (US$40-55, in eight to nine seater, 2½ to four hours, cheaper in a five-seater, fix the price before embarking; in midweek few people go so there is no chance of negotiating, but boat owners are more flexible on where they go; at weekends it is very busy, so it may be easier to get a party together and reduce costs). Check before going whether the flamingos are there; they usually nest here during May and June and stay through July and August (although salt mining is disturbing their habitat).

Listings Valladolid and around *map p236*

Tourist information

Tourist office
Southeast corner of the plaza.
Maps, general information and flyers.

Where to stay

$$$ Casa Tía Micha
Calle 39 No 197, T985-856 0499, www. casatiamicha.wix.com/casatiamicha.
Boutique colonial-style hotel with 1 room and 2 suites, very intimate and romantic; 1 'luxury suite' with jacuzzi and wine, 1 'honeymoon suite' with 4-poster bed. Very helpful staff and hospitable hosts. Recommended.

$$$ Hotel Las Hamacas
Calle 49 No 202-A, T985-100 4270, www.casahamaca.com.

Denis Larsen has done an extraordinary and commendable job with his friendly and hospitable B&B, which is set in verdant grounds, with a pool, 8 comfortable suites and an English-language library. It's adorned with indigenous art and artefacts; shamanic therapies are available. A storehouse of information on the area.

$$$ Mesón del Marqués
Calle 39 with Calle 40 and 42, north side of Plaza Principal, T985-856 2073, www.mesondelmarques.com.
Housed in a handsome colonial edifice, this hotel has 90 tasteful rooms, all with a/c and cable TV. There's a pool, Wi-Fi, garden and laundry service. Check the room before accepting. Recommended.

$$ Hotel Zaci
Calle 44 No 191, between Calles 37 and 39, T985-856 2167, www.hotel zaci.com.mx.

Large hotel with good-value rooms overlooking a narrow central courtyard, with a small pool, 48 standards, 12 premier, solid wood furniture, simple, comfortable.

$$ San Clemente
Calle 42 No 206, T985-856 2208, www.hotelsanclemente.com.mx.
Located right on the plaza, rooms are large, comfortable and overlook a central courtyard. They are cleaned daily, although some are a bit musty. It's good value and a great price for the location. There's also a pool and a café.

$ Antonio 'Negro' Aguilar
Rents rooms for 2, 3 or 4 people. The best budget deal in the town for 2 or more, clean, spacious rooms on a quiet street, garden, volleyball/ basketball court. The rooms are on Calle 41 No 225, but you need to book them at Aguilar's shop (Calle 44 No 195, T985-856 2125). If the shop's closed, knock on the door of the house on the right of the shop.

$ Hostel Candelaria
Calle 35 No 201F, between Calles 42 and 44, Parque de Candelaria, T985-856 2267, www.hostel valladolidyucatan.com.
Fantastic location on the lovely Plaza Candelaria, townhouse with a great garden, benches, tree growing through the centre. Best hostel in town.

Río Lagartos and around

$$ Villa de Pescadores
Calle 14 No 93, on the Malecón T986-862 0020, www.hotelrio lagartos.com.mx.
The best option in town, functional, simple and clean. They have 11 rooms, some with balconies, breezes and expansive views over the harbour, worth the extra pesos.

Restaurants

$$$ Conato
Calle 40 No 226, between Calles 45 y 47.
Atmospheric bohemian bar-restaurant with Frida Kahlo artwork, antiques and vibrant Mexican folk art. They serve Mexican staples, hearty and reasonable international fare too. Kitsch place, mellow vibe.

$$$ La Casona de Valladolid
Calle 41 and 44, T985-100 7040.
People come for the lunch buffet ($$$), which includes Yucatec specialities. Good setting and atmosphere with a splendid colonial building and lots of folk art. Seating is on a large outdoor patio, many tables, frequent tour groups.

$$$ Taberna de los Frailes
Calle 49 No 235, www.tabernadelos frailes.com.
Romantic setting near the Convent of San Bernardino, lots of character, fabulous building and garden. They serve Yucatec and Mayan specialities, a bit pricey for the town, but very beautiful.

$$ Las Campanas
Calle 42, Parque Central.
Reasonable Mexican fare, some of it good. An atmospheric building and lots of diners in the evenings.

$$-$ Squimz
Calle 39 No 219, between Calles 44 and 46, www.squimz.com.mx.
Modern, airy café with casual booth seating up front and a relaxing patio out back. They serve good breakfasts, coffee, smoothies, sandwiches and some international fare. Wi-Fi and attentive service.

$$-$ Yerbabuena del Sisal
Calle 54A No 217.
Lovely lunch café serving Yucatec treats and staple snacks made with healthy fresh ingredients, including revitalizing fruit and juices, spicy salsas, hot tortillas and salads prepared with love.

$ Bazar
Northeast corner of Plaza Principal, next to Mesón del Marqués.
Wholesome grub, a bit hit and miss, it's best to choose a popular kitchen and ignore the excitable waiters trying to lure you in.

Río Lagartos and around

For a fishing village, the seafood is not spectacular, as most of the good fish is sold to restaurants in Mérida and Cancún.

$$ Isla Contoy
Calle 19 No 134.
Average seafood, not cheap for the quality.

$$ Los Negritos
Off the plaza.
Moderately priced seafood.

Río Lagartos and around

17 Jul A big local fiesta, with music, food and dancing in the plaza.
12 Dec Virgen de Guadalupe. The whole village converges on the chapel built in 1976 on the site of a vision of the Virgin Mary by a local non-believer, who suddenly died, along with his dog, shortly after receiving the vision.

Bus

The **ADO** bus terminal is on Calle 39 and 46, 2 blocks from the main plaza. To **Cancún**, **ADO**, frequent, 2½ hrs, US$12.50; and many 2nd class, 3-4 hrs, US$6. To **Chichén Itzá**, **ADO**, 4 daily, 30 mins; US$5.25; and many 2nd class, US$2.50. To **Mérida**, ADO, 16 daily, 2½ hrs, US$13. To **Playa del Carmen**, 6 daily, 3 hrs, US$12.50. To **Tizimín** (for Río Lagartos), frequent 1 hr, US$2. To **Tulum**, 4 daily, US$7.50.

Río Lagartos and around
Bus

There are 2 terminals side by side in Tizimín. If coming from Valladolid en route to Río Lagartos, you will need to walk to the other terminal. Tizimín–Río Lagartos, 7 per day, 1½ hrs, US$2. To **Valladolid**, frequent, 1 hr, US$2. To **Mérida**, several daily, 4 hrs, US$4. There are also buses to **Cancún**, **Felipe Carrillo Puerto** and **Chetumal**.

It is possible to get to Río Lagartos and back in a day from **Valladolid**, if you leave on the 0630 or 0730 bus (taxi Tizimín–Río Lagartos US$25, driver may negotiate). Last bus back from Río Lagartos at 1730.

Campeche State

The state of Campeche embraces the torpid Gulf coast of the Yucatán Peninsula. It enjoys a special prosperity thanks to its offshore oil reserves, exploited by Pemex since the 1970s. Despite its huge potential as a destination, next to the big tourist hubs of Quintana Roo and Yucatán states, relatively few travellers take the time to explore Campeche. But those who do invariably discover a land steeped in history and legends, as vivid and compelling as any of the Yucatán's hot spots.

The state capital, Campeche City, recalls the age of seafarers and pirates with its crumbling city walls and defensive forts, a bastion of colonial grandeur standing sentinel on the coast. Inland, the landscape alternates between savannah and rainforest, the setting for scores of distinctive Mayan ruins. The Chenes, Puuc and Río Bec architectural styles are all represented, triumphs of extraordinary aesthetic form, but nothing beats the mighty Calakmul for sheer size, its behemoth pyramids and temples testament to the vast power of the early Mayan city states. South of the capital, the sweltering Gulf coast is a lesser visited stretch of windswept beaches, sluggish mangroves, yawning estuaries and wildlife-rich lagoons, including Laguna de Términos.

For those willing to get off the beaten track, Campeche promises adventure and intrigue, blissfully free from crowds.

Oil profits have gone a long way to revitalizing the economy of the ancient fortified city of Campeche: neatly hidden behind traffic-choked streets, its Centro Histórico has enjoyed an extensive programme of restoration since the 1980s. It is now rapidly becoming gentrified and has been a UNESCO World Heritage Site since 1999. Replete with cafés and art galleries, the area also has pretty pastel-shaded town houses and cobblestone streets. Beyond the city walls, the seafront *malecón* is an extensive promenade where people stroll, cycle, walk and relax in the evening in the light of the setting sun.

Like many Yucatán towns, Campeche's streets in the Old Town are numbered rather than named. Even numbers run north–south beginning at Calle 8 (no one knows why) near the Malecón, east to Calle 18 inside the walls; odd numbers run east (inland) from Calle 51 in the north to Calle 65 in the south. Most of the points of interest are within this compact area. Connecting sea and land gates, Calle 59 has now been pedestrianized with great success. A full circuit of the walls is a long walk; buses marked 'Circuito Baluartes' provide a regular service around the perimeter.

Sights

Of the original walls, seven of the *baluartes* and an ancient fort (now rather dwarfed by two big white hotels on the seafront) remain; some house museums (see below).

The heart of the city is the Zócalo, where the austere Franciscan **cathedral** (1540-1705) has an elaborately carved façade; inside is the Santo Entierro (Holy Burial), a sculpture of Christ on a mahogany sarcophagus with a silver trim. There is plenty of shade under the trees in the Zócalo and a small pagoda with a snack bar.

Right in front of the Zócalo is the **Baluarte de Nuestra Señora de la Soledad**, the central bulwark of the city walls, from where you can do a walking tour of the **Circuito Baluartes**, the remains of the city walls. Heading east, you will come to the **Puerta del Mar**, formerly the entrance for those permitted to enter the city from the sea, which used to come up to this point. Next along the *circuito* is a pair of modern buildings, the **Palacio de Gobierno** and the **Congreso**. The latter looks like a flying saucer and makes for a bizarre sight when viewed with the 17th-century **Baluarte de San Carlos** in the background. Baluarte de San Carlos now houses the **Museo de la Ciudad**. Heading west on the continuation of the *circuito*, you will come to **Templo de San José**, on Calle 10, an impressive baroque church with a beautifully tiled façade. It has been de-consecrated and is now an educational centre. Back on to the *circuito*, you will next reach the **Baluarte de Santa Rosa**, now the home of the tourist information office. Next is **Baluarte de San Juan**, from which a large chunk of the old city wall still extends, protecting you from the noisy traffic on the busy road beyond. The wall connects with **Puerta de la Tierra** ⓘ *Tue, Fri and Sat 2000 (for information, contact the tourist office), US$4*, where a *Luz y Sonido* (Light and Sound) show takes place. The continuation of the *circuito* will take you past the **Baluarte de San Francisco** and then past the market, just outside the line of the city walls. **Baluarte de San Pedro** flanks the northeast corner of the city centre and now houses a museum. The *circuito* runs down to the northwest tip of the old city, where the **Baluarte de Santiago** houses the Botanical Gardens.

There are a few cultural centres in Campeche. The **Casa del Teniente de Rey** ⓘ *Calle 59 No 38 between 14 and 16, T981-811 1314, www.inah.gob.mx*, houses the **Instituto Nacional** de Antropología e Historia (INAH), dedicated to the restoration of Mayan ruins in the state of Campeche, as well as supporting local museums. INAH can be visited for information regarding any of the sites in the state. The **Centro Cultural Casa 6** ⓘ *Calle 57, between Calle 8 and 10, daily 0900-2100, US$0.35*, is housed in a handsome building on the main plaza. It conjures the opulence and splendour of Campeche's golden days.

Further from the city walls is the **Batería de San Luis**, 4 km south from the centre along the coast road. This was once a lookout post to catch pirates as they approached the city from a distance. The **Fuerte de San Miguel**, 600 m inland, is now a museum. A 20-minute walk along Avenida Miguel Alemán from Baluarte de Santiago is the 16th-century **San Francisco** church, with wooden altars painted in vermilion and white. Nearby is the **Portales de San Francisco**, a beautifully restored old entrance to the city, with several good restaurants in its shadow.

The **Museo de Arquitectura Maya** ⓘ *Baluarte de Nuestra Señora de la Soledad, Tue-Sun, 0800-1930, US$2.70*, has three well-laid-out rooms of Mayan stelae and sculpture.

Campeche

Where to stay
Castelmar 1
Don Gustavo 2
H177 3
Hostal Casa Balche 4
López Campeche 5
Socaire 6

Viatager Inn 7

Restaurants
Ambigú 1
Anchor's 59 3
Chocol Ha 5
Don Gustavo 8

El Bastión de Campeche 9
Fresh 'n Green 10
La Parroquia 7
La Pigua 4
Luz de Luna 11
Marganzo 2

BACKGROUND

Campeche

Highway 180 enters the city as the Avenida Resurgimiento, passing either side of the huge **Monumento al Resurgimiento**, a stone torso holding aloft the Torch of Democracy. Originally the trading village of Ah Kim Pech, it was here that the Spaniards, under Francisco Hernández de Córdoba, first disembarked on Mexican soil (22 March 1517) to replenish their water supply. For fear of being attacked by the native population, they quickly left, only to be attacked later by the locals further south in Champotón, where they were forced to land by appalling weather conditions at sea. It was not until 1540 that Francisco de Montejo managed to conquer Ah Kim Pech, founding the city of Campeche on 4 October 1541, after failed attempts in 1527 and again in 1537.

The export of local dyewoods, *chicle*, timber and other valuable cargoes soon attracted the attention of most of the famous buccaneers, who constantly raided the port from their bases on Isla del Carmen, then known as the Isla de Tris. Combining their fleets for one momentous swoop, they fell upon Campeche on 9 February 1663, wiped out the city and slaughtered its inhabitants. Five years later the Crown began fortifying the site, the first Spanish colonial settlement to be completely walled. Formidable bulwarks, 3 m thick and 'a ship's height', and eight bastions (*baluartes*) were built in the next 36 years. All these fortifications soon put a stop to pirate attacks and Campeche prospered as one of only two Mexican ports (the other was Veracruz) to have had the privilege of conducting international trade.

After Mexican Independence from Spain, the city declined into an obscure fishing and logging town. Only with the arrival of a road from the 'mainland' in the 1950s and the oil boom of the 1970s has Campeche begun to see visitors in any numbers, attracted by its historical monuments and relaxed atmosphere (*campechano* has come to mean an easy-going, pleasant person).

Jardín Botánico Xmuch'Haltun ⓘ *Baluarte de Santiago, Mon-Sat 0900-2100, Sun 0900-1600, US$0.80*, is a small but perfectly formed collection of tropical plants and flowers in a peaceful setting. The **Fuerte de San Miguel** ⓘ *Tue-Sun 0900-1930, US$2.50*, on the Malecón 4 km southwest, is the most atmospheric of the forts (complete with drawbridge and a moat said to have once contained either crocodiles or skin-burning lime, take your pick!); it houses the **Museo de Cultura Maya** ⓘ *Tue-Sun 0900-1730*, with a well-documented display of pre-Columbian exhibits including jade masks and black funeral pottery from Calakmul and recent finds from Jaina.

Around Campeche

Lerma is virtually a small industrial suburb of Campeche, with large shipyards and fish-processing plants; the afternoon return of the shrimping fleet is a colourful sight. The **Fiesta de Polk Kekén** is held on 6 January, with traditional dances. The nearest decent beaches are at Seybaplaya (see page 250), 20 km south of Campeche. There, the beaches are clean and deserted; take your own food and drink as there are no facilities. Crowded, rickety buses marked 'Lerma' or 'Playa Bonita' run from Campeche, US$1.50, 8 km.

Tourist information

For a good orientation take the Centro Histórico tour, a regular tourist tram running daily from the main plaza on the hour 0900-1200 and 1700-2000, 45 mins, US$7.50, English and Spanish spoken.

Municipal tourist office
Calle 55 No 3, T019 816 3989,
www.campeche.travel.
Located next to the cathedral and supplemented by an information booth on the plaza.

State tourist office
Av Ruiz Cortines s/n, T981-127 3300,
www.campeche.travel. On the malecón.

Where to stay

$$$$ Don Gustavo
Calle 59 No 4, T01800-839 0959,
www.casadongustavo.com.
Classic colonial beauty at this upmarket boutique hotel, a converted townhouse. Suites are simple and elegant, crisply attired and adorned with delicate antiques. Pleasant patios, spa facilities and a superb restaurant. The best in town.

$$$$ Hacienda Uayamon
Carretera Uayamon–China–Edzná
Km 20, T981-813 0530, www.hacienda
uayamon.com.
This beautiful old hacienda has been tastefully restored to its former elegance and now serves as a luxury hotel. Rooms are handsome, combining traditional and contemporary flourishes. The grounds, setting and architecture are superb.

$$$ Castelmar
Calle 61, between Calle 8 and 10, T981-
811 1204, www.castelmar hotel.com.
Fantastic early 19th-century building, a former military barracks, now one of the oldest hotels in town and decorated in

grand colonial style. Its 26 rooms are smart, clean, spacious and decorated with solid wooden furniture and fine tiled floors.

$$$ Hotel Socaire
Calle 55 No 22, between Calles 12 and 14,
T981-811 2130, www.hotelsocaire.com.mx.
A youthful new hotel with 8 good, clean, well-equipped rooms, simple, stylish and modern. There's also a decent restaurant attached, friendly staff and a small pool. Calm and welcoming colours. Recommended.

$$$-$$ Hotel H177
Calle 14 No 177, between Calles 59 and 61,
T981-816 4463, www.h177hotel.com.mx.
A modern lodging with a trendy look. Brand new rooms include comfortable singles, doubles and suites, all crisply attired with white linen and red curtains. Facilities include spa and jacuzzi.

$$ Hotel López Campeche
Calle 12 No 189 between Calles 61 and 63,
T981-816 3344, www.hotellopezcampeche.
com.mx.
An interesting art deco building with 50 clean, simple, comfortable rooms overlooking an inner courtyard. Facilities include a small pool, café and all modern conveniences. Central and good value.

$$-$ Hostal Casa Balche
Calle 57 No 6, T981-811 0087,
www.casabalche.com.
A bit more expensive than your usual hostel, but very new, comfortable, stylish and unique, and a superb location overlooking the plaza. There's just 1 private room (**$$**) and a few small clean dorms with bunks. Services include free Wi-Fi, breakfast and laundry. Attractive, hospitable and recommended.

$ Viatger Inn
Calle 51 No 28, between Calles 12 and 14,
T981-811 4500, www.viatgerinn.com.

A small, crisp, clean and stylish youth hostel with mixed and single-sex dorms. Coffee and Wi-Fi included. Brand new and in great shape.

Restaurants

Campeche is known for its seafood, especially *camarones* (large shrimps), *esmedregal* (black snapper) and *pan de cazón* (baby hammerhead shark sandwiched between corn tortillas with black beans). Food stands in the market serve *tortas*, tortillas, *panuchos* and *tamales* but hygiene standards vary widely; barbecued venison is also a marketplace speciality.

$$$ Anchor's 59
Calle 59 between Calles 10 and 12.
A plush new seafood restaurant, recommended chiefly for its stock of wine. Smart, pleasant interior and a tempting menu of grilled coconut prawns, seafood tostadas, snapper, pasta and more.

$$$ Don Gustavo
Calle 59 No 4, T01800-839 0959, www.casadongustavo.com.
Don Gustavo's is the place for a romantic evening meal. They serve creatively prepared local specialities, steaks, pasta and fusion cuisine. The setting, inside the hotel, is a handsome colonial house with an elegant dining room and intimate patio seating. Attentive service.

$$$ La Pigua
Av Miguel Alemán 179A, www.lapigua.com.mx.
La Pigua is well-established, modern and clean. It has a traditional kitchen specializing in fresh fish, prawn cocktails, calamari, Campeche caviar and other seafood. Pleasant dining, open for lunch and dinner.

$$$-$$ Ambigú
Calle 59 between Calles 10 and 12.
A cool place with a friendly atmosphere and a simple but elegant interior and additional al fresco seating on the pedestrian street.

They serve home-cooked regional cuisine and great cocktails made with traditional plants, fruits and nance liquor.

$$$-$$ El Bastión de Campeche
Calle 57 No 2a, www.elbastion.mx.
A good spot on the plaza, clean and pleasant. They serve Mexican, Yucatec and international cuisine, specialities include chicken stuffed with cream cheese and chaya, filet mignon and shrimp in mango sauce. Breakfast, lunch and dinner.

$$$-$$ Luz de Luna
Calle 59 No 6, between Calles 10 and 12.
A good Mexican restaurant serving national and local classics, including flavourful burritos, tacos, enchiladas and fish fillet with lemon and pepper. Friendly, attentive service and al fresco seating.

$$$-$$ Marganzo
Calle 8, www.marganzo.com.
Highly regarded by the locals, **Marganzo** is a colonial-style restaurant serving good seafood and Mexican fare, including Yucatec specialities. They regularly lay on music with a trio of musicians and regional dancing. Good evening atmosphere. Recommended.

$$-$ La Parroquia
Calle 55 No 8, part of the hotel with the same name.
This busy locals' joint – staffed by smartly attired and friendly waiters – is open 24 hrs and packed at breakfast time. They serve reliable grub, reasonable and casual, but not gourmet.Free Wi-Fi.

$ Fresh 'n Green
Calle 59 No 5.
A simple sandwich and salad bar, very casual and cheap, fast food, and popular with students.

Cafés

Chocol Ha
Calle 59 No 30.
A chilled-out little patio, great for after-dinner crêpes, frappés and hot chocolate.

They have some tasty local produce on sale too, including honey and chocolate.

Festivals

Feb/Mar Good **Carnival.**
7 Aug State holiday.
Sep **Feria de San Román**, 2nd fortnight.
4-13 Oct **Fiesta de San Francisco**.

Shopping

Handicrafts

Excellent cheap Panama hats (*jipis*), finely and tightly woven so hat they retain their shape even when crushed into your luggage (within reason); cheaper at the source in Becal. Handicrafts are generally cheaper than in Mérida. There are souvenir shops along Calle 8, such as **Artesanía Típica Naval**, Calle 8 No 259, with exotic bottled fruit like *nance* and *marañón*. Many high-quality craft items are available from the **Exposición** in the Baluarte San Pedro and **Casa de Artesanías Tukulná**, Calle 10 No 333, between C59 and C31, www.tukulna.com.mx, open daily 0900-2000.

The market, from which most local buses depart, is beside Alameda Park at the south end of Calle 57. There are plenty of bargains here. Try the ice cream, although preferably from a shop rather than a barrow.

What to do

Tour operators

Kankabi'Ok, *Calle 59 No 3, between Calles 8 and 10, T981-811 2792, www.kankabiok.com.* Eco and adventure tours, including kayaking, camping and ruins. A tour to Edzná is around US$25 per person (2-person minimum), including transport and guide. Other popular excursions include the 'Camino Real', a half-day tour of rural villages and workshops, including a traditional meal.
Viajes Xtampak Tours, *Calle 57 No 14, T981-816 6473, www.xtampak.com.* Daily transport to ruins including Edzná, Calakmul, Uxmal

and Palenque – they'll collect you from your hotel with 24 hrs' notice. There's a discount for groups and guide services at an extra cost. Recommended.

Transport

Air

The modern, efficient airport (**CPE**) on Porfirio is 10 km northeast of town. If on a budget, walk 100 m down service road (Av Aviación) to Av Nacozari, turn right (west) and wait for 'China–Campeche' bus to the Zócalo.

Aeroméxico direct daily to **Mexico City**, T981-816 3109.

Bus

Long-distance buses arrive at the **ADO** bus terminal on Av Casa de Justicia 237, 3 km from downtown; buses to the centre pass outside, US$0.70, taxis cost US$3.

Buses to **Seybaplaya** leave from the tiny Cristo Rey terminal opposite the market, 9 a day from 0615, 45 mins, US$1.50.

Long distance See above for the location of the 1st-class **ADO** terminal. The 2nd-class bus terminal is about 1 km east of the centre along Av Gobernadores, but services are steadily moving to the main terminal. To **Cancún**, 8 daily with **ADO** and **ADO GL**, 7 hrs, US$38-45. To **Chetumal**, 1400, 6 hrs, US$38. To **Ciudad del Carmen**, frequent **ADO** services, 3 hrs, US$16. To **Escárcega**, 6 daily, 2 hrs, US$11. To **Mérida**, frequent **ADO** services, 2½ hrs, US$14. To **San Cristóbal de las Casas**, OCC at 2145, 11 hrs, US$36. To **Veracruz**, luxury only, **ADO GL** at 2010, 11½ hrs, US$62. To **Villahermosa**, frequent **ADO** services, 6-7 hrs, US$31.

Car

Car hire **Maya Nature**, Av Ruiz Cortines 51, inside Hotel del Mar, T981-811 9191. **Hertz** and **Autorent** car rentals at airport.

A number of city remains (mostly in the Chenes architectural style) are scattered throughout the rainforest and scrub to the east of Campeche; little excavation work has been done and most receive few visitors. Getting to them by the occasional bus service is possible in some cases, but return trips can be tricky. The alternatives are one of the tours run by travel agencies in Campeche (see Tour operators, above) or renting a vehicle (preferably with high clearance) in Campeche or Mérida. Whichever way you travel, you are strongly advised to carry plenty of drinking water.

Edzná

Tue-Sun 0800-1700, US$3.50; local guides available. The easiest way to reach Edzná is on a tourist minibus. They depart hourly and operators include Xtampak, Calle 57 No 14, between Calle 10 and 12, T981-812 8655, xtampac_7@ hotmail.com, US$21.50 (prices drop depending on number of passengers); and Transportadora Turística Jade, Av Díaz Ordaz No 67, T981-827 4885, Jade_tour@hotmail.com, US$14. To get there on public transport, catch a morning bus to Pich and ask to be let out at Edzná – it's a 15-min walk from the highway. Ask the driver about return schedules, as services are quite infrequent and subject to change. There's no accommodation at Edzná and hitchhiking isn't recommended.

The closest site to the state capital is Edzná ('House of Grimaces'), reached by the highway east to Cayal, then a right turn onto Highway 261, a distance of 61 km. A paved shortcut southeast through China and Poxyaxum (good road) cuts off 11 km; follow Avenida Nacozari out along the railway track.

Gracefully situated in a lovely, tranquil valley with thick vegetation on either side, Edzná was a huge ceremonial centre, occupied from about 600 BC to AD 200, built in the simple Chenes style mixed with Puuc, Classic and other influences. The centrepiece is the magnificent, 30-m-tall, 60-sq-m **Temple of the Five Storeys**, a stepped pyramid with four levels of living quarters for the priests and a shrine and altar at the top; 65 steep steps lead up from the Central Plaza. Opposite is the **Paal U'na**, Temple of the Moon. Excavations are being carried out on the scores of lesser temples by Guatemalan refugees under the direction of Mexican archaeologists, but most of Edzná's original sprawl remains hidden away under thick vegetation. Imagination is still needed to picture the network of irrigation canals and holding basins built by the Maya along the valley below sea level. Some of the stelae remain in position (two large stone faces with grotesquely squinting eyes are covered by a thatched shelter); others can be seen in various Campeche museums. There is also a good example of a *sacbé* (sacred road).

Edzná is well worth a visit especially in July, when a Mayan ceremony to honour Chac is held, to encourage or to celebrate the arrival of the rains (exact date varies). There is a small *comedor* at the entrance.

Hochob

Daily 0800-1700, US$2.70.

Of the more remote and less-visited sites beyond Edzná, Hochob and Dzibilnocac are the best choices for the non-specialist. Hochob is reached by turning right at Hopelchén on Highway 261, 85 km east of Campeche. This quiet town has an impressive fortified 16th-century church but only one hotel. From here a narrow paved road leads 41 km south to the village of **Dzibalchén**.

Don Willem Chan will guide tourists to Hochob (he also rents bikes), is helpful and speaks English. Directions can be obtained from the church here (run by Americans); you need to travel 18 km southwest on a good dirt road (no public transport, hopeless quagmire in the rainy season) to the village of **Chenko**, where locals will show the way (4 km through the jungle). Bear left when the road forks; it ends at a small *palapa* and, from here, the ruins are 1 km uphill with a magnificent view over the surrounding forest.

Hochob once covered a large area but, as at Edzná, only the hilltop ceremonial centre (the usual plaza surrounded by elaborately decorated temple buildings) has been properly excavated; although many of these are mounds of rubble, the site is perfect for contemplating deserted, yet accessible Mayan ruins in solitude and silence. The one-room temple to the right (north) of the plaza is the most famous structure: deep-relief patterns of stylized snakes moulded in stucco across its façade were designed to resemble a mask of the ferocious rain god Chac. A door serves as the mouth. A fine reconstruction of the building is on display at the Museo de Antropología in Mexico City. Early morning second-class buses serve Dzibalchén, but returning to Campeche later in the day is often a matter of luck.

Dzibilnocac
Daily 0800-1700, free.

Some 20 km northeast of Dzibalchén at Iturbide, this site is one of the largest in Chenes territory. Only three temples have been excavated here (many pyramidal mounds in the forest and roadside *milpas*); the first two are in a bad state of preservation, but the third is worth the visit: a unique narrow edifice with rounded corners and remains of a stucco façade, primitive reliefs and another grim mask of Chac on the top level. Much of the stonework from the extensive site is used by local farmers for huts and fences.

Several buses daily travel to Iturbide, three hours, US$6.70, and there is no accommodation. If driving your own vehicle, well-marked 'km' signs parallel the rocky road to Iturbide (no accommodation); bear right around the tiny Zócalo and its attendant yellow church and continue (better to walk in the wet season) for 50 m, where the right branch of a fork leads to the ruins. Other sites in the region require 4WD transport and appeal mostly to archaeologists.

Becal
Becal is the centre for weaving Panama hats, here called *jipis* (pronounced 'hippies') and ubiquitous throughout the Yucatán. Many of the town's families have workshops in cool, moist backyard underground caves, which are necessary for keeping moist and pliable the shredded leaves of the *jipijapa* palm from which the hats are made. Most vendors give the visitor a tour of their workshop, but are quite zealous in their sales pitches. Prices are better for *jipis* and other locally woven items (cigarette cases, shoes, belts, etc) in the **Centro Artesanal, Artesanías de Becaleña** ① *Calle 30 No 210*, than in the shops near the plaza, where the hat is honoured by a hefty sculpture of three concrete *sombreros*! More celebrations take place on 20 May during the **Feria del Jipi**.

Listings Mayan sites east of Campeche

Festivals

3 May **Día de la Santa Cruz**.

13-17 Apr A traditional **Honey and Corn Festival** is held in Holpechén.

Opening to expansive views of the ocean, Campeche's Gulf coast sweeps south from Campeche City. The Highway 180 clings to the narrow shore, crumbling into the sea in places and usually ignored by tourists, but scenic. Running parallel, the toll road connecting Campeche City to Champotón is rapid, but bypasses Seybaplaya and Sihoplaya.

Seybaplaya and Sihoplaya

The low-key Mexican resort of **Seybaplaya**, 32 km south of Campeche City, is a dusty, mellow place where fishermen mend nets and pelicans dry their wings along the beach. On the highway there are open-air restaurants serving red snapper, but in general there's little to explore. Only the **Balneario Payucán** at the north end of the bay makes a special trip worthwhile; it is the closest decent beach to Campeche, but quite isolated. A short distance further south of Seybaplaya is the smaller resort of **Sihoplaya** (regular buses from Campeche US$1).

Champotón

Run-down but relaxed, Champotón, 66 km south of Campeche City, is a fishing and shrimping port sprawled at the mouth of the Río Champotón. In pre-Hispanic times, it was an important trade link between Guatemala and Central Mexico. Toltec and Maya mingled here, followed by the Spaniards, including ill-fated Francisco Hernández de Córdoba, fatally wounded in a skirmish with the inhabitants in 1517. The remnants of the 1719 San Antonio fort, built as a defence against the pirates, can be seen the south side of town. The **Feast of the Immaculate Conception** (8 December) is celebrated with a joyous festival lasting several days. At Champotón, Highway 261 runs 86 km due south to Escárcega, joining Highway 186, giving access to southern Campeche State and Chetumal in Quintana Roo.

Ciudad del Carmen → *Colour map 3, B5.*

Perched between the Gulf of Mexico and Laguna de Términos (named during the first Spanish expedition when it thought it had reached the end of the 'island' of Yucatán), Ciudad del Carmen is the hot, bursting-at-the-seams principal oil port of the region.

The site was established in 1588 by a pirate named McGregor, as a lair from which to raid Spanish shipping; it was infamous until the pirates were wiped out in 1717 by Alfonso Felipe de Andrade, who named the town after its patroness, the Virgen del Carmen. The patroness is honoured with a cheerful fiesta each year between 15 and 30 June.

The attractive, cream-coloured **cathedral** (Parroquia de la Virgen del Carmen), begun 1856, is notable for its stained glass. **La Iglesia de Jesús** (1820) opposite Parque Juárez is surrounded by elegant older houses. Nearby is the Barrio del Guanal, the oldest residential quarter, with the church of the **Virgen de la Asunción** (1815) and houses with spacious balconies and tiles brought from Marseille. There are several good beaches with restaurants and water sports, the most scenic being **Playa Caracol** (southeast of the centre) and **Playa Norte**, which has extensive white sand and is safe for bathing. The lagoon is rich in tarpon (*sábalo*) and bonefish.

West of Ciudad del Carmen

A few kilometres west of Ciudad del Carmen, the **Zacatal** bridge crosses the lagoon to connect with the mainland; at 3.2 km it is the longest bridge in Latin America (celebrated with a light and sound show every evening). Near the exit, the lighthouse of **Xicalango** stands at the site of an important pre-Columbian trading centre. Cortés landed near here in 1519 on his way to Veracruz and was given 20 female slaves, including 'La Malinche', the indigenous princess baptized as Doña Marina who, as the Spaniards' interpreter, played an important role in the Conquest. A series of lagoons lie further west on Highway 180, good for birdwatching. Thereafter, the highway crosses the state border into Tabasco, skirting the Gulf up to the US border.

Listings Ciudad del Carmen

Where to stay

Hotel accommodation is generally poor value and can be difficult to come by Mon-Thu; book in advance and arrive early. You'll find a handful of 'economical' hotels opposite the ADO bus station.

$$$ EuroHotel
Calle 22 No 208, T938-382 3044,
reganem@prodigy.net.mx.
Large and modern, 2 restaurants, pool, a/c, disco, built to accommodate the flow of Pemex traffic.

$ Lino's
Calle 31 No 132, T938-382 0788.
A/c, pool, restaurant, also has 10 RV spaces with electricity hook-ups.

Restaurants

$$ El Kiosco Calle 33 s/n
Between Calle 20 and 22, in Hotel del Parque
with view of the Zócalo.
Modest prices, eggs, chicken, seafood and Mexican dishes.

$$-$ El Pavo
Tucked away down Calle 36A,
in Col Guadalupe.
This superb, family-run restaurant serves excellent seafood dishes at cheap prices. Very popular with the locals.

$$-$ La Fuente
Calle 20.
24-hr snack bar with view of the Laguna.

$ La Mesita
Outdoor stand across from the old
ferry landing.
Well-prepared shrimp, seafood cocktails, extremely popular all day.

Transport

Air
Carmen's airport (CME, 5 km east of the plaza) currently only has direct flights to **Mexico City**, from where there are connections to the rest of the country.

Bus
The **ADO** bus terminal is some distance from the centre. Take bus or *colectivo* marked 'Renovación' or 'ADO'; they leave from around the Zócalo. There are frequent **ADO** and **ATS** services to **Campeche**, 2½-3 hrs, US$16. To **Mérida**, frequent, 6 hrs, US$29. To **Villahermosa** via the coast, 3 hrs, US$14, where connections can be made to **Palenque**. Buses also travel via **Escárcega**, where you can connect to **Chetumal** and **Belize**.

Car
Car hire Budget, Calle 31 No 117, T938-382 0908. **Auto-Rentas del Carmen**, Calle 33 No 121, T938-382 2376.

a remote forested area concealing scores of unexplored Mayan ruins

This region encompasses part of the vast lowland forest that reaches into northern Guatemala's Petén, much of it inaccessible without a guide and a good machete. For vehicles, the Escárcega–Chetumal highway bisects the region and eventually connects with Chetumal in Quintana Roo. From the hamlet of Xpujil, 150 km east of Escárcega, you can access the sites of Xpujil, Becán and Chicanná, all intriguing examples of the Río Bec architectural style, which is characterized by heavy masonry towers simulating pyramids and temples, usually found rising in pairs at the ends of elongated buildings. Encompassing a densely forested wilderness, the Calakmul Biosphere Reserve is an exceptional destination, home to one of the most powerful capitals in Mayan history, a site of monumental proportions.

Francisco Escárcega → Colour map 4, B1.

The town of Francisco Escárcega grew up on the Coatzacoalcos–Mérida railway line, which once transported the state's bounty of precious wood, rubber and gum. Today, at the junction of Highways 261 and 186, it is a major hub for travellers on their way to and from Mayan sites in southern Campeche, as well as south to Tabasco and Chiapas and north to Campeche City. The town itself is not particularly enticing, set on a busy highway with a dusty Wild West atmosphere. If stuck here overnight, there are a few hotels, a bank and several cheap restaurants (see Listings, below).

★Calakmul → Colour map 4, B2.

Daily 0800-1700, US$3.70, cars US$4, entrance to biosphere reserve US$4. Calakmul is only accessible by car; take Route 186 until Km 95, then turn off at Conhuás, where a paved road leads to the site, 60 km.

Some 300 km southeast from Campeche town and a further 60 km off the main Escárcega–Chetumal road are the ruins of Calakmul. The site has been the subject of much attention in recent years, due to the previously concealed scale of the place. It is now believed to be one of the largest archaeological sites in Mesoamerica, and certainly the biggest of all the Mayan cities, with somewhere in the region of 10,000 buildings in total, many of them as yet unexplored. The scale of the site is vast and many buildings are still under excavation, which means that information on Calakmul's history is continually being updated. There is evidence that Calakmul was begun in 300 BC, and continually added to until AD 800.

At the centre of the site is the **Gran Plaza**, overlooked by Structure II, a massive 45-m-high pyramid built in several phases; its core dates to the middle pre-Classic era (200-400 BC) with numerous reconstructions and layers added over the centuries until the end of the Classic era (AD 900). One of the buildings grouped around the Gran Plaza is believed, due to its curious shape and location, to have been designed for astronomical observation. The **Gran Acrópolis**, the largest of all the structures, is divided into two sections: **Plaza Norte**, with the ball court, was used for ceremonies; **Plaza Sur** was used for public activities.

Chicanná → *Colour map 4, B3.*
Daily 0800-1700. US$3.40.

Located 12 km from Xpujil, Chicanná was named upon its discovery in 1966 in reference to Structure II: *chi* (mouth), *can* (serpent) and *ná* (house), 'House of the Serpent's Mouth'. Due to its dimensions and location, Chicanná is considered to have been a small residential centre for the rulers of the ancient regional capital of Becán. It was occupied during the late pre-Classic period (300 BC-AD 250); the final stages of activity at the site have been dated to the post-Classic era (AD 1100). Typical of the Río Bec style are numerous representations of the Maya god Itzamná, or Earth Mother. One of the temples has a dramatic entrance in the shape of a monster's mouth, with fangs jutting out over the lintel and more fangs lining the access stairway. A taxi will take you from Xpujil bus stop to Becán and Chicanná for US$10, including waiting time.

Becán → *Colour map 4, B3.*
Daily 0800-1700, US$3.70.

Seven kilometres west of Xpujil, Becán is another important site in the Río Bec style. Its most outstanding feature is a moat, now dry, which surrounds the entire city and is believed to be one of the oldest defence systems in Mesoamerica. Seven entrance gates cross the moat to the city. The large variety of buildings on the site are a strange combination of decorative towers and fake temples, as well as structures used as shrines and palaces. The twin towers, typical of the Río Bec style, feature on the main structure, set on a pyramid-shaped base supporting a cluster of buildings that seem to have been used for many different functions.

Xpujil → *Colour map 4, B3.*
Tue-Sun 0800-1700, US$3.40, US$3 to use a camcorder. To get there, see Transport, below.

The name means a type of plant similar to a cattail. The main building at Xpujil features an unusual set of three towers, with rounded corners and steps that are so steep they are unscalable, suggesting they may have been purely decorative. The façade features the open jaws of an enormous reptile in profile on either side of the main entrance, possibly representing Itzamná, the Maya god of creation. Xpujil's main period of activity was AD 500-750; it began to go into decline around 1100. Major excavation on the third structure was done as recently as 1993, and there are still many unexcavated buildings dotted about the site. It can be very peaceful and quiet in the early mornings, compared with the throng of tourist activity at the more accessible sites such as Chichén Itzá and Uxmal.

Hormiguero
Daily 0800-1700, free.

Some 20 km southwest of Xpujil, Hormiguero is the site of one of the most important buildings in the Río Bec region, whose elaborate carvings on the façade show a fine example of the serpent's-mouth entrance, with huge fangs and a gigantic eye.

Río Bec → *Colour map 4, B3.*
Río Bec is south off the main highway, some 10 km further along the road to Chetumal. Although the site gave its name to the architectural style seen in this area, there are better examples of the style at the ruins listed above. Río Bec is a cluster of numerous small sites, all of which are difficult to reach without a guide.

Where to stay

Francisco Escárcega

$$ Escárcega
Justo Sierra 86, T982-824 0187, around the corner from the bus terminal (turn left twice).
Clean, bath, parking, hot water, good restaurant, small garden.

$$ María Isabel
Justo Sierra 127, T982-824 0045.
A/c, restaurant, comfortable, back rooms noisy from highway.

Restaurants

Francisco Escárcega

There are few places used to serving tourists, but there is a good and cheap *lonchería* opposite the bus terminal.

$$ Titanic
Corner of the main highway and the road to the train station (1st turning on the right after turning right out of the bus terminal).
For a more expensive meal with a/c.

Transport

Francisco Escárcega
Bus

Most buses from Chetumal or Campeche drop you off at the 2nd-class terminal on the main highway. To buy tickets, you have to wait until the outgoing bus has arrived; sit near the ticket office and wait for them to call out your destination, then join the scrum at the ticket office. There is an **ADO** terminal west of the 2nd-class terminal, a 20-min walk. From there, 1st-class buses go to **Palenque**, 5 daily, 3-4 hrs, US$15. To **Chetumal**, 7 daily, 4 hrs, US$18. To **Campeche**, 9 daily, 2 hrs, US$11. To **Mérida**, frequent, 4½ hrs, US$24.

From the 2nd-class terminal, there are buses to **Campeche**, 16 a day, 2½ hrs, US$8. To **Chetumal**, 7 daily, 4 hrs, US$15. To **Playas de Catazajá**, connecting with *colectivos* to **Palenque**, frequent, US$7. To **Villahermosa**, 12 a day, 4 hrs, US$16. *Colectivos* to **Palenque** leave from outside the 2nd-class terminal, US$11.

Xpujil

You are strongly advised to use your own transport when exploring southern Campeche as passing buses on Highway 186 (Escárcega–Chetumal) are infrequent (every 3-4 hrs). From Xpujil, you must hire a taxi to visit the ruins.

Bus

2nd-class buses from **Chetumal** and **Escárcega** stop on the highway in the centre of Xpujil, some 800 m east of the 2 hotels. There are 4 buses a day to **Escárcega**, between 1030 and 1500, 3 hrs, US$8. 8 buses a day to **Chetumal**, 2 hrs, US$7. Change at Escárcega for buses to **Palenque** or **Campeche**. 1st-class buses will not stop at Xpujil.

This is
Belize

Belize is a smorgasbord of landscapes, from mountainous jungle with abundant wildlife to fertile subtropical foothills where cattle are reared, and sugar, rice and fruit trees are cultivated, or coastal wetlands filled with birds and small islands – known as cayes – with beautiful beaches.

Measuring 174 miles north to south and just 80 miles across, the country nestles on the coast between Mexico and Guatemala, with a land area of about 8860 sq miles, including hundreds of cayes. The reefs and cayes form a 184-mile barrier reef with crystal-clear water and are a major attraction for world-class diving, snorkelling and sport fishing. And hidden beneath the depths is the magnificent Blue Hole, one of the world's best dives.

Inland, rivers and rainforest invite you to head out, trekking, paddling and biking, to visit the ancient ruins of the Maya, or to cave in their spiritual underworld. For the beginner and the specialist birdwatching is an endless pleasure.

With a Caribbean history and a Central American geography, Belize is a subtle blend of cultures that encourages the laid-back attitude of the small (just 311,000) but ethnically diverse population, who paint an intriguing picture in this culturally different, English-speaking Central American nation.

Footprint
picks

1 **Northern cayes**, page 270
2 **Blue Hole**, page 283
3 **Actun Tunichil Muknal Cave**, page 291
4 **Caracol**, page 297
5 **Crooked Tree Wildlife Sanctuary**, page 300
6 **Cockscomb Basin Wildlife Sanctuary**, page 320

Footprint picks

★ **Northern cayes**, page 270

Sling a hammock, pour yourself a glass of rum and soak up the easy-going Caribbean vibe on these palm-fringed paradise islands.

★ **Blue Hole**, page 283

Marvel at the incredible underwater wonders of this subterranean sinkhole, one of the world's most famous dive sites.

★ **Actun Tunichil Muknal Cave**, page 291

Descend into the shimmering Mayan underworld, filled with haunting rock formations, ancient ritual artefacts and crystallized sacrificial remains.

★ **Caracol**, page 297

Scramble over the ruins of Caracol, a major power centre during the Classic era of Mayan civilization.

★ **Crooked Tree Wildlife Sanctuary**, page 300

Admire the Jaribu stork – the largest flying bird in the Western Hemisphere – and many other avian species in this sanctuary managed by the Belize Audubon Society.

★ **Cockscomb Basin Wildlife Sanctuary**, page 320

Promising an unforgettable encounter with neo-tropical fauna, this superb reserve is the world's premier destination for jaguar observation.

Essential Belize City

Getting around

Belize City is small enough to walk around when exploring. If going further afield, jump in a cab.

Best places to stay

Radisson Fort George, page 264
Villa Boscardi, page 264
D'Nest, page 264
Red Hut Inn, page 265

Safety

Tourist police wearing dark green uniforms patrol the city centre in an attempt to control crime and give advice; their introduction has been encouraging and crime in the city is greatly reduced.

Tip...

Try the local drink, anise and peppermint, known as 'A and P'; also the powerful Old Belizeno rum. The local beer, Belikin, is good, as is the stout, strong and free of gas.

Best restaurants

De Barcelona, page 265
Sumathi Indian, page 265
Bird's Isle, page 265

A common-sense approach is needed and a careful eye on your possessions recommended. Watch out for conmen. Guides have to be licensed and should carry a photo ID. Street money changers are not to be trusted. It is wise to avoid small, narrow sidestreets and stick to major thoroughfares, although even on main streets you can be the victim of unprovoked threats and racial abuse. Travel by taxi is advisable, particularly at night and in the rain.

Cars should only be left in guarded car parks. For a tip, the security officer at hotels with secure parking will look after cars for a few days while you go to the cayes.

When to go

Humidity is high, but the summer heat is offset by the northeast trades.

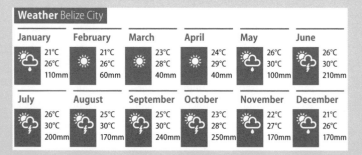

Weather Belize City

January	February	March	April	May	June
21°C 26°C 110mm	21°C 26°C 60mm	23°C 28°C 40mm	24°C 29°C 40mm	26°C 30°C 100mm	26°C 30°C 210mm

July	August	September	October	November	December
26°C 30°C 200mm	25°C 30°C 170mm	25°C 30°C 240mm	23°C 28°C 250mm	22°C 27°C 170mm	21°C 26°C 170mm

Belize City

Clapboard houses line dusty streets while people huddle in groups as the world drifts idly by. Hardly large enough to warrant the title 'city', in any other country Belize City would be a dusty backwater, but here, it is the country's largest settlement, home to a quarter of Belize's population, and an enticing blend of Latin American and Caribbean influences. It is the main centre for maritime communications with boat services to the northern cayes and it is also a flight hub, home to the country's only international airport. For many years, Belize City functioned as the capital of British Honduras, as the country was then known. After it was levelled by Hurricane Hattie in 1961, the government was transferred to the planned city of Belmopan, now the official capital, 80 km west in Cayo District.

Many of the houses are wooden, with galvanized-iron roofs. Most stand on 2-m-high piles – signs of when the city was regularly flooded. The city has improved greatly in recent years. Reclaimed land and building around the Eyre Street area, the Museum of Belize, renovation of the Bliss Institute and the House of Culture show plans to improve the city are well underway.

Hurricane Iris hit in 2002 and Hurricane Richard in 2010, acting as reminders of the inherent risks of Belize City's lowland location. *Colour map 8, B2.*

Sights

Haulover Creek divides the city and is crossed by the antiquated **swing-bridge**, which opens to let large vessels pass, if required, usually between 1730 and 1800. Three narrow canals further divide the city. The main commercial area is either side of the swing-bridge, with most shops on the south side, many being located on Regent and Albert streets and with offices and embassies generally on the northern side.

The area around **Battlefield Park** (formerly Central Park) is always busy, with the former colonial administration and court buildings bordering the overgrown park adding to the sense of mischief in the area. At the southern end of Regent Street, the **Anglican Cathedral** (St John's) and **Government House** nearby are interesting. Both were built in the early 19th century and draw on the romantic and grand memories of colonialism. In the days before the foundation of the Crown Colony, the kings of the Mosquito Coast were crowned in the cathedral, which was built with bricks brought from England as ships' ballast. In the **cathedral** ① *Mon-Fri 0900-1500 and during Sun services, donation requested*, note the 19th-century memorial plaques that give a harrowing account of early deaths from 'country fever' (yellow fever) and other tropical diseases.

In Government House, the **museum** ① *Mon-Fri 0830-1630, US$5*, contains some interesting pictures of colonial times, displays of furniture and silver and glassware, as well as a one showing fishing techniques and model boats. There are pleasant gardens surrounding the museum if you are looking for somewhere quiet.

The **jail building** (1857) in front of the Central Bank on 8 Gabourel Lane has been beautifully renovated and is now the **National Museum of Belize** ① *T223-4524, www. nichbelize.org, Mon-Thu 0830-1700, Fri 0830-1630, US$5*, with exhibits on the history of Belize City and a permanent exhibit on the Maya sites of Belize.

Continuing to the right, pop into the **Image Factory Art Foundation** ① *91 North Front St, www.imagefactorybelize.com, Mon-Fri 0900-1700, free*, for a peek at exhibitions by local artists – more grassroots than the other galleries. Moving towards the end of the peninsula is the **Tourism Village** consisting of souvenir and gift shops and snack bars, along with several handicraft shops. This development caters to tourists arriving from cruise ships. A little further on, at the tip of the peninsula on Marine Parade, is **Memorial Park**, with a small obelisk, two cannon and concrete benches peppered with the holes of land crabs. The views across the bay can be spectacular in the early morning. The park by the **Fort George Lighthouse** has a children's play area and is a popular meeting place. Baron Bliss' tomb is also here. **Belize Zoo** (see page 287) is definitely worth a visit and not far from Belize City. The trip is very easy with buses from Belize City passing the entrance every half hour.

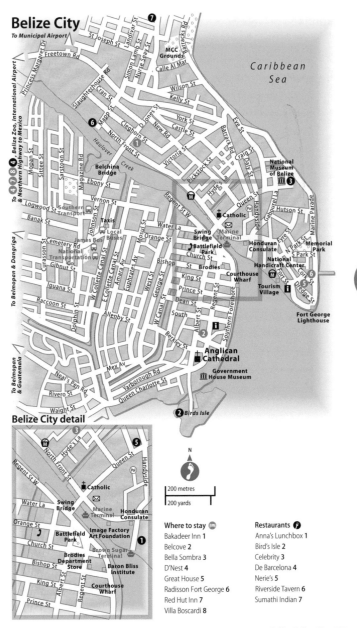

Belize City

To Municipal Airport

Caribbean Sea

St Joseph St
Freetown Rd
Simon Lamb St
Landivar St
Surge Sea St
Barracks Rd
MCC Grounds
Calle Al Mar
Wilson St
Slaughterhouse
Cran St
Kelly St
Cleghorn St
Jones St
York St
Castle St
Mapp St
New Rd
North Front St
Victoria St
Eve St
Barrack Rd
Craig St
Daly St
National Museum of Belize
Pickstock St
Hyde St
Queen St
Handyside St
Hutson St
Gabourel La
Regent St W
Catholic
Marine Terminal
Swing Bridge
Battlefield Park Church St
Honduran Consulate
National Handicraft Center
Memorial Park
N Park St
Cork St
Dedge St
Tourism Village
Fort George Lighthouse

Princess Margaret Dr
To Belize Zoo, International Airport & Northern Highway to Mexico

Belchina Bridge
Haulover Creek
Ebony St
Vernon St
Southern Transport
Magazine Rd
Mopan St
Sarstoon St
Sittee St
Logwood St
Banak St
Johnson St
Taxis
Local Buses
Water La
Mosul St
Orange St
Bishop St
Taxis
James Bus
National Transportation Co
Cemetery Rd
Gibnut St
Curasson St
Iguana St
Raccoon St
Dolphin St
Gibnut St
Brodies
Courthouse Wharf
King St
Prince St
Dean St
South St
Berkley St
Southern Foreshore
Albert St
Regent St
E Collette Canal St
W Collette Canal St
Amara Av
Euphrates Av
West St
George St
Allenby St

To Belmopan & Dangriga

To Belmopan & Guatemala

Mex Av
Neal's Pen Rd
Rivero St
Waight St
Yarborough Rd
Queen Charlotte St

Anglican Cathedral
Government House Museum

Birds Isle

Belize City detail

Regent St W
North Front St
Hyde's La
Queen St
Handyside
Pol
Catholic
Water La
Swing Bridge
Marine Terminal
Honduran Consulate
Orange St
Battlefield Park
Church St
Bishop St
Brodies Department Store
King St
Albert St
Regent St
Prince St
Image Factory Art Foundation
Brown Sugar Terminal
Baron Bliss Institute
Courthouse Wharf

N

200 metres
200 yards

Where to stay
Bakadeer Inn **1**
Belcove **2**
Bella Sombra **3**
D'Nest **4**
Great House **5**
Radisson Fort George **6**
Red Hut Inn **7**
Villa Boscardi **8**

Restaurants
Anna's Lunchbox **1**
Bird's Isle **2**
Celebrity **3**
De Barcelona **4**
Nerie's **5**
Riverside Tavern **6**
Sumathi Indian **7**

Tourist information

Belize Tourist Board
64 Regent St, T227-2420, www.travelbelize.
org. Mon-Thu 0800-1200, 1300-1700, Fri
0800-1200, 1300-1630.
Provides a bus schedule with a map of Belize
City, as well as hotel lists. There's also an
office in the Tourism Village.

Where to stay

On the north side of the swing-bridge,
turn left up North Front St for some of the
cheaper hotels. Most places can arrange
airport pick-up with advance notice, but
clarify costs carefully.

$$$$ Radisson Fort George
2 Marine Parade, T223-3333,
www.radisson.com.
A large and well-attired hotel spread across
3 wings, including the Club Wing, where
rooms have marble floors and panoramic
views of the Caribbean; and the Colonial
Section with balconies overlooking the sea.
Rooms are excellent, the staff are helpful,
and the service is good. Amenities include a
main restaurant (and **Stonegrill Restaurant**
where food is cooked on hot, volcanic
stones), 2 lovely pools, bar, coffee shop,
fitness room and small garden.

$$$$ The Great House
13 Cork St, T223-3400,
www.greathousebelize.com.
Built in 1927, this beautifully maintained
4-storey colonial mansion claims to be the
largest intact classic wooden structure in
Belize. Lodgings here include 16 spacious
rooms with homey furnishings and mod
cons; some have ocean view. Facilities
include a bar-restaurant, **The Smoky
Mermaid**, in the colonial courtyard on
the lower floor.

$$$ D'Nest
475 Cedar St, Belama Phase II, T223-5416,
www.dnestinn.com.
D'Nest is a very hospitable and
accommodating B&B. Located 3 miles out
of the city centre in a very safe middle class
neighbourhood, it features a selection of
cosy rooms with comfortable king-size
beds and interesting Belizean antiques.
The garden is lush and tranquil and the
thoughtful hosts are very knowledgeable
about the country.

$$$ Villa Boscardi
6043 Manatee Dr, Buttonwood Bay,
T223-1691, www.villaboscardi.com.
Secluded, gracious, friendly and tasteful,
Villa Boscardi is a European-style B&B
situated in a safe residential neighbourhood,
a short distance from downtown. It has 7
spacious rooms fully kitted with large beds,
Wi-Fi, a/c, cable TV and attractive tropical
hardwood furnishings. Pleasant garden,
good cooked breakfast included.

$$$-$$ Bella Sombra
36 Hydes Lane, T223-0223,
www.lasbrisasdelmar.net.
This place has an excellent downtown
location very close to the water taxi
terminals. Rooms are spacious, clean and
well-equipped with Wi-Fi, cable TV, ice cold
a/c and small kitchenettes with microwaves
and fridges (no cookers). There's also a
communal area and parking. Good and safe.

$$ Bakadeer Inn
74 Cleghorn St, T223-0659,
www.bakadeerinn.com.
Located in an area of the city once known
as the **Bakadeer**, this friendly downtown
inn near the riverside has 12 small but
comfortable rooms with hot water, a/c, and
cable TV. The property also includes a large
central lobby area with tables and chairs,
good for hanging out. Simple, quiet, and
well-kept.

$$ Red Hut Inn
90 Bella Vista, T223-1907, www.red-hut-inn-belize.50megs.com.

Located 6 miles from the international airport in a safe residential district, **Red Hut Inn** is good option for those who don't want to contend with the hustle of downtown Belize City. Rooms are quiet and simple, equipped with cable TV, hot water and Wi-Fi. They also have a deck, hammock and loungers, and can organize connections to the domestic airport and the water taxis.

$$-$ Belcove Hotel
9 Regent St West, T227-3054, www.belcove.com.

Overlooking the waterfront near the swing bridge, the **Belcove Hotel** is a good, safe downtown option for those on a budget. Rooms are modest, with ($$) or without ($) private bath. Popular with international travellers. There's free coffee in the morning, and it's within easy walking distance of the water taxis.

Restaurants

It can be difficult to find places to eat between 1500-1800.

$$$ Riverside Tavern
2 Mapp St.

Not a locals' joint, but an upscale American-style bar-restaurant with sports TV, beer, burgers, onion rings and other artery-hardening comfort food. This place will suit those seeking safe shelter or familiar flavours. So-so ambience but the burgers are something special. It's perched on the riverside, as the name suggests.

$$$-$$ Celebrity
Marine Parade Blvd, Volta Building, T223-7272, www.celebritybelize.com.

This reliable middle class restaurant might be considered upmarket for Belize City. It serves local and international food in large portions, including salads, burgers, pastas, meat, and seafood. Popular with families, couples and local businessmen.

$$$-$$ De Barcelona
Buttonwood Bay Blvd, T666-4680.

The best Catalan and Spanish cuisine in town with tasty paella, red tuna, beef tenderloin and tapas. Smart, hip interior and cool outdoor seating under a *palapa*. They also host live regular live music and serve delicious sangria. Excellent, creative and authentic. Recommended for a special evening out.

$$$-$$ Sumathi Indian
19 Baymen Av, T223-1172.

Weary Brits will not be able to resist this authentic curry house. Their menu includes a tempting array of Indian specialities such as chicken, mutton, and shrimp biryani, 4 varieties of naan bread, papadums, chicken tikka and madras, and many more flavourful curries to invigorate even the most jaded taste buds. Good and wholesome, the taste of home.

$$ Bird's Isle
90 Albert St.

Bird's Isle features an open-air deck with panoramic ocean views, ideal for taking in the sunset. Its name refers to the small islet located off the city's southeastern shore. They serve reasonable seafood, salads, burgers, steaks and chicken; you pay for the setting. A great lunch spot; however, take a taxi as the neighbourhood is sketchy.

$$ Nerie's
Corner Queen and Daly St, T223-4028, www.neries.bz. Open for breakfast, lunch, and dinner.

A family-owned business for over 15 years, **Nerie's** serves up home-cooked Belizean cuisine (including 'the best rice and beans in the country'), along with international fare such as burgers, salads, and fresh fruit juices. They have an extensive menu. At their Douglas Jones St branch there is also a bar.

$ Anna's Lunchbox
North Front St. Open for breakfast and lunch.

Managed by Miss Anna, this friendly locals' place is conveniently located near the San

Pedro Water Taxi, great for a quick bite en route to the island. They serve tasty home-cooked Belizean grub, including fresh Johnny cakes, fry jacks, jerk chicken and, to wash it down, ice-cold Belikin beer.

Bars and clubs

There are lots of bars, some with jukeboxes, poolrooms and karaoke nights.

Fri night is the most popular night for going out. Clubs often have a cover charge of US$5 and drinks are expensive. Happy hour on Fri starts at 1600 at **Radisson Fort George** and continues at **Biltmore**, **Calypso** and elsewhere. The best and safest bars are at major hotels: **Fort George**, **Biltmore Plaza**, **Bellevue** and **Princess**.

Club Calypso
At the Princess Hotel, see Where to stay.
Top bands at weekends.

The Wet Lizard
Near the Tourism Village.
Good American/Creole fare, great view.

Entertainment

Cinema
Princess Hotel, *see Where to stay*. A 2-theatre modern cinema, showing recent movies for US$7.50.

Shopping

The whole city closes down on Sun except for a few shops open in the morning, eg Brodies in the centre of town. Banks and many shops and offices are also closed on Sat afternoons.

Books
Brodies, *Albert St*. Decent selection of books on Belize and some paperback novels. It is now the only bookshop in the city.

Markets and supermarkets
The market is by the junction of North Front St and Fort St.

Brodies. *Closed Sun*. The widest grocery selection, though prices are slightly higher.

Souvenirs
Handicrafts, woodcarvings and straw items are all good buys. Zericote (or Xericote) wood carvings can be bought at **Brodies**, Central Park end of Regent St (which also sells postcards), the **Fort George Hotel**, see Where to stay, above, or **Egbert Peyrefitte**, 11a Cemetery Rd. Such wood carvings are the best buy, but to find a carver rather than buy the tourist fare in shops, ask a taxi driver. The wood sculpture of **Charles Gabb**, who introduced carving into Belize, can be seen at the Art Centre, near Government House. Wood carvers sell their work in front of the main hotels.
Belize Audubon Society, *see box, page 284*. A small but good selection of posters, T-shirts, gifts, and jewellery, all locally made in villages, and all at very reasonable prices.
National Handicraft Center, *South Park St*. The Belize Chamber of Commerce's showcase promotes craftspeople from all over Belize; come here first for an overview of Belizean art and crafts.

What to do

Cultural centres
Audubon Society, see box, page 284.
Baron Bliss Institute, public library, temporary exhibitions and 1 stela and 2 large discs from Caracol on display.
Belize National Handicraft Center, *sales room on South Park St*. A good supply of books about Belize culture.
Programme for Belize, *1 Eyre St, T227-5616, www.pfbelize.org*. A conservation organization that manages land reserves including Río Bravo.
Society for the Promotion of Education and Research (SPEAR), *5638 Gentle Av, T223-1668, www.spear.org.bz*. A great reference library for everything Belizean.

Diving

Hugh Parkey's Belize Dive Connection, *www.belizediving.com*. Based at the **Radisson's** dock, this is a professional outfit.

Tour operators

Discovery Expeditions, *5916 Manatee Dr, Buttonwood Bay, T223-0748, www.discovery belize.com*. An efficient and professional company offering interesting cultural and adventure tours out of the city and across the country. Recommended.

Green Dragon, *based out near Belmopan, but covering most of the country, T822-2124, www.greendragonbelize.com*. Very helpful and will arrange hotel bookings and tours all over Belize.

Island Expeditions Co, *Canada-based, in UK toll-free T0800-404 9535, www. islandexpeditions.com*. Adventure and multi-sport wilderness, rainforest and reef trips. Also run **Belize Kayaking**, www.belizekayaking.com.

Maya Travel Services, *42 Cleghorn St, T223-1623, www.mayatravelservices.com/contact. php*. Gets positive reports.

S&L Guided Tours, *91 North Front St, T227-7593, www.sltravelbelize.com*. Recommended group travel (groups of 4 people for most tours, 2 people for Tikal). If booking tours in Belize from abroad it is advisable to check prices and services offered with a reputable tour operator in Belize first.

Air

International flights arrive at **Phillip Goldson International Airport** on the Northern Highway, Ladyville, T225-2045, www. pgiabelize.com, 10½ miles from Belize City. Taxi to town US$25, 30 mins; see also below. It's a 1½-mile walk to the junction of the Northern Highway where buses pass to the centre (US$1). **Belize City Municipal Airport** for local flights is 2 miles north of the city centre on the seafront, 15 mins' drive away. Taxi to the centre US$5, no bus service.

The international airport has facilities in the check-in area including toilets, a restaurant, internet, bank (daily 0830-1200 and 1230-1800), viewing deck and duty-free shop. There are no facilities on the arrivals side but you can just walk round to the check-in area. If getting a taxi into the centre, be aware that taxi drivers strongly discourage sharing so team up, if need be, before getting outside. Make sure your taxi is legitimate by checking for the green licence plates. Taxis operate on a fixed rate, so you should get the same price quoted by every driver. Ask to see a rate sheet if you have doubts about the price. If transferring direct to or from the islands or elsewhere in Belize with a domestic carrier be sure to stipulate that you would like a connection through the international airport. This will

cost an extra US$20 or so, offset by avoiding an unnecessary transit through Belize City to the municipal airport or boat dock (and an associated US$25 taxi fare).

Domestic services, including the island hops operated by **Maya Island** and **Tropic Air**, arrive at the pocket-sized municipal airstrip, flights every 30 mins, 0700-1630. Flights to and from the islands can be taken from the international airport and companies link their flights to international arrivals and departures; flights from the international airport cost extra (see above). **Maya** and **Tropic** also have services to **Flores**, Guatemala.

Boat

Boats to **Caye Caulker** continuing to **San Pedro** (Ambergris Caye) and **Chetumal in Mexico** leave from 3 principal boat terminals in Belize City, with sailings at regular times between around 0700 and 1730 each day. As long as you check schedules beforehand you are never more than 30 mins from a boat during the day. The **Water Jets Express** (T226-2194, www.sanpedrowatertaxi. com) dock lies on Bird's Isle at the far end of Albert St in the southside of Belize City, just beyond St John's Cathedral. The company has services 4 times daily to Caye Caulker (US$12 one way, 30-45 mins), San Pedro (US$18 one way, 60-80 mins) and once daily on to Chetumal in Mexico (US$35 from San Pedro and US$40 from Caye Caulker, both one way). The company is also an official agent for Mexican ADO buses, and can book tickets from Chetumal or all along the Riviera Maya to Cancún, and connections beyond, including Guatemala.

Belize's other 2 boat terminals both lie on North Front St, about 200 m southeast of the swing bridge in the city centre. Closest to the bridge is the **Marine Terminal**, home to the Caye Caulker Water Taxi Association (T226-0992, www.cayecaulkerwatertaxi. com) also with 4 times daily to Caye Caulker (US$10 one way, 45 mins), San Pedro (US$15 one way, about 90 mins).

A little further on up the same road right next to the cruise ship tourist facility in the **Brown Sugar Terminal**, is the San Pedro Belize Express Water Taxi (Brown Sugar Market Square, 111 North Front St, T223-2225, http://belizewatertaxi.com). They have the same number of sailings to the same destinations as the Caye Caulker Water Taxi Association, for the same price, and once daily, on to Chetumal in Mexico (US$35 from San Pedro and US$40 from Caye Caulker, both one way). Terminals have areas where you can leave a bag and the Caye Caulker Water Taxi Association terminal has a few shops and cafés.

For further information on border crossings to Mexico and Guatemala, see box, page 511.

Bus

The main **bus station** is on West Collette Canal St to the west of town, an area that requires some caution. If arriving after dark, arrange for a taxi as walking through this part of town in darkness with luggage can be dangerous; a taxi costs around US$3 to the centre.

Within the city the fare is US$0.50 run by **Belize in Transit** services. They originate next to the taxi stand on Cemetery Rd.

There are bus services to all the main towns. The **National Transportation Co** operates Northern Transport from West Collette Canal St (can store luggage, US$0.50).

North to **Chetumal** (see Mexico, page 207), about 15 daily each way, roughly every 30 mins, starting at 0500 until 1800, 3 hrs, US$2.50, express buses from 0600 stopping at **Orange Walk** and **Corozal** only, US$6.50, 2½ hrs. If taking a bus from Chetumal which will arrive in Belize City after dark, decide on a hotel and go there by taxi.

West towards **Guatemala** by bus to **Belmopan** and **San Ignacio**, express bus 0900, US$3, with a/c and refreshments, ordinary bus every 30 mins, Mon-Sat frequent 0600-1900, Sun 0630-1700. The 0600, 0630 and 1015 buses connect at the border with services to **Flores**, Guatemala.

To **San Ignacio**, **Benque Viejo** and the **Guatemalan border** via Belmopan, US$2.50 to Belmopan, US$4 to San Ignacio, US$4.50 to Benque, hourly Mon-Sat, 1100-1900. The last possible bus connection to **Flores** leaves the border at 1600, but it is better to get an earlier bus to arrive in daylight. Many buses leave for **Melchor de Mencos**, 0600-1030. To **Flores**, Guatemala, minibuses leave the Marine Terminal on Front St in Belize City; make reservations the previous day. See also box, page 514.

1st-class express buses from Belize City to **Flores/Tikal** with **Mundo Maya/Línea Dorada**, www.tikalmayanworld.com, leave from Belize City daily at 1000 and 1700, with buses connecting to Guatemala City and beyond. Also with services heading north to **Chetumal**. Check the **Mundo Maya** counter in the Marine Terminal on North Front St.

South to Dangriga, via Belmopan and the Hummingbird Hwy. **Southern Transport** (T227-3937), from the corner of Vernon and Johnson St near the Belchina Bridge, several daily on the hour 0800-1600, plus Mon 0600, US$5. **James** (T702-2049), to **Punta Gorda** via **Dangriga**, **Cockscomb Basin Wildlife Sanctuary** and **Independence**, every hour from 0515 to 1015 and 1215 to 1515 with the last bus at 1545, 6-8 hrs, US$14.

Car
Car hire Cars start at US$75 plus insurance of around US$15 a day. Most rental firms have offices in Belize City and opposite the international airport terminal building.

Avis, T203-4619, avisbelize@btl.net. **Budget**, 2½ miles, Northern Hwy, T223-2435, www.budget-belize.com. **Crystal Auto Rental**, Mile 5 Northern Hwy, T223-1600, www.crystal-belize.com, cheapest deals in town, but not always most reliable, wide selection of vehicles, will release insurance papers for car entry to Guatemala and Mexico. **Hertz**, 11a Cork St, beside Radisson Fort George Hotel, T223-5395, www.hertz belize.com, and International Airport, T225-3300. **Pancho's**, 5747 Lizarraga Av, T224-5554, www.panchosrentalbelize.com, locally owned rental company.

Taxi
Official cabs have green licence plates (drivers have ID card); within Belize, US$4 for 1 or 2 people; slightly more for 3 or more. There is a taxi stand on Central Park, another on the corner of Collet Canal St and Cemetery Rd, and a number of taxis on Albert St, Queen St and around town. Outside Belize City, US$1.75 per mile, regardless of number of passengers. Belize City to the resorts in Cayo District approximately US$100-125, 1-4 people. No meters, so beware of overcharging and make sure fare is quoted in BZ$ not US$.

Northern
cayes

★The cayes off the coast are attractive, relaxing, slow and very 'Caribbean', an excellent place for diving, sea fishing or just lazing about. Palm trees fringe the coastline, providing day-long shade for resting in your hammock looking out at the stunning azure seas. They are popular destinations, especially in August and between December and May.

There are some 212 sq miles of cayes. The cayes and atolls were home to fishermen and resting points to clean the catch or grow coconuts. But they have always been valued. The Maya built the site of Marco Gonzalez on the southwestern tip of Ambergris Caye, the largest and most populated of the islands.

Nearby Caye Caulker is a popular destination for the budget travellers, while serious divers head for the Turneffe Islands. Other smaller cayes are home to exclusive resorts or remain uninhabited, many being little more than mangrove swamps. St George's Caye, nine miles northeast of Belize, was once the capital and the scene of the battle in 1798 that established British possession.

This island (pronounced Am-*ber*-gris, population 10,445), along with the town of San Pedro, has grown rapidly over the last couple of years, with over 50 hotels and guesthouses on the island. Buildings are still restricted to no more than three storeys in height, and the many wooden structures retain an authentic village atmosphere.

The very helpful **Ambergris tourist information office** ⓘ *Mon-Sat 1000-1300, 1400-1900*, is next to the town hall.

Although sand is in abundance, there are few beach areas around San Pedro town. You cannot, in practice, walk north along the beach from San Pedro to Xcalak, Mexico. The emphasis is on snorkelling on the nearby barrier reef and Hol Chan Marine Park, and the fine scuba diving, sailing, fishing and board sailing. The main boat jetties are on the east (Caribbean Sea) side of San Pedro. It can be dangerous to swim near San Pedro as there have been serious accidents with boats. Boats are restricted to about 5 mph within the line of red buoys about 25 yards offshore, but this is not always adhered to. There is a 'safe' beach in front of the park, just to the south of the government dock. A short distance to the north and south of San Pedro lie miles of deserted beachfront, where picnic barbecues are popular for day-tripping snorkellers and birders who have visited the nearby small cayes hoping to glimpse rosets, spoonbills or white ibis. If you go north you have to cross a small inlet with hand-pulled ferry, US$0.50 for foreigners. **Note** Only very experienced snorkellers should attempt to swim in the cutting between the reef and the open sea.

Around Ambergris Caye

Just south of Ambergris Caye, and not far from Caye Caulker, is the **Hol Chan Marine Park** ⓘ *US$12 entry fee; the park office (with reef displays and information on Bacalar Chico National Park to the north) is on Caribeña St, T226-2247, www.holchanbelize.org.* This underwater natural park is divided into three zones: Zone A is the reef, where fishing is prohibited; Zone B is the sea grass beds, where fishing can only be done with a special licence (the **Boca Ciega** blue hole is here); Zone C is mangroves where fishing also requires a licence. Only certified scuba divers may dive in the reserve. Fish feeding, although prohibited, takes place at Shark Ray Alley, where about 15 sharks and rays are fed for the entertainment of tourists. Not the most natural of experiences.

San Pedro is well known for its diving. Long canyons containing plenty of soft and hard coral formations start at around 50-60 ft going down to 120 ft. Often these have grown into hollow tubes, which make for interesting diving. **Tackle Box**, **Esmeralda**, **Cypress**, **M & Ms** and **Tres Cocos** are only some of the dive sites. The visibility in this area is usually over 100 ft. There is a recompression chamber in San Pedro and a US$1 tax on each tank fill insures treatment throughout the island.

Although offshore, Ambergris Caye airport makes arranging tours to visit places on the mainland very easy (for example, Altun Ha US$60 per person; Lamanai US$125 per person) while still being able to enjoy other water experiences (catamaran sailing, deep-sea fishing, manatee and Coco Solo).

Where to stay

Accommodation is generally upscale and poor value relative to the mainland.

San Pedro

$$$$ Changes in Latitude
36 Coconut Dr, T226-2986, www. changesinlatitudesbelize.com.
Located 150 m from the sea, this sweet B&B has 6 rooms decorated in retro style. Guests have free use of bikes, a golf cart and the yacht club pool. Local artists occasionally hang out in the courtyard. Lots of good reports, popular, book in advance.

$$$$ Ramon's Village
Coconut Dr, T226-2071, www.ramons.com.
Nestled amid bougainvillea and hibiscus flowers, this popular dive resort features upscale cabanas styled after the Tahitian cottages on the Polynesian island of Bora Bora. Even if you're not diving it's well worth staying here as there are plenty additional activities of fishing, swimming, boating and snorkelling. Amenities include a pool with a beach-club atmosphere. Highly recommended.

$$$$ Sun Breeze Hotel
Coconut Dr, T226-2191, www.sunbreeze.net.
The **Sun Breeze** is a modern, villa-style resort with architecture reminiscent of Spain's Costa del Sol. Its dive shop is a branch of Hugh Parkey's (www.belizediving. com), one of the best on the island. Good service and comfortable rooms, nice pool and restaurant. Their sister establishment, Sun Breeze Suites, offer 12 ocean view and 8 ocean front suites with fully equipped kitchen. Recommended.

$$$$-$$$ Holiday Hotel
Barrier Reef Dr, T+1 713 893-3825, www.sanpedroholiday.com.
This locally owned landmark establishment is built in traditional Caribbean style.

With a convenient central location, it has 16 rooms including suites and a *casita*. Fun atmosphere with good facilities including a bar-grill, spa and tour desk.

$$$ Conch Shell Inn
11 Foreshore St, T226-2062, www. ambergriscaye.com/conchshell.
Established in 1973, this beachfront favourite has 10 rooms with a shared veranda overlooking the ocean, ideal for chilling out in a hammock. All rooms feature mini-bar, Wi-Fi and slumber-inducing tempurpedic mattresses; some have a full kitchenette. Cheery, friendly, and pink.

$$$ Mayan Princess
Pelican St and seafront, T226-2778, www.mayanprincesshotel.com.
Right on the beach and close to the heart of the action, the Mayan Princess boasts a great downtown location. Its suites are good value for the island and include a fully equipped kitchen, living area, a/c, cable TV and veranda-balcony. Rooms on the 3rd floor catch the best views and sea breezes. Ask about deals and discounts. Dive packages available with their affiliated shop.

$$ Hotel San Pedrano
T226-2054, sanpedrano@btl.net.
Modest family-run lodgings, low-key and economical for the island. Rooms are fairly no frills, but they feature a/c, fan, Wi-Fi, private bath and hot water. It's not luxurious, but is adequate for those who intend to spend most of their time on the beach. Friendly, helpful management.

$$-$ Pedro's Inn
Seagrape Dr, T226-3825, www.backpackersbelize.com.
Starting at US$10 per person per night, this is the only true budget place on the island, aimed squarely at the backpacker market. Their private rooms ($$) are fairly good. There's a bar, barbecue and pools.

$$-$ Ruby's
On the beach, T226-2063.
Ramshackle and basic with paper thin walls and an air of decay, Ruby's is fairly typical of cheap Central American lodgings. Its 26 rooms have a/c or fan and private or shared bath. Good views, low prices (for the island) and a central location.

Outside San Pedro
Several resort-style complexes outside the town offer seclusion and an ambience that borders on paradise.

$$$$ El Pescador
On Punta Arena beach 3 miles north of San Pedro, access by boat, T226-2398, www.elpescador.com.

This award-winning sports fishing lodge offers a range of packages to suit anglers, couples and families. Lodgings include 8 wood-built private villas with all mod cons. There's a restaurant-bar, 3 pools, gym, massage, complimentary kayaks and bicycles and scuba lessons. Good reputation and service.

$$$$ Mata Chica Resort
5 miles north of town, T226-5010, www.matachica.com.
This tasteful, tranquil, European-owned resort features 26 beautiful and stylish stucco cabins with thatched roofs, original art from around the world, mosaic bathrooms, a/c and Matouk and Frette linens. Located on a lovely beach with amenities that include

spa treatments, jacuzzi, infinity pool and the award-winning **Mambo** Restaurant. Romantic and indulgent.

$$$$ Portofino
6 miles north, access by boat,
T888 240 1923 (toll free), T678-5096,
www.portofinobelize.com.
Overlooking the sea, Portofino offers a series of spacious and very comfortable thatched roof beach cabins gathered around a jewel-like pool. The Belgian owners organize excursions, diving and run one of the best kitchens on the island. Rustic chic and romantic.

$$$$ Victoria House
2 miles south of town, T226-2067, T1-800-247-5159 (US toll free), www.victoria-house.com.
This lavish, crisp-white exclusive resort has received praise from luxury travel media such as Condé Nast. It offers 4 different types of stylishly decorated lodgings, including *casitas*, 'plantation rooms', suites and private villas. Excellent facilities, including a lovely pool and a good dive shop. Highly recommended.

$$$$-$$$ Corona del Mar
Coconut Dr, ½ mile south of San Pedro,
T226-2055, www.coronadelmarhotel.com.
Located within easy walking distance of the town (15 mins), but far enough to enjoy some peace and quiet, the beachfront Corona del Mar offers a variety of accommodation, including standard rooms with ocean, pool or garden views, fully kitted apartments, a master suite and a cottage. A good option for couples, groups or families. Free rum punch all day.

$$$ The Turtleman's House
Bacalar Chico Marine Reserve, north end of the island, www.turtlemanshouse.com.
A Robinson Crusoe-style wooden shack over the water, extremely basic and adventurous. Managed by a marine biologist, Greg Smith, aka the Turtleman, this intriguing accommodation promises up close wilderness encounters with the reef in front of the cabana and options for excellent turtle, manatee and jungle tours. Something different. Recommended for nature lovers.

$$$-$$ Ak'bol Yoga Retreat and Eco-Resort
1 mile north of town past the bridge,
T226-2073, www.akbol.com.
The epitome of rustic chic, this attractive yoga retreat has a range of accommodation, including economical 'village rooms' (**$$**) and beautiful thatched cabanas (**$$$**) with mosaic work, carved mahogany sinks and private porches. In addition to yoga, they offer snorkelling, diving, massage and tours.

Restaurants

San Pedro

$$$ Elvi's Kitchen
www.elviskitchen.com.
Upmarket restaurant with live music and a roof built around flamboyant tree. It's popular, so can get very busy, and has won international awards.

$$$ Hidden Treasure
4088 Sarstoon St, T226-4111, www.hidden treasurebelize.com. Open for dinner only.
Awarded 'Restaurant of the Year' by the Belize Tourism Board, **Hidden Treasure** promises a truly magical and romantic dining experience. It serves culinary delights such as roasted lamb chops with wild mushrooms and Madeira wine; fresh snapper fillet seasoned with Mayan spices and cooked in banana leaf; and coconut chicken breast served with orange and ginger sauce. Meals are served in a beautiful garden setting. Highly recommended.

$$$ Wild Mango's
South of main strip, T226-2859. Closed Mon.
Run by Amy Knox, former chef at **Victoria House**, this place is in a rustic setting overlooking the sea. The delicious meals are tastefully presented; try the rum-soaked bacon-wrapped shrimp. Recommended.

$$$-$$ Blue Water Grill
At the Sunbreeze Hotel, www. bluewatergrillbelize.com.
Owned by Kelly McDermott Kanabar, who was born and raised in San Pedro but educated in the US, the popular Blue Water grill overlooks the beach with an open front. They serve an eclectic range of international cuisine including ceviche, buffalo wings, tacos, salads, sandwiches and more. Pizzas are available in the evening and a sushi menu for dinner on Tue and Thu. Recommended.

$$$-$$ El Fogon
2 Trigger Fish St, north of Tropic Air Terminal.
This very presentable and busy restaurant serves delicious Belizean cuisine prepared on a traditional hearth fire. Their seafood is particularly recommended, including dishes such as fish, shrimp and lobster kebabs in mango sauce; lime and garlic shrimp; and conch fritters with honey mustard dipping sauce. A great family place. Recommended.

$$$-$$ Hurricane's Ceviche Bar and Grill
Foreshore Beachfront, Coconut Dr.
Perched at the end of a wooden pier over the waves, this popular seafood restaurant serves very good ceviche, shrimp, conch, lobster and catch of the day. A fine place for quaffing cold beers and rum. Casual and fun, but not cheap; you pay for the ocean views and friendly ambience.

$$ Estel's Dine by the Sea
On the beach close to water taxi terminal.
Good food and 1940s-50s music.

$$-$ My Secret Deli
Caribeña St. Open for breakfast and lunch.
Managed by the amiable Don Oscar from El Salvador, this fantastic locals' joint serves a selection of flavourful daily specials inspired by local recipes and old favourites from the homeland. Offerings include stewed pork with coconut rice and conch soup with corn tortillas. Eat in or take-away. Large

portions, good value and friendly service. Recommended.

$ Dande's Frozen Custard
Middle St, www.dande.bz.
Popular place for an ice cream cone, sorbet or frozen custard.

Outside San Pedro

$$$ Aji Tapa Bar & Restaurant
2½ miles north of San Pedro, T226-4047.
Nestled among palm trees behind a creek, **Aji Tapa** enjoys prime ocean views from its location on the edge of the beach. They serve tapas and beautifully presented seafood, including good paella, conch ceviche and fish fillets. Candlelit and close to nature with a rustic, romantic atmosphere.

$$$ Lazy Croc BBQ
2½ miles north of San Pedro, T226-4015.
Hidden among the mangroves, this breezy family restaurant with a rustic wooden deck serves good comfort food, hearty platters of barbecue grub, including sweet baby back ribs and succulent pulled pork. Look out for the crocodiles which live in the pond, easy to spot from the bridge and the balcony. A fun place, but not cheap.

$$$-$$ Palapa Bar and Grill
1½ miles north of San Pedro.
This young party place consists of a large wooden *palapa* on the water. They serve hearty grilled grub including smoked barbecue chicken wings, sausage dip, fish platter and a 'kickass humungous hamburger'. They also supply inner tubes so you can float on the water and drink Belikin beers lowered to you in a bucket.

Bars and clubs

Big Daddy's Disco, open evenings but cranks up at midnight. Try also 'Chicken Drop' in Pier Lounge at **Spindrift Hotel** on a Thu night: you bet US$1 on which square the chicken will leave its droppings. **Jaguar's**

Temple and **Barefoot Iguana** are current popular nightspots.

Shopping

There are many gift shops in the centre of San Pedro town. It is better to shop around the smaller shops and groceries where prices are clearly marked. When paying check that the bill is correct.

Fidos has **Belizean Arts** (paintings and prints by local artists) and **Ambar Jewelry**. **Kasbah** and **Orange** sell local crafts and jewellery.

What to do

Diving and snorkelling
Park fees are not included in prices quoted. US$10 for Hol Chan, US$30 for Blue Hole, US$10 Half Moon Caye and US$10 for Bacalar Chico. Be clear on what's included. You will likely be charged extra for equipment. Instruction to PADI Open Water level available, from US$350. Local 2-tank dive US$60, Turneffe US$140-160, Blue Hole US$185. Many operators practice chumming to attract fish and sharks; divers should discourage operators from doing this. Accommodation and dive packages at some hotels are very good value. All dive operators offer snorkelling trips from US$25 for Shark Ray Alley to US$125 for the Blue Hole.

   Note Check the diving shop's recent safety record before diving.
Ambergris Divers, *T226-2634, www.amber grisdivers.com*. Will collect divers from Caye Caulker for Blue Hole trip. Very good-value dive and accommodation packages with a number of hotels on the island.
Amigos del Mar, *opposite Lily's, T226-2706, www.amigos dive.com*. Gets a lot of return customers and has been recommended, but practices chumming at the Blue Hole.
Ramon's Village, *T226 2071, www.ramons. com*. A bit more expensive than other operators. Check the diving shop's recent safety record before diving.

Fishing
Extreme Reef Adventures, *office by the dock at Fido's, T226-3513*. Parasailing, banana tubing and other sport tours.
Sailsports, **Holiday Hotel**, *T226-4488, www. sailsportsbelize.com*. Windsurfing, sailing, kitesurfing lessons and rentals.

Tour operators
Tanisha Tours, *T226 2314, www.tanishatours. com*. Trips to the Maya sites on the north of the caye in the Bacalar Chico National Park.
Travel and Tour Belize, *in town, T226-2031*. Helpful, all services and can arrange flights, with a request stop at Sarteneja (for the Shipstern Nature Reserve).

Transport

Air
Tropic Air, T226-2012, and **Maya Island Air**, T226-2435, have flights to/from both **Belize City** airports, many hourly, to **Caye Caulker** and **Corozal**. Charter services are available.

Bicycle and golf cart
Bicycles US$2.50 per hour, negotiate for long-term rates. Golf carts from US$15 per hour and up to US$300 per week, battery or gas powered, driver's licence needed.

Boat
More interesting than going by air are the boats. All these call at **Caye Caulker** and San Pedro. **San Pedro Belize Express water taxi**, http://belizewatertaxi.com, to **Caye Caulker** and **Belize City** at 0700 (express to Belize City), 1130, 1430, 1630 and 1800. With **San Pedro Jet Express** at 0600, 1030, 1500 and 1730. Many regular boats to Caye Caulker. Daily services to **Chetumal** in Mexico.

   The *Island Ferry*, T226-3231, from Fido's dock, services the north of the island every 2 hrs from 0700-1700 then hourly 1800-2200. Also at 2400 and 0200 on Wed, Fri and Sat. Returns 0600-2200 every 2 hrs, US$10-25.

On Caye Caulker, a thin line of white sandy beach falls to a sea of blue and green, while the reef can be seen a mile and a half from the shore. By day on this tranquil island, it's diving and snorkelling, sea and sand; at dusk everyone heads up to the Split to watch the sunset. By night it's eating, drinking and dancing. A quiet lobster-fishing island (closed season 15 February to 14 June) until fairly recently, its relaxed atmosphere, gentle climate, postcard-perfect views and the myriad small restaurants and bars have drawn increasing numbers of tourists.

The caye is actually two islands separated by a small channel (the Split); swimming is possible here but beware of fishing and powerboats. All services are on the southern island and, in the north, there is a **marine reserve** ⓘ *free for school parties, tourists are asked for a US$2 donation to help expansion and to increase the work in ecology education.* In the south, next to **Shirley's**, is the **Caye Caulker Mini Reserve**.

Tour operators and hotels on the island have worked hard to improve services for visitors. The atmosphere is friendly and easy-going, but the usual common sense rules apply with regards to personal safety. Drugs are readily available, but they are illegal and you shouldn't expect any sympathy should you get into difficulties. Some think the atmosphere is more relaxed out of high season. Sandflies can be ferocious in season (December to February); take long trousers and a good repellent. Make sure you fix prices before going on trips or hiring equipment and, if you pay the night before, get a receipt.

A walk south along the shore takes you to the airstrip, the Caye Caulker Mini Reserve and to mangroves where the rare black catbird can be seen and its sweet song heard.

Around Caye Caulker

Reef trips are the same as those found on Ambergris Caye; for more details see What to do, above, under San Pedro.

Generally all trips are offered at the same price by agreement between tour operators, eliminating the need to shop around for a good price. Tour operators share clients if numbers are not sufficient. This means that you can be certain there is always a trip, but make sure that the boat operator is reliable. Tour organizers must be licensed by the **Belize Tourist Board** and should have a licence to prove it. To encourage high standards, and for your own safety, insist on seeing proof that your guide is licensed.

Protect against sunburn on reef trips, even while snorkelling. Tours are slightly cheaper from Caye Caulker than Ambergris Caye; see What to do, below.

Listings Caye Caulker *map p278*

Where to stay

In all accommodation, take precautions against theft. The arrival pier is just about in the centre of town, with all the accommodation on or within a 15-min walk of the main street. The southern end of town is slightly quieter and has a smattering of mangrove and bird life, but it's quite a walk from the Split for swimming or snorkelling. Camping on the beach is forbidden.

$$$$ Iguana Reef Inn
Near the football field, T226-0213, www.iguanareefinn.com.

Caye Caulker

Located near the water's edge, a secluded and upscale resort with rooms that are spacious and decorated with local art and furniture. One of the best places on the island, relaxing and quiet.

$$$$-$$$ Sea Dreams
At north end of the island, T226-0602, www.seadreamsbelize.com.
This popular family-run boutique hotel offers a range of cosy and tastefully attired rooms ($$$) overlooking a lush courtyard with a Banyan tree, as well as lodging in a colourful cabana, modern apartments and a house ($$$$). 10% of profits go to a community school established by co-owner Heidi Curry. Recommended.

$$$$-$$$ Seaside Cabanas
First place you reach off the boat, T226-0498, www.seasidecabanas.com.
Adorned with earthy Moroccan furnishings, **Seaside Cabanas** offers comfortable rooms and cabins designed in Mexican-Belizean style. The best ones have their own roof terraces, kitchenettes, sea views and private hot tubs. Amenities include pool and funky bar. Excellent tours and very helpful.

$$$ Lazy Iguana
Southwest side of the island, a block from the cemetery, T226-0350, www.lazyiguana.net.

This beautifully designed B&B has a commanding rooftop terrace with 360-degree views, ideal for yoga, sunsets or simply lolling in a hammock. Guestrooms are spacious and homely, and downstairs you'll find 2 communal areas. Also offers onsite massages for guests. Tranquil.

$$$ Oasi
9 Av Mangle, T226 0384, www.oasi-holidaysbelize.com.
This popular apartment complex has modern, convenient and tastefully decorated units, with fully equipped kitchens, access to verandas with hammocks, Wi-Fi, cable TV and drinking water. Facilities include a bar, barbecue and complimentary use of bikes. A great option for couples and small families, but book in advance.

$$$ Rainbow Hotel
T226-0123, www.rainbowhotel-cayecaulker.com.
This long-standing family-owned hotel enjoys a great central location on a street front facing the beach. Its deluxe suites overlook the ocean and enjoy modern conveniences such as TVs, fridge, a/c and safe. Other options include junior suites, a cabana and a *casita* with 2 apartments. Friendly and helpful.

$$$ Tree Tops Guesthouse
T226-0240, www.treetopsbelize.com.
A long-standing Caye Caulker favourite built in Caribbean-Mediterranean style, This friendly guesthouse offers a range of spotless, spacious boutique rooms and suites, all decorated with intriguing art and craft pieces that reflect the travel experiences of the owners, Terry and Doris Creasy. German spoken, children over 10 only. Recommended.

$$$-$$ Barefoot Beach
Playa Asuncion, T226-0205, www.barefootbeachbelize.com.
Painted in candy coloured shades of pink, yellow and blue, this cheery and inviting establishment has a range of

accommodation including modern cabanas, cottages, bungalows and oceanfront and ocean-view suites equipped with fridges, cable TV, and a/c. Their most economical lodgings are clean and comfortable 'mini-huts' ($$).

$$$-$$ Colinda Cabanas
On the beach facing the reef, T226-0383, www.colindacabanas.com.
Enjoying almost constant cool breezes on the east side of the island, these inviting cabanas and suites have a plethora of mod cons including well-equipped kitchens, purified water, Wi-Fi and, most essentially, coffee grinders with Belizean beans. They also have a private pier with a palapa and hammocks, and can supply bicycles at no extra charge.

$$$-$ Marin's Guest House
Estrella St, 1½ blocks from the beach at the southern end, T226-0444, www.marinsguesthouse.com.
Established in 1970, Marin's is one of the oldest lodgings on the island. The new extension features 4 spacious, simple, comfortable and well-equipped suites in hacienda-style. There are also more economical rooms with private or shared facilities ($) in wooden cabins on stilts. Friendly and hospitable.

$$$-$ PAW Animal Sanctuary
1 Pasero St, T624-7076, www.pawanimalsanctuarybelize.
Lovers of felines will enjoy staying at the **PAW Animal Sanctuary**, home to many dozens of cats and a few dogs too. Lodging includes fully equipped self-catering suites ($$$-$$) and rustic beach cabanas ($). Your money goes to a good cause and volunteers get reduced rates. Contact in advance of your stay.

$$ Mara's Place
27 Hicaco Av, T600-0080.
Simple, tidy and good value, this reliable budget hotel has several wood-built duplexes with units on both levels. Each has

their own fridge and porch with a hammock, but no a/c. Located near the Split, guests can also enjoy the private pier and sun loungers, and there's a shared kitchen too. Funky, colourful and fun.

$$ Maxhapan Cabanas
55 Av Pueblo Nuevo, T226-0118, maxhapan04@hotmail.com.
Nestled amid coconut trees in a quiet neighbourhood in the south of the island, **Maxhapan** is a very hospitable establishment offering tranquil lodging in well-maintained Caribbean-style duplexes. Suites have fridges, cable TV and great private verandas for chilling out. A small, friendly place with lovely management. Recommended.

$$-$ Sandy Lane
Corner of Chapoose St and Langosta St, T226-0117.
Run by Rico and Elma Novelo, an interesting couple who have been active in the local community for decades, **Sandy Lane** offers several simple bungalow-type cabins, clean and economical, and cheapest with shared bathrooms. Their best units feature kitchen and TV for longer stays. Recommended.

$$-$ Yuma's House
Playa Asuncion, T206-0019, www.yumashousebelize.com.
Lots of good reports about this popular backpackers' hostel, one of the cheapest places on the caye and in a great beachfront location. Accommodation includes 6 small dorms ($) and 6 private rooms ($$), or you can sling a hammock. Good amenities, including 2 shared kitchens, chilled-out garden with sitting areas, and a private dock. Arty, funky, and well-maintained. Recommended.

Restaurants

Beer is sold by the crate at the wholesaler on the dock by the generator; ice for sale at Tropical Paradise.

$$$ Pasta per Caso
Av Hicaco.
Managed by Anna and Armando, this delightful little Italian joint is very low-key, casual and authentic. They make their own pasta by hand and serve a changing menu of delicious home-cooked fare such as spaghetti with calamari, vegetable lasagne and fettuccine with mushroom sauce. There's just a handful of seats out front and they also sell their pasta and sauce in packets to take at home. Great wine and desserts too. Recommended.

$$$-$$ Aladdin's
Corner of Front St and Hattie St, just before the Split. Closed Tue.
Fresh, tasty and fully authentic Lebanese cuisine including falafel, pitta wraps, lamb kebabs, hummus and vegetarian options. A casual joint with just a few picnic tables out front. Friendly, popular and lots of good reports.

$$$-$$ Paradiso Café
Av Hicaco.
Located near the Split where it enjoys ocean breezes, this little café on the seafront serves healthy and hearty breakfasts, good hot and cold coffee (try the frozen cappuccino), smoothies and an array of gourmet sandwiches, including grilled paninis and BLTs. A bit pricey but portions are large. Eat in or take away.

$$$-$$ Rainbow Bar and Restaurant
On its own jetty.
This restaurant has a beautiful view and serves good-value delicious burritos.

$$$-$$ Syd's Restaurant
Middle St. Closed Sun.
Family-run restaurant which is very popular with locals.

$$$-$$ Terry's Grill
On the beach by the Split.
Tempting passersby with its smoky barbecue aromas, this simple beachside grill cooks up a tantalizing array of seafood.

The menu changes with seasons and the fishermen's haul, but often includes lemon and garlic lobster, whole fish or honey mustard fillet, curried conch, shrimp sticks, pork ribs and jerk chicken.

$$ Amor y Cafe
Av Hicaco. Tue-Sun 0600-1130.
Reportedly the best place on the island for breakfast.

$$ Glenda's
Back St. Open mornings only.
An old-time island favourite, serving good breakfast and lunches.

$$ The Little Kitchen
Marvin Gainy St, back street on south-western side of the island, ask around.
Managed by a friendly mother and daughter team, **The Little Kitchen** serves up a changing menu of home-cooked local fare prepared with love. Offerings include coconut fish fillet, lemon ginger snapper and creole lobster, washed down with fruit juice, rum or Belikin beer.

$$ Rose's Bar & Grill
Front St.
A great grill with good seafood and burgers.

$$-$ Caribbean Colors Art Café
Av Hicaco, www.caribbean-colors.com. Open 0700-1500.
Adorned with vibrant local artwork, this cute little café with an upstairs balcony makes a great breakfast or lunch stop. They serve good value burritos, pancakes, fruit and granola, tasty bagels and other fresh-baked goodies such as triple chocolate espresso brownies. For lunch there's salads, soups and sushi.

$ Chan's Take Out
Corner of Dock and 2nd St. Open late.
Although it's not much to look at, this hole in the wall is hugely popular with locals and backpackers for its cheap and hearty grub. Offerings include chicken wings, shrimps, pork chops and burgers served with fries. They also do Chinese.

Coffee shops

Ice and Beans
Front St inside the Remax building, www.iceandbeans.com.
Good coffee, hot or iced, but everyone loves the mini-doughnuts coated in cinnamon, chocolate and sugar. They also do shaved ice and home-made rum balls.

Bars and clubs

Many of the restaurants become bars in the evenings.

Herbal Tribes
Near the north end of the island.
Bar and restaurant with a good atmosphere.

I and I Bar.
Used to be the **Swing Bar** and still has the swings. Should be tried later at night.

Lazy Lizard
Right at the north tip of the island at the Split.
An excellent place to watch the sunset.

Shopping

There are at least 4 small 'markets' on the island where a variety of food can be bought; prices are 20-50% higher than the mainland. There are a couple of gift shops and a gallery in the same building as Coco Loco.

Chan's Mini Mart, *Middle St, 1 street back from main street.* Daily including Christmas and New Year's Day.

What to do

Diving and snorkelling
Mask and snorkel hire from several dive and tour operators; normally US$2.50 per day. **Belize Diving Services**, *T226-0143, www. belizedivingservice.com.* A dive shop on the island with similar prices to **Frenchie's**. **Big Fish Dive Center**, *T226-0450, bigfish dive@btl.net.* Go to the Blue Hole, US$175, Lighthouse Reef and Turneffe. Also does PADI refresher courses and works with **Frenchie's**.

Frenchie's Diving, *T226-0234, www. frenchiesdivingbelize.com.* Charges US$310 for a 4-day PADI course, friendly and effective, 2-tank dive US$90, also advanced PADI instruction. Day excursion diving Blue Hole, etc, US$190, snorkellers welcome.

Fishing

Fishing can be arranged through tour operators or by ringing Eloy Badillo T226-0270.

Kayaking

Tour agencies on the main street rent kayaks.

Manatee watching

Available with most tour operators.

Sailing

See also **Ras Creek** and **E-Z Boy Tours**, below, for their sailing trips.
Raggamuffin Tours, *T226-0348, www. raggamuffintours.com.* Do a fun sunset cruise, US$25 per person, with booze and music on a sail boat as well as offering a 3-day all-inclusive sailing tour to Placencia leaving Tue and Fri, US$300 per person, minimum 8 people including all food and 2 nights' camping on Rendezvous Caye and Tobacco Caye. Beats travelling by bus and is an increasingly popular excursion.

Tour operators

Prices are consistent across all operators, so find someone you connect with and feel you can trust. The main excursion is snorkelling in Hol Chan Marine Park and visiting Shark Ray Alley and San Pedro, US$45, equipment included. Further afield there are other snorkelling trips, river and Maya site tours. Manatees and Goff Caye (a paradise-perfect circular island with good snorkelling around), US$60; fishing trips US$175. Snorkelling excursions to the Turneffe Islands, Half Moon Caye, Bird Sanctuary and Blue Hole on request. **Sunset Tours** are popular with snorkelling until dusk, US$30.

E-Z Boy Tours, *on main street, T226-0349.* As well as the usual snorkelling tours, **E-Z** offers a seahorse, a Maya archaeology and croc-spotting tour.
Javier Novelo *at Anwar Tours, T226-0327, www.anwartours.com.* Locally recommended for a range of snorkelling tours.
Raggamuffin Tours, *see Sailing, above.* Trips to the Caye Caulker Marine Reserve and Hol Chan. They can also arrange fishing tours with local fishermen, full day, US$275.

Guides Recommended guides include **Ras Creek**, 'a big man with a big heart', in his boat, based at the water taxi dock, US$27.50 including lunch and entrance fee to the Caye Caulker Marine Reserve; seahorse trips, fishing trips, US$37.50; booze cruise, US$10 per person; canoe and snorkel rental. **Neno Rosado**, of Tsunami Adventures, T226-0462, www.tsunamiadventures.com, has been approved by the guide association and is reliable and knowledgeable.

Transport

Air

Maya Island Air flies to/from **Belize City**, **Corozal** and **San Pedro**, several daily. Also flights with **Tropic Air**, T226-2439.

Bicycle and golf cart hire

Island Boy Rentals, T226-0229. Golf cart rental for US$10 per hr. Bike hire for US$7.50 per day.

Boat

Boats leave from the main dock in front of **Seaside Cabanas** to **Belize City** with the **Caye Caulker Water Taxi Association** at 0630, 0730, 0830, 1000, 1100, 1200, 1330, 1500, 1600, 1700, 45 mins 1 way (can be 'exciting' if it's rough). To **San Pedro** 0700, 0820, 0845, 0950, 1120, 1250, 1420, 1550 and 1720. **Triple J** leave from the **Rainbow Hotel** dock. Daily services to **Chetumal** in Mexico also available.

Lighthouse Reef is the outermost of the three north–south reef systems off Belize and is some 45 miles to the east of Belize City. Trips out here are not cheap, but if you like diving and have the money, this is well worth the expense. On arrival you must register near the lighthouse with the warden who will provide maps and tell you where you can camp.

There are two cayes of interest: Half Moon Caye (on which the lighthouse stands) and **Long Caye**, where there is accommodation with Huracan Diving (see page 285). Between the two are some of the most pristine coral reefs in the Western hemisphere, including the diving shrine of the **Blue Hole** (see below) is found. **Half Moon Caye** is the site of the **Red-Footed Booby Sanctuary** ① *US$20*, a national reserve. Besides the booby, magnificent frigate birds also nest on the island. The seabirds nest on the western side, which has denser vegetation (the eastern side is covered mainly in coconut palms). Of the 98 other bird species recorded on Half Moon Caye, 77 are migrants. The iguana, the wish willy (smaller than the iguana) and the Anolis allisoni lizard inhabit the caye, and hawksbill and loggerhead turtles lay their eggs on the beaches. The **Belize Audubon Society** in Belize City (see box, page 284) maintains the sanctuary, providing a lookout tower and a trail. The lighthouse on the caye gives fine views of the reef. It was first built in 1820: the present steel tower was added to the brick base in 1931 and nowadays the light is solar powered. Around sunset you can watch the boobies from the lookout as they return from fishing. They land beside their waiting mates at the rate of about 50 a minute, seemingly totally unperturbed by humans.

★Blue Hole
US$20, US$40 to snorkel or dive.

On Lighthouse Reef is this National Monument, a circular sinkhole which is 1000 ft across and has depths exceeding 400 ft. The crater was probably formed by the collapsed roof of a subterranean cave, and was studied by Jacques Cousteau in 1984. Stalagmites and stalactites can be found and it is rated as one of the best dives in the world. Scuba diving is outstanding at Lighthouse Reef, and includes two walls that descend almost vertically from 30-40 ft to a depth of almost 400 ft.

Caye Chapel
This was once a small, quiet caye dotted with palms and devoid of sandflies, close to its busier neighbour Caye Caulker, where you could escape to a bit of quiet and solitude. That has all changed, as it is now exclusive as well as secluded.

Conservation is a high priority in Belize. Tourism vies for the top spot as foreign currency earner in the national economy, and is the fastest-growing industry. Nature reserves are supported by a combination of private and public organizations including the Belize Audubon Society, the government and international agencies.

The Belize Audubon Society, PO Box 1001, 12 Fort Street, Belize City, T223-5004, www.belizeaudubon.org, manages seven protected areas including Half Moon Caye Natural Monument (3929 ha), Cockscomb Basin Wildlife Sanctuary (41,800 ha – the world's only jaguar reserve), Crooked Tree Wildlife Sanctuary (6480 ha – swamp forests and lagoons with wildfowl), Blue Hole National Park (233 ha), Guanacaste National Park (20.25 ha), Tapir Mountain Nature Reserve (formerly known as Society Hall Nature Reserve; 2731 ha – a research area with Maya presence) and the Shipstern Nature Reserve (8910 ha – butterfly breeding, forest, lagoons, mammals and birds, contact BAS or the International Tropical Conservation Foundation, through www.shipstern.org).

The Río Bravo Management and Conservation Area (105,300 ha) bordering Guatemala to the northwest of the country, covers some 4% of the country and is managed by the Programme for Belize, PO Box 749, 1 Eyre Street, Belize City, T227-5616, www.pfbelize.org.

Other parks include the Community Baboon Sanctuary at Bermudian Landing, Bladen Nature Reserve (watershed and primary forest) and Hol Chan Marine Reserve (reef ecosystem). More recently designated national parks and reserves include: Five Blue Lakes National Park, based on an unusually deep karst lagoon, and a maze of exotic caves and sinkholes near St Margaret Village on the Hummingbird Highway; Kaax Meen Elijio Panti National Park, at San Antonio Village near the Mountain Pine Ridge Reserve; Vaca Forest Reserve (21,060 ha); and Chiquibul National Park (107,687 ha – containing the Maya ruins of Caracol). There's also Laughing Bird Caye National Park (off Placencia), Glovers Reef Marine Reserve, and Caye Caulker, which now has a marine reserve at its north end.

Belize Enterprise for Sustained Technology (BEST), Mile 54 Hummingbird Highway, PO Box 35, Belmopan, T822-3043, www.best.org.bz, is a non-profit organization committed to the sustainable development of Belize's disadvantaged communities and community-based ecotourism, for example Gales Point and Hopkins Village.

On 1 June 1996 a National Protected Areas Trust Fund (PACT), www.pactbelize.org, was established to provide finance for the "protection, conservation and enhancement of the natural and cultural treasures of Belize". Funds for PACT come from a US$3.75 conservation fee paid by all foreign visitors on departure by air, land and sea, and from 20% of revenues derived from protected areas entrance fees, cruise ship passenger fees, etc. Visitors pay only one PACT tax every 30 days, so if you go to Tikal for a short trip from Belize, show your receipt in order not to pay twice.

Where to stay

Many cayes have package deals for a few days or a week.

$$$$ Blackbird Caye Resort
Turneffe Islands, T223-2767,
www.blackbirdresort.com.
An ecological resort on this 4000-acre island is used by the **Oceanic Society** and is a potential site for a biosphere reserve underwater project. Weekly packages arranged. Diving or fishing packages available, no bar, take your own alcohol.

$$$$ Huracan
Lighthouse Reef, T603 2930,
www.huracandiving.com.
Simple but elegant accommodation in a small chalet with polished wooden floors on a tiny island on the Lighthouse Reef. The sea views from the islands beaches and jetties are unforgettable, with a real sense of remoteness, the diving the best on the reef (this is the only dive operator within 20 mins of the Blue Hole) and the cooking and hospitality from Ruth and her husband Karel warm and welcoming. Prices include transfers from Belize, full board and dives, making this a very good-value option.

$$$$ Turneffe Flats
Turneffe Islands, T220-4046, www.tflats.com.
In a lovely location, offers week-long packages for fishing and scuba; takes 20 guests.

$$$$ Turneffe Island Resort
Big Caye Bokel, Turneffe Islands, T532-2990,
www.turnefferesort.com.
Can accommodate 16 guests for week-long fishing and scuba packages.

What to do

Diving
The main dive in the Blue Hole is very deep, at least 130 ft; the hole itself is 480 ft deep. Check your own qualifications as the dive operator probably will not; you should be experienced and it is advisable to have at least the Advance Open Water PADI course, although an Open Water qualification is fine if you feel confident and don't have major problems equalizing.
Huracan Diving, *T603-2930, www. huracandiving.com.* The only hotel and dive operation on Lighthouse Reef itself. Excellent value (see Where to stay).

Dive operators on Ambergris and on Caye Caulker run trips to Half Moon Caye, the Blue Hole and Turneffe Islands, see above. It's also possible to go from Belize City with:
Hugh Parkey's Belize Dive Connection, *based at the Radisson's dock, www.belize diving.com.*
Sunrise Travel, *Belize City, T227-2051 or T223-2670.* Helps arrange trips, advance book.

Belmopan
& Cayo District

A procession of impressive sights – artificial and natural – line the route from Belize City to Cayo District in Western Belize, starting with Belize Zoo, a pleasant break from the norm. Monkey Bay Wildlife Sanctuary and Guanacaste National Park are both worth a visit. From the bustling town of San Ignacio, there are canoe trips down the Macal River and dramatic cave systems, journeys into the impressive limestone scenery of Mountain Pine Ridge, and the spectacular Maya ruins of Caracol, Xunantunich and Cahal Pech to explore. Day trippers can also cross the border for a quick visit to Tikal in Guatemala. At the heart of the region stands Belmopan, a sterile planned city, business hub and the capital of the nation.

Belmopan → Colour map 8, B1.

quiet and ordered, the planned capital of the nation

As capital of Belize, Belmopan has been the seat of government since 1970. It is 50 miles inland to the west of Belize City, near the junction of the Western Highway and the Hummingbird Highway to Dangriga (Stann Creek Town). Following the devastation caused in Belize City by Hurricane Hattie in 1961, plans were drawn up for a town that could be a centre for government, business and study away from the coast: Belmopan is the result.

The hurricanes of recent years have prompted a renewed interest in plans to develop the Belmopan, and several government organizations are in the process of relocating to the city, injecting a desperately needed 'heart' to this most eerie of capitals. One possible site of interest would be the **Department of Archaeology** in the government plaza, which has a vault containing specimens of the country's artefacts. Unfortunately, the vault is currently closed and there are no plans to open it in the near future, although there is a small display and plans to build a museum. Part of the collection is displayed in the **National Museum of Belize** in Belize City (see page 262).

Belmopan has the National Assembly building, two blocks of government offices (with broadly Maya-style architecture), the national archives, police headquarters, a hospital, over 700 houses for civil servants, a non-governmental residential district to encourage expansion, and a market. The Western Highway from Belize City is now good (a one-hour drive), continuing to San Ignacio, and there is an airfield (for charter services only).

Travelling from Belize City to Belmopan by road, the Western Highway passes the cemetery, where burial vaults stand elevated above the boggy ground, running through palmetto scrub and savannah landscapes created by 19th-century timber cutting. At Mile 16 is **Hattieville**, originally a temporary settlement for the homeless after Hurricane Hattie in 1961. The highway runs roughly parallel to the Sibun River, once a major trading artery where mahogany logs were floated down to the coast in the rainy season; the place name 'Boom' recalls spots where chains were stretched across rivers to catch logs being floated downstream.

Around Belmopan

The small but excellent **Belize Zoo** ⓘ *daily 0900-1700, US$7.50, www.belizezoo.org, take any bus from Belize City along the Western Highway (1 hr)*, is at Mile 28½; watch out for the sign or tell the driver where you're going. It is a wonderful collection of local species (originally gathered for a wildlife film), lovingly cared for and displayed in wire-mesh enclosures amid native trees and shady vegetation, including jaguar and smaller cats, pacas (called gibnuts in Belize), snakes, monkeys, parrots, crocodile, tapir (mountain cow), peccary (wari) and much more. Get there early to miss the coach party arrivals. There are tours by enthusiastic guides, and T-shirts and postcards are sold for fundraising. A visit is highly recommended, even for those who hate zoos.

At Mile 31½, the **Monkey Bay Wildlife Sanctuary** ⓘ *www.belizestudyabroad.net*, protects 1070 acres of tropical forest and savannah between the highway and the Sibun River (great swimming and canoeing). Birds are abundant and there is a good chance of seeing mammals.

Forty-seven miles from Belize City, a minor road runs 2 miles north to **Banana Bank Lodge and Jungle Equestrian Adventure** (see Where to stay, below). A mile beyond is the highway junction for Belmopan and Dangriga.

At the confluence of the Belize River and Roaring Creek is the 50-acre **Guanacaste National Park** ⓘ *US$2.50*, protecting a parcel of neotropical rainforest and a huge 100-year-old *guanacaste* (tubroos) tree, which shelters a wide collection of epiphytes including orchids. Many mammals (jaguarundi, kinkajou, agouti etc) and up to 100 species of bird may be seen from the 3 miles of nature trails cut along the river. This is a particularly attractive swimming and picnicking spot at which to stop or break the journey if travelling on to Guatemala. It has a visitor centre, where luggage can be left. To get there, take an early morning bus from Belize City, see the park in a couple of hours, then pick up a bus going to San Ignacio or Dangriga.

Soon after the junction to Belmopan is **Roaring Creek**, once a thriving town but now rather overshadowed by the barely illuminated capital nearby. At Camelote, a dirt road southwards takes you to **Roaring River**. At Teakettle, turn south along a dirt road for 5 miles to **Pook's Hill Reserve** (see Where to stay, below).

The important but unimpressive **Floral Park** archaeological site is just beyond the bridge over **Barton Creek** (Mile 64). Just 2 miles further is **Georgeville**, from where a gravel road runs south into the Mountain Pine Ridge Forest Reserve (see page 296). The highway passes the turn-off at Norland for **Spanish Lookout**, a Mennonite settlement area 6 miles north (**B & F Restaurant**, Centre Road, by Farmers' Trading Centre, is clean and excellent value). The **Central Farm Agricultural College**, the village of **Esperanza** and other small settlements along the way keep the road interesting until it reaches **Santa Elena**. Formerly only linked by the substantial Hawkesworth suspension bridge to its twin town of San Ignacio, it now has a small, one-lane 'temporary bridge' you must take to cross the river to San Ignacio.

Listings Belmopan

Where to stay

Belmopan has been described as a 'disaster' for the budget traveller.

$$$ Bull Frog Inn
25 Half Moon Av, T822-2111,
www.bullfroginn.com.
A 15-min walk east of the market through the parliament complex or a short taxi ride from the bus station. A/c, good, reasonably priced, laundry, karaoke nights on Thu (popular with locals).

$$ El Rey Inn
23 Moho St, T822-3438, www.elreyhotel.com.
A central, basic place offering big, clean rooms with fan and hot and cold water. Friendly staff, laundry on request.

Around Belmopan

$$$$ Pook's Hill Lodge
Pook's Hill Reserve, T820-2017,
www.pookshilllodge.com.
A 120-ha nature reserve on Roaring Creek, 6 cabanas, horses and rafting.

$$$ Orchid Garden Eco-Village Hotel
Western Highway Mile 14.5, T225-6991,
www.trybelize.com.
For those who would prefer to give the city a wide berth (or simply wish to be immersed in exuberant natural surroundings), the **Orchid Garden** boasts wonderfully verdant grounds with nature trails. Located 20 mins outside the city, accommodation is offered as part of all-inclusive packages that include day trips to surrounding natural attractions (contact in advance).

$$$-$$ Banana Bank Lodge and Jungle Equestrian Adventure
Guanacaste National Park, T820-2020,
www.bananabank.com.
Resort accommodation with meals, horse riding along the river and jungle trails, birding and river trips.

$$ Belize Savanna Guesthouse
Pine Savanna Nature Reserve,
signed off the Western Highway at
Mile 28.5, near Belize Zoo, T822-8005,
www.belizesavannaguesthouse.co.
This down-to-earth and intimate B&B is managed by 2 Emmy-winning natural history film-makers, Carol and Richard Foster, who use their house as a production base and studio. It is some distance from the airport and nearer Belmopan than Belize City, but worth the effort for the unique hospitality and verdant surroundings of the wild savanna. Rooms are cosy and decked with wood in typical Caribbean style. Book in advance. Recommended.

$ Monkey Bay Wildlife Sanctuary
Mile 31 Western Highway, T820-3032,
www.belizestudyabroad.net.
Dorm accommodation or you can camp on a wooden platform with thatched roof; showers are available. You can swim in the river, and meals are eaten with the family.

Restaurants

Eating options are limited in Belmopan. There are several cheap *comedores* at the back of the market and a couple of bakeries near Constitution Dr Cafés are closed on Sun.

$$ Caladium
At Market Square in front of bus terminal.
Limited fare, moderately priced,
small portions.

$$ Pasquales Pizza
Forest Dr and Slim Lane, T822-4663.
Also serves pasta and hot and
cold sandwiches.

$$ Perkup Café
Shopping Center, T822 0001,
www.perkupcoffeeshop.com.
Good coffee, snacks and ice cream.

Transport

Bus
To **San Ignacio**, hourly on the hour 0500-2100, 1 hr, US$2.50. To **Belize City**, Mon-Sat, every 30 mins, 0600-1900, hourly on Sun, 1 hr, US$3.50. Heading south hourly buses Mon-Sat 0830-1630 (fewer on Sun) to **Dangriga**, 1 hr, US$3, **Mango Creek**, 3 hrs, US$8 and **Punta Gorda**, 4½ hrs, US$9. **James Bus** leaves for **Belize City** and **Punta Gorda** from opposite the **National Transportation Co** bus station. To **Orange Walk** and **Corozal** take an early bus to Belize City and change.

San Ignacio and around → *Colour map: 8, B1. See map, page 290.*

an appealing agricultural town, a good base for local trips

Some 68 miles from Belize City and 10 miles from the border, San Ignacio (locally called Cayo) is the capital of Cayo District and Western Belize's largest town, serving the citrus, cattle and peanut farms of the area, and a good base for excursions into the Mountain Pine Ridge and other places in Western Belize. A convenient town to rest in if coming from Guatemala, it stands amid attractive wooded hills from 200-550 ft and has a pleasant climate.

The town is on the eastern branch of the Old, or Belize, River, known as the Macal. The 180-mile river journey down to Belize City is internationally famous as the route for the annual Ruta Maya Belize River Challenge, a gruelling three-day canoe race held the weekend of Baron Bliss Day, 9 March; see box, page 291.

Dr Rosita Arvigo, a Maya healer, runs the **Ix Chel Wellness Center** ⓘ *25 Burns Av, T804-0264, by appointment only*, offering herbology and traditional Maya healing. She also sells a selection of herbs (the jungle salve, US$5, has been found effective against mosquito bites) and a book on medicinal plants used by the Maya. The herbs and books are also sold in most local gift shops. For local medicines you could also talk to the García sisters (see San Antonio, page 324).

The San Ignacio Resort Hotel (see Where to stay, below) houses the **Green Iguana Exhibit and Medicinal Jungle Trail** ⓘ *0700-1600, US$5.45 for a guided tour of the medicinal trail*, where you will learn about the life and habits of this vibrantly coloured reptile. Entrance fees are used to provide scholarships for local pupils. From March to May you're likely to see iguanas in the wild if you take the pleasant half hour walk from San Ignacio to where the Mopan and Macal rivers meet.

A short walk from San Ignacio (800 m from **Hotel San Ignacio**) is **Cahal Pech** ⓘ *daily 0600-1700, US$5*, an interesting Maya site and nature reserve on a wooded hill overlooking the town, with a visitor centre and small museum.

Around San Ignacio
Four miles west of San Ignacio on a good road is **Bullet Tree Falls**, a pleasant cascade amid relaxing surroundings on the western branch of the Belize River, here in its upper course

known as the Mopan River. On a similarly good road 9 miles southwest of San Ignacio is the tranquil town of **Benque Viejo del Carmen**, near the Guatemalan border. Many of the inhabitants are Maya Mopan. For information on the Benque Viejo–Melchor de Mencos border crossing, see box, page 514.

Near Benque Viejo is the **Che Chem Ha Cave** ⓘ *T820-4063*, on the private property of the Moralez family on the Vaca Plateau. In contrast to Barton Creek and Actun Tunichil Muknal this is a so-called dry cave, and it has Maya artefacts. The family offers trips into the cave, a 30-minute hike to the entrance, followed by a one- to 1½-hour walk in the cave. The view from the property is stunning and the family serves lunch. Tours start at 0900 and 1300. If you go by private transport be there in time for the tour and call the family in advance or, better still, book a tour with an agency in San Ignacio.

Twelve miles north of San Ignacio is **El Pilar**, an archaeological site that straddles the border with Guatemala. Although it is a large site (about 94 acres), much of it has been left intentionally uncleared so that selected architectural features are exposed within the rainforest. The preserved rainforest here is home to hundreds of species of birds and animals. There are five trails – three archaeological, two nature – the longest of which is 1½ miles. There are more than a dozen pyramids and 25 identified plazas. Unusually for Maya cities in this region, there is an abundance of water (streams and falls). Take the Bullet Tree Road north of San Ignacio, cross the Mopan River Bridge and follow the signs to El Pilar. The reserve is 7 miles from Bullet Tree on an all-weather limestone road. It can be reached by vehicle, horse or mountain bike (hiking is only recommended for the

San Ignacio

Where to stay 🛏
Casa Blanca Guesthouse 1
Hi-Et 3
Martha's Guest House 4
Midas Resort 2

San Ignacio Resort 11

Restaurants 🍴
Eva's Bar 2
Martha's Kitchen 1

Mr Greedy's Pizzeria 4
Serendib 6

Paddling the great Macal River

Time it right and you can paddle down the length of the Macal River taking part in La Ruta Maya canoe race. It's a gruelling three-day open canoe race, starting in San Ignacio covering 180 miles along the river before ending in Belize City on Baron Bliss Day (early March). All food and water is provided for the trip, but you'll need to be fit and healthy. You'll struggle to compete at the racing end of the field unless you're a top athlete and have a canoe of modern design, but plenty of people enter the race for the challenge and with a bit of luck it's possible to turn up, talk with people around town and find yourself a place on a boat. For information, visit www.larutamayabelize.com.

experienced; carry lots of water). The caretakers, who live at the south end of the site in a modern green-roofed house, are happy to show visitors around. The **Cayo Tour Guides Association** works in association with the **Belize River Archaeological Settlement Survey** (BRASS) and can take visitors. See also *Trails of El Pilar: A Guide to the El Pilar Archaeological Reserve for Maya Flora and Fauna*.

South of San Ignacio, halfway between the Clarissa Falls turn-off and Nabitunich, is Chial Road, gateway to adventure. A half-mile down the road is a sharp right turn that takes you through Negroman, the modern site of the ancient Maya city of **Tipu** which has the remains of a Spanish Mission from the 1500s. Across the river from here is **Guacamallo Camp**, a rustic jungle camping and the starting point for canoe trips on the Macal River (see below). Two miles further up, also across the river, is **Ek Tun** (see Where to stay, below). The **Belize Botanic Gardens** ⓘ *T824-3101, www.belizebotanic.org, daily 0700-1700, US$2.50, guided walks 0730-1500, US$7.50*, on 50 acres of rolling hills, is next to the duPlooy's lodge (see Where to stay, below) with hundreds of orchids, dozens of named tree species, ponds and lots of birds. Recommended.

Canoe trips up the **Macal River** are worthwhile. They take about three hours upstream, 1½ hours on return. Hiring a canoe to go upstream without a guide is not recommended unless you are highly proficient as there are Grade II rapids one hour from San Ignacio. Another trip is to **Barton Creek Cave**, a 1½-hour drive followed by a 1½-hour canoe trip in the cave. The cave vault system is vast, the rock formations are beautiful, the silence is eerily comforting and all can be explored for a considerable distance by canoe (US$55 per person, minimum two people). Tours can be arranged at almost every place in San Ignacio.

★**Actun Tunichil Muknal (ATM) Cave** For an adventurous caving tour, you shouldn't leave without going to Actun Tunichil Muknal (ATM) Cave (the Cave of the Stone Sepulchre), a one-hour drive east of San Ignacio to the Tapir Mountain Nature reserve, a 45-minute jungle hike in the reserve and then 3½ hours of adventurous, exhilarating caving, US$75. Besides the beautiful rock formations, this cave is full of Maya artefacts and sacrificial remains. The guides from both **Emilio Awe's Pacz Tours** and **Mayawalk** (see What to do, below) are recommended. Mayawalk also run an overnight ATM tour (US$180); under eights and pregnant women are discouraged from taking this tour.

Xunantunich → *Colour map 8, B1.*

Daily 0730-1600, US$5; a leaflet on the area is available from the site for US$4. Apart from a small refreshment stand, there are no facilities for visitors, but a museum has been built and a couple of stelae have been put on display in a covered area. It is an extremely hot walk up the hill, with little or no shade, so start early. Last ferry (free) back is at 1630. See also Transport, below.

At Xunantunich ('Maiden of the Rock') there are Classic Maya remains in beautiful surroundings. The heart of the city was three plazas aligned on a north-south axis, lined with many temples, the remains of a ball court, and surmounted by the Castillo. At 130 ft, this was thought to be the highest artificial structure in Belize until the Sky Palace at Caracol was measured. The impressive view takes in the jungle, the lowlands of Petén and the blue flanks of the Maya Mountains. Maya graffiti can still be seen on the wall of Structure A-16; friezes on the Castillo, some restored in modern plaster, represent astronomical symbols. Extensive excavations took place in 1959-1960 but only limited restoration work has been undertaken.

Just east of the ferry, **Magaña's Art Centre** and the **Xunantunich Women's Group** sell locally made crafts and clothing in a shop on a street off the highway. About 1½ miles further north are the ruins of **Actuncan**, probably a satellite of Xunantunich. Both sites show evidence of earthquake damage.

Listings San Ignacio and around *map p290*

Where to stay

Some hotels in town and on Cahal Pech Hill may be noisy at weekends from loud music, and during the day from traffic and buses. In the area surrounding San Ignacio there are many jungle hideaways. Ranging from secluded and exclusive cottages to full activity resorts, and covering a wide range of budgets, these places are normally an adventure on their own. Before going, make sure you know what's included in the price; food is often extra.

$$$$ San Ignacio Resort Hotel
18 Buena Vista Rd, T824-2125,
www.sanignaciobelize.com.
At the southern end of town, on the road to Benque Viejo, this hotel has clean rooms with bath, a/c and hot water; some have balconies. Helpful staff, pool, tennis court, tour agency and excellent restaurant. Live music every weekend at the **Stork Club**. The **Green Iguana Exhibit** is on site, see page 289.

$$$ Martha's Guest House
10 West St, T804-3647,
www.marthasbelize.com.
This friendly place has 10 comfortable, clean rooms with TV, a/c, cheaper without; 2 have balconies. There's also a lounge area, a good restaurant and kitchen facilities.

$$$ Midas Resort
Branch Mouth Rd, T824-3172,
www.midasbelize.com.
An attractive 7-acre family-run resort, located on the edge of town, yet with a more remote wilderness feel. Cabana accommodation with Wi-Fi service and access to the river for swims.

$$$-$$ Casa Blanca Guesthouse
10 Burns Av, T824-2080, www.
casablancaguesthouse.com.
A friendly place with 8 clean rooms (2 beds in each), private shower, fan or a/c and TV. Use of kitchenette and free coffee.

$$-$ Hi-Et
12 West St, T824-2828, thehiet@ yahoo.com.
Lovely, red and cream old wooden building
with 10 rooms and private shower, cheaper
without. It's reportedly noisy, but it has a
nice balcony, and is friendly, helpful and
family-run. There are stunning orchids in
the patio, and free coffee.

Around San Ignacio

$$$$ duPlooy's
*South of San Ignacio, past the Chaa Creek
road, then follow (including 1 steep hill)
to its end above the Macal River, T824-3101,
www.duplooys.com.*
Choices of accommodation and packages
are available, enjoy the **Hangover Bar** with
cool drinks on the deck overlooking trees
and river. The **Belize Botanic Gardens** (see
above) is also run by the duPlooy family.

$$$$ Ek Tun
*South of San Ignacio, T820-3002, in USA
T303-4426150, www.ektunbelize.com.*
A 500-acre private jungle retreat on the
Macal River, boat access only. There are
2 very private deluxe thatched guest
cottages in a spectacular garden setting, and
excellent food. It's a great spot for romantic
adventurers. Advance reservations only, no
drop-ins, adults only and 3-night minimum.

$$$$ The Lodge at Chaa Creek
*On the Macal River, south of San Ignacio off
the Chial Rd, after the turn to Ix Chel Farm,
T824-2037, www.chaacreek.com, or hotel
office at 56 Burns Av, San Ignacio.*
Upscale accommodation, amenities and
tours, with spa, conference centre, butterfly
breeding centre, natural history movement
and an adventure centre. Strong supporters
of environmental groups and projects. Tours
and excursions offered.

$$$ Cahal Pech Village
*South of town, near Cahal Pech, T824-3740,
www.cahalpech.com.*
Thatched cabins or a/c rooms, restaurant
and bar.

$$$ Clarissa's Falls
*On Mopan River, down a signed track on the
Benque road, around Mile 70, T824-3916,
www.clarissafallsresort.aguallos.com.*
Owned by Chena Galvez, thatched
cottages on riverbank by a set of rapids,
also bunkhouse with hammocks or beds,
camping space ($) and hook-ups for RVs,
rafting, kayaking and tubing available,
wonderful food in the restaurants.

$$$ Maya Mountain Lodge (Bart and Suzi Mickler)
*¾ mile east of San Ignacio at 9 Cristo
Rey Rd, Santa Elena, San Ignacio,
T824-2164, www.mayamountain.com.*
Welcoming place offering special weekly,
monthly and family rates. There's a
restaurant, expensive excursions, a self-
guided nature trail and pool. Hiking, riding,
canoeing and fishing can be arranged.

$$$ Windy Hill Resort
*2 miles west of San Ignacio, on Graceland
Ranch, T824-2017, www.windyhillresort.com.*
14 cottages, all with bath and dining room.
There's also a small pool and nature trails.
Horse riding and river trips can be arranged,
but they are expensive.

$$ Aguada Hotel
*Santa Elena, across the river, T804-3609,
www.aguadabelize.com.*
Full-service hotel in a quiet part of town
with 12 rooms, private baths; a/c costs more.
There's a freshwater pond, a heart-shaped
pool and an excellent restaurant and bar.

$$ Parrot Nest
*Near village of Bullet Tree Falls, 3 miles
north of San Ignacio, T820-4058,
www.parrot-nest.com.*
Family-run with small, comfortable tree
houses in beautiful grounds by the river.
Breakfast and dinner are available, as well
as free tubing. Can arrange local tours.

$$-$ Cosmos Camping & Cabanas
*Branch Mouth Rd, T824-2116,
cosmoscamping@btl.net.*

4 very simple units, or camp on the site alongside the Macal River. Tents for rent, washing and cooking facilities, run by friendly Belizean family, good breakfasts, canoe and bikes for hire. Cabins available ($).

Camping

$ Inglewood Camping Grounds
West of San Ignacio at Mile 68¼, T824-3555, www.inglewoodcampingground.com.
Palapas, camping, RV hook-ups, hot and cold showers, maintained grounds, some highway noise.

Restaurants

$$$ Running W
In the San Ignacio Resort Hotel (see Where to stay above).
One of the best restaurants in town, with live music every 2nd Sat in the hotel bar.

$$ Eva's Bar
22 Burns Av, T804-2267. Mon-Sat 0800-1500 and 1800-late.
Good diner-style restaurant, local dishes, helpful with good local information, bike rental, internet facilities and tours.

$$ Mr Greedy's Pizzaria
5 Burns Av. Daily 0600-2100.
Popular with locals and foreigners. Italian style oven-cooked pizza, beach sand floor and bamboo bar.

$$ Sanny's Grill
Several blocks down the hill off the Western Hwy past the Texaco station.
Serves the 'world's best conch ceviche' and a full dinner menu in a charming setting.

$$ Serendib
27 Burns Av, T824-2302. Mon-Sat, 1030-1500 and 1830-1100.
Good-value excellent Indian-style food, Sri Lankan owners.

$$-$ Martha's Kitchen
Below Martha's Guest House (see Where to stay, above).
Very good breakfasts and Belizean dishes, plus pizzas and burgers, served in a garden patio.

$ Hode's Place
Savannah Rd across park, just outside town. Open daily.
Popular with locals and good value, Belizean food arrives in huge portions, and there's a pleasant yard to sit outside.

$ Old French Bakery
JNC building.
Good pastries for days out exploring.

Bars and clubs

Cahal Pech
www.cahalpech.com, on a hill, with TV station, beside the road to Benque Viejo before the edge of town.
Music and dancing at weekends, *the* place to be, live bands broadcast on TV and radio. Good views, opposite Cahal Pech archaeological site.

Culture Club
Same building as Pitpan, upstairs.
Live reggae Thu-Sat night, popular with foreigners and the local Rasta crowd.

Legends 200
Bullet Tree Rd.
Disco, popular with locals.

Pitpan
Right turn off King St to river. Daily.
A popular spot with an open-air bar is at the back of the building.

Stork Club
San Ignacio Resort Hotel, see Where to stay, above.
Live music every 2nd Sat in the bar.

Shopping

There's a fruit and veg market every Fri and Sat morning.
Black Rock Gift Shop, *near Flavias, linked to Black Rock Lodge.* Luggage can be left here

if canoeing from Black Rock to San Ignacio, arts and crafts, workshop.

Celina's Supermarket, *Burns Av, next to the bus station. Mon-Sat 0730-1200, 1300-1600 and 1900-2100*. Not the cheapest but it does have a wide selection.

Maxim's, *West St*. Small, cheap supermarket.

Snooty Fox, *Waights Av (opposite Martha's)*. Book exchange.

What to do

Many resorts and lodges in this area organize a variety of tours and expeditions. Local tour operators generally offer similar tours at similar prices. Trips to the nearby ruins of Xunantunich (see above) are very easy by bus, with regular traffic going to the Guatemalan border. Tours of Mountain Pine Ridge (see below) are available, but shop around carefully; if you decide to go with a taxi you probably won't get far in the wet season. Trips to Caracol are best arranged from San Ignacio, and if you only want to visit Tikal in Guatemala, you can arrange a day trip that will maximize your time spent at the ruins.

Body and soul

Dr Rosita Arvigo, *see page 289*.
Therapeutic Massage Studio, *38 West St, T604-0314. Mon-Fri 0800-1200, 1300-1630. Sat 0830-1200*.

Tour operators

David's Adventure Tours, *near bus terminal, T804-3674*. Recommended for visits to Barton's Creek Cave, US$37, Mountain Pine ridge and Barton, US$67, Caracol, US$75, or guided canoe trips along the Macal River, including the medicinal trail and overnight camping, US$127. Always gets a good report.

Easy Rider, *Bullet Tree Rd, T824-3734*. Full-day horse-riding tours for US$40 with lunch.

Hun Chi'ik Tours, *Burns Av, T670-0746, www. hunchiiktours.com*. Cave and other tours, specializing in small groups but providing discounts for groups of more than 6 people.

Maya Mystic Tours, *Savannah St, T804-0055*. All trips organized including El Pilar, US$45 per person and river canoeing. Shuttles arranged.

Mayawalk Tours, *19 Burns Av, T824-3070, www.mayawalk.com*. Has received good recommendations. Similar rates to **Pacz**, also offers overnight rainforest and cave packages if you're looking for some true adventure.

Pacz Tours, *30 Burns Av, T824-0536, www. pacztours.net*. Offers great trips to Actun Tunichil Muknal Cave for US$75 including lunch and reserve fee of US$30. Excellent guides. Bob, who runs the bar, is the best starting point for information on any of the trips and is very helpful. Your hotel will also have details and suggestions. Canoe trips on the Macal River, with bird and wildlife watching, medicinal plant trail, good value, US$65; Barton Creek Cave, US$55 for ½-day tour, Mountain Pine Ridge, US$65, Caracol and trip to pools, US$75, Tikal, US$135. Highly recommended.

Transport

For more information on crossing the border to Guatemala, see box, page 514.

Bus

National Transport Company Bus Station is on Burns Av. To **Belize City**, Mon-Sat 0430-1800 every hour, Sun hourly 0700-1800, 3½-4 hrs, US$2.50. To **Belmopan**, same schedule as Belize City, 1 hr, US$1.70. To **Benque Viejo**, every 2 hrs, Mon-Sat 0730-2300 (less on Sun), 30 mins, US$0.75. Change at Belmopan for Dangriga and the south. From the bus station at Benque, you need to get a taxi to the immigration post at **Melchor de Mencos**, US$1.25, 2 mins. See also box, page 514.

Minibuses also run to **Tikal**, making a day trip possible. Organized tours cost about US$70.

Taxi

Savannah Taxi Drivers' Co-op, T824-2155, T606-7239 (Manuel, 24 hrs). To **Guatemalan border**, US$15 (*colectivo* US$2.50), on the road, but US$12.50 if you pick them up from their base opposite David's). See also box, page 514. To **Xunantunich** US$30 return, to **Belize City** US$75, to **Tikal** US$175 return, to **Mountain Pine Ridge**, US$75, **Chaa Creek**, US$30, **Caracol**, US$175 return.

Xunantunich

Bus

Bus from San Ignacio towards the border as far as **San José Succotz** (7 miles), US$0.75, where a hand-operated ferry takes visitors and cars across the Mopan River (0800-1600, free); it is then a 20-min walk uphill on an all-weather road. Return buses to San Ignacio pass throughout the afternoon.

Mountain Pine Ridge → *Colour map 8, B1.*

undulating landscape of protected forest with waterfalls and limestone caves

The easiest way of visiting is on a trip from San Ignacio. Try contacting the Forestry Conservation Officer, T824-3280, who may be able to help. See also Transport, below.

Mountain Pine Ridge is a forest reserve that covers 146,000 acres of the northwestern Maya Mountains. It's comprised of a largely undisturbed pine and gallery forest, and valleys of lush hardwood forests filled with orchids, bromeliads and butterflies. The devastation to large swathes of the pine forest first caused by an infestation of the southern pine bark beetle in 2001 continues to impact on the area. Note the frequent changes of colour of the soil and look out for the fascinating insect life. If lucky, you may see deer. There's river scenery to enjoy, high waterfalls, numerous limestone caves and shady picnic sites; it's a popular excursion despite the rough roads.

Two roads lead into the reserve: from Georgeville to the north and up from Santa Elena via Cristo Rey. These meet near **San Antonio**, a Mopan Maya village with many thatched-roof houses and the nearby Pacbitun archaeological site (where stelae and musical instruments have been unearthed). At San Antonio, the García sisters have their workshop, museum and shop where they sell carvings in local slate; this is a regular stop on tours to the Mountain Pine Ridge. The sisters also have a guesthouse ($). You can sample Maya food and learn about the use of medicinal plants. A donation of US$0.50 is requested; US$12.50 is charged to take photos of the sisters at work. There are two buses a day from San Ignacio, 1000 and 1430, from market area; check times of return buses before leaving San Ignacio.

The falls

The main forest road meanders along rocky spurs, from which unexpected and often breathtaking views emerge of jungle far below and streams plunging hundreds of feet over red-rock canyons. A lookout point (with a small charge) has been provided to view the impressive falls, said to be 1000 ft high (often shrouded in fog October to January). On a clear day you can see Belmopan from this viewpoint. It is quite a long way from the main road and is probably not worth the detour if time is short, particularly in the dry season (February to May) when the flow is restricted. At this time of year, there is an ever-present danger of fire and open fires are strictly prohibited. Eighteen miles into the reserve the road crosses the **Río On**. Here, where the river tumbles into inviting pools over huge granite boulders; is one of Belize's most beautiful picnic and swimming spots. The rocks form little water slides and are fun for children.

Augustine

Five miles further on is the tiny village of Augustine (also called Douglas D'Silva or **Douglas Forest Station**), the main forest station where there is a shop, accommodation in two houses (bookable through the Forestry Departttment in Belmopan, the Area Forestry Office is in San Antonio) and a **camping ground**, see Where to stay, below. A mile beyond Augustine is a cluster of caves in rich rainforest. The entrance to the **Río Frío Cave** (in fact a tunnel) is over 65 ft high, and there are many spectacular rock formations and sandy beaches where the river flows out. Trees in the parking area and along the Cuevas Gemelas nature trail, which starts one hour from the Río Frío cave, are labelled. It's a beautiful excursion and highly recommended.

Forestry roads continue south further into the mountains, reaching **San Luis** (6 miles), the only other inhabited camp in the area, with a post office, sawmill and forest station, and continuing on over the granite uplands of the Vaca Plateau into the **Chiquibul Forest Reserve** (460,000 acres).

The four forest reserves that cover the Maya Mountains are the responsibility of the Forestry Department, who have only about 20 rangers to patrol over a million acres of heavily forested land. A hunting ban prohibits the carrying of firearms. Legislation, however, allows for controlled logging; all attempts to have some areas declared national parks or biosphere reserves have so far been unsuccessful. You can stay in the area at **Las Cuevas Research Station and Explorers Lodge** (see Where to stay, below).

★ Caracol

About 24 miles south-southwest of Augustine, about one hour by 4WD, Caracol is a rediscovered Maya city. The area is now a National Monument Reservation. Caracol was established about 300 BC and continued well into the Late Classic period (glyphs record a victorious war against Tikal). Why Caracol was built in such a poorly watered region is not known, but Maya engineers showed great ingenuity in constructing reservoirs and terracing the fields. The **Sky Palace** (*Caana*) pyramid, which climbs 138 ft above the site, is being excavated by members of the University of Central Florida. Excavations take place between February and May, but there are year-round caretakers who will show you around. Very knowledgeable guides escort groups around the site twice daily, there's an information centre and an exhibition hall has been built. The road has been improved and is passable for much of the year with normal vehicles and year-round with 4WD. It is an interesting journey as you pass through the Mountain Pine Ridge, then cross the Macal River and immediately enter a broadleaf tropical forest. Take your own food as there is none at the site. Otherwise **Pine Ridge Lodge, Gaia River Lodge** or **Blancaneaux Lodge** are open for lunch (see Where to stay).

Listings Mountain Pine Ridge

Where to stay

$$$$ Hidden Valley Inn
Cooma Cairn Rd, Mountain Pine Ridge,
T822-3320, www.hiddenvalleyinn.com.
This romantic, intimate luxury wilderness lodge has a series of spacious, very comfortable cabins set in a flower-filled garden in one of the remotest and wildest stretches of Mountain Pine Ridge. It offers a broad range of tours and excursions.

$$$ Mountain Equestrian Trails
Mile 8, Mountain Pine Ridge Rd (from
Georgeville), Central Farm PO, T699 1124,
www.metbelize.com.

Accommodation is in 4 double cabanas with bath, no electricity, hot water and mosquito nets; good food is served in the *cantina*. Half-day, full-day and 4-day adventure tours on horseback in Western Belize, packages, birdwatching tours and other expeditions offered; excellent guides and staff.

Augustine

$$$ Las Cuevas Research Station and Explorer's Lodge
In the Chiquibul Forest, T822-2149, www.lascuevas.org.
This is a genuine wilderness experience, in an isolated research station open to non-researchers. Rivers, caves and archaeological sites are nearby.

Camping
Campsite, *US$1*. No mattresses (see rangers for all information on the area), keep your receipt, a guard checks it on the way out of Mountain Pine Ridge.

Caracol

$$$$ Blancaneaux Lodge
Mountain Pine Ridge Rd, east of San Ignacio, Central Farm, Cayo District, T824-3878, www.blancaneaux lodge.com.
Once the mountain retreat of Francis Ford Coppola and his family, now 1 villa and wonderful, huge cabanas decorated in Guatemalan textiles. There's horse riding, croquet, spa, hot pool, overlooking a stream, and a private air strip. Access to Big Rock Falls. Italian restaurant and bar. Recommended.

$$$$ Gaia River Lodge
East of San Ignacio, 2½ miles beyond Blancaneaux Lodge, T820-4005, www.gaiariverlodge.com.
Formerly **Five Sisters Lodge**, rustic cottages lit by oil lamps, with great views and a good-value restaurant. Recommended.

$$$ Pine Ridge Lodge
East of San Ignacio, on the road to Augustine, just past turning to Hidden Valley Falls, T606-4557, www.pineridgelodge.com.
Cabanas in the pinewoods, price includes breakfast.

Transport

Taxi
There's no public transport. Apart from tours, the only alternatives are to take a taxi or hire a vehicle or mountain bike. Everything is well signposted. The private pickups that go into San Ignacio from Augustine are usually packed, so hitching is impossible. Taxis charge around US$75-80 for 5 people. Roads are passable but rough Jan-May, but after Jun they are marginal and are impossible in the wet (Sep-Nov). It's essential to seek local advice at the time.

North Belize

North Belize is notable for the agricultural production of sugar, fruit and vegetables and for providing much of the country's food. But among the fields of produce are some well-hidden sights and wildlife magnets. The Maya ruins of Lamanai are just about visible in the spectacular setting of the dense jungle. Wildlife can easily be seen at the Community Baboon Sanctuary, the Crooked Tree Wildlife Sanctuary – home to thousands of beautiful birds – and the wildlife reserve of Shipstern near Sartaneja. The vast Río Bravo Conservation Area nudges up to the Guatemalan border and contains the truly isolated ruins and lodge of Chan Chich.

Heading north out of Belize City, the Northern Highway leads to the Mexican border. You can do the journey in just a few hours, passing through Orange Walk and Corozal, but you won't see a thing. It's definitely worth stopping off if you have time.

Bermudian Landing

About 15 miles out of Belize City a road heading west leads to the small Creole village of Bermudian Landing (12 miles on a rough road from the turn-off), which has been thrust into the global conservation spotlight. This was once a transfer point for the timber that floated down the Belize River, but now there's a local wildlife museum sponsored by the WWF, and the **Community Baboon Sanctuary** ⓘ *daily 0900-1700, www.howlermonkeys. org, 45- to 60-min guided tours from US$7, including a visit to the small museum; guided wildlife walks are available when booked ahead and simple homestay accommodation is available,* where visitors can see black howler monkeys, many of whom are so used to people that they come very close.

★Crooked Tree Wildlife Sanctuary

US$4; you must register at the visitor centre, drinks are on sale, but take food. There is a helpful, friendly warden, Steve, who will let you sleep on the porch of the visitor centre. It is easy to get a lift to the sanctuary, and someone is usually willing to take visitors back to the main road for a small charge.

The Northern Highway continues to **Sand Hill**, and a further 12 miles to the turn-off for the Crooked Tree Wildlife Sanctuary, which was set up in 1984 and is a rich area for birds. The network of lagoons and swamps is an internationally protected wetland under the RAMSAR programme, and attracts many migrating birds. The dry season, October to May, is a good time to visit. You may see the huge jabiru stork, the largest flying bird in the Western Hemisphere at a height of 5 ft and a wingspan of 11-12 ft, which nests here, as well as herons, ducks, vultures, kites, ospreys, hawks, sand pipers, kingfishers, gulls, terns, egrets and swallows. In the forest you can also see and hear howler monkeys. Other animals include coatimundi, crocodiles, iguanas and turtles. Glenn Crawford is a good guide.

The turn-off to the sanctuary is signposted but keep an eye out for the intersection, which is 22 miles from Orange Walk and 33 miles from Belize City. There is another sign further south indicating the sanctuary but this just leads to the park boundary, not to the Wildlife Sanctuary. The mango and cashew trees in the village of Crooked Tree are said to be 100 years old. Birdwatching is best in the early morning but, as buses do not leave Belize City early, for a day trip take an early Corozal bus, get off at the main road (about 1¼ hours from Belize City) and hitch to the sanctuary. The village is tiny and quaint, occupied mostly by Creoles. Boats and guides can be hired for approximately US$80 per boat (maximum four people). It may be worth bargaining as competition is fierce. Trips include a visit to an unexcavated Maya site.

Altun Ha

Daily 0900-1700, US$5, insect repellent necessary.

The Maya remains of Altun Ha, 31 miles north of Belize City and 2 miles off the Old Northern Highway, are worth a visit. Altun Ha was a major ceremonial centre in the Classic period (AD 250-900) and also a trading station linking the Caribbean coast with Maya centres in the interior. There are two central plazas surrounded by 13 partially excavated pyramids and temples. What the visitor sees now is composite, not how the site would have been at any one time in the past. The largest piece of worked Maya jade ever found, a head of the Sun God Kinich Ahau weighing 9½ lb (4.3 kg), was found here in the main temple (B-4) in 1968. It is now in a bank vault in Belize City. Nearby is a large reservoir, now called **Rockstone Road**.

Where to stay

Bermudian Landing

$$$$-$$$ Black Orchid Resort
T225 9158, www.blackorchidresort.com.
Selection of rooms with shared bath through to luxury villas on the banks of the Belize River. Restaurant, freshwater swimming pool, and very good tours along the Belize River in search of history, howler monkeys and crocodiles, with friendly owner Doug Thompson. A great alternative choice to Belize City or Crooked Tree. Airport transfers easily arranged.

$$$ Howler Monkey Resort
400 m from museum, T607-1571, www.howlermonkeyresort.bz.
Cabins with screened windows, fans, shared bath cheaper. Camping US$5 per person, bring your own tent. Transport from Belize City in pickup US$40, 1-4 people, on request. Breakfast, lunch and dinner, US$5-9. Many good tours including river tours US$25 per person, recommended, and night-time crocodile adventures US$40. Canoe rentals in Burrell Boom for trips on Belize River to see birds, howler monkeys, manatee and other wildlife. Student discount, and TCs, Visa and MasterCard accepted.

$ Community Baboon Sanctuary.
Cabanas are available alongside the visitor centre, with bath and hot water. Basic lodging is also available with families in the village and can be arranged through the Baboon Sanctuary office.

Crooked Tree Wildlife Sanctuary

$$$-$$ Bird's Eye View Lodge
T203-2040, www.birdseyeviewbelize.com.
Owned by the Gillett family. Single and double rooms, shower, fan, meals available, boat trips, horse riding, canoe rental, nature tours with licensed guide. Ask for information at the **Belize Audubon Society** (see box, page 284).

$$$-$$ Crooked Tree Lodge
T626 3820, www.crookedtreelodgebelize.com.
Relaxing birdwatching on the lagoon, and wildlife- and nature-related tours. Run by Mick and Angie Webb.

Transport

Bermudian Landing
Bus
From **Belize City**, **Mcfadzean Bus** from corner of Amara Av and Cemetery Rd at 1215 and 1715 Mon-Fri; 1200 and 1400 Sat. **Rancho Bus** (**Pook's Bus**) from Mosul St, 1700 Mon-Fri, 1300 Sat, check details, US$1.50-2, 1 hr. Alternatively, any bus travelling the Northern Highway can drop you off at the turn-off to Bermudian Landing where you can wait for a bus, or hitch a ride. A day trip giving any meaningful time in the sanctuary is difficult by public transport, so it's best to stay the night.

Crooked Tree Wildlife Sanctuary
Bus
Buses from **Belize City** with **JEX** (1035); return from Crooked Tree at 0600-0700.

Altun Ha
Bus
With little transport on this road, hitching is not recommended; it's best to go in a private vehicle or a tour group. Vehicles leave **Belize City** for the village of **Maskall**, 8 miles north of Altun Ha, several days a week, but same-day return is not possible.

agricultural town near one of Belize's most important Maya sites

The Northern Highway runs to Orange Walk (population 15,990), the centre of a district where Creoles, Mennonites and Maya earn their living from timber, sugar planting and general agriculture. Nearby, the impressive ruins of Lamanai make a good day trip; see below. This is also the departure point for Sartaneja and the Shipstern Peninsula and for the long overland trip to Río Bravo Conservation Area, Chan Chich and Gallon Jug.

There is little to draw the visitor for an extended stay in Orange Walk. The country's second city, it is busy with the comings and goings of a small town. Orange Walk is a truly multicultural centre with inhabitants from all over Central America, making Spanish the predominant language. Originally from Canada, Mennonites live in nearby colonies using the town as their marketing and supply centre. The only battle fought on Belizean soil took place here, during the Yucatecan Caste Wars (1840-1870s): the Maya leader, Marcus Canul, was shot in the fighting in 1872. The **House of Culture** on Main Street shows a history of the town's development.

Buses plying the route from Belize City to the Mexican border stop on Queen Victoria Avenue, the main street, close to the town hall. While a few pleasant wooden buildings remain on quiet side streets, most are worn out and badly in need of repair. Many have been pulled down and replaced by the standard concrete box affairs, which lack both inspiration and style.

A toll bridge now spans the New River a few miles south of the town at Tower Hill. There is a market overlooking New River, which is well organized with good food stalls and interesting architecture.

West and south of Orange Walk

From Orange Walk a road heads west, before turning south, running parallel to the Mexican and then Guatemalan border, where it becomes unpaved. Along this road are several archaeological sites. First is **Cuello**, 4 miles west on San Antonio road, behind Cuello Distillery (ask there for permission to visit); taxi about US$3.50. The site dates back to 1000 BC, but, although it has yielded important discoveries in the study of Maya and pre-Maya cultures, there is little for the layman to appreciate and no facilities for visitors. At **Yo Creek** the road divides, north to San Antonio, and south through miles of cane fields and tiny farming settlements as far as **San Felipe** (20 miles via San Lázaro, Trinidad and August Pine Ridge). At August Pine Ridge there is a daily bus to Orange Walk at 1000. You can camp at the house of Narciso Novelo or 'Chicho' (T323-3019), a little-known secret and a relaxing place to stay set amongst bananas, pine tres, bushes and flowers; no fixed cost, just pay what you think. Chicho will meet you off the bus if you call ahead. At San Felipe, a branch leads southeast to Indian Church/Lamanai, 35 miles from Orange Walk (one hour driving, 4WD needed when wet). Another road heads west to Blue Creek village on the Mexican border (see below).

Lamanai
US$5.

Near Indian Church on the west side of New River Lagoon, 22 miles by river south of Orange Walk, is one of Belize's largest archaeological sites, Lamanai. Difficult to get to and hidden in the jungle, it is a perfect setting to hide the mysteries of the Maya and definitely worth a visit. While the earliest buildings were erected about 700 BC, culminating in the completion of the 112-ft major temple, N10-43, about 100 BC (the tallest known pre-Classic Maya structure), there is evidence the site was occupied as long ago as 1500 BC. As a Maya site, it is believed to have the longest history of continuous occupation and, with the Spanish and British sites mentioned below and the present-day refugee village nearby, Lamanai's history is impressive.

The Maya site has been partially cleared, but covers a large area so a guide is recommended. The views from temple N10-43, dedicated to Chac, are superb; look for the Yin-Yang-like symbol below the throne on one of the other main temples, which also has a 12-ft-tall mask overlooking its plaza. Visitors can wander freely along narrow trails and climb the stairways. There is a very informative museum housing the only known stela found at the site. There is also a fine jungle lodge; see Where to stay, below.

At nearby **Indian Church**, a Spanish mission was built over one of the Maya temples in 1580, and the British established a sugar mill here. The remains of both buildings can still be seen. The archaeological reserve is jungle and howler monkeys are visible in the trees. There are many birds and the best way to see them is to reach Lamanai by boat, easily arranged in Orange Walk or by taking a day trip from Belize City, see Tour operators, page 305. The earlier you go the better, but the trips from Orange Walk all leave at pretty standard times. The mosquitoes are vicious in the wet season (wear trousers and take repellent). The community phone for information on Indian Church, including buses, is T309-3015.

Blue Creek and around

West of San Felipe is Blue Creek (10 miles), the largest of the Mennonite settlements. Many inhabitants of these close-knit villages arrived in 1959, members of a Canadian colony that had migrated to Chihuahua, Mexico, to escape encroaching modernity. They preserve their Low German dialect, are exempt from military service, and their industry now supplies the country with most of its poultry, eggs, vegetables and furniture. Some settlements, such as Neustadt in the west, have been abandoned because of threats by drug smugglers in the early 1990s.

Belize and Mexico have signed an agreement to build an international bridge from Blue Creek across the river to La Unión, together with a river port close to the bridge. It is not known when work will start; at present there is a canoe-service for foot passengers across the Blue Creek. See also box, page 514.

A vast area to the south along the **Río Bravo** has been set aside as a conservation area (see box, page 284). Within this, there is a study and accommodation centre near the Maya site of **La Milpa**. The site is at present being excavated by a team from the University of Texas and Boston University, USA.

A good road can be followed 35 miles south to **Gallon Jug**, where a jungle tourism lodge has been built in the **Chan Chich** Maya ruin, see Where to stay, below. The journey to Chan Chich passes through the Río Bravo Conservation Area, is rarely travelled and offers some of the best chances to see wildlife. Chan Chich is believed to have the highest number of jaguar sightings in Belize, and is also a birdwatchers' paradise. Another road has been cut south through Tambos to the main road between Belmopan and San Ignacio, but travel in this region is strictly a dry-weather affair.

Where to stay

Orange Walk
Parking for vehicles is very limited at hotels.

$$$-$$ Hotel de la Fuente
14 Main St, T322-2290,
www.hoteldelafuente.com.
Suites of rooms, with kitchenettes, simple
wooden desks and wildlife paintings by a
local artist. Tours to Lamanai available.

$$ D'Victoria
40 Belize Rd (Main St), T322-2518,
www.dvictoriabelize.com.
A reasonably comfortable but somewhat
run-down place with a/c rooms that have a
shower and hot water. There's a pool
and parking.

$$ St Christopher's
12 Main St, T302-1064, www.stchristophers
hotelbze.com.
The best place in town, with beautiful clean
rooms and bathrooms. Highly recommended.

$ Akihito Japanese Hotel
22 Belize Corozal Rd, T302-0185,
akihitolee@ hotmail.com.
An affordable place in the centre of town.

Lamanai

$$$$ Lamanai Outpost Lodge
At Indian Church, T223-3578,
www.lamanai.com.
Run by the incredibly friendly Howells, this
beautiful lodge is a short walk from Lamanai
ruins, overlooking New River Lagoon. The
thatched wooden cabins have a bath, hot
water, fan and 24-hr electricity. There's also a
restaurant, and day tours with excellent and
well-informed guides. A juvenile crocodile
study is underway and guests are invited to
participate. Package deals are available.

Camping
Nazario Ku, the site caretaker, permits
camping or hammocks at his house,
opposite path to Lamanai ruins, good value
for backpackers.

Blue Creek and around

$$$$ Chan Chich
Chiun Chah, T223-4419, www.chanchich.com.
This beautifully sited lodge is in the midst
of Maya ruins with an extensive trail system
in the grounds and fantastic birdwatching
and wildlife-watching opportunities with
very good guides. Delicious food is served,
and there's a pool. Phone before setting out
for Chan Chich for information on the roads.
Recommended.

$$$ La Milpa Field Station
La Milpa, for information call T323-0011, or
contact the Programme for Belize in Belize
City (T227-5616, www.pfbelize.org).
A good base for exploring trails in the region
and birdwatching. The reserve is privately
owned and you will need proof of booking
to pass the various checkpoints. There are
4 spacious and comfortable double cabanas
with a thatched roof overhanging a large
wooden deck, or a dorm sleeping up to 30.
To reach La Milpa, go 6 miles west from Blue
Creek to Tres Leguas, then follow the signs
south towards the Río Bravo Escarpment.

$$ Hill Bank Field Station
On the banks of the New River Lagoon.
Also a good base for exploring trails in
the region and birdwatching, and with a
dorm sleeping up to 30. See **La Milpa Field
Station** above for contact details.

Restaurants

Orange Walk
Most restaurants in town are Chinese. We've
received encouraging reports about **La
Hacienda Steakhouse** and **Marvias**.

$$ Nahil Mayab
www.nahilmayab.com, closed Sun.
The best in town, serving contemporary
Mexican cuisine, grilled meat and
vegetarian dishes.

$ Central Plaza Restaurant
Behind the main bus terminal.
A popular choice in a handy location.

$ Diner
Clarke St, behind the hospital.
Good meals, very friendly; to get
there, take a taxi (US$4) or walk.

What to do

Orange Walk
Jungle River Tours, *20 Lovers Lane, T302-
2293, lamanaimayatour@btl.net*. In **Lovers'
Café** on the southeastern corner of the
park. Organize and run trips to Lamanai
(US$40 plus entrance of US$5, including
lunch, departing 0900 returning 1600),
Altun Ha and New River area, regular trips,

the specialists on the region and consistently
recommended. They also provide trips to
any destination in Belize with a minimum
of 4 people.

Transport

Orange Walk
Bus
The bus station is on street beside the fire
station, on the main road. All buses travelling
from Belize City to Corozal and beyond to
Chetumal stop in Orange Walk; from **Belize**,
US$3. From **Corozal**, US$1.50, 50 mins. For
Lamanai take bus to Indian Church (Mon,
Wed, Fri 1600). Buses to **Sarteneja** (which is
40 miles away) outside **Zeta's Store** on Main
St, 5 between 1300 and 1900, US$2.50. Also
to **Progresso** at 1100 and 1130.

Blue Creek and around
Air
Flights to Chan Chich from **Belize City** can
be chartered.

North of Orange Walk → *Colour map 8, A2.*

wildlife reserve, fishing villages and archaeological sites

Sarteneja and the northeast

From Orange Walk a complex network of roads and tracks converge on **San Estevan** and
Progresso to the north. The Maya ruins near San Estevan have reportedly been flattened
to a large extent and are not very impressive. Ten miles from San Estevan is a road junction;
straight on is **Progresso**, a village picturesquely located on the lagoon of the same name.
The right turn, signposted, runs off to the Mennonite village of **Little Belize** and continues
(in poor condition) to **Chunox**, a village with many Maya houses of pole construction. In
the dry season it is possible to drive from Chunox to the Maya site of Cerros (see below).

Three miles before Sarteneja is the visitor centre for Shipstern Nature Reserve, which
covers 22,000 acres of this northeastern tip of Belize. Hardwood forests, saline lagoon
systems and wide belts of savannah shelter a wide range of mammals (coatis and foxes,
and all the fauna found elsewhere in Belize, except monkeys), reptiles and 200 species of
bird. There are mounds of Maya houses and fields everywhere. The most remote forest,
south of the lagoon, is not accessible to short-term visitors. There is a botanical trail
leading into the forest with trees labelled with Latin and local Yucatec Maya names; a
booklet is available. At the visitor centre is the **Butterfly Breeding Centre** ⓘ *daily 0800-
1700, US$5 including excellent guided tour*. Visit on a sunny day if possible; on dull days the
butterflies hide themselves in the foliage. There is rather poor dormitory accommodation
at the visitor centre, US$10 per person. A day-trip by private car is possible from Sarteneja
or Orange Walk. Mosquito repellent is essential.

Leaving the Northern Highway, a road heads east to **Sarteneja**, a small fishing and former boat-building settlement founded by Yucatán refugees in the 19th century. The main catch is lobster and conch. On Easter Sunday there is a popular regatta, with all types of boat racing, dancing and music. There are the remains of an extensive Maya city scattered throughout the village, and recent discoveries have been made and are currently being explored to the south around the area of Shipstern Lagoon.

Corozal and around

The Northern Highway continues to Corozal (96 miles from Belize City, population 9110), formerly the centre of the sugar industry, now with a special zone for the clothing industry and garment exports. Much of the old town was destroyed by Hurricane Janet in 1955 and it is now a mixture of modern concrete commercial buildings and Caribbean clapboard seafront houses on stilts. Like Orange Walk it is economically depressed but Corozal is much the safer place. It is open to the sea with a pleasant waterfront where the market is held. There is no beach but you can swim in the sea and lie on the grass. You can check out the local website at www.corozal.com.

Between Orange Walk and Corozal, in San José and San Pablo, is the archaeological site of **Nohmul**, a ceremonial centre whose main acropolis dominates the surrounding cane fields (the name means 'Great Mound'). Permission to visit the site must be obtained from Estevan Itzab, whose house is opposite the water tower.

From Corozal, a road leads 7 miles northeast to **Consejo**, a quiet, seaside fishing village on Chetumal Bay. There's no public transport; a taxi costs about US$10.

Six miles northeast of Corozal, to the right of the road to Chetumal, is **Four Mile Lagoon**, about a quarter of a mile off the road (buses will drop you there). There is clean swimming, better than at Corozal bay, and some food and drinks available; it is often crowded at weekends.

Across the bay to the south of Corozal stand the mounds of **Cerros**, once an active Maya trading port whose central area was reached by canal. Some of the site is flooded but one pyramid, 69-ft-high with stucco masks on its walls, has been partially excavated. Take a boat from Corozal, walk around the bay (a boat is needed to cross the mouth of the New River) or do the dry-season vehicular trail from Progresso and Chunox (see above). Trips can be arranged with **Hotel Maya** and **Hok'Ol K'in Guest House**, from US$60 for a water taxi carrying up to six people.

Listings North of Orange Walk

Where to stay

Sarteneja

$ Backpacker's Paradise
T423-2016, http://backpackers.blue greenbelize.com, 5 mins from the village.
Cabins and camping, kitchen and restaurant and a range of activities. Attracts a young and boisterous crowd.

Corozal

$$$ Copa Banana
409 Corozal Bay Rd, T422-0284, www.copabanana.bz.
Newest place in town, with 5 suites all with private bathrooms. US-owned so complimentary coffee each morning. Ask the bus driver to drop you off.

$$$ Tony's
South End, T422-2055, www.tonysinn.com.
With a/c, clean, comfortable units in landscaped grounds. Recommended, but restaurant overpriced.

$$$-$$ Las Palmas Hotel
123, 5th Av South, T422-0196, www.laspalmashotelbelize.com.
With bath and fan, OK, *refrescos* available, good food, lively bar downstairs.

$$ Hok'Ol K'in Guest House
4th Av and 4th St South, T422-3329, www.corozal.net.
Immaculate rooms. Runs tours to Cerros.

$ Caribbean Village Resort
South End, T422 2725.
Hot water, US$5 camping, US$12 trailer park, restaurant. Recommended.

Camping

Caribbean Motel and Trailer Park
See Caribbean Village Resort, above.
Camping possible (US$4 per person) but not very safe, shaded sites, restaurant.

Corozal
There are many Chinese restaurants in town.

$$ Cactus Plaza
5th Av South.
A loud bar with lots of fluorescent lighting and great a/c. Worth trying if you're stuck in town for the night.

$ Corozal Garden
4th Av, 1 block south.
Good, quick local food.

$ Gongora's Pastry
Southwest corner of main square.
Hot pizza pieces, cakes and drinks.

$ RD's Diner
7-4th Av, T422-3796.
Burgers and American-style food.

Sartaneja
Bus
Bus from **Belize City** at 1200, US$4.50, from the corner of Victoria and North Front St. Buses also leave from **Corozal** (1400), via Orange Walk (1530).

Corozal
Air
Maya Island Air, daily from Belize City via Caye Caulker and San Pedro (Ambergris Caye); **Tropic Air** daily from San Pedro. Airstrip 3 miles south, taxi US$1.50. Private charters to **Sartaneja** cost about US$75 for the 30-min journey (compared with 3 hrs by road).

Boat
To **Orange Walk**, leaving at 1400.

Bus
Heading south, buses leave every 30 mins, starting at 0400 running until 1830. Regular service 3 hrs, US$2.50, faster express service, 2½ hrs, US$3.50, leaves at 0600, 0700, 1200, 1500 and 1800. If heading north, buses from **Belize City** continue north to **Chetumal** terminal, with stopping time to allow for immigration procedures.

For those coming from Mexico who are interested in **Tikal** in Guatemala, it is possible to make the journey border to border in a day, with a change of bus in Belize City.

For further information on border crossings to Mexico and Guatemala, see box, page 511.

Taxi
Leslie's Taxi Service, T422-2377. Transfers from Corozal to the Mexican border, US$22 for a 4-person taxi. Ask for a quote for other services. Reliable and professional.

South Belize
& the southern cayes

Southern Belize is the most remote part of the country and has poor roads, but it is worth exploring. Dangriga is the largest of several Garífuna settlements that burst into life every year on Settlement Day. The paradise beaches of Hopkins and Placencia are perfect for watersports and relaxing. Cockscomb Basin Wildlife (Jaguar) Sanctuary offers one of the best chances of seeing a big cat in the wild, while the sparsely populated far south around Punta Gorda has many Maya settlements to visit in a region dotted with impressive Maya ruins.

South to Dangriga → Colour map 8, B2.

beautiful verdant route lined with jungle and citrus plantations

About 2 miles beyond the Belize Zoo on the Western Highway, the Coastal Highway (a good dirt road) runs southeast to Gales Point, a charming fishing village on a peninsula at the south end of Manatee Lagoon, 15 miles north of Dangriga. The villagers are keen to preserve natural resources and there are still significant numbers of the endangered manatee and hawksbill turtles. Boat tours of the lagoon are recommended.

Along the Hummingbird Highway

The narrow Hummingbird Highway branches off the Western Highway 48 miles west of Belize City, passes Belmopan and heads south. Skirting the eastern edge of Mountain Pine Ridge, the highway meanders through lush scenery of cohune palms, across vast flood plains filled with citrus trees, which provide a spectacular backdrop for the 52-mile journey southeast to Dangriga.

The Hummingbird Highway climbs through rich tropical hardwood forest until reaching Mile 13, where a visitor centre marks a track leading off to **St Herman's Cave**. Two paths, with good birdwatching, lead through shady ferns before descending in steps to the cave entrance with its unique microclimate. You can walk for more than a mile underground but it can be slippery if wet; torch and spare batteries essential. There is a 3-mile trail to a campsite from the visitor centre.

Two miles further on is the **Blue Hole National Park** ⓘ *daily 0800-1600, US$4, visitor centre at entrance,* an azure blue swimming hole fringed with vines and ferns, fed by a stream that comes from St Herman's Cave. This is typical karst limestone country with sinkholes, caves and underground streams. After its long journey underground, the water here is deliciously cool until it disappears again into the top of a large underwater cavern. Eventually this joins the Sibun River which enters the sea just south of Belize City. There is a rough 2½-mile trail (good hiking boots are required), through low secondary forest, between St Herman's Cave and the Blue Hole itself. A sign on the roadway warns visitors against thieves; lock your car and leave someone on guard if possible when swimming. An armed guard and more wardens have been hired to prevent further theft and assaults.

The peaks of the mountains dominate the south side of the highway until about Mile 30, when the valley of Stann Creek begins to widen out into Belize's most productive agricultural area, where large citrus groves stretch along the highway.

Canoeing or tubing trips can be organized down Indian Creek, visiting the imaginatively named Caves Five, Four and Three and then Daylight Cave and Darknight Cave, from **Over-the-Top Camp** on the Hummingbird Highway, or **Kingfisher/Belize Adventures** in Placencia. Vehicle support is brought round to meet you on the Coastal Highway near Democracia.

Turn east at Mile 32 for 4 miles along a gravel road to **Tamandua**, a wildlife sanctuary in **Five Blue Lakes National Park** ⓘ *Friends of 5 Blues, PO Box 111, Belmopan, T809-2005, or the warden, Lee Wengrzyn, a local dairy farmer, or else Augustus Palacio.* Follow the track opposite **Over-the-Top Camp**, turning right and crossing the stream for Tamandua, then for another 2 miles or so straight on following the signs for the national park, 1½ miles, where there is camping.

Listings South to Dangriga

Where to stay

$$$$ Caves Branch Jungle Lodge
Hummingbird Highway Mile 41.5, T610-3451, www.cavesbranch.com.
Reached along a ½-mile track, signed on the left, any bus between Belmopan and Dangriga will stop. A secluded spot on the banks of Caves Branch River, comfortable treehouses and cabanas with private baths, delicious meals served buffet style. More than just accommodation, this is very much an activity centre. Great trips through caves, 7-mile underground floats, guided jungle trips, overnight trips as well, tubing, kayaking, mountain biking and rappelling, including the adrenalin-busting **Black Hole Drop**. Excellent guides, pricey for some budgets but highly recommended.

$$$$ Sleeping Giant Lodge
Hummingbird Highway Mile 36.5, T707-6986, www.sleepinggiantbelize.com.
Situated on a sloping terrace by the Sibun river, this beautiful rainforest resort enjoys unrivalled views of Sleeping Giant Mountain and the surrounding range. Luxury lodgings include tasteful and tranquil rooms and *casitas* with mahogany woodwork, marble and granite finishes, and hand-crafted furniture. The grounds are lush and leafy and feature a bubbling creek, hot tub and pool. All-inclusive packages available.

$$ Yamwits
Hummingbird Highway Mile 35.5, T822-2906, www.yamwits.com.
Nestled in the fragrant grounds of a citrus orchard, **Yamwits** is a locally owned, family-run lodging with 6 simple, clean and economical rooms with a wide veranda

overlooking the fruit trees and mountains. They serve local cuisine in their restaurant; worth a stop if you're driving through. Friendly hosts, classic Belizean hospitality.

What to do

There is a wide variety of day and overnight excursions to Gales Point, from US$30 per boat holding 6-8 people. Contact Kevin Andrewin of **Manatee Tour Guides Association** on arrival. Community phone, T02-12031, minimum 48 hrs' notice is advisable, ask for Alice or Josephine.

Transport

Boat

Gales Point can be reached by inland waterways from **Belize City**, but buses have largely superseded boat services.

Bus

At least 2 daily **Southern Transport** buses run between **Belize City** and Dangriga on the coastal road.

Dangriga and around → Colour map 8, B2.

cheerful and busy seafront town with a largely Garífuna population

The chief town of the Stann Creek District, Dangriga (population 11,600) is on the seashore, and has the usual Belizean aspect of wooden clapboard houses elevated on piles. North Stann Creek meets the sea at Dangriga, coming alive with flotillas of boats and fishermen.

There are several petrol stations, a good hospital and an airfield with regular flights. The beach has been considerably cleaned up and extended, being particularly pleasant at the far north of town at the Pelican Beach Hotel, where it is raked and cleaned daily. Palm trees have been planted by Pal's Guest House where the beach has been enlarged. Dangriga means 'standing waters' or 'sweet water' in Garífuna. It's possible to take a boat from Dangriga to Honduras; see box, page 516.

To understand more about the Garífuna culture, visit the **Gulisi Garífuna Museum** ① *Stann Creek Valley Rd, T502-0639, www.ngcbelize.org, Mon-Fri 1000-1700, Sat 0800-1200, US$5.* The museum includes information about the origins of the Garífuna people, history and customs, with music and a working garden of traditional plants and herbs.

Cayes near Dangriga

Tobacco Caye ① *US$15, 35 mins by speedboat from Dangriga*, is a tiny and quite heavily populated island, but has lots of local flavour and charm and, though becoming a little commercialized, still has an authentic feel. It sits right on the reef and you can snorkel from the sandfly-free beach although there are no large schools of fish; snorkelling gear for rent. Boats go daily, ask at Riverside Café ① *US$12-15 per person*.

South Water Caye, the focus of a marine reserve, is a lovely palm-fringed tropical island with beautiful beaches, particularly at the south end.

South of Dangriga

The Southern Highway (now completely paved except for a stretch of a mile or so) connects Dangriga with Punta Gorda in the far south. Six miles inland from Dangriga the road branches off the Hummingbird Highway and heads south through mixed tropical forests, palmettos and pines along the fringes of the Maya Mountains. West of the road, about 5 miles from the junction with the Hummingbird Highway, a track leads to

Mayflower, a Maya ruin. Some minimal work has begun on opening it up and some say it will eventually be the biggest archaeological site in southern Belize.

Fifteen miles from Dangriga, a minor road forks off 4 miles east to the Garífuna fishing village of Hopkins. Watch out for sandflies when the weather is calm. The villagers throw household slops into the sea and garbage on to the beach.

Turning east towards the Caribbean just before Kendal a road leads down the Sittee River to **Sittee River Village** and **Possum Point Biological Station**.

Glover's Reef

Glover's Reef, part of North East Cay and about 45 miles offshore, is an atoll with beautiful diving and has been a **Marine Reserve** ① US$10, since 1993. The reef here is pristine and the cayes are generally unspoilt, but yellow blight has hit the area killing most of the existing palm trees, especially on **Long Caye**. The combination of Hurricane Mitch and high water temperatures has damaged the coral, and the snorkelling is not as good as it once was.

Listings Dangriga and around

Where to stay

Dangriga

$$$ Pelican Beach
Outside town, on the beach north of town, T522-2044, www.pelicanbeachbelize.com.
This Belizean-owned hotel overlooking the ocean has 20 rooms with private bath, hot water, a/c, veranda, hammocks. Amenities include restaurant, bar, games lounge, gift shop and tours. Friendly and helpful. Take a taxi from town, or it's a 15-min walk from North Stann Creek.

$$$-$$ Chaleanor
35 Magoon St, T522-2587, www.chaleanorhotel.com.
Managed by Chad and Eleanor Usher, this comfortable guesthouse has fairly large rooms, some with TV and fan and a/c, some with sea views, and a rooftop restaurant.

$$ Pal's Guest House
868 A Magoon St, Dangriga, T522-2095, www.palsbelize.com.
These 19 units on the beach, all have balconies, sea views, bath, fan and cable TV; cheaper rooms in main building, shared bath downstairs, private upstairs. **Dangriga Dive Centre** runs from next door (see What to do, below).

$ D's Hostel
Corner Mahogany St and Sharp St, T502-3324, www.valsbackpackerhostel.com.
Formerly Val's place, D's is the only backpacker hostel in town. It's a chilled, friendly place, with a family atmosphere, and has 24 dorm beds, hot and cold water, Wi-Fi (extra), lockers and a book exchange. A waffle breakfast and hot coffee are included.

Cayes near Dangriga
Tobacco Caye

There is no electricity on the island, but it has a good family atmosphere and is great fun.

$$$ Reef's End Lodge
T522-2419, www.reefsendlodge.com.
The new Swedish owners have spruced this simple but appealing place up, now probably the best place on the island. Accommodation includes sea view rooms with veranda and wood-built beach cabanas. Minimum 3 nights and rates include full board.

$ Tobacco Caye Paradise Cabins
North Point, T532-2101, www.tobacocayeparadisecabin.com.
Formerly a holiday lodge belonging to a Belizean family, this accommodation includes 6 simple, rustic, traditionally

Caribbean clapboard cabins, suitable for budget travellers. Rates are per person, and meals are available (**$$**).

South Water Caye

$$$$ Blue Marlin Lodge
T522-2243, www.bluemarlinlodge.com.
Excellent dive lodge with a host of accommodation include beachside cabins, 'island igloos' and rooms. Offers various packages, small sandy island with snorkelling off the beach, good accommodation and food, runs tours.

$$$$ Pelican's Beach Resort
T522-2044, www.pelicanbeachbelize.com.
Rooms in a 2-storey colonial building, and 3 secluded cottages. **Pelican University** is ideal for groups housing up to 23 people at US$60 per person per day including 3 meals.

Other Cayes

$$$$ Coco Plum Island Resort
T1-800-763-7360, www.cocoplumcay.com.
Set on a private caye, this adults-only private resort would suit couples seeking seclusion and romance. Lodgings include 14 Caribbean-style oceanfront cabanas with well-attired interiors. Various packages available from 'no frills' to 'lover's getaway'. Exclusive and professional.

$$$$ Thatch Caye Resort
T532-2414, www.thatchcayebelize.com.
Located in the heart of the South Water Caye Marine Reserve, this exclusive private island resort promises access to some great dive and snorkel sites. Lodgings consist of cabanas and *casitas* on the edge of the water. Expensive and rustic-chic.

South of Dangriga

$$$$ Hamanasi
Sittee Point, T1-877-552-3483, www.hamanasi.com.
This boutique beachside resort is set in 17-acre gardens bursting with tropical

flowers and orchids. Accommodation includes 13 private treehouses on stilts, 2 honeymoon suites and 8 beachfront deluxe rooms. Amenities include pool, kayaks, bikes and a full dive operation.

$$$$ Jaguar Reef Lodge
South of Hopkins, just north of Sittee River, T822-3851, www.jaguarreef.com.
18 a/c rooms with fridges. Central lodge on sandy beach, pool, diving, snorkelling, kayaking, mountain bikes, birdwatching and wildlife excursions.

$$$$-$$$ Beaches and Dreams
Sittee Point, T523-7259, www.beaches anddreams.com.
4 extremely well-furnished beachfront rooms. Price includes full breakfast, Dangriga transfer, use of bikes and kayaks.

$$$ Hopkins Inn
On beach south of centre, T523-7283, www.hopkinsinn.com.
White cabins with private bathroom, very clean and friendly, German spoken. Price includes breakfast, knowledgeable owners.

$$$-$$ Jungle Jeanie's by the Sea
About 1 mile south of Hopkins Village, T533-7047, www.junglebythesea.com.
Perched between the jungle and the ocean, comfortable wooden beachfront cabanas fully equipped with fan, fridge and coffee-maker. For families there's a beach house and jungle loft. Budget-orientated travellers may prefer the 'mini-cabanas' (**$$**). Simple, natural and pleasant.

$$ Tipple Tree Beya Inn
Just before Sandy Beach Lodge, T520-7006, www.tippletree.com.
English-American run, 4 rooms in a wooden house and small cabin apartment, camping possible.

$$-$ Windschief Cabanas
Hopkins Village, T523-7249, www.windsurfing-belize.com.
Windschief has 2 simple, wood-built cabanas. The small one (**$**) has a double

bed, hot shower, balcony facing the sea, fan, fridge and coffee-maker. The large one (**$$**) has the same facilities but sleeps up to 4. They also manage a beach bar with Wi-Fi.

$ The Funky Dodo
Hopkins Village, T667-0558, www.thefunkydodo.com.
Accommodation at this funky backpacker hostel include a 14-bed dorm and 6 private rooms. Amenities include a small plunge pool, hammocks, shared kitchen, Wi-Fi and a treetop bar under a thatched roof. It's cosy and a bit rustic.

Glover's Reef

$$-$ Glover's Atoll Resort
North East Caye, T532-2916, www.glovers.com.bz.
8 cabins with wood-burning stoves, you can also choose dorm or camping. Weekly rates include round-trip transportation from Sittee River. Occasional rice and seafood meals, bring food, some groceries and drinking water (US$2.50 a gallon) available. Best to bring everything you will need. Facilities are very simple and basic. Guests are sometimes invited to help out.

Restaurants

$ Riverside Café
South bank of river, just east of main road.
Better inside than it looks from the outside, good breakfast, good service and food, best place to get information on boats to Tobacco Caye.

Bars and clubs

Listen for local music punta rock, a Garífuna/African-based Carib sound, now popular throughout Belize. Home-made instruments are a Garífuna speciality, particularly drums. Studios can be visited.

Local Motion Disco
Next to Cameleon. Sat-Sun.
Punta rock, reggae, live music.

Riviera Club
Between bridge and Bank of Nova Scotia.
Popular nightclub at weekends.

Festivals

18-19 Nov Garífuna, or **Settlement Day**, celebrating the landing of the Black Caribs in 1823. Dancing all night and next day; very popular. Booking advisable for accommodation. Private homes rent rooms, though. Boats from Puerto Barrios to Punta Gorda (see Transport, page 323) tend to be full, but launches take passengers for US$10 per person.

What to do

Dangriga Dive Centre, *T522-3262*. Derek Jones arranges fabulous trips to the cayes.
Pelican Beach Hotel, runs tours to Cockscomb Basin, Gales Point and citrus factories.
Rosado's Tours, *35 Lemon St, T522-2119*. Government services.
Treasured Travels, *64 Commerce St, T522-2578*. Very helpful, run by Diane.

South of Dangriga
Second Nature Divers, *T523-7038, divers@ btl.net, or enquire at Hamanasi*. English-owned, good guides and equipment; a recommended spot to visit is Sharks' Cave.

Glover's Reef
Off The Wall Dive Center, *Dangriga, T614-6348, www.offthewallbelize.com.*
Offers dive courses. Friendly owners Jim and Kendra Schofield offer packages that include transport, accommodation, meals and diving.

small seaside community and good base for exploring cayes

Placencia, a former Creole fishing village 30 miles south of Dangriga, is on a thin sandy peninsula and makes a good jumping-off point for the cayes and their marine life, as well as inland tours. Continuing down the Southern Highway a couple of hotel signs indicate a turning (nothing official, look carefully) to a road that heads east to Riversdale (after 9 miles) turning south to follow the peninsula to Maya Beach, Seine Bight and, eventually, Placencia. The peninsula road is very rough from Riversdale to Seine Bight, with sand mixed with mud; a 4WD is advisable.

Placencia is becoming more popular among people looking for a remote adventure. It's a relaxing combination of chilling out on the beach, fishing, snorkelling and diving. If you time the trip right or get lucky, your visit may coincide with the migrations of the whale shark – the largest fish in the world at up to 55 ft – that passes through local waters from

Placencia

Where to stay
Deb & Dave's Last Resort **2**
Lydia's Guesthouse **5**
Miramar Apartments **15**
Paradise Resort **6**
Ranguana Lodge **7**
Robert's Grove **14**
Sea Glass Inn **3**

Seaspray **8**
Trade Winds **12**
Turtle Inn **10**
Yellow House **11**

Restaurants
BJ's **1**
Cozy Corner **6**

De Tatch Café **2**
La Dolce Vita **8**
Omar's Creole Grub **13**
Pickled Parrot Bar & Grill **7**
Rumfish **14**
Secret Garden **15**
Tutti-frutti Ice Cream
  Parlour **9**

50 metres
50 yards

March to May. And, between January and March, hundreds of scarlet macaws gather at nearby Red Bank. Also worth hitting if you can time it right is the **Lobster Fest** – on the last full weekend in June, with two days of music, dancing and lobster – and the **Sidewalk Arts Festival,** held the weekend before or after Valentine's Day. Placencia is a natural base for one- and two-day trips to **Cockscomb Basin Wildlife Sanctuary**; see page 320. **Big Creek,** on the mainland opposite Placencia, is 3 miles from Mango Creek.

There are no streets, just a network of concrete footpaths connecting the wooden houses that are set among the palms. The main sidewalk through the centre of the village is reported to be in the *Guinness Book of Records* as the world's narrowest street. There is a laid-back atmosphere, with lots of Jamaican music, particularly after the Easter and Christmas celebrations.

The local **Placencia Tourism Center** ① *T523-4045, www.placencia.com, Mon-Fri 0900-1700, closed public holidays, and 1130-1300 during low season,* is in Placencia Village Square, with lots of useful information. It also produces the local monthly newssheet, *Placencia Breeze* (www.placenciabreeze.com).

Around Placencia

Trips can be made to local cayes and the **Barrier Reef**, approximately 18 miles offshore. Day trips include snorkelling, with a beach barbecue lunch of lobster and conch. Offshore cayes include **Laughing Bird Caye**, **Gladden Spit** and **Silk Cayes Marine Reserve** (reserve fee US$10), also protected by **Friends of Nature**. Whale sharks visit the spit in March, April, May and June for 10 days after the full moon to feed on the spawn of aggregating reef fish.

Several hotels and guide services have kayaks that can be rented to explore some of the nearer islands or the quieter waters of the **Placencia Lagoon**. Those who want to keep their feet dry can go mountain biking on the peninsula or use it as a base for trips to **Cockscomb Basin Wildlife Sanctuary** and Maya ruins.

Day tours by boat south along the coast from Placencia to **Monkey River** and **Monkey River Village** are available. Monkey River tours, US$20 per person, feature howler monkeys, toucans, manatees and iguanas. Monkey River Village can be reached by a rough road, which is not recommended in wet weather. The road ends on the north side of the river and the town is on the south side, so call over for transport. Trips upriver can also be arranged here with locals but kayaking is best organized in Placencia. Trips can be arranged to Red Bank for the scarlet macaws, which gather in their hundreds between January and March. North of Placencia is the Garífuna community of **Seine Bight**.

Cayes near Placencia

Ranguana Caye is a private caye reached from Placencia (US$5). Getting there is free if it fits in with one of the regular trips, otherwise it costs US$150 each way for up to four people. Divers must bring their own scuba equipment. Day trips for diving, snorkelling or just relaxing cost US$45-50, and include lunch. For longer stays, see Where to stay, below.

At the southernmost end of the Mesoamerican Barrier Reef are the **Sapodilla Cayes**, US$10. Tours are arranged from Guatemala (see Río Dulce and Lívingston, pages 440 and 436) or can be made from Placencia. There are settlements on a few of the Cayes including **Hunting Caye**.

The **Silk Cayes**, also known as the **Queen Cayes**, is a small group of tiny, picture-perfect islands, which sits on the outer barrier reef and, together with Gladdens Spit, has become the core zone of the country's newest marine reserve. The Silk Cayes have superb diving, especially on the North Wall. Coral in the deeper areas is in good condition with many tube and barrel sponges and sharks, turtles and rays often seen cruising the reef wall. The

Silk Cayes are a popular destination for Placencia-based dive operators; however, it's not possible to dive in this area during periods of rough weather. The rainy season lasts from June to January.

Laughing Bird Caye ⓘ *reserve fee US$4, www.friendsofnaturebelize.org*, used to be the home of the laughing gull (*Larus articilla*) but now is home to other sea birds and has an exciting array of underwater life around its shores.

Listings Placencia and around *map p314*

Where to stay

Rooms may be hard to find in the afternoon (after the arrival of the bus from Dangriga). Usually several houses to rent, US$200-550 per week; see the ads at the tourist information centre.

$$$$ Robert's Grove
North of the air strip and Rum Point Inn, T523-3565, www.robertsgrove.com.
Luxury resort with 2 pools, massage service, boats and jacuzzis set on a white-sand beach shaded by the odd palm. Rooms are spacious, comfortable and quiet and the restaurant serves good, filling food. Entertainment and tours, including PADI diving from its own marina, are organized. Friendly bar staff.

$$$$ Turtle Inn
On beach close to airstrip, T364-3451, www.turtleinn.com.
Completely destroyed by Hurricane Iris, owner Francis Ford Coppola rebuilt this impressive resort in local and Balinese style set around a circular pool with restaurant and spa.

$$$$-$$$ Miramar Apartments
T523 3658, www.miramarbelize.com.
Immaculate, fully equipped apartments close to the beach that range from 1-bed studios to 3-bed apartments. Lots of amenities, very comfortable and recommended for families.

$$$ Paradise Resort
Down by the piers, T523-3179, www.paradisevacation belize.com.

Formerly the **Paradise Vacation Hotel**, Paradise resort has 12 rooms with a/c and private baths. Facilities include pool, restaurant, roof deck with hot tub and views of the harbour. Located on the water at the southern end of Placencia.

$$$ Ranguana Lodge
T523-3112, www.ranguanabelize.com.
Ranguana Lodge has 5 lovely little wooden cabins, some with sea views. All are well-equipped with hammock, balcony, hot shower, cable TV; those situated in the garden have a full kitchen. Simple, comfortable and very clean. Wi-Fi and barbecue available.

$$$ Sea Glass Inn
Garden Grove, T523-3098, www.seaglassinnbelize.com.
Formerly known as **Dianni's Guest House**, this affordable boutique hotel has 6 spacious, modern, recently renovated rooms with a/c, hot water and Wi-Fi. There's also a nice balcony with hammocks.

$$$ Trade Winds Hotel
South Point, T523-3122, trdewndpla@btl.net.
This no-frills place has 9 very colourful cabins in a spacious private plot on the south beach in a great location.

$$$ The Yellow House
T523-3481, www.ctbelize.com.
A bright yellow building, directly behind **Serenade**, with 4 very comfortable rooms with communicating doors, so excellent for a family or group of friends. Front rooms have microwaves, coffee machines and

fridges. They also run several other lodgings in the village.

$$ Deb and Dave's Last Resort
T523-3207, www.toadaladventure.com.
4 very good budget rooms with shared bathroom and hot water. There's kayak and bike rental, as well as tours of the local area. Walk-ins only, no advance reservations.

$$-$ Lydia's Guesthouse
T523-3117, www.lydiasguesthouse.com.
Situated across the sidewalk on a quiet part of the beach, this simple but very relaxing place has 8 double rooms with shared toilet and shower. There are kitchen facilities, free Wi-Fi and a PC for hire. Recommended.

$$-$ Seaspray
T523-3148, www.seasprayhotel.com.
Very nice, comfortable and friendly, with good-value rooms for range of prices, from beachside cabanas to small doubles in the original building. The popular **De Tatch Café** is on the beach; see Restaurants, below.

Camping
Sea Kunga, *www.seakunga.com.*
Organizes camping tours on the beach.

Around Placencia
Maya Beach

$$$$ Green Parrot Beach Houses
T533-8188, www.greenparrot-belize.com.
This very chilled place has thatched beach houses on stilts, all with sea view and sleeping up to 5, with kitchenettes. There's also an open-air restaurant and bar.

$$$$-$$$ Maya Breeze Inn
T601-9695.
4 cottages on the beach, 2 with a/c, restaurant across the road.

$$$$-$$$ Singing Sands Inn
T533-3022, www.singingsands.com.
Set in beautifully landscaped tropical gardens, **Singing Sands** has 6 simple, comfortable thatched cabins with Guatemalan bedspreads and Mexican

tilework, hot water, fans and an ocean view. There's snorkelling in front of the resort at False Caye, and a restaurant and bar on the beach.

$$$ Barnacle Bill's
T533-8110, www.barnaclebills-belize.com.
Deluxe wood-built cabanas with queen-sized bed, sleeper/sofa in the living/dining area, full kitchen, private bath and fans.

Mango Creek/Independence

$$ Ursella's Guest House
T503-2062.
9 simple rooms with shared or private bath and TV.

$ Hotel above People's Restaurant
A very basic place. Ask to borrow a fan and lamp; the shower is a bucket of water in a cabin. There's a simple restaurant.

Cayes near Placencia

$$$$ Hatchet Caye Resort
T533-4446, www.hatchetcaye.com.
Secluded and exclusive, **Hatchet Caye** is a luxurious private island resort with a range of excellent cabanas, all immaculately attired and very expensive. First class.

$$$$ Ranguana Caye
Reservations through Robert's Grove, T523-3565, www.robertsgrove.com.
3 cabanas, each with a double and single bed, gas stove, private hot showers and toilet in a separate building. There are barbecue pits so bring food, but meals are also available.

Restaurants

$$$ La Dolce Vita
Near Wallen's Market, T523-3115.
Italian restaurant who claim to have the best wine selection in town.

$$$ The Secret Garden
Near Wallen's Market, T523-3617.

International cuisine served in a relaxed, chilled out atmosphere.

$$$-$$ Rumfish
T523-3293, rumfish@btl.net.
Good-quality restaurant, popular with locals.

$$ Cozy Corner
On the beach, T523-3280.
Very good beachside bar and restaurant. Good, mid-priced barbecue and grilled seafood.

$$ De Tatch Café
Just before the north end of the sidewalk. Closed Wed.
Said to be the best coffee in town and it's certainly hugely popular, with excellent seafood specials at night and snappy service; a winner.

$$ Pickled Parrot Bar and Grill
Close to Wallen's Market. Closed Sun.
Good pizza, chicken and seafood.

$$-$ BJ's Restaurant
See map, T523-3131.
Good fried chicken and traditional Creole food. Owners Percy and Betty offer good Asian stir-fries and pizza. It's inexpensive and popular with the locals.

$ Omar's Creole Grub
Main St, T624-7168.
Creole diner.

$ Tutti-frutti Ice Cream Parlour
Placencia Village Square.
Great Italian ice cream, made by real Italians!

Around Placencia

$$ Goyo's Inn/Restaurant Independence
Mango Creek.
Family-owned, good food.

$ Lola's Café and Art Gallery
Sign at south end of Seine Bight.
For an entertaining evening with dinner, run by local artist Lola Delgado.

$ White house with green shutters
Mango Creek, behind People's.
Better than at **People's**. Book 2 hrs in advance if possible.

Bars and clubs

Barefoot Beach Bar
At Tipsy Tuna. Closed Mon.
A very popular joint on the beach with live music and a happy hour 1700-1800.

Tipsy Tuna Sports Bar
Open from 1900.
Popular sports and karaoke beachside bar.

What to do

Fishing
Fishing, especially saltwater fly-fishing, is excellent, with recognized world-class permit fishing. Reputable licensed guides and tour operators include **Kurt Godfrey**, T523-3277, and **Earl Godfrey**, T523-3433, lgodfrey@ btl.net.
Bruce Leslie, *from Tutti-frutti, T523-3370.* Rates for a full day of light tackle and fly fishing, including lunch, average US$325, maximum 2 anglers per boat for fly-fishing.
Destinations Belize, *T523-4018, www. destinationsbelize.com.* Offers combination cayes camping and fishing/snorkelling trips, plus whale shark interaction tours.

Kayaking
Toadal Adventures, *T523-3207, www. toadala dventure.com.* A reputable tour operator for multi-day kayaking trips to the cayes and Monkey River.

Scuba-diving and snorkelling
Full PADI scuba-diving courses are available at most local dive shops for around US$350. Some dive operators listed below base themselves out of high-end resorts. Of the in-town operators **Seahorse**, **Joy Tours** and **Splash** enjoy solid reputations. However, environmental standards and genuine concern for the reef is somewhat

lacking; this could be improved with a little encouragement. Prices are from about US$70, plus 9% sales tax, for 2-tank dives, US$105 to outer reef (gear extra). Snorkel trips generally cost US$60-70 for a full day and US$30-45 for a half day, including gear. There is a whale shark and snorkelling fee of US$15 from 1 Mar-3 Jul charged by **Friends of Nature**.

Joy Tours, *T651-0464, www.njoybelize.com.* Locally recommended.

Ocean Motion Guide Service, *T523-3363, www.oceanmotion placencia.com.* A reputable snorkelling tour operator.

Seahorse Dive Shop, *T523-3166, www. belize scuba.com.* Ask for Brian Young. Good selection of gear.

Splash, *T523-3058, www.splashbelize.com.* Helpful owners who specialize in dive training and courses.

Transport

Air
Placencia has its own airstrip. **Maya Island Air** and **Tropic Air** (T523-3410) fly several times a day to **Belize City** (international and municipal), also to **Dangriga** and **Punta Gorda**.

Boat
The **Hokie Pokie Water Taxi**, T523-2376, www.aguallos.com/hokeypokey. In Placencia leaves from the water taxi fuel station terminal behind the **M'n M** store. In Mango Creek the terminal is across the lagoon to **Independence**. US$5, check

website for schedule (regular departures). From here, buses depart for **Punta Gorda** and **Belize City**.

The **Belize–Honduras Boat**, T632-0083, www.belizeferry.com, provides a regular weekly service linking Placencia and **Puerto Cortés** in Honduras. The journey can be quite choppy. From Placencia the boat leaves the dock near the petrol station at 0930 every Fri, passing Big Creek at 1000 to complete immigration formalities. It arrives in Puerto Cortés from1200, US$50. Buy tickets in the Placencia Tourism Center, US$55. Return service leaves Puerto Cortés on Mon at 1100 arriving 1330.

See also box, page 516.

Bus
Placencia Peninsula Shuttle, T607-2711, runs from the Placencia dock to the **Zeboz Hotel** 5 times daily each way, US$2.50-5. See the tourist office for schedule. Buses to **Dangriga** direct at 0600, 0630, 1400, 3 hrs, US$5. Express, US$6. Direct busess to **Punta Gorda**, from Placencia with **Southern Transport** or **James Buses**. Alternatively, take the **Hokie Pokie Water Taxi**, see above, to catch the **James Bus Line** buses from Independence Village, at 0930, 1045, 1500, 1630, 1645, 1½-2½ hrs. For buses to **Dangriga**, 1 hr, **Belmopan**, 2½ hrs and **Belize City**, 3½ hrs, also catch the boat to Independence. Buses leave at 0715, 0815, 1015, 1415 and 1645. Check times and fares at the Placencia tourist centre at the dock next to the **Shell** petrol station.

★Some 20 miles south of Dangriga, the Southern Highway crosses the Sittee River at the small village of Kendal (ruins nearby). One mile beyond is the village of Maya Centre from where a poor seven-mile track winds west through Cabbage Haul Gap to the Cockscomb Basin Wildlife Sanctuary (21,000 acres, US$5), worth an extended visit if you have two to three days. The sanctuary was created out of the Cockscomb Basin Forest Reserve in 1986 to protect the country's highest recorded density of jaguars (*Panthera onca*), and their smaller cousins the puma (red tiger), the endangered ocelot, the diurnal jaguarundi and that feline cutey, the margay.

Many other mammals share the heavily forested reserve, including coatis, collared peccaries, agoutis, anteaters, Baird's tapirs and tayras (a small weasel-like animal). There are red-eyed tree frogs, boas, iguanas and fer-de-lances, as well as over 290 species of bird, including king vultures and great curassows. The sanctuary is a good place for relaxing, showering under waterfalls, tubing down the river, or listening to birds – hundreds of bird species have been spotted and there are several types of toucan, hummingbirds and scarlet macaws to be seen by early risers. The reserve is sponsored by the Belizean government, the Audubon Society, the Worldwide Fund for Nature and various private firms. Donations are very welcome.

Park HQ is at the former settlement of Quam Bank (whose milpa-farming inhabitants founded the **Maya Centre** outside the reserve). Here there is an informative visitor centre. An 18-mile network of jungle trails spreads out from the centre, ranging in distance from a few hundred yards to 2½ miles. Walkers are unlikely to see any of the big cats as they are nocturnal, but if you fancy a walk in the dark you may be lucky. Note that the guards leave for the day at 1600. You will see birds, frogs, lizards, snakes and spiders. Longer hikes can be planned with the staff.

Nearby is one of Belize's highest summits, **Victoria Peak** (3675 ft), which is an arduous four- or five-day return climb and should not be undertaken lightly. There is virtually no path, a guide is essential; February to May are the best months for the climb. For guides, see What to do, below.

Listings Cockscomb Basin Wildlife Sanctuary and around

Where to stay

To guarantee accommodation, contact the Belize Audubon Society; see box, page 284.

$$$$ Bocawina Rainforest Resort and Adventures
T+1-604-894-2311, in UK toll-free T0800-404 9535, www.bocawina.com.
Formerly **Mama Noots Backabush Resort**, this great adventure lodge has traditional cabanas and rooms nestled in the heart of the rainforest. They offer scores of onsite

activities including jungle hiking, zip-lining, birdwatching and rappelling. They are ecologically aware, with electricity from solar, wind and hydro systems, and most fruits and veg are grown organically here.

$$-$ Park HQ.
Purpose-built cabins and dorms (**$** per person) with a picnic area. Drinking water is available as are compost toilets, but you must bring all your own food, drinks, matches, torch, sleeping bag, eating utensils

and insect repellent. The nearest shop is at Maya Centre.

What to do

The **Belize Audubon Society**, see box on page 284, runs the reserve. The most knowledgeable guides to the reserve live in Maya Centre; contact **Julio Saqui**, of Julio's Cultural Tours, T608-4992, www.cockscomb mayatours.com, who runs the village shop and can look after any extra luggage. At Greg's Bar, on the main road in the middle of the village, you can contact **Greg Sho**, an experienced river and mountain guide who can arrange kayak trips.

Full-day Mopan Mayan cultural tours of Maya Centre Village are available including visits to workshops on traditional Mayan cooking, crafts, language and natural tropical medicines. Contact **Liberato** or **Araceli Saqui** at Maya Centre Village. Tour operators in Placencia run day trips for US$65.

Transport

Bus

Buses can be booked at time of reservation, or locals will drive you from Maya Centre, otherwise it is a 6-mile, uphill walk from Maya Centre to the reserve – allow 2 hrs for the walk to Maya Centre. If you leave early in the morning going either way you are likely to see quite a lot of wildlife. All buses going south from **Dangriga** go through Maya Centre, 40 mins, US$4; and north from Placencia, return buses from 0700 onwards to Dangriga. If walking, leave all unwanted gear in Dangriga in view of the uphill stretch from Maya Centre, or you can leave luggage at Julio's little store in Maya Centre for a daily fee.

Taxi

A taxi from **Dangriga** will cost about US$50; it's not difficult to hitch back.

Punta Gorda and around → *Colour map 8, C1.*

culturally diverse market town and fishing port

The turn-off from the Southern Highway for Mango Creek, Independence and Big Creek comes 15 miles after the Riversdale turn-off, and the road runs 4 miles east through the Savannah Forest Reserve to the mangrove coast opposite Placencia. About 35 miles beyond the junction, 10½ miles north of the T-junction for Punta Gorda, half a mile west of the road, is the Nim Li Punit archaeological site which has a visitor centre and clean spacious housing for the stelae. Nim Li Punit ('The Big Hat') was only discovered in 1974. A score of stelae, 15-20 ft tall, were unearthed, dated AD 700-800, as well as a ball court and several groups of buildings. The site is worth visiting – look for the sign on the highway. Day trips are also offered from Placencia.

Nearby, the highway passes Big Falls Village, almost completely destroyed by Hurricane Iris. Take a short hike back to the hot springs for a swim, camp or sling a hammock, but first seek permission from the landowner, Mr Peter Aleman.

Four miles from Big Falls, the Highway reaches a T-junction, known locally as the 'Dump', marked by a Shell station; the road to San Antonio branches right (west), the main road turns sharp left and runs down through a forest reserve for 13 miles to Punta Gorda. The road is paved from Big Falls to Punta Gorda.

Punta Gorda (population 5255) is the southernmost settlement of any size in Belize, with a varied ethnic makeup of Creoles, Q'eqchi', Mopan, Chinese, East Indians and descendants of the many races brought here over the years as labourers in ill-fated settlement attempts. Three miles north of **Toledo** are the remains of the sugar cane settlement founded by Confederate refugees after the American Civil War. The coast, about 10 ft above sea level, is fringed with coconut palms. The seafront is clean and enjoyable – once you get away from Front Street, where the lively and colourful market on Wednesday, Friday and Saturday comes with the associated smells of fish and rotting vegetables. The *Voice of America* has an antenna complex to the south of town.

At **Toledo Visitor Information Center**, also called **Dem Dats Doin** ① *in booth by pier, PO Box 73, T722-2470, demdatsdoin@btl.net, free, irregular opening hours*, Alfredo and Yvonne Villoria provide information on travel, tours, guiding, accommodation with indigenous families (under the Homestay Programme), message service and book exchange, for the whole of Toledo district. The **Tourist Information Centre** ① *Front St, T722-2531, Mon-Sat 0800-1200 and 1300-1700*, provides a wealth of information about the area, including bus schedules to local Maya villages, and can organize flight reservations, hotels, tours and boat trips to Honduras. The **Toledo Ecotourism Association** has an office in the same building, with information on the **Village Guesthouse** and **Ecotrail** programme, and transport to the villages, see also box, page 326.

Around Punta Gorda

Rainfall in this region is particularly heavy, with more than 170 inches annually, and the vegetation is consequently luxuriant. There are many tours that can be enjoyed on the numerous rivers in the Toledo District. Countless species of birds make their homes along the rivers, as do troops of howler monkeys and other wildlife. Kayaking is a good way to view wildlife on the rivers. There are many white-sand beaches on the cayes off Punta Gorda for the beachcomber, or camper. Fly fishing is becoming a popular sport and sport fishing, snorkelling and scuba-diving are available. Toledo is off the beaten path and has some of the most spectacular views, waterfalls, rainforest, cayes and friendly people.

Listings Punta Gorda and around

Where to stay

$$$$ Cotton Tree Lodge
T670-0557, www.cottontreelodge.com.
11 charming thatched *cabanas* at the woody bank of Moho River, built and run in an eco-friendly manner. Guests can visit local Mayan farmers and have a taste of their culture. The restaurant serves 3 meals a day. Families are welcome.

$$$ Hickatee
T622-4475, www.hickatee.com.
English breakfast, afternoon tea and wonderful, comfortable accommodation in wooden chalets set in a bird-filled glade in the heart of the rainforest. The helpful and knowledgeable owners can organize trips around Toledo.

$$$ Sea Front Inn
4 Front St, T722-2300, www.seafrontinn.com.
This place offers 14 rooms with private bath hot water, a/c and TV, and a restaurant with great views. **Maya Island Air** and **Tropic Air** agents.

$$-$ Tate's Guest House
34 José María Nuñez St, T722-0147, tatesguesthouse@yahoo.com.
Friendly guesthouse with clean rooms that have a/c, cheaper without, hot water, bathroom and TV. There's breakfast before 0730, parking and laundry.

$ Nature's Way Guest House
65 Front St, T702-2119.
Clean, friendly place, with good breakfast, and camping gear for rent. Recommended.

$ St Charles Inn
23 King St, T722-2149, stcharlespg@btl.net.
Super-clean, a good budget choice. All rooms are spacious, with bath, fan or a/c, cable TV.

$ Wahima
On waterfront, T722-2542.
Clean and safe, with private bath. The owner Max is friendly and informative. Also rents kitchenettes.

Restaurants

Several cafés around the market area have good views over the bay.

$$ Bobby's
Main St.
Serves excellent fish dishes. Bobby is a local fishing guide and arranges trips.

$$ Earth Runnings Café and Bukut Bar
Main Middle St, T702-2007, bukutbar@ hotmail.com. Closed Tue.
Great, idiosyncratic bar and café with regular live music that also provides tourist information, internet and occasional yoga and therapeutic massage.

$$ Gomier's
Behind the Sea Front Inn.
For vegan meals and soya products.

$$ Marian's Bayview Restaurant
76 Front St, T722-0129.
Serves traditional Belizean and East Indian dishes. Serves good ice cream and food as well.

What to do

Green Iguana Eco Adventures, *T722-2475.* Provides a wide range of tours and services. **Sun Creek Tours**, *suncreek@hughes.net.* **Tide Tours**, *Main St, T722-2129, www. tidetours.org.* Organizes ecotours.

Transport

Air
Airstrip 5 mins' walk east of town. Daily flights with **Maya Island Air** and **Tropic Air**, T722-2008, from Dangriga, Placencia, Belize City (both airports). Tickets at **Alistair King's** (at Texaco station), **Bob Pennell's** hardware store on Main St, the **Sea Front Inn** on Front St or the offices alongside the airstrip. Advance reservations recommended.

Boat
Requena's Charter Services, T722-2070, leaves Punta Gorda for **Puerto Barrios, Guatemala**, at 0900 every day, US$20, 1 hr, return journey leaves at 1400. Guatemalan operator **Pichilingo** provides a similar service, leaving Puerto Barrios for Punta Gorda at 1000, returning at 1400. See also box, page 514.

Bus
James bus line to **Belize City** (6½ hrs, longer in heavy rain), daily at 0400, 0500, 0600, 0800, 1000 and 1200. **James** bus returns from Belize City daily, leaving hourly between 0515 and 1015, then 1215, 1315, 1515 and 1545. To **San Antonio** from square, see below; buses to **San Pedro Columbia** and **San José**, Wed and Sat 1200, return Wed and Sat morning. Buses can be delayed in the wet season. For the latest information on schedules, contact the Tourist Information Centre or Dem Dats Doin at the pier by the Customs House.

San Pedro Columbia

Inland from Punta Gorda there are several interesting villages in the foothills of the Maya Mountains. Take the main road as far as the 'Dump', the road junction with the Southern Highway. Take the road west to San Antonio. After nearly 2 miles, there is a branch to San Pedro Columbia, a Q'eqchi' village where the Maya inhabitants speak the Q'eqchi language and the women wear colourful costumes, including Guatemalan-style *huipiles*. There are many religious celebrations, at their most intense on **San Luis Rey Day** (5 August).

Lubaantun

0800-1600 daily, beyond San Pedro, continuing left around the church, then right and downhill to the concrete bridge, then left for a mile, a caretaker will point out things of interest. Take refreshments.

Lubaantun ('Fallen Stones') was the major ceremonial site of southern Belize. The site has a visitor centre and has undergone extensive work to restore a large part of the ruins. It was found to date from AD 800-900, late in the Maya culture and therefore unique. A series of terraced plazas surrounded by temples and palaces ascend along a ridge from south to north. The buildings were constructed with unusual precision and some of the original lime-mortar facings can still be discerned. Excavation revealed whistle figurines, iron pyrite mirrors, obsidian knives, conch shells from Wild Cane Caye, etc. One of the great controversies of the site was the discovery in 1927 of the Crystal Skull by the daughter of the explorer FA Mitchell-Hedges (see box, opposite). This whole region is a network of hilltop sites, mostly unexcavated and unrecognizable to the untrained eye.

Blue Creek

Blue Creek is another attractive indigenous village which has a marked trail to **Blue Creek Caves** ① *US$12.50 per person, the caretaker is the guide,* and their Maya drawings. The trail leads through forest and along rock-strewn creeks. Swimming nearby is good but choose a spot away from the strong current. Turn off 3 miles before San Antonio at **Roy's Cool Spot** (good restaurant; daily truck and all buses pass here).

Pusilhá

Pusilhá is one of the most interesting Maya cities, only accessible by boat. Many stelae have been found here dating from AD 573-731, and carvings are similar to those at Quiriguá, Guatemala. Rare features are a walled-in ball court and the abutments remaining from a bridge that once spanned the Moho River. Swimming in the rivers is safe. There are plenty of logging trails and hunters' tracks penetrating the southern faces of the Maya Mountains but if hiking in the forest, do not go alone.

San Antonio

San Antonio, 21 miles from Punta Gorda, was founded by refugees from San Luis in Guatemala in the late 19th century. Nearby there are Maya ruins of mainly scientific interest. There's a community phone for checking buses and other information, T702-2144. **Dem Dats Doin** in Punta Gorda (see page 322) will also be able to give information. There's a medical centre in the village.

There are no roads to the southern border with Guatemala along the Sarstún River. The **Sarstoon-Temash National Park** is a wilderness of red mangroves and unspoilt rainforest.

ON THE ROAD

The Crystal Skull of Lubaantun

In 1927, a young woman by the name of Anna Mitchell-Hedges woke for her 17th birthday. For her it proved more eventful than most as she explored the recently excavated Maya site of Lubaantun to discover a finely crafted crystal skull made of pure quartz – setting off a tale of intrigue that remains to this day.

The size of a small watermelon, the translucent skull of reflected light weighs just over 5 kg. The skull is one of only two ever found in Central America. Its date of manufacture is unknown – but some put it at over 3600 years old – and its purpose is equally curious. Local Maya people gave the skull to Anna's father, the British explorer FA Mitchell-Hedges as a gift, saying it was used for healing and, more sinisterly, for willing death.

Dating the skull precisely is difficult because of the purity of the crystal, but the details of the finding are equally mysterious,with speculation that the skull was 'placed' to make that birthday so special.

There are no visitor facilities at present. At **Barranco**, the only coastal hamlet south of Punta Gorda, there is a village guesthouse (part of TEA, see box, page 326). A dirt road goes to Barranco through the village of Santa Ana, or you can go by boat.

Listings South of Punta Gorda

Where to stay

Accommodation is restricted to community-based ecotourism projects where you can stay in the indigenous villages. There are 2 main projects: TEA (Toledo Ecotourism Association), T722-2096, www.teabelize.org, where you can stay in your private accommodation within the village, and the Homestay Programme, where you stay with the family in their house. The Homestay Programme can be arranged via Blue Creek Rainforest Lodge; see below. See also box, page 326.

\$\$ Blue Creek Rainforest Lodge
www.ize2belize.com.
Simple wooden bungalows in the middle of the forest and just 15 mins' walk from Blue Creek Village. Pack full with adventure, trekking around the jungle, exploring caves and learning about local culture.

\$ Maya Mountain Research Farm
www.mmrfbz.org.
An organization that promotes forestry research and welcome internship researches and volunteers from a week to a semester. You pay for your accommodation.

San Antonio

\$ Bol's Hilltop Hotel
This clean hotel has rooms with showers and toilets. Meals are available.

Restaurants

San Antonio

\$ Theodora or Clara
Next to the hotel.
Both do meals with advance notice. Local specialities are *jippy jappa/kula*, from a local plant, and chicken *caldo*.

ON THE ROAD

Guesthouse programme

An interesting alternative to Punta Gorda is to stay in indigenous villages as part of the Guesthouse Programme, run by villagers and the non-competitive cooperative the Toledo Ecotourism Association (TEA).

A number of villages have joined together and developed a visitor scheme. Each has built a well-appointed guesthouse, simple, but clean, with sheets, towels, mosquito nets, oil lamps, ablutions block, and a total of eight bunks in two four-bunk rooms. Visitors stay here, but eat in the villagers' houses on rotation, so each household gains equal income and only has to put up with intrusive foreigners for short periods. Villages taking part include San Miguel, San José (Hawaii), Laguna and Blue Creek. Santa Elena is an isolated village beyond the Dump towards San Ignacio. Medina Bank is more accessible as its location is just off the southern highway. Barranco is a Garífuna village south of Punta Gorda, accessible by boat or poor road.

Local attractions include: San Antonio waterfall; caves at San José (Hawaii); Uxbenka ruins and caves 2½-hour walk from San Antonio (turn right just before Santa Cruz), with commanding view from ruins; and Río Blanco waterfalls, 10 minutes beyond the village. For Uxbenka and Santa Cruz, take Chun's bus on Wednesday and Saturday at 1300 from San Antonio and arrange return time. Do not take Cho's bus, it does not return. Many village men and children speak English. The local indigenous people have been relearning old dances from elderly villagers and are trying to rescue the art of making and playing the harp, violin, marimba and guitar for evening entertainments. Home-made excursions

Transport

San Antonio
Bus and car
From **Punta Gorda**, 1-1½ hrs, US$1.50, Mon, Wed, Fri, Sat 1230, from west side of Central Park, also 1200 on Wed and Sat, continuing to **Santa Cruz**, **Santa Elena** and **Pueblo Viejo** (1 hr from San Antonio). Or, hire a pickup van in **Dangriga**; or get a ride in a truck from the market or rice cooperative's mill in Punta Gorda (1 leaves early afternoon); or go to the road junction at Dump, where the northern branch goes to Independence/Mango Creek, the other to San Antonio; 6 miles, either hitch or walk. Bus from San Antonio to **Punta Gorda**, Mon, Wed, Fri and Sat 0530, also 0500 Wed and Sat (having left Pueblo Viejo at 0400). If going to **Dangriga**, take the 0500, get out at Dump to catch 0530 **Southern Transport** bus going north. This area is full of places to explore and it is worth hiring a vehicle.

are arranged; these vary from a four-hour trek looking at medicinal plants and explaining agriculture, to seeing very out-of-the- way sights like caves and creeks (take boots, even in dry season). The village tour could be skipped, although by doing this on your own you deprive the 'guide' of income.

One night for two people, with a forest tour and three meals, costs US$43; all profits go direct to the villages, with no outsiders as middlemen. Dorms are US$11 per person. Profits are ploughed back into the villages' infrastructure, schools and other community projects. A US$5 registration fee is payable at the TEA Office at the Tourist Information Center (BTB Building) in Punta Gorda, T722-2096, before visiting the village. The staff provide information about participating villages, key attractions, tours and courses, and take bookings and arrange transport. You may have to arrange your own transport, or a vehicle can be hired. Staff at TEA will be able to advise. Hitching is not recommended as some villages are remote. 'Market' buses leave Punta Gorda every Monday, Wednesday, Friday and Saturday at 1130 or 1200 depending on the village. They come from the villages on the morning of the same days departing early at 0400, 0500 or 0600, depending on the village.

Additionally, there are cultural exchange and tourism programmes operating in several villages that are not part of the TEA co-op, including Na Luum Ca and Aguacate. Accommodation is no frills and there is full immersion in tribal life. Guests sleep with the family in one- or two-room palm-thatch and adobe houses. There's little privacy with shared outhouse 'bathrooms' with no warm water. Meals of corn tortillas, beans and fish or meat are eaten communally. Men are expected to help work the *milpa* fields and women to grind corn and attend to other traditional duties. See Belize Explorer, www.belizeexplorer.com, a good general guide to community tourism in Belize.

This is
Guatemala

Guatemala has a monopoly on colour: from the red lava tongues of volcanoes in the western highlands to the creamy shades of caves in the Petén, and from the white sand of the Caribbean coast near Lívingston to the black sand and orange sunsets over the Pacific.

Completing this work of art are traditional Maya fiestas, where idol worship and Roman Catholicism merge, and jungle temples where ancient ruins tell of long-lost civilizations. Deep in Guatemala's jungle, the majestic cities of the Maya are buried, with temples and plazas, and evidence of human sacrifice and astronomical genius.

Antigua is the colonial centre of the New World. Gracefully ruined after an 18th-century earthquake, its cobbled streets are lined with columned courtyards, toppled church arches, preserved pastel-coloured houses, flowers and fountains galore.

Formed by a volcanic explosion, Lake Atitlán and its three volcanoes are truly breathtaking. Further west, the bustling city of Quetzaltenango makes an excellent base from which to explore volcanoes, markets and villages. In the Verapaces, rivers run through caves stuffed with stalagmites and stalactites. On the humid Pacific coast, Olmec-influenced ruins are buried among coffee bushes and turtles nest on the shore, while on the Caribbean shores, the Garífuna rock to the sound of punta and dolphins frolic in the sea.

Pacific Ocean

Footprint picks

Footprint picks

★ **Antigua**, page 347

Dramatically located at the foot of three volcanoes, with grand colonial ruins and excellent Spanish schools.

★ **Lake Atitlán**, page 365

A spectacular and sacred lake protected on all sides by silent volcanic peaks.

★ **Todos Santos Cuchumatán**, page 403

Mountain community famous for the distinctive colourful clothes of its indigenous Mam inhabitants and its All Saints' Day horse race.

★ **Around Quetzaltenango**, pages 407, 409 and 411

Maya villages, hot springs and volcanoes dot the mountains around the highland town of Quezaltenango.

★ **Lívingston and Río Dulce**, pages 436 and 440

The relaxed Caribbean village of Lívingston is home to the Guatemalan Garífuna, and the starting point for boat trips up the Río Dulce.

★ **Parque Nacional Tikal**, page 466

The jungle-shrouded ruins of Tikal made up the Mayan world's most enigmatic metropolis.

Essential Guatemala City

Finding your feet

Any address not in Zona 1 – and it is absolutely essential to quote zone numbers in addresses – is probably some way from the centre. Addresses themselves, being purely numerical, are usually easy to find. For example, 19 Calle, 4-83 is on 19 Calle between 4 Avenida and 5 Avenida at No 83.

If driving, Avenidas have priority over calles (except in Zona 10, where this rule varies).

Best places to stay

Posada Belén, page 338
La Inmaculada, page 339
Quetzalroo, page 339

Getting around

You can walk between the main sights in central Zona 1 but will need to take a bus or taxi to Zonas 9, 10 and 14. Cheap city buses run all day until 2000. Otherwise, take a taxi but for safety reasons make sure it's an official one; see page 346 for more information.

Safety

As with any big city, take precautions, especially on public transport or in crowded areas such as markets or bus stations. Be vigilant in all zones of the city, even in upmarket areas, and after dark, when it's advisable to take a radio taxi (see also Getting around above) rather than walk. Avoid withdrawing large sums of money from the bank. Don't wear jewellery or display valuable items such as cameras or phones. It may be best to avoid the Carretera Salvador from the city to the El Salvador border as car-jackings and holdups are becoming increasingly common on that route. To report an incident, contact INGUAT's tourist assistance on T1500, or the police on T110 or T120.

When to go

Temperatures normally average around the mid-20°Cs, but it can be chilly due to the high altitudes. Wet season is May to October.

Time required

Two days.

Best restaurants

Gracia Cocina de Autor, page 340
Hotel Pan American restaurant, page 340
Restaurante Vegetariano Rey Sol, page 340

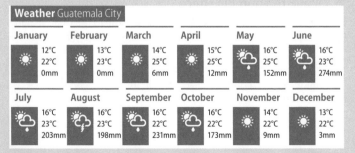

Weather Guatemala City					
January 12°C 22°C 0mm	**February** 13°C 23°C 0mm	**March** 14°C 25°C 6mm	**April** 15°C 25°C 12mm	**May** 16°C 25°C 152mm	**June** 16°C 23°C 274mm
July 16°C 23°C 203mm	**August** 16°C 23°C 198mm	**September** 16°C 22°C 231mm	**October** 16°C 22°C 173mm	**November** 14°C 22°C 9mm	**December** 13°C 22°C 3mm

Guatemala City

Smog-bound and crowded, Guatemala City, known simply as 'Guate', is the commercial and administrative centre of the country. Sketchy in parts and rarely rated by visitors, this is the beating heart of Guatemala and is worth a couple of days if you have time and can bear the noise and pollution in Zona 1. Guatemala City is surrounded by active and dormant volcanoes easily visited on day trips. *Colour map 6, B4.*

Sights

industrial sprawl sprinkled with architectural treasures and urban sculpture

The old centre of Guatemala City (population 1.2 million, altitude 1500 m) is Zona 1. It is still a busy shopping and commercial area, with some good hotels and restaurants, and many of the cheaper places to stay. However, the main activity of the city has been moving south, first to Zona 4, now to Zonas 9, 10 and 14. With the move have gone commerce, banks, embassies, museums and the best hotels and restaurants. The best residential areas are in the hills to the east, southeast and west.

Around Zona 1

At the city's heart lies the **Parque Central**. It is intersected by the north–south-running 6 Avenida, the main shopping street. The eastern half has a floodlit fountain; on the west side is **Parque Centenario**, with an acoustic shell in cement used for open-air concerts and public meetings. The Parque Central is popular on Sunday with many *indígenas* selling textiles.

To the east of the plaza is the **cathedral**. It was begun in 1782 and finished in 1815 in classical style with notable blue cupolas and dome. Inside are paintings and statues from ruined Antigua. Solid silver and sacramental reliquary are in the east side chapel of the Sagrario. Next to the cathedral is the colonial mansion of the Archbishop. Aside from the cathedral, the most notable public buildings constructed between 1920 and 1944, after the 1917 earthquake, are the **Palacio Nacional** ① *Mon-Sat 0900-1200 and 1400-1700, entrance and guided tour US$4*, built of light green stone and concealing a lavish interior filled with murals and chandeliers, the police headquarters, the Chamber of Deputies and the post office, which is now home to a small cultural centre. To the west of the cathedral are the Biblioteca Nacional and the Banco del Ejército. Behind the Palacio Nacional is the Presidential Mansion.

Museums in Zona 1 include the **Museo Nacional de Historia** ① *9 Calle, 9-70, T2253-6149, www.mcd.gob.gt, Mon-Fri 0900-1700, US$1.50*, which has historical documents and objects from Independence onward. The **Museo de la Universidad de San Carlos**

Zona 1

Guatemala City maps
1 Guatemala City: Zona 1, page 334
2 Guatemala City: Zona 9, 10, 13, page 337

N

300 metres
300 yards

Where to stay
Ajau 2 *D2*
Pan American 7 *A2*
Pensión Meza 8 *B3*
Posada Belén 1 *C3*
Theatre International 3 *C2*

Restaurants 🍴
Altuna 1 *C2*
Café de Imeri 3 *A1*
Helados Marylena 5 *A1*
Rey Sol 7 *A2*

Bars & clubs 🍸
El Portal 12 *A2*
Europa 4 *B2*
La Bodeguita del Centro 10 *B1*
Las Cien Puertas 14 *A2*

Transport 🚌
ADN to Santa Elena 5 *C2*
Escobar y Monja Blanca to Cobán 1 *C2*
Fuente del Norte to Río Dulce & Santa Elena/Flores 2 *D2*
Línea Dorada to Río Dulce & Flores 3 *D3*
Marquensita to Quetzaltenango 6 *E1*

Rutas Orientales to Chiquimula & Esquipulas 7 *D3*
Transportes Galgos to Mexico 12 *D2*
Transportes Litegua to Puerto Barrios & Río Dulce 13 *C3*

de Guatemala (MUSAC) ① *9 Av, 9-79, T2232-0721, www.musacenlinea.org, Mon, Wed-Fri 0930-1730, Sat 0930-1700, US$1; guided tours at 1000 and 1400,* charts the history of the university. The Salón Mayor is where Guatemala signed its Independence from Mexico in 1823, and in 1826 the Central American Federation, with Guatemala as the seat of power, abolished slavery in the union. Also, Doctor Mariano Gálvez, the country's president from 1831-1838, is buried behind part of the salon wall and a marble bust of him sits outside the door. The Universidad de San Carlos was the first university in Guatemala City. **Casa MIMA** ① *8 Av, 14-12, T2253-6657, casamima@hotmail.com, Mon-Sat 0900-1230, 1400-1500, US$1, no photography,* is the only authentic turn-of-the-19th-century family home open to the public, once owned by the family Ricardo Escobar Vega and Mercedes Fernández Padilla y Abella. It is furnished in European-influenced style with 15th- to mid-20th-century furniture and ornaments.

Churches Most of the churches worth visiting are in Zona 1. **Cerro del Carmen** ① *11 Av y 1 Calle A,* was built as a copy of a hermitage destroyed in 1917-1918, containing a famous image of the Virgen del Carmen. Situated on a hill with good views of the city, it was severely damaged in the earthquake of 1976 and remains in poor shape. **La Merced** ① *11 Av y 5 Calle,* dedicated in 1813, has beautiful altars, organ and pulpit from Antigua as well as jewellery, art treasures and fine statues. **Santo Domingo** ① *12 Av y 10 Calle,* built between 1782 and 1807, is a striking yellow colour, reconstructed after 1917, with an image of Nuestra Señora del Rosario and sculptures. **Sagrado Corazón de Jesús,** or **Santuario Expiatorio** ① *26 Calle y 2 Av,* holds 3000 people; the colourful, exciting modern architecture was by a young Salvadorean architect who had not qualified when he built it. Part of the complex, built in 1963 (church, school and auditorium) is in the shape of a fish. The entrance is a giant arch of multicoloured stained glass, wonderfully illuminated at night. The walls are lined with glass confessionals. **Las Capuchinas** ① *10 Av y 10 Calle,* has a very fine St Anthony altarpiece, and other pieces from Antigua. **Santa Rosa** ① *10 Av y 8 Calle,* was used for 26 years as the cathedral until the present building was ready. The altarpieces are from Antigua (except above the main altar). **San Francisco** ① *6 Av y 13 Calle,* a large yellow and white church that shows earthquake damage outside (1976), has a sculpture of the Sacred Head, originally from Extremadura in Spain. **Carmen El Bajo** ① *8 Av y 10 Calle,* was built in the late 18th century; again the façade was severely damaged in 1976.

North of the centre

Parque Minerva ① *Av Simeón Cañas, Zona 2, www.mapaenrelieve.org, 0900-1700, US$4,* has a huge relief map of the country made in 1905 to a horizontal scale of 1:10,000 and a vertical scale of 1:2,000. The park has basketball and baseball courts, bar and restaurant and a children's playground (unsafe at night). To get there, take bus V21 from 7 Avenida, Zona 4. Just beyond is a popular park, the **Hipódromo,** which is packed on Sundays with bumper cars and mechanical games, and a great little train for kids.

South of the centre: Avenida La Reforma

The modern **Centro Cívico,** which links Zona 1 with Zona 4, includes the Municipalidad, Palacio de Justicia, Ministerio de Finanzas Públicas, Banco de Guatemala, the mortgage bank, the social-security commission and the tourist board. The curious **Teatro Nacional** ① *Mon-Fri 0800-1630 for tours, US$4,* with its blue and white mosaic, dominates the hilltop of the west side of the Centro Cívico. There is an excellent view of the city and surrounding mountains from the roof. An old Spanish fortress provides a backdrop to the open-air theatre adjoining the Teatro Nacional.

BACKGROUND

Guatemala City

Guatemala City was founded by decree of Carlos III of Spain in 1776 to serve as capital after earthquake damage to the earlier capital, Antigua, in 1773. Almost completely destroyed by earthquakes in 1917-1918, it was rebuilt in modern fashion, or in copied colonial, only to be further damaged by earthquake in 1976. Most of the affected buildings have been restored.

Cuatro Grados Norte, located on Vía 5 between Ruta 1 and Ruta 2, is a pedestrianized area that has grown up around the IGA theatre and bookshop (a cultural centre, which sometimes has interesting concerts and exhibitions). Cafés and bars have tables on the street and it's safe and fun to wander around at night. The **Centro Cultural de España** is located here with live music, films, exhibitions and conferences, and there is also a branch of **Sophos**, an excellent bookshop. On Saturdays there is a street market with craft and jewellery stalls, often cultural events in the street. On Sundays there are clowns and events for children. It's a strange mix of wealthy Guatemalans strolling with their poodles and alternative street-market types; sit back and enjoy watching the people.

To see the finest residential district go south down 7 Avenida to Ruta 6, which runs diagonally in front of Edificio El Triángulo, past the orange **Capilla de Yurrita** (Ruta 6 y Vía 8). Built as a private chapel in 1928 on the lines of a Russian Orthodox church, it has been described as an example of "opulent 19th-century bizarreness and over-ripe extravagance". There are many woodcarvings, slender white pillars, brown/gold ornamentation and an unusual blue sky window over the altar. Ruta 6 runs into the wide tree-lined Avenida La Reforma.

To the east, in Zona 10, are some excellent museums. **Museo Ixchel del Traje Indígena** ⓘ *Campus of Universidad Francisco Marroquín, 6 Calle Final, T2331-3623, www.museoixchel. org, Mon-Fri 0900-1700, Sat 0900-1300, US$4.60*, has a collection of indigenous dress. In addition to the clothes there are photos from the early 20th century, paintings and very interesting videos. A shop sells beautiful textiles that aren't available on the tourist market, prices are fixed, and quality costs. **Museo Popol Vuh de Arqueología** ⓘ *6 Calle Final, T2338-7896, www.popolvuh.ufm.edu.gt, Mon-Fri 0900-1700, Sat 0900-1300, US$4.60, US$3 for photos*, has an extensive collection of pre-Columbian and colonial artefacts, as well as a replica of the Dresden Codex, one of the only Maya parchment manuscripts in existence. **Museo de Historia Natural de la USAC y Jardín Botánico** ⓘ *Calle Mcal Cruz 1-56, T2334-6065, Mon-Fri 0800-1600, Sat 0830-1230, US$1.30*, has gardens, stuffed animals and live snakes.

In **Parque Aurora**, Zona 13, in the southern part of the city, are La Aurora International Airport, the Observatory, racetrack and **Parque Zoológico La Aurora** ⓘ *T2472-0507, www.aurorazoo.org.gt, Tue-Sun 0900-1700, US$3.30*. The newer areas show greater concern for the animals' wellbeing. There are also several museums: the **Museo Nacional de Antropología y Etnología** ⓘ *Salón 5, Parque Aurora, Zona 13, T2475-4406, www. munae.gob.gt, Tue-Fri 0900-1600, Sat-Sun 0900-1200, 1330-1600, US$7.90, no photos*, has outstanding Maya pieces including stelae from Piedras Negras and typical Guatemalan dress, as well as good models of Tikal, Quiriguá and Zaculeu. There are sculptures, murals, ceramics, textiles, a collection of masks and an excellent jade collection. Around the corner is the **Museo Nacional de Historia Natural** ⓘ *6 Calle, 7-30, Zona 13, T2472-0468, Mon-Fri*

0900-1600, Sat-Sun 0900-1200, 1400-1600, US$6.50, which houses a collection of national fauna, including stuffed birds, animals, butterflies, geological specimens, etc. Opposite the archaeology museum, the **Museo de Arte Moderno** ① *Salón 6, Parque Aurora, Zona 13, T2472-0467, US$4, Tue-Fri 0900-1600*, has a modest but enjoyable collection. Next door is the **Museo de los Niños** ① *T2475-5076, Tue-Fri 0830-1200, 1300-1630, US$4*, an interactive museum with a gallery of Maya history and the Gallery of Peace which houses the world's largest single standing artificial tree – a *ceiba*.

➡ **Guatemala City maps**
1 Guatemala City: Zona 1, page 334
2 Guatemala City: Zona 9, 10, 13, page 337

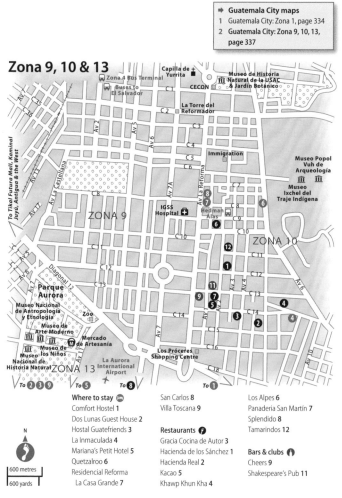

Zona 9, 10 & 13

Where to stay 🛏
Comfort Hostel **1**
Dos Lunas Guest House **2**
Hostal Guatefriends **3**
La Inmaculada **4**
Mariana's Petit Hotel **5**
Quetzalroo **6**
Residencial Reforma
  La Casa Grande **7**
San Carlos **8**
Villa Toscana **9**

Restaurants 🍴
Gracia Cocina de Autor **3**
Hacienda de los Sánchez **1**
Hacienda Real **2**
Kacao **5**
Khawp Khun Kha **4**
Los Alpes **6**
Panadería San Martín **7**
Splendido **8**
Tamarindos **12**

Bars & clubs 🍸
Cheers **9**
Shakespeare's Pub **11**

Tourist information

INGUAT
7 Av, 1-17, Zona 4 (Centro Cívico), 24 hrs
T1801-464-8281, T2421-2800, www.
visitguatemala.com. Mon-Fri 0800-1600.
They are very friendly and English is
sometimes spoken. They provide a hotel list,
a map of the city, and general information
on buses, market days, museums, etc. There
is also an office in the airport arrivals hall
(T2331-4256, open 0600-2100) where staff
are exceptionally helpful and on the ball.

Where to stay

You can get better prices in the more
expensive hotels by booking corporate
rates through a travel agent or simply
asking at the desk if any lower prices are
available. Hotels are often full at Easter
and Christmas. At the cheaper hotels,
single rooms are not always available.
There are many cheap *pensiones* near bus
and railway stations and markets; those
between Calle 14 and Calle 18 are not
very salubrious.
 Hoteles Villas de Guatemala,
reservations 8 Calle 1-75 Zona 10, T2223-
5000, www.villasdeguatemala.com, rents
luxury villas throughout Guatemala.

Zona 1

$$ Pan American
9 Calle, 5-63, T2232-6807,
www.hotelpanamerican.com.gt.
This one time art deco jewel of the Centro
Histórico is well past its heyday, but worth
a look nonetheless. They offer quiet,
comfortable, reasonable rooms with TV,
but try to avoid those on the main-road
side. Award-winning restaurant with good
food (see Restaurants, below). Parking, and
breakfast included.

$$ Posada Belén
13 Calle "A", 10-30, T2232-9226,
www.posadabelen.com.
A colonial-style house run by the friendly
Francesca and René Sanchinelli, who
speak English. Quiet, comfy rooms with
good hot showers. Laundry, email service,
luggage store and good meals. Parking.
Tours available. A lovely place to stay.
Highly recommended.

$ Ajau
8 Av, 15-62, T5205-5137, www.hotelajau.com.
This converted early 20th-century house has
45 simple, adequate, economical rooms set
around a central courtyard, with or without
private bath. Services include Wi-Fi, internet
terminal, airport transfer, laundry and meals.
A typical old school cheapie, helpful, secure
and no frills.

$ Pensión Meza
10 Calle, 10-17, T2232-3177.
A large ramshackle place with beds in dorms.
It's popular with helpful staff and English
is spoken. It's sometimes noisy and some
rooms are damp. Other rooms are darker
than a prison cell, but cheered by graffiti,
poetry and paintings. There is table tennis,
book exchange, internet at US$8 per hr and
or free Wi-Fi.

$ Theatre International
8 Av, 14-17, T4202-5112,
www.theatreihostel.com.
Located to the side of the Teatro Abril,
this 70-bed party hostel features 2 patios,
kitchen, Wi-Fi and complimentary
pancake breakfasts. There is a range of
accommodation to suit all budgets, include
thrifty 8- and 14-bed dorms, and private
rooms with or without private bath. One for
the whippersnappers and sadly a bit stuck
up ("entrance is not allowed for people older
than 45").

South of the centre: Avenida La Reforma

$$$ Comfort Hostel
17 Calle, 14-35, Zona 10, T2367-0754, www.comforthostel.com.
This small, secluded and professionally managed B&B features a very reasonable restaurant and a small patio where you can relax or work. Rooms are spacious, tranquil, tasteful and well-equipped with cable TV, clock radio, Wi-Fi, safety boxes and sparkling bathrooms with hot water. Simple but personal.

$$$ La Inmaculada
14 calle 7-88, Zona 10, T2314-5100, www.inmaculadahotel.com.
With Egyptian cotton linens, complimentary L'Occitane toiletries and slick contemporary design, **La Inmaculada** is indeed immaculately stylish, a great option for couples or hip young things. Services include spa treatments and business centre. Highly tasteful and highly recommended.

$$$ Residencial Reforma La Casa Grande
Av La Reforma, 7-67, Zona 10, T2332-0914, www.casagrande-gua.com.
Near the US embassy, a very attractive colonial-style house dating to the early 20th century, complete with whitewashed courtyard and lavish statues. Rooms and suites are comfortable but also rather simple and pricey for what you get. Good, small restaurant, open 0630-2100, also a bar and internet service.

$$$ San Carlos
Av La Reforma, 7-89, Zona 10, T2362-9076, www.hsancarlos.com.
A small, charming hotel set in a sumptuous historical property with a small pool and leafy garden. Rooms are modern, middle-of-the-road and fully equipped with Wi-Fi and cable TV; suites and apartments are more luxurious. Rates includes breakfast and airport transfer.

$$ Villa Toscana
16 Calle 8-20, Zona 13, Aurora I, T2261-2854, www.hostalvillatoscana.com.
Stylish B&B adorned in tones of gold and cream. Rooms come with cable TV, Wi-Fi, handmade hardwood furniture and floral wall sculptures. The garden, where breakfast is served under a canopy, features a trim green lawn and well-tended flowers. Lovely and relaxing. Airport shuttle included.

$$-$ Hostal Guatefriends
16 Calle, 7-40, Zona 13, Aurora I, T5308-3275, www.hostalguatefriends.com.
Brightly painted hostel accommodation by the night or the month, including 4-person dorms ($, but still a bit pricey for Guatemala) and private rooms ($$) with cable TV and Wi-Fi. Rates include breakfast and airport shuttle. Friendly, safe and helpful.

$$-$ Mariana's Petit Hotel
20 Calle, 10-17, Zona 13, Aurora II, www.marianaspetithotel.com.
Located close to the airport with free pickup and drop-off, this simple and homely B&B has a range of comfortable, quiet and unpretentious rooms, all with cable TV and Wi-Fi. Upstairs there's a lovely roof terrace where you can soak up the sun. Great breakfasts. Helpful and hospitable.

$$-$ Quetzalroo
6 Av, 7-84, Zona 10, T5746-0830, www.quetzalroo.com.
This successful Australian/Guatemalteco-owned youth hostel is recommended as the best of its kind in the city. The staff are super-friendly and helpful; rooms are simple, comfortable and cosy ($$); dorms are low-key ($). They do a city tours by bike and a basic breakfast is included. Sociable, quiet and relaxed.

$ Dos Lunas Guest House
21 Calle, 10-92, Zona 13, T2261-4248, www.hoteldoslunas.com.
Private rooms and dorms in a comfy B&B. Very close to the airport with free transport to or from the airport. Storage service, free

breakfast and water and tourist information. Lorena, the landlady, also organizes shuttles and taxis and tours. English spoken. Reservations advisable as often full.

Restaurants

Zona 1

There are all kinds of food available in the capital, from the simple national cuisine to French, Chinese and Italian food. There is a plethora of fast-food restaurants and traditional *comedores* where you will get good value for money; a reasonable set meal will cost no more than US$3. The cheapest places to eat are at street stalls and the various markets – take the normal precautions.

$$$ Altuna
5 Av, 12-31, www.restaurantealtuna.com.
This establishment has a beautiful traditional Spanish bar interior and serves tasty Spanish food in huge portions, including paella and seafood. Lobster is available but expensive. Delicious coffee. There is a branch in Zona 10 at 10 Calle, 0-45.

$$$-$$ Hotel Pan American
See Where to stay, above.
Regional and international cuisine served in the central courtyard of this hotel, a faded but distinctive art deco beauty that was once the haunt of the rich and famous. An award-winning establishment with lots of ambience and an affordable lunchtime menu.

$$-$ Café de Imeri
6 Calle, 3-34. Closed Sun.
Sandwiches, salads, soups and pastries in a patio garden. Set lunch and excellent cakes. It's popular with young professional Guatemalans. Try the *pay de queso de elote* (maize cheesecake). Its bakery next door has a rare selection of granary breads, birthday cakes, etc.

$ Restaurante Vegetariano Rey Sol
8 Calle, 5-36. Closed Sun.
A prize vegetarian find – wholesome food and ambience oasis amid the fumes of Zona 1, and popular with the locals. Delicious veggie concoctions at excellent prices served canteen-style by friendly staff. Breakfasts and *licuados* also available. Newer, larger and brighter branch at 11 Calle, 5-51.

Ice cream parlours

Helados Marylena
6 Calle, 2-49. Daily 1000-2200.
Not quite a meal but almost. This establishment has been serving up the weirdest concoctions for 90 years. From the probably vile – fish, chilli, yucca and cauliflower ice cream – to the heavenly – beer and sputnik (coconut, raisins and pineapple). The *elote* (maize) is good too. This city institution is credited with making children eat their vegetables! Anyone travelling with fussy eaters should stop by here.

South of the centre: Avenida La Reforma
Most of the best restaurants are in the **Zona Viva**, within 10 blocks of the Av La Reforma on the east side, between 6 Calle and 16 Calle in Zona 10. **Zona 9** is just across the other side of Av La Reforma.

There are several options in the area around **Cuatro Grados Norte** providing tapas, sushi, *churros* and chocolate. Lively, especially on Fri and Sat nights.

$$$ Gracia Cocina de Autor
14 Calle y 4 Av, Zona 10, T2366 8699.
Modern and minimalist, Gracia Cocina de Autor serves an eclectic menu of flavourful gourmet dishes by chef Pablo Novales in a stylish setting. Recipes are international fusion with smoked salmon bagels and eggs benedict among the offerings for brunch, lamb chops and roast pork for lunch or dinner. Recommended.

$$$ Hacienda de los Sánchez
12 Calle, 2-25, Zona 10.
Good steaks and local dishes, but seriously crowded at weekends, and so not the most pleasant of settings compared with other steakhouses in the vicinity. Well-established and something of a classic on the scene.

$$$ Hacienda Real
5 Av 14-67, Zona 10, www.hacienda-real.com.
An excellent selection of grilled meats with a hint of smokiness. Great ambience, often buzzing, and the candles and palms create a garden-like setting. There's also a nice little bar with Mexican leather chairs on one side.

$$$ Kacao
1 Av, 13-51, Zona 10, www.kacao.com.gt.
A large variety of delicious local and national dishes, which are attractively prepared and served in ample portions. The setting is fantastic: a giant thatched room, *huipiles* for tablecloths and beautiful candle decorations. Some options are expensive.

$$$ Khawp Khun Kha
13 Calle A, 7-19, Zona 10, Plaza Tiffany.
If the flavours of Central America have grown tired and old, try this hip Thai restaurant, serving spicy *panang* and green curries, pad Thai and other specialities sure to liven up your taste buds. Good and tasty, but definitely fusion cuisine and not quite authentically Thai (close enough though).

$$$ L'Osteria
Cuatro Grados Norte, Vía 5 between Ruta 1 and Ruta 2.
Popular Mediterranean restaurant on the corner, complete with a pleasant outdoor terrace. They serve tasty Greek fare, hummous and pitta bread, along with solid Italian favourites such as pizza and lasagne.

$$$ Splendido
12 Calle, 4-15, Zona 14, www. restaurantesplendido.com.
A very presentable bistro-style restaurant with impeccable service and delicious and predominantly French-flavoured fusion

cooking. Main courses include scallops, shrimps, steaks and a selection of pasta. Specialities include sweet chilli tuna, chicken curry, peppered steak and key lime cheesecake.

$$$ Tamarindos
11 Calle, 2-19A, Zona 10, T2360-2815.
Mixed Asian, sushi, Vietnamese rolls, mushrooms stuffed with almonds and crab are some of the tantalizing options at this very smart Asian restaurant with spiral shades and soothing bamboo greens.

$$ Los Alpes
10 Calle, 1-09, Zona 10. Closed Mon.
A Swiss-Austrian place with light meals and a smorgasbord of excellent cakes and chocolates. Popular with Guatemalan families.

$$-$ Panadería San Martin
2 Av, Zona 10, www.sanmartinbakery.com.
San Martín is a very popular bakery with branches across Guatemala and El Salvador. In addition to baked goods, they offer cooked breakfasts and reliable international fare such as pizzas, salads, soups and sandwiches. Not outstanding, but easy and tasty enough.

Bars and clubs

Cheers
13 Calle, 0-40, Zona 10. Mon-Sat 0900-0100, Sun 1300-2400ish.
A basement sports bar with pool tables, darts and large cable TV. Happy hour until 1800. The awning outside features the logo from the hit TV show.

El Portal
Portal del Comercio, 8 Calle, 6-30, Zona 1. Mon-Sat 1000-2200.
This was a favourite spot of Che Guevara and you can imagine him sitting here holding court at the long wooden bar. A stuffed bull's head now keeps watch over drinkers. To get there, enter the labyrinths of passageways facing the main plaza at No 6-30 where

there is a Coke stand. At the first junction bear round to the left and up on the left you will see its sign. *Comida típica* and marimba music, beer from the barrel.

Europa
11 Calle, 5-16, Zona 1. Mon-Sat 0800-0100.
Popular peace-corps/travellers' hangout. A sports bar, showing videos, with books for sale. They also serve grub.

La Bodeguita del Centro
12 Calle, 3-55, Zona 1, T2239-2976.
The walls of this hip place in an old stockhouse are adorned with posters of Che Guevara, Bob Marley and murdered Salvadorean Archbishop Romero. There's live music Thu-Sat at 2100, talks, plays, films, and exhibitions upstairs. Wooden tables are spread over 2 floors; seriously cheap nachos and soup are on the menu. It's an atmospheric place to spend an evening. Call in to get their **Calendario Cultural** leaflet.

Las Cien Puertas
Pasaje Aycinea, 7 Av, 8-44, just south of Plaza Mayor, Zona 1. Daily 1600-2400.
Has a wonderful atmosphere with political, satirical and love missives covering its walls. There's excellent food and outdoor seating and it's friendly.

Shakespeare's Pub
13 Calle, 1-51, Zona 10. Mon-Fri 1100-0100, Sat and Sun 1400-0100.
English-style basement bar with a good atmosphere, American owner, a favourite with expats and locals, safe for women to drink.

Entertainment

Cinema and theatre
There are numerous cinemas and they often show films in English with Spanish subtitles. Teatro Nacional, *Centro Cívico, see page 338.* Most programmes are Thu-Sun.

Shopping

Bookshops
Museo Ixchel, *see page 336.* This museum has a bookshop.
Museo Popol Vuh bookshop, *see page 336.* Has a good selection of books on pre-Columbian art, crafts and natural history.

Maps
Maps can be bought from the **Instituto Geográfico Nacional (IGN)**, Av Las Américas, 5-76, Zona 13, T2332-2611. Mon-Fri 0900-1730. The whole country is covered by about 200 1:50,000 maps available in colour or photocopies of out-of-print sections. None is very up to date. There is, however, an excellent 1996, 1:15,000 map of Guatemala City in 4 sheets. A general *Mapa Turístico* of the country is available here, also at INGUAT, see Tourist information above.

Markets
The **Central Market** operates underground behind the cathedral, from 7 to 9 Av, 8 Calle, Zona 1. One floor is dedicated to textiles and crafts, and there is a large, cheap basketware section on the lower floor. Silverware is cheaper at the market than elsewhere in Guatemala City. Other markets include the **Mercado Terminal** in Zona 4, and the **Mercado de Artesanía** in the Parque Aurora, near the airport, which is for tourists. Large shopping centres are good for a wide selection of local crafts, artworks, funky shoes, and clothes. Don't miss the *dulces*, candied fruits and confectionery.

Shopping centres and supermarkets
The best shopping centres are **Centro Comercial Los Próceres**, 18 Calle and 3 Av, Zona 10, the **Centro Comercial La Pradera**, Carretera Roosevelt and Av 26, Zona 10. There is a large **Paiz** supermarket on 18 Calle and 8 Av and a vast shopping mall **Tikal Futura** at Calzada Roosevelt and 22 Av, Zona 11. *Artesanías* for those who shop with a conscience at the fair-trade outlet **UPAVIM**,

Calle Principal, Col La Esperanza, Mesquital Zona 12, T2479-9061, www.upavim.org, Mon-Fri 0800-1800, Sat 0800-1200.

What to do

Clark Tours, *Plaza Clark, 7 Av 14-76, Zona 9, T2412-4700, www.clarktours.com.gt, and several other locations*. Long-established, very helpful, tours to Copán, Quiriguá, etc.
Four Directions, *1 Calle, 30-65, Zona 7, T2439-7715, www.fourdirections.travel*. Recommended for Maya archaeology tours. English spoken.
Maya Expeditions, *13 Av, 14-70, Zona 10, T2366-9950, www.mayaexpeditions.com*. Very experienced and helpful, with varied selection of short and longer river/hiking tours, whitewater rafting, bungee jumping, cultural tours, tours to Piedras Negras.
Trolley Tour, *T5907-0913, Tue-Sat 1000-1300, Sun 1000*. Pick-ups from Zona 10 hotels for 3-hr city tours, US$20, children US$10.
Turismo Ek Chuah, *3 Calle 6-24, Zona 2, T2220-1491, www.ekchuah.com*. Nationwide tours as well as some specialist and tailor-made tours on bicycle and horseback.

Transport

Air
The airport is in the south part of the city at La Aurora, 4 km from the Plaza Central, T2331-8392. It has banks, ATMs, internet, bars and restaurants. A taxi to Zona 10 is US$8, Zona 1, US$10, and from Antigua, US$25-30. Shuttles from outside airport to Antigua meet all arriving flights, US$10.

Flights to **Flores** with **Grupo Taca** 0820, 1605 and 1850, and **TAG** at 1630 daily. For the following domestic airlines, phone for schedules: **Aerocharter**, T5401-5893, to **Puerto Barrios**. **Aeródromo**, T5539-9364, to **Huehuetenango**. **Aerolucía**, T5959-7008 to **Quetzaltenango**.

Bus
Local
Buses operate between 0600-2000, after which you'll have to rely on taxis.

In town, US$0.13 per journey on regular buses and on the larger red buses known as *gusanos* (worms) except on Sun and public holidays when they charge US$0.16. One of the most useful bus services is the **101**, which travels down 10 Av, Zona 1, and then cuts across to the 6 Av, Zona 4, and then across Vía 8 and all the way down the Av La Reforma, Zona 10. The **82** also travels from Zona 1 to 10 and can be picked up on the 10 Av, Zona 1 and the 6 Av, Zona 4. Bus **85**, with the same pickup points, goes to the cluster of museums in Zona 13. Buses **37**, **35**, **32** all head for the INGUAT building, which is the large blue and white building in the Centro Cívico complex. **R40** goes from the 6 Av, Zona 4, to the Tikal Futura shopping complex; a good spot to catch the Antigua bus, which pulls up by the bridge to the complex. Buses leaving the 7 Av, Zona 4, just 4 blocks from the Zona 4 bus terminal, for the Plaza Mayor, Zona 1, are *gusano* **V21**, **35**, **36**, **82**, and **101**.

Long distance
The Zona 4 chicken bus terminal between 1-4 Av and 7-9 C serves the Occidente (west), the Costa Sur (Pacific coastal plain) and El Salvador. The area of southern Zona 1 contains many bus offices and is the departure point for the Oriente (east), the Caribbean zone, Pacific coast area towards the Mexican border and the north, to Flores and Tikal. 1st-class buses often depart from company offices in Zona 1 (see map, page 334).

There are numerous bus terminals in Guatemala City. The majority of 1st-class

> **Tip...**
>
> Watch your bags everywhere, but like a hawk in the Zona 4 terminal.

buses have their own offices and departure points around Zona 1. Hundreds of chicken buses for the south and west of Guatemala leave from the Zona 4 terminal, as well as local city buses. Note that some companies have been moved from Zona 1 and Zona 4 out to Zona 7 and 12. There was a plan, at the time of writing, to redirect all buses for the southern region to leave from Central Sur, Col Villalobos.

International buses (see below) have their offices scattered about the city. (The cheaper Salvador buses leave from near the Zona 4 terminal.) The Zona 4 bus terminal has to be the dirtiest and grimmest public area in the whole of the city.

The main destinations with companies operating from Guatemala City are:

Antigua, every 15 mins, 1 hr, US$1, until 2000 from Av 23 and 3 Calle, Zona 3. To **Chimaltenango** and **Los Encuentros**, from 1 Av between 3 y 4. Calle, Zona 7. **Chichicastenango** hourly from 0500-1800, 3 hrs, US$2.20 with **Veloz Quichelense**. **Huehuetenango**, with **Los Halcones**, Calzada Roosevelt, 37-47, Zona 11, T2439-2780, 0700, 1400, 1700, US$7, 5 hrs, and **Transportes Velásquez**, Calzada Roosevelt 9-56, Zona 7, T2440-3316, 0800-1630, every 30 mins, 5 hrs, US$7.

Panajachel, with **Transportes Rebulí**, 41 Calle, between 6 y 7 Av, Zona 8, T2230-2748, hourly from 0530-1530, 3 hrs, US$2.20; also to **San Lucas Tolimán** 0530-1530, 3 hrs US$2.10 **San Pedro La Laguna** with **Transportes Méndez**, 41 C, between 6 y and Av, Zona 8, 1300, 4 hrs. **Santiago Atitlán**, with various companies, from 4 C, between 3 y 4 Av, Zona 12, 0400-1700, every 30 mins, 4 hrs, US$4.

Quetzaltenango (Xela) and **San Marcos**. 1st-class bus to Xela with **Transportes Alamo**, 12 Av "A", 0-65, Zona 7, T2471-8626, from 0800-1730, 6 daily 4 hrs, US$7. **Líneas Américas**, 2 Av, 18-47, Zona 1, T2232-1432, 0500-1930, 7 daily, US$7. **Galgos**, 7 Av, 19-44, Zona 1, T2232-3661, between 0530-1700, 5 daily, 4 hrs, US$7 to **Tapachula** in Mexico

through the El Carmen border; see also box, page 512. **Marquensita**, 1 Av, 21-31, Zona 1, T2230-0067. From 0600-1700, 8 a day, US$6.10, to Xela and on to San Marcos. To **Tecpán**, with **Transportes Poaquileña**, 1 Av corner of 3 and 4 Calle, Zona 7, 0530-1900, every 15 mins, 2 hrs, US$1.20.

To **Santa Cruz del Quiché**, Sololá and Totonicapán, buses depart from 41 Calle between 6 and 7 Av, Zona 8.

To **Biotopo del Quetzal** and **Cobán**, 3½ hrs and 4½ hrs respectively, hourly from 0400-1700, US$6 and US$7.50, with **Escobar y Monja Blanca**, 8 Av, 15-16, Zona 1, T2238-1409. **Zacapa**, **Chiquimula** (for **El Florido**, on the Honduran border) and **Esquipulas** with **Rutas Orientales**, 19 Calle, 8-18, Zona 1, T2253-7282, every 30 mins 0430-1800. To **Zacapa**, 3¼ hrs, to **Chiquimula**, 3½ hrs, to **Esquipulas**, 4½ hrs, US$6.

Puerto Barrios, with **Transportes Litegua**, 15 Calle, 10-40, Zona 1, T2220-8840, www.litegua.com, 0430-1900, 31 a day, 5 hrs, US$6.80, 1st class US$12 and **Río Dulce** 0600, 0900, 1130, 5 hrs, US$6.20.

El Petén with **Fuente del Norte** (same company as **Líneas Máxima de Petén**), 17 Calle, 8-46, Zona 1, T2251-3817, going to **Río Dulce** and **Santa Elena/Flores**. There are numerous departures 24 hrs; 5 hrs to Río Dulce, US$6.50; to Santa Elena, 9-10 hrs, US$12; buses vary in quality and price, breakdowns not unknown. The 1000 and 2130 departures are a luxury bus **Maya del Oro** with snacks, US$18, the advantage being it doesn't stop at every tree to pick up passengers. **Línea Dorada**, 16 Calle, 10-03, Zona 1, T2220-7990, www.tikalmayan world. com, at 1000, US$16 to **Flores**, 8 hrs and on to **Melchor de Mencos**, 10 hrs. To **Santa Elena ADN**, 8 Av, 16-41, Zona 1, T2251-0050, www.adnautobuses delnorte.com, luxury service, 2100 and 2200, returns at 2100 and 2300, US$19, toilets, TV and snacks.

To **Jalapa** with **Unidos Jalapanecos**, 22 Calle 1-20, Zona 1, T2251-4760, 0430-1830, every 30 mins, 3 hrs, US$2.50 and with **Transportes Melva Nacional**, T2332-6081,

0415-1715, every 30 mins, 3 hrs 30 mins, US$2.50. Buses also from the Zona 4 terminal. To **San Pedro Pinula** between 0500-1800.

To **Chatia Gomerana**, 4 Calle y 8 Av, Zona 12, to **La Democracia**, every 30 mins from 0600-1630 via Escuintla and Siquinala, 2 hrs. **Transportes Cubanita** to **Reserva Natural de Monterrico** (La Avellana), 4 Calle y 8 Av, Zona 12, at 1030, 1230, 1420, 3 hrs, US$2.50. To **Puerto San José** and **Iztapa**, from the same address, 0430-1645 every 15 mins, 1 hr. To **Retalhuleu** (Reu on bus signs) with **Transportes Fortaleza del Sur**, Calzada Aguilar Batres, 4-15, Zona 12, T22230-3390, between 0010-1910 every 30 mins via Escuintla, Cocales and Mazatenango, 3 hrs, US$6.80. Numerous buses to **Santa Lucía Cotzumalguapa** go from the Zona 4 bus terminal.

International buses
Reserve the day before if you can. Taking a bus from Guatemala City as far as, say, San José, is tiring and tiresome (the bus company's bureaucracy and the hassle from border officials all take their toll). For crossings to Honduras and El Salvador, see also boxes, pages 517 and 518. For Belize border information, see box, page 514, and for Mexico, see box, page 512.

To **Honduras** avoiding El Salvador, take a bus to **Esquipulas**, then a minibus to the border. **Hedman Alas**, 2 Av, 8-73, Zona 10, T2362-5072, www.hedmanalas.com, to **Copán** via El Florido, at 0500 and 0900, 5 hrs, US$30. Also goes on to **San Pedro Sulas**, US$45, and **La Ceiba**, US$52. **Pullmantur** to **Tegucigalpa** daily at 0700 via San Salvador, US$66 and US$94. **Ticabus** to **San Pedro Sula**, US$34 and **Tegucigalpa**, US$34 via San Salvador. **Rutas Orientales**, 19 C, 8-18, T2253-7282 goes to **Honduras** at 0530 via Agua Caliente, 8 hrs, US$28; see also box, page 517, for more on crossing into Honduras.

To **Mexico** with **Trans Galgos Inter**, 7 Av, 19-44, Zona 1, T2223-3661, www.transgalgosinter.com.gt, to **Tapachula** via **El Carmen**, 0730, 1330, and 1500, 7 hrs; see also box, page 512. **Línea Dorada**, address above, to **Tapachula** at 0800, US$24. **Transportes Velásquez**, 20 Calle, 1-37, Zona 1, T2221-1084, 0800-1100, hourly to **La Mesilla**, 7 hrs, US$5. **Transportes Fortaleza del Sur**, Calzada Aguilar Batres, 4-15, T2230-3390 to **Ciudad Tecún Umán**, 0130, 0300, 0330, 0530 via **Retalhuleu**, 5 hrs.

To **Chetumal** via **Belize City**, with **Línea Dorada** change to a minibus in Flores. Leaves 1000, 2100, 2200 and 2230, 2 days, US$42. Journey often takes longer than advertised due to Guatemala–Belize and Belize–Mexico border crossings.

To **El Salvador** via **Valle Nuevo**, border crossing, with **Ticabus**, 0600 and 1300 daily to San Salvador, US$17 1st class, 5 hrs. From **Ticabus** terminal, Calzada Aguilar Batres 22-25, T2473-0633, www.ticabus.com, clean, safe, with waiting area, café, toilets, no luggage deposit.

Car
Car hire companies Budget, at the airport; also at 6 Av, 11-24, Zona 9, www.budget.co.uk. **Hertz**, at the airport, T2470-3800, www.hertz.com. **Tabarini**, 2 Calle "A", 7-30, Zona 10, T2331-2643, airport T2331-4755, www.tabarini.com. **Tally**, 7 Av, 14-60, Zona 1, T2232-0421, very competitive, have pickups. Recommended.

Car and motorcyle repairs Mike and Andy Young, 27 Calle, 13-73, Zona 5, T2331-9263, Mon-Fri 0700-1600. Excellent mechanics for all vehicles, extremely helpful. Honda motorcycle parts from **FA Honda**, Av Bolívar, 31-00, Zona 3, T2471-5232. Some staff speak English. Car and motorcycle parts from **FPK**, 5 Calle, 6-75, Zona 9, T2331-9777. **David González**, 32 Calle, 6-31, Zona 11, T5797-2486, for car, bike and bicycle repairs. Recommended.

Shuttle
Shuttles are possible between Guatemala City and all other destinations, but reserve in advance. Contact shuttle operators in Antigua (see Antigua Transport, page 361).

Guatemala City to **Antigua**, US$15, **Panajachel** US$30, Chichicastenango US$30, **Copán Ruinas**, US$40, **Cobán**, US$30 and **Quetzaltenango**, US$25.

Taxi

If possible call a taxi from your hotel or get someone to recommend a reliable driver; there are hundreds of illegal taxis in the city that should be avoided.

There are 3 types of taxis: **Rotativos**, **Estacionarios** and the ones that are metered, called **Taxis Amarillos**. *Rotativos* are everywhere in the city cruising the length and breadth of all zones. You will not wait more than a few minutes for one to come along. They are numbered on their sides and on their back windscreen will be written TR (*Taxi Rotativo*) followed by 4 numbers. Most of them have a company logo stamped on the side as well. *Estacionarios* also have numbers on the sides but are without logo. On their back windscreen they have the letters TE (*Taxi Estacionario*) followed by 4 numbers. They are to be found at bus terminals and outside hotels or in other important places. They will always return to these same waiting points (good to know if you leave something in a taxi). Do not get in a taxi that does not have either of these labels on its back windscreen. *Rotativos* and *Estacionarios* are unmetered, but *Estacionarios* will always charge less than *Rotativos*. The fact that both are unmetered will nearly always work to your advantage because of traffic delays. You will be quoted an inflated price by *Rotativos* by virtue of being a foreigner. *Estacionarios* are fairer. It is about US$8 from the airport to Zona 1. From Zona 1 to 4 is about US$4. The metered *Taxi Amarillo* also moves around but less so than the *Rotativos*, as they are more on call by phone. They only take a couple of minutes to come. **Amarillo Express**, T2332-1515, are available 24 hrs.

Antigua
& around

★Antigua is rightly one of Guatemala's most popular destinations. It overflows with colonial architecture and fine churches on streets that are linked by squat houses, painted in ochre shades and topped with terracotta tiles, basking in the fractured light of the setting sun. Antigua is a very attractive city and is the cultural centre of Guatemala; arts flourish here. Maya women sit in their colourful clothes amid the ruins and in the Parque Central. In the late-afternoon light, buildings such as Las Capuchinas are beautiful, and in the evening the cathedral is wonderfully illuminated as if by candlelight.

If the city was not treasure enough, the setting is truly memorable. Volcán Agua (3766 m) is due south and the market is to the west, behind which hang the imposing peaks of Volcán Acatenango (3976 m) and Volcán Fuego (3763 m), which still emits the occasional column of ash as a warning of the latent power within.

Also around Antigua are a cluster of archaeological sites and highland villages to explore.

Essential Antigua

Getting around

Avenidas run north to south and calles run from east to west. House numbers do not give any clue about how far from the Parque Central a particular place is.

Best places to stay

Casa Florencia, page 352
Hostel Tropicana, page 353
Yellow House, page 353

Safety

Unfortunately, despite its air of tranquillity, Antigua is not without unpleasant incidents. Take care and advice from the tourist office on where to go or not to go. There are numerous tourist police (green uniforms) who are helpful and conspicuous; their office is at 4 Avenida Norte at the side of the Municipal Palace. If you wish to go to Cerro de la Cruz (see page 351), or the cemetery, they will escort you, leaving 1000 and 1500 daily. Antigua is generally safe at night, but it's best to keep to the well-lit area near the centre. Report incidents to police and the tourist office. Tourist assistance 24 hours, T2421-2810.

Best restaurants

Caffé Mediterráneo, page 354
Hector's, page 354
Micho's Gastropub, page 354
Rainbow Café, page 355
Típico Antigüeño, page 355

Sights → *Colour map 6, B3,*
colonial buildings and volcano backdrop

Parque Central and around

In the centre of the city is the Parque Central, the old Plaza Real, where bullfights and markets were held in the early days. The present park was constructed in the 20th century though the fountain dates back to the 18th century. The **cathedral** ⓘ *US$0.40*, to the east, dates from 1680 (the first cathedral was demolished in 1669). Much has been destroyed since then and only two of the many original chapels are now in use. The remainder can be visited. The **Palacio de los Capitanes Generales** is to the south. The original building dates from 1558, was virtually destroyed in 1773, was partly restored in the 20th century, and now houses police and government offices. The **Cabildo**, or **Municipal Palace**, is to the north and an arcade of shops to the west. You can climb to the second floor for a great view of the volcanoes (Monday to Friday 0800-1600). The **Museo de Santiago** ⓘ *Tue-Fri 0900-1600, Sat-Sun 0900-1200, 1400-1600, US$4*, is in the municipal offices to the north of the plaza, as is the **Museo del Libro Antiguo** ⓘ *same hours and price*, which contains a replica of a 1660 printing press (the original is in Guatemala City), old documents and a collection of 16th- to 18th-century books (1500 volumes in the library). The **Museo de Arte Colonial** ⓘ *Tue-Fri 0900-1600, Sat-Sun 0900-1200, 1400-1600, US$6.60*, is half a block from Parque Central at Calle 5 Oriente, in the building where the San Carlos University was first housed. It now has mostly 17th- to 18th-century religious art, well laid out in large airy rooms around a colonial patio.

Hotel Casa Santo Domingo

Hotel Casa Santo Domingo is one of Antigua's most beautiful sights: a converted old Dominican church and also monastery property. Archaeological excavations have turned up some unexpected finds at the site. During the cleaning out of a burial vault in September 1996, one of the greatest finds in

Antigua's history was unearthed. The vault had been filled with rubble, but care had been taken in placing stones a few feet away from the painted walls. The scene is in the pristine colours of natural red and blue, and depicts Christ, the Virgin Mary, Mary Magdalene and John the Apostle. It was painted in 1683, and was only discovered with the help of ultraviolet light. Within the monastery grounds are the **Colonial Art Museum**, with displays of Guatemalan baroque imagery and silverware and the **Pre-Columbian Art Museum**, **Glass Museum**, **Museum of Guatemalan Apothecary** and the **Popular Art and Handicrafts of Sacatepequez Museum** ① *3 Calle Ote 28, 0900-1700, US$5.25, 1 ticket covers all admissions.*

Colonial religious buildings

There are many fine religious buildings dating from the colonial era: 22 churches, 14 convents and 11 monasteries, most ruined by earthquakes and in various stages of restoration. Top of the list are the cloisters of the convent of **Las Capuchinas** ① *2 Av Norte y 2 Calle Ote, 0900-1700, US$3.90,* with immensely thick round pillars (1736) adorned with bougainvillea. The church and convent of **San Francisco** ① *1 Av Sur y 7 Calle Ote, 0800-1200, 1400-1700, US$0.40,* with the tomb of Hermano Pedro, is much revered by all the local communities. He was canonized in 2002. The church has been restored and now includes the **Museo de Hermano Pedro** ① *Tue-Sun 0900-1200, 1300-1630, US$0.40.* The convent of **Santa Clara** ① *6 Calle Ote y 2 Av Sur, 0900-1700, US$3.90,* was founded in about 1700 and became one of the biggest in Antigua, until the nuns were forced to move to Guatemala City. The adjoining garden is an oasis of peace. **El Carmen** ① *3 Calle Ote y 3 Av Norte,* has a beautiful façade with strikingly ornate columns, tastefully illuminated at night, but the rest of the complex is in ruins. Likewise **San Agustín** ① *5 Calle Pte y 7 Av Norte,* was once a fine building, but only survived intact from 1761 to 1773; earthquake destruction continued until the final portion of the vault collapsed in 1976, leaving an impressive ruin. **La Compañía de Jesús** ① *3 Calle Pte y 6 Av Norte, 0930-1700,* at one time covered the whole block. The church is today in ruins but the rest of the complex was recently restored by the Spanish government and now houses a cultural centre, **Centro de Formación de la Cooperación**

Antigua

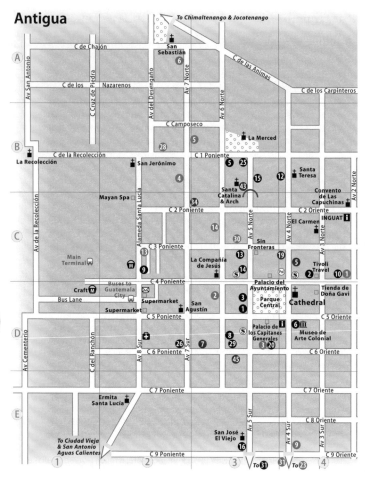

N

100 metres
100 yards

Where to stay 🛏
Aurora **1** *C4*
Base Camp **7** *D5*
Casa Encantada **31** *E4*
Casa Florencia **6** *A2*
Casa Rustica **2** *D3*
Casa Santo Domingo **8** *C6*
Hostel Tropicana **3** *D3*
Jungle Party Hostal **14** *C3*
Los Encuentros **4** *B2*
Mesón de María **30** *C3*
Posada del Angel **23** *E4*

Posada Juma Ocag **13** *C2*
Posada La Merced **5** *B3*
San Jorge **9** *E4*
Yellow House **28** *B2*

Restaurants 🍴
Bagel Barn **1** *D3*
Café Condesa **3** *D3*
Café Flor **6** *D4*
Caffé Mediterráneo **20** *D3*
Doña Luisa
  Xicoténcatl **10** *C4*

El Sabor del Tiempo **13** *C3*
El Sereno **12** *B4*
Fonda de la Calle Real **14** *C3*
Frida's **15** *B3*
Hector's **5** *B3*
La Antigua Viñería **16** *E3*
La Casserole **41** *C5*
Micho's Gastropub **2** *C4*
Quesos y Vinos **25** *B3*
Rainbow Café &
  Travel Center **26** *D2*
Sabe Rico **8** *D3*

Española ⓘ *www.aecid-cf.org.gt, 0900-1800, free*, with occasional exhibitions and workshops. The church and cloisters of **Escuela de Cristo** ⓘ *Calle de los Pasos y de la Cruz*, a small independent monastery (1720-1730), have survived and were restored between 1940 and 1960. The church is simple and has some interesting original artwork. **La Recolección** ⓘ *Calle de la Recolección, 0900-1700, US$5.25*, despite being a late starter (1700), became one of the biggest and finest of Antigua's religious institutions. It is now the most awe-inspiring ruin in the city. **San Jerónimo** ⓘ *Calle de la Recolección, 0900-1700, US$4*, was a school (early 1600s) for La Merced, three blocks away, but later became the local customs house. There is an impressive fountain in the courtyard. **La Merced** ⓘ *1 Calle Pte y 6 Av Norte, 0800-1700*, with its white and yellow façade dominates the surrounding plaza. The church (1767) and cloisters were built with earthquakes in mind and survived better than most. The church remains in use and the **cloisters** ⓘ *US$0.65*, are being further restored. Antigua's finest fountain is in the courtyard. **Santa Teresa** ⓘ *4 Av Norte*, was a modest convent, but the church walls and the lovely west front have survived. It is now the city's men's prison.

Other ruins including **Santa Isabel**, **Santa Cruz**, **La Candelaria**, **San José El Viejo** and **San Sebastián** are to be found round the edges of the city, and there is an interesting set of the Stations of the Cross, each a small chapel, from San Francisco to **El Calvario** church, which was where Pedro de Betancourt (Hermano Pedro) worked as a gardener and planted an esquisuchil tree. He was also the founder of the **Belén Hospital** in 1661, which was destroyed in 1773. However, some years later, his name was given to the **San Pedro Hospital**, which is one block south of the Parque Central.

There is a fabulous panorama from the **Cerro de la Cruz**, which is 15 minutes' walk from the northern end of town along 1 Avenida Norte.

Tourist information

The monthly magazine *The Revue* is a useful source of tourist information in English with articles, maps, events and advertisements; it's free and widely available in hotels and restaurants.

INGUAT office

2a Calle Ote,11 (between Av 2 and Av 3 Norte), T7832-3782, www.visit guatemala.com. Mon-Fri 0800-1700, Sat and Sun 0900-1700.
Very helpful, with maps and information; occasional exhibitions in rooms around courtyard behind office. Information available about volunteer work. English, Italian and a little German spoken.

Where to stay

In the better hotels, advance reservations are advised for weekends and Dec-Apr. During Holy Week, hotel prices are significantly higher, sometimes double for the more expensive hotels. In the Jul-Aug period, find your accommodation early in the day.

$$$$ Casa Santo Domingo
3 Calle Ote 28, T7820-1220, www.casasantodomingo.com.gt.
This is a beautifully designed hotel with 126 rooms in the ruins of a 17th-century convent with prehispanic archaeological finds. Good service, beautiful gardens, a magical pool, excellent restaurant with breakfast included. Worth seeing just to dream. See also page 348.

$$$$ Posada del Angel
4 Av Sur 24-A, T7832-0260, www.posadadelangel.com.
Bill Clinton is among the former guests of this famous, sumptuous and award-winning hotel. Lodging is in boutique suites and rooms set around a central courtyard, all with own fireplaces and consistently tasteful

decor. Amenities include dining room, exercise pool and roof terrace. Romantic, exclusive and private.

$$$ Aurora
4 Calle Ote 16, T7832-0217, www.hotelauroraantigua.com.
The oldest hotel in the city with old plumbing (but it works), antique furnishings and 1970s features. Quieter rooms face a colonial patio overflowing with beautiful flowers. Continental breakfast included, English spoken.

$$$ Casa Encantada
9 Calle Pte1, esq Av 4 Sur, T7832-7903, www.casa encantada-antigua.com.
This sweet colonial boutique hotel with 10 rooms is a perfect retreat from the centre of Antigua. It has a small rooftop terrace where breakfast is served and a comfortable sitting room with open fire, books, lilies and textile-lined walls. 2 rooms are accessed by stepping stones in a pond. The suite, with jacuzzi, enjoys views of the 3 volcanoes.

$$$ Casa Florencia
7 Av Norte 100, T7832-0261, www.cflorencia.net.
A sweet little colonial-style hotel enjoying views towards Volcán Agua. They offer 10 pleasant rooms set around a central courtyard with all the usual mod cons including TV, safe and Wi-Fi. The 2nd-floor balcony has *cola de quetzal* plants lining it. Staff are very welcoming. Recommended.

$$$ Hotel Mesón de María
3 Calle Pte 8, T7832-6068, www.hotelmesonde maria.com.
Great little place with a wonderful roof terrace. Their 20 stylish rooms are decorated with local textiles and earthy colours. Free internet and breakfast included at a local restaurant. Friendly and attentive service. Showers have large skylights.

$$ Hotel Casa Rústica
6 Av Nte 8, T7832-0694,
www.casarusticagt.com.
Casa Rústica has bright, comfortable rooms, each equipped with hand-carved furniture and Guatemalan textiles; cheaper rooms have shared bath (**$**). There are good communal areas, including kitchen, garden and sun terrace with views. Pleasant, but on the pricey side. Ask to see a few rooms before accepting as size and quality vary.

$$ Hotel Los Encuentros
7 Av Norte 60, T4114-5400,
www.hotelosencuentros.com.
This guesthouse offers quiet, comfortable and occasionally quirky rooms with hand-carved wooden furniture, Guatemalan art, textiles and antiques. The hostess Irma is very sweet and helpful. There are cooking facilities and breakfast is included. Rooms vary, ask to see a few.

$$ Hotel San Jorge
4 Av Sur 13, Calle del Conquistador, T7832-3132, www.hotelsanjorgeantigua.com.
Established in 1989, Hotel San Jorge has lovely green gardens with wide lawns and flowery beds. Rooms are understated but have thoughtful touches like wall-to-wall carpets, There is Talavera tilework, fireplaces, cable TV and handwoven bedspreads.

$$ Posada La Merced
7 Av Nte 43, T7832-3197,
www.posadalamercedantigua.com.
Located 1 block from La Merced church, this well-established colonial-style guesthouse features a beautiful patio with a fountain and plenty of leafy potted plants. Upstairs, a sun terrace has fine views. Rooms are smallish and simple, but comfortable. Quiet, relaxing and central.

$$-$ Hostel Tropicana
6 Calle Pte, between Av 4 and 5, T7832-0462, www.tropicanahostel.com.
This new addition to Antigua's party hostel scene is a cut above the rest with its small but refreshing outdoor pool, a

sun deck and a hot tub. There's a well-stocked bar too, and for chilling out, a leafy garden framed by ruined colonial walls. Accommodation includes a range of large and small dorms (**$**), and private rooms (**$$**). Promising and recommended.

$ Base Camp
7 Calle Pte 17, T 7832-0468,
www.guatemalavolcano.com.
Nice views of Volcán Agua from the roof terrace at this fun, young, energetic hostel marketed to adventure travellers. Accomodation includes 6 dorm beds and 2 double rooms with lots of shared space and all the usual hostel facilities. Runs adventure tours through **Outdoor Excursions** (see Tour operators, below).

$ Jungle Party Hostal and Café
6 Av Norte 20, T7832-0463,
www.junglepartyhostal.com.
Buzzing with backpakers in its onsite bars, this fun and sociable party hostel enjoys a great central location and impressive views of the volcanoes. Accommodation consists of dorm beds with hot water, lockers, small patio, TV, hammocks, swings, bean bags, Wi-Fi, free breakfast and movies. There's an all-you-can-eat barbecue on Sat.

$ Posada Juma Ocag
8 Av Norte 13 (Alameda Santa Lucía), T7832-3109, www.posadajumaocag.com.
This modest, family-run guesthouse is small but very clean, and nicely decorated using local textiles as bedspreads. It has an enclosed roof terrace and rooms come with or without private bath. Quiet and friendly with Wi-Fi, and free coffee in the morning.

$ Yellow House
1 Calle Pte 24, T7832-6646,
www.guatetravel.com.
There are 8 clean rooms in this hostel run by the welcoming Ceci. Breakfast included. Colonial style, laundry service, free internet. 3 rooms with bath, kitchen, patio, parking. Recommended.

Apartments

Look on the notice boards in town. Rooms and apartments are available from about US$25 a week up to US$500 per month. One recommended family is **Estella López**, 1 Calle Pte 41A, T7832-1324, who offer board and lodging on a weekly basis. The house is clean, and the family friendly.

Restaurants

For the cheapest of the cheap go to the stalls on the corner of 4 Calle Pte and 7 Av Norte, and those at the corner of 5 Calle Pte and 4 Av Sur. During the Easter period, the plaza in front of La Merced is transformed into a food market. At all these places you can pick up *elote, tortillas, tostadas* and *enchiladas*.

$$$ El Sereno
4 Av Norte 16, T7832-0501. Open 1200-1500 and 1800-2300.
International/Italian cuisine. Grand entrance with massive heliconia plants in the courtyard. It has a lovely terrace bar up some stone steps and a cave for romantic dining; it's popular at weekends.

$$$ La Casserole
Callejón de Concepción 7, T7832-0219 close to Casa Santo Domingo. Tue-Sat 1200-1500 and 1900-2200, Sun 1200-1500.
Sophisticated French cooking with fresh fish daily served at tables set in a beautiful courtyard, exclusive. Rigoberta Menchú dined with Jacques Chirac here.

$$$ Micho's Gastropub
4 Calle Ote 10, Edif Jaulon, T7832-3522.
Micho's stands out as one of the city's better establishments with its top-notch international cuisine, creatively prepared and beautifully presented. They serve lunchtime specials, along with breakfast and dinner, good cocktails and wine by the glass. Romantic ambience in the tranquil courtyard. Recommended.

$$$-$$ Caffé Mediterráneo
6 Calle Pte 6A, T7832-7180. Wed-Mon 1200-1500 and 1830-2200.
1 block south of the plaza. Mouth-watering Italian cuisine with great candlelit ambience. Recommended.

$$$-$$ Fonda de la Calle Real
5 Av Norte 5 and No 12, T7832 0507, also at 3 Calle Pte 7 (which wins over the others for the setting).
This place's speciality is *queso fundido*. It also serves local dishes including *pepián* (and a vegetarian version) and *kak-ik*, a Verapaz speciality.

$$ El Sabor del Tiempo
Calle del Arco and 3 Calle Poniente, T7832 0516.
Good steaks, burgers, seafood and pasta in tastefully converted former warehouse, with polished wood and glass cabinets. A bit pricey but full of antiquey character.

$$ Frida's
5 Av Norte 29, Calle del Arco, T7832-0504. Daily 1200-0100.
Ochre and French navy colours decorate this restaurant's tribute to Mexico's famous female artist. It is quite dark inside but Frida memorabilia and colander-like lampshades lighten the interior. Efficient service. 2nd-floor pool table, Wed and Thu ladies' night.

$$ Hector's
1 Calle Poniente No 9, T7832-9867.
Small, busy and welcoming restaurant that serves wonderful food at good prices. Highly recommended.

$$ La Antigua Viñería
5 Av Sur 34A, T7832-7370. Mon-Thu 1800-0100, Fri-Sun 1300-0100.
Owned by Beppe Dángella, next door to San José ruins. Amazing photographic collection of clients in various stages of inebriation, excellent selection of wines and grappa, you name it. Very romantic, feel free to write your comments on the walls, very good food, pop in for a reasonably priced *queso*

fundido and glass of wine if you can't afford the whole hog.

$$ Quesos y Vinos
Calle Poniente 1, T7832-7785. Wed-Mon 1200-1600 and 1800-2200.
Authentic Italian food and owners, good selection of wines, wood-fired pizza oven, sandwiches, popular.

$$ Sabe Rico
6 Av Sur No 7, 7832-0648.
Herb garden restaurant and fine food deli that serves healthy, organic food in tranquil surroundings.

$$-$ Café Flor
4 Av Sur 1, T7832-5274. Open 1100-2300.
Full-on delicious Thai/Guatemalan-style and tandoori food. The stir-fries are delicious, but a little overpriced. Discounts sometimes available. Friendly staff.

$$-$ Rainbow Café
7 Av Sur, on the corner of 6 Calle Pte.
Consistently delicious vegetarian food served in a pleasant courtyard surrounded by hanging plants, good filling breakfasts, indulgent crêpes, popular, live music evenings, good book exchange. Bar at night with happy hour and ladies' nights. Recommended.

$$-$ Travel Menu
6 Calle Pte 14.
Buzzing and bohemian, **Travel Menu** serves fresh, hearty, reasonably priced international fare in large portions, including big fat juicy sandwiches and tofu stir-fry. Candlelit ambience and regular live music. Friendly and sociable.

$ Típico Antigüeño
Alameda Sta Lucía 4, near the PO, T7832-5995.
This locally run place offers an absolute bargain of a *menú del día* (fish, chicken), which includes soup and sometimes a drink. It is extremely popular and can get ridiculously busy, so best to turn up before 1300 for lunch. Recommended.

Cafés and delis

Bagel Barn
5 Calle Pte 2. Open 0600-2200.
Popular, breakfast, snack deals with bagels and smoothies, videos shown nightly, free.

Café Condesa
5 Av Norte 4. Open 0700-2100.
West side of the main plaza in a pretty courtyard, popular, a little pricey for the portions, breakfast with free coffee fill-ups, desserts, popular Sun brunches.

Doña Luisa Xicoténcatl
4 Calle Ote 12, 1½ blocks east of the plaza. Daily 0700-2130.
Popular meeting place with an excellent bulletin board, serving breakfasts, tasty ice cream, good coffee, burgers, large menu, big portions. Good views of Volcán Agua upstairs. Shop sells good selection of wholemeal, banana bread, yogurts, etc. Don't miss the chocolate and orange loaf if you can get it.

Vivero y Café de La Escalonia
5 Av Sur Final 36 Calle, T7832-7074. Daily 0900-1800.
This delightful place is well worth the walk – a café amid a garden centre with luscious flowers everywhere, including bird of paradise flowers and tumbergia, a pergola and classical music. They serve *postres*, herb breads, salads and cold drinks.

Bars and clubs

Café No Sé
1 Av Sur 11 C, www.cafenose.com.
Grungy and bohemian, an interesting place with live music every night, and a range of high-powered mescal cocktails. Good.

Casbah
5 Av Norte 30. Mon-Sat 1800-0100.
Cover charge includes a drink. Gay night Thu. Has a medium-sized dance floor with a podium and plays a mix of good dance and

Latin music, the closest place to a nightclub atmosphere in Antigua.

La Chimenea
7 Av Norte 18. Mon-Sat 1700-2430.
Happy hour every day, seriously cheap, relaxed atmosphere, mixed young crowd, dance floor, salsa, rock.

La Sala
6 Calle Pte, T5671-3008.
One of the most popular salsa dancing and watering holes in town.

Ocelot
4 Av Nte 3.
A splendid watering hole full of interesting characters. They do happy hour, pub quizzes, American grub from the taco cart. Good crowd, popular on the expat scene.

Riki's Bar
4 Av Norte 4, inside La Escudilla.
Usually packed with gringos, but attracts a young Guatemalan crowd as well, and popular with the gay fraternity. Good place to meet people. A good mix of music, including jazz.

The Snug
6 Calle Pte 14, next to Travel Menu.
The Snug proves good things do come in small packages. A hit with expats and travellers, this intimate and fully authentic Irish bar does cold beer, rum, occasional live music and interesting conversation. Cosy, friendly and fun.

Entertainment

Cinemas
Antigua must be the home of the lounge cinema. All show films or videos in English, or with subtitles.
Café 2000, *6 Av Sur.* Free films daily and the most popular spot in town to watch movies.
Cine Sin Ventura, *5 Av Sur 8.* The only real screen in town, auditorium can get cold, and they need to hit the brightness button.

Festivals

Feb **International Culture Festival**: dance, music and other top-quality performers from around the globe come to Antigua.
Mar/Apr **Semana Santa**: see box, opposite.
21-26 Jul The feast of **San Santiago**.
31 Oct-2 Nov **All Saints** and **All Souls**, in and around Antigua.
7 Dec **Quema del Diablo** (burning of the Devil) by lighting fires in front of their houses and burning an effigy of the Devil in the Plazuela de La Concepción at night, thereby starting the Christmas festivities.
15 Dec The start of what's known as the **Posadas**, where a group of people leave from each church, dressed as Mary and Joseph, and seek refuge in hotels. They are symbolically refused lodging several times, but are eventually allowed in.

Shopping

Antigua is a shopper's paradise, with textiles, furniture, candles, fabrics, clothes, sculpture, candies, glass, jade and ceramics on sale. The main municipal market is on Alameda Santa Lucía next to the bus station, where you can buy fruit, clothes and shoes. The *artesanía* market is opposite, next to the bus lane.

Art
Galería de Arte Antigua, *4 Calle Ote 27 y 1 Av. Tue-Sat.* Large art gallery.

Bookshops
Numerous bookshops sell books in English and Spanish, postcards, posters, maps and guides, including **Footprint Handbooks**.
Casa del Conde, *5 Av Norte 4.* Has a full range of books from beautifully illustrated coffee-table books to guides and history books.
Hamlin and White, *4 Calle Ote 12A.* Books on Guatemala are cheaper here than at Casa del Conde.
Rainbow Cafe, *7 Av Sur 18.* Sells second-hand books.

Semana Santa

This week-long event in Antigua is a spectacular display of religious ritual and floral design. Through billowing clouds of incense, accompanied by music, processions of floats carried by purple-robed men make their way through the town. The cobbled stones are covered in *alfombras* (carpets) of coloured sawdust and flowers.

The day before the processions leave from each church, Holy Vigils (*velaciones*) are held, and the sculpture to be carried is placed before the altar (*retablo*), with a backdrop covering the altar. Floats (*andas*) are topped by colonial sculptures of the cross-carrying Christ. He wears velvet robes of deep blue or green, embroidered with gold and silver threads, and the float is carried on the shoulders by a team of 80 men (*cucuruchos*), who heave and sway their way through the streets for as long as 12 hours. The processions, arranged by a religious brotherhood (*cofradía*), are accompanied by banner and incense carriers, centurions, and a loud brass band.

The largest processions with some of the finest carpets are on Palm Sunday and Good Friday. Not to be missed are: the procession leaving from La Merced on Palm Sunday at 1200-1300; the procession leaving the church of San Francisco on Maundy Thursday; the 0200 sentencing of Jesus and 0600 processions from La Merced on Good Friday; the crucifixion of Christ in front of the cathedral at noon on Good Friday; and the beautiful, candlelit procession of the crucified Christ which passes the Parque Central between 2300 and midnight on Good Friday.

This is the biggest Easter attraction in Latin America so accommodation is booked far ahead. If you plan to be here and haven't reserved a room, arrive a few days before Palm Sunday. If unsuccessful, commuting from Guatemala City is an option. Don't rush; each procession lasts up to 12 hours. The whole week is a fantastic opportunity for photographs – and if you want a decent picture remember the Christ figure always faces right. Arm yourself with a map (available in kiosks in the Parque Central) and follow the processional route before the procession to see all the carpets while they are still intact. (There are also processions into Antigua from surrounding towns every Sunday in Lent.)

Un Poco de Todo, *near Casa del Conde on the plaza.*

Crafts, textiles, clothes and jewellery
Many other stores sell textiles, handicrafts, antiques, silver and jade on 5 Av Norte between 1 and 4 Calle Pte and 4 Calle Ote.
Casa Chicob, *Callejón de la Concepción 2, www.casachicob.com.* Beautiful textiles, candles and ceramics for sale.
Casa de Artes, *4 Av Sur 11, www. casadeartes.com.gt.* For traditional textiles and handicrafts, jewellery, etc, but very expensive.

Casa de los Gigantes, *7 Calle Ote 18.* For textiles and handicrafts.
Diva, *5 Av Norte 16.* For Western-style clothes and jewellery.
El Telar, *Loom Tree, 5 Av Sur 7.* All sorts of coloured tablecloths, napkins, cushion covers and bedspreads are sold here.
Guate Es, *4 Calle Ote 10, Edif El Jaulón, www.guate-es.com.* Guate Es has an interesting and attractive stock of clothing, shoes, jewellery and handbags which incorporate colourful Mayan textiles and designs. A new concept, fresh and innovative.

Huipil market, *held in the courtyard of La Fuente every Sat 0900-1400*. The display is very colourful and if the sun is out this is an excellent place for photos.

Mercado de Artesanías, *next to the main market at the end of 4 Calle Pte.*

Nativo's, *5 Av Norte, 25 "B", T7832-6556*. Sells some beautiful textiles from places like Aguacatán.

Nim P'ot, *5 Av Norte 29, T7832-2681, www.nimpot.com*. A mega-warehouse of traditional textiles and crafts brought from around the country. Excellent prices.

Textura, *5 Av Norte 33, T7832-5067*. Lots of bedroom accessories.

Food

Doña María Gordillo, *4 Calle Ote 11*. Famous throughout the country. It is impossible to get in the door most days but, if you can,

take a peek, to see the *dulces*, as well as the row upon row of yellow wooden owls keeping their beady eyes on the customers.

La Bodegona, *5 Calle Pte 32, opposite Posada La Quinta, on 5 Calle Pte and with another entrance on 4 Calle Pte*. Large supermarket.

Tienda de Doña Gavi, *3 Av Norte 2, behind the cathedral*. Sells all sorts of lovely potions and herbs, candles and home-made biscuits. Doña Gaviota also sells Guatemala City's most famous ice creams in all sorts of weird and wonderful flavours (see **Helados Marylena**, page 340).

What to do

Horse riding

Ravenscroft Riding Stables, *2 Av Sur 3, San Juan del Obispo, T7830-6669*. You can also hire horses in Santa María de Jesús.

Language schools

Footprint has received favourable reports from students for the following language schools:

Academia Antigüeña de Español, 1 Pte 10, T7832-7241, www.spanishacademyantiguena.com.

Alianza Lingüística 'Cano', Av El Desengaño 21A, T7832-0370. Private classes are also available.

Amerispan, 6 Av Norte 40 and 7 Calle Ote, T7832-0164, www.amerispan.com. In the US, 1334 Walnut St, 6th floor, Philadelphia PA 19107.

Centro Lingüístico Maya, 5 Calle Pte 20, T7832-1342, www.clmmaya.com.

CSA (Christian Spanish Academy), 6 Av Norte 15, Aptdo Postal 320, T7832-3922, www.learncsa.com.

Don Pedro de Alvarado, 6 Av Norte 39, T5872-2469, www.donpedrospanishschool.com. 25 years' experience.

Proyecto Bibliotecas Guatemala (PROBIGUA), 6 Av Norte 41B, T7832-2998, www.probigua.org. Gives a percentage of profits towards founding and maintaining public libraries in rural towns; frequently recommended.

Proyecto Lingüístico Francisco Marroquín, 6 Av Norte, www.plfm-antigua.org.

Sevilla Academia de Español, 1 Av Sur 8, T7832-5101, www.sevillantigua. com.

Tecún Umán, 6 Calle Pte 34A, T7832-2792, www.tecunuman.centramerica.com.

For private lessons check the ads in Doña Luisa's and others around town and the tourist office. Recommended teachers are: Julia Solís, 5 Calle Pte 36, T7832-5497, julisar@hotmail. com (she lives behind the tailor's shop); and Armalia Jarquín, Av El Desengaño 11 (there are, unbelievably, numerous No 11s on this road), T7832-2377. Armalia's has a sign up and is opposite No 75, which has a tiled plaque.

ON THE ROAD

Learning the lingo

Antigua is overrun with language students and so some say it is not the most ideal environment in which to learn Spanish. There are about 70-plus schools, open year round. At any one time there may be 300-600 overseas students in Antigua. Not all schools are officially authorized by INGUAT and the Ministry of Education. INGUAT has a list of authorized schools in its office. Rates depend on the number of hours of tuition per week, and vary from school to school. As a rough guide, the average fee for four hours a day, five days a week is US$120-200, at a reputable school, with homestay, though many are less and some schools offer cheaper classes in the afternoon. You will benefit more from the classes if you have done a bit of study of the basics before you arrive. There are guides who take students around the schools and charge a high commission (make sure this is not added to your account). They may approach tourists arriving on the bus from the capital.

All schools offer one-to-one tuition; if you can meet the teachers in advance, so much the better, but don't let the director's waffle distract you from asking pertinent questions. Paying more does not mean you get better teaching and the standard of teacher varies within schools as well as between schools. Beware of 'hidden extras' and be clear on arrangements for study books. Some schools have an inscription fee. Several schools use a portion of their income to fund social projects and some offer a programme of activities for students such as dance classes, Latin American film, tours, weaving and football. Before making any commitment, find somewhere to stay for a couple of nights and shop around at your leisure. Schools also offer accommodation with local families, but check the place out if possible before you pay a week in advance. Average accommodation rates with a family with three meals a day are US$75-100 per week. In some cases the schools organize group accommodation; if you prefer single, ask for it.

Spas

Antigua Spa Resort, *San Pedro El Panorama, lote 9 and 10 G, T7832-3960. Daily 0900-2100*. Swimming pool, steam baths, sauna, gym, jacuzzi and beauty salon. Reservations advised.
Mayan Spa, *Alameda Sta Lucía Norte 20, T7832-3537. Mon-Sat 0900-1800*. Massages and pampering packages, including sauna, steam baths and jacuzzi, are available.

Swimming

Porta Hotel Antigua, non-residents may use the pool for a charge.

Villas de Antigua, *Ciudad Vieja exit, T7832-0011-15*. For buffet lunch, swimming and marimba band.

Tour operators

Adrenalina Tours, *3a Calle Poniente, T7882 4147, www.adrenalinatours.com*. Xela's respected tour operator has opened up in Antigua too. As well as shuttles all around Guatemala, there are minibuses to San Cristóbal de las Casas, Mexico, US$55. Also customized packages, weekend trips to Xela and discounted Tikal trips. Recommended.
Adventure Travel Center Viareal, *5 Av Norte 25B, T7832-0162*. Daily trips to Guatemalan destinations (including Río Dulce sailing, river

and volcano trips), Monterrico, Quiriguá, El Salvador and Honduras.

Antigua Tours, *Casa Santo Domingo, 3 Calle Ote 22, T7832-5821, www.antiguatours.net*. Run by Elizabeth Bell, author of 4 books on Antigua. She offers walking tours of the city (US$20 per person), book in advance, Mon, Thu 1400-1700, Tue, Wed, Fri, Sat 0930-1230. During Lent and Holy Week there are extra tours, giving insight into the processions and carpet making. Highly recommended.

Aventuras Naturales, *Col El Naranjo No 53, Antigua, T5381-6615, http://aventuras naturales.tripod.com*. Specialized trips including guided birding tours.

Aventuras Vacacionales, *T5306-3584, www.sailing-diving-guatemala.com*. Highly recommended sailing trips on *Las Sirenas* owned by Captain John Clark and sailed by Captain Raúl Hernández (see also under Río Dulce, page 442).

CA Tours, *6 Calle Oriente Casa 14, T7832-9638, www.catours.co.uk*. British-run motorbike tour company. Recommended.

Eco-Tour Chejo's, *3 Calle Pte 24, T832-5464, ecotourchejos@hotmail.com*. Well-guarded walks up volcanoes. Interesting tours also available to coffee fincas, flower plantations, etc, shuttle service, horse riding, very helpful.

Gran Jaguar, *4 Calle Pte 30, T7832-2712, www.guacalling.com/jaguar/*. Well-organized fun volcano tours with official security. Also shuttles and trips to Tikal and Río Dulce. Very highly recommended for the Pacaya trip.

Guatemala Reservations, *3 Av Norte 3, T7832-3293, www.guatemalareservations. com. Closed Sun*. A wide range of tours and transport services. Frequently recommended. Also has guidebooks for reference or to buy, along with a water bottle-filling service to encourage recycling. Cheap phone call service. Shuttles and tours.

Old Town Outfitters, *5 Av Sur 12 "C", T7832-4171, www.adventureguatemala.com*. Action adventure specialists, with mountain bike tours (½-day tour, US$39), kayak tours hiking and climbing, outdoor equipment on sale, maps, very helpful.

Outdoor Excursions, *1 Av Sur 4b, T7832-0074, www.guatemalavolcano.com*. Professional, knowledgeable and fun volcano tour company with private security. Overnight tours to Fuego (US$79), Acatenango (US$79) and Pacaya (US$59).

Rainbow Travel Center, *7 Av Sur 8, T7931-7878, www.rainbowtravelcenter.com*. Full local travel service, specialists in student flights and bargain international flights, they will attempt to match any quote. It also sells ISIC, Go25 and teachers' cards. English, French, German and Japanese spoken.

Sin Fronteras, *5a Av Norte 15 "A", T7720-4400, www.sinfront.com*. Local tours, shuttles, horse riding, bicycle tours, canopy tours, national and international air tickets including discounts with ISIC and Go25 cards. Also sells travel insurance. Agents for rafting experts **Maya Expeditions**. Reliable and highly recommended.

Tivoli Travel, *4 Calle Ote 10, T7832-4274, antigua@tivoli.com.gt. Closed Sun*. Helpful with any travel problem, English, French, Spanish, German, Italian spoken, reconfirm tickets, shuttles, hotel bookings, good-value tours. Useful for organizing independent travel as well as tours.

ViaVenture, *2 Calle Ote 2, T7832-2509, www.viaventure.com*. Professional tour operator offering special interest and tailor-made tours.

Transport

Bus

To **Guatemala City**: buses leave when full between 0530 and 1830, US$1, 1-1½ hrs, depending on the time of day, from the Alameda Santa Lucía near the market, from an exit next to **Pollo Campero** (not from behind the market). All other buses leave from behind the market. To **Chimaltenango**, on the Pan-American Hwy, from 0600-1600, every 15 mins, US$0.65, for connections to **Los Encuentros** (for Lake Atitlán and **Chichicastenango**), **Cuatro Caminos** (for **Quetzaltenango**) and **Huehuetenango** (for the Mexican border). It is possible to get to Chichicastenango and back by bus in a day, especially on Thu and Sun, for the market. Get the bus to Chimaltenango and then change. It's best to leave early. See Chimaltenango for connections. The only direct bus to **Panajachel** is Rebuli, leaving at 0700, from 4 Calle Pte, in front of **La Bodegona** supermarket, US$5, 2½ hrs, returning 1100. Other buses to **Pana** via Chimaltenango with **Rebuli** and **Carrillo y Gonzalez**, 0600-1645, US$2.50. To **Escuintla**, 0530-1600, 1 hr, US$1.25.

To **Ciudad Vieja**, US$0.30, every 30 mins, 20 mins. **San Miguel de las Dueñas**. Take a bus marked 'Dueñas', every 30 mins, 20 mins, US$0.30. To **San Antonio Aguas Calientes**, every 30 mins, 30 mins, US$0.30. To **Santa María de Jesús** every 30 mins, 45 mins, US$0.50.

International To **Copán** and other cities in Honduras, including **Tegucigalpa**, with **Hedman Alas**, www.hedmanalas.com, from Posada de Don Rodrigo to its terminal in Guatemala City for a connection to Copán. Leaves at 0330 and 0630 from Antigua, US$41, US$77 return and 0500 and 0900 from Guatemala City, US$35, US$65 return. Return times are 1330 and 1800 to Guatemala City; the earlier bus continues to Antigua. See also box, page 517.

Shuttles Hotels and travel agents run frequent shuttle services to and from **Guatemala City** and the **airport** (1 hr) from 0400 to about 2000 daily, US$10-15 depending on the time of day: details from any agency in town. There are also shuttles to **Chichicastenango**, US$5-18, **Panajachel**, US$5-12, **Quetzaltenango**, US$16, **Monterrico**, US$15, **Flores**, US$20-40, **Copán**, US$8-25 and other destinations, but check for prices and days of travel. **Plus Travel** (www.plustravelguate.com) has some of the best prices and range of destinations, with offices in Antigua (6a Calle Pte No 19, T7832-3147) and Copán Ruinas. Recommended.

Around Antigua

former colonial capital, village fiestas and coffee farm

Ciudad Vieja – the former capital – is 5.5 km southwest of Antigua at the foot of Volcán Agua. Today Ciudad Vieja is itself a suburb of Antigua, but with a handsome church, founded in 1534, and one of the oldest in Central America. There's a fiesta on December 8.

In 1527, Pedro de Alvarado moved his capital, known then as Santiago de Los Caballeros, from Iximché to San Miguel Escobar, now a suburb of Ciudad Vieja. On 11 September 1541, after days of torrential rain, an immense mudslide came down the mountain and swallowed up the city. Alvarado's widow, Doña Beatriz de la Cueva, newly elected governor after his death, was among those drowned.

Between Ciudad Vieja and San Miguel de las Dueñas is the **Valhalla macadamia nut farm** ⓘ *T7831-5799, www.exvalhalla.net, free visits and nut tasting, 0800-1700.*

About 3 km northwest of Ciudad Vieja is **San Antonio Aguas Calientes**. The hot springs unfortunately disappeared with recent earthquakes, but the village has many small shops selling locally made textiles. **Carolina's Textiles** is recommended for a fine selection, while on the exit road **Alida** has a shop. You can watch the weavers in their homes by the roadside. Local fiestas are 16-21 January, Corpus Christi (a moveable feast celebtrated around June) and 1 November.

Beyond San Juan del Obispo, beside Volcán Agua, is the charming village of **Santa María de Jesús**, with its beautiful view of Antigua. In the early morning there are good views of all three volcanoes from 2 km back down the road towards Antigua. Colourful *huipiles* are worn, made and sold from a couple of stalls, or ask at the shops on the plaza. The local fiesta is on 10 January.

Just north of Antigua is **Jocotenango**. The music museum, **Casa K'ojom** ⓘ *Mon-Fri 0830-1630, Sat 0830-1600, US$4*, is in the **Central Cultural La Azotea**, with displays of traditional Maya and colonial-era instruments. The village also has public saunas at the **Fraternidad Naturista Antigua**.

Five kilometres beyond San Lucas Sacatepéquez, at Km 29.5, Carretera Roosevelt (the Pan-American Highway), is **Santiago Sacatepéquez**, whose fiesta on 1 November, *Día de los Muertos* (All Souls' Day), is characterized by colourful kite-flying (*barriletes*). They also celebrate 25 July. Market days are Wednesday and Friday.

Visiting a **coffee farm** is an interesting short excursion. **Tour Finca Los Nietos** ⓘ *on the outskirts of Antigua, near the Iglesia San Felipe de Jesús, T7728-0812, www.filadelfiaresort. com*, runs two-hour tours (US$18) three times a day. They are very informative and interesting with expert multilingual guides, in beautiful manicured grounds and restored colonial buildings; also with restaurant and shop.

North of Guatemala City is **Mixco Viejo**, the excavated site of a post-Classic Maya fortress, which spans 14 hilltops, including 12 groups of pyramids. Despite earthquake damage it is worth a visit and is recommended. It was the 16th-century capital of the Pokomam Maya. There are a few buses a day between Mixco Viejo and the Zona 4 terminal, Guatemala City. The bus goes to Pachalum; ask to be dropped at ruins entrance.

Volcanoes

active volcanoes, lava fields and spectacular views

Each of the four volcanoes that are immediately accessible from Antigua provides a unique set of challenges and rewards. Agua, Fuego and Acatenango volcanoes directly overlook Antigua whilst Volcan Pacaya is about an hour's drive away. All of these volcanoes can be experienced either as part of a day trip (a cheaper and faster option that requires only lightweight packs) or with an overnight excursion (heavier packs making climbing times longer, but with better light conditions for lava viewing and enhancing already spectacular views with beautiful sunset and sunrises).

Whatever option you choose, it is important to prepare properly for the unique features of each volcano (Pacaya is a relatively quick climb in a secure national park, while the three volcanoes on Antigua's perimeter are longer climbs with much greater risk of robberies and attacks). At a minimum, ensure that you have appropriate clothing and footwear (as summits are cold and volcanic ash is sharp bring fleeces and ideally use climbing boots), enough water (very important) and snacks for the trip and make informed decisions about safety. Although you can climb each of these volcanoes independently, you will significantly decrease your risks of getting lost, attacked or not finding shelter by using a professional guiding service; **Outdoor Excursions** (see Tour operators, page 360), which runs trips with expert guides and armed security, is particularly recommended. Remember that altitude takes its toll and for the longer hikes it is important to start early in the morning to allow enough time to ascend and descend in daylight. As a general rule, descents take from a third to a half of the ascent time.

Volcán Pacaya

Tours are available for US$6 upwards and are sold by most tour companies in Antigua. The popular and best time for organized trips is to leave Antigua at 1300 and return at 2100. Departures also 0600 returning 1300. There is also a US$3.50 fee to be paid at the entrance to the Volcán Pacaya National Park in San Francisco de Sales (toilets available).

At 2552 m, the still-active Volcán Pacaya can't be missed and is the most exciting volcano to climb. Pacaya has erupted about 20 times since 1565, but since the mid-1960s it has been continuously active, meaning it can reward climbers with some spectacular lava flows. The cone – now split in two since the most recent eruption, in 2010 – is covered in black basaltic rock, shed from the crater. The rocks get warm and are lethally sharp. One of the results of the eruption is that shallow tunnels have formed, creating natural open-air saunas. They offer quite a spectacular experience, though for obvious safety reasons you should only enter these at the advice of an experience guide.Take a torch/flashlight refreshments and water and – it may sound obvious – wear boots or trainers, not sandals. Walking sticks are also offered at the park entrance – don't be too proud, on the steeper slopes, the crumbly lava screes can be very tricky to climb up or down. If you bring marshmallows to toast on the lava, make sure you have a long stick – lava is (rather unsurprisingly) very hot! Security officers go with the trips and police escorts ensure everyone leaves the area after dark. Check the situation in advance for **camping** (well below the crater lip). Sunrise comes with awesome views over the desolate black lava field to the distant Pacific (airborne dust permitting) and the peaks of Fuego, Acatenango and Agua. And as the sun sets on the horizon, Agua is silhouetted in the distance, a weak orange line streaked behind it.

Volcán Agua

Most organized tours with Antigua tour operators are during the day; you should enure that costs include both a guide and security. Trips normally leave Antigua about 0500.

At 3760 m, Agua is the easiest but least scenic of the three volcanoes overlooking Antiqua. The trail, which can be quite littered, begins at **Santa María de Jesús**. Speak to Aurelio Cuy Chávez at the **Posada El Oasis**, who offers a guide service or take a tour with a reputable agency. You have to register first at the Municipalidad; guides are also available in the main square, about US$50 a day per guide. For Agua's history, see Ciudad Vieja above. The crater has a small shelter (none too clean), which was a shrine, and about 10 antennae. There are great views of Volcán Fuego. It's a three- to five-hour climb if you are fit, and at least two hours down. To get the best views before the clouds cover the summit, it is best to stay at the radio station at the top. Agua can also be climbed from **Alotenango**, a village between Agua and Fuego, south of Ciudad Vieja. It's 9 km from Antigua and its name means 'place surrounded by corn'. Alotenango has a fiesta from 18-20 January.

Volcán Acatenango

If you do this climb independently of a tour agency, ask for a guide in La Soledad. However, it is strongly recommended that you use a professional guiding service, ideally with security.

Acatenango is classified as a dormant volcano and is the third tallest in the country (3975 m) with two peaks to its name. Its first recorded eruption was in 1924. Two other eruptions were reported in 1924-1927 and 1972. The best trail heads south at **La Soledad**, 2300 m (15 km west of Ciudad Vieja), which is 300 m before the road (Route 5) turns right to Acatenango (see Where to stay, below). A small plateau, La Meseta on maps, known locally as **El Conejón**, provides a good camping site half way up (three or four hours). From here it is a further three or four hours' harder going to the top. The views of the nearby (lower) active crater of Fuego are excellent.

Volcán Fuego
This is an active volcano with trails that are easy to lose; it is recommended that you use a guiding service and do not venture up to the crater.

This volcano (3763 m) can be climbed via Volcán Acatenango, sleeping between the two volcanoes, then climbing for a further two to three hours before stopping a safe distance from the crater. This one is for experienced hikers only. Do not underestimate the amount of water needed for the climb. It is a seven-hour ascent with a significant elevation gain; it's a very hard walk, both up and down. There are steep, loose cinder slopes, which are very tedious, in many places. It is possible to camp about three-quarters of the way up in a clearing. Fuego has regular eruptions that shoot massive boulders from its crater, often without warning. Check in Antigua before attempting to climb. If driving down towards the south coast you can see the red volcanic rock it has thrown up.

Listings Volcanoes

Where to stay

$ Pensión
Volcán Acatenango.
Basic, with good cheap meals.

Transport

Volcán Agua
Bus
From Antigua to **Alotenango** from 0700-1800, 40 mins.

Volcán Acatenango
Bus
To reach **La Soledad**, take a bus heading for Yepocapa or Acatenango village and get off at La Soledad.

Car
Tabarini, 6 Av Sur 22, T7832-8107, also at the **Hotel Radisson Villa Antigua**, T7832-7460, www.tabarini.com.

Horse-drawn carriage
Available at weekends and during fiestas around the plaza.

Motorcycle hire
La Ceiba, 6 Calle Pte 15, T7832-0077.

Taxi
Servicio de Taxi 'Antigua', Manuel Enrique Gómez, T5417-2180, has been recommended.

Tuk-tuk
Motorbike taxis with a seat for 2 will whizz you around town for US$1.50.

Lake Atitlán
& around

★In the Central Highlands volcano landscapes are dotted with colourful markets and the Maya wearing traditional clothes in the towns and villages. Aldous Huxley called Lake Atitlán "the most beautiful lake in the world" and attractive villages flank its shores. Further north you can explore the streets of Chichicastenango as the town fills with hawkers and vendors at the weekly markets serving tourists and locals alike. North of Chichicastenango, the Quiché and Ixil Triangle regions have small and very traditional hamlets set in beautiful countryside and are easily explored by bus.

Towards Lake Atitlán → Colour map 6, B3.

beautiful scenery stretching west of the capital

The Pan-American Highway heads west out of the capital passing through Chimaltenango and on to Los Encuentros where it turns north for Chichicastenango, Santa Cruz del Quiché, Nebaj and the Ixil Triangle, and south for Sololá and the Lake Atitlán region. It continues to the western highland region of Quetzaltenango, Totonicapán, Huehuetenango and the Cuchumatanes Mountains.

Chimaltenango and around

Chimaltenango is busy with traffic. Here, another road runs south for 20 km to Antigua. This tree-lined road leads to Parramos where it turns sharp left. Straight on through the village, in 1.5 km, is a well known inn and restaurant, **La Posada de Mi Abuelo** (see Where to stay, below). This road continues through mountains to Pastores, Jocotenango and finally to Antigua. Some 6 km south of Chimaltenango, **San Andrés Itzapa** is well worth a visit; there is a very interesting **chapel to Maximón** ① *open till 1800 daily.* Shops by the chapel sell prayer pamphlets and pre-packaged offerings. Beyond Chimaltenango is **Zaragoza**, a former Spanish penal settlement, and beyond that a road leads 13 km north to the interesting village of **Comalapa**. This is the best place to see *naíf* painting and there are plenty of galleries. The **tourist information office** ① *Av 3-76, T5766-3874,* is in the house of Andrés Curuchich, a popular artist. There's a colourful market on Monday and Tuesday.

Routes west: La Mesilla, Tecpán and Los Encuentros

Returning to the Pan-American Highway the road divides 6 km past Zaragoza. The southern branch, the old Pan-American Highway, goes through Patzicía and Patzún (see below) to Lake Atitlán, then north to Los Encuentros. The northern branch, the new Pan-American Highway, which is used by all public transport, goes past Tecpán (see below) and then to Los Encuentros. From Los Encuentros there is only the one road west to San Cristóbal Totonicapán, where it swings northwest to La Mesilla/Ciudad Cuauhtémoc, at the Mexican border; see box, page 512.

From Zaragoza the Pan-American Highway runs 19 km to near **Tecpán**, which is slightly off the road at 2287 m. It has a particularly fine church with silver altars, carved wooden pillars, odd images and a wonderful ceiling that was severely damaged by the 1976 earthquake. There is accommodation, restaurants and banks. Near Tecpán are the important Maya ruins of **Iximché** ⓘ *5 km of paved road south of Tecpán, 0800-1700, US$3.25*, once capital and court of the Cakchiqueles. The first capital of Guatemala after its conquest was founded near Iximché; followed in turn by Ciudad Vieja, Antigua and

Lake Atitlán

To Quetzaltenango & Mexico

To El Cuchillo, Los Encuentros & Chichicastenango

To Las Trampas, Guatemala City & Zaragoza

To El Cuchillo, Los Encuentros (Pan-American Highway) & Chichicastenango

Km 149

Río Panajachel

San José Chacayá

Sololá

Santa Lucía Utatlán

San Jorge La Laguna

Cerro San Marcos (2918m)

María Linda

Río Quixtab

San Andrés Semetabaj

Tzanjucup

Chaquichoy

Santa Cruz La Laguna

Las Canoas

San Marcos La Laguna

Jaibalito

Tzununá

Panajachel

Santa María Visitación

Lake Atitlán (1558m)

Santa Catarina Palopó

Santa Clara La Laguna

San Pablo La Laguna

Cerro Cristalino (2251m)

Godínez

San Juan La Laguna

San Pedro La Laguna

San Antonio Palopó

To Patzún

Tzampetey

Finca Tzantziapa

Cerro de Oro (1892m)

Volcán San Pedro (3020m)

Cerro Chuitinamit

Cerro de Oro

Agua Escondida

Cerro Chuichumil

Pachitulúl

Panaranjo

Cerro Paquixtán (2455m)

Cerro Paquisís (2831m)

Santiago Atitlán

San Lucas Tolimán

San Gabriel

N

2 km

2 miles

To Chicacao

Volcán Tolimán (3158m)

Volcán Atitlán (3535m)

To Cocales & Pacific Highway

Guatemala City. The ruins are well presented with three plazas, a palace and two ball courts on a promontory surrounded on three sides by steep slopes.

The old and new Pan-American highways rejoin 11 km from Sololá at the **El Cuchillo** junction. About 2 km east is **Los Encuentros**, the junction of the Pan-American Highway and the paved road 18 km northeast to Chichicastenango.

To Lake Atitlán along the old Pan-American Highway

With amazing views of Lake Atitlán and the surrounding volcanoes, travellers of the southern road from Zaragoza to Lake Atitlán encounter a much more difficult route than the northern option, with several steep hills and many hairpin bends. Nevertheless, if you have both the time and a sturdy vehicle, it is an extremely rewarding trip. Note that there is no police presence whatsoever along the old Pan-American Highway.

The route goes through **Patzicía**, a small Maya village founded in 1545 (no accommodation). Market days are Wednesday and Saturday and the local fiesta is 22-27 July. The famous church, which had a fine altar and beautiful silver, was destroyed by the 1976 earthquake. Beyond is the small town of **Patzún**; its church, dating from 1570, is severely damaged and is not open to the public. There is a Sunday market, which is famous for the silk (and wool) embroidered napkins and for woven *fajas* and striped red cotton cloth; other markets are on Tuesday and Friday and the town fiesta is 17-21 May. For accommodation, ask at the *tiendas*.

The road leaves Patzún and goes south to Xepatán and on to **Godínez**, the highest community overlooking the lake. From Godínez, a good paved road turns off south to the village of San Lucas Tolimán and continues to Santiago Atitlán.

The main (steep, paved) road continues straight on for Panajachel. The high plateau, with vast wheat and maize fields, now breaks off suddenly as though pared by a knife. From a viewpoint here, there is an incomparable view of Lake Atitlán, 600 m below. The very picturesque village of **San Antonio Palopó** is right underneath you, on slopes leading to the water. It is about 12 km from the viewpoint to Panajachel. For the first 6 km you are close to the rim of the old crater and, at the point where the road plunges down to the lakeside, is **San Andrés Semetabaj** which has a beautiful ruined early 17th-century church. Market day is Tuesday. Buses go to Panajachel.

Sololá

On the road down to Panajachel is Sololá (altitude 2113 m), which has superb views across Lake Atitlán. Outside the world of the tourist, this is the most important town in the area. A fine, modern, white church, with bright stained-glass windows and an attractive clocktower dominates the west side of the plaza. Sololá is even more special for the bustling market that brings the town to life every Tuesday and Friday, when the Maya gather from surrounding commuities to buy and sell local produce. Women and particularly men wear traditional dress. While it is primarily a produce market, there is also a good selection of used *huipiles*. Even if you're not in the market to buy, it is a colourful sight. Markets are mornings only; Friday market gets underway on Thursday. There's a fiesta 11-17 August.

From Sololá the old Pan-American Highway weaves and twists through a 550-m drop in the 8 km to Panajachel. The views are impressive at all times of day, but particularly in the morning. Time allowing, it is quite easy to walk down direct by the road (two hours); you also miss the unnerving bus ride down (US$0.40).

Where to stay

Chimaltenango and around

$$ La Posada de Mi Abuelo
Carretera a Yepocapa, Parramos, T7849-5930,
see Facebook.
A delightful inn, formerly a coffee farm,
with a good restaurant. Packages with
horse riding, biking and meals are available.

$ Pixcayá
0 Av, 1-82, Comalapa, T7849-8260.
Hot water, parking.

Sololá

$ Del Viajero
7 Av, 10-45, on Parque Central (also annexe
around the corner on Calle 11), T7762-3683.
Rooms with bath, cheaper without, spacious,
clean and friendly, good food in restaurant
on the plaza (**El Cafetín**).

$ El Paisaje
9 Calle, 5-41, 2 blocks from Parque Central,
T7762-3820.
Pleasant colonial courtyard, shared baths
and toilets, clean, hot water, restaurant, good
breakfast, family-run, laundry facilities.

Transport

Chimaltenango and around
Bus
Any bus heading west from Guatemala City
stops at Chimaltenango. To **Antigua** buses

leave from the corner of the main road and
the road south to Antigua where there is a
lime green and blue shop, Auto Repuestos
y Frenos Nachma, 45 mins, US$0.34. To
Chichicastenango, every 30 mins, 0600-
1700, 2 hrs, US$2. To **Cuatro Caminos**,
2½ hrs, US$2.50. To **Quetzaltenango**, every
45 mins, 0700-1800, 2½ hrs, US$2.80. To
Tecpán every 30 mins, 0700-1800, 1 hr.

Routes west: La Mesilla, Tecpán and Los Encuentros
Bus
From Tecpán to **Guatemala City**, 2¼ hrs,
buses every hour, US$2.20; easy day trip from
Panajachel or **Antigua**.

To Lake Atitlán along the old Pan-American Highway
Bus
To and from **Godínez** there are several
buses to Panajachel, US$0.45 and 1 bus
daily Patzún–Godínez. To **San Andrés**
Semetabaj, bus to Panajachel, US$0.40.

Sololá
Bus
To **Chichicastenango**, US$0.50, 1½ hrs; to
Panajachel, US$0.38, every 30 mins, 20 mins,
or 1½-2 hrs' walk. To **Chimaltenango**,
US$1.20. To **Quetzaltenango**, US$1.8.
Colectivo to **Los Encuentros**, US$0.20.
To **Guatemala City** direct US$2.50, 3 hrs.

The old town of Panajachel is pretty and quiet but the newer development, strung
along a main road, is a tucker and trinket emporium. It's busy and stacked cheek by jowl
with hundreds of stalls and shops along the principal street. Some of the best bargains
are here and textiles and crafts from across the country can be found. Panajachel is a
gringo magnet, and if you want to fill up on international cuisine and drink then it's a
good place to stay for a few days. There are also stunning views from the lakeshore.

The town centre is the junction of Calle Principal and Calle (or Avenida) Santander. The main bus stop is here, stretching south back down Calle Real, and it marks the junction between the old and the modern towns. It takes about 10 minutes to walk from the junction to the lakeshore. Calle Rancho Grande is sometimes called Calle del Balneario and

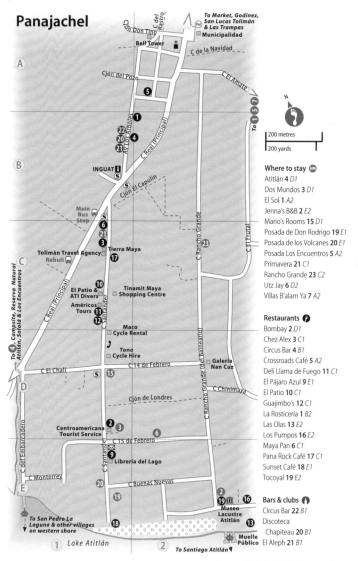

Panajachel

Where to stay 🛏
Atitlán **4** *D1*
Dos Mundos **3** *D1*
El Sol **1** *A2*
Jenna's B&B **2** *E2*
Mario's Rooms **15** *D1*
Posada de Don Rodrigo **19** *E1*
Posada de los Volcanes **20** *E1*
Posada Los Encuentros **5** *A2*
Primavera **21** *C1*
Rancho Grande **23** *C2*
Utz Jay **6** *D2*
Villas B'alam Ya **7** *A2*

Restaurants 🍴
Bombay **2** *D1*
Chez Alex **3** *C1*
Circus Bar **4** *B1*
Crossroads Café **5** *A2*
Deli Llama de Fuego **11** *C1*
El Pájaro Azul **9** *E1*
El Patio **10** *C1*
Guajimbo's **12** *C1*
La Rosticería **1** *B2*
Las Olas **13** *E2*
Los Pumpos **16** *E2*
Maya Pan **6** *C1*
Pana Rock Café **17** *C1*
Sunset Café **18** *E1*
Tocoyal **19** *E2*

Bars & clubs 🍸
Circus Bar **22** *B1*
Discoteca
  Chapiteau **20** *B1*
El Aleph **21** *B1*

BACKGROUND

Panajachel

The original settlement of Panajachel was tucked up against the steep cliffs to the north of the present town, about 1 km from the lake. Virtually all traces of the original Kaqchikel village have disappeared, but the early Spanish impact is evident with the narrow streets, public buildings, plaza and church. The original Franciscan church was founded in 1567 and used as the base for the Christianization of the lake area. Later, the fertile area of the river delta was used for coffee production, orchards and many other crops, some of which are still grown today and can be seen round the back of the tourist streets or incorporated into the gardens of the hotels.

Tourism began here in the early 20th century with several hotels on the waterfront, notably the Tzanjuyú and the Monterrey, the latter originally a wooden building dating from about 1910, rebuilt in 1975. In the 1970s came an influx of young travellers, quite a few of whom stayed on to enjoy the climate and the easy life. Drugs and the hippy element eventually gave Panajachel a bad name, but rising prices and other pressures have encouraged this group to move on, some to San Pedro across the lake. Others joined the commercial scene and still run services today.

other streets have variants. The **tourist information office**, INGUAT ① *Calle Real Principal and Av Los Arboles, T7762-1106, daily 0900-1300 and 1400-1700*, is helpful with information about buses and boats and offer good local knowledge. Also see www.atitlan.com.

Safety There have been reports from travellers who have suffered robbery walking around the lake between San Juan and San Pablo and between San Marcos and Tzununá. Seek local advice from INGUAT, other travellers and local hotels/hostels before planning a trip.

Sights

The old town is 1 km from the lake and dominated by the **church**, originally built in 1567, but now restored. It has a fine decorated wooden roof and a mixture of Catholic statues and Maya paintings in the nave. A block up the hill is the daily market, worth a visit on Sunday mornings especially for embroideries. The local fiesta runs from 1-7 October; the main days are at the weekend and on 4 October.

In contrast, the modern town, almost entirely devoted to tourism, spreads out towards the lake. Calle Santander is the principal street, leading directly to the short but attractive **promenade** and boat docks. The section between Calle Santander and Calle Rancho Grande has been turned into a park, which delightfully frames the traditional view across the lake to the volcanoes. Near the promenade, at the **Hotel Posada de Don Rodrigo**, is the **Museo Lacustre Atitlán** ① *daily 0900-1200, 1400-1800, US$4.40*, created by Roberto Samayoa, a prominent local diver and archaeologist, to house some of the many items found in the lake. The geological history is explained and there is a fine display of Maya classical pottery and ceremonial artefacts classified by period. A submerged village has been found at a depth of 20 m, which is being investigated. It has been named **Samabaj** in honour of Don Roberto. For those interested in local art, visit **La Galería** (near Rancho

Grande Hotel), where Nan Cuz, an indigenous painter, sells her pictures evoking the spirit of village life. She has been painting since 1958 and has achieved international recognition.

On the road past the entrance to Hotel Atitlán is the **Reserva Natural Atitlán** ① *T7762-2565, www.atitlanreserva.com, daily 0800-1800, US$8.30 entrance, US$29-45 zip-line (including entrance)*, a reserve with a bird refuge, butterfly collection, monkeys and native mammals in natural surroundings, with a picnic area, herb garden, waterfall, visitor centre, café, zip-lines and access to the lakeside beach. Camping and lodging are available ($).

Listings Panajachel *map p369*

Where to stay

$$$$ Villas B'alam Ya
Outside Panajachel, Carretera a Catarina Palopó Km 2, T7762-2522, www.panzaverde.com.
The sister property of the swish Meson Panza Verde in Antigua, **Villas B'alam Ya** includes 4 luxury villas on the hillside and lakeshore, all tastefully attired and equipped with all mod cons. Guests can enjoy plentiful services and facilities including kayaks, gourmet room service, tours and yoga classes. Very peaceful, secluded and romantic.

$$$ Atitlán
1 km west of centre on lake, 2nd turning off the road to Sololá, T7762-1441, www.hotelatitlan.com.
Full board available, colonial style, excellent rooms and service, beautiful gardens with views across lake, pool, private beach and top-class restaurant.

$$$ Posada de Don Rodrigo
Final Calle Santander, overlooks the lake, T7762-2326, www.posadadedonrodrigo.com.
Pool, sauna, terrace, gardens, good restaurant, excellent food and service, comfortable and luxurious bathrooms, and fireplaces.

$$$ Rancho Grande
Calle Rancho Grande, Centro, T7762-1554, www.ranchogrande inn.com.
Cottages in charming setting, 4 blocks from beach, popular for long stay, good, including breakfast with pancakes. Pool

with café in spacious gardens which have good children's play equipment. Staff are helpful. Recommended.

$$$-$$ Jenna's B&B
Casa Loma, Calle Rancho Grande, T5458-1984, www.jennasriverbedandbreakfast.com.
This quirky B&B has 7 cosy guest rooms decorated with local antiques, Guatemalan art and textiles. There is also a basement apartment available by the week or month and, for those seeking something different, a yurt (**$$$**). Amenities include garden, TV, Wi-Fi, living room and full bar. Breakfast included, additional meals on request.

$$ Dos Mundos
Calle Santander 4-72, Centro, T7762-2078, www.hoteldosmundos.com.
Pool, cable TV, some rooms surround pool, good Italian restaurant (**La Lanterna**). Breakfast included.

$$ Posada de los Volcanes
Calle Santander, 5-51, Centro, T7762-0244, www.posadadelosvolcanes.com.
12 rooms with bath, hot water, clean, comfortable, quiet, friendly owners, Julio and Jeanette Parajón.

$$ Posada Los Encuentros
Barrio Jucany, a 15-min walk from town, T7762-1603, www.losencuentros.com.
Off-the-beaten track in Panajachel, **Los Encuentros** boasts a lovely medicinal herb garden, wood-fuelled sauna, thermally heated mineral pool, and a well-equipped fitness centre. They have links to local

healers and offer Mayan cultural tours. Accommodation includes 7 pleasant rooms.

$$ Primavera
Calle Santander, Centro, T7762-2052, www.primaveratitlan.com.
Clean, bright rooms, with TV, cypress wood furniture, gorgeous showers, washing machine available, friendly. Recommended. **Chez Alex** next door serves French food in a lovely patio setting at the back. Don't get a room overlooking the street at weekends.

$$ Utz Jay
5 Calle, 2-50, Zona 2, T7762-0217, www.hotelutzjay.com.
This small hotel has 13 rooms overlooking a lush tropical garden replete with leafy foliage and birds. Rooms are clean and tranquil, equipped with hot water and decorated with Mayan textiles. Services available at extra cost include breakfast, laundry, sauna, jacuzzi and packed lunch.

$ Hotel El Sol
Barrio Jucanya, a 15-min walk from town, T7762-6090, www.hotelelsolpanajachel.com.
Hotel El Sol is a Japanese-owned hostel, which is quiet, good value, economical and suitable for backpackers or families. Lodgings include immaculately clean private rooms and an 8-bed dorm. There is a small garden outside and a sun terrace with views of the hills. Inside there is a restaurant and lounges for watching DVDs. Pleasant and restful.

$ Mario's Rooms
Calle Santander esq Calle 14 de Febrero, Centro, T7762-1313.
Cheaper without bath, with garden, clean, bright rooms, hot showers, good breakfast, but not included, popular and friendly.

Apartments
Ask around for houses to rent; available from US$125 a month for a basic place, to US$200, but almost impossible to find in Nov and Dec. Break-ins and robberies of tourist houses are not uncommon. Water supply is variable. **Apartamentos Bohemia**, Callejón Chinimaya, rents furnished bungalows.

Camping
Possible in the grounds of **Hotel Visión Azul** and **Tzanjuyú**.

Restaurants

$$$ Chez Alex
Calle Santander, centre, T7762-0172.
Open 1200-1500 and 1800-2000.
French menu, good quality, mainly tourists, credit cards accepted.

$$$ Tocoyal
Annexe to Hotel del Lago.
A/c, groups welcome, buffet on request but tourist prices.

$$ Circus Bar
Av Los Arboles 0-62, T7762-2056.
Open 1200-2400.
Italian dishes including delicious pasta and pizzas, good coffee, popular. Live music from 2030, excellent atmosphere. Recommended.

$$ Crossroads Café
Calle de Campanario 0-27. Tue-Sat 0900-1300 and 1500-1900.
Global choice of quality coffee, but you can't go wrong with Guatemalan! Excellent cakes.

$$ El Patio
Calle Santander.
Good food, very good large breakfasts, quiet atmosphere but perfect for people-watching from the garden. Try the amaretto coffee.

$$ Guajimbo's
Calle Santander.
Good atmosphere, excellent steaks, fast service, popular, live music some evenings. Recommended.

$$ La Rostería
Av Los Arboles 0-42, T7762-2063.
Daily 0700-2300.
Good food, try eggs 'McChisme' for breakfast, good fresh pasta, excellent banana cake, good atmosphere, popular,

a bit pricey. Live piano music at weekends, friendly service.

$$ Los Pumpos
Calle del Lago.
Varied menu, bar, good fish and seafood dishes.

$$ Pana Rock Café
With Pana Arte upstairs, Calle Santander 3-72.
Buzzing around happy hour (2 for 1), salsa music, very popular, international food, pizza.

$$ Sunset Café
Superb location on the lake. Open 1100-2400.
Excellent for drinks, light meals and main dishes, live music evenings, but you pay for the view.

$$-$ Bombay
Calle Santander near Calle 15 Febrero, T7762-0611. Open 1100-2130.
Vegetarian recipes, including spicy curries, German beer, Mexican food, good food and wines, set lunch popular, good service. Very highly recommended.

$$-$ El Pájaro Azul
Calle Santander 2-75, T7762-2596. Open 1000-2200.
Café, bar, crêperie with gorgeous stuffed sweet or savoury crêpes, cakes and pies. Vegetarian options available. Reasonable prices, good for late breakfasts. Recommended.

$ Deli Llama de Fuego
Calle Santander, T7762-2586. Thu-Tue 0700-2200.
Sweet little café with a giant cheese plant as its focus. Breakfasts, muffins, bagels, pizzas, pasta, Mexican food and vegetarian sandwiches.

$ Restaurante Las Olas
Overlooking the lake at the end of Calle Santander, down by the dock.
Serves the absolute best nachos, great for just before catching the boat.

Bakeries

Maya Pan
Calle Santander 1-61.
Excellent wholemeal breads and pastries, banana bread comes out of the oven at 0930, wonderful, cinnamon rolls and internet too. Recommended.

Bars and clubs

Circus Bar
Av los Arboles. Daily 1200-0200.
Good live music from 2030.

Discoteca Chapiteau
Av los Arboles 0-69.
Nightclub Thu-Sat 1900-0100.

El Aleph
Av los Arboles. Thu-Sat 1900-0300.
One of a number of bars.

Shopping

Bartering is the norm. There are better bargains here than in Chichicastenango. The main tourist shops are on Calle Santander.

Librería del Lago, *Calle Santander Local A-8, T7762-2788. Daily 0900-1800.* Great bookshop selling a good range of quality English-language and Spanish books.
Tinamit Maya Shopping Centre, *Calle Santander.* Bargain for good prices. Maya sell their wares cheaply on the lakeside; varied selection, bargaining is easy/expected.

What to do

Cycling
There are several rental agencies on Calle Santander, eg **Maco Cycle Rental** and **Tono Cycle Rental**. Also **Alquiler de Bicicletas Emanuel**, on Calle 14 de Febrero. Prices start at US$2 per hr or about US$10 for a day.

Diving
ATI Divers, *round the back of El Patio, Calle Santander, T5706-4117, www.laiguanaperdida. com.* A range of options including PADI Open

Water US$220, fun dive US$30, 2 for US$50. PADI Rescue and Dive Master also available. Altitude speciality, US$80. Dives are made off Santa Cruz La Laguna and are of special interest to those looking for altitude diving. Here there are spectacular walls that drop off, rock formations you can swim through, trees underwater and, because of its volcanic nature, hot spots, which leaves the lake bottom sediment boiling to touch. Take advice on visibility before you opt for a dive.

Fishing

Lake fishing can be arranged, black bass (*mojarra*) up to 4 kg can be caught. Boats for up to 5 people can be hired for about US$15. Check with INGUAT, see page 370, for latest information.

Hang-gliding

Rogelio, *contactable through Americo's Tours, Calle Santander, and other agencies will make arrangements, at least 24 hrs' notice is required.* Jumps are made from San Jorge La Laguna or from above Santa Catarina, depending on weather conditions.

Kayaking and canoing

Kayak hire is around US$2 per hr. Ask at the hotels, INGUAT and at lakeshore. Watch out for strong winds that occasionally blow up quickly across the lake; these are potentially dangerous in small boats.
Diversiones Acuáticos Balán, *in a small red and white tower on the lakeshore.* Rent out kayaks.

Tour operators

All offer shuttle services to Chichicastenango, Antigua, the Mexican borders, etc, and some to San Cristóbal de las Casas (see Transport, below) and can arrange most activities on and around the lake. There are a number of tour operators on Calle Santander, including those listed below.
Americo's Tours, *T7762-2021.*
Centroamericana Tourist Service, *T7832-5032.*

Tierra Maya, *T7725-7320.* Friendly and reliable tour operator, which runs shuttles to San Cristóbal de las Casas as well as within Guatemala.
Toliman Travel, *T7762-1275.*

Waterskiing

Arrangements can be made with **ATI Divers** at **Iguana Perdida** in Santa Cruz.

Transport

Boat

There are 2 types of transport – the scheduled ferry service to Santiago Atitlán and the *lanchas* to all the other villages. The tourist office has the latest information on boats. The boat service to **Santiago Atitlán** runs from the dock at the end of Calle Rancho Grande (Muelle Público) from 0600-1630, 8 daily, 20 mins in launch, US$3.10, 1 hr in the large **Naviera Santiago** ferry, T7762-0309 or 20-35 mins in the fast *lanchas*. Some *lanchas* to all the other villages leave from here, but most from the dock at the end of Calle Embarcadero run by **Tzanjuyú** from 0630-1700 every 45 mins or when full (minimum 10 people). If you set off from the main dock the *lancha* will pull in at the Calle Embarcadero dock as well. These *lanchas* call in at **Santa Cruz, Jaibalito, Tzununá, San Marcos, San Pablo, San Juan** and **San Pedro**, US$1.20 to US$2.50 to **San Marcos** and beyond. To **San Pedro** US$3.10. There are no regular boats to Santa Catarina, San Antonio or San Lucas: pickups and buses serve these communities, or charter a *lancha*, US$30 return to Santa Catarina and San Antonio.

The 1st boat of the day is at 0700. If there is a demand, there will almost always be a boatman willing to run a service but non-official boats can charge what they like. Virtually all the dozen or so communities round the lake have docks, and you can take a regular boat to any of those round the western side. The only reliable services back to Panajachel are from **Santiago** or

San Pedro up to about 1600. If you wait on the smaller docks round the western side up to this time, you can get a ride back to Panajachel, flag them down in case they don't see you, but they usually pull in if it's the last service of the day.

Note that, officially, locals pay less. Only buy tickets on the boat; if you buy them from the numerous ticket touts on the dockside, you will be overcharged. Bad weather can, of course, affect the boat services. Crossings are generally rougher in the afternoons, worth bearing in mind if you suffer from sea-sickness.

Boat hire and tours *Lanchas* can be hired to go anywhere round the lake, about US$100 for 5 people for a full day. For round trips to **San Pedro** and **Santiago** and possibly **San Antonio Palopó**, with stopovers, go early to the lakefront and bargain. Trip takes a full day, eg 0830-1530, with stops of 1 hr or so at each, around US$6-7, if the boat is full. If on a tour, be careful not to miss the boat at each stage; if you do, you will have to pay again.

Bus
Rebuli buses leave from opposite Hotel Fonda del Sol on Calle Real, otherwise, the main stop is where Calle Santander meets Calle Real. **Rebuli** to **Guatemala City**, 3½ hrs, US$3.30, crowded, hourly between 0500 and 1500. To **Guatemala City** via **Escuintla** south coast, 8 a day plus 3 **Pullman** a day. Direct bus to **Quetzaltenango**, 7 a day between 0530 and 1415, US$2.70, 2½ hrs. There are direct buses to **Los Encuentros** on the Pan-American Hwy (US$0.75). To **Chichicastenango** direct, Thu and Sun, 0645, 0700, 0730 and then hourly to 1530. Other days between 0700-1500,

US$2, 1½ hrs. There are 4 daily direct buses to **Cuatro Caminos**, US$1.60 from 0530, for connections to Totonicapán, Quetzaltenango, Huehuetenango, etc. To **Antigua** take a bus up to Los Encuentros through Sololá. Change for a bus to **Chimaltenango** US$3.10, and change there for Antigua. There is also a direct bus (Rebuli) to **Antigua** leaving 1030-1100, daily, US$4.40. To **Sololá**, US$0.40, 20 mins, every 30 mins. You can wait for through buses by the market on Calle Real. The fastest way to southern **Mexico** is probably by bus south to Cocales, 2½ hrs, 5 buses between 0600 and 1400, then many buses along the Pacific Highway to **Tapachula** on the border. For **La Mesilla**, take a bus up to Los Encuentros, change west for Cuatro Caminos. Here catch a bus north to La Mesilla; see also box, page 512. Some travel agencies go direct to **San Cristóbal de las Casas** via La Mesilla, daily at 0600. See Tour operators, above.

Shuttles Services are run jointly by travel agencies, to **Guatemala City**, **Antigua**, **Quetzaltenango**, **Chichi** and more. Around 4 a day. **Antigua**, US$14, **Chichicastenango**, on market days, US$15, **Quetzaltenango** US$20 and the **Mexican border** US$40. **Atitrans**, Calle Santander, next to Hotel Regis, T7762-0146, is recommended.

Motorcycle
Motorcycle hire About US$6 per hour, plus fuel and US$100 deposit. Try **Maco Cycle** near the junction of Calle Santander and 14 de Febrero, T7762-0883.

Motorcycle parts **David's Store**, opposite Hotel Maya Kanek, has good prices and also does repairs.

Villages around the lake are connected to Panajachel by boat services. Some are served by buses. Travelling round the lake is the best way to enjoy the stunning scenery and the effect of changing light and wind on the mood of the area. The slower you travel the better, and walking round the lake gives some fantastic views (but take advice on safety). With accommodation at towns and villages on the way, there is no problem finding somewhere to bed down for the night if you want to make a complete circuit. The lake is 50 km in circumference and you can walk on or near the shore for most of it. Here and there the cliffs are too steep to allow for easy walking and private properties elsewhere force you to move up 'inland'.

For boat information see Transport, page 374. At almost any time of year, but especially between January and March, strong winds (*El Xocomil*) occasionally blow up quickly across the lake. This can be dangerous for small boats.

Santa Catarina Palopó

The town, within easy walking distance (4 km) of Panajachel, has an attractive adobe church. Reed mats are made here, and you can buy *huipiles* (beautiful, green, blue and yellow) and men's shirts. Watch weaving at **Artesanías Carolina** on the way out towards San Antonio. Bargaining is normal. There are hot springs close to the town and an art gallery. Houses can be rented and there is at least one superb hotel (see Where to stay, below). The town fiesta is 25 November.

San Antonio Palopó

Six kilometres beyond Santa Catarina, San Antonio Palopó has another fine 16th-century church. Climbing the hill from the dock, it lies in an amphitheatre created by the mountains behind. Up above there are hot springs and a cave in the rocks used for local ceremonies. The village is noted for the clothes and head dresses of the men, and *huipiles* and shirts are cheaper than in Santa Catarina. A good hike is to take the bus from Panajachel to Godínez; take the path toward the lake 500 m south along the road to Cocales, walk on down from there to San Antonio Palopó (one hour) and then along the road back to Panajachel via Santa Catarina Palopó (three hours). You can walk on round the lake from San Antonio, but you must eventually climb steeply up to the road at Agua Escondida. The local fiesta is 12-14 June.

San Lucas Tolimán

San Lucas is at the southeastern tip of the lake and is not as attractive as other towns. It is known for its fiestas and markets especially Holy Week with processions, arches and carpets on the Thursday and Friday, and 15-20 October. Market days are Tuesday, Friday and Sunday (the best). There are two banks and an internet centre. **Comité Campesino del Altiplano** ⓘ *T5804-9451, www.ccda.galeon.com*, is based in the small village of Quixaya, 10 minutes from San Lucas. This Campesino Cooperative now produces fairtrade organic coffee buying from small farmers. You can visit its organic processing plant on a small coffee finca and learn about its *café justicia*, and political work. Long-term volunteers welcome, Spanish required.

Volcán Atitlán and Volcán Tolimán

Ask Father Gregorio at the Parroquia church, 2 blocks from the Central Plaza, or at the Municipalidad for information and for available guides in San Lucas. Father Greg has worked in the area for more than 40 years so has a vested interest in recommending safe and good guides. One guide is Carlos Huberto Alinan Chicoj, leaving at 2400 with torches to arrive at the summit by 0630 to avoid early cloud cover.

From San Lucas the cones of **Atitlán**, 3535 m, and **Tolimán**, 3158 m, can be climbed. The route leaves from the south end of town and makes for the saddle (known as Los Planes, or Chanán) between the two volcanoes. From there it is south to Atitlán and north to the double cone (they are 1 km apart) and crater of Tolimán. Though straightforward, each climb is complicated by many working paths and thick cover above 2600 m. If you are fit, either can be climbed in seven hours, five hours down. Cloud on the volcano is common, but least likely from November to March. There have been reports of robbery so consider taking a guide, and ask local advice before setting out.

Santiago Atitlán

Santiago is a fascinating town, as much for the stunningly beautiful embroidered clothing of the locals, as for the history and character of the place with its mix of Roman Catholic, evangelical and Maximón worship. There are 35 evangelical temples in town as well as the house of the revered idol Maximón. The Easter celebrations here rival Antigua's for interest and colour. These are some of the most curious and reverential ceremonies in the world. If you only visit Guatemala once in your lifetime and it's at Easter and you can't bear to leave Antigua, come to Santiago at least for Good Friday. Commemorative events last all week and include Maximón as well as Christ.

You will be taken to the house of Maximón for a small fee. The fine church, with a wide nave decorated with colourful statues, was founded in 1547. The original roof was lost to earthquakes. There is a plaque dedicated to priest Father Francis Aplas Rother who was assassinated by the government in the church on 28 August 1981. At certain times of the year, the square is decked with streamers gently flapping in the breeze. The Tz'utujil women wear fine clothes and the men wear striped, half-length embroidered trousers (the most beautiful in Guatemala). There is a daily market, best on Friday and all sorts of artwork and crafts can be bought. **Asociación Cojol ya weaving centre** ① *T5499-5717, Mon-Fri 0900-1600, Sat 0900-1300, free, weaving tours also.* As well as Holy Week, the local fiesta takes place 23-27 July.

Near town is the hill, **Cerro de Oro**, with a small village of that name on the lake. The summit (1892 m) can be reached from the village in 45 minutes.

For more information on the **Lake Atitlán Medical project** and volunteer opportunities, see www.puebloapueblo.org.

San Pedro La Laguna

San Pedro is a small town set on a tiny promontory with coffee bushes threaded around tracks lined with hostels and restaurants on the lakeside fringes. The tourists and long-term gringos have colonized the lakeside while the **Tz'utujil Maya** dominate the main part of the town up a very steep hill behind. San Pedro is now the favourite spot to hang out in for a couple of days or longer. It's a place to relax, to soak in hot baths, learn a bit of Spanish, horse ride and trek up Nariz de Maya. Some of the semi-permanent gringo inhabitants run bars and cafés or sell home-made jewellery and the like. The cobbled road from the dock facing Panajachel (known as the *muelle)* climbs up to the centre and another goes down, more or less at right angles, to the other dock (known as the *playa* or beach) facing Santiago with the town arranged around. There's a mazy network of *callejones* and paths that fringe the shoreline between the two ferries. Market days are Thursday and Sunday (better) and there's a fiesta 27-30 June with traditional dances.

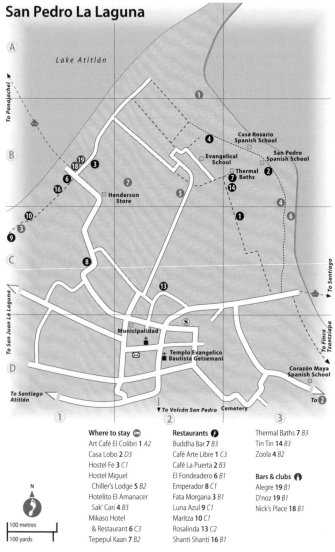

San Pedro La Laguna

Where to stay		Restaurants		Thermal Baths 7 *B3*
Art Café El Colibri **1** *A2*		Buddha Bar **7** *B3*		Tin Tin **14** *B3*
Casa Lobo **2** *D3*		Café Arte Libre **1** *C3*		Zoola **4** *B2*
Hostel Fe **3** *C1*		Café La Puerta **2** *B3*		
Hostel Miguel		El Fondeadero **6** *B1*		**Bars & clubs**
Chiller's Lodge **5** *B2*		Emperador **8** *C1*		Alegre **19** *B1*
Hotelito El Amanacer		Fata Morgana **3** *B1*		D'noz **19** *B1*
Sak' Cari **4** *B3*		Luna Azul **9** *C1*		Nick's Place **18** *B1*
Mikaso Hotel		Maritza **10** *C1*		
& Restaurant **6** *C3*		Rosalinda **13** *C2*		
Tepepul Kaan **7** *B2*		Shanti Shanti **16** *B1*		

The town lies at the foot of the **Volcán San Pedro** (3020 m), which can be climbed in four to five hours, three hours down. It is now in the Parque Ecológico Volcán San Pedro, and the US$15 entrances includes the services of a guide. **Politur** also work in the park and there have been no incidents of robbery since the park's inauguration. Camping is possible. Go early (0530) for the view, because after 1000 the top is usually smothered in cloud; also you will be in the shade all the way up and part of the way down.

Descubre San Pedro has set up a museum of local culture and coffee, with natural medicine and Maya cosmovision tours.

Evangelical churches are well represented in San Pedro, and you can hardly miss the yellow and white **Templo Evangélico Bautista Getsemaní** in the centre. A visit to the rug-making cooperative on the beach is of interest and backstrap weaving is taught at some places. A session at the **thermal baths** ⓘ *about US$10, Mon-Sat 0800-1900, best to reserve in advance*, is a relaxing experience. Note that the water is solar heated, not chemical hot springs. Massage is also available, US$10.

Canoes are made in San Pedro and hire is possible.

San Juan La Laguna and Santa Clara La Laguna

The road north from San Pedro passes around a headland to San Juan La Laguna (2 km), a traditional lakeside town. Look for **Los Artesanos de San Juan** ⓘ *8 Av, 6-20, Zona 2, T5963-9803*, and another image of Maximón displayed in the house opposite the Municipalidad. **Rupalaj Kistalin** ⓘ *close to the textile store, LEMA, T5964-0040, daily 0800-1700*, is a highly recommended organization run by local guides. LEMA ⓘ *T2425-9441, lema@sanjuanlalaguna.com*, the women weavers' association that uses natural dyes in their textiles, is also in town. Weaving classes (T7759-9126) are possible too. On the road towards San Pablo there's a good viewpoint from the hilltop with the cross; a popular walk. A more substantial walk, about three hours, is up behind the village to Santa Clara La Laguna, 2100 m, passing the village of **Cerro Cristalino** with its attractive, white church with images of saints around the walls.

Santa María Visitación and San Pablo La Laguna

A short distance (500 m) to the west, separated by a gully, is a smaller village, Santa María Visitación. As with Santa Clara La Laguna, this is a typical highland village, and unspoilt by tourism. San Juan is connected to San Pablo by the lakeshore road, an attractive 4-km stretch mainly through coffee plantations. San Pablo, a busy village set 80 m above the lake, is known for rope making from *cantala* (maguey) fibres, which are also used for bags and fabric weaving.

San Marcos La Laguna

San Marcos' location is deceptive with the main part of the community 'hidden' up the hill. The quiet village centre is set at the upper end of a gentle slope that runs 300 m through coffee and fruit trees down to the lake, reached by two paved walkways. If arriving by boat and staying in San Marcos, ask to be dropped at the Schumann or the Pirámides dock. The village has grown rapidly in the last few years with a focus on the spiritual and energy; there is a lot of massage, yoga, and all sorts of other therapies. It is the ideal place to be pampered. Beyond the centre 300 m to the east is the main dock of the village down a cobbled road. Down the two main pathways are the hotels; some with waterfront sites have their own docks. There is a slanting trail leaving the village up through dramatic scenery over to Santa Lucía Utatlán, passing close to Cerro San Marcos, 2918 m, the highest point in the region apart from the volcanoes.

San Marcos to Santa Cruz

From the end of San Marcos where the stone track goes down to the dock, a rough track leads to **Tzununá**, passable for small trucks and 4WD vehicles, with views across the lake all the way. The village of Tzununá is along the tree-lined road through coffee plantations with a few houses up the valley behind. There is also a hotel with wonderful views (see Where to stay, below). There is a dock on the lakeside but no facilities. From here to Panajachel there are no roads or vehicular tracks and the villages can only be reached by boat, on horse or on foot. Also from here are some of the most spectacular views of the lake and the southern volcanoes. **Jaibalito** is smaller still than Tzununá, and hemmed in by the mountains with wonderful accommodation (see Where to stay, below). Arguably the best walk in the Atitlán area is from Jaibalito to Santa Cruz.

Santa Cruz La Laguna

Santa Cruz village is set in the most dramatic scenery of the lake. Three deep ravines come down to the bay separating two spurs. A stone roadway climbs up the left-hand spur, picks up the main walking route from Jaibalito and crosses over a deep ravine (unfortunately used as a rubbish tip) to the plaza, on the only flat section of the right spur, about 120 m above the lake. The communal life of the village centres on the plaza. The hotels, one of them overflowing with flowers, are on the lakeshore. Behind the village are steep, rocky forested peaks, many too steep even for the locals to cultivate. The fiesta takes place 7-11 May.

There is good walking here. Apart from the lake route, strenuous hikes inland eventually lead to the Santa Lucía Utatlán–Sololá road. From the left-hand (west) ravine reached from the path that runs behind the lakeshore section, a trail goes through fields to an impossible looking gorge, eventually climbing up to Chaquijchoy, **Finca María Linda** and a trail to San José Chacayá (about four hours). In the reverse direction, the path southwest from San José leads to the Finca María Linda, which is close to the crater rim from where due south is a track to Jaibalito, to the left (east) round to the trail to Santa Cruz. Others follow the ridges towards San José and the road. These are for experienced hikers, and a compass (you are travelling due north) is essential if the cloud descends and there is no one to ask. From Santa Cruz to Panajachel along the coast is difficult, steep and unconsolidated, with few definitive paths. If you do get to the delta of the Río Quiscab, you may find private land is barred. The alternatives are either to go up to Sololá, about 6 km and 800 m up, or get a boat.

Listings Around Lake Atitlán map p378

Where to stay

Santa Catarina Palopó
You can stay in private houses (ask around) or rent rooms (take a sleeping bag).

$$$$ Casa Colibri
Carretera a San Antonio Palopó Km 6.7, entrada a Tzampoc Casa 4, T5353-5823, www.lacasacolibri.com.

Beautifully designed and decorated, this plush vacation rental boasts an extravagant infinity pool overlooking the lake, sauna, fireplaces, and 5 luxurious guestrooms, all with en suite bathrooms. Tasteful and tranquil with space for 12 people.

$$$$ Casa Palopó
Carretera a San Antonio Palopó, Km 6.8, less than 1 km beyond Santa Catarina, on the left up a steep hill, T5773-7777, www.casapalopo.com.

One of the finest hotels in the country, 9 beautiful rooms all richly furnished, flowers on arrival, excellent service, heated pool, spa, gym and a top-class restaurant overlooking the lake. Reservations necessary.

$$$$ Tzam Poc Resort
Vía Rural Km 6.5, T7762-2680,
www.atitlanresort.com.
Resort on the slopes above Santa Catarina with an amazing infinity pool. Lovely villas and spa. There's also an archery range.

$$$ Villa Santa Catarina
T7762-1291, www.villasdeguatemala.com.
36 comfortable rooms with balconies around the pool, most with view of the lake. Good restaurant.

$$ Hotel Terrazas del Lago
T7762-0157, www.hotelterrazasdellago.com.
On the lake with view, bath, clean, restaurant, a unique hotel built up over the past 30 plus years.

San Lucas Tolimán

$$$ Toliman
Av 6, 1 block from the lake, T7722-0033.
18 rooms and suites in colonial style washed in terracotta colours with some lovely dark wood furniture. Suite No 1 is very romantic with lit steps to a sunken bath, good but expensive restaurant (reservations), fine gardens, pool, partial lake views. Recommended.

$ Casa Cruz Inn
Av 5 4-78, a couple of blocks from the park.
Clean, comfortable beds, run by an elderly couple, garden, quiet, good value.

$ Hotel y Restaurante Don Pedro
Av 6, on lakeside, T7722-0028.
An unattractive building in a sort of clumsy rustic style, a little rough around the edges, with 12 rooms, restaurant, bar.

$ La Cascada de María
Calle 6, 6-80, T7722-0136.

With bath, TV, parking, garden, restaurant, good.

Santiago Atitlán
Book ahead for Holy Week.

$$$$ Lake Villa Guatemala
Between Santiago and Cerro de Oro,
5 km from Santiago Atitlán, T5050-0767,
www.lakevillaguatemala.com.
This private villa with just 2 cosy guestrooms would particularly suit those seeking a spiritual retreat. With hilltop and lakeside views, the property offers numerous meditation spaces, including rooms, terraces and gardens. The food is gourmet vegan and the owners can arrange Mayan ceremonies and consultations with local healers. Minimum 2-night stay.

$$$-$$ Posada de Santiago
1.5 km south of town, T7721-7366,
www.posadade santiago.com.
Relaxing lakeside lodge with comfortable stone cottages (some cheaper accommodation), restaurant with home-grown produce and delicious food, tours and a pool. Massage and language classes arranged. Friendly and amusing management – David, Susie and his mum, Bonnie – quite a trio. Has its own dock or walk from town. Highly recommended.

$$ Bambú
On the lakeside, 500 m by road towards San
Lucas, T7721-7332, www.ecobambu.com.
10 rooms, 2 bungalows and 1 *casita* in an attractive setting with beautifully tended gardens, restaurant, a secluded pool, a few minutes by *lancha* from the dock. Kayaks available.

$$ Mystical Yoga Farm
Bahia de Atitlán, a 5-min boat
ride from Santiago, T4860-9538,
www.mysticalyogafarm.com.
There are surely few better places to practice asanas than on the shores of Lake Atitlán. Part of the **School Yoga Institute**, which has properties and yoga schools all over

the world, the Mystical Yoga Farm offers all-inclusive packages which cover lodging, food, meditation, workshops, ceremonies and more. 3-night minimum stay.

$ Chi-Nim-Ya
Walk up from the dock, take the 1st left, walk 50 m and it's there on the left, T7721-7131.
Clean, comfortable and friendly, cheaper without bath, good value, good café, cheap, large helpings.

$ Tzutuhil
On left up the road from the dock to centre, above Ferretería La Esquina, T7721-7174.
With bath and TV, cheaper without, restaurant, great views, good.

Camping
Camping is possible near **Bambú**.

San Pedro La Laguna
Accommodation is mostly cheap and laid back; it's worth bringing your own sleeping bag.

$$$ Casa Lobo
6 Av, Callejón B, on the lakeshore, 200 m after Villa Cuba, 15 mins' walk out of town, www.casalobo.org.
Set in verdant grounds overlooking the lake, German-owned Casa Lobo is a secluded colonial-style property with a range of bungalows, apartments and houses, all tastefully furnished and fully equipped with Wi-Fi, stove, fridge and cable TV. 2-night minimum stay.

$$-$ Mikaso Hotel Resto
Callejon A, I-82, T7721-8232, www.mikasohotel.com.
Owned and managed by a family from Quebec, **Mikaso** has great lake views and a good restaurant serving wood-fired pizzas and crêpes. Private rooms are clean and cosy (**$$**) and for the thrifty there's 6 and 8-bed dorms (**$**). Facilities include a hot tub, roof terrace, pool table, shared kitchen and Swedish massage. Occasional live music.

$ Art Café El Colibri
Behind Colegio Bethel, in front of the museum Tzununya, T7721-8378, www.colibrisanpedro.com.
Colibri offers Spanish and painting classes and is also home to an art gallery, restaurant-cafe and a small B&B with 3 quiet, no-frills rooms, all equipped with hot showers. Owned by a local artist, very chilled place, simple and down to earth, lovely atmosphere complete with friendly dogs.

$ Hostel Fe
Calle Principal, turn right from the boat dock, then 60 m along the lake on the left, T3486-7027, www.hostelfe.com.
If you're in San Pedro to party, try **Hostel Fe**. Perched on the edge of the water, their restaurant-bar is buzzing with action every most evening; Tue is Ladies' Night, Fri is quiz night. Other sources of entertainment include a diving platform, board games, darts and live music. Accommodation is in basic dorms and private rooms.

$ Hostel Miguel Chiller's Lodge
Opposite Yo Mama Hostel.
Managed by the friendly Miguel and his family, this quiet, low-key hostel has a handful of simple private rooms and dorm accommodation. Amenities include Wi-Fi, shared kitchen, lounge and barbecue. There are great views of San Pedro volcano from the roof terrace. Relaxed and hospitable. Good breakfast included.

$ Hotelito El Amanacer Sak' Cari
T7721-8096, www.hotelsakcari.com.
With bath, hot water, lovely rooms with great garden, ask for those with fabulous lake views. Extremely good value. Recommended.

$ Tepepul Kaan
6 Calle 5-10, take the 2nd left heading up from the Pana boat dock, T4301-2271, www.hoteltepepulkaan.com.
This ultra-economical hotel offers basic rooms with bath for about US$10 a night and donates 25% of the rates to scholarship funds

for local students. Facilities include kitchen, hammocks, lawn and lake view. They claim to offer the 'best deal' in San Pedro and they may be right.

San Juan La Laguna

$$$-$$ Hotel Uxlabil
T5990-6016/2366-9555 (in Guatemala City), www.uxlabil.com.
This is an eco-hotel set up on the hill with its own dock (flooded, like all the village shore, in 2010), a short walk from the town centre. It's run by very friendly people with a small restaurant, and beautiful views from its rooftop terrace. It is a perfect, relaxing getaway, with a Maya sauna and tended gardens, in this most unassuming and interesting of towns. It has links with the ecotourism association in town. Recommended.

San Marcos La Laguna

$$$-$$ Aaculaax
Las Pirámides dock, on a path from the Centro Holístico, T5287-0521, www.aaculaax.com.
A Hansel-and-Gretel affair on the lakeshore, run by German Niels. It is a blend of cave work with Gaudí-type influence from the stained-glass work down to the sculptures and lamp shades. A corner of artistic nirvana on Lake Atitlán. Each of the 7 rooms with private bathroom is different, with quirky decor. It is run on an eco-basis, with compost toilets and all. There is a restaurant, bar, bakery and massage room, as well as glass and papier mâché workshops. Highly recommended.

$$ Posada del Bosque Encantado
Barrio 3, T4146-1050, www.hotel posadaencantado.com.
Rustic and arty, this colonial-style guesthouse features spacious, earthy, brick-built rooms with solid wood doors, red tile roofs, terracotta floors, Mayan textiles and stonework. The garden is so verdant and lush it is like a mini-jungle. Their restaurant serves *comida típica*.

$ Hotel Jinava
2nd dock, left at the top of 1st pathway, T5299-3311, www.hoteljinava.com.
This is heaven on a hill. With fabulous views, this German-owned place clings to a steep slope with lovely rooms, restaurants, terraces and a patio. There are books and games or solitude if you want it. It's close to the lakeshore with its own dock where launches will drop you. There are only 5 rooms, breakfast included. Recommended.

$ Hotel Paco Real
Barrio 3, T4688-3715, www.pacorealatitlan.com.
Located 50 m from the lake, Paco Real has simple but comfortable rooms inside wood and stone-built *cabañas*, with or without private bath. Also on site is a *temazcal* sauna, lush garden, Wi-Fi, bar-restaurant, movie projector and book exchange.

$ Las Pirámides del Ka
Las Pirámides dock, www.laspiramidesdelka.com.
A residential meditation centre. See also What to do, below.

$ Unicornio
Las Pirámides dock, 2nd pathway.
With self-catering, bungalows, shared kitchen and bathrooms. It also has a little post office.

San Marcos to Santa Cruz

$$$ Lomas de Tzununá
Tzununá, T7820-4060, www.lomasdetzununa.com.
This hotel enjoys a spectacular position high up above the lake. The views from the restaurant terrace are magnificent. The 10 spacious rooms, decorated with local textiles, have 2 beds each with lake views and a balcony. The hotel, run by a friendly Belgian family, offers walking, biking, kayaking and cultural tours. The restaurant (**$$-$**) uses home-made ingredients, the hotel is run on solar energy and the pool does not use chlorine. Board games,

internet, bar and giant chess available. The family are reforesting a hill. Breakfast and taxes included.

$$ La Casa del Mundo
Jaibalito, T5218-5332,
www.lacasadelmundo.com.
Enjoys one of the most spectacular positions on the entire lake. Room No 15 has the best view followed by room No 1. Cheaper rooms have shared bathrooms. Many facilities, standard family-style dinner, lakeside hot tub, a memorable place with fantastic views. Repeatedly recommended.

Santa Cruz La Laguna

$$$$ Laguna Lodge
1 Tzantizotz, Santa Cruz La Laguna,
T4066-8135, www.thelagunalodge.com.
Overlooking the lake, this luxury boutique hotel features tasteful suites beautifully decorated with hand-made furniture and antiques. A stunning setting, exquisite design and impeccably executed. Spa services available. Romantic and restful. Recommended.

$$$ La Fortuna
Patzisotz Bay, between Panajachel and Santa Cruz, T5203-1033, www.lafortunaatitlan.com.
A truly green venture with solar energy and all natural building materials, this self-described 'nano boutique hotel' is a very romantic option with its 4 luxury bungalows set in beautifully landscaped grounds. Secluded and tranquil, the perfect getaway.

$$$-$$ Villa Sumaya
Paxanax, beyond the dock, about 15 mins' walk, T5810-7199, www.villasumaya.com.
With its own dock, this comfortable, peaceful place has a sauna, massage and healing therapies and yoga. Rates include breakfast.

$$-$ Arca de Noé
To the left of the dock, T5515-3712.
Bungalows, cheaper rooms with shared bathrooms, good restaurant, barbecue, lake activities arranged, nice atmosphere,

veranda overlooking a really beautiful flower-filled gardens and the lake. Low-voltage solar power.

$$-$ La Casa Rosa
To the right as you face the dock from the water, along a path, T5416-1251, www.atitlanlacasarosa.com.
Bungalows and rooms, with bath, cheaper without, home-made meals, attractive garden, sauna. Candlelit dinners at weekends.

$$-$ La Iguana Perdida
Opposite dock, T5706-4117, www.laiguanaperdida.com.
Rooms with and without bathroom and dorm ($ per person) with shared bath, lively, especially weekends, delicious vegetarian food, barbecue, popular, friendly, great atmosphere. **ATI Divers** centre (see What to do, below), waterskiing; kayaks and snorkelling. Bring a torch.

Restaurants

San Lucas Tolimán

$ La Pizza de Sam
Av 7, 1 block down from the plaza towards the lake.
Pizzas and spaghetti.

$ Restaurant Jardín
Orange building on corner of plaza.
Comida típica and *licuados.*

Santiago Atitlán
There are many cheap *comedores* near the centre. The best restaurants are at the hotels.

$$$ El Pescador
On corner 1 block before Tzutuhil.
Full menu, good but expensive.

$$$ Posada de Santiago
1.5 km south of town, T7721-7167.
Delicious, wholesome food and excellent service in lovely surroundings. Highly recommended.

$ Restaurant Wach'alal
Close to Gran Sol. Daily 0800-2000.
A small yellow-painted café serving breakfasts, snacks and cakes. Airy and pleasant.

San Pedro La Laguna
Be careful of drinking water in San Pedro; both cholera and dysentery exist here.

$$-$ Café Arte Libre
Up the hill from Hotel San Pedro.
All meals, vegetarian dishes, good value.

$$-$ Luna Azul
Along shore.
Popular for breakfast and lunch, good omelettes.

$$-$ Restaurant Maritza
With commanding views over lake. Chilled place to hang out with reggae music. Service is slow though. 5 rooms also to rent with shared bath ($).

$$-$ Tin Tin.
Good value. Thai food, delightful garden. Recommended.

$ Buddha Bar
Shows movies every night and has a rooftop and sports bar.

$ Café La Puerta
On the north shore coastal path.
Daily 0800-1700.
Cheap, tasty dishes, with tables in a quirky garden, or looking out over the lake. Beautiful setting.

$ Comedor Sta Elena
Near Nick's Italian.
Seriously cheap and filling breakfasts.

$ El Fondeadero
Good food, lovely terraced gardens, reasonable prices.

$ Emperador
Up the hill.
Comedor serving good local dishes.

$ Fata Morgana
Near the Panajachel dock.
Great focaccia bread sandwiches, with pizza and fine coffee too.

$ Rosalinda
Near centre of village.
Friendly, breakfasts (eg *mosh*), local fish and good for banana and chocolate cakes.

$ Shanti Shanti
Run by Israelis, Italian dishes.

$ Thermal Baths
Along shore from playa.
Good vegetarian food and coffee, but it's expensive.

$ Zoola
Close to the north shore. Open 0900-2100.
A quiet, hideaway with pleasant garden. A great spot.

San Marcos La Laguna
All hotels and hostels offer food.

$$-$ Il Giardino
Up the 2nd pathway.
Attractive garden, Italian owners, good breakfasts.

Bars and clubs

San Pedro La Laguna
Nick's Place, overlooking the main dock, is popular, and well frequented in the evening. Nearby are **Bar Alegre**, a sports bar (www.thealegrepub.com) and **D'noz**. **Ti Kaaj** is another popular spot.

What to do

Santiago Atitlán
Aventura en Atitlán, *Jim and Nancy Matison, Finca San Santiago, T7811-5516. 10 km outside Santiago.* Riding and hiking tours.
Francisco Tizná *from the* **Asociación de Guías de Turismo**, *T7721-7558.* Extremely informative. Ask for him at the dock or at any of the hotels. Payment is by way of donation.

San Pedro La Laguna
There is a growing list of activities available in San Pedro, from hiking up the Nariz de Maya (5 hrs, US$13) and other local trips, through to local crafts. Yoga for all levels is available down towards the shore (US$5 for 1½ hrs).

San Juan La Laguna
Rupalaj Kistalin, *T5964-0040, rupalajkistalin@yahoo.es*. Offers interesting cultural tours of the town visiting painters, weavers, *cofradías* and traditional healers. As well as this cultural circuit there is an adventure circuit taking in Panan forest and a canopy tour at Park Chuiraxamolo' or a nature circuit taking in a climb up the Rostro de Maya and fishing and kayaking. Some of the local guides speak English. Highly recommended.

San Marcos La Laguna
Body and soul
Casa Azul Eco Resort, *T5070-7101, www. casa-azul-ecoresort.com*. A gorgeous little place offering yoga and reiki, among other therapies and writers' workshops hosted by Joyce Maynard. There's also a sauna, campfire and café/restaurant serving

vegetarian food. You can reach it from the first dock, or from the centre of the village.
Kaivalya Yoga and Ashram, *50 m on the left after the Lion's gate at the entrance to San Marcos, T3199-1344, www. yogaretreatguatemala.com*. Spiritual seekers may find illumination at this interesting ashram which offers everything from yoga and meditation classes to 'dark retreats'.
Las Pirámides del Ka, *www.laspiramides delka.com*. The month-long course costs US$420, or US$15 by the day if you stay for shorter periods, accommodation included. Courses are also available for non-residents. In the grounds are a sauna, a vegetarian restaurant with freshly baked bread and a library. This is a relaxing, peaceful place.
San Marcos Holistic Centre, *up the 2nd pathway, beyond Unicornio, www. sanmholisticcentre.com. Mon-Sat 1000-1700*. Offers iridology, acupuncture, kinesiology, Indian head massage, reflexology and massage. Classes in various techniques can also be taken.

Transport

Santa Catarina Palopó
There are frequent pickups from Panajachel and boat services.

San Antonio Palopó
Frequent pickups from Panajachel. Enquire about boats.

San Lucas Tolimán
Boat
Enquire about boats. Private *lancha*, US$35.

Bus
To **Santiago Atitlán**, hourly and to **Guatemala City** via **Panajachel**.

Santiago Atitlán
Boat
4 sailings daily to Pana with *Naviera*, 1¼ hrs, US$1.80, or by *lancha* when full, 20-35 mins, US$1.30-2. To **San Pedro** by

lancha several a day, enquire at the dock for times, 45 mins, US$1.80.

Bus
To **Guatemala City**, US$2.60 (5 a day, first at 0300). 2 **Pullmans** a day, US$3.40. To **Panajachel**, 0600, 2 hrs, or take any bus and change on main road south of San Lucas.

San Pedro La Laguna
Boat
Up to 10 *lanchas* to **Panajachel**. To **Santiago**, leave when full (45 mins, US$2.50). To **San Marcos**, every 2 hrs. Private *lanchas* (10 people at US$2 each).

Bus
There are daily buses to **Guatemala City**, several leave in the early morning and

early afternoon, 4 hrs, US$4.50, to **Antigua** and to **Quetzaltenango**, in the morning, 3½ hrs, US$3.

San Marcos La Laguna
Boat
Service roughly every ½ hr to **Panajachel** and to **San Pedro**. Wait on any dock. Fare US$1.80 to either.

Bus
San Pedro to Pan-American Hwy can be boarded at San Pablo. **Pickup** Frequent pickups from the village centre and anywhere along the main road. To **San Pedro**, US$0.50, less to villages en route.

Chichicastenango → *Colour map 6, B3.*
famous for its market where hundreds come for a bargain

Chichicastenango (altitude 2071 m) is a curious blend of mysticism and commercialism. On market mornings the steps of the church are blanketed in flowers as the women, in traditional dress, fluff up their skirts, amid baskets of lilies, roses and blackberries. But, with its mixture of Catholic and indigenous religion readily visible, it is more than just a shopping trolley stop. On a hilltop peppered with pine, villagers worship at a Mayan shrine; in town, a time-honoured tradition of brotherhoods focuses on saint worship. Coupled with the mist that encircles the valley in the late afternoon, you can sense an air of intrigue.

A large plaza is the focus of the town, with two white churches facing one another: **Santo Tomás** the parish church and **Calvario**. Santo Tomás, founded in 1540, is open to visitors, although photography is not allowed, and visitors are asked to be discreet and enter by a side door (through an arch to the right). Next to Santo Tomás are the cloisters of the Dominican monastery (1542). Here the famous *Popol Vuh* manuscript of the Maya creation story was found. A human skull wedged behind a carved stone face, found in Sacapulas, can be seen at the **Museo Arqueológico Regional** ① *main plaza, Tue, Wed, Fri, Sat 0800-1200, 1400-1600, Thu 0800-1600, Sun 0800-1400, closed Mon, US$0.70, photographs and video camera not permitted*. There's also a jade collection once owned by 1926-1944 parish priest Father Rossbach. The **tourist office** ① *5 Av and Teatro Municipalidad, 1 block from church, T7756-2022, daily 0800-2000*, is helpful and provides a free leaflet with map, and local tour information.

The Sunday and Thursday markets are both very touristy, and bargains are harder to come by once shuttle-loads of people arrive mid-morning. Articles from all over the Highlands are available: rugs, carpets and bedspreads; walk one or two streets away from the main congregation of stalls for more realistic prices, but prices are cheaper in Panajachel for the same items and you won't find anything here that you can't find in Panajachel.

The idol, **Pascual Abaj**, a god of fertility, is a large black stone with human features on a hill overlooking the town. Crosses in the ground surrounding the shrine are prayed in front of for the health of men, women and children, and for the dead. Fires burn and the wax of a thousand candles, flowers and sugar cover the shrine. One ceremony you may see is that of a girl from the town requesting a good and sober husband. If you wish to undergo a ceremony to plead for a partner, or to secure safety from robbery or misfortune, you may ask the *curandero* (US$7 including photographs). To reach the deity, walk along 5 Avenida, turn right on 9 Calle, down the hill, cross the stream and take the second track from the left going steepest uphill, which passes directly through a farmhouse and buildings. The farm now belongs to a mask-maker whom you can visit and buy masks from. Follow the path to the top of the pine-topped hill where you may well see a Maya ceremony in progress. It's about 30 minutes' walk. The site can be easily visited independently (in a small group), or an INGUAT-approved guide arranged through the local tourist committee can take you there and explain its history and significance (US$6.50, one or two hours, identified by a license in town).

Chichicastenango

Where to stay		
Chalet House **3**	Salvador **6**	La Villa de los Cofrades **4**
Chugüilá **4**	Santo Tomás **11**	Las Brasas Steak House **5**
Mayan Inn **8**	Tuttos **2**	Tu Café **3**
Pensión Girón **9**		Tziguan Tinamit **6**
Posada Belén **1**	Restaurants	
Posada El Arco **5**	La Fonda de Tzijolaj **4**	
	La Parrillada **2**	

BACKGROUND

Chichicastenango

Often called 'Chichi' but also known as Santo Tomás, Chichicastenango is the hub of the Maya-K'iche' highlands. The name derives from the *chichicaste*, a prickly purple plant-like a nettle, which grows profusely, and *tenango*, meaning 'place of'. Today the locals call the town 'Siguan Tinamit' meaning 'place surrounded by ravines'. The townsfolk are also known as Masheños, which comes from the word Max, also meaning Tomás. About 1000 ladinos live in the town, but 20,000 Maya live in the hills nearby and flood the town for the Thursday and Sunday markets. The town itself has winding streets of white houses roofed with bright red tiles, which wander over a little knoll in the centre of a cup-shaped valley surrounded by high mountains.

The men's traditional outfit is a short-waisted embroidered jacket and knee breeches of black cloth, a woven sash and an embroidered kerchief around the head. The cost of this outfit, now over US$200, means that fewer and fewer men are wearing it. Women wear *huipiles* with red embroidery against black or brown and their *cortes* skirts have dark blue stripes.

Listings Chichicastenango *map p388*

Where to stay

You won't find accommodation easily on Sat evening, when prices are increased. As soon as you get off the bus, boys will swamp you and insist on taking you to certain hotels.

$$$ Mayan Inn
*Corner of 8 Calle, 1-91, T7756-1176,
www.mayaninn.com.gt.*
A classic, colonial-style courtyard hotel, filled with plants, polished antique furniture, beautiful dining room and bar with fireplaces. Gas-heated showers and internet. The staff are very friendly and wear traditional dress. Secure parking.

$$$ Santo Tomás
7 Av, 5-32, T7756-1061.
A very attractive building with beautiful colonial furnishings and parrots in patios. There's a pool, sauna, good restaurant and bar. It is often full at weekends. Buffet

lunch (US$14) is served on market days in the stylish dining room, with attendants in traditional dress.

$$ Posada El Arco
4 Calle, 4-36, T7756-1255.
Clean, very pretty, small, friendly, garden, washing facilities, negotiate lower rates for stays longer than a night, some large rooms, good view, parking, English spoken.

$$-$ Chalet House
*3 Calle, 7-44, T7756-1360,
www.chalethotelguatemala.
com.* A clean, guesthouse with family atmosphere, hot water. Don't be put off by the dingy street.

$ Chugüilá
*5 Av, 5-24, T7756-1134,
hotelchuguila@yahoo.com.*
Some rooms have fireplaces. Avoid the front rooms, which are noisy. There's also a restaurant.

$ Pensión Girón
Edif Girón on 6 Calle, 4-52, T7756-1156.
Clean rooms with bath, cheaper without, hot water, parking.

$ Posada Belén
12 Calle, 5-55, T7756-1244.
With bath, cheaper without, hot water, clean, will do laundry, fine views from balconies and hummingbirds in attractive garden, good value. Recommended.

$ Salvador
10 Calle, 4-47.
Large rooms with bath, a few with fireplaces (you can buy wood in the market), good views over town, parking. Cheaper, smaller rooms without bath available.

$ Tuttos
12 Calle, near Posada Belén, T7756-7540.
Reasonable rooms.

Restaurants

The best food is in the top hotels, but is expensive. On market days there are plenty of good food stalls and *comedores* in the centre of the plaza that offer chicken in different guises or a set lunch for US$1.50.

There are several good restaurants in the Centro Comercial Santo Tomás, on the north side of the plaza (market).

$$ La Fonda de Tzijolaj
On the plaza.
Great view of the market below, good meals, pizza, prompt service, reasonable prices.

$$ Las Brasas Steak House
6 Calle 4-52, T7756-2226.
Nice atmosphere, good steak menu, accepts credit cards.

$$-$ La Villa de los Cofrades
On the plaza.
Café downstairs, breakfasts, cappuccinos, espressos, good value. There is a 2nd restaurant 2 blocks up the street towards Arco Gucumatz, which is more expensive but has a great people-watching upstairs location. An escape during market days, and popular for breakfast.

$$-$ Tziguan Tinamit
On the corner of 5 Av, esq 6 Calle.
Some local dishes, steaks, tasty pizzas, breakfasts, good pies but a little more expensive than most places, good.

$ Caffé Tuttos
See Where to stay. Daily 0700-2200.
Good breakfast deals, pizzas, and *menú del día*, reasonable prices.

$ La Parrillada
6 C 5-37, Interior Comercial Turkaj.
Escape the market bustle, courtyard, reasonable prices, breakfast available.

$ Tu Café
5 Av 6-44, on market place, Santo Tomás side. Open 0730-2000.
Snacks, budget breakfast, sandwiches, set lunch, good value.

Festivals

1 Jan Padre Eterno.
20 Jan San Sebastián.
19 Mar San José.
Feb/Apr Jesús Nazareno and María de Dolores (both Fri in Lent).
Mar/Apr Semana Santa (Holy Week).
29 Apr San Pedro Mártir.
3 May Santa Cruz.
29 Jun Corpus Christi.
18 Aug Virgen de la Coronación.
14 Sep Santa Cruz.
29 Sep San Miguel.
30 Sep San Jerónimo Doctor.
1st Sun of Oct Virgen del Rosario.
2nd Sun in Oct Virgen de Concepción.
1 Nov San Miguel.
13-22 Dec Santo Tomás, with 21 Dec being the main day. There are processions, traditional dances, the *Palo Volador* (19, 20, 21 Dec) marimba music, well worth a visit – very crowded.

Markets

Market days in Guatemala are alive with colour and each community is characterized by unique clothes and crafts. Simply wandering through the labyrinthine stalls amid the frenetic throng of colour, noise, aromas and movement is a potent and memorable experience.

Markets run the gamut from low-key indoor bazaars to massive, sprawling outdoor events that draw traders from across the country. The most famous takes place in the town of **Chichicastenango**, an hour north of Lake Atitlán, where Maya and visitors converge in a twice-weekly frenzy of produce and textile shopping. It is a superb venue for souvenir purchases and the quintessential Guatemala market experience. **Sololá**, 20 minutes from Panajachel, hosts a Friday market that is always crowded with locals but rarely visited by foreigners, so it's an authentic slice of Mayan culture. For sheer size and scope, don't miss the Friday market at **San Francicso de Alto**, the largest, busiest and best stocked open-air market in Central America.

When shopping, bartering is the norm and almost expected; sometimes, unbelievable discounts can be obtained. You won't do better anywhere else in Central America, but getting the discount is less important than paying a fair price. Woven goods are normally cheapest bought in the town of origin. Try to avoid middlemen and buy direct from the weaver. Guatemalan coffee is highly recommended, although the best is exported; coffee sold locally is not vacuum-packed.

Shopping

Chichicastenango's markets are on Sun and Thu. See box, above.

Ut'z Bat'z, *5a Avenida and 5a Calle, T5008-5193*. Women's Fair Trade weaving workshop, with free demonstrations; high-quality clothes and bags for sale.

What to do.

Chichicastenango
Maya Chichi Van, *6 Av, 6-45, T7756-2187, mayachichivan@yahoo.com*. Shuttles and tours ranging from US$10-650.

Transport

Bus
Buses passing through Chichi all stop at 5 Av/5 Calle by the **Hotel Chugüilá**, where there are always police and bus personnel to give information. To **Guatemala City**, every 15 mins 0200-1730, 3 hrs, US$3.70. To **Santa Cruz del Quiché**, every ½ hr 0600-2000, US$0.70, 30 mins or 20 mins, if the bus driver is aiming for honours in the graduation from the School of Kamikaze Bus Tactics. To **Panajachel**, ½ hr, US$2, several until early afternoon or take any bus heading south and change at Los Encuentros. Same goes for **Antigua**, where you need to change at Chimaltenango. To **Quetzaltenango**, 5 between 0430-0830, 2½ hrs, US$3.80. To **Mexico**, and all points west, take any bus to Los Encuentros and change. To **Escuintla** via Santa Lucía Cotzumalguapa, between 0300 and 1700, 3 hrs, US$2.80. There are additional buses to local villages especially on market days.

Shuttles These operate to **Guatemala City**, **Xela**, **Panajachel**, **Huehuetenango** and **Mexican border**. See Maya Chichi Van, in What to do, above.

Santa Cruz del Quiché (population 7750, altitude 2000 m), often simply called Quiché, attracts few tourists here and prices are consequently reasonable. Its main attraction is Utatlán, the remains of the Maya K'iche' capital. The large Parque Central has a military garrison on the east side with a jail on the lower floor and a sinister military museum with reminders of recent conflicts above. The date of the town's fiesta varies around the Assumption but is usually held around 14-20 August.

Three kilometres away are the remains of temples and other structures of the former Quiché capital, **Gumarcaj**, sometimes spelt **K'umarkaaj**, and now generally called **Utatlán** ① *0800-1700, US$1.30, from the bus station, walk west along 10 Calle for 40 mins until you reach a small junction with a blue sign (SECP), take the right lane up through gates to the site.* The city was largely destroyed by the Spaniards, but the stonework of the original buildings can be seen in the ruins, which can be reached on foot; the setting is very attractive and well maintained. There are two subterranean burial chambers (take a torch, as there are unexpected drops) still used by the Maya for worship and chicken sacrifices. The seven plazas, many temples, ball court, gladiator's archway and other features are marked.

There is a paved road east from Quiché to (8 km) **Santo Tomás Chiché**, a picturesque village with a fine, rarely visited Saturday market (fiesta 25-28 December). There is also a road to this village from Chichicastenango. Although it is a short-cut, it is rough and virtually impassable in any vehicle. It makes a good, three- to four-hour walk, however. Further east (45 km) from Chiché is **Zacualpa**, where beautiful woollen bags are woven. The church has a remarkably fine façade and there is an unnamed *pensión* near the plaza. Market days are Sunday and Thursday.

At **Joyabaj** women weave fascinating *huipiles* and there is a colourful Sunday market, followed by a procession at about noon from the church led by the elders with drums and pipes. This was a stopping place on the old route from Mexico to Antigua. There is good walking in the wooded hills around, for example north to Chorraxaj (two hours), or across the Río Cocol south to Piedras Blancas to see blankets being woven. During fiesta week (9-15 August) Joyabaj has a *Palo Volador* and other traditional dances. There is a restaurant next to the Esso station on the Santa Cruz end of the plaza with a bank opposite (will change US dollars cash).

The road east to Cobán
The road east from **Sacapulas** is one of the most beautiful mountain roads in all Guatemala, with magnificent scenery in the narrow valleys. There is accommodation in **Uspantán** and this is the place to stay for the night enroute to Cobán. The road is not paved beyond Uspantán.

It's a five-hour walk from Uspantán south to **Chimul**, the birthplace of **Rigoberta Menchú**, Nobel Peace Prize winner in 1992. The village was virtually wiped out during the 1980s, but the settlement is coming to life again. Only pickups go to the village.

Where to stay

There are several very basic options around the bus arrival/departure area.

$ Rey K'iché
8 Calle, 0-9, 2 blocks from bus terminal.
Clean, comfortable, hot water, parking, restaurant, TV.

$ San Pascual
7 Calle, 0-43, 2 blocks south of the central plaza, T5555-1107.
Good location, with bath, cheaper without, quiet, locked parking.

The road east to Cobán
There are a couple of *hospedajes* in Uspantán.

$ Galindo
4 blocks east of the Parque Central.
Clean, friendly, recommended.

Restaurants

Try *sincronizadas*, hot tortillas baked with cubed ham, spiced chicken and cheese.

$ La Cabañita Café
1 Av, 1-17.
Charming, small café with pinewood furniture, home-made pies and cakes, excellent breakfasts (pancakes, cereals, etc), eggs any way you want 'em, and great snacks, such as *sincronizadas*.

$ La Toscan
1 Av just north of the church, same road as La Cabañita.
A little pizza and *pastelería* with checked cloth-covered tables. Lasagne lunch a bargain with garlic bread and pizza by the slice also.

Transport

Bus
Terminal at 10 Calle y 1 Av, Zona 5.
To **Guatemala City**, passing through **Chichicastenango**, at 0300 until 1700, 3 hrs, US$4.50. To **Nebaj** and **Cotzal**, 8 a day, US$3.20, 2 hrs. Buses leave, passing through Sacapulas (1 hr, US$2.50), roughly every hour from 0800-2100. To **Uspantán**, via **Sacapulas**, for **Cobán** and **San Pedro Carchá** every hour, 2 hrs, US$3.90. To **Joyabaj**, several daily, via Chiché and Zacualpa, US$1.80, 1½ hrs. 1st at 0800 with buses going on to the capital. Last bus back to Quiché at 1600. It is possible to get to **Huehuetenango** in a day via Sacapulas, then pickup from bridge to **Aguacatán** and bus from there to Huehuetenango. Last bus to Huehue from Aguacatán, 1600. Daily buses also to **Quetzaltenango**, **San Marcos**, and to **Panajachel**. To **Joyabaj**, **Joyita** bus from Guatemala City, 10 a day between 0200 and 1600, 5 hrs, US$1.80. There are buses from Quiché to **San Andrés Sajcabaja**.

The road east to Cobán
Bus and truck
Several trucks to Cobán, daily in the morning from **Sacapulas**; 7 hrs if you're lucky, usually much longer. Start very early if you wish to make it to Cobán the same day. **Transportes Mejía** from Aguacatán to **Cobán** stops in Sacapulas on Tue and Sat mornings. Also possible to take Quiché–Uspantán buses (0930, 1300, 1500), passing Sacapulas at about 1030, 1400, 1600. Then take the early morning buses at 0300 and 0500 from Uspantán to Cobán or the **Transportes Mejía** buses. After that, pickups leave when full. Hitchhiking to Cobán is also possible. Buses to **Quiché** 0300, 2200, other early morning departures.

The Ixil Triangle is made of up of the highland communities of Nebaj, Chajul and Cotzal set in the beautiful Cuchumatanes mountains, although sadly, out of local necessity, many of the slopes have been badly deforested and the wood burnt for fires. The traditional dress of the Nebaj women – an explosion of primary colours – is spectacular. Much of this area was decimated during the Civil War and then repopulated with the introduction of 'model villages' established by the government. Evidence of wartime activities can still be seen and more remote Maya Ixil-speaking villages are gradually opening up to visitors with the introduction of hostel and trekking facilities.

Nebaj and around

The town of Nebaj is high in the Cuchumatanes Mountains and its green slopes are often layered with mist. It is coloured by the beautiful dress worn by the local women, in an extravaganza of predominantly green, with red, yellow, orange, white and purple. The *corte* is mainly maroon with vertical stripes of black and yellow; some are bright red, and the *huipil* is of a geometric design. The women also wear a headdress with colourful bushy pom-poms on them. The men hardly ever wear the traditional costume; their jacket is red and embroidered in black designs. The main plaza is dominated by a large, simple white church. At the edge of the plaza there are weaving cooperatives selling *cortes, huipiles* and handicrafts from the town and the surrounding area – bargaining is possible. When you arrive, boys will meet you from incoming buses and will guide you to a *hospedaje* – they expect a tip. Nebaj has Sunday and Thursday markets and a fiesta on 12-15 August with traditional dancing. There is an excellent website for Nebaj, www.nebaj.com, run by **Solidaridad Internacional**, with useful phrases in Ixil and your daily Maya horoscope. There's a **tourist office** ⓘ *6a Av and 8a Calle Cantón Vitzal, T7755-8337.*

La Tumba de la Indígena Maya is a shrine a 15-minute walk outside Nebaj where some of those massacred during the war were buried. Take the same route as to Ak'Tzumbal, but at the bottom of the very steep hill, immediately after the bridge over the river, take a left, walk straight on over a paved road, then you come to a small junction – carry straight on until you see a minor crossroads on a path with an orange house gate to your left. Look up and you will see a small building. This is the shrine. Walk to your right where you will see a steep set of stairs leading to the shrine.

There is a walk to **Ak'Tzumbal**, through fields with rabbits, and through long, thin earth tunnels used by the military and guerrillas during the war. You need a guide to walk this cross-country route. Alternatively, you can take the road to Ak'Tzumbal, where the new houses still display signs warning of the danger of land mines. Walk down 15 Avenida de Septiembre away from the church, and take a left just before **El Triangulo** gas station past **El Viajero Hospedaje**, then left and then right down a very steep hill and keep walking (1½ hours). When you reach a small yellow tower just before a fork take the right (the left goes to Salquil Grande) to reach the model village. Above the village of Ak'Tzumbal is **La Pista**, an airstrip used during the war. Next to it bomb craters scar the landscape. Only a few avocado trees, between the bomb holes, survive, and the *gasolinera* to refuel planes, is still there, although it is now covered in corrugated iron. Ask around for directions.

Chajul and Cotzal

Chajul, the second largest village in the Ixil Triangle, is known for its part in the Civil War, where Rigoberta Menchú's brother was killed in the plaza, as relayed in her book *I, Rigoberta Menchú*. According to the Nobel Peace Prize winner, on 9 September 1979 her 16-year-old brother Petrocinio was kidnapped after being turned in for 15 quetzales. He was tortured in the plaza by the army along with numerous others. Villagers were forced to watch the torture under threat of being branded communists. People were set on fire, but the onlookers had weapons and looked ready to fight. This caused the army to withdraw. Chajul's main fiesta is the second Friday in Lent. There is also a pilgrimage to Christ of Golgotha on the second Friday in Lent, beginning the Wednesday before (the image is escorted by 'Romans' in blue police uniforms). Market day is Tuesday and Friday. It is possible to walk from Chajul to Cotzal. It's a six-hour walk from Nebaj to Chajul.

Cotzal is spread over a large area on a number of steep hills. The village's fiesta is 22-25 June, peaking on the day of St John the Baptist (24 June). Market days are Wednesday and Saturday. You can hire bikes from **Maya Tour** on the plaza next to the church. Nebaj to Cotzal is a pleasant four-hour walk. There's no accommodation or restaurants in other small villages and it is difficult to specify what transport is available in this area as trucks and the occasional pickup or commercial van are affected by road and weather conditions. For this reason, be prepared to have to spend the night in villages.

Listings The Ixil Triangle

Where to stay

$ Solidaridad Internacional
Supports 6 hostels in the villages of **Xexocom**, **Chortiz**, **Xeo**, **Cocop**, **Cotzol** and **Párramos Grande** where there is room for 5 people. Contact them at the PRODONT-IXIL office, Av 15 de Septiembre, Nebaj.

Nebaj and around

$$-$ Hotel Turansa
1 block from plaza down 5 Calle, T7755-8219.
Tiny rooms, but very clean, soap, towels, 2nd-floor rooms are nicer, cable TV and parking, little shop in entrance, phone service.

$ Hospedaje Esperanza
6 Av, 2-36.
Very friendly, clean, hot showers in shared bathroom, noisy when evangelical churches nearby have activities, hotel is cleaner than it looks from the outside.

$ Hostal Ixil Don Juan
0 Av A, 1 Calle B, Canton Simocol. Take Av 15 de Septiembre and take a left at Comedor Sarita, opposite grey office of PRODONT-IXIL, then it's 100 m to the right, on the right, T7755-4014/1529.
Part of **Programa Quiché**, run with the support of the EU, there are 6 beds in 2 rooms, each bed with a locked strongbox, and hot showers. The colonial building has a traditional sauna, *chuj*.

$ Hotel Mayan Ixil
On north side of main square, T7755-8168.
Just 5 rooms with private bath and gas hot water. Small restaurant overlooking the plaza, internet service downstairs.

$ Ilebal Tenam
Cantón Simecal, bottom of Av 15 de Septiembre, road to Chajul, T7755-8039.
Hot water, shared and private bath, very clean, friendly, parking inside, attractive decor.

$ Media Luna MediaSol
T5749-7450, www.nebaj.com/hostel.htm.
A backpackers' hostel close to **El Descanso** restaurant with dorms and private rooms. The hostel's also got a little kitchenette, DVD player and Wi-Fi.

Chajul
There are a couple of very basic *hospedajes* in town.

Cotzal

$ Hostal Doña Teresa.
Has a sauna, patio and honey products for sale.

Restaurants

Nebaj and around
Boxboles are squash leaves rolled tightly with *masa* and chopped meat or chicken, boiled and served with salsa and fresh orange juice.

$ El Descanso.
Popular volunteer hang-out, good food and useful information about their other community-based projects (see www.nebaj.com).

$ Maya Ixil
On the Parque Central.
Substantial food, local and international dishes, pleasant family atmosphere.

$ Pizza del César
Daily 0730-2100.
Breakfasts, mouth-wateringly good strawberry cake, and hamburgers as well as pizzas.

Cotzal

$ Comedor and Hospedaje El Maguey.
Bland meals, but a decent size, plus drink, are served up for for US$1.70. Don't stay here though, unless you're desperate.

What to do.

Nebaj and around
Guías Ixiles *(El Descanso Restaurant), www. nebaj.com.* ½- to 3-day hikes, bike rental. There's also a 3-day hike to Todos Santos.

Solidaridad Internacional, *Av 15 de Septiembre, www.nebaj.org. Inside the PRODONT-IXIL (Proyecto de Promoción de Infraestructuras y Ecoturismo) office, in a grey building on the right 1 block after the Gasolinera El Triángulo on the road to Chajul.* For further information call in to see the director Pascual, who is very helpful. 2-, 3- and 4-day hikes, horses available. Options to stay in community *posadas*, with packages available, from 1 to 4 days, full board, from about US$100-200 per person.

Chajul and Cotzal
Ask Teresa at **Hostal Doña Teresa** about trips from the Cotzal or ask for Sebastián Xel Rivera who leads 1-day camping trips.

Transport

Nebaj and around
Bus
The bus ride to Quiché is full of fabulous views and hair-raising bends but the road is now fully paved. Buses to **Quiché** (US$3.20, 2½ hrs) passing through **Sacapulas** (1¾ hrs from Nebaj, US$1.30) leave hourly from 0500-1530. Bus to **Cobán** leaves Gasolinera Quetzal at 0500, 4-5 hrs, US$6.50. Cobán to Nebaj at 1300. Alternatively get to Sacapulas on the main road, and wait for a bus.

Chajul and Cotzal
Bus
Buses to Chajul and Cotzal do not run on a set schedule. It is best to ask the day before you want to travel, at the bus station. There are buses and numerous pickups on Sun when villagers come to Nebaj for its market, which would be a good day to visit the villages. Alternatively, bargain with a local pickup driver to take you on a trip.

Western
highlands

Just before the volcanic highlands reach their highest peaks, this part of the western highlands takes the form of scores of small market towns and villages, each with its own character: the loud animal market at San Francisco El Alto, the extra-planetary landscape at Momostenango, and its Maya cosmovision centre, and the dancing extravaganzas at Totonicapán. The modern *ladino* town of Huehuetenango sits at the gateway to the Sierra de los Cuchumatanes, within which hides, in a cold gash in a sky-hugging valley, the indigenous town and weaving centre of Todos Santos Cuchumatán.

North to Huehuetenango → *Colour map 6, B2.*

highland Mayan towns with colourful markets

Nahualá and Cuatro Caminos

Before the major four-way junction of Cuatro Caminos, the Pan-American Highway runs past Nahualá, a Maya village at 2470 m. The traditional *traje* is distinctive and best seen on market days on Thursday and Sunday, when finely embroidered cuffs and collars are sold, as well as very popular *huipiles*. The **Fiesta de Santa Catalina** is on 23-26 November (25th is the main day).

There is an unpaved all-weather road a little to the north and 16 km longer, from Los Encuentros (on the Pan-American Highway) through Totonicapán (40 km) to San Cristóbal Totonicapán. The route from Chichicastenango to Quiché, Xecajá and Totonicapán takes a day by car or motorcycle, but is well worth taking and recommended by cyclists. There are no buses. There is also a scenic road from Totonicapán to Santa Cruz del Quiché via San Antonio Ilotenango. It takes one hour by car or motorcycle and two hours by pickup truck. There are no buses on this route either.

Cuatro Caminos is a busy junction with roads, east to Totonicapán, west to Los Encuentros, north to Huehuetenango and south to Quetzaltenango. Buses stop here every few seconds so you will never have to wait long for a connection. There is a petrol station and lots of vendors to keep you fed and watered. Just north of Cuatro Caminos is **San Cristóbal Totonicapán**, noted for its *huipiles*.

Totonicapán

The route to San Miguel Totonicapán (altitude 2500 m), the capital of its department, passes through pine-forested hillsides, pretty red-tiled roofs and *milpas* of maize on the roadside. The 18th-century beige church stands on one of the main squares, unfortunately now a car park, at 6 y 7 Avenida between 3 and 4 Calle. The market is considered by Guatemalans to be one of the cheapest, and it is certainly very colourful. Saturday is the main market noted for ceramics and cloth, with a small gathering on Tuesdays. There is a traditional dance fiesta on 12-13 August, music concerts and a chance to see *cofradía* rituals. The annual **feria** is on 24-30 September in celebration of the Archangel San Miguel, with the main fiesta on 29 September. The **Casa de Cultura** ① *8 Av, 2-17, T5630-0554, www.larutamayaonline.com/aventura.html*, run by Carlos Humberto Molina, displays an excellent collection of fiesta masks, made on site at the mask factory, and for sale. It has a cultural programme with a number of tour options, cultural activities and bicycle adventures. You need to reserve in advance.

San Francisco El Alto

San Francisco stands high on a great big mound in the cold mountains at 2640 m above the great valley in which lie Totonicapán, San Cristóbal and Quetzaltenango. It is famous for its market, which is stuffed to capacity, and for the animal market held above town, where creatures from piglets to kittens to budgies are for sale. The town's fiesta is on 1-6 October, in honour of St Francis of Assisi.

The market is packed to bursting point on Fridays with locals buying all sorts, including woollen blankets for resale throughout the country. It's an excellent place for buying woven and embroidered textiles of good quality, but beware of pickpockets. Go early to see as much action as possible. Climb up through the town for 10 minutes to see the animal market (ask for directions all the time as it's hard to see 5 m ahead, the place is so packed).

The **church** on the main square is magnificent; notice the double-headed Hapsburg eagle. It is often full on market days with locals lighting candles, and their live purchases ignoring the 'Silencio' posters. The white west front of the church complements the bright colours of the rest of the plaza, especially the vivid green and pink of the Municipalidad.

Momostenango

Momostenango is set in a valley with ribbons of houses climbing higgledy-piggledy out of the valley floor. Momostenango, at 2220 m, represents *Shol Mumus* in K'iche', meaning 'among the hills', and on its outlying hills are numerous altars and a hilltop image of a Maya god. Some 300 medicine men are said to practise in the town. Their insignia of office is a little bag containing beans and quartz crystals. Momostenango is the chief blanket-weaving centre in the country, and locals can be seen beating the blankets (*chamarras*) on stones, to shrink them. There are also weird stone peaks known as the *riscos* – eroded fluted columns and draperies formed of volcanic ash – on the outskirts of town.

The town is quiet except on Wednesday and Sunday market days, the latter being larger and good for weaving, especially the blankets. On non-market days try **Tienda Manuel de Jesús Agancel** ① *1 Av, 1-50, Zona 4, near bank*, for good bargains, especially blankets and carpets. There is also **Artesanía Paclom** ① *corner of 1 Calle and 3 Av, Zona 2*, just five minutes along the road to Xela. This family have the weaving looms in their back yard and will show you how it's all done if you ask.

The **Feast of Wajshakib Batz' Oj** (pronounced 'washakip'), is celebrated by hundreds of *Aj Kij* (Maya priests) who come for ceremonies. New priests are initiated on this first day of the ritual new year; the initiation lasting the year. The town's very popular fiesta is between 21 July and 4 August, with the town's patron saint of Santiago Apóstol celebrated on 25 July. The **Baile de Convites** is held in December with other dances on 8, 12 and 31 December and 1 January. At **Takilibén Maya Misión** ① *3 Av 'A', 6-85, Zona 3, T7736-5537, wajshakibbatz13@yahoo.es*, just after the Texaco garage on the right on the way in from Xela, Chuch Kajaw (day keeper/senior priest) Rigoberto Itzep welcomes all interested in learning more about Maya culture and cosmology. He offers courses in culture and does Maya horoscope readings. He also has a **Maya sauna** (*Tuj*).

Just outside town are three sets of *riscos* (eroded columns of sandstone with embedded quartz particles), creating a strange eerie landscape of pinnacles that look like rocket lollipop ice creams. To get there, take the 2 Calle, Zona 2, which is the one to the right of the church, for five minutes until you see a sign on a building pointing to the left. Follow the signs until you reach the earth structures (five to 10 minutes).

Listings North to Huehuetenango

Where to stay

Totonicapán

$ Hospedaje San Miguel
3 Calle, 7-49, Zona 1, T7766-1452.
Rooms with or without bath, hot water, communal TV.

$ Pensión Blanquita
13 Av and 4 Calle.
20 rooms, hot showers, good. Opposite this *pensión* is a Shell station.

San Francisco El Alto

$ Hotel Vásquez
4 Av, 11-53, T7738-4003.
Rooms all with private bathroom. Parking.

$ Vista Hermosa
2 Calle, 2-23, T7738-4010.
36 rooms, cheaper without bathroom, hot water, TV.

Momostenango

$ Estiver Ixcel
1 Calle, 4-15, Zona 4, downhill away from plaza, T7736-5036.
12 rooms, hot water, cheaper without bath, clean.

$ Hospedaje y Comedor Paclom
Close to central plaza, at 1 Calle, 1-71, Zona 4.

Pretty inner courtyard with caged birds and plants, hot water in shared bathrooms.

$ La Villa
1 Av, 1-13, Zona 1, below bank, T7736-5108.
6 rooms, warm water only, clean and nicely presented.

Restaurants

Totonicapán

$ Comedor Brenda 2
9 Av, 3-31.
Good, serving local food.

$ Comedor Letty
3 Calle, 8-18.
Typical Guatemalan fare.

Momostenango

$ Comedor Santa Isabel
Next door to Hospedaje y Comedor Paclom.
Friendly, cheap and good breakfasts.

$ Flipper
1 Calle y 2 Av A.
Good *licuados* and a range of fruit juices.

$ Hospedaje y Comedor Paclom
Close to the central plaza and where buses arrive from Xela, 1 Calle, 1-71, Zona 4.
Cheap meals, including snacks in a pretty inner courtyard.

Transport

Totonicapán

Bus Every 15 mins to **Quetzaltenango**, US$0.40, 45 mins. To **Los Encuentros**, US$2.20. To **Cuatro Caminos**, 30 mins, US$0.30.

San Francisco El Alto

Bus 2 km along the Pan-American Hwy heading north from Cuatro Caminos is a paved road, which runs to San Francisco El Alto (3 km) and then to Momostenango (19 km). Bus from **Quetzaltenango**, 50 mins on Fri, US$0.75. The last bus back is at 1800.

Momostenango

Bus From **Cuatro Caminos** (US$0.50) and **Quetzaltenango**, 1-1½ hrs. Buses to **Xela** every 30 mins from 0430-1600.

Huehuetenango and around → *Colour map 6, B2.*

a pleasant, large town and a busy transport hub

Huehuetenango (altitude 1905 m) – colloquially known as Huehue – offers little to detain you. However, it is an important transport centre serving the Cuchumatanes Mountains and the Mexican border. Its bus terminal, 2 km from town, is one of the busiest in the country. There are Maya ruins near the town, which were badly restored by the infamous United Fruit Company, and new adventure tourism opportunities opening up nearby. Trips, including horse rides, to more remote spots in the Huehuetenango region to see forests, haciendas and lakes are organized by Unicornio Azul. A useful website is www.interhuehue.com.

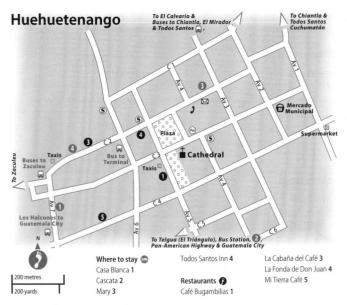

Huehuetenango

To El Calvario & Buses to Chiantla, El Mirador & Todos Santos

To Chiantla & Todos Santos Cuchumatán

Mercado Municipal

Plaza

Cathedral

Supermarket

Taxis

Bus to Terminal

Buses to Zaculeu

Taxis

To Zaculeu

Los Halcones to Guatemala City

To Telgua (El Triángulo), Bus Station, Pan-American Highway & Guatemala City

200 metres
200 yards

Where to stay
Casa Blanca 1
Cascata 2
Mary 3
Todos Santos Inn 4

Restaurants
Café Bugambilias 1

La Cabaña del Café 3
La Fonda de Don Juan 4
Mi Tierra Café 5

The neoclassical **cathedral** was built between 1867 and 1874, destroyed by earthquake in 1902, and took 10 years to repair. In 1956, the image of the patron saint, the Virgen de la Concepción was burnt in a fire. Then, during the 1976 earthquake, 80% of it was damaged, save the bells, façade and cupola. The skyline to the north of the city is dominated by the Sierrra de los Cuchumatanes, the largest area over 3000 m in Central America.

The ruins of **Zaculeu** ⓘ *0800-1800, US$6.40*, the old capital of the Mam Maya, are 5 km west of Huehuetenango on top of a rise with steep drops on three sides – a site chosen because of these natural defence measures. Its original name in Mam was *Xinabajul*, meaning 'between ravines'. In K'iche' it means 'white earth'. It was first settled in the Early Classic period (AD 250-600), but it flourished during the late post-Classic (AD 1200-1530). In July 1525, Gonzalo de Alvarado, the brother of Guatemala's conqueror, Pedro de Alvarado, set out for Zaculeu with 80 Spaniards, 40 horses and 2000 indigenous fighters, passing Mazatenango and Totonicapán on the way. The battle lasted four months, during which time the soldiers and residents of Zaculeu were dying of hunger, and eating their dead neighbours. The weakened Kaibil Balam, the Zaculeu *cacique* (chief), called for a meeting with Gonzalo. Gonzalo told the Mam chief that peace was not on the cards. Negotiations followed with the outcome being that Kaibil Balam be instructed in Christianity, obey the Spanish king and leave the city, whereupon Gonzalo de Alvarado would take possession of the Mam kingdom settlement in the name of the Spanish crown.

Aguacatán

The women of Aguacatán (altitude 1670 m) wear the most stunning headdresses in the country. On sale in *tiendas* in town, they are a long, slim belt of woven threads using many colours. The women also wear beautiful clothes: the *cortes* are dark with horizontal stripes of yellow, pink, blue and green. The town fiesta is 40 days after Holy Week, Virgen de la Encarnación.

Towards Todos Santos Cuchumatán

To get to Todos Santos, you have to climb the front range of the Cuchumatanes Mountains above Chiantla by a steep road from Huehuetenango. **Chiantla** has the **Luna Café** with art gallery and the nearby paleontological site of **El Mamutz**. Looking down on a clear day the cathedral at Huehuetenango resembles a blob of orange blancmange on the plain. At the summit, at about 3300 m, there is **El Mirador**.

The paved road continues over bleak moorland to Paquix where the road divides. The unpaved road to the north continues to Soloma. The other to the west goes through Aldea Chiabel, noted for its outhouses, more obvious than the small dwellings they serve. Here, giant agave plants appear to have large pom-poms attached, reminiscent of the baubles on Gaudí's Sagrada Familia in Barcelona. On this journey you often pass through cloud layer, eventually surfacing above it. On cloudier days you will be completely submerged until descending again to Huehuetenango. The road crosses a pass at 3394 m before a difficult long descent to Todos Santos, about 50 km from Huehuetenango.

The walk northwest from Chiantla to Todos Santos Cuchumatanes can be done in around 12-14 hours, or better, two days, staying overnight at **El Potrillo** in the barn owned by Rigoberto Alva. This route crosses one of the highest parts of the sierra at over 3500 m. Alternatively, cycle the 40-km part-gravel road, which is steep in places, but very rewarding.

Where to stay

Huehuetenango

$$ Casa Blanca
7 Av, 3-41, T7769-0777.
Comfortable, good restaurant in a pleasant garden, buffet breakfast, set lunch, very popular and good value, parking.

$$ Cascata
Lote 4, 42, Zona 5, Col Alvarado, Calzada Kaibil Balam, close to the bus station, T7769-0795, www.hotelcascata.ya.st.
Newish hotel with 16 rooms with Wi-Fi and private bathrooms. It is owned by Dutch, French and English folk and the service is excellent.

$ Mary
2 Calle, 3-52, T7764-1618.
With bath, cheaper without, good beds, hot water, cable TV, parking, clean, quiet, safe, well-maintained, good value. Recommended.

$ Todos Santos Inn
2 Calle, 6-74, T7764-1241.
Shared bath and private bath available, hot water, TV, helpful, clean, laundry, some rooms a bit damp, luggage stored. Recommended.

Restaurants

Huehuetenango

$$-$ La Cabaña del Café
2 Calle, 6-50.
Log cabin café with to-die-for cappuccino, snack food and good *chapín* breakfasts, good atmosphere. Recommended.

$ Café Bugambilias
5 Av 3-59, on the plaza.
Large, unusual 4-storey building, most of which is a popular, cheap, restaurant, very good breakfasts, *almuerzos*, sandwiches. Recommended.

$ La Fonda de Don Juan
2 Calle, 5-35.
Italian restaurant and bar (try the *cavatini*), sandwiches, big choice of desserts, *licuados*, coffees, good pizzas, also *comida típica*, with reasonable prices all served in a bright environment with red and white checked tablecloths.

$ Mi Tierra Café
4 Calle, 6-46, T7764-1473.
Good drinks and light meals, Mexican offerings; try the *fajitas*, nice setting, popular with locals and travellers. Recommended.

What to do

Unicornio Azul, *based in Chancol, T5205-9328, www.unicornioazul.com*. Horse-riding trips, trekking, mountain biking and birdwatching in the Cuchumatanes.

Transport

Huehuetenango
Bus and taxi
Local From the terminal to town, take 'Centro' minibus, which pulls up at cathedral, 5 mins. Taxis from behind the covered market. Walking takes 20-25 mins. Bus leaves Salvador Osorio School, final Calle 2, every 30 mins, 15 mins, to **Zaculeu**, last return 1830. Taxi, US$8, including waiting time. To walk takes about 1 hr; either take 6 Av north, cross the river and follow the road to the left, through Zaculeu modern village to the ruins, or go past the school and turn right beyond the river. The signs are barely visible.

Long distance To **Guatemala City**, 5 hrs, US$11, **Los Halcones**, 7 Av, 3-62, Zona 1 (they do not leave from the terminal) at 0430, 0700, 1400, reliable. From the bus terminal there are numerous services daily to the capital from 0215-1600 via **Chimaltenango**, 5 hrs, US$4. Via **Mazatenango** there are 5 daily.

North To **Todos Santos Cuchumatán**, 10 daily until 1630, 2-3 hrs, US$3.60. To **Barillas**, via **San Juan Ixcoy** (2½ hrs), **Soloma** (3 hrs), and **San Mateo Ixtatan** (7 hrs), 10 daily from 0200-2330, US$7. There are also buses to **San Rafael la Independencia** passing through Soloma and **Sta Eulalia**.

Northwest To **La Mesilla** for Mexico, frequent buses between 0530-1800, US$3.50, 2½ hrs, last bus returning to Huehue, 1800. To **Nentón**, via La Mesilla twice a day. To **Gracias a Dios**, several times a day.

South To **Quetzaltenango**, 13 a day from 0600-1600, US$3, 2-2¼ hrs. To **Cuatro Caminos**, US$2, 2 hrs. To **Los Encuentros**, for Lake Atitlán and Chichicastenango, 3 hrs.

East To **Aguacatán**, 12 daily, 0600-1900, 1 hr 10 mins, US$1.20. To **Nebaj** you have to get to Sacapulas via Aguacatán. To **Sacapulas**, 1130, 1245. To **Cobán**, take the earliest bus/pickup to Aguacatán and then Sacapulas and continue to Uspantán to change for Cobán.

Aguacatán

Bus

From **Huehue**, 1 hr 10 mins. It is 26 km east of Huehuetenango on a semi-paved route (good views). Returning between 0445 and 1600. Buses and pickups for **Sacapulas** and for onward connections to Nebaj and Cobán leave from the main street going out of town. Wait anywhere along there to catch your ride. It is 1½ hrs from Aguacatán to Sacapulas. To **Guatemala City** at 0300, 1100.

Todos Santos Cuchumatán and around → *Colour map 6, A2.*

indigenous village in a spectacular mountain setting

★High in the Cuchumatanes, the Mam-speaking Todos Santeros maintain a traditional way of life with their striking, bright, indigenous dress and their adherence to the 260-day Tzolkin calendar. Todos Santos (altitude 2470 m) is hemmed in by 3800-m-high mountains either side that squeeze it into one long, 2-km street down the valley. The town is famous for its weaving, and even more famous for the horse race, see box, page 404.

Some of Guatemala's best weaving is done in Todo Santos. Fine *huipiles* may be bought in the cooperative on the main street and direct from the makers. The men wear the famous red-and-white striped trousers. Some wear a black wool over-trouser piece. Their jackets are white, pink, purple and red-striped with beautifully coloured, and intricately embroidered, collars and cuffs. Their straw hat is wrapped with a blue band. You can buy the embroidered cuffs and collars for men's shirts, the red trousers, and gorgeous colourful crocheted bags made by the men. The women wear navy blue *cortes* with thin, light blue, vertical stripes.

There is a colourful Saturday market and a smaller one on Wednesday. The **church** near the park was built in 1580.

Around Todos Santos

The closest walk is to **Las Letras**, where the words 'Todos Santos' are spelt out in white stone on a hillside above the town. The walk takes an hour. To get there take the path down the side of **Restaurant Cuchumatlán**. The highest point of the Cuchumatanes, and the highest non-volcanic peak in the country, **La Torre** at 3837 m, is to the northeast of Todos Santos and can be reached from the village of **Tzichem** on the road to Concepción Huista. When clear, it's possible to see the top of Volcán Santa María, one of the highest volcanoes in Guatemala. The hike takes about five hours. The best way to do it is to start in the afternoon and spend the night near the top. It is convenient for camping, with wood

ON THE ROAD

Todos Santos festival

The horse racing festival of Todos Santos is one of the most celebrated and spectacular in Central America – it is also a frenzied day that usually degenerates into a drunken mess. Quite simply riders race between two points, having a drink at each turn until they fall off.

According to Professor Margarito Calmo Cruz, the origins of the fiesta lie in the 15th or 16th century with the arrival of the *conquistadores* to Todos Santos. They arrived on horses wearing large, colourful clothes with bright scarves flowing down their backs and feathers in their hats. The locals experimented, imitating them, enjoyed it and the tradition was born.

When the day begins, the men are pretty tipsy, but sprightly and clean. The race is frantic and colourful with scarves flying out from the backs of the men. As the day wears on, they get completely smashed, riding with arms outstretched – whip in one hand and beer bottle in the other. They are mudspattered, dishevelled and are moaning and groaning from the enjoyment and the alcohol which must easily have reached near comatose level. At times the riders fall, and look pretty lifeless. They are dragged by the scruff of the neck, regardless of serious injury or death, to the edge of the fence as quickly as possible, to avoid trampling.

The men guzzle gallons of beer and the aim is to continue racing all day. A fall means instant dismissal from the race. There are wardens on the side lines with batons, whose primary job is the welfare of the horses, changing them when they see necessary. But they also deal with protesting fallen riders, who try and clamber back onto their horses. By the end of the day the spectacle is pretty grotesque. The horses are drenched with sweat and wild-eyed with fear. The men look hideous and are paralytic from booze. The edge of the course and the town is littered with bodies.

The race takes place on the road that winds its way out of town, not the incoming road from Huehue. It starts at 0800. There are about 15 riders on the course at any one time. It continues until noon, stops for *cerveza* guzzling and begins again at 1400, ending at 1700.

---

but no water. A compass is essential in case of mist. From Todos Santos, you can also hike south to **San Juan Atitán**, four to five hours, where the locals wear an interesting *traje típico*. Market days are on Mondays and Thursdays. From there you can hike to the Pan-American Highway; it's a one day walk. The local fiesta is 22-26 June.

Jacaltenango to the Mexican border

The road from Todos Santos continues northwest through **Concepción Huista**. Here the women wear towels as shawls and Jacalteco is spoken. The fiesta, 29 January-3 February, has fireworks and dancing. The hatmaker in Canton Pilar supplies the hats for Todos Santos, he welcomes viewers and will make a hat to your specifications (but if you want a typical Todos Santos leather *cincho*, buy it there).

Beyond Jacaltenango is **Nentón**, and **Gracias a Dios** at the Mexican border. When the road north out of Huehue splits at Paquix, the right fork goes to **San Mateo Ixtatán**, with ruins nearby. The road from Paquix crosses the roof of the Cuchumatanes, before descending to **San Juan Ixcoy, Soloma** and **Santa Eulalia**, where the people speak O'anjob'al as they do in Soloma. East along a scenic route is **Barillas**. There are several *pensiones* in these places and regular buses from Huehue.

Where to stay

Reservations are necessary in the week before the Nov horse race, but even if the town is full, locals offer their homes.

$ Casa Familiar
Up the hill, close to central park, T7783-0656.
Run by the friendly family of Santiaga Mendoza Pablo. Hot shower, sauna, breakfast, dinner, delicious banana bread, spectacular view, popular. The Mendoza family give weaving lessons.

$ Hotel La Paz
Friendly, great view of the main street from balconies, excellent spot for the 1 Nov fiesta, shared showers not great, enclosed parking.

$ Hotel Mam
Above the central park, next to Hotelito Todos Santos.
Friendly, clean, hot water, but needs 1 hr to warm up, not too cold in the rooms as an open fire warms the building, good value.

$ Hotelito Todos Santos
Above the central park.
Hot water, clean, small café, but beware of boys taking you to the hotel quoting one price, and then on arrival, finding the price has mysteriously gone up.

Around Todos Santos

$ Hospedaje San Diego
San Juan Atitán.
Only 3 beds, basic, friendly, clean, food available.

Restaurants

There are *comedores* on the 2nd floor of the market selling very cheap meals.

$ Comedor Katy
Will prepare vegetarian meals on request, good-value *menú del día*.

$ Cuchumatlán
Has sandwiches, pizza and pancakes, and is popular at night.

Festivals

1 Nov Horse race. The festival begins on 21 Oct. See box, opposite.
2 Nov Day of the Dead, when locals visit the cemetery and leave flowers and food.

Shopping

The following shops all sell bags, trousers, shirts, *huipiles*, jackets and clothes. The best bargains are at **Tienda Maribel**, up the hill from Casa Familiar, and **Cooperativa Estrella de Occidente**, on the main street. **Casa Mendoza**, just beyond Tienda Maribel, is where Telésforo Mendoza makes clothes to measure. **Domingo Calmo** also makes clothes to measure. His large, brown house with tin roof is on the main road to the Ruinas (5 mins); follow the road up from Casa Familiar. Ask for **Casa de Domingo**.

Transport

Bus
To **Huehuetenango**, 2-3 hrs, crowded Mon and Fri, 0400, 0500, 0600, 0615-0630, 1145, 1230, 1300. Possible changes on Sat so ask beforehand. For petrol, ask at **El Molino**.

Jacaltenango to the Mexican border
Bus
From **Huehuetenango** at 0330, 0500, returning at 1130 and 1400; also pickups.

Quetzaltenango
& around

Quetzaltenango (commonly known as Xela, pronounced 'shayla') is the most important city in western Guatemala. It is set among a group of high mountains and volcanoes, one of which, Santa María, caused much death and destruction after an eruption in 1902. The bulk of the city is modern, but its 19th-century downtown revamp and its narrow streets give the centre more of a historic feel. There is a pleasant park with its beautifully restored façade of the colonial church. It is an excellent base from which to visit nearby hot springs, religious idols, volcanoes and market towns.

Quetzaltenango → *Colour map 6, B2.*
Guatemala's second city, with a colonial cathedral and breathtaking views

The central park, Parque Centro América, is the focus of Quezaltenango (altitude 2335 m). It is surrounded by the cathedral, with its beautifully restored original colonial façade, and a number of elegant neoclassical buildings, constructed during the late 19th and early 20th century.

The modern cathedral, **Catedral de la Diócesis de los Altos**, was constructed in 1899 and is set back behind the original. The surviving façade of the 1535 **Catedral del Espíritu Santo** is beautiful, intricately carved and with restored portions of murals on its right side. On the south side of the park is the **Casa de la Cultura**. Inside are the **Museo de la Marimba** with exhibits and documents relating to the 1871 Liberal Revolution. On the right-hand side of the building is the totally curious **Museo de Historia Natural** ① *Mon-Fri 0800-1200, 1400-1800, US$0.90.* Deformed stuffed animals are cheek by jowl with pre-Columbian pottery, sports memorabilia, fizzy drink bottles, a lightning-damaged mirror and dinosaur remains. It satisfies the most morbid of curiosities with displays of a two-headed calf, Siamese twin pigs, an eight-legged goat, and a strange sea creature that looks like an alien, known as *Diabillo del Mar* (little sea devil). On the park's southwest side is the **Museo de Arte**, with a collection of contemporary Guatemalan art, and the **Museo del Ferrocarril Nacional de los Altos** ① *7 Calle y 12 Av, Mon-Fri 0800-1200, 1400-1800, US$0.90,* recounting the story of an electric railway between Xela and the Pacific slope.

Getting around

The town centre is compact and all sites and most services are within walking distance. The Santa Fe city bus goes between the terminal, the rotonda and the town centre. Out of town destination buses stop at the rotonda and it is quicker to get here from the town centre than to the Minerva Terminal. City buses for the terminal leave from 4 Calle and 13 Avenida, Zona 1, and those straight for the rotonda leave from 11 Avenida and 10 Calle, Zona 1, US$0.15.

A taxi within Zona 1, or from Zona 1 to a closer part of Zona 3, is about US$3.20.

The **Banco de Occidente**, founded in 1881, and the first bank to opened in Guatemala, dominates the northern edge of the park. The overly wired-up **Municipalidad** straddles the eastern edge of the park with its neoclassical columns. Its first building blocks were laid in 1881, but it wasn't completed until 1897.

The stately **Teatro Municipal** (1892-1896) is on 14 Avenida y 1 Calle and can be visited outside of performance hours. Restored at a cost of four million quetzales, it has an imposing presence. To its left, on Avenida 14 "A", is the **Teatro Roma**. Building began in 1898, but was not completed until 1931, when it became the first cinema to open in Guatemala. It was restored in 2000 as a theatre with a capacity for 1400 and is open for performances.

There is a sickly green modern church, the **Sagrado Corazón**, on the Parque Benito Juárez near the market. Inside is a gigantic, freestanding, Chagall-influenced painting with swooping angels, and Christ in a glass box, built into the picture. The church of **La Transfiguración** ① *near the corner of 11 Calle and 5 Av, Zona 1*, houses the largest crucified Christ figure (San Salvador del Mundo) to be found in Central America – it is almost 3 m in height and now housed behind glass. At 20 Avenida and 4 Calle is the city's **Cementerio** ① *0700-1900*. Inside are the remains of the Quetzalteco President, Estrada Cabrera (1898-1920) in a small cream neoclassical temple. Behind his tomb are the unmarked graves of a large number of cholera victims wiped out in a 19th-century epidemic. Manuel Lisandra Barillas (Guatemalan President 1885-1892) is also entombed here. There is a small patio area known as Colonia Alemana lined with graves of German residents; a large area where those that died as martyrs in the civil war lie; and a memorial to those that perished in the September Revolution of 1897. The town's fiestas are 9-17 September, Holy Week and the October fiesta of La Virgen del Rosario.

★ North of Quetzaltenango

Between Quetzaltenango and Cuatro Caminos is the small *ladino* town of **Salcajá**, where *jaspé* skirt material has been woven since 1861. If you fancy a taste or a whiff of some potent liquor before bracing yourself for an entry into Quetzaltenango, then this is the place to halt. It is worth a visit not only for the booze but its famous church – the oldest

Quetzaltenango

To Estado Mario Camposeco & Olintepeque
To Transportes Alamo
Calzado Rodolfo Robles
La Democracia Market & Sagrado Corazón
Parque Gabriel Pinillos
C 0a

To **12**, Transportes Galgos, Mont Blanc Shopping Centre, Templo de Minerva, Market & Minerva Bus Terminal

Teatro Roma
ZONA 1
C Cajolá
Av 15
Av 14A
Teatro Municipal
C 0C
C 2
Agencia de Viajes SAB
C 1
Av 10
To Lineas América Buses, La Rotonda, Cuatro Caminos & Guatemala City
C 3
15 Av A
To Cementerio
Vrisa
Av 13
Av 11
Av 9
Av 8
C 4
C 5
Museo de Ferrocarril Nacional de los Altos & Museo de Arte
Parque Centro América
Municipalidad
Cine
Despensa Familiar Supermarket
Cathedral
C 6
To 14
Diagonal 13
C an 15
To 18
Casa de la Cultura
Centro Comercial Municipal
C 8
C 9
Buses to Almolonga & Zunil
C 10
Av 8

N
100 metres
100 yards

Where to stay
7 Orejas Hostal 1 *A1*
Black Cat Hostel 10 *B2*
Casa Doña Mercedes 4 *C1*
Casa Mañen 6 *C3*
Casa Renaissance 5 *D2*
Casa San Bartolomé 14 *C3*
Casa Seibel 7 *D3*
Casa Xelajú 8 *D1*
Hostel Nim Sut 9 *B3*
Kiktem-Ja 11 *C2*
Modelo 12 *B1*
Villa del Centro 13 *B2*

Restaurants
Asados Puente 17 *C2*
Bakeshop 12 *A1*
Blue Angel Café 2 *C1*
Café Baviera 1 *C2*
Café y Chocolate La Luna 8 *C3*
Cardinali 20 *B2*
Chocolate Doña Pancha 18 *D1*
El Apaste 4 *C2*
El Deli Crepe 5 *B2*
La Chatia Artesana 3 *C1*
Las Calas 9 *B1*
Royal París & Guatemaya Intercultural Travel Agency 10 *B1*
Sabor de India 7 *B1*
Salón Tecún 16 *C2*
Tertulianos Villas Lesbia 6 *B2*
Ut'z Hua 11 *B2*

Bars & clubs
El Duende 14 *A1*
El Zaguán 13 *A1*
La Taberna de Don Rodrigo 15 *A2*
Ojalá 19 *B1*

The most important battle of the Spanish conquest took place near Quetzaltenango when the great K'iche' warrior Tecún Umán was slain. In October 1902 the Volcán Santa María erupted, showering the city with half a metre of dust. An ash cloud soared 8.6 km into the air and some 1500 people were killed by volcanic fallout and gas. A further 3000 people died a short while later from malaria due to plagues of mosquitoes which had not been wiped out by the blast. Some 20 years on, a new volcano, born after the 1902 eruption, began to erupt. This smaller volcano, Santiaguito, spews clouds of dust and ash on a daily basis and is considered one of the most dangerous volcanoes in the world. The city's prosperity, as seen by the grand neoclassical architecture in the centre, was built on the back of the success of the coffee fincas on the nearby coastal plain. This led to the country's first bank being established here.

in Central America – and for its textiles, often seen being produced in the streets. In 1524 the first church in Central America was founded by the conquering Spaniards. **San Jacinto** is a small church on 6 Avenida y 2 Calle; it may not always be open. *Caldo de frutas*, a highly alcoholic drink with quite a kick, is not openly sold but is made in the town and drunk on festive occasions. It is illegal to drink it in public places. It is a concoction of nances, cherries, peaches, apples and quinces and is left to ferment in rum. There is also *rompope*, a drink made with eggs. Salcajá is a town that also revolves around textiles, with shops on every street. Yarn is tied and dyed, untied, and wraps are then stretched around telephone poles along the road or on the riverside. One of these can be seen outside San Jacinto church. Market day is Tuesday.

San Andrés Xecul is a small village in stunning surroundings with an extraordinarily lurid-coloured church, 8 km north of Xela. Painted a deep-mustard yellow in 1900, its figurines, including angels, have been given blue wings and pastel-pink skirts. Climb the hill a bit above the town and catch a glimpse of the fantastic dome – mulitcoloured like a beach ball. With your back to the church climb the cobbled street leading up the right-hand side of the plaza to a yellow and maroon chapel peering out across the valley. The view from here is spectacular. Market day is Thursday, opposite the church. The town's fiestas are on 21 November, 30 November and 1 December.

★South of Quetzaltenango

Souteast of Xela is Cantel which has the largest and oldest textile factory in the country. Sunday is market day and the town's fiesta is 12-18 August (main day 15 August). At Easter a passion play is performed. A little further on, on the outskirts of town, on the right-hand side (one minute on the bus), is the white **Copavic glass factory** ① *T7763-8038, www. copavic.com, Mon-Fri 0500-1300, Sat 0500-1200*, where you can watch and photograph the workers blow the recycled glass.

Zunil Pinned in by a very steep-sided valley is the town of Zunil, 9 km from Quetzaltenango. It is visited for the nearby hot thermal baths that many come to wallow in, and for its worship of its well-dressed idol San Simón (Maximón). The market is held on Mondays. The town's fiesta is 22-26 November (main day 25) and there is a very colourful Holy Week. The **church** is striking both inside and out. It has a large decorated altarpiece and a small shrine to murdered Bishop Gerardi at the altar. The façade is white with serpentine columns wrapped in carved ivy.

San Simón (Maximón) is worshipped in the town and is often dressed in different clothes at different times. A small charge is made for the upkeep and to take photos; ask anyone in the town to escort you to his house. To the left of the church is the **Santa Ana Cooperative**, which sells beautiful *huipiles*, shirt and skirt materials, as well as bags and bookmarks.

The nearby extinct **Volcán Pico Zunil**, rises to 3542 m to the southeast of the town. On its slopes are the **thermal baths of Fuentes Georginas** ① *0700-1900, US$2.70*, which you'll know you're approaching by the wafts of sulphurous fumes that come your way. There are several different-sized pools set into the mountainside surrounded by thick, luscious vegetation and enveloped in the steam that continuously rises up in wafts from the hot pools. There are spectacular views on the way to the baths.

The thermal baths of **Aguas Amargas** ① *0800-1700, US$2, children, US$1.30*, are on Zunil Mountain below Fuentes Georginas. They are reached by following the road south and heading east (left) by Estancia de La Cruz. This road passes fields of flowers and would make a great trip on a bike.

El Viejo Palmar This is Guatemala's Pompeii. The river that cuts through here flows directly down from the active Santiaguito volcanic cone following a series of serious lahars (mudflows of water and volcanic material) that took place in the 1990s. The small town of 10,000 was evacuated, leaving an extraordinary legacy. In August 1998, the whole south end of the ghost town was destroyed by a massive lahar that crushed the church. This also shifted the course of the Río Nimá I, which began to flow directly through the centre of the church remains. Very heavy erosion since has left the west front and the altar separated by a 30-m-deep ravine – an unbelievable sight.

Volcán Santa María and Santiaguito Santiaguito's mother, Santa María (3772 m), is a rough 5½-hour climb (1500 m). You can see Santiaguito (2488 m) below, erupting mostly with ash blasts and sometimes lava flows from a mirador. It is possible to camp at the summit of Santa María, or on the saddle west of the summit, but it is cold and windy, but worth it because dawn provides views of the entire country's volcanic chain and an almighty shadow is cast across the area by Santa Maria's form. Santiaguito is a fairly new volcano that formed after the eruption of Santa María out of its crater. Do not attempt to climb Santiaguito: it erupts continuously on a daily basis throwing up ash and is considered one of the most dangerous volcanoes in the world. To see it erupting you need to climb Santa María, where you can look down on this smaller volcano. ►► *See Tour operators, page 416.*

Laguna Chicabal San Martín rangers' station ① *0700-1800, US$2*, is where the two-hour climb to Laguna Chicabal starts. This is a lime-green lake, at 2712 m, in the crater of the extinct volcano (2900 m) of the same name, with wild white lilies, known as *cartucho*, growing at the edges. The Maya believe the waters are sacred and it is thought that if you swim in the lake you will become ill. The highlight of a trip here is the sight of the clouds tumbling down over the circle of trees that surround the lake, and then appearing to bounce on the surface before dispersing. Ceremonies of Maya initiation are held at the lake in early May, known as *Jueves de la Ascensión*. The walk from San Martín takes about two hours.

★ West of Quetzaltenango

It takes 30 minutes to reach **San Juan Ostuncalco**, 15 km away. It's a pleasant, prosperous town with a big white church noted for its good weekly market on Sunday and beautiful sashes worn by men. Its fiesta, Virgen de la Candelaria, is held on 29 January to 2 February. The road, which is paved, switchbacks 37 km down valleys and over pine-clad mountains to a plateau looking over the valley in which are San Pedro and San Marcos. **San Marcos** has a few places to stay and eat. It is a transport hub with little to see. **San Pedro Sacatepéquez** has a huge market on Thursday. The Maya women wear golden and purple skirts.

The extinct **Volcán Tajumulco**, at 4220 m, is the highest in Central America. Start very early in the day if you plan to return to San Marcos by nightfall. It's about a five-hour climb and a three-hour descent. Once you have reached the ridge on Tajumulco, turn right along the top of it; there are two peaks, the higher is on the right. The peak on the left (4100 m) is used for shamanistic rituals.

Dormant **Volcán Tacaná** (4093 m) on the Mexican border may be climbed from the village of Sibinal. Its last eruption was 1949, but there was activity in 2001, so check before climbing. It is the second highest volcano in Guatemala with a 400-m-wide crater and fumaroles on its flanks. Take a bus to Sibinal from San Marcos. It is a six-hour difficult climb to the summit and it's recommended that you ask for a guide in the village. About 15 km west of San Marcos the road begins its descent from 2500 m to the lowlands. In 53 km to **Malacatán** it drops to 366 m. It is a winding ride with continuous bends, but the scenery is attractive. There is accommodation.

The road to the coastal plain from San Juan Ostuncalco is the most attractive of all the routes down from the highlands, bypassing most of the small towns through quickly changing scenery as you lose height. After San Juan, go south for 1.5 km to **Concepción Chiquirichapa**, with a bright blue and yellow church, which is one of the wealthiest villages in the country. It has a small market early every Thursday morning and a fiesta on 5-9 December. About 6 km beyond is **San Martín Sacatepéquez**, which used to be known as San Martín Chile Verde, and is famous for its hot chillies. This village appears in Miguel Angel Asturias' *Mulata de Tal*. It stands in a windy, cold gash in the mountains. The slopes are superbly steep and farmed, giving fantastic vistas on the climb up and down from Laguna Chicabal (see above). The men wear very striking long red and white striped tunics, beautifully embroidered around the hem. Market day is Sunday. The fiesta runs from 7-12 November (main day 11 November).

Listings Quetzaltenango and around *map p408*

Tourist information

General information can be found at www.xelapages.com and www.xela who.com, which has good listings.

INGUAT
7 Calle, 11-35, on the park, T7761-4931.
Mon-Fri 0900-1600, Sat 0900-1300.
Not recommended. Try the recommended tour operators (see What to do, below) for information instead.

Where to stay

At Easter, 12-18 Sep and Christmas, rooms need to be booked well in advance.

$$ Casa Mañen
9a Av, 4-11, Zona 1, T7765-0786.
Reports are consistently good, serves great breakfasts and friendly staff offer a very warm welcome. Room 2 is a great option with a bed on a mezzanine. Some rooms have microwave, fridge and TV. All are

comfortable, and furnished with attractive wooden accessories. There is a small, pretty courtyard area and secure parking.

$$ Casa San Bartolomé
2 Av, 71-17, T7761-9511,
www.casasanbartolome.com.
Located in a historical neighbourhood near the Parque Central, **Casa San Bartolomé** is a colonial-style B&B with 7 simple and unpretentious rooms, all equipped with Wi-Fi, cable TV, hot water and heating. There's a small garden and mountain views from the shared balcony. Breakfast included.

$$ Hotel Modelo
14 Av A, 2-31, T7761-2529,
www.hotelmodelo1892.com.
This comfortable colonial-style option enjoys a convenient central location and a handsome interior furnished with antiques and abundant potted plants. They offer 19 spacious rooms complete with hot water, cable TV, private bath and Wi-Fi.

$$-$ 7 Orejas Hostal
2 Calle, 16-92, T7768-3218, www.7orejas.com.
Set in a handsome colonial building, this hotel is well maintained and professionally managed. They offer simple but attractive rooms with cable TV, private bath, and solid hand-carved furniture, as well as a cheaper option in their 8-bed dorm. Upstairs you can enjoy breakfast (US$4) on their pleasant open-air terrace. There are also furnished apartments for long stays. Recommended.

$$-$ Casa Doña Mercedes
6 Calle y 14 Av, 13-42, T5687-3305,
www.hostalcasadonamercedes.com.gt.
Good value, hospitable and affordable, this modest little guesthouse has a range of tidy, spacious and pleasant rooms with hot water and cable TV. There's also a fully equipped kitchen and cheery communal areas.

$$-$ Villa del Centro
12 Av, 3-61, T7761-1767,
www.hotelvilladelcentro.com.

Quiet, clean and friendly, **Villa del Centro** has a great central location less than a block from the Parque Central. It offers simple, pleasant, recently renovated rooms with firm beds, Wi-Fi and TV.

$ Black Cat Hostel
13 Av, 3-33, Zona 1, T7761-2091,
www.blackcathostels.net.
A hostel in the old Casa Kaehler. Dorms and private rooms all with shared bathrooms. Breakfast included.

$ Casa Renaissance
9 Calle, 11-26, T3121-6315,
www.casarenaissance.com.
Bright, cosy, and full of character, **Casa Renaissance** is a colonial-style guesthouse that is over a century old. It boasts lots of homey enclaves including 2 patios with hammocks and a living room with sofas and a TV. Rooms are simple but comfortable. Additional facilities include Wi-Fi, kitchen, free coffee and tea.

$ Casa Seibel
9 Av, 8-10, T5958-7529, www.casaseibel.com.
Featuring wooden floors, 2 leafy courtyards and an old piano, this charming hostel and guesthouse has lots of character and history. Accommodation includes simple dorms and spacious rooms and there are dining rooms, communal lounges and an open kitchen. Friendly hostess. Economical and recommended.

$ Casa Xelajú
Callejón 15, Diagonal 13-02, T7761-5954,
www.casaxelaju.com.
Part of a Spanish school but also available to non-students, Casa Xelajú has several nice little 1-bed apartments complete with fully equipped kitchens, Wi-Fi, cable TV, hot water and bath tubs. Very quiet and comfortable, a great deal if you're in town for a while. Weekly or monthly rental. Recommended.

$ Hostel Nim Sut
4 Calle, 9-42, T7761-3083, www.hostelnim sutquetzaltenango.weebly.com.

A nice little hostel with a pleasant courtyard and good mountain views from the roof terrace. They have economical private rooms and dorms, with or without private bath. Rates include drinking water, Wi-Fi, use of kitchen, but breakfast is extra.

$ Kiktem-Ja
13 Av, 7-18, Zona 1, T7761-4304.
A central location with 16 colonial-style rooms, nicely furnished, locally made blankets on the beds, wooden floors, all with bath, hot water, open fires, car parking inside gates.

Zunil

$$$-$$ Las Cumbres Eco-Saunas y Gastronomía
T5399-0029, www.las cumbres.com.gt. Daily 0700-1800.
Beyond Zunil on the left-hand side of the road heading to the coast (Km 210). This is the place for some R&R with saunas emitting natural steam from the geothermal activity nearby. There are 12 rooms with sauna, cheaper without, and separate saunas and jacuzzis for day visitors (US$2.50 per hr) and a restaurant serving good regional food and natural juices. Highly recommended. See Transport, below, for transfers.

$ Turicentro Fuentes Georginas.
6 cold bungalows with 2 double beds and 2 bungalows with 3 single beds. They have cold showers, fireplaces with wood, electricity 1700-2200 and barbecue grills for guests' use near the baths. Guests can use the baths after public closing times. Reasonably priced restaurant with breakfasts, snacks and drinks, 0800-1800.

Restaurants

$$$-$$ Cardinali
14 Av, 3-25, Zona 1.
Owned by Benito, a NY Italian, great Italian food, including large pizzas with 31 varieties: 2 for 1 on Tue and Thu; tasty pastas of 20 varieties, extensive wine list.

Recommended. Also does home delivery in 30 mins (T7761-0924).

$$$-$ Las Calas
14 Av "A", 3-21, Zona 1. Mon-Sat.
Breakfasts, salads, soups, paella and pastas served around a courtyard with changing art hanging from walls. The food is tasty with delicious bread to accompany, but small portions are served. The breakfast service is far too slow. Adjoining bar.

$$$-$ Restaurante Royal París
14 Av "A", 3-06, Zona 1.
Delicious food (try the fish in a creamy mushroom sauce), excellent choices, including vegetarian. Also cheap options. Run by Stéphane and Emmanuelle. Recommended. Live music from 2000 on Fri.

$$$-$ Restaurante Tertulianos Villa Lesbia
14 Av, 5-26, Zona 3, T7767-4666.
Gourmet quality, specializing in meat, cheese and chocolate fondues, and scrumptious desserts. Recommended.

$$ El Apaste
5 Calle, 14-48, Zona 3, T7776-6249.
Local Xela cuisine, rich stews and meats, traditionally served in the eponymous *apaste* (terracotta dish).

$$ Sabor de India
15 Avenida, 3-64.
Don't miss this fully authentic Indian restaurant. It serves wholesome, flavourful, good value curries complete with naan bread. Lovely sweet mango lassis, good service and relaxed ambience. Recommended.

$$ Ut'z Hua
Av 12, 3-02, Zona 1.
This prettily decorated restaurant with purple tablecloths does typical food, which is always very good and filling. Ask for the *pollo con mole* or fish. Recommended.

$$-$ Asados Puente
7 Calle, 13-29.

Lots of veggie dishes with tofu and tempeh. Also ceviche. Popular with expats. Run by Ken Cielatka and Eva Melgar. Some profits go towards helping ill children.

$$-$ Salón Tecún
Pasaje Enríquez, off the park at 12 Av y 4 Calle, Zona 1.
Bar, local food, breakfasts also, TV. Always popular with gringos and locals.

$ El Deli Crepe
14 Av, 3-15, Zona 1.
Good tacos, *almuerzo* with soup, great milkshakes, savoury and sweet crêpes, juicy *fajitas* that arrive steaming.

Cafés and bakeries

Bakeshop at 18 Av
1-40, Zona 3. Tue and Fri 0900-1800.
Mennonite bakery that is Xela's answer to *dulce* heaven. They bake a whole range of cookies, muffins, breads and cakes and sells fresh yoghurt and cheeses. Get there early as the goodies go really fast.

Blue Angel Café
7 Calle, 15-79, Zona 1.
Great salads, light meals, service a little slow though, movies shown on a monthly rotation, useful noticeboard.

Café Baviera
5 Calle, 13-14, Zona 1. Open 0700-2000.
Good cheap meals and excellent pies, huge cake portions (try the carrot cake) and coffee in large premises, with walls lined from ceiling to floor with old photos and posters. Good for breakfasts, but a little on the expensive side. Popular, but lacks warmth.

Café y Chocolate La Luna
8 Av, 4-11, Zona 1.
Delicious hot chocolate with or without added luxuries, good cheap snacks, also top chocolates and *pasteles* (the strawberry and cream pie is recommended), pleasant atmosphere in a colonial house decorated with moon symbols, fairy lights, and old photos; a good meeting place.

Chocolate Doña Pancha
10a Calle 16-67 Zona 1, T7761-9700.
High-quality chocolate factory, with great range of drinks, cakes and pastries, also chocolate products to take away.

La Chatia Artesana
7 Calle, 15-18, www.lachatia-artesana.com.
This wonderful café-restaurant serves superb gourmet sandwiches, such as chicken teriyaki and portobello mushrooms, on a variety of artisanal breads. There's also delicious cookies, brownies and other snacks, along with fresh coffee and juice. Lovely outdoor courtyard. Recommended.

Bars and clubs

El Duende
14 Av 'A,' 1-42, Zona 1. Open 1800-2330.
Popular café-bar. A favourite among Guatemalans and gringos.

El Zaguán
14 Av 'A', A-70, Zona 1. Wed, Thu 1900-2430, Fri, Sat 2100-2430.
A disco-bar, US$3.25, drink included; plays salsa music.

La Taberna de Don Rodrigo
14 Av, Calle C-47, Zona 1.
Cosy bar, reasonable food served in dark wood atmosphere, draught beer.

Ojalá
15 Av 'A', 3-33.
An entertainment venue, popular with both locals and gringos, which also shows films.

Entertainment

See also Blue Angel Café and Ojalá in Cafés and bakeries and Bars and clubs, above.

Cinemas
Cine Sofía, 7 Calle 15-18. Mon-Fri 1800.
La Pradera, in shopping mall in Zona 3, next to bus terminal. 5 screens, latest releases.

Dance

Trópica Latina, *5 Calle 12-24, Zona 1, T5892-8861, tropicalatina@xelawho.com.* Classes Mon-Sat.

Theatre

Teatro Municipal, *14 Av and 1 Calle.* Main season May-Nov, theatre, opera, etc.

Shopping

Bookshops

Vrisa, *15 Av, 3-64, T7761-3237.* A good range of English-language second-hand books.

Markets

The **main market** is at Templo de Minerva on the western edge of town (take the local bus, US$0.10); at the southeast corner of Parque Centro América is the **Centro Comercial Municipal**, a shopping centre with craft and textile shops on the upper levels, food, clothes, etc below. There is another **market** at 2 Calle y 16 Av, Zona 3, south of Parque Benito Juárez, known as La Democracia. Every first Sun of the month there also is an art and handicrafts market, around Parque Centro América.

Language schools

See also box, page 359. Many of Xela's schools can be found at www.xelapages.com/schools.htm. There are many schools offering individual tuition, accommodation with families, extra-curricular activities and excursions. Some also offer Mayan languages. Several schools fund community-development projects, and students are invited to participate with voluntary work. Some schools are non-profit making; enquire carefully. Extra-curricular activities are generally better organized at the larger schools. Prices start from US$130 per week including accommodation, but rise in June-August to US$150 and up. The following have been recommended:

Centro de Estudios de Español Pop Wuj, 1 Calle, 17-72, T7761-8286, www.pop-wuj.org.
Guatemalensis, 19 Av, 2-14, Zona 1, T7765-1384, www.geocities.com/spanland/.
Sol Latino, Diagonal 12, 6-58, Zona 1, T5613-7222, www.spanishschoollatino.com.
Instituto Central América (ICA), 19 Av, 1-47 Calle, Zona 1, T7763-1871.
INEPAS (Instituto de Estudios Español y Participación en Ayuda Social), 15 Av, 4-59, T7765-1308, www.inepas. org. Keen on social projects and has already founded a primary school in a Maya village, extremely welcoming.
Juan Sisay Spanish School, 15 Av, 8-38, Zona 1, T7761-1586, www.juansisay.com.
Kie-Balam, Diagonal 12, 4-46, Zona 1, T7761-1636, kie_balam@hotmail.com. Offers conversation classes in the afternoon in addition to regular hours.
La Paz, Diagonal 11, 7-36, T7761-2159, xela.escuela lapaz@gmail.com.
Minerva Spanish School, 24 Av, 4-39, Zona 3, T7767-4427, www.minervaspanishschool.com.
Proyecto Lingüístico Quetzalteco de Español, 5 Calle, 2-40, Zona 1, T7765-2140, hermandad@plqe.org. Recommended.
Proyecto Lingüístico 'Santa María', 14 Av "A", 1-26, T7765-1262. Volunteer opportunities and free internet access.
Sakribal, 6 C, 7-42, Zona 1, T7763-0717, www.sakribal.com. Community projects are available.
Ulew Tinimit, 4 C, 15-23, Zona 1, T7761-6242, www.spanish guatemala.org. Utatlán, 12 Av, 14-32, Pasaje Enríquez, Zona 1, T7763-0446, utatlan_xela@hotmail.com. Voluntary work opportunities, one of the cheaper schools.

Supermarkets

Centro Comercial Mont Blanc, *Paiz, 4 Calle between 18-19 Av, Zona 3*.
Despensa Familiar, *13 Av, 6-94*.
La Pradera, *near the Minerva Terminal*.

North of Quetzaltenango

The smallest bottle of bright yellow *rompope* is sold in various shops around Salcajá, including the **Fábrica de Pénjamo**, 2 Av, 4-03, Zona 1, US$1.55, and it slips down the throat very nicely!

What to do

When climbing the volcanoes make sure your guides stay with you all the time; it can get dangerous when the cloud rolls down.

Adrenalina Tours, *inside Pasaje Enríquez, T7761-4509, www.adrenalinatours.com.* Numerous tours are on offer including bike, fishing, rafting, horse riding, rock climbing and volcano tours as well as packages to Belize, Honduras and the Petén and trips to Huehue and Todos Santos. Specializes in hikes and treks all over Guatemala. Highly recommended.
Agencia de Viajes SAB, *1 Calle, 12-35, T7761-6402.* Good for cheap flights.
Guatemaya Intercultural Travel Agency, *14 Av "A", 3-06, T7765-0040.* Very helpful.
Mayaexplor, *T7761-5057, www.maya explor. com.* Run by Thierry Roquet, who arranges a variety of trips around Xela and around the country. He can also arrange excursions into Mexico, Belize and Honduras and treks, eg Nebaj–Todos Santos. French-speaking. His website offers useful info for travellers. A proportion of funds goes towards local development projects. Recommended.
Quetzaltrekkers, *based inside Casa Argentina at Diagonal 12, 8-37, T7765-5895, www.quetzaltrekkers.com.* This recommended, established, non-profit agency is known for its 3-day hike (Sat morning to Monday afternoon) from Xela across to Lake Atitlán. Proceeds go to the **Escuela de la Calle School**

for children at risk, and a dorm for homeless kids. Also offers trek from Nebaj–Todos Santos, 6 days, full-moon hike up Santa María and others. Hiking volunteers are also needed for a 3-month minimum period: hiking experience and reasonable Spanish required.
Tranvia de los Altos, *www.tranviadelos altos.com.* Provides daytime and nighttime walking tours in Xela as well as excursions. Guided city tour is only US$4. Recommended.

Zunil

See **Las Cumbres Eco-Saunas y Gastronomía**, T5399-0029, under Where to stay, above.

Transport

Bus

Most visitors arrive by bus, a 30-min (14.5 km) journey southwest of Cuatro Caminos. Buses pull into the Zona 3 Minerva Terminal. To get a bus into the city centre, take a path through the market at its far left or its far right, which brings you out in front of the Minerva Temple. Watch out for very clever pickpockets walking through this market. Buses for the town centre face away (left) from the temple. All Santa Fe services go to Parque Centro América, US$0.15. Alternatively take a taxi.

Local City buses run between 0600 and 1900. Between the town centre and Minerva Terminal, bus No 6, Santa Fe, US$0.20, 15-30 mins, depending on traffic. Catch the bus at the corner of 4 Calle and 13 Av by Pasaje Enríquez. Buses to the Rotonda leave from the corner of 11 Av and 10 Calle, US$0.20, or catch bus No 6, 10 or 13, from Av 12 y 3 Calle as they come down to the park, 15 mins. To catch buses to **San Francisco El Alto**, **Momostenango**, the **south coast** and Zunil, get off the local bus at the Rotonda, then walk a couple of steps away from the road to step into a feeder road where they all line up.

Long distance To **Guatemala City**, **Galgos**, Calle Rodolfo Robles, 17-43, Zona 1, T7761-2248, 1st-class buses, at 0400, 1230, 1500, US$5, 4 hrs, will carry bicycles; **Marquensita** several a day (office in the capital 21 Calle, 1-56, Zona 1), leaves from the Minerva Terminal, US$4.60, comfortable, 4 hrs. **Líneas América**, from 7 Av, 3-33, Zona 2, T7761-2063, US$5, 4 hrs, between 0515-2000, 6 daily. **Línea Dorada**, 12 Av and 5 C, Zona 3, T7767-5198, 0400 and 1530, US$9. **Transportes Alamo** from 14 Av, 5-15, Zona 3, T7763-5044, between 0430 and 1430, 7 a day, US$5, 4 hrs.

The following destinations are served by buses leaving from the Minerva Terminal, Zona 3 and the Rotonda. For **Antigua**, change at Chimaltenangoby either taking a chicken bus or Pullman. To **Almolonga**, via **Cantel**, every 30 mins, US$0.50, 10 mins. (Buses to Almolonga and Zunil not via Cantel, leave from the corner of 10 Av and 10 Calle, Zona 1.) To **Chichicastenango** with **Transportes Veloz Quichelense de Hilda Esperanza**, several from 0500 to 1530, US$3.80, 2½ hrs. To **Cuatro Caminos** US$0.50, 30 mins. To **Huehuetenango** with **Transportes Velásquez**, every 30 mins 0500-1730, US$2.50, 2½ hrs. To **La Mesilla** at 0500, 0600, 0700, 0800, 1300, 1400 with **Transportes Unión Fronteriza**, US$3.60, 4 hrs. To **Los Encuentros**, US$2.20. To **Malacatán**, US$3.60, 5 hrs. To **Momostenango**, US$1.20, 1½ hrs. To **Panajachel**, with **Transportes Morales**, at 0500, 0600, 1000, 1200, 1500, US$3.20, 2½-3 hrs. To **Retalhuleu**, US$1.20, 1½ hrs. To **Salcajá**, every 30 mins, US$0.40, 15 mins. To **San Andrés Xecul** every 2 hrs, US$0.60, 30 mins. To **San Cristóbal Totonicapán**, every 30 mins, US$0.40, 20 mins. To **San Francisco El Alto**, US$0.70. **San Marcos**, every 30 mins, US$1, 1 hr. **San Martín Sacatepéquez/San Martín Chile Verde**, US$0.70, 1 hr. **Santiago Atitlán**, with **Ninfa de Atitlán** at 0800, 1100, 1230, 1630, 4½ hrs. To **Ciudad Tecún Umán** every 30 mins, 0500-1400, US$3.60, 4 hrs. To **Totonicapán**,

every 20 mins, US$1.20, 1 hr. To **Zunil**, every 30 mins, US$0.70, 20-30 mins.

Shuttle **Adrenalina Tours**, see Tour operators, above, runs shuttles. To **Cobán**, US$45, Panajachel, US$20 and Antigua, US$25. Adrenalina also runs a shuttle to and from **San Cristóbal de las Casas**, Mexico, US$35.

Car
Car hire **Tabarini Renta Autos**, 9 Calle, 9-21, Zona 1, T7763-0418.

Mechanic José Ramiro Muñoz R, 1 Calle, 19-11, Zona 1, T7761-8204. Also **Goodyear Taller** at the Rotonda and for motorbikes **Moto Servicio Rudy**, 2 Av, 3-48, Zona 1, T7765-5433.

Taxi
Found all over town, notably lined up along Parque Centro América.
Taxis Xelaju, T7761-4456.

North of Quetzaltenango
Bus
All buses heading to Quetzaltenango from Cuatro Caminos pass through **Salcajá**, 10 mins. From Xela to **San Andrés Xecul**, US$0.60, 30 mins. Or take any bus heading to Cuatro Caminos and getting off at the Esso station on the left-hand side, and then almost doubling back on yourself to take the San Andrés road. There are pickups from here.

South of Quetzaltenango
Bus
Cantel is 10-15 mins by bus (11 km), and US$0.24 from Xela on the way to Zunil, but you need to take the bus marked for Cantel Fábrica and Zunil, not Almolonga and Zunil. From **Zunil** to Xela via Almolonga leaves from the bridge. Walk down the left-hand side of the church to the bottom of the hill, take a left and you'll see the buses the other side of the bridge, US$0.60. **Fuentes Georginas** is reached either by walking the 8 km uphill just to the south of Zunil, 2 hrs

(300-m ascent; take the right fork after 4 km, but be careful as robbery has occurred here), by pickup truck in 15 mins (US$10 return with a 1-hr wait), or hitch. If you come by bus to Zunil and are walking to the Fuentes, don't go down into town with the bus, but get off on the main road at the Pepsi stand and walk to the entrance road, which is visible 100 m away on the left. See also Shuttles, above, for transfer to the thermal pools.

El Viejo Palmar
Bus
Just before San Felipe, and just before the Puente Samalá III, if you're heading south, is the turn to the right for El Viejo Palmar. Take any bus heading to the south coast, and asked to be dropped off at the entrance and walk. Or, take a pickup from San Felipe park. Ask for Beto or Brígido.

Taxi
From Xela round trip is US$25, or take a tour from town.

Volcán Santa María and Santiaguito
Bus
To reach the volcano take the bus to **Llano del Pinal**, 7 km away, from the Minerva Terminal (every 30 mins, last bus back 1800). Get off at the crossroads and follow the dirt road towards the right side of the volcano until it sweeps up the right (about 40 mins), take the footpath to the left (where it is marked for some distance); bear right at the saddle where another path comes in from the left, but look carefully as it is easily missed.

Laguna Chicabal
Bus/car
The last bus to **Quetzaltenango** leaves at 1900, 1 hr. Parking at the entrance, US$2. It is a 40-min walk from the car park (and you'll need a sturdy vehicle if you attempt the steep first ascent in a car).

West of Quetzaltenango
Bus
Volcán Tajumulco can be reached by getting to the village of **San Sebastián** from San Marcos, which takes about 2 hrs.

Southern
Guatemala

The southern coastal plain of Guatemala supports many plantations of coffee, sugar and tropical fruit trees and its climate is unbearably hot and humid. Amid the fincas some of the most curious archaeological finds have been unearthed, a mixture of monument styles such as Maya and Olmec, including Abaj Takalik, the cane field stones at Santa Lucía Cotzumalguapa and the big 'Buddhas' of Monte Alto.

On the coast are the black-sand beaches and nature reserves of the popular and laid-back Monterrico and Sipacate resorts, where nesting turtles burrow in the sand and masses of birds take to the skies around. Casting a shadow over the coast, the Central Highland volcanoes of Lake Atitlán, and the Antigua trio of Fuego, Acatenango and Agua, look spectacular, looming on the horizon above the lowlands.

Routes to El Salvador
Three routes pass through Southern Guatemala to El Salvador. The main towns are busy but scruffy with little to attract the visitor. See also box, page 512, for more information on crossing into El Salvador.

Route 1 The Pan-American Highway: The first route heads directly south along the paved Pan-American Highway from Guatemala City (CA1) to the border at **San Cristóbal Frontera**. **Cuilapa**, the capital of Santa Rosa Department, is 65 km along the Highway. About 9 km beyond Los Esclavos is the El Molino junction. Further east, just off the Pan-American Highway, is the village of **El Progreso**, dominated by the imposing Volcán Suchitán, at 2042 m, now part of the Parque Regional Volcán Suchitán run by La Fundación de la Naturaleza. There is accommodation. The town fiesta with horse racing is from 10-16 November. From El Progreso, a good paved road goes north 43 km to Jalapa through open, mostly dry country, with volcanoes always in view. There are several crater lakes including **Laguna del Hoyo** near Monjas that are worth visiting. The higher ground is forested. Beyond Jutiapa and El Progreso the Pan-American Highway heads east and then south to Asunción Mita. Here there is a turning left to Lago de Güija. Before reaching the border at **San Cristóbal Frontera**, the Pan-American Highway dips and skirts the shores (right) of **Lago Atescatempa**, with several islands set in heavy forest.

Route 2 Via Jalpatagua: The second, quicker way of getting to San Salvador is to take a highway that cuts off right from the first route at El Molino junction, about 7 km beyond the Esclavos bridge. This cut-off goes through El Oratorio and Jalpatagua to the border at **Valle Nuevo**, continuing then to Ahuachapán and San Salvador.

Route 3 El Salvador (La) via the border at Ciudad Pedro de Alvarado: This coastal route goes from **Escuintla** (see below) to the border bridge over the Río Paz at La Hachadura (El Salvador). It takes two hours from Escuintla to the border. At **Taxisco,** there is a white church with a curious hearts and holly design on the façade. Further east is Guazacapán, which merges into **Chiquimulilla**, 3 km to the north, the most important town of the area, with good-quality leather goods available. There is accommodation available. A side excursion can be made from Chiquimulilla up the winding CA 16 through coffee fincas and farmland. About 20 km along there is a turning to the left down a 2- to 3-km steep, narrow, dirt road that goes to **Laguna de Ixpaco**, an impressive, greenish-yellow lake that is 350 m in diameter. It is boiling in some places, emitting sulphurous fumes and set in dense forest. This trip can also be made by heading south off the Pan-American Highway after Cuilapa (just before Los Esclavos) towards Chiquimulilla on the CA 16, with old trees on either side, some with orchids in them, where you will reach the sign to Ixpaco, after 20 km. Thirty kilometres beyond on the Pacific Highway is **Ciudad Pedro de Alvarado** on the border.

Guatemala City to the Pacific coast → *Colour map 6, B2/C3.*
tranquil lake and Pacific ports

Amatitlán
Heading south from the capital on Highway CA19, the town of Amatitlán is perched on the banks of a lake of the same name. Sadly, the lake is too polluted for swimming, but rowing boats ply its waters, US$5 per hour. Less demanding is the **teleférico** ① *Fri-Sun 0900-1700, US$2 return*, climbing from its station on the lakeshore to supply commanding views of the surroundings. The main reason for coming to Amatitlán, however, is the **Day of the Cross** on 3 May, when the Christ figure is removed from the church and floated out of a boat amid candles and decorations. South of Amatitlán, the village of **Palín** has a Sunday market in a plaza under an enormous ceiba tree. The textiles are exceptional, but are increasingly difficult to find. There are great views of Pacaya to the east as you head down to the coast, Volcán Agua to the northwest, and the Pacific lowlands to the west.

Escuintla
Highway CA19 from Guatemala City and Highway 14 from Antigua converge in Escuintla: a large, unattractive provincial centre set in a rich tropical valley. This town acts a major transport hub for the Pacific slope with connections to all the main ports, as well as the international borders with Mexico and El Salvador via Highway CA2, which runs east–west through the region. There are cheap lodgings if you get stuck. For entertainment, you could head 25 km southeast to admire the beasts at the **Autosafari Chapín** ① *Carretera a Taxisco Km 87.5, www.autosafarichapin.com, Tue-Sun, 0900-1730, US$8*. Any bus to Taxisco should be able to drop you at the entrance.

Puerto San José, Chulamar and Iztapa

South of Escuintla, a fast paved highway heads to Puerto San José, which first opened for business (especially the coffee trade) in 1853 and was once upon a time the country's second largest port. The climate is hot, the streets and most of the beaches are dirty, and at weekends the town fills up with people from the capital. There are swimming beaches nearby, but beware of the strong undercurrent. One of the more popular ones is **Chulamar**, some 5 km to the west. Iztapa, 12 km east of Puerto San José, is world renowned for deep-sea fishing. Sail fish, bill fish, marlin, tuna, dorado, roosterfish, yellowfin and snapper are to be found in large numbers here. The **Chiquimulilla Canal** runs either side of Puerto San José parallel to the coast for close to 100 km.

Listings Guatemala City to the Pacific coast

Where to stay

Puerto San José, Chulamar and Iztapa
There are a number of *comedores* in town.

$$$$ Soleil Pacífico
Chulamar, T7879-4444, www. hotelessoleilguatemala.com.
Set in rambling landscaped grounds, this large all-inclusive resort is the only accommodation of its type in the area. It boasts luxury rooms, suites and bungalows in addition to all the usual luxuries, including 2 jacuzzis, pools, volleyball courts, football fields, restaurants and lounges. There have been a few mixed reports and maintenance issues.

$$$ Hotel y Turicentro Eden Pacific
Barrio El Laberinto, Puerto San José, T7881-1605, www.hot900edenpacific.com.
Overlooking the beach, a family-run hotel with a self-contained chalet for 12 guests and 35 reasonable a/c rooms with TV. Facilities include pool and restaurant. Various packages are available.

$$-$ Hotel Club Sol y Playa Tropical
1 Calle, 5-48, on the canal, Iztapa, T7881-4365.
Adequate lodgings with restaurant, pool, friendly staff and fair standard rooms with fans.

Transport

Bus
To and from Guatemala City to **Amatitlán** (every 30 mins, US$0.50) from 0700-2045 from 14 Av, between 3 y 4 Calle, Zona 1, Guatemala City. From **Escuintla** (1½ hrs) to the capital from 8 Calle and 2 Av, Zona 1, near the corner of the plaza in Escuintla. Buses that have come along the Pacific Highway and are going on to the capital pull up at the main bus terminal on 4 Av. From the terminal there are buses direct to **Antigua** every 30 mins, 1-1½ hrs, US$1.20. To **Taxisco** from Escuintla, every 30 mins, 0700-1700, 40 mins, for connections onwards (hourly) to La Avellana, for boats to Monterrico. Frequent buses to **Iztapa** with the last bus departing at 2030.

If you are changing in Escuintla for **Santa Lucía Cotzumalguapa** to the west, you need to take a left out of the bus terminal along the 4 Av up a slight incline towards the police fortress and take a left here on its corner, 9 Calle, through the market. Head for 3 blocks straight, passing the Cinammon Pastelería y Panadería on the right at 9 Calle and 2 Av. At the end here are buses heading to Santa Lucía and further west along the Pacific Highway. It is a 5- to 10-min walk. Buses leave here every 5 mins. To **Santa Lucía Cotzumalguapa** (the bus *ayudantes* shout 'Santa'), 35 mins, US$1.20. On the return, buses pull up at the corner of the 8 Calle and 2 Av, where Guatemala City buses also pass.

Puerto San José, Chulamar and Iztapa
Bus
Regular buses from the capital passing through **Escuintla**, 2-3 hrs. If you are

heading further east by road from Iztapa along the coast to **Monterrico** (past loofah plantations), see page 424.

Monterrico → *Colour map 6, C4.*

a small black-sand resort backed by languid mangroves

Monterrico is a beachside village where the sunsets are a rich orange and the waves crash spectacularly on to the shore. Due to powerful riptides even strong swimmers can get into trouble here, so take care. The village itself is hot and sleepy during the week, but increasingly popular at the weekends. If you are in the area between September and January, thanks to the efforts of local hatcheries, you can sponsor a baby turtle's waddle to freedom.

The landing stage is 10 minutes' walk from the ocean front, where you'll find the main restaurants and places to stay. When you step off the dock take the first left, and keep left, which heads directly to the main cluster of beach hotels. This road is known as Calle del Proyecto or Calle del Muelle. Walking straight on from the dock takes you to the main drag in town. When you get to the main drag and want to walk to the main group of hotels, take a left along the beach or take the sandy path to the left one block back from the beach where the sand is a tiny bit easier to walk on.

Although Monterrico's popularity is growing fast, its views are undisturbed by high-rise blocks. All the hotels, mostly rustic and laid-back, are lined up along the beach, and there are a few shops and *comedores* not linked to hotels, in this village of just 1500 people. The village is surrounded by canals carpeted in aquatic plants and mangrove swamps with bird and turtle reserves in their midst. These areas make up the **Biotopo Monterrico-Hawaii** (also known as the **Monterrico Nature Reserve**), which can be explored by *lancha* with the turtle hatchery (see below), around US$10 per person for a one- to two-hour tour. Anteater, armadillo, racoon and weasel live in the area, but it is worth taking the boat trip at sunrise or sunset to see migratory North and South American birds, including flamingo.

However, the real stars in this patch are the olive ridleys *Parlama blanca* and *Parlama negra* turtles, which lay eggs between July and October, and the Baule turtle, which lays between between October and February. There is a turtle hatchery in the village, the **Tortugario Monterrico** ⓘ *daily 0800-1200, 1400-1700, US$6.50,* which offers night tours and volunteer opportunities. Just behind the hatchery there are 300 breeding crocodiles, 150 turtles and iguanas. The turtle liberation event takes place every Saturday night between October and February. Around 8 km east of Monterrico is another hatchery, also offering tours and volunteering. It is run by **Arcas Guatemala** ⓘ *inside Parque Hawaii, T4743-4655, www.arcasguatemala.com; buses from Monterrico every 1-2 hrs, 30 mins, US$0.65.*

Where to stay

Most hotels are fully booked by Sat
midday and prices rise at weekends
so book beforehand.

$$$$-$$$ Isleta de Gaia
*East of Monterrico on a small island near Las
Lisas, T7885-0044, www.isleta-de-gaia.com.*
Managed by a French-American team, an
exclusive boutique hotel located on a private
island between the Chiquimulilla Canal
and the Pacific ocean. Accommodation is
in tasteful, traditional bungalows. A great
hideaway and the most interesting lodging
for miles, but accessible only by private
lancha; contact in advance to organize
transport. Rustic-chic. Recommended.

$$$ Atelie del Mar
*Just off the beach, west of Calle Principal,
5752-5528, www.hotelateliedelmar.com.*
This personable boutique hotel has a
secluded, colourful, well-tended garden,
an art gallery featuring work by the owner,
Violeta Marroquín, a restaurant and 2 pools.
Accommodation includes 16 rooms of
different sizes, all equipped with a/c, TV, and
private bath. Rates include breakfast and
Wi-Fi. Hospitable and helpful. Good service.

$$$ Dos Mundos
*8901 Monterrico Rd, east of Calle Principal,
T7823-0820, www.hotelsdosmundos.com.*
One of Monterrico's more upmarket options,
The resort-style **Dos Mundos** boasts
14 well-attired bungalows with a/c and a
rather beautiful infinity pool overlooking the
ocean. Other amenities include restaurant,
bar, and tours. Breakfast included.

$$$-$ Café del Sol
*250 m west of Calle Principal, T5810-0821,
www.cafe-del-sol.com.*
Quiet, simple and comfortable beachside
lodgings, including 13 pleasant rooms. The
newest ones are the most comfortable
($$$); those across the road in an annexe

are much more spartan ($). There is also a
bar area, pool, jacuzzi and restaurant. Part of
their profits go to Eternal Spring Foundation,
a sustainable development organization.
Recommended.

$$ Hotel Pez de Oro
*At the end of main strip to the east,
T2368-3684, www.pezdeoro.com.*
18 spacious bungalows with traditional
thatched roofs, terraces, and hammocks, all
attractively set around a pool. All rooms have
private bathroom, mosquito lamps, hand-
woven bedspreads, pretty bedside lights and
fan; some have a/c. Secluded and tranquil.
Recommended.

$$ Hotel Restaurante Dulce y Salado
*Some way away from the main cluster
of hotels and a 500-m hard walk east
through sand if you are on foot, T4154-0252,
www.dulceysaladoguatemala.com.*
The sea breezes and uninterrupted view of
the highland volcanoes at this secluded hotel
are fantastic. Set around a pool, the thatched
cabins are nice and clean, with bath, fans
and mosquito nets. Run by a friendly Italian
couple, Fulvio and Graziella. Breakfast
included, good Italian food in the restaurant.

$$-$ Johnny's Place
*Main strip, T4369-6900,
www.johnnysplacehotel.com.*
Very popular with locals and gringos,
Johnny's Place is a buzzing social space
(especially at weekends) with a wide range of
accommodation including bungalows ($$$),
rooms ($$), suites, economy 'backpacker'
rooms with shared bath, and for the very
thrifty, dorms ($). There is internet, table
tennis, pools and a beachside restaurant with
free coffee fill-ups. A good place for groups.
Recommended.

$ El Delfín
*On the beachfront, 20 m from Calle Principal,
T4661-9255, www.hotel-el-delfin.com.*

Lots of good reports about this cheery no-frills option, popular with backpackers and families. Accommodation includes a range of good value bungalows and rooms with deals sometimes available if staying more than 3 nights. The restaurant and bar overlook the beach and serve vegetarian food. Organizes shuttles at any hour. Relaxing and recommended.

Restaurants

Be careful, especially with *ceviche*. There are lots of seafood joints and local *comedores* along Calle Principal, which leads to the beach. The best and most popular of the bunch appears to be:

$$$-$$ Taberna El Pelicano
On the seafront past Johnny's Place. Wed-Sat.
Named after a rescued pelican called Pancho, this relaxed and well-established haunt offers a diverse and creative menu of steaks, pastas, salads and seafood, all very fresh and prepared according to flavourful Swiss and Italian recipes. Try the catch of the day or the toasted camembert salad. Recommended.

Bars and clubs

For drinking and dancing, try Johnny's Place (see Where to stay, above), thronging with party-loving Guatemaltecos on Fri and Sat nights. Also worth a look is Mañanitas Beach Lounge, overlooking the beach at the end of Calle Principal.

What to do

Tour operators
Those preferring to stay on land can rent horses for a jaunt on the beach. *Lancha* and turtle-searching tours are operated by a couple of agencies in town.

Transport

Bus and boat
There are 3 ways of getting to Monterrico: 2 by public transport and 1 by shuttle.

The **1st route** to Monterrico involves heading direct to the Pacific coast by taking a bus from the capital to **Puerto San José**, 1 hr, and changing for a bus to **Iztapa**. Or take a direct bus from Escuintla to Iztapa. Then cross river by the toll bridge to **Pueblo Viejo** for US$1.60 per vehicle (buses excluded), or US$0.80 per foot passenger, 5 mins. The buses now continue to Monterrico, about 25 km east, 1 hr. Buses run to and from Iztapa between 0600-1500, from the corner of main street and the road to Pueblo Viejo to the left, 3 blocks north of the beach, just past the Catholic church on the right.

The **2nd route** involves getting to Taxisco first and then La Avellana. There are also direct buses to La Avellana from Guatemala City, see page 345. If you are coming from Antigua, take a bus to **Escuintla** 1-1½ hrs. From there, there are regular departures to **Taxisco**, 40 mins. From Taxisco to La Avellana, buses leave hourly until 1800, US$1, 20 mins. If you take an international bus from Escuintla (45 mins), it will drop you off just past the Taxisco town turn-off, just before a bridge with a slip road. Walk up the road (5 mins) and veer to the right where you'll see the bus stop for **La Avellana**. At La Avellana take the **motor boats** through mangrove swamps, 20-30 mins, US$0.60 for foot passengers, from 0630 and then hourly until 1800. The journey via this route from Antigua to Monterrico takes about 3¼ hrs if your connections are good. Return boats to La Avellana leave at 0330, 0530, 0700, 0800, 0900, 1030, 1200, 1300, 1430, 1600. Buses leave La Avellana for Taxisco hourly until 1800. Buses pull up near the **Banco Nor-Oriente** where numerous buses heading to Guatemala and Escuintla pass.

Shuttles Alternatively, numerous travel agencies in **Antigua** run shuttles, US$10-12 one way. You can book a return shuttle journey in Monterrico by going to the language school on the road that leads to the dock. There are also mini buses operating from Monterrico to **Iztapa** and vice-versa.

Amid the sugar-cane fields and fincas of this coastal town lie an extraordinary range of carved stones and images with influences from pre-Maya civilizations, believed mostly to be ancient Mexican cultures, including the Izapa civilization from the Pacific coast area of Mexico near the Guatemalan border.

Four main points of interest entice visitors to the area: **Bilbao, El Baúl, Finca El Baúl** and the **Museo de Cultura Cotzumalguapa**. The town is just north of the Pacific Highway, where some of the hotels and banks are.

Bilbao, El Baúl, Finca El Baúl and Museo de Cultura Cotzumalguapa

You can visit all the sites on foot. However, you are advised not to go wandering in and out of the cane fields at the Bilbao site as there have been numerous assaults in the past. You can walk along the tarmacked road north to the El Baúl sites (6 km and 8 km respectively from town), but there is no shade, so take lots of water. Ask for directions. There is an occasional 'Río Santiago' bus, which goes as far as Colonia Maya, close to the El Baúl hilltop. Only workers' buses go to Finca El Baúl in the morning, returning at night. Alternatively, take a taxi from town (next to the plaza) and negotiate a trip to all 4 areas. They will charge around US$20. Note Do not believe any taxi driver who tells you that Las Piedras (the stones) have been moved from the cane fields to the museum because of the increasing assaults.

There is considerable confusion about who carved the range of monuments and stelae scattered around the town. It is safe to say that the style of the monuments found in the last 150 years is a blend of a number of pre-Columbian styles. Some believe the prominent influence is Toltec, the ancestors of the Maya K'iche', Kaqchikel, Tz'utujil and Pipiles. It is thought the Tolteca-Pipil had been influenced in turn by the Classic culture from Teotihuacán, a massive urban state northeast of the present Mexico City, which had its zenith in the seventh century AD. However, some experts say that there is no concrete evidence to suggest that the Pipiles migrated as early as AD 400 or that they were influenced by Teotihuacán. All in all, the cultural make-up of this corner of Guatemala may never be known.

The remnants at **Bilbao**, first re-discovered in 1860, are mainly buried beneath the sugar cane but monuments found above ground show pre-Maya influences. It is thought that the city was inhabited 1200 BC-AD 800. There are four large boulders – known as Las Piedras – in sugar-cane fields, which can be reached on foot from the tracks leading from the end of 4 Avenida in town. **El Baúl** is a Late Classic ceremonial centre, 6 km north of Santa Lucía, with two carved stone pieces to see; most of its monuments were built between AD 600 and 900. **Finca El Baúl** has a collection of sculptures and stelae gathered from the large area of the finca grounds.

The **Museo de Cultura Cotzumalguapa** ⓘ *Finca Las Ilusiones, Mon-Fri 0800-1600, Sat 0800-1200, US$1.30, less than 1 km east of town, ask the person in charge for the key,* displays numerous artefacts collected from the finca and a copy of the famous Bilbao Monument 21 from the cane fields. To get to the museum, walk east along the Pacific Highway and take a left turn into the finca site.

Santa Lucía Cotzumalguapa to the Mexican border

Beyond Santa Lucía Cotzumalguapa is **Cocales**, where a good road north leads to Patulul and after 30 km, to Lake Atitlán at San Lucas Tolimán. The Pacific Highway continues through San Antonio Suchitepéquez to **Mazatenango** (where just beyond are the crossroads for Retalhueleu and Champerico) and on to Coatepeque and Ciudad Tecún Umán for the Mexican border; see box, page 512. Mazatenango is the chief town of the Costa Grande zone. While not especially attractive, the Parque Central is very pleasant with many fine trees providing shade. There is a huge fiesta in the last week of February, when hotels are full and double their prices. At that time, beware of children carrying (and throwing) flour.

Retalhuleu and around

Retalhuleu, normally referred to as 'Reu' (pronounced 'Ray-oo') is the capital of the department. The entrance to the town is grand with a string of royal palms lining the route, known as Calzada Las Palmas. It serves a large number of coffee and sugar estates and much of its population is wealthy. The original colonial church of **San Antonio de Padua** is in the central plaza. Bordering the plaza to the east is the neoclassical **Palacio del Gobierno**, with a giant quetzal sculpture on top. The **Museo de Arqueología y Etnología** ① *Tue-Sat 0830-1300, 1400-1800, Sun 0900-1230, US$1.30, next to the palacio*, is small. Downstairs are exhibits of Maya ceramics.

If you fancy cooling off, near Reu are the **Parque Acuático Xocomil** ① *Km 180.5 on the road from Xela to Champerio, T7722-9400, www.irtra.org.gt, Thu-Sun 0900-1700, US$9.60*. Nearby is the enormous theme park with giant pyramids of **Xetulul** ① *T7722-9450, www.irtra.org.gt, Thu-Sun 100-1800, US$26*.

Abaj Takalik

Daily 0700-1700, US$3.25, guides are volunteers so tips are welcomed.

One of the best ancient sites to visit outside El Petén is Abaj Takalik, a ruined city that lies, sweltering, on the southern plain. Its name means 'standing stone' in K'iche'. The site was discovered in 1888 by botanist Doctor Gustav Brühl. It is believed to have flourished in the late pre-Classic period of 300 BC to AD 250 strategically placed to control commerce between the highlands and the Pacific coast. There are some 239 monuments, which include 68 stelae, 32 altars and some 71 buildings, all set in peaceful surroundings. The environment is loved by birds and butterflies, including blue morphos, and by orchids, which flower magnificently between January and March. The main temple buildings are mostly up to 12 m high, suggesting an early date before techniques were available to build Tikal-sized structures.

Towards the Mexican border

The main road runs 21 km east off the Pacific Highway to **Coatepeque**, one of the richest coffee zones in the country. There is a bright, modern church in the leafy Plaza Central. The local fiesta takes place from 11-19 March. There are several hotels, *hospedajes* and restaurants. **Colomba**, an attractive typical village east of Coatepeque in the lowlands, has a basic *hospedaje*.

Where to stay

Santa Lucía Cotzumalguapa

$$ Santiaguito
Pacific Highway at Km 90.4, T7882-5435,
hsantiaguito@yahoo.com.mx.
Located on the highway on the west side
of Santa Lucía, probably the best option in
town (which isn't saying much). Rooms have
a/c, TV and hot and cold water. Nice leafy
grounds with a pool and restaurant. Non-
guests can use the pool for US$2.60.

$$-$ Hotel El Camino
Diagonally opposite Santiaguito across the
highway at Km 90.5, T7882-5316.
Large if fairly simple rooms with bath, TV,
tepid water and fan. Some have a/c (more
expensive). Restaurant attached.

$ Hospedaje La Reforma
A stone's throw from the park on 4 Av, 4-71,
T7882-1731.
Lots of dark box rooms and dark shared
showers, ask to see before accepting. Clean,
ultra-cheap and basic, would suit budget
travellers with modest needs.

Retalhuleu and around

$$ Astor
5 Calle 4-60, T7957-8300,
www.hotelastorguatemala.com.
Constructed in the late 19th century and
converted to a hotel in 1923 by the Ruiz
Javalois family, this handsome colonial-style
lodging offers 27 clean, comfortable rooms
set around a pretty courtyard. Amenities
include a pool, jacuzzi, parking, bar and
restaurant. Non-guests can use the pool
(better than the one at **Posada de Don José**)
for a fee. A good option, recommended.

$$ La Colonia
1.5 km to the north at Km 180.5,
T7772-2048, www.hlacoloniareu.com.
This good value highway lodging boasts
a relaxing garden space and patio with
leafy tropical plants and pools for adults
and children. The lodgings encompass a
variety of rooms equipped with a/c and
cable TV; ask to see a few. Good food is
served in the restaurant.

$$ Posada de Don José
5 Calle, 3-67, T7962-2900,
www.posadadonjose.com.
Don Jose's is a well-established colonial-style
option with 2 floors of comfortable, spacious
well-attired rooms overlooking a central
courtyard with a pool; some are newer
than others, ask to see a few. The restaurant
is possibly the best in town, serving such
mouth-watering temptations as lobster
sautéed in cognac. Non-guests can use the
pool for a small fee.

$$ Siboney
5 km northwest of Reu in San Sebastián,
Km 180.5, T7772-2174, www.hotelsiboney.com.
A very reasonable 3-star option on the
highway, motel-style with comfortable
rooms set around pool. There's a water slide
for the kids and a jacuzzi for the adults.
Try the *caldo de mariscos* or *paella* in the
excellent restaurant. Non-guests can pay to
use the pool.

Restaurants

Retalhuleu and around
There are lots of pizzerias and a few fast
food joints in town. For a quality dining
experience, head to **Hotel Astor** or **Posada
de Don José** (see Where to stay, above).
Alternatively, for something cheap and
low-key, try:

$$ Restaurante La Luna
8a Av and 5a Calle, a block from the main plaza.
Well-established and popular, La Luna is the place for good value, hearty, home-cooked *típico* meals.

Transport

Santa Lucía Cotzumalguapa
Bus
Regular departures to the capital. Buses plying the Pacific Highway also pass through, so if you are coming from Reu in the west or Escuintla in the east you can get off here.

Car
If you are driving, there are a glut of 24-hr **Esso** and **Texaco** gas stations here. See under Guatemala City to the Pacific coast, page 421, for catching transport from **Escuintla**.

Santa Lucía Cotzumalguapa to the Mexican border
Bus
5 a day **Cocales-Panajachel**, between 0600 and 1400, 2½ hrs. Frequent buses to **Mazatenango** from Guatemala City, US$5. To the border at **Ciudad Tecún Umán**, US$2.10, an irregular service with Fortaleza del Sur.

Retalhuleu and around
Bus
Services along the Pacific Highway to Mexico leave from the main bus terminal, which is beyond the city limits at 5 Av 'A'. To **Coatepeque** (0600-1800), **Malacatán**, **Mazatenango** and **Champerico** (0500-1800). Buses also leave from here to **El Asintal**, for Abaj Takalik, 30 mins, every 30 mins from 0600-1830, last bus back to Reu 1800. Or catch them before that from the corner of 5 Av 'A' and the Esso gas station as they turn to head for the village. Leaving from a smaller terminal at 7 Av/10 Calle, there are regular buses to **Ciudad Tecún Umán**, **Talismán** and **Guatemala City** via the Pacific route, and to **Xela** (1¾ hrs, every hour 0500-1800).

Abaj Takalik
Bus
Take a bus to El from **Retalhuleu** and walk the hot 4 km to the site entrance. Or, take any bus heading along the Pacific Highway and get off at the **El Asintal** crossroads. Take a pickup from here to El Asintal; then a pickup from the town square to Abaj Takalik. As there are only fincas along this road, you will probably be on your own, in which case it is US$5 to the site or US$10 round trip, including waiting time. Bargain hard.

Taxi and tour
A taxi from central plaza in Reu to the site and back including waiting time is US$13. Alternatively, take a tour from Xela.

Towards the Mexican border
Bus
From Quetzaltenango to **Coatepeque**, catch any bus heading to Ciudad Tecún Umán from Reu.

Guatemala City
to the Caribbean

From the capital to the Caribbean, the main road passes through the Río Motagua Valley, punctuated by cacti and bordered by the Sierra de Las Minas mountains rising abruptly in the west. Dinosaur remains, the black Christ and the Maya ruins of Quiriguá can be found on or close to the highway. The banana port of Puerto Barrios is a large transport and commercial hub and jumping-off point for the Garífuna town of Lívingston. Trips down the lush gorge of the Río Dulce are a highlight; nearby are some great places to see and stay on its banks, as well as accommodation around Lago de Izabal.

The Carretera al Atlántico, or Atlantic Highway, stretches from Guatemala City all the way to Puerto Barrios on the Caribbean coast in the department of Izabal. Most worthwhile places to visit are off this fast main road, along the Río Motagua valley, where cactus, bramble, willow and acacia grow. There are numerous buses plying the route.

Along the Atlantic Highway

Before Teculután is **El Rancho** at Km 85, the jumping-off point for a trip north to Cobán (see page 448). There are a few places to stay here. Geologists will be interested in the **Motagua fault** near Santa Cruz, between Teculután and Río Hondo. Just before Río Hondo (Km 138), a paved road runs south towards Estanzuela. Shortly before this town you pass a monument on the right commemorating the 1976 earthquake, which activated a fault line that cut across the road. It can still be seen in the fields on either side of the road. The epicentre of this massive earthquake, which measured 7.5 on the Richter scale, and killed 23,000 people, was at **Los Amates**, 65 km further down the valley towards Puerto Barrios.

Estanzuela

Estanzuela is a small town fronting the highway. Its **Museo de Palaeontología, Arqueología y Geología** ① *daily 0800-1700, free*, displays the incredible reconstructed skeletal remains of a 4-m prehistoric giant sloth found in Zone 6, Guatemala City and a giant armadillo, among others. To get there, either take a **Rutas Orientales** bus from Guatemala City to Zacapa (every 30 minutes 0430-1800, 2¾ to three hours), or take a minibus south from Río Hondo and ask to be dropped at the first entrance to the town on the right. Then walk right, into the town, and continue for 600 m to the museum, 10 minutes. When you reach the school, walk to the right and you will see the museum. Moving on to Esquipulas, take the same Rutas Orientales service that continues from Zacapa, US$6, 1½ hours.

Chiquimula, Volcán de Ipala and the Honduran border → *Colour map 6, B5.*
volcanic lake and impressive Mayan site

Chiquimula is a stop-off point for travellers who stay here on their way to or from Copán Ruinas, Honduras, if they can't make the connection in one day. The town's fiesta, which includes bullfighting, is from 11-18 August.

An alternative route to Chiquimula and Esquipulas is from the southeast corner of Guatemala City (Zona 10), where the Pan-American Highway heads towards the Salvadorean border. After a few kilometres there is a turning to **San José Pinula** (fiesta: 16-20 March). After San José, an unpaved branch road continues for 203 km through fine scenery to **Mataquescuintla**, **Jalapa** (several *hospedajes*, good bus connections; fiesta: 2-5 May), **San Pedro Pinula**, **San Luis Jilotepeque** and **Ipala** to Chiquimula.

   Southwest of Chiquimula, the extinct Volcán de Ipala (1650 m) can be visited. The crater lake is cool and good for swimming. To get here, take an early bus to **Ipala** from Chiquimula; stay on the bus and ask the driver to let you off at Aldea El Chaparroncito (10 minutes after Ipala). From here it's a 1½-hour ascent, following red arrows every now and then. Another ascent goes via Municipio Agua Blanca. Take a minibus to **Agua Blanca** from Ipala and get out at the small village of El Sauce, where the trail starts. The last bus from Ipala to Chiquimula is 1700.

   At **Vado Hondo**, 10 km south of Chiquimula on the road to Esquipulas, a smooth dirt road branches east to the Honduran border (48 km) and a further 11 km to the great Maya ruins of Copán. The border is 1 km after the village. For more on crossing to Honduras, see box, page 517.

Esquipulas

Esquipulas is dominated by a large, white basilica, which attracts millions of pilgrims from across Central America to view the image of a Black Christ. The town has pulled out the stops for visitors, who, as well as a religious fill, will lack nothing in the way of food, drink and some of the best kitsch souvenirs on the market. If it's possible, stop at the mirador, 1 km from the town, for a spectacular view on the way in of the basilica, which sits at the end of a 1.5-km main avenue. The history of the famous *Cristo Negro* records that in 1735 Father Pedro Pardo de Figueroa, suffering from an incurable chronic illness, stood in front of the image to pray, and was cured. A few years later, after becoming Archbishop of Guatemala he ordered a new church to be built to house the sculpture. The **basilica** ⓘ *open until 2000*, was completed in 1758 and the *Cristo Negro* was transferred from the parish church shortly after that. Inside the basilica, the Black Christ is on a gold cross, elaborately engraved with vines and grapes. It was carved by Quirio Cataño in dark balsam wood in 1595. The image attracts over 1,000,000 visitors per year, some crawling on their hands and knees to pay homage. The main pilgrimage periods are 1-15 January (with 15 January being the busiest day), during Lent, Holy Week and 21-27 July.

Quiriguá → *Colour map 6, B6.*

Daily 0730-1630, US$4. Take insect repellent. There are toilets, a restaurant, a museum and a jade store and you can store your luggage with the guards. There is no accommodation at the site (yet). The site is reached by a paved road from the Atlantic Highway. The village of Quiriguá is about halfway between Zacapa and Puerto Barrios on the highway, and about 3 km from the entrance road to the ruins.

The remarkable Late Classic ruins of Quiriguá include the tallest stelae found in the Maya world. The UNESCO World Heritage Site is small, with an excavated acropolis to see, but the highlight of a visit is the sight of the ornately carved tall stelae and the zoomorphic altars. The Maya here were very industrious, producing monuments every five years between AD 751 and 806, coinciding with the height of their prosperity and confident rule. The earliest recorded monument dates from AD 480.

It is believed that Quiriguá was an important trading post between Tikal and Copán, inhabited since the second century, but principally it was a ceremonial centre. The Kings of Quiriguá were involved in the rivalries, wars and changing alliances between Tikal, Copán and Calakmul. It rose to prominence in the middle of the eighth century, around the time of Cauac Sky who ascended to the throne in AD 724. Cauac Sky was appointed to the position by 18 Rabbit, powerful ruler of Copán (now in Honduras), and its surrounding settlements. It seems that he was fed up with being a subordinate under the domination of Copán, and during his reign, Quiriguá attacked Copán and captured 18 Rabbit. One of the stelae tells of the beheading of the Copán King in the plaza at Quiriguá as a sacrifice after the AD 738 battle. After this event 18 Rabbit disappears from the official chronicle and a 20-year hiatus follows in the historical record of Copán. Following this victory, Quiriguá became an independent kingdom and gained control of the Motagua Valley, enriching itself in the process. And, from AD 751, a monument was carved and erected every five years for the next 55 years.

The tallest stelae at Quiriguá is **Stelae E**, which is 10.66 m high with another 2.5 m or so buried beneath. It is 1.52 m wide and weighs 65 tonnes. One of its dates corresponds with the enthronement of Cauac Sky, in AD 724, but it's thought to date from AD 771. All of the stelae, in parkland surrounded by ceiba trees and palms, have shelters, which makes photography difficult. Some monuments have been carved in the shape of animals, some mythical, all of symbolic importance to the Maya.

Thirteen kilometres from Quiriguá is the turn-off for **Mariscos** and Lago de Izabal (see page 440). A further 28 km on are the very hot twin towns of Bananera/Morales. From Bananera there are buses to Río Dulce, Puerto Barrios and the Petén.

Puerto Barrios → *Colour map 7, C5.*

Puerto Barrios, on the Caribbean coast, is a hot and dusty port town, still a central banana point, but now largely superseded as a port by Santo Tomás. The launch to the Garífuna town of Lívingston leaves from the municipal dock here. While not an unpleasant town, it is not a destination in itself, but rather a launch pad to more beautiful and happening spots in Guatemala. It's also the departure point for the Honduran Caribbean. On the way into town, note the cemetery on the right-hand side, where you will pass a small Indian mausoleum with elephant carvings. During the 19th century, *culi* (coolies) of Hindu origin migrated from Jamaica to Guatemala to work on the plantations. The fiesta is 16-22 July.

Listings Chiquimula, Volcán de Ipala and the Honduran border

Where to stay

Chiquimula

$$-$ Posada Perla del Oriente
2 Calle between 11 and 12 Av, T7942-0014.
Near the bus station, this quiet place has plain but spacious rooms with TV and fan ($); some have a/c ($$). There is parking, a restaurant and a pool; grounds are verdant and tranquil. A good deal. Recommended.

$ Hernández
3 Calle, 7-41, T7942-0708.
Enjoying a convenient central location, this reliable cheapie offers basic, spartan rooms with fan or a/c, cheaper with shared bath. A pool adds to its attraction. Family-run (the owner, Henry, speaks fluent English), quiet and friendly.

$ Hotel Posada Don Adán
8 Av, 4-30, T7942-0549.
A good, cheap option. **Don Adán** has tidy little rooms with private bath, fan, a/c, TV. Run by a friendly, older couple.

Esquipulas

There are plenty of cheap hotels, *hospedajes* and *comedores* all over town, especially in and around 11 Calle, also known as Doble Vía Quirio Cataño. Prices tend to double before the Jan feast day. They also rise at Easter and at weekends. When quiet, midweek, bargain for lower room prices.

$$$ Hotel El Gran Chortí
On the outskirts of town at Km 222, T6685-9696, www.realgranchorti.com.
Rack rates are on the pricey side, but the grounds are lovely. Rooms are dated, restful and OK. They come complete with cable TV, Wi-Fi, a/c, phone and *frigobar*. There is also a great pool with slides, a restaurant serving meat, pasta and seafood dishes, and a bar.

$$$ Legendario
3 Av and 9 Calle, T7943-1824, www.hotellegendario.com.
The most expensive place in town, comfortable enough but not great value. Rooms are simple, fine, well-equipped and unremarkable. The real draw is the leafy garden and the massive pool, but check it is open before checking in.

$$$ Payaquí
2 Av, 11-26, T7943-1143, www.hotelpayaqui.com.
The 40 rooms are fair and fine (the suites are comfortable too, if a bit grandiose), with *frigobars*, full of beers for the pilgrims to guzzle, hot-water showers and free drinking water. Facilities include a pool, jacuzzi, spa services, business centre, parking, restaurant

and bar. Credit cards, Honduran lempiras and US dollars accepted.

$$ Hotel El Peregrino
2 Av, 11-94, T7943-1054,
www.elperegrinoesquipulas.com.
A small, quiet, comfortable hotel, nothing fancy but quite adequate. Their unique selling point is the rooftop terrace with a small pool and unobstructed views of the basilica. Ask to see rooms before accepting.

$$ Hotel Real Santa María
2 Av y 10a Calle, 20-1, T7943-0214,
www.hotelrealsantamaria.com.
Situated a block from the basilica with fine views from its terrace, **Real Santa María** boasts sumptuous antiques and elaborate wood carved panels in the reception area. Rooms are simple and pleasant. They feature the usual conveniences including Wi-Fi, a/c, and hot water, but avoid those facing the street. There is also a pool and parking area.

$ Hotel Real Esquipulas
10a Calle, 3-25, T7943-3293,
www.realesquipulashotel.com.
This uninspired cheapie has plain windowless rooms with hot water, cable TV and a/c. Not really royal, but perfectly adequate for thrifty sorts.

Quiriguá

$$ Hotel Restaurante Santa Mónica
In Los Amates, 2 km south of Quiriguá village on the highway, T7947-3838.
17 rooms all with private bath, TV and fan, pool, restaurant. It is opposite a 24-hr Texaco gas station and convenient if you don't want to walk the 10-15 mins into Quiriguá village. There are a couple of shops, banks, and *comedores* here.

$$-$ Posada de Quiriguá
Km 204, Barrio Toltec, Aldea Quiriguá, Los Amates, T5349-5817,
www.geocities.jp/masaki_quirigua.
Designed and managed by Masaki Kuwada from Japan, **Posada de Quiriguá**

is an attractive guesthouse with a lovely tropical garden and a range of simple but restful rooms, easily the best place to stay in the area. The restaurant serves hearty Guatemalan breakfasts and authentic sushi for dinner. Recommended, but tricky to find – ask around town.

$ Hotel y Restaurante Royal
T7947-3639.
Basic budget lodgings with a restaurant attached. Rooms have bath, cheaper without, clean, mosquito netting on all windows. A good place to meet other travellers.

Puerto Barrios
There is not much reason to stay and good options are thin on the ground. The following are OK for a night:

$$ El Reformador
16 Calle and 7 Av 159, T7948-5489.
Set around shaded patios, 51 rooms with bathroom, fan and TV, some with a/c, restaurant, laundry service, clean, quiet, accepts credit cards. The same management run the **Oguatour** travel agency across the road. OK.

$$-$ Hotel del Norte
At the end of 7 Calle, T7948-2116.
A rickety, old wooden structure with sloping landings on the seafront side. All rooms have bath, some with a/c. There's a pool and expensive restaurant, but worth it for the English colonial tearoom atmosphere, no credit cards, but will change dollars. Ask to see a few different rooms, some have great views. The newest are the most comfortable, but lack the dilapidated style that makes this hotel an attraction.

$ Hotel Europa 2
3a Av, between 11a and 12a Calle, T7948-1292.
Located in a quiet neighbourhood near the dock, acceptable budget lodgings with clean, simple rooms with brick walls, wandering chickens in the grounds.

Recommended chiefly for its friendly and helpful Cuban management.

Restaurants

Chiquimula

$ Magic
Corner of 8 Av and 3 Calle.
A good place from which to watch the world go by, and most of what's on offer is seriously cheap. Sandwiches, *licuados* and burgers.

$ Pastelería Las Violetas
7 Av, 4-80, and another near Hotel Victoria.
An excellent cake shop with a fine spread, good-value sandwiches too, plus great cappuccino, and a/c. Next door is its bakery.

Esquipulas
There are plenty of restaurants, but prices are high for Guatemala.

$$$ La Hacienda
2 Av, 10-20.
Delicious barbecued chicken and steaks. Kids' menu available, breakfasts available. One of the smartest restaurants in town.

$$ Restaurante Payaquí
2 Av, 11-26, inside the hotel of the same name.
Specialities include turkey in *pipián*, also lunches and breakfasts. A poolside restaurant makes a pleasant change.

$ Café Pistachos
Close to Hotel Calle Real.
Clean, cheap snack bar with burgers, hotdogs, etc.

Puerto Barrios

$$$-$$ Restaurante Safari
At the north end of 5 Av and 1 Calle, overlooking the bay with views all around.
Basically serving up oceans of fish, including whole fish, *ceviche* and fishburgers.

$$ La Fonda de Quique
An orange and white wooden building at 5 Av and corner of 12 Calle.

Nicely a/c with hand-made wooden furniture, serving lobster, fish and meats, plus snacks.

Bars and clubs

Puerto Barrios

Mariscos de Izabal
Open until 0100.
One of the most popular spots in Puerto Barrios, this thatched bar is mostly a drinking den but also has tacos, tortillas and burgers served amid beating Latin rhythms.

The Container
Just past the Hotel del Norte overlooking the sea. Open 0700-2300.
An unusual bar constructed from the front half of an old ship equipped with portholes, and a number of banana containers from the massive banana businesses just up the road.

Transport

Chiquimula
Bus
There are 3 terminals in Chiquimula, all within 50 m of each other. To **Guatemala City**, **Transportes Guerra** and **Rutas Orientales**, hourly, US$4, 3¼-3½ hrs, leave from 11 Av between 1 and 2 Calle, as do buses for **Puerto Barrios**, several companies, every 30 mins, between 0300-1500, 4 hrs, US$6.50. To **Quiriguá**, US$3.20, 1 hr 50 mins. Take any Puerto Barrios-bound bus. On to **Río Dulce** take the Barrios bus and get off at La Ruidosa junction and change, or change at Bananera/Morales. To **Flores** with **Transportes María Elena**, 8 hrs, 0400, 0800, 1300. Buses to **Ipala** and **Jalapa** also leave from here; 4 buses daily to Jalapa between 0500-1230, 4½ hrs, US$5.80; to Ipala, US$2.20. Supplemented by minibuses 0600-1715 to Ipala. To **Zacapa**, 25 mins, from the terminal inside the market at 10 Av between 1 and 2 Calle. Same for those to **Esquipulas**, every 10 mins, US$2.70, until 1900. To and from **Cobán** via El Rancho (where a change must be made). Buses to **El Florido** (on the

Honduras border) leave with **Transportes Vilma** from inside the market at 1 Calle, between 10 and 11 Av, T7942-2253, between 0530-1630, US$2.70, 1½ hrs. Buses return from the border at 0530, 0630 and then hourly 0700-1700. For more on crossing to Honduras, see box, page 517.

Esquipulas
Bus
Rutas Orientales. Leaving Esquipulas, 1 Av "A" and 11 Calle, T7943-1366, for **Guatemala City** every 30 mins from 0200-1700, 4½ hrs, US$8.50. To **Chiquimula** by minibus, every 30 mins, 0430-1830, US$1.40.

Quiriguá
Bus
Emphasize to the bus driver if you want Quiriguá *pueblo* and not the *ruinas*. Countless travellers have found themselves left at the ruins and having to make a return journey to the village for accommodation.

To get to the **ruins** directly, take any bus heading along the highway towards Puerto Barrios and ask to be let off at the *ruinas*. At this ruins crossroads, take a pickup (very regular), 10 mins, US$0.50, or bus (much slower and less regular) to the ruins 4 km away. The last bus back to the highway is at 1700. You can walk, but take lots of water, as it's hot and dusty with little shade.

To get to the **village** of Quiriguá, 3 km south from the ruins entrance entrance, it is only a 10-min walk to the **Hotel Royal**. Keep to the paved road, round a left-hand bend, and it's 100 m up on the left. Or take a local bus heading from the highway into the village. The **Hotel Edén** is a further 5 mins on down the hill. There is a frequent daily bus service that runs a circular route between Los Amates, Quiriguá village and then on to the entrance road to the ruins. You can also walk through the banana plantations from Quiriguá village to the ruins as well. From **Hotel Royal** walk past the church towards the old train station and the **Hotel Edén**, and follow the tracks branching to the right, through the plantation to the ruins.

Puerto Barrios
Boat
It's a 10-min walk to the municipal dock at the end of Calle 12, from the **Litegua** bus station. Ferries *(barca)* leave for **Lívingston** at 1030 and 0500 (1½ hrs, US$2.50). *Lanchas* also leave when a minimum of 12 people are ready to go, 30 mins, US$3.80. The only scheduled *lanchas* leave at 0630, 0730, 0900 and 1100, and the last will leave, if there are enough people, at 1800. **Transportes El Chato**, 1 Av, between 10 and 11 Calle, T7948-5525, pichilingo2000@yahoo.com, also does trips from here to **Punta de Manabique**, and other places near and far.

To Belize *Lanchas* leave for **Punta Gorda** at 1000 with **Transportes El Chato**, address above, returning at 1400, 1 hr 20 mins, US$22. Also services with **Requena** to Punta Gorda at 1400, returning at 0900. See also Border crossing box, page 514.

Bus
To **Guatemala City**, with **Litegua**, 6 Av between 9 and 10 Calle, T7948-1002, www.litegua.com. 18 a day, 5 hrs, US$11-7.50. Bus to **El Rancho** (turn-off for Biotopo del Quetzal and Cobán), 4 hrs, take any bus to Guatemala City. To **Quiriguá**, 2 hrs, take any capital-bound bus. To **Chiquimula**, operated by **Carmencita**, 4 hrs. Alternatively, catch a bus to Guatemala City, getting off at Río Hondo, and catch a *colectivo* or any bus heading to Chiquimula. For **Río Dulce**, take any bus heading for Guatemala City and change at **La Ruidosa** (15 mins). For minibuses to **Entre Ríos**, for the El Cinchado border crossing to **Honduras** (**Corinto**), with connections to **Omoa**, **Puerto Cortés** and **La Ceiba**. See also box, page 517, for more information on crossing into Honduras.

★Lívingston, or La Buga, is populated mostly by Garífuna, who bring a colourful flavour to this corner of Guatemala. With its tropical sounds and smells, it is a good place to hang out for a few days, sitting on the dock of the bay, or larging it up with the locals, *punta*-style.

Coco pan and *cocado* (a coconut, sugar and ginger *dulce*) and locally made jewellery are sold in the streets. The town is the centre of fishing and shrimping in the Bay of Amatique and only accessible by boat. It is nearly 23 km by sea from Puerto Barrios and there are regular daily boat runs that take 35 minutes in a fast *lancha*.

The bulk of the town is up a small steep slope leading straight from the dock, which is at the mouth of the Río Dulce estuary. The other part of town is a linear spread along the river estuary, just north of the dock and then first left. The town is small and everything is within walking distance. The Caribbean beach is pretty dirty nearer the river estuary end, but a little further up the coast, it is cleaner, with palm trees and accommodation. Closer to the town are a couple of bars and weekend beach discos. The town's **Centro Cultural Garífuna-Q'eqchi'** is perched on a hillock, and has the best views in the whole of Lívingston. The town's fiestas are 24-31 December, in honour of the Virgen del Rosario, with dancing including the *punta*, and Garífuna Day, 26 November. The small but helpful **tourist office** ⓘ *on the east side of the Parque Municipal, www.livingston.com.gt, daily 0600-1800*, with a café and exhibition space behind.

Around Lívingston

Northwest along the coastline towards the Río Sarstún, on the border with Belize (where manatee can be seen), is the **Río Blanco beach** (45 minutes by *lancha* from Lívingston), followed by **Playa Quehueche** (also spelt Keueche). Beyond Quehueche, about 6 km (1½ hours) from Lívingston, are **Los Siete Altares**, a set of small waterfalls and pools hidden in the greenery. They are at their best during the rainy season when the water cascades down to the sea. In the drier seasons much of the water is channelled down small, eroded grooves on large slabs of grey rock, where you can stretch out and enjoy the sun. Early *Tarzan* movies were filmed here. Don't stroll on the beach after dark and be careful of your belongings at the Siete Altares end. Police occasionally accompany tourists to the falls; check on arrival what the security situation is. Boats can be hired in Lívingston to visit beaches along the coast towards San Juan and the Río Sarstún.

For one of the best trips in Guatemala take a boat up the **Río Dulce** through the sheer-sided canyon towards El Golfete, where the river broadens. Trees and vegetation cling to the canyon walls, their roots plunging into the waters for a long drink below. The scenery here is gorgeous, especially in the mornings, when the waters are unshaken. Tours can be arranged from Lívingston for US$12. You can also paddle up the Río Dulce gorge on *cayucos*, which can be hired from some of the hotels in Lívingston.

The **Biotopo Chocón Machacas** ⓘ *0700-1600, US$2.50 (private hire at US$125 is the only transport option)*, is one place where the elusive manatee (sea cow) hangs out, but you are unlikely to see him munching his way across the lake bottom, as he is very shy and retreats at the sound of a boat motor. The manatee is an aquatic herbivore, which can be up to 4 m long when adult, and weigh more than 450 kg. It eats for six to eight hours daily and can consume more than 10% of its body weight in a 24-hour period. Administered by CECON, the reserve is a mangrove zone, halfway between Río Dulce town and

Lívingston, on the northern shore of **El Golfete**, an area where the Río Dulce broadens into a lake 5 km across. Four Q'eqchi' communities of 400 people live on land within the 6245-ha reserve. Within the reserve are carpets of water lilies, dragonflies, blue morpho butterflies, pelicans and cormorants. On land, spot army ants, crabs, mahogany trees and the *labios rojos* ('hot lips') flower.

Proyecto Ak' Tenamit ⓘ www.aktenamit.org, meaning 'new village' in Q'eqchi', is 15 minutes upriver from Lívingston. It was set up to help 7000 Q'eqchi' Maya displaced by the civil war. Volunteers are needed for a minimum of a month's work (board and transport are available, and volunteers get weekends off). A working knowledge of Spanish is required. There's also a shop and restaurant, with excursions, run by locally trained volunteer guides. Near here is the **Río Tatín tributary** the wonderfully sited **Finca Tatín** and **Hotelito Perdido**; see Where to stay, below. **Reserva Ecológica Cerro San Gil**, with its natural pools, karstic caves and biostation, can be visited from here, or from Río Dulce. Contact **FUNDAECO** ⓘ www.fundaeco.org.gt.

Punta de Manabique

Punta de Manabique is a fine, finger-shaped peninsula northeast of Puerto Barrios and just visible across the bay from Lívingston, coated in a beach of white sand on its eastern side, and by mangrove on the other. Travelling north to the point of the peninsula, you pass the Bahía de Graciosa, where dolphins frolic and manatees silently graze under the surface. In its virgin tropical forest live howler monkeys, parrots, snakes, pizote, tapirs and peccary and, on its beaches, turtles. There is a visitor centre, scientific station and a hotel. For more information contact the **Fundación Mario Dary** ⓘ www.guate.net/fundary manabique/fundacion.htm, which operates conservation, health, education and ecotourism projects.

Listings Lívingston and around

Where to stay

$$$ Hotel Villa Caribe
Up Calle Principal from the dock on the right,
T7947-0072, www.villasdeguatemala.com.
Part of an upscale Guatemalan hotel chain, **Villa Caribe** enjoys a privileged vantage from its hillside perch. All rooms have views of the Río Dulce or the Caribbean, there is also a pool (available to non-guests when the hotel is not busy for US$6.50), bar and a large restaurant. The best in town, popular with tour groups, but needs some maintenance.

$$ Posada El Delfín
T7947-0976, www.posadaeldelfin.com.
Located at the mouth of the Río Dulce on a long pier that juts out into the sea, **El Delfín** promises tranquil views of the local wildlife and boat traffic. They offer 24 reasonable

rooms and suites, chill-out areas with hammocks, and a restaurant. Tours available.

$$ Vecchia Toscana
Barrio Paris, T7947-0884,
www.livingston-vecchiatoscana.com.
This Italian-owned lodging on the beach features a leafy garden with a refreshing pool, breezy rooftop terraces, private pier and a decent Italian restaurant with sea views. Accommodation is in a variety of simple, tranquil, comfortable and occasionally brightly painted rooms, most of them equipped with a/c.

$ Casa de la Iguana
Calle Marcos Sánchez Díaz,
5 mins from the dock, T7947-0064,
www.casadelaiguana.com.
A very cool party hostel with ultra-cheap dorms, private rooms with shared bath, and economical 'jungle huts' set around

well-tended garden, as well as space for tents and hammocks. Hot showers, Wi-Fi, bar, daily happy hour and a pub quiz on Sun; what more could you need?

$ Casa Nostra
Near the river, T7947-0842, www.casanostralivingston.com.
Rooms at this simple little bed and breakfast are clean, cheap and colourful. It is recommended chiefly for its friendly host, Stuart Winand, and for its good food, which includes excellent pizza and fresh seafood prepared with international flavours. Very hospitable, good reports.

$ Casa Rosada
600 m from the dock, T7947-0303, www.hotelcasarosada.com.
This pastel-pink house set on the waterfront offers 10 bungalows furnished with attractive hand-painted furniture. The room upstairs overlooks the bay. Meals are set for the day, ranging from pasta to delicious shrimps bathed in garlic. Good, friendly and chilled out, but reservations advisable.

$ Flowas
Barrio Compoamor, on the beach, T7947-0376, infoflowas@gmail.com.
Rustic beach bungalows for those who like to be up close to the lapping ocean. Each unit has a porch and hammock. Tranquil and secluded with a hippy backpacker vibe.

$ Hotel Ríos Tropicales
T7947-0158, www.mctropic.webs.com.
This place has some nice touches to distinguish it from the majority of other places in town, like terracotta-tiled floors. They offer 11 rooms, with fans, 5 with private bath, book exchange and the **McTropic** restaurant up the road with internet and a tour operator.

Around Lívingston

$$-$ Q'ana Itz'am
Lagunita Salvador, T5992-1853, www.lagunitasalvador.com.

This excellent Q'eqchi community tourism project includes an ecolodge with rustic wooden cabins and a lovely jungle setting. Activities include kayaking, hiking, nature observation and traditional dances. Advance reservation absolutely necessary. Highly recommended.

$ Finca Tatín
Río Tatín tributary, with great dock space to hang out on, T5902-0831, www.fincatatin. centroamerica.com.
This lovely, rustic, wood-built B&B offers a range of Robinson Crusoe lodgings including dorms, private rooms and simple bungalows nestled in the jungle. The Casa Grande (main house) is the focal point for evening gatherings where you can enjoy games, books, table tennis and music. Tours and kayak rental available.

$ Hotel Ecológico Salvador Gaviota
Along the coast, towards Siete Altares, beyond Hotel Ecológico Siete Altares, T7947-0874, www.hotelsalvadorgaviota.com.
The beach here is lovely, hummingbirds flit about and the owner Lisette is friendly. Rooms have shared bath, but the bungalows for 2 or 4 people have private bath. Rooms available for monthly rent, all set in lush surroundings. There is a bar and restaurant (0730-2200), and free *lancha* service; ring beforehand. Tours available. Highly recommended.

$ Hotelito Perdido
On the Río Lampara, can be dropped off on the Lívingston–Río Dulce boat service, T5725-1576, www.hotelitoperdido.com.
This quiet, rustic very attractive hideaway is located across the river from the mineral hot springs. Grounds include tropical gardens, winding pathways, bar-restaurant and 5 types of wood-built jungle lodgings. They also rent kayaks and wooden *cayucos*. Ecologically oriented with solar power, recycling and organic vegetable plots. Recommended.

$ The Roundhouse
La Pintada, 20 mins by boat from Livingston, T4294-9730, www. roundhouseguatemala.com.
The Roundhouse is a popular party hostel with a great setting on the riverbank. It has an environmentally aware ethos with solar hot water, a natural feed water system and bio-sand purification. Accommodation is in dorms or private rooms, both very affordable.

Restaurants

Fresh fish is available everywhere; in restaurants ask for *tapado*, a rich soup with various types of seafood, banana and coconut. Women sell *pan de coco* on the streets.

$$ Bahía Azul
Calle Principal.
Serving excellent breakfasts but dreadful coffee, this place specializes in salsas, *camarones* and *langosta*. There You can sit at tables on the street or in the dining room. There is also a tourist service and the **Exotic Travel Agency**.

$$ Buga Mama
An excellent example of an innovative development project and well worth checking out. Local Mayan young people staff this large restaurant located next to the water as part of their training with the Ak'Tenamit project (www.aktenamit.org). The food is OK, the service excellent, and it's in a great spot too.

$$ El Malecón
50 m from the dock on the left.
Serves *chapín* and Western-style breakfasts, seafood and chicken *fajitas*, all in a large, airy wooden dining area.

$$ Happy Fish
Just along from the Hotel Río Dulce.
A popular restaurant with an internet café. Serves a truckload of fish (not quite so happy now) with good coffee. Occasional live music at weekends.

$ McTropic
Opposite the Hotel Río Dulce.
This popular place offers great breakfasts and cocktails at street tables, with good service.

$ Rasta Mesa Restaurant
In Barrio Nevago, just past the cemetery, www.site.rasta mesa.com.
Garífuna cultural centre and restaurant with music, history, and classes in cooking and drumming. A great place to hang out.

$ Tiburón Gato
Far end of Calle Principal.
A simple open-fronted place, serving a good range of fish, seafood and pasta. It's open for breakfasts too.

Bars and clubs

Lugudi Barana
Sun 1500-0100 only.
A disco that's also on the beach and popular with visitors and locals.

Festivals

26 Nov Garífuna Day.
24-31 Dec In honour of the **Virgen del Rosario**, with traditional dancing.

What to do

Tour operators
Captain Eric, *located at the Pitchi Mango snack bar on the main street, T4265-5278*. Will arrange 1- to 2-day boat tours for groups of up to 5 people to the surrounding region.
You can also contract any of the *lancheros* at the dock to take you to Río Dulce, Playa Blanca and Siete Altares.

Transport

Boat
Ferry to **Puerto Barrios** to (22.5 km), 1½ hrs, US$1.60 at 0500 and 1400 Mon-Sat. Private *lanchas* taking 16-25 people also sail this route, 30 mins, US$4. They leave at 0630 and 0730 each day and at 0900 and 1100

Mon-Sat to Puerto Barrios and then when full. Lívingston to **Río Dulce**, with short stops at **Aguas Calientes** and the **Biotopo Chacón Machacas**, US$15.50 1 way. *Lanchas* definitely leave at 0900 and 1430 for **Río Dulce**, but these make no stops. To **Honduras** (Omoa, Puerto Cortés, La Ceiba), *lanchas* can be organized at the dock or through tour operators, see above. See also box, page 517. To **Belize** (Punta Gorda, Placencia, Cayos Zapotillos), check with tour operators, see above, about boats to Belize. Anyone who takes you must have a manifest with passengers' names, stamped and signed at the immigration office. On Tue and Fri fast *lanchas* make the trip to Punta Gorda (US$22). Enquire at the dock and negotiate a fare with the *lanchero* association. See also Border crossings box, page 514, for more information on crossing into Belize. Boats to Placencia and the Zapotilla cayes can also be arranged.

Lago de Izabal → *Colour map 6, A6.*

beautiful riverside and lakeside places to stay

The vast Lago de Izabal, the largest lake in Guatemala at 717 sq km, narrows to form a neck at the town of Fronteras. Better known as Río Dulce, it is famed for its riverside setting. Just south of Río Dulce on the lake is the restored Castillo de San Felipe, while on the northern shore of the lake is the town of El Estor, and on its southern shore the smaller town of Mariscos. Further east, beyond Río Dulce, the river broadens out to El Golfete, where there is the Biotopo Chacón Machacas, see above. It then narrows into one of the finest gorges in the world, and opens out at its estuary, with Lívingston at its head. This area can be wet in the rainy season, but it experiences a lull in July, known as the *canícula*.

★Fronteras/Río Dulce and around

Río Dulce is a good place to stop and kick back for a couple of days. Allow yourself to be tempted to laze on a boat for the afternoon, walk in the nearby jungle, or eat and drink at one of several dockside restaurants. Río Dulce, www.mayaparadise.com, is 23 km upstream from Lívingston at the entrance to Lago de Izabal, is easily accessible from Puerto Barrios by road, and is the last major stop before the Petén. It's also a good place to collect information about the area stretching from El Estor to Lívingston.

On the shore of Lago de Izabal is **Casa Guatemala** ① *14 Calle, 10-63, Zona 1, Guatemala City, T2231-9408, www.casa-guatemala.org* (also known as **Hotel Backpacker's**), an orphanage where you can work in exchange for basic accommodation and food. At the entrance to Lago de Izabal, 2 km upstream, is the old Spanish fort of **Castillo de San Felipe** ① *0800-1700, US$3.30*. The fortification was first built in 1643 to defend the coast against attacks from pirates; it has been well preserved and in lovely grounds; great views from the battlements. Between Río Dulce and El Estor is **Finca El Paraíso**, a hot waterfall with waters that plunge into a cool-water pool below.

El Estor and around

Strung along the northwest shore of Lago de Izabal, backed by the Santa Cruz mountain range and facing the Sierra de las Minas, El Estor enjoys one of the most beautiful vistas in Guatemala. It's a great place to relax, swim (down a nearby canyon), go fishing and spot manatee. Some businesses are expecting the new road to bring a surge of tourist visitors. For the next few years though you'll still have the place mostly to yourself. The town dates back to the days when the Europeans living in the Atlantic area got their provisions from a store situated at this spot, now the **Hotel Vista al Lago**. Briton Skinner and Dutchman Klee supplied the region from *el store* 1815-1850. Nickel mining began just outside town in 1978, but was suspended at the **Exmibal plant** after the oil crisis of 1982, because the process depended on cheap sources of energy.

You can hire a boat from Río Dulce to El Estor, passing near the hot waterfall, inland at Finca El Paraíso, which can be reached by a good trail in about 40 minutes. The Río Sauce cuts through the impressive **Cañón El Boquerón**, where you can swim with the current all the way down the canyon, which is brilliant fun. It's a deep canyon with lots of old man's beard hanging down, strange rock formations and otters and troops of howler monkeys whooping about. One of the locals will paddle you upstream for about 800 m (US$1). Exploring the Río Zarco, closer to town, also makes for a good trip, with cold swimming. The **Refugio de Vida Silvestre Bocas del Polochic** (Bocas del Polochic Wildlife Reserve) is a 23,000-ha protected area on the western shores of the lake. Howler monkeys are commonly seen. In addition to over 350 bird species, there are iguanas, turtles and the chance of sighting crocodiles and manatees. The NGO **Defensores de la Naturaleza** ① *2 Calle and 5 Av, El Estor, T2440-8138 in the capital, www.defensores.org.gt*, has a research station at Selempim with bunk beds ($ per person), food, showers and kitchen. It's a two- or three-hour boat ride from El Estor to Ensenada Los Lagartos. Tours are available from town for US$30 for two people. Contact the office in El Estor or ask at a hotel about boat services.

Mariscos is on the southern shore of Lago de Izabal. The best reason to come here is the nearby **Denny's Beach**; see Where to stay, below.

Listings Lago de Izabal

Where to stay

Fronteras/Río Dulce and around
All the establishments below are located out of town on the water. If you need to stay in the less attractive locale of Río Dulce itself, try **Hotel Vista al Río** ($), just past **Bruno's** under the bridge, T7930-5665, www.hotelvistario.com.

$$$-$$ Hacienda Tijax
T7930-5505, www.tijax.com. 2 mins by lancha from the dock, yacht moorings available.
There is a beautiful jungle trail with canopy walkway at the tranquil **Hacienda Tijax**, also a rubber plantation, bird sanctuary, pool with whirlpool and jacuzzi, and natural swimming pools. Activities include horse riding, kayaking, sailing and rowboat hire and a medicine trail. Accommodation is in well-built wooden cabins with mod cons, including a/c. There is excellent food in the riverside bar and restaurant. Highly recommended.

$$-$ Tortugal Hotel and Marina
T5306-6432, www.tortugal.com.
Beautifully presented bungalows with gorgeous soft rugs on the floor and various other types of accommodation including open-air ranchos and a *casita*. There is plentiful hot water. Also there is a riverside restaurant and bar, pool table in a cool upstairs attic room with books, satellite TV, internet, phone and fax service. Very highly recommended.

$ Hotel Backpacker's
Just out of town by the bridge on the south bank of the river, T7930-5169, www.hotelbackpackers.com.
Profits of **Hotel Backpacker's** go to the Casa Guatemala Orphanage and guests have the option of working for their lodging as

part of a volunteer holiday. There are basic dorms with lockers and simple private rooms with bathroom, as well as a restaurant and bar, and internet and telephone service. Recommended.

$ Hotel Kangaroo
On the Río La Colocha, T5363-6716, www.hotelkangaroo.com.
Perched on the water's edge, this Mexican-Australian owned river lodge has rustic wood-built rooms, dorms and bungalows, all very simple and close to nature. There's a bar-restaurant on the decking serving Aussie and Mexican grub, and an unheated jacuzzi.

El Estor and around

$$$-$$ Denny's Beach
T5398-0908, www.dennys beach.com.
This remote place offers resort-style lodgings with a gorgeous lakeside location, accessible by *lancha* from Río Dulce (minimum fee US$41), or free from Mariscos if you call ahead. Tours, wake boarding and horse riding can be arranged. Internet service.

$ Hotel Vista al Lago
6 Av, 1-13, T7949-7205.
21 clean rooms with private bath and fan. Ask for the lakeview rooms, where there is a pleasant wooden balcony on which to sit. Friendly owner Oscar Paz will take you fishing, and runs ecological and cultural tours.

$ Villela
6 Av, 2-06, T7949-7214.
With a flower-filled garden with chairs to sit out in, this place has 9 big, clean rooms with bath, although some are quite dark. Recommended.

Restaurants

Fronteras/Río Dulce and around
There are restaurants in the hotels and a couple along the main road.

$$-$ Ranchón Mary
El Relleno, T7930-5103.
Thatch-roofed waterfront deck with tables, serving delicious fish and seafood and ice-cold beer.

$$-$ Rosita's Restaurant
San Felipe de Lara, T5054-3541.
Lovely waterfront location with open deck, overlooking the bridge, 5 mins by *lancha* from Río Dulce. Great seafood, nachos and home-made banana pie.

El Estor and around

$ Dorita.
Popular with the locals, this *comedor* serves good seafood meals which are excellent value.

$ Marisabela
8 Av and 1 Calle.
Good and cheap spaghetti, as well as fish and chicken, with lake views.

$ Restaurant del Lago
West side of main square.
This popular restaurant overlooks the main square and offers local dishes.

$ Restaurant Elsita
2 blocks north of the market on 8 Av.
This is a great people-watching place with a large menu and good food.

What to do

Fronteras/Río Dulce
Sailing
Captain John Clark's sailing trips on his 46-ft Polynesian catamaran, *Las Sirenas*, are highly recommended. Food, taxes, snorkelling and fishing gear, and windsurf boards included. Contact **Aventuras Vacacionales SA**, Antigua, www.sailing-diving-guatemala.com; see page 360.

Coastguard For emergencies, call Guarda Costa on VHF channel 16, T4040-4971.

Tour operators

Atitrans Tours, *on the little road heading to the dockside*. To **Finca Paraíso** for US$20. **Otiturs**, *opposite Tijax Express*, T5219-4520. Run by the friendly and helpful Otto Archila. Offers a minibus service as well as tours to local sites, internal flights and boat trips. **Tijax Express**, *opposite Atitrans*, T7930-5505, *info@tijax.com*. Agent for Hacienda Tijax (over the river).

Lancheros offer trips on the river and on Lago de Izabal. They can be contacted at the *muelle principal*, under the bridge. Ask for Cesár Mendez, T5819-7436, or ask at **Atitrans** for collection.

Transport

Fronteras/Río Dulce and around
Boat
Lanchas colectivas leave for **Lívingston** at 0930 and 1300, US$15.50. Private *lanchas* can be arranged at the dock to any of the river or lakeside hotels.

Bus
Local To get to **Castillo de San Felipe**, take a boat from Río Dulce, or *camioneta* from the corner of the main road to Tikal, and the first turning left after the bridge by **Pollandia**, 5 mins, or a 5-km walk. From Río Dulce to **Finca El Paraíso**, take the same road, 45 mins, US$1.70. Buses to Río Dulce pass the finca between 40 and 50 mins past the hour. To **El Estor**, from the same Pollandia turn-off, US$2.50, 1½ hrs on a paved road, 0500-1600, hourly, returning 0500-1600. To **Puerto Barrios**, take any bus to **La Ruidosa** and change, 35 mins to junction then a further 35 mins to Puerto Barrios.

Long-distance To **Guatemala City** and **Flores**: through buses stop at Río Dulce. To

Guatemala City with **Litegua**, T7930-5251, www.litegua.com, 7 a day between 0300 and 1515, US$7.54, 6 hrs. **Fuente del Norte**, T5692-1988, 23 services daily, US$6.30. Luxury service 1300, 1700 and 2400, US$13. **Línea Dorada**, at 1300, luxury service, 5 hrs, US$13. To **Flores** from 0630-0300, 25 buses daily, 4½ hrs with **Fuente del Norte**, US$8. Luxury service, 1430, US$13. This bus also stops at **Finca Ixobel** and **Poptún**, US$3.90. **Línea Dorada**, to Flores, 1500, 3 hrs, luxury service with a/c, TV and snacks, US$13, and on to **Melchor de Mencos** for Belize; see also Border crossing box, page 514, for more information on crossing into Belize. **Fuente del Norte**, also to **Melchor de Mencos**, at 1300, 2130 and 2330, 6 hrs, US$12.50. Also to, **Sayaxché** at 2200 and one to **Naranjo** at 2100.

Shuttles Atitrans, T7930-5111, www.atitrans.com, runs shuttles to **Antigua**, **Flores**, **Copán Ruinas** and **Guatemala City**.

El Estor and around
Bus The ferry from Mariscos no longer runs, but a private *lancha* can be contracted.

To **Río Dulce**, 0500-1600, hourly, 1 hr, US$2.20. Direct bus to **Cobán**, at 1300, 7 hrs, US$5.60. Also via either Panzós and Tactic, or Cahabón and Lanquín. For the **Cañón El Boquerón**, take the Río Dulce bus and ask to be dropped at the entrance. Or hire a bike from town (8 km) or a taxi, US$6.50, including waiting time.

To **Cobán**, with **Transportes Valenciana**, 1200, 0200, 0400 and 0800, 8 long and dusty hrs, with no proper stop. To **Guatemala City**, 0100 direct, via Río Dulce, 7 hrs, US$6.30, or go to Río Dulce and catch one. At 2400 and 0300 via Río Polochic Valley. For **Santa Elena, Petén** take a bus to Río Dulce and pick on up from there.

The Verapaces

Propped up on a massive limestone table eroded over thousands of years, the plateau of the Verapaz region is riddled with caves, underground tunnels, stalagtites and stalagmites. Cavernous labyrinths used by the Maya for worship, in their belief that caves are the entrances to the underworld, are also now visited by travellers who marvel at the natural interior design of these subterranean spaces.

Nature has performed its work above ground too. At Semuc Champey, pools of tranquil, turquoise-green water span a monumental limestone bridge; beneath the bridge a river thunders violently through. The quetzal reserve also provides the opportunity to witness a feather flash of red or green of the elusive bird, and dead insects provide curious interest in Rabinal, where their body parts end up on ornamental gourds.

The centre of this region – the imperial city of Cobán – provides respite for the traveller with a clutch of museums honouring the Maya, coffee and orchid, and a fantastic entertainment spectacle at the end of July with a whirlwind of traditional dances and a Maya beauty contest.

Baja Verapaz region is made up of a handful of Achi'-Maya speaking towns, namely Salamá, Rabinal, San Jerónimo and Cubulco. The department is known for the quetzal reserve, the large Dominican finca and aqueduct, and the weird decorative technique of the crafts in Rabinal.

Sierra de las Minas Biosphere Reserve → *Colour map 6, B5.*

To visit, get a permit in San Augustín from the office of La Fundación de Defensores de la Naturaleza, Barrio San Sebastián, 1 block before the Municipalidad, T7936-0681, ctot@ defensores.org.gt, www.defensores.org.gt. The contact is César Tot. Alternatively, contact the Fundación offices in Santa Elena, Petén, at 5 Calle, 3 Av "A", Zona 2, T7926-3095, lacandon@ defensores.org.gt, or in the capital at 7 Av, 7-09, Zona 13, T2440-8138.

Just north of El Rancho, in the Department of El Progreso, is **San Agustín Acasaguastlán**, an entrance for the Sierra de las Minas Biosphere Reserve, one of Guatemala's largest conservation areas with peaks topping 3000 m and home to the quetzal, harpy eagle and peregrine falcon, puma, jaguar, spider monkey, howler monkey, tapir and pizote.

Biotopo del Quetzal

Daily 0700-1600, US$2.60, parking, disabled entrance. Run by Centro de Estudios Conservacionistas (CECON), Av Reforma, 0-63, Zona 10, Guatemala City, T2331-0904, cecon@usac.edu.gt.

The Biotopo del Quetzal, or **Biosphere Mario Dary Rivera**, is between Cobán and Guatemala City at Km 160.5, 4 km south of Purulhá and 53 km from Cobán. There are two trails. Increasing numbers of quetzals have been reported in the Biotopo, but they are still very elusive. Ask for advice from the rangers. The area around the Biotopo has been protected as a **Corredor Biológico Bosque Nuboso**, with numerous privately run reserves and restaurants by the roadside offering birdwatching trails, waterfalls, natural swimming holes and caves. For more information, see www.bosquenuboso.com.gt.

Salamá, Rabinal and Cubulco

Just before Salamá is **San Jerónimo**, with a Dominican church and convent, from where friars tended vineyards, exported wine and cultivated sugar. There is an old sugar mill (*trapiche*) on display at the finca and a huge aqueduct of 124 arches to transport water to the sugar cane fields and the town. Salamá sits in a valley with a colonial cathedral, containing carved gilt altarpieces as its centrepiece. The town also has one of a few remaining **Templos de Minerva** in the country, built in 1916. Behind the Calvario church is the hill Cerro de la Santa Cruz, from where a view of the valley can be seen. Market day is Monday and is worth a visit.

The village of **Rabinal** was founded in 1537 by Fray Bartolomé de las Casas. It has a 16th-century church, and a busy Sunday market, where lacquered gourds, beautiful *huipiles* and embroidered napkins are sold. The glossy lacquer of the gourd is made from the body oil of a farmed scaly insect called the *niij*. The male *niij* is boiled in water to release its oil, which is then mixed with soot powder to create the lacquer. The **Museo Rabinal Achí** ① *2 Calle y 4 Av, Zona 3, T5311-1536, museoachi@hotmail.com*, displays historical exhibits and has produced bilingual books about the Achí culture.

West of Rabinal, set amid maize fields and peach trees, Cubulco is known for its tradition of performing the pole dance, *Palo Volador,* which takes place every 20-25 July. Men,

BACKGROUND

The Verapaces

Before the Spanish conquest of the region, Las Verapaces had a notorious reputation; it was known as Tezulutlán (land of war) for its aggressive warlike residents, who fought repeated battles with their neighbours and rivals, the K'iche' Maya. These warring locals were not going to be a pushover for the Spanish conquerors and they strongly resisted when their land was invaded. The Spanish eventually retreated and the weapon replaced with the cross. Thus, Carlos V of Spain gave the area the title of Verdadera Paz (true peace) in 1548.

The region's modern history saw it converted into a massive coffee- and cardamom-growing region. German coffee fincas were established from the 1830s until the Second World War, when the Germans were invited over to plough the earth by the Guatemalan government. Many of the fincas were expropriated during the war, but some were saved from this fate by naming a Guatemalan as the owner of the property. The area still produces some of Guatemala's finest coffee – served up with some of the finest cakes. The Germans also introduced cardamom to the Verapaces, when a *finquero* requested some seeds for use in biscuits. Guatemala is now the world's largest producer of cardamom.

attached by rope, have to leap from the top of the pole and spiral down, accompanied by marimba music. There are three basic *hospedajes* in town.

Listings Baja Verapaz

Where to stay

Biotopo del Quetzal

$$ Posada Montaña del Quetzal
At Km 156, T7823-9636,
www.hposadaquetzal.com.
Rustic and remote, this tranquil highland *posada* offers modest bungalows or rooms with spartan furnishings, private bathrooms and hot water; try to get one with a fireplace so you can get good and toasty after dark. There's also café, bar, pool and gardens. Simple, romantic and rugged.

$$ Ram Tzul
Km 158, T5908-4066, www.ramtzul.com.
Set in rambling 100-ha grounds, the wood-built cabins at **Ram Tzul** are very beautiful and creatively rendered, some of them featuring stained-glass windows, lovely

stonework and superb views of the forested hills. The restaurant is equally interesting and serves hearty *comida típica*. Dozens of excursions can be arranged. Recommended.

$ Hospedaje Ranchitos del Quetzal
Km 160.8, T7823-5860.
Conveniently located just 200 m from the Biotopo entrance, this economical place has clean and simple rooms in old and new buildings, with shared or private bathrooms and hot water. There's also a *comedor*. It's good for early morning foray.

Transport

Biotopo del Quetzal
Bus
From **Guatemala City**, take a Cobán bus with **Escobar-Monja Blanca** and ask to be let out at the Biotopo, hourly from

0400-1700, 3½ hrs, US$3.50. From **Cobán**, 1 hr, US$0.80, take any capital-bound bus or a minibus from Campo 2 near football stadium every 20 mins, US$0.80. From **El Rancho**–Biotopo, 1¼ hrs. Cobán–Purulhá, local buses ply this route between 0645-2000 returning until 1730, 1 hr 20 mins.

Salamá, Rabinal and Cubulco
Bus
Salamá–Rabinal, 1-1½ hrs. Rabinal is reached by travelling west from Salamá on a paved road. From **Guatemala City**, 5½ hrs, a beautiful, occasionally heart-stopping ride, or via El Progreso, and then Salamá by bus. Buses leave 0330-1600 to Guatemala City via Salamá from Cubulco. There is a bus between Rabinal and Cubulco, supplemented by pickup rides.

Alta Verapaz
mountainous limestone region with caves and a mystical lake

The region of Alta Verapaz is based on a gigantic mountain, Sierra de Chamá. Dinosaurs roamed the area more than 65 million years ago before it was engulfed by sea. It later emerged, covered with limestone rock, which over millions of years has left the area riddled with caves, and dotted with small hills. In the far northwest of the department are the emerald-green waters of Laguna Lachuá.

Santa Cruz Verapaz and around → *Colour map 6, B4.*
Santa Cruz Verapaz has a fine white 16th-century church with a fiesta between 1-4 May when you can see the wonderful Danza de los Guacamayos (scarlet macaws). This **Poqomchi' Maya** village is 15 km northwest of Tactic, at the junction with the road to Uspantán. To get there, take the San Cristóbal Verapaz bus, 25 minutes, or take a bus heading to the capital, get off at the junction and walk 200 m into town. The local fiestas are 15, 20 January, 21-26 July with the *Palo Volador*. The devil-burning dance can be seen on 8 December. Six kilometres west towards Uspantán is **San Cristóbal Verapaz**, which has a large, white, colonial church. From the church, a 1-km long, straight, road (Calle del Calvario) slopes down and then curves upwards to a hilltop **Calvario Church**. At Easter, the whole road is carpeted in flowers that rival those on display in Antigua at this time of year. There is **Museo Katinamit** ⓘ *T7950-4039, cecep@intelnet. net.gt, Mon-Fri 0900-1200, 1500-1700, run by the Centro Comunitario Educativo Poqomchi'*, dedicated to the preservation and learning of the Poqomchi' culture.

Listings Alta Verapaz

Where to stay

$$$-$$ Casa Kirvá
Km 204.4, Tontem village, T4693-4800, www.casakirva.com.
Perched on a hill, **Casa Kirvá** is a reasonably new, beautifully constructed lodge with fine stone and woodwork, wonderful landscaped grounds and a striking architectural design that successfully blends contemporary and colonial styles. Rooms veer toward comfort and simplicity rather than ostentatiousness.

$$$-$$ Hotel Park
Km 196, on the main road south of the junction to the Poqomchi' Maya village, Santa Cruz, T7955-3600, www.parkhotelresort.com.

This Italian-owned resort on the highway has a lavish and immaculately landscaped garden, restaurants, gym, tennis court, heated pool, convention centre, wildlife rescue centre and, should you require it for a dramatic entrance or exit, a helipad. Accommodation includes 158 rooms and *casitas* spread across 7 complexes.

$ Eco Hotel Chi' Ixim
Km 182.5, just beyond Tactic, T7953-9198.
Simple and rustic, **Chi' Ixim** offers economical rooms and cabins with private bath, hot water and fireplaces. There is also a restaurant, garden and lots of wandering livestock.

$ Hotel El Portón Real
4 Av, 1-44, Zona 1, Santa Cruz Verapaz, T7950-4604.
This hotel may look dreary from the outside, but inside it's lovely, with lots of wood furnishings and run by a very friendly *señora*. There are rooms with bath, cheaper without, as well as hot water and free drinking water. The hotel closes its doors at 2130.

Transport

Bus
From **Cobán** between 0600-1915 every 15 mins, US$0.700, 40 mins. All capital-bound buses from Cobán run through **Tactic**, or take a local bus between 0645-2000, returning between 0500-1730, 40 mins, US$0.80. Bus from Cobán to **Senahú**, 6 hrs, from opposite INJAV building, from 0600-1400, 4 daily, US$2.90. If you are coming from El Estor, get off at the Senahú turn-off, hitch or wait for the buses from Cobán. Trucks take this road, but there is little traffic, so you have to be at the junction very early to be in luck.

Cobán and around → *Colour map 6, B4.*
attractive colonial town surrounded by coffee plantations

The cathedral and centre of the Imperial City of Cobán (www.cobanav.net, altitude 1320 m), is perched on a long, thin plateau with exceptionally steep roads climbing down from the plaza. To the south the roads are filled with the odd, well-preserved colonial building and a coffee finca.

There is year-round soft rainfall, known as *chipi-chipi*, which is a godsend to the coffee and cardamom plants growing nearby. Most visitors use the city as a base for visiting sights in the surrounding area, trips to Semuc Champey, Languin and as a stepping-off point for rafting trips on the Río Cahabón. English is spoken at the **city tourist office** ① *Parque Central*, where they have lots of information and can help organize tours. The **INGUAT office** ① *7 Av 1-17, in Los Arcos shopping centre, T7951-0216, Mon-Fri 0800-1600, Sat 0900-1300*, is very helpful with leaflets and maps on the whole Verapaz region. For online information on northern Alta Verapaz and the southern Petén, check www.puertamundomaya.com.

The **cathedral** is on the east side of the Parque Central and dates from the middle of the 16th century. The chapel of **El Calvario**, in the northwest, has its original façade still intact. On the way up to the church are altars used by worshippers who freely blend Maya and Roman Catholic beliefs. It's worth climbing the 142 steps to get a bird's-eye view of Cobán. The **Museo El Príncipe Maya** ① *6 Av, 4-26, Zona 3, Mon-Sat 0900-1300, 1400-1800, US$1.30*, is a private museum of pre-Columbian artefacts. The **Parque Nacional Las Victorias** ① *just west of El Calvario, daily 0700-1800, US$0.80*, has two little lagoons in its 84 ha. There are paths and you can picnic and camp, toilets but no showers, but check with the tourist office about safety before going. The daily market is near the bus terminal.

Starbucks coffee fans can check out where their mug of the old bean comes from, direct from **Finca Santa Margarita** ① *on the edge of town, 3 Calle, 4-12, Zona 2, T7951-3067,*

Mon-Fri 0800-1230, 1330-1700, Sat 0800-1200, 45-min tour with English/Spanish-speaking guides, US$2.50. Don't miss a visit to the flower-filled world of **Vivero Verapaz** ⓘ *2.5 km southwest of town, 40-min walk, or taxi ride, 0900-1200, 1400-1700 daily, US$1.30; US$1.30 for guided tour*, an orchid farm with more than 23,000 specimens, mostly flowering from December to February – the best time to go – with the majority flowering in January.

Around Cobán

Southeast of Cobán (8 km) is **San Juan Chamelco** with an old colonial church. A one-hour walk from here is **Aldea Chajaneb** (see Where to stay, below). Along this road are the caves of **Grutas Rey Marcos** ⓘ *US$1.30,* and **Balneario Cecilinda** ⓘ *0800-1700.* **San Pedro Carchá** is 5 km east of Cobán on the main road and used to be famous for its pottery, textiles, wooden masks and silver, but only the pottery and silver are available now. The local food speciality here is *kaq Ik*, a turkey broth.

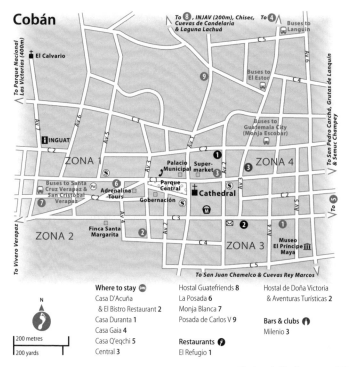

Cobán

Where to stay 🛏
Casa D'Acuña
& El Bistro Restaurant **2**
Casa Duranta **1**
Casa Gaia **4**
Casa Q'eqchi **5**
Central **3**

Hostal Guatefriends **8**
La Posada **6**
Monja Blanca **7**
Posada de Carlos V **9**

Restaurants 🍴
El Refugio **1**

Hostal de Doña Victoria
& Aventuras Turísticas **2**

Bars & clubs 🍸
Milenio **3**

Where to stay

Accommodation is extremely hard to find on the Fri and Sat of Rabin Ajau (last week of Jul) and in Aug. For Rabin Ajau you need to be in town a few days beforehand to secure a room, or ring and reserve.

$$ Casa Duranta
3 Calle, 4-46, Zona 3, T7951-4188, www.casaduranta.com.
With a convenient central location near the plaza, **Casa Duranta** has 10 large, simple rooms with hot water, cable TV, Wi-Fi, hardwood furnishings and hand-woven Guatemalan bedspreads. The leafy garden and interior courtyard are popular with hummingbirds, a definite plus. Ask for a quieter room away from reception and the street.

$$ Casa Gaia
9 Av Final, Zona 10, Barrio San Jorge, T7941-7021, www.hotelcasagaia.com.
Surrounded by native pine forests on the edge of the city, 14 blocks from central park (20 mins' walk), **Casa Gaia** is a lovely secluded lodge set in well-tended 10-ha grounds. Rooms are simple, tasteful and tranquil, and their restaurant overlooks the trees with a pleasant open-air veranda.

$$ Casa Q'eqchi
4 Calle, 7-29, Zona 3, T3295-9169, www.hotelencoban.com.
Family-owned and operated, **Casa Q'eqchi** is a very helpful, friendly and personable boutique B&B. The emphasis is on service and hospitality, and they are also quite knowledgeable about Mayan culture. The rooms are attractive and comfortable, tastefully combining colonial and modern styles. There is a pleasant courtyard too. Recommended.

$$ La Posada
1 Calle, 4-12, Zone 2, T7952-1495, www.laposadacoban.com.gt.

One of Cobán's best, this handsome colonial hotel offers 16 atmospheric rooms decorated with popular and religious art, antique furnishings, tiled bathrooms and fireplaces. The gardens are flourishing and well-kept. Featuring a terrace and fireplace, the restaurant is stylish too; stop by for a drink, if nothing else. Credit cards accepted.

$$-$ Hostal Guatefriends
Carretera Cobán-Guatemala Km 205, T4715-3508.
Located 10 mins out of the city, this very restful and highly appealing B&B is in a beautiful and unusual building reminiscent of an Alpine lodge with its fine stonework, slanted ceilings and cosy wood-panelled enclaves. It's set in verdant grounds, with expansive views of the hills. The owners are lovely and helpful, and it's a great choice for couples and families. There are economical dorms too (**$**). Recommended.

$$-$ Posada de Carlos V
1 Av, 3-44, Zona 1, T7951 3501, www.hotelcarlosvcoban.com.
This is a calm oasis hidden from the chaos of the market outside. The attractive landscaped grounds include a rocky hillside and walking trail laden with flowers and trees. Accommodation spans 22 rooms with pine furniture, cable TV, Wi-Fi and hot water.

$ Casa D'Acuña
4 Calle, 3-11, Zona 2, T7951-0482, www.casadeacuna.com.
Housed by a fine colonial edifice, **Casa D'Acuña** is a decent hostel with 4 small dorms and 2 private rooms, shared ultra-clean bathrooms with hot water, laundry service, internet, excellent meals, tempting goodies and coffee in **El Bistro** restaurant, which overlooks a pretty courtyard (see Restaurants, below). The owners also run a tourist office, shop and tours. Recommended.

$ Central
1 Calle, 1-79, T7952-1442.
A stone's throw from the cathedral in a great location, **Hotel Central** has 15 very clean large rooms with hot shower, all set around a central patio. Rooms with TV cost a little extra. A good budget option.

$ Monja Blanca
2 Calle, 6-30 Zona 2, T7952-1712.
The peaceful, simple, comfortable place is run by a slightly eccentric *señora* and looks shut from the outside. Once inside, all rooms are set around a tranquil leafy courtyard, which is great for chilling out. There is also an old-fashioned dining room serving good value breakfast. Recommended.

Restaurants

$$$-$$ El Bistro
In Casa D'Acuña, see Where to stay, above.
Excellent menu and massive portions. Try the blueberry pancakes. There's also great yogurt, and don't walk through the restaurant without putting your nose into the cake cabinet! Recommended.

$$ El Refugio
2 Av, 2-28, Zona 4, T7952-1338.
Open 1030-2300.
Excellent service and substantial portions at good-value prices of steaks, fish, chicken and snacks, as well as set lunch. There are also cocktails, a big screen TV and a bar.

$$ Hostal de Doña Victoria
See Where to stay, above.
Serves breakfast, lunch and supper in a semi-open area with a pleasant, quiet ambience. Good Italian food, including vegetarian options, is the speciality of the house. There is also a mini cellar bar.

Cafés

Café Fantasia
1 Calle, 3-13, western end of the main park.
A handy spot open for breakfast.

Café La Posada
Part of La Posada (see Where to stay).
Open afternoons.
Divine brownies and ice cream, sofas with a view of the Parque Central.

Bars and clubs

Milenio
3 Av 1-11, Zona 4.
A popular place with a mature crowd and 5 rooms, a dance floor, live music weekends, beer by the jug, pool table and big screen TV. There's a minimum consumption of US$3 at weekends.

Entertainment

Cinema
Plaza Magdalena, *a few blocks west of town.* Multi-screen cinema usually showing the latest releases.

Festivals

Mar/Apr Holy Week.
Last week of Jul Rabin Ajau, the election of the Maya Beauty Queen. Around this time the **Paa banc** is also performed, when the chiefs of brotherhoods are elected for the year.
1-6 Aug Santo Domingo, the town's fiesta in honour of its patron.

What to do

Adrenalina Tours, *west of the main square*. Reliable tour operator, with a national presence.
Aventuras Turísticas, *3 Calle, 2-38, Zona 3, T7952-2213, www.aventurasturisticas.com.* Also offers tourist information.
Proyecto Ecológico Quetzal, *2 Calle, 14-36, Zona 1, Cobán, T7952-1047, www. ecoquetzal.org.* Contact David Unger. Trips are organized to the multicoloured Río Ikbolay, northwest of Cobán, see page 453, and the mountain community of Chicacnab.

Bus

The central bus terminal has attempted to group the multitude of bus stations into one place. While many now depart from this bus terminal, there are still a number of departure points scattered around town. Seek local advice for updates or changes.

To **Guatemala City** with **Transportes Escobar-Monja Blanca**, T7951-3571, every 30 mins from 0200-1600, 4-5 hrs, US$7, from its own offices near the terminal. **El Estor**, 4 daily from Av 5, Calle 4, 1st at 0830, and mostly morning departures, but check in the terminal beforehand, 7 hrs, US$5.60.

To **Fray Bartolomé de las Casas**, 0600-1600 by bus, pickup and trucks, every 30 mins. Route **Raxrujá–Sayaxché–Flores** there are minibuses **Micro buses del Norte** that leave from the terminal del norte near INJAV 0530 and 0630, 5 hrs, US$7.20. In Sayaxché you take a passenger canoe across the river (there is also a car ferry) where minibuses will whisk you to Flores on a tarmacked road in 45 mins. To **Uspantán**, 1000 and 1200, 5 hrs, US$2 from 1 Calle and 7 Av, Zona 2. Cobán can be reached from **Santa Cruz del Quiché** via Sacapulas and Uspantán, and from **Huehuetenango** via Aguacatán, Sacapulas and Uspantán.

Around Cobán
Bus

Every 20 mins from Cobán to **San Juan Chamelco**, US$0.25, 20 mins from Wasen Bridge, Diagonal 15, Zona 7 To **San Pedro Carchá**, every 15 mins, US$0.25, 20 mins from 2 Calle and 4 Av, Zona 4.

Lanquín and Semuc Champey → Colour map 6, A5.
limestone caves and green-and-blue coloured pools

Lanquín is surrounded by mountainous scenery reminiscent of an Alpine landscape. It nestles in the bottom of a valley, where a river runs. With this mountain ambience, caves and the clear water pools at Semuc Champey, it is worth kicking back for a few days and inhaling the high-altitude air.

Lanquín is 56 km east of Cobán, 10 km from the Pajal junction. Just before the town are the **Grutas de Lanquín** ① *0800-1600, US$3, 30-min walk from town*. The caves are lit for 200 m and strange stalactite shapes are given names, but it's worth taking a torch. The cave, whose ceiling hangs with thousands of stalactites, is dangerously slippery from guano mud, although handrails will help you out. The sight of the bats flying out at dusk is impressive. Outside the cave you can swim in the river and camp for free.

From Lanquín you can visit the natural bridge of **Semuc Champey** ① *0600-1800, US$6, parking available*, a liquid paradise stretching 60 m across the Cahabón Gorge. The limestone bridge is covered in stepped, glowing blue and green water pools which span the length and breadth of it. Upstream you can see the water being channelled under the bridge. As it thunders through, it is spectacular. At its voluminous exit you can climb down from the bridge and see it cascading. You can swim in all the pools and little hot flows pour into some of them. Tours of Semuc Champey from Cobán cost around US$31.

Parque Nacional Laguna Lachuá → Colour map 6, A3.
T5704 1509 to hire a guide for the day, US$4, main entrance, US$5.20, Mon-Sat 0900-1700.

Near **Playa Grande**, northwest of Cobán, is Parque Nacional Laguna Lachuá. The deep velvet-green lake, formed by a meteor impact, is 5 sq km and 220 m deep in places. It is surrounded by virtually unspoilt dense jungle, and the chances of seeing wildlife at dawn and dusk are high. There is a guided nature trail and camping and a basic guesthouse. In this area is the **Río Ikbolay**, a green river that runs underground through caves. When it emerges the other side it is blue. The river has changed its course over time leaving some of its run-through caves empty, making it possible to walk through them. The **Proyecto Ecológico Quetzal**, see page 451, runs jungle hikes in this area.

Listings Lanquín and Semuc Champey

Where to stay

Semuc Champey

$$-$ Greengo's
400 m from Semuc Champey, T3020-8016, www.greengoshotel.com.
A good Israeli-run hostel in a natural setting and a convenient location near the pools. There are simple dorms, rooms and brightly painted wooden cabins with slanted roofs. The interiors are very rustic, but feature comfy enough beds and an electrical socket. Facilities include a volleyball court, table football, Wi-Fi, backgammon and a shared kitchen.

$$-$ Utopia
By the river, 11 km from Lanquín and 3 km from Semuc Champey, T3135-8329, www.utopiaecohotel.com.
In great natural surrroundings a 30- to 60-min hike to the pools, this relaxed, rustic eco-hotel has a friendly and sociable atmosphere. It offers a wide range of accommodation including riverside *cabañas* with stone walls and floors (**$$**), simple wood-built cabins (**$**), semi-private 'nooks' in the dormitory loft, bunk beds and hammocks. There is also a restaurant-bar and Spanish school.

$ El Muro
Calle Principal, Lanquín, T5413-6442, www.elmurolanquin.com.
Although not exactly a party hostel, this place has a bar, and sometimes can get lively. Accommodation includes simple rooms, dorms, and for the ultra-thrifty, open-air hammocks. There is an attractive porch overlooking the jungle foliage. It's

conveniently located for early morning or late night transport connections in Lanquín, or any other amenities you might need in town.

$ El Portal de Champey
At the entrance to Semuc Champey, T4091-7878, www.elportaldechampey.com.
Built from local materials on the banks of the Río Cahabón, this is the closest accommodation to Semuc Champey itself and located at the end of the road. Accommodation include very simple and rustic cabins and dorms. Like many other places in the area, electricity is limited. There's no hot water and you'll need insect repellent.

$ El Retiro
5 mins from Lanquín on the road to Cahabón, T3225 9251, www.elretirolanquin.com.
Campsite, *cabañas*, rooms, dorms and restaurant, all in a gorgeous riverside location. There's an open fire for cooking, hammocks to chill out in, a sauna for detoxing, and inner tubes for floating on the river. A fun, relaxing, sociable place which is very popular, with a summer camp feel. To get there don't get off in town, continue for 5 mins and ask to be dropped off. Recommended.

$ Hostal Oasis
Just outside Lanquín by the river, a 5-min tuk-tuk ride, T5870-9739, www.carlosmeza2.wix.com/hostaloasis.
Recommended as one of the few locally owned lodgings in the area and a friendly, low-key alternative to the party places. Like most other hostels around Lanquín, it has rustic dorms and *cabañas*, and offers filling fare at its restaurant, along with very occasional evening shindigs. The guys

running the place are great and stand out for their helpfulness. Located steps from the river, you can go inner tubing too.

Lanquín and Semuc Champey
Bus
From **Cobán** there are minibuses that leave from the 3 Av, 5-6 Calle, 9 a day 0730-1745, US$3.80. From Lanquín to Semuc Champey hire a pickup, see below. From Lanquín to **Flores**, take a Cobán-bound bus to **Pajal**, 1 hr, then any passing bus or vehicle to **Sebol**, 2-2½ hrs (there are Las Casas–Cobán buses passing hourly in the morning only) and then pickup, hitch or bus to Sayaxché and then Flores.

Semuc Champey is a 10-km walk to the south from Lanquín, 3 hrs' walking along the road, which is quite tough for the first hour as the road climbs very steeply out of Lanquín. If planning to return to Lanquín the same day, start very early to avoid the midday heat.

To get there in a pickup start early (0630), US$0.85, or ask around for a private lift (US$13 return). Transport is very irregular so it's best to start walking and keep your fingers crossed. By 1200-1300 there are usually people returning to town to hitch a lift with. If you are on your own and out of season, it would be wise to arrange a lift back.

Car
There is a petrol station in Lanquín near the church.

Car hire Inque Renta Autos, T7952-1431, **Tabarini**, T7952-1504.

Parque Nacional Laguna Lachuá
Heading for **Playa Grande** from Cobán, also known as **Ixcán Grande**, ask the bus driver to let you off before Playa Grande at 'la entrada del parque', from where it's a 4.2-km (1-hr) walk to the park entrance. Minibuses leave Cobán every 30 mins via Chisec, 4 hrs, US$8 opposite INJAV.

North of Cobán and southern Petén crossroads → Colour map 6, A5.
rugged karst landscapes and subterranean marvels

About 100 km northeast of Cobán is Sebol, reached via Chisec and unappealing Raxrujá. From here roads go north to Sayaxché and east to Modesto Méndez via Fray Bartolomé de las Casas.

West of Raxrujá are the **Grutas de Candelaria** ① *US$5.35 including a guided tour*, an extensive cavern system with stalagmites. Tubing is available. Take the road to Raxrujá and look for the Candelaria Camposanto village at Km 310 between Chisec and Raxrujá or look for a sign saying 'Escuela de Autogestión Muqbilbe' and enter here to get to the caves and eco-hotel. Camping is possible. Both points of access offer activities for visitors. North of Raxrujá is the Maya site of **Cancuén** ① *www.puertamundomaya.com, ask in Cobán about tours*, reached by *lancha* in 30 minutes (US$40 for one to 12 people), from the village of La Unión (camping and meals are available at the site). Ten kilometres east of Sebol, and 15 minutes by bus, is **Fray Bartolomé de las Casas**, a town that is just a stop-off for travellers on the long run between Poptún and Cobán or Sayaxché. A road (that is nearly all tarmacked) links Fray Bartolomé de las Casas, Sebol and Sayaxché via Raxrujá. The scenery is beautiful with luscious palms, solitary sheer-sided hills and thatched-roofed homes.

Where to stay

$$$-$$ Complejo Cultural y Ecoturístico Cuevas de Candelaria
T7861-2203, www.cuevasdecandelaria.com.
Set in 40 ha of grounds, including pleasant walking paths where you can admire the tropical flora and fauna, accommodation in La Candelaria includes very comfortable thatched *cabañas* and private rooms. There's a good restaurant and café on site. Full board is available.

$ Las Diamelas
Fray Bartolomé de las Casas, just off park, T5810-1785.
This place offers the cleanest rooms in town. The restaurant food is OK and cheap.

$ Rancho Ríos Escondidos
Near Grutas de Candelaria, on the main road.
Camping is possible at this farmhouse. Ask for Doña América.

Transport

Bus
Local transport in the form of minibuses and pickups connects most of the towns in this section before nightfall.

Bus to **Poptún** from Fray Bartolomé de las Casas leaves at 0300 from the central park, 5¾ hrs, US$5.10. This road is extremely rough and the journey is a bone-bashing, coccyx-crushing one. Buses to **Cobán** at 0400 until 1100 on the hour. However, do not be surprised if one does not turn up and you have to wait for the next one. To **Flores** via Sebol, Raxrujá and Sayaxché at 0700 (3½ hrs) a further 30 mins to 1 hr to Flores. The road from **Raxrujá** via Chisec to Cobán is very steep and rocky. **Chisec** to Cobán, 1½ hrs. The Sayaxché–Cobán bus arrives at Fray Bartolomé de las Casas for breakfast and continues between 0800 and 0900. You can also go from here to Sebol to Modesto Méndez to join the highway to **Flores**, but it is a very slow, a killer of a journey. Buses leave from Cobán for Chisec from Campo 2 at 0500, 0800, 0900.

El Petén

Deep in the lush lowland jungles of the Petén lie the lost worlds of Maya cities, pyramids and ceremonial centres, where layers of ancient dust speak ancient tales. At Tikal, where battles and burials are recorded in intricately carved stone, temples push through the tree canopy, wrapped in a mystical shroud.

Although all human life has vanished from these once-powerful centres, the forest is humming with the latter-day lords of the jungle: the howler monkeys that roar day and night. There are also toucans, hummingbirds, spider monkeys, wild pig and coatimundi. Jaguar, god of the underworld in Maya religion, stalks the jungle but remains elusive, as does the puma and tapir.

Further into the undergrowth away from Tikal, the adventurous traveller can visit El Mirador, the largest Maya stronghold, as well as El Zotz, El Perú, El Ceibal and Uaxactún by river, on foot and on horseback.

Poptún → _Colour map 6, A5._

Poptún is best known for its association with Finca Ixobel; see Where to stay, below. Otherwise, it is just a staging-post between Río Dulce and Flores, or a stop-off to switch buses for the ride west to Cobán.

Listings Poptún

Where to stay

$$-$ Finca Ixobel
T5410-4307, www.fincaixobel.com.
A working farm owned by Carole Devine, widowed after the assassination of her husband in 1990. This highly acclaimed 'paradise' has become the victim of its own reputation and is frequently crowded especially at weekends. However, you can still camp peacefully and there are great treehouses, dorm beds, private rooms and bungalows. One of the highlights is the food. The finca offers a range of trips that could keep you there for days. Recommended.

Transport

Bus
Take any **Fuente del Norte** bus or any bus heading to the capital from **Flores**, 2 hrs. To Flores catch any Flores-bound bus from the capital. To **Río Dulce**, 2 hrs. Buses will drop you at the driveway to **Finca Ixobel** if that's your destination, just ask. From there it's a 15-min walk. Or, get off at the main bus stop and arrange a taxi there or through **Finca Ixobel**. To **Guatemala City** there are plenty daily, 7-8 hrs, US$10-13. The only bus that continues to **Fray Bartolomé de las Casas** (Las Casas on the bus sign) leaves at 1030, 5¾ hrs, US$8.

Essential El Petén

When to go

The dry season and wet season offer different advantages and disadvantages. In the months of November through to early May, access to all sites is possible as tracks are bone-dry. There are also less mosquitoes and if you are a bird lover, the mating season falls in this period. In the rainy winter months, from May to November, tracks become muddy quagmires making many of them impassable, also bringing greater humidity and mosquitoes. Take plenty of repellent, and reapply frequently. It's also fiercely hot and humid at all times in these parts so lots of sun screen and drinking water are essential.

Safety

Roadside robbery used to be a problem on the road to Tikal and to Yaxhá. Get independent, up-to-date advice before visiting these places and leave all valuables at your hotel. Asistur, see Safety, page 529, can assist and have a base at Tikal.

Best places to stay
Finca Ixobel, Poptún, see left column
Flores Hotel Boutique, Flores, page 460
Hostal Los Amigos, Flores, page 461
La Lancha, Lake Petén Itzá, page 462
Posada del Cerro, near El Remate, page 462

BACKGROUND

El Petén

Predominantly covered in jungle, the Petén is the largest department of Guatemala although it has the smallest number of inhabitants. This jungle region was settled by the Maya Itzá Kanek in about AD 600, with their seat then known as La Isla de Tah Itzá (Tayasal in Spanish), now modern-day Flores. The northern area was so impenetrable that the Itzás were untouched by Spanish inroads into Guatemala until the Mexican conquistador Hernán Cortés and Spanish chronicler Bernal Díaz del Castillo dropped by in 1525 on their way from Mexico to Honduras. In 1697 Martín Urzua y Arismendi, the governor of the Yucatán, fought the first battle of the Itzás, crossing Lake Petén Itzá in a galley killing 100 indigenous people in the ensuing battle, and capturing King Canek. He and his men destroyed the temples and palaces of Tayasal and so finished off the last independent Maya state.

In 1990, 21,487 sq km of the north of the Petén was declared a Reserva de la Biósfera Maya (Maya Biosphere Reserve), by CONAP, the National Council for Protected Areas. It became the largest protected tropical forest area in Central America. Inside the boundaries of the biosphere are the Parque Nacional Tikal, Parque Nacional Mirador–Río Azul and Parque Nacional Laguna del Tigre.

Flores and Santa Elena → *Colour map 7, B3.*

a colourful island town and its less elegant mainland counterpart

Flores is perched on a tiny island in Lake Petén Itzá. Red roofs and palm trees jostle for position as they spread up the small hill, which is topped by the white twin-towered cathedral. Some of the streets of the town are lined with houses and restaurants that have been given lashings of colourful paint, giving Flores a Caribbean flavour. A pleasant new lakeshore *malecón* has been built around the island, with benches, street lamps and jetties for swimming. *Lanchas*, drifting among the lilies and dragonflies, are pinned to the lake edges.

Santa Elena is the dustier and noisier twin town on the mainland where the cheapest hotels, banking services and bus terminal can be found.

Sights

The **cathedral**, Nuestra Señora de los Remedios y San Pablo del Itzá, is plain inside, and houses a Cristo Negro, part of a chain of Black Christs that stretches across Central America, with the focus of worship at Esquipulas. **Paraíso Escondido** is home to the **zoo** ① *US$2.70*. A dugout to the island costs US$16 round trip. Near the zoo is **ARCAS (Asociación de Rescate y Conservación de Vida Silvestre)** ① *T5208-0968, www.arcasguatemala.com, US$2*, where they care for rescued animals and release them back into the wild. Volunteers are welcome. There is a centre and interactive trails at the site. Boat tours of the lake depart from the end of the causeway in Flores, around US$20 for one hour, but it's worth bargaining. There is also a longer tour that costs around U$50 for three to four hours, calling at the zoo and **El Mirador** on the Maya ruin of **Tayasal** ① *US$2.70*.

Actún Kan caves ① *0800-1700, US$2.70*, are a fascinating labyrinth of tunnels where, legend has it, a large serpent lived. They are 3 km south of Santa Elena and a 30- to 45-minute walk. To get there take the 6 Avenida out of Santa Elena to its end, turn left at a small hill, then take the first road to the right where it is well marked. South of Santa Elena at Km 468 is **Parque Natural Ixpanpajul** ① *T2336-0576, www.ixpanpajul.com*, where forest canopy Tarzan tours, zip-wire, night safari, birdwatching and horse riding and more are on offer. Local fiestas include 12-15 January, the Petén *feria*, and 11-12 December in honour of the Virgen de Guadalupe.

Around Lake Petén Itzá

San Andrés, 16 km by road from Santa Elena, enjoys sweeping views of Lake Petén Itzá, and its houses climb steeply down to the lakeshore. There is a language school, **Eco-Escuela Español** ① *T5940-1235, www.ecoescuelaespanol.org*, which offers 20 hours of

Flewers

N

50 metres
50 yards

Where to stay 🛏
Casa Amelia **13**
Casazul **3**

Flores Hotel Boutique **1**
Hospedaje Doña Goya **4**
Hostal Los Amigos **5**
Isla de Flores **6**
La Casona de la Isla **2**
Sabana **8**
Santana **10**
Villa del Lago **12**

Restaurants 🍴
Café Arqueológico Yax-há **1**
Café Uka **12**
Capitán Tortuga **11**
Cool Beans **2**
El Mirador **3**
Hacienda del Rey **4**
La Albahaca **10**
La Canoa **5**

La Galería del Zotz **6**
La Luna **7**
Las Puertas Café Bar **8**
La Villa del Chef **9**
Mayan Princess Restaurant
  Café Bar & Cinema **14**
Raíces **13**
Suica **15**

classes, homestay and extra-curricular activities for a week, US$150. Adonis, a villager, takes good-value tours to El Zotz and El Mirador and has been recommended. Ask around for him; his house is close to the shoreline. You can also volunteer in the village with **Volunteer Petén** ⓘ *Parque Nueva Juventud, T5711-0040, www.volunteerpeten.com*, a conservation and community project.

The attractive village of **San José**, a traditional Maya Itzá village, where efforts are being made to preserve the Itzá language and revive old traditions, is 2 km further northeast on the lake from San Andrés. Its painted and thatched homes huddling steeply on the lakeshore make it a much better day trip than San Andrés. It also has a Spanish school, the **Escuela Bio-Itzá** ⓘ *www.ecobioitza.org*, which offers classes, homestay and camping for US$150 a week. Some 4 km beyond the village a signed track leads to the Classic period site of **Motul**, with 33 plazas, tall pyramids and some stelae depicting Maya kings. It takes 20 minutes to walk between the two villages. On 1 November San José hosts the **Holy Skull Procession**.

At the eastern side of Lake Petén Itzá is **El Remate**. The sunsets are superb and the lake is flecked with turquoise blue in the mornings. You can swim in the lake in certain places away from the local women washing their clothes and the horses taking a bath. There are many lovely places to stay, as it is also a handy stop-off point en route to Tikal. West of El Remate is the 700-ha **Biotopo Cerro Cahuí** ⓘ *daily 0800-1600, US$2.70, administered by CECON*. It is a lowland jungle area where three species of monkey, deer, jaguar, peccary, ocellated wild turkey and some 450 species of bird can be seen. If you don't want to walk alone, you can hire a guide. Ask at your *posada*.

Listings Flores and Santa Elena *map p459*

Tourist information

If you wish to make trips independently to remote Maya sites, check with ProPetén to see if they have vehicles making the journey.

CINCAP (Centro de Información sobre la Naturaleza Cultura y Artesanía de Petén
On the plaza, T7926-0718, housed in the same building is the Alianza Verde. Closed Mon.
An organization promoting sustainable ecotourism. Free maps of Tikal, and other local information.

INGUAT
In the airport, T7956-0533. Daily 0700-1200 and 1500-1800.

ProPetén
Calle Central, T7867-5155, www.propeten.org.
Associated with Conservation International.

Where to stay

There are hotels in Santa Elena and Flores across the causeway (10 to 15 mins from Santa Elena).

Flores

$$$$ Flores Hotel Boutique
Calle Fraternidad, T7867-7568, www.floreshotelboutique.com.
The chic modern suites at **Flores Hotel Boutique** are impeccably attired with classy furnishings and all mod cons including LCD satellite TVs, high-speed internet and fully equipped kitchens. Spa services are also available, including massage and shiatsu, along with tours, transport and room service. Attentive and hospitable: the best luxury option on the island.

$$$ Isla de Flores
Av La Reforma, T7867-5176, www.hotelisladeflores.com.

Bright, young and stylish, **Hotel Isla de Flores** partly occupies a traditional island townhouse, recently renovated with several extensions and tasteful modern decor. Amenities include wooden sun deck and jacuzzi overlooking the lake and a restaurant downstairs. Rooms are comfortable, airy and tranquil.

$$ Hotel Casa Amelia
Calle La Unión, T7867-5430,
www.hotelcasamelia.com.
Cheerful and friendly hotel with 15 comfortable, a/c rooms, 6 of which have lake views. There's also a terrace and a pool table.

$$ Hotel Casazul
Calle Fraternindad, T7867-5451,
www.hotelesdepeten.com.
The 9 rooms are all blue and most have a lakeside view. All come with cable TV, a/c and fan.

$$ Hotel Santana
Calle 30 de Junio, T7867-5123,
www.santanapeten.com.
Clean rooms, all with their own terrace a/c, and TV. There's also a lakeside restaurant and a pool.

$$ La Casona de la Isla
Callejón San Pedrito, on the lake, T7867-5163,
www.hotelesdepeten.com.
This friendly place has elegant, clean rooms with fans and TV. Good restaurant, nice breakfasts, bar, garden and pool.

$$ Sabana
Calle La Unión, T7867-5100,
www.hotelsabana.com.
Huge, airy rooms, good service, clean, pleasant, with funky green wavy paintwork in lobby. Good views, lakeside pool and restaurant. Caters for European package tours.

$$ Villa del Lago
Calle 15 de Septiembre, T7867-5181,
www.hotelvilladelago.com.gt.

Very clean rooms with a/c and fan, cheaper with shared bath, some rooms have a lake view and balcony. Breakfast is served on a terrace overlooking the lake, but the service is excruciatingly slow. Breakfast is open to non-guests, but avoid it in high season unless you don't mind a long wait.

$ Chal Tun Ha Hostel
San Miguel peninsula, 3 mins by boat from Flores, T4219-0851, www.chaltunhahostel.com.
This family-owned hostel offers cheap dorm beds and a variety of basic wooden *cabañas* on stilts, each with screens and private porch, and surrounded by trees. There is a restaurant-bar with fine views and refreshing breezes. Overlooking the lake, the garden has sun loungers, hammocks and a small pool. There is a sister hostel, **Chal Tun Ha Hostel Flores Island**, on the island but it's not quite as good as this one.

$ Hospedaje Doña Goya
Calle Unión, T7926-3538, http:// hospedajedonagoya.weebly.com.
A friendly, family-run place with 6 basic but clean rooms, 3 with private bath (cheaper without), 3 with balcony. The terrace has superb views, and there's internet, a book exchange, kitchen and hammocks on a thatched roof terrace.

$ Hostal Los Amigos
Calle Central and Av Barrios, T7867-5075,
www.amigoshostel.com.
This hostal is very popular with backpackers but can be crowded and noisy. There's a choice of a private rooms, dorms with 20 beds, luxury dorms and hammocks with a funky courtyard. Good, cheap restaurant; bar and internet available. Staff are very helpful and friendly. Highly recommended. It also rents out hammocks and mosquito nets for tours to Tikal.

Santa Elena

$$$$ Hotel Casona del Lago
Overlooking the lake, T7952-8700,
www.hotelesde peten.com.

32 spacious rooms, some with balcony, in this lovely duck-egg blue and white hotel. Pool, restaurant, internet and travel agency.

$ San Juan
Calle 2, close to the Catholic church, T7926-0562, sanjuanttravel@hotmail.com.gt.
Full of budget travellers in the older rooms, cheaper with shared bath, but not always spotless. Some remodelled rooms have a/c and TV. Exchanges US dollars and Mexican pesos and buys Belizean dollars. It's not the best place to stay but it's safe, and there's a public phone inside and parking. Note that the Tikal minibuses leave from 0500 so you will probably be woken early.

Around Lake Petén Itzá
To reach the lodgings along the north shore of the lake can be up to a 2-km walk from El Remate centre, depending on where you stay (turn left, west on the Flores–Tikal main road). There is street light up to the Biotopo entrance until 2200.

$$$$ Bahía Taitzá Hotel and Restaurant
Barrio El Porvenir, San José, T7928-8125, www.taitza.com.
The 8 lovely rooms are decorated with local furnishings and set behind a beautiful lawn that sweeps down to the lakeshore. Rates include breakfast and transfer, and there's a restaurant on site.

$$$$-$$$ La Lancha
T7928-8331, www.blancaneaux.com.
Francis Ford Coppola's attractive, small hotel is quiet and friendly, and in a lovely setting. It has 10 rooms which have been tastefully furnished and are decorated using local arts and crafts. 4 rooms have lake views from their balconies. There's a pool and the terrace restaurant serves excellent local cuisine. Horse riding and kayaking trips are available.

$$$ El Sombrero
Laguna Yax-Ha, T4215-8777, www.ecolodgeelsombrero.com.
Hidden in the jungle on the shores of Yaxhá lagoon, **El Sombrero** is a well-established and family-run ecolodge, Italian owned with a good social and ethical philosophy. Accommodation is in simple but comfortable stone cabins with their own porches. Expect the usual jungle facilities, including limited electricity.

$$$ Hotel Ni'tun
2 km from San Andrés on the Santa Elena road, T5201-0759, www.nitun.com.
These luxury *cabañas* on a wooded hillside above the lake are run by a friendly couple, Bernie and Lore, who cook fantastic vegetarian meals and organize expeditions to remote sites.

$$$-$$ Posada del Cerro
Just west of El Remate near the entrance of the Biotopo Cerro Cahuí, T5376-8722, www.posadadelcerro.com.
The epitome of rustic chic, **Posada del Cerro** incorporates contemporary decor, furnishings and finishes with traditional rancho architecture. Their cosy apartments ($$$) feature a double bed, a sofa bed and a fully equipped kitchen. Rooms ($$) include attractive stonework, hardwood furniture and thatched roofs. Very relaxing, comfortable, natural and ecologically aware.

$$ La Mansión del Pajaro Serpiente
El Remate, T5967-9816, www.30minutesfromtikal.com.
Set in lush tropical grounds replete with palms, orchids, peacocks and walking trails, this traditional B&B features very reasonable stone-built cabins with mahogany furniture, hand-woven bedspreads and views of the lake; some have a/c. There's a large pool with a waterfall, tours and a dining room. A secluded natural retreat perched on a hilltop.

$ Hotel y Restaurante Mon Ami
On the El Remate side, T7928-8413, www.hotelmon ami.com.
Lovely bungalows, dorms and hammocks for sleeping. The conservationist owner organizes guided tours to Yaxhá and Nakum. English, French and Spanish are spoken. The restaurant (0700-2130) serves seriously cheap

chicken, pasta and other dishes, and offers a selection of wines.

$ La Casa de Don David
20 m from the main road, on the El Remate side, T7928-8469, www.lacasadedondavid.com.
Clean and comfortable; all rooms with private bath and some with a/c. There's a great view from the terrace restaurant, which serves cheap food. Transport to Tikal and other tours are available and there's free bike hire. They have a wealth of information and can offer helpful advice.

$ Las Gardenias
El Remate, T5936-6984, www.hotelasgardenias.com.
A quiet family-run guesthouse on the way to Tikal. Rooms are simple, clean, airy, bright, and fully equipped with hot shower, TV and a/c. They have a restaurant serving breakfast, *comida típica* and an à la carte menu, and the communal terrace has hammocks and views of Lake Petén Itza. Shuttles and tours can be arranged. There's limited internet in the lobby.

$ Sun Breeze Hotel
Exactly on the corner, on the El Remate side, T7928-8044.
Run by the very friendly Humberto Castro, this place has little wooden rooms with views over the lake. Fans and *mosquiteros* are in each room, and 2 rooms have a private bathroom. Humberto runs a daily service to Tikal, as well as other trips.

Restaurants

Flores

$$$-$$ Raíces
T5521-1843, raicesrestaurante@gmail.com.
Excellent waterfront restaurant beside the *lanchas* near the far west end of Calle Sur. Specialities include *parillas* and kebabs. Great seafood.

$$ La Villa Del Chef
T4366-3822, lavilladelchefguatemala@ yahoo.com.
Friendly German-owned restaurant at the south end of Calle Unión that specializes in *pescado blanco*. It has a happy hour and also rents canoes for lake tours. Recommended.

$$ Mayan Princess Restaurant Café Bar and Cinema
Reforma and 10 de Noviembre. Closed Sun.
Has the most adventurous menu on the island including daily specials, many with an Asian flavour, relaxed atmosphere, with bright coloured textile cloths on the tables. Internet and free films.

$$-$ Café Arqueológico Yax-há
Calle 15 de Septiembre, T5830-2060, www.cafeyaxha.com.
Cheap daily soups, Maya specialities, such as chicken in tamarind sauce, great smoothies, and home-made nachos. German owner Dieter (who speaks English too) offers tours to little-known Maya sites and works with local communities to protect them.

$$-$ Capitán Tortuga
Calle 30 de junio.
Pizzas, pasta and bar snacks, with dayglo painted walls and lakeside terrace.

$$-$ Hacienda del Rey
Calle Sur.
Expensive Argentine steaks are on the menu, but the breakfasts are seriously cheap.

$$-$ La Albahaca
Calle 30 de Junio.
First-class home-made pasta and chocolate cake.

$$-$ La Galería del Zotz
15 de Septiembre.
A wide range of food, delicious pizzas, good service and presentation, popular with locals.

$$-$ La Luna
Av 10 de Noviembre. Closed Sun.
Refreshing natural lemonade, range of fish, meat and vegetarian dishes. The restaurant

has a beautiful courtyard with blue paintwork set under lush pink bougainvillea. Recommended.

$$-$ Las Puertas Café Bar
Av Santa Ana and Calle Central, T7867-5242. Closes at 2300 for food and 2400 completely. Closed Sun.
Cheap breakfasts, huge menu, good, large pasta portions. It's popular at night with locals and travellers and is in an airy building, chilled atmosphere, games available.

$ Café Uka
Calle Centro América. Open from 0600.
Filling breakfasts and meals.

$ Cool Beans
Calle Fraternidad, T5571-9240, coolbeans@itelgua.com.
Cheap food with home-made bread and pastries.

$ El Mirador
Overlooking the lake but view obscured by restaurant wall.
Seriously cheap food and snacks but service is slow.

$ La Canoa
Calle Centro América.
Good breakfasts (try the pancakes), dinners start at US$1.50, with good *comida típica*, very friendly owners.

$ Suica
Calle Fraternidad. Mon-Sat 1200-1900.
Small place serving an unusual mix of sushi, tempura and curries.

Santa Elena

$$ El Rodeo
1 Calle.
Excellent restaurant serving reasonably priced food. Plays classical music and sometimes there's impromptu singing performances.

$ El Petenchel
Calle 2.
Vegetarian food served here as well as conventional meats and meals. Excellent breakfasts and a good-value *menú del día*. Music played, prompt service.

$ Restaurante Mijaro
Calle 2 and Av 8.
Great filling breakfasts and a bargain *menú del día* at US$1.70, all in a thatched-roofed roadside location.

What to do

Tour operators
Beware 'helpful' touts, especially those on buses, and don't be pressured into buying tours, transport or accommodation; there's plenty to choose from in Flores.
Martsam Travel, *Calle 30 de Junio, Flores, T7867-5377, www.martsam.com.* Guided tours to Tikal, El Zotz, El Mirador, El Perú, Yaxhá, Nakum, Aguacate, Ceibal and Uaxactún. Guides with wildlife and ornithological knowledge in addition to archaeological knowledge. Highly recommended.
Mayan Adventure, *Calle 15 de Septiembre, Flores, T5830-2060, www.the-mayan-adventure.com.* Led by German archaeologist Dieter Richter, this company offers insightful expeditions and tours to a range of sites under excavation. An insider look at the scientific work of archaeology.
San Juan Travel Agency, *T7926-0042.* Offers transport (US$7.50 return) to Tikal and excursions to Ceibal, Uaxactún, and Yaxhá (US$80). Mixed reports, not a first choice.
Tikal Connection, *international airport, T7926-1537, www.tikalcnx.com.* Runs tours to El Perú, El Mirador, Nakbé, El Zotz, Yaxhá, Dos Aguadas, Uaxactún. It also sells bus tickets.

Transport

Air
Flores is 2 km from the international airport on the outskirts of Santa Elena. A taxi from the airport into Santa Elena or Flores costs US$1.30 and takes 5 mins, but bargain hard.
Be early for flights, as overbooking is common. The airport departures hall has an internet place. Tour operator and

hotel representatives are based in the arrival halls. The cost of a return flight is between US$180-220, shop around. **Grupo Taca**, T2470-8222, www.taca.com, leaves **Guatemala City** daily at 0645, 0955, 1725, 1 hr, returns 0820, 1605 and 1850. **Tag**, T2360-3038, www.tag.com.gt, flies at 0630 returning 1630. To **Cancún**, Grupo Taca. To **Belize City**, Tropic Air, www.tropicair.com.

Boat

Lanchas moor along Calle Sur, Flores; behind the **Hotel Santana**; from the dock behind **Hotel Casona de Isla**; and beside the arch on the causeway.

Bus

If you arrive by long-distance bus from Guatemala City, Mexico or Belize, the terminal is 10 blocks south of the causeway, which links Flores and Santa Elena. Chicken buses run between the two, US$0.35. Tuk-tuks charge US$0.90 for journeys between them.

Local Local buses (chicken buses), US$0.26, Flores to Santa Elena, leave from the end of the causeway in Flores.

Long distance All long-distance buses leave from the relocated bus terminal, 6 blocks south of the Calle Principal in Santa Elena. It has a snack bar, toilets, seating and ATM. Opposite are restaurants, *comedores*, and a bakery. Banrural is down the side. To **Guatemala City**, Línea Dorada, daily office hours 0500-2200, www.tikalmayan world.com, leaves 1000, 2100, 1st class, US$30; 2200, US$16, 8 hrs. **Autobuses del Norte (ADN)**, T7924-8131, www.adnauto busesdelnorte.com, luxury service, 1000, 2100, 2300, US$23. **Fuente del Norte**, T7926-0666, office open 24 hrs, buses every 45 mins-1 hr, 0330-2230, US$12, 9 hrs. At 1000, 1400, 2100, 2200, US$20, 7-8 hrs. 2nd-class buses, **Rosita**, T7926-5178 and **Rápidos del Sur**, T7924-8072, also go to the capital, US$13. If you are going only to **Poptún**, 2 hrs, or **Río Dulce**, 3½-4 hrs, make sure you do

not pay the full fare to Guatemala City. To **Sayaxché** with Pinita, T9926-0726, at 1100, returns next day at 0600, US$2.50. With **Fuente del Norte** at 0600, US$1.70, returning 0600. *Colectivos* also leave every 15 mins 0530-1700, US$2.40. Buses run around the lake to **San Andrés**, with one at 1200 with Pinita continuing to **Cruce dos Aguadas,** US$2.90 and **Carmelita**, US$3.30 for access to El Mirador. Returning from Carmelita at 0500 the next day. Minibuses also run to San Andrés. To **Chiquimula**, take Transportes **María Elena**, T5550-4190, at 0400, 0800, 1300, US$3. The **María Elena** bus continues onto **Esquipulas**, 9 hrs, US$12. **Fuente del Norte** to **Cobán**, 0530, 0630, 1230, 1330, 5 hrs, US$8. Or take a minibus to Sayaxché and change. Shuttle transfers may also be possible. To **Jutiapa**, 0500, 0530, 7 hrs, returning 0900, US$10-12.

International To **Melchor de Mencos** at the Belize border, 0500, 0600, 1630, 2300, 1½ hrs, US$3.30. Returning 0200, 0500, 0600, 1630, 2300. See also Border crossing box, page 514, for more information on crossing into Belize. Also with **Línea Dorada** and on to **Chetumal, Mexico.** See also Border crossing box, page 512.

To **Copán Ruinas**, **Honduras**, take **Transportes María Elena**, T5550-4190, to Chiquimula at 0400, 0800, 1300, US$13 then from Chiquimula to El Florido and finally on to Copán Ruinas. Alternatively, take any bus to the capital and change at Río Hondo. See also box, page 517, for more on crossing to Honduras. To **San Salvador**, 0600, 8 hrs, US$26.70; see also box, page 518, for crossing into El Salvador.

Car

There are plenty of agencies at the airport, mostly Suzuki jeeps, which cost about US$65-80 per day. **Hertz**, at the airport, T7926-0332. **Garrido** at Sac-Nicte Hotel, Calle 1, Santa Elena, T7926-1732.

Petrol Available in Santa Elena at the 24-hr Texaco garage on the way to the airport.

Around Lake Petén Itzá
Boat

Public *lanchas* from San Benito have virtually come to a stop. Visitors can still charter a *lancha* from Flores for about US$10.

Bus

There's a bus ticket and internet office opposite the turning to El Remate. Any bus/

shuttle heading for Tikal can stop at El Remate, US$2.50, last bus around 1600; taxi around US$10. Returning to **Flores**, pick up any shuttle heading south (this is a lot easier after 1300 when tourists are returning). There is a bus service heading to **Flores** from El Remate at 0600, 0700, 0830, 0930, 1300 and 1400. Shuttles leave every 30 mins for San Andrés, US$0.70, 30 mins and go on to San José.

Parque Nacional Tikal → *Colour map 7, A4.*
Mayan skyscrapers pushing up through the jungle canopy

★Tikal will have you transfixed. Its steep-sided temples for the mighty dead, stelae commemorating the powerful rulers, inscriptions recording the noble deeds and the passing of time, and burials that were stuffed with jade and bone funerary offerings, make up the greatest Mayan city in this tropical pocket of Guatemala.

The ruins → *Numbers in brackets refer to the map, page 468.*

The **Great Plaza (3)** is a four-layered plaza with its earliest foundations laid around 150 BC and its latest around AD 700. It is dwarfed by its two principal temples – Temples I and II. On the north side of the plaza between these two temples are two rows of monuments. It includes Stela 29, erected in AD 292, which depicts Tikal's emblem glyph – the symbol of a Mayan city – and the third century AD ruler Scroll Ahau Jaguar, who is bearing a two-headed ceremonial bar.

Temple I (Temple of the Great Jaguar) (1), on the east side of the Great Plaza, rises to 44 m in height with nine stepped terraces. It was ordered to be built by the ruler Ah Cacao, who ruled between AD 682 to around AD 720-724, who probably planned it for use as his shrine. His tomb, the magnificent Burial 116, was discovered beneath Temple I in 1962 with a wealth of burial goods on and around his skeleton. The display is reconstructed in the Museo Cerámico/Tikal.

Temple II (Temple of the Masks) (2) faces Temple I on the Great Plaza and rises to 38 m, although with its roof comb it would have been higher. It's thought Ah Cacao ordered its construction as well. The lintel on the doorway here depicted a woman wearing a cape, and experts have suggested that this could be his wife.

ON THE ROAD
Wildlife

Tikal is a fantastic place for seeing animal and bird life of the jungle. Wildlife includes spider monkeys, howler monkeys, three species of toucan (most prominent being the keel-billed toucan), deer, foxes and many other birds and insects. Pumas have been seen on quieter paths and coatimundis (pizotes), in large family groups, are often seen rummaging through the bins. The ocellated turkeys with their sky-blue heads with orange baubles attached are seen in abundance at the entrance, and at El Mundo Perdido.

Essential Parque Nacional Tikal

Getting there

From Flores, it's possible to visit Tikal in a day. San Juan Travel Agency minibuses leave hourly between 0500 and 1000, one at 1400 and return at 1230 and hourly between 1400 and 1700 (though on the way back from Tikal, buses are likely to leave 10-15 minutes before scheduled), one hour, US$7.50 return. Several other companies also run trips such as Línea Dorada at 0500, 0830, 1530, returning 1400 and 1700. If you have not bought a return ticket you can often get a discounted seat on a returning bus if it's not full. Minibuses also meet Guatemala City–Flores flights. A taxi to Tikal costs US$60 one way. You can also visit Tikal with a one-day or two-day package tour from Guatemala City or Antigua.

Opening times and entry fee

Daily 0600-1800, US$20 per day, payable at the national park entrance, 18 km from the ruins (park administration, T7920-0025).

Time required

An overall impression of the ruins may be gained in five hours, but you need at least two days to see them properly. If you enter after 1600 your ticket is valid for the following day. To enter the site before or after closing time costs US$13 and you must be accompanied by a guide. If you stay the night in the park hotels, you can enter at 0500 once the police have scoured the grounds. This gives you at least a two-hour head start on visitors coming in from Flores.

Tourist information

A guide is highly recommended as outlying structures can otherwise be missed. The official Tourist Guide Association offers tours of varying natures and in different languages, US$40 for four people plus US$5 for each additional person, just turn up at the visitor centre. A private guide can be hired for US$60 or you can join up with a group for US$15 per person. Tours are available in Spanish, English, Italian, German and French. The guidebook *Tikal*, by WR Coe, in several languages, has an excellent map; or you can buy a reasonable leaflet/map at the entrance, US$2.50. Free transport around the site is available for elderly and disabled visitors, in an adapted pickup truck, with wheelchair access.

Facilities

At the park's visitor centre there is a post office, which stores luggage, a tourist guide service (see under Tourist information), exchange facilities, toilets, a restaurant and a few shops that sell relevant guidebooks.

When to go

Try to visit the ruins after 1400, or before 0900, as there are fewer visitors. From April to December it rains every day for a while; it is busiest November to January, during the Easter and summer holidays and most weekends. The best time for birdwatching tours is December to April, with November to February being the mating season. Mosquitoes can be a real problem even during the day if straying away from open spaces.

What to take

Bring a hat, mosquito repellent, water and snacks with you as it's extremely hot, drinks at the site aren't cheap and there's a lot of legwork involved.

The **North Acropolis (4)** contains some 100 buildings piled on top of earlier structures in a 1-ha area and is the burial ground of all of Tikal's rulers until the break with royal practice made by Ah Cacao. In 1960, the prized Stelae 31, now in the Museo Cerámico/Tikal, see below, was found under the Acropolis. It was dedicated in AD 445. Its base was deliberately burnt by the Maya and buried under Acropolis buildings in the eighth century. This burning was thought to be like a 'killing', where the burning ritual would 'kill' the power of the ruler depicted on the monument, say, after death. It's thought to depict the ruler Siyah Chan K'awil (Stormy Sky), who died sometime around AD 457 having succeeded to the throne in AD 411. Yax Moch Xok (Great Scaffold Shark) is thought to be entombed in the first century

Tikal

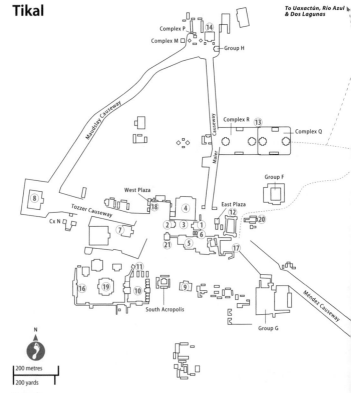

To Uaxactún, Río Azul & Dos Lagunas

Sights ○

Temple I (Temple of the
  Great Jaguar) **1**
Temple II (Temple of the
  Masks) **2**
Great Plaza **3**
North Acropolis **4**
Central Acropolis **5**

Ball Court **6**
Temple III (Temple of the
  Jaguar Priest) **7**
Temple IV (Temple of the
  Double-Headed Serpent) **8**
Temple V **9**

Plaza of the Seven
  Temples **10**
Triple Ball Court **11**
Market **12**
Twin Pyramid Complexes
  Q & R **13**

North Group **14**
Temple VI (Temple of
  Inscriptions) **15**
El Mundo Perdido (Lost
  World) **16**

AD grave, Burial 85. Surrounding the headless male body were burial objects and a mask bearing the royal head band. Under a building directly in the centre of this acropolis Burial 22 – that of ruler Great Jaguar Paw, who reigned in the fourth century, and died around AD 379 – was discovered. Also found here was Burial 10, thought to be the tomb of Nun Yax Ayin I (Curl Nose), who succeeded to the throne in AD 379 after Great Jaguar Paw. Inside were the remains of nine sacrificed servants as well as turtles and crocodile remains and a plethora of pottery pieces. The pottery laid out in this tomb had Teotihuacán artistic influences, demonstrating Tikal's links to the powers of Teotihuacán and Teotihuacán-influenced Kaminal Juyú. Burial 48 is thought to be the tomb of Curl Nose's son, Siyah Chan K'awil (Stormy Sky).

Central Acropolis (5) is made up of a complex of courts connected by passages and stairways, which have expanded over the centuries to cover 1.6 ha. Most of the building work carried out took place between AD 550-900 in the late-Classic era. The **East Plaza** behind Temple I is the centre of the highway junctions of the Maler Causeway in the north, and the Méndez Causeway heading southeast.

On the western side of the **West Plaza** is structure 5D II under which Burial 77 was brought to light. The skeleton was adorned with a jade pendant, which was stolen from the site museum in the 1980s.

Temple III (Temple of the Jaguar Priest) (7) is so called because of the scene of a figure in a glamorous jaguar pelt on a lintel found on the temple. Some experts believe this figure is Ah Chitam (Nun Yax Ayin II, Ruler C), son of Yax Kin, and grandson of the great Ah Cacao, and so propose that this is his shrine, although there has been no confirmation of this. Temple III was constructed around AD 810 and is 55 m tall.

Temple IV (Temple of the Double-Headed Serpent) (8) is the highest building in Tikal at 70 m. It was built in the late-Classic period around AD 741, as proven by hieroglyphic inscriptions and carbon dating. It's thought it was built to honour Yax Kin, the son of Ah Cacao, who became ruler in AD 734. A date on the lintel is AD 741, the same year that Temple I was dedicated.

Temple V (9), constructed between AD 700-750 during the reign of Yax Kin, is 58 m high. It is the mortuary temple of an unknown ruler.

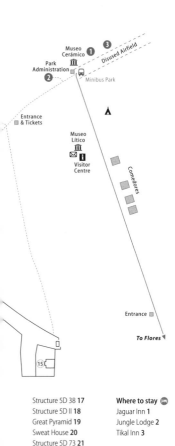

Structure 5D 38 **17**
Structure 5D II **18**
Great Pyramid **19**
Sweat House **20**
Structure 5D 73 **21**

Where to stay
Jaguar Inn **1**
Jungle Lodge **2**
Tikal Inn **3**

BACKGROUND

Tikal

At its height, the total 'urban' area of Tikal was more than 100 sq km, with the population somewhere between 50,000 and 100,000. The low-lying hill site of Tikal was first occupied around 600 BC during the pre-Classic era, but its buildings date from 300 BC. It became an important Maya centre from AD 300 onwards, which coincided with the decline of the mega power to the north, El Mirador. It was governed by a powerful dynasty of 30-plus rulers between about the first century AD until about AD 869, with the last known named ruler being Hasaw Chan K'awill II.

Tikal's main structures, which cover 2.5 sq km, were constructed from AD 550 to 900 during the late-Classic period. These include the towering mega structures of temples – shrines to the glorious dead – whose roof combs were once decorated with coloured stucco figures of Tikal lords. Doorways on the temple rooms were intricately carved – using the termite-resistant wood of the sapodilla tree – with figures and symbols, known as lintels.

Tikal's stelae tell of kings and accessions and war and death. Its oldest stela dates from AD 292. Many Central Mexican influences have been found on the stelae imagery, in burial sites at Tikal and in decorative architectural technique, which led archaeologists to conclude that the city was heavily influenced from the west by forces from the great enclave of Teotihuacán, now just outside Mexico City. This war-like state bred a cult of war and sacrifice and seemed intent on spreading its culture. After the collapse of Teotihuacán in AD 600, a renaissance at Tikal was achieved by the ruler Ah Cacao (Lord Cocoa, Ruler A, Moon Double Comb, Hasaw Chan K'awil I, Sky Rain) who succeeded to the throne in AD 682 and died sometime in the 720s.

However, in the latter part of the eighth century the fortunes of Tikal declined. The last date recorded on a stela is AD 889. The site was finally abandoned in the 10th century. Most archaeologists now agree the collapse was due to warfare with neighbouring states, overpopulation, which resulted in environmental destruction, and drought. Tikal's existence was first reported by Spanish monk Andrés de Avendaño, but its official discovery is attributed to Modesto Méndez, commissioner of the Petén, and Ambrosio Tut, governor of the Petén, in 1848. They were both accompanied by the artist Eusebio Lara.

El Mundo Perdido (The Lost World) (16). The **Great Pyramid** is at the centre of this lost world. At 30 m high, it is the largest pyramid at Tikal. It is flat topped and its stairways are flanked by masks. From the top a great view over the canopy to the tops of other temples can be enjoyed. Together with other buildings to the west, it forms part of an astronomical complex. The Lost World pyramid is a pre-Classic structure, but was improved upon in the Early Classic. East of El Mundo Perdido is the **Plaza of the Seven Temples (10)**, constructed during the Late Classic period (AD 600-800). There is a triple ball court lying at its northern edge.

Temple VI (Temple of the Inscriptions) (15) was discovered in 1951. The 12-m-high roof comb is covered on both sides in hieroglyphic text and is the longest hieroglyphic recording to date. It was carved in AD 766, but the temple was built under the rule of Yax Kin some years before. Altar 9 is at the base of the temple as is Stela 21, said to depict the sculptured foot of the ruler Yax Kin to mark his accession as ruler in AD 734. Unfortunately because of the location of this temple away from the rest of the main structures it has become a hideout for robbers and worse. Some guides no longer take people there. Take advice before going, if at all.

The North Group has several twin pyramid complexes, including Complexes Q and R, marking the passing of the *katun* – a Maya 20-year period.

The Museo Cerámico (Museo Tikal) ① *near the Jungle Lodge, Mon-Fri 0900-1700, Sat and Sun, 0900-1600, US$1.30*, has a collection of Maya ceramics, but its prize exhibits are Stela 31 with its still clear carvings, and the reconstruction of the tomb of Tikal's great ruler, Ah Cacao. In the Museo Lítico ① *inside the visitor centre, Mon-Fri 0900-1700, Sat and Sun, 0900-1600*, there are stelae and great photographs of the temples as they were originally found, and of their reconstruction, including the 1968 rebuild of the Temple II steps. Note Photography is no longer permitted in either of these museums.

Listings Parque Nacional Tikal *map p468*

Where to stay

You are advised to book when you arrive; in high season, book in advance. Take a torch: 24-hr electricity is not normally available.

$$$-$$ Jungle Lodge
T5361-4098, www.quik.guate.com/jltikal/index.html.
These spacious, comfortable bungalows have bath, 24-hr hot water and a fan (electricity 0700-2100); it's cheaper without bath. There's also a pool and they can cash TCs. Full board is available (although we've had consistent reports of unsatisfactory food, slow service and small portions). Jungle Lodge's Tikal tours have been recommended.

$$$-$$ Tikal Inn
T7926-1917.
This place has bungalows and rooms, hot water 1800-1900, electricity 0900-1600 and 1800-2200, and helpful staff. The beautiful pool is for guest use only. Natural history tours at 0930 for US$10 for a minimum 2 people.

$$ Jaguar Inn
T7926-0002, www.jaguar tikal.com.
Full board is available, less without food. There is also a dorm with 6 beds, hammocks with mosquito nets, and lockers. Electricity is available 1800-2200 and there's hot water in the morning or on request Mar-Oct and Nov-Feb, 0600-2100. They will provide a picnic lunch and can store luggage.

Camping

$ Camping Tikal
Run by the Restaurante del Parque, reservations T2370-8140, or at the Petén Espléndido, T7926-0880.
If you have your own tent or hammock it's US$5; if you need to rent the gear it's US$8. There are also *cabañas* with mattresses and mosquito nets for US$7 per person. It also does deals that include breakfast, lunch and dinner ranging from US$15-30 for a double. Communal showers available. Take your own water as the supply is very variable.

There are literally hundreds of Mayan sites in the Petén. Below is a handful of sites, whose ruins have been explored, and of whose histories something is known.

Uaxactún → Colour map 7, A4.

In the village of Uaxactún (pronounced Waash-ak-tún) are ruins, famous for the oldest complete Maya astronomical complex found, and a stuccoed temple with serpent and jaguar head decoration. The village itself is little more than a row of houses either side of a disused airstrip. The site is 24 km north of Tikal on an unpaved road. It is in fairly good condition taking less than one hour in any vehicle.

Uaxactún is one of the longest-occupied Mayan sites. Its origins lie in the middle pre-Classic (1000-300 BC) and its decline came by the early post-Classic (AD 925-1200) like many of its neighbouring powers. Its final stelae, dated AD 889, is one of the last to be found in the region. The site is named after a stela, which corresponds to Baktun 8 (8 x 400 Maya years), carved in AD 889; uaxac means 8, tun means stone.

South of the remains of a ball court, in **Group B**, a turtle carving can be seen, and Stela 5, which marks the takeover of the city, launched from Tikal. Next door to this stela under Temple B-VIII were found the remains of two adults, including a pregnant woman, a girl of about 15 and a baby. It is believed this may have been the governor and his family who were sacrificed in AD 378. From Group B, take the causeway to **Group A**. In Group A, Structure A-V had 90 rooms and there were many tombs to be seen. The highest structure in the complex is Palace A-XVIII, where red paint can still be seen on the walls. In **Group E** the oldest observatory (E-VII-sub) ever found faces structures in which the equinoxes and solstices were observed. When the pyramid (E-VII) covering this sub-structure was removed, fairly well preserved stucco masks of jaguar and serpent heads were found flanking the stairways of the sub-structure.

The ruins lie either side of the village, the main groups (**Group A** and **Group B**) are to the northwest (take a left just before **Hotel El Chiclero** and follow the road round on a continuous left to reach this group). A smaller group (**Group E**) with the observatory is to the southwest (take any track, right off the airstrip, and ask. This group is 400 m away.

El Zotz → Colour map 7, A4.

El Zotz, meaning bat in Q'eqchi', is so called because of the nightly flight from a nearby cave of thousands of bats. There is an alternative hiking route as well (see below). Incredibly, from Temple IV, the highest in the complex at 75 m, it is possible to see in the distance, some 30 km away, Temple IV at Tikal. The wooden lintel from Temple I (dated AD 500-550) is to be found in the Museo Nacional de Arqueología y Etnología in the capital. Each evening at about 1850 the sky is darkened for 10 minutes by the fantastic spectacle of tens of thousands of bats flying out of a cave near the camp. The 200-m-high cave pock-marked with holes is a 30-minute walk from the camp. If you are at the cave you'll see the flight above you and get doused in falling excrement. If you remain at the campsite you will see them streaking the dark blue sky with black in straight columns. It's also accessible via Uaxactún. There is some basic infrastructure for the guards, and you can camp.

One of the best trips you can do in the Petén is a three-day hike to El Zotz and on through the jungle to Tikal. The journey, although long, is not arduous, and is accompanied by birds, blue morpho butterflies and spider monkeys chucking branches at you all the way.

El Perú and the Estación Biológica Guacamayo → *Colour map 7, A3.*

A visit to El Perú is included in the **Scarlet Macaw Trail**, a two- to five-day trip into the **Parque Nacional Laguna del Tigre**, through the main breeding area of the scarlet macaw. There is little to see at the Mayan site, but the journey to it is worthwhile. In 2004 the 1200-year-old tomb and skeleton of a Maya queen were found. A more direct trip involves getting to the isolated Q'eqchi'-speaking community of **Paso Caballos** (1¾ hours). Here, the **Comité de Turismo** can organize transport by *lancha* along the Río San Pedro. From Paso Caballos it is one hour by *lancha* to the El Perú campsite and path.

It's possible to stop off at the **Estación Biológica Guacamayo** ① *US$1.30, volunteers may be needed, contact Propeten, www.propeten.org*, where there is an ongoing programme to study the wild scarlet macaws (*ara macao*). The chances of seeing endangered scarlet macaws during March, April and May in this area is high because that's when they are reproducing.

A couple of minutes upriver is the landing stage, from where it's a 30-minute walk to the campsite of El Perú: howler monkeys, hummingbirds, oropendola birds and fireflies abound. From there, it is a two-hour walk to the El Perú ruins. Small coral snakes slither about, howler monkeys roar, spider monkeys chuck branches down on the path. White-lipped peccaries, nesting white turtles, eagles, fox and kingfishers have also been seen. The trip may be impossible between June and August because of rising rivers during the rainy season and because the unpaved road to Paso Caballos may not be passable. Doing it on your own is possible, although you may have to wait for connections and you will need a guide, about US$20 per day.

El Mirador, El Tintal and Nakbé → *Colour map 7, A3/A4.*

El Mirador is the largest Mayan site in the country. It dates from the late pre-Classic period (300 BC-AD 250) and is thought to have sustained a population of tens of thousands. It takes five days to get to El Mirador. From Flores it is 2½ to three hours to the village of Carmelita by bus or truck, from where it is seven hours walking, or part horse riding to El Mirador. It can be done in four days – two days to get there and two days to return. The route is difficult and the mosquitoes and ticks and the relentless heat can make it a trying trip. Organized tours are arranged by travel agents in Flores; get reassurance that your guides have enough food and water. If you opt to go to El Mirador independently, ask in Carmelita for the **Comité de Turismo**, which will arrange mules and guides. Take water, food, tents and torches.

It is about 25 km to El Tintal, a camp where you can sling a hammock, or another 10 km to El Arroyo, where there is a little river for a swim near a *chiclero* camp. It takes another day to El Mirador, or longer, if you detour via Nakbé. You will pass *chiclero* camps on the way, which are very hospitable, but very poor. In May, June and July there is no mud, but there is little chance of seeing wildlife or flora. In July to December, when the rains come, the chances of glimpsing wildlife is much greater and there are lots of flowers. It is a lot fresher, but there can be tonnes of mud, sometimes making the route impassable. The mosquitos are also in a frenzy during the rainy season. Think carefully about going on the trip (one reader called it "purgatory").

The site, which is part of the Parque Nacional Mirador-Río Azul, is divided into two parts with the **El Tigre Pyramid** and complex in the western part, and the **La Danta** complex, the largest in the Maya world, in the east, 2 km away. The larger of two huge pyramids – La Danta – is 70 m high; stucco masks of jaguars and birds flank the stairways of the temple complex. The other, El Tigre, is 55 m in height and is a wonderful place to be on top of at night, with a view of endless jungle and other sites, including Calakmul, in Mexico. In **Carmelita** ask around for space to sling your hammock or camp. There is a basic *comedor*. **El Tintal**, a day's hike from El Mirador, is said to be the second largest site in Petén, connected by a causeway to El Mirador, with great views from the top of the pyramids. **Nakbé**, 10 km southeast of El Mirador, is the earliest known lowland Maya site (1000-400 BC), with the earliest examples of carved monuments.

Río Azul and Kinal → *Colour map 7, A4.*

From Uaxactún a dirt road leads north to the *campamento* of **Dos Lagunas**. It's a lovely place to camp, with few mosquitoes, but swimming will certainly attract crocodiles. The guards' camp at **Ixcán Río**, on the far bank of the Río Azul, can be reached in one long day's walk, crossing by canoe if the water is high. If low enough to cross by vehicle you can drive to the Río Azul site, a further 6 km on a wide, shady track. It is also possible to continue into Mexico if your paperwork is OK. A barely passable side track to the east from the camp leads to the ruins of Kinal. The big attraction at Río Azul are the famous black and red painted tombs, technically off limits to visitors without special permission, but visits have been known.

Yaxhá, Topoxte, Nakum and Melchor de Mencos → *Colour map 7, A4/B4.*
T7861-0250, www.conap.com.gt. Yaxhá is open 0800-1700. Entry to each site US$9.

This group of sites has been designated as a national park. About 65 km from Flores, on the Belize road ending at Melchor de Mencos, is a turning left, a dry weather road, which brings you in 8.5 km to Laguna Yaxhá. On the northern shore is the site of Yaxhá (meaning Green Water), the third largest known Classic Maya site in the country, accessible by causeway. This untouristy site is good for birdwatching and the views from the temples of the milky green lake are outstanding. The tallest structure, **Templo de las Manos Rojas**, is 30 m high. In the lake is the unusual Late post-Classic site (AD120-1530) of Topoxte. (The island is accessible by boat from Yaxhá, 15 minutes.) About 20 km further north of Yaxhá lies Nakum, which is thought to have been both a trading and ceremonial centre. You will need a guide and your own transport if you have not come on a tour.

Northwest Petén and the Mexican border → *Colour map 7, A2.*
An unpaved road runs 151 km west from Flores to **El Naranjo** on the Río San Pedro, near the Mexican border. Close by is **La Joyanca**, a site where the chance of wildlife spotting is high. You can camp at the *cruce* with the guards.

Parque Nacional Laguna del Tigre and Biotopo → *Colour map 7, A2.*
The park and biotope is a vast area of jungle and wetlands north of El Naranjo. The best place to stay is the CECON camp, across the river below the ferry. This is where the guards live and they will let you stay in the bunk house and use their kitchen. Getting into the reserve is not easy and you will need to be fully equipped, but a few people go up the Río Escondido. The lagoons abound in wildlife, including enormous crocodiles and spectacular bird life. Contact **CECON** ⓘ *Centro de Estudios Conservacionistas (CECON), Av Reforma, 0-63, Zona 10, Guatemala City, T2331-0904, cecon@usac.edu.gt,* for more information.

Sayaxché → *Colour map 7, B3.*
Sayaxché, south of Flores on the road to Cobán, has a frontier town feel to it as its focus is on a bend on the Río de la Pasión. It is a good base for visiting the southern Petén

including a number of archaeological sites, namely El Ceibal. You can change US dollar bills and traveller's cheques at **Banoro**.

El Ceibal → *Colour map 7, B3.*

This major ceremonial site is reached by a 45-minute *lancha* ride up the Río de la Pasión from Sayaxché. It is about 1.5 km from the left bank of Río de la Pasión hidden in vegetation and extending for 1.5 sq km. The height of activity at the site was from 800 BC to the first century AD. Archaeologists agree that it appears to have been abandoned in between about AD 500 and AD 690 and then repopulated at a later stage when there was an era of stelae production between AD 771 and 889. It later declined during the early decades of the 10th century and was abandoned. You can sling a hammock at El Ceibal and use the guard's fire for making coffee if you ask politely – a mosquito net is advisable, and take repellent for walking in the jungle surroundings. Tours can be arranged in Flores for a day trip to Sayaxché and El Ceibal (around US$65) but there is limited time to see the site. From Sayaxché the ruins of the **Altar de los Sacrificios** at the confluence of the Ríos de la Pasión and Usumacinta can also be reached. It was one of the earliest sites in the Péten, with a founding date earlier than that of Tikal. Most of its monuments are not in good condition. Also within reach of Sayaxché is **Itzán**, discovered in 1968.

Piedras Negras → *Colour map 7, A1.*

Still further down the Río Usumacinta in the west of Petén is Piedras Negras, a huge Classic period site. In the 1930s Tatiana Proskouriakoff first recognized the periods of time inscribed on stelae here coincided with human life spans or reigns, and so began the task of deciphering the meaning of Maya glyphs. Advance arrangements are necessary with a rafting company to reach Piedras Negras. **Maya Expeditions** (see page 343) run expeditions, taking in Piedras Negras, Bonampak, Yaxchilán and Palenque. This trip is a real adventure. The riverbanks are covered in the best remaining tropical forest in Guatemala, inhabited by elusive wildlife and hiding more ruins. Once you've rafted down to Piedras Negras, you have to raft out. Though most of the river is fairly placid, there are the 30-m **Busilhá Falls**, where a crystal-clear tributary cascades over limestone terraces and two deep canyons, with impressive rapids to negotiate, before reaching the take-out two days later.

Petexbatún → *Colour map 7, B3.*

From Sayaxché, the Río de la Pasión is a good route to visit other Maya ruins. From **Laguna Petexbatún** (16 km), a fisherman's paradise can be reached by outboard canoe from Sayaxché. Excursions can be made from here to unexcavated ruins that are generally grouped together under the title Petexbatún. These include **Arroyo de la Piedra**, Dos Pilas and Aguateca. **Dos Pilas** has many well-preserved stelae, and an important tomb of a king was found here in 1991 – that of its Ruler 2, who died in AD 726. Dos Pilas flourished in the Classic period when as many as 10,000 lived in the city. There are many carved monuments and hieroglyphic stairways at the site, which record the important events of city life. **Aguateca**, where the ruins are so far little excavated, gives a feeling of authenticity. The city was abandoned in the early ninth century for unknown reasons. Again, a tour is advisable. It's a boat trip and a short walk away. The site was found with numerous walls (it's known the city was attacked in AD 790) and a chasm actually splits the site in two. The natural limestone bridge connects a large plaza with platforms and buildings in the west with an area of a series of smaller plazas in the east. These places are off the beaten track and an adventure to get to.

Uaxactún

$ Aldana's Lodge
T5801-2588, edeniaa@yahoo.com.
Run by a friendly family, **Aldana's Lodge**
has small, white, clean *casitas*, as well as tent
and hammock space behind **El Chiclero**.
Just before **El Chiclero** take a left on the
road to the ruins and then take the 1st right
until you see a whitewashed *casita* on the
right (2 mins).

$ El Chiclero
T7926-1095.
Neat and clean, hammocks and rooms in a
garden, also good food by arrangement.

Sayaxché

$ Guayacán
Close to ferry, T7928-6111.
Owner Julio Godoy is a good source
of information.

$ Hotel Posada Segura
*Turn right from the dock area and then
1st left, T7928-6162.*
One of the best options in town, clean,
and some rooms have a bath and TV.

Petexbatún

$$$ Chiminos Island Lodge
T2335-3506, www.chiminosisland.com.
Remote, small ecolodge close to a Maya
site on a peninsula on the river, in a great
for exploring local sites, fishing and wildlife
spotting. Rates includes all food.

$$$ Posada Caribe
T7928-6117.
Comfortable *cabañas* with bathroom and
shower. They offer trips to **Aguateca** by
launch and a guide for excursions. Rates
include 3 meals.

Camping
Camping is possible at Escobado,
on the lakeside.

Restaurants

Uaxactún

$ Comedor Imperial
At the village entrance.
Bargain *comida típica* for US$1.30.

Sayaxché

$$$ El Botanero Café Restaurante
and Bar
Straight up from the dock and 2nd left.
A funky wooden bar with logs and seats
carved from tree trunks.

$ Restaurant La Montaña
Near dock.
Cheap food, local information given.

$ Yakín
Near dock.
Cheap, good food; try the *licuados*.

What to do

Uaxactún
For guided walks around the ruins ask
for one of the trained guides, US$10. For
expeditions further afield, contact Elfido
Aldana at **Posada Aldana**. Neria Baldizón
at **El Chiclero** has high-clearance pickups
and plenty of experience in organizing
both vehicle and mule trips to any site. She
charges US$200 per person to go to Río Azul.

Sayaxché
Viajes Don Pedro, *on the river front near the
dock, T7928-6109.* Runs launches to El Ceibal
(US$35 for up to 3), Petexbatún and Aguateca
(US$60 for up to 5), Dos Pilas (US$50 for
small group). Trip possible by jeep in the
dry season, Altar de los Sacrificios (US$100
minimum 2 people) and round trips to
Yaxchilán for 3 days (US$400). Mon-Sat 0700-
1800, Sun 0700-1200.

Transport

Uaxactún
Bus
To Uaxactún from **Santa Elena** at 1200 arriving between 1600-1700, US$2.60, returning 0500 with **Transportes Pinita**. Foreigners have to pay US$2 to pass through Parque Nacional Tikal on their way to Uaxactún, payable at the main entrance to Tikal.

El Mirador, El Tintal and Nakbé
Bus
1 bus daily with **Transportes Pinita** to **Carmelita**. See Flores for information.

Northwest Petén and the Mexican border
Boat and bus
To **El Naranjo** at 0500 and 1000, returning at 0500, 1100 and 1300, US$4. Or hire a *lancha* from Paso Caballos.

Sayaxché
Bus
There are buses to **Flores**, 0600, 0700, 1-2 hrs, and microbuses every 30 mins. To **Raxrujá** and on to **Cobán** via **Chisec** at 0400, US$.80, 6½ hrs direct to Cobán. There are pickups after that hourly and some further buses direct and not via Chisec. For **Lanquín** take the bus to Raxrujá, then a pickup to Sebol, and then a pickup to Lanquín, or the Lanquín *cruce* at Pajal, and wait for onward transport. If you are heading to **Guatemala City** from here it could be quicker to head north to Flores rather than take the long road down to Cobán. However, this road has now been entirely tarmacked.

Petaxbatún
Boat
It is 30-40 mins in *lancha* from Sayaxché to the stop for **Dos Pilas** to hire horses. It's 50 mins-1 hr to **Chiminos** lodge and 1 hr 20 mins to the **Aguateca** site. To Dos Pilas and Aguateca from Chiminos, US$27 return to each site.

Background

History

While controversy exists around the precise date humans arrived in the Americas, the current prevailing view suggests the first wave of emigrants travelled across the Bering Strait ice bridge created in the last Ice Age between Siberia and Alaska approximately 15,000 years ago. Small groups of peoples quickly moved through the region as the migratory lifestyle of the hunter-gather explored the Americas. In fertile lands the development of farming and the reduced reliance on hunting and migrating encouraged groups to settle. By 1500 BC villages were developing and growing in many parts of the Americas.

Pre-Columbian civilizations

The Aztec Empire that Spanish conqueror Hernán Cortés encountered in 1519 and subsequently destroyed was the third major power to have dominated what is now known as Mexico. Before it, the empires of Teotihuacán and Tula each unified what had essentially been an area of separate indigenous groups. All three, together with their neighbours such as the Maya (dealt with below) and their predecessors, belong to a more or less common culture called Mesoamerica. Despite the wide variety of climates and terrains that fall within Mesoamerica's boundaries, from northern Mexico to El Salvador and Honduras, the civilizations that developed were interdependent, sharing the same agriculture (based on maize, beans and squash) and many sociological features. They also shared an enormous pantheon, with the god of rain and the feathered serpent-hero predominant; the offering of blood to the gods, from oneself and from sacrificial victims usually taken in war; pyramid-building; a team game played with a rubber ball; trade in feathers, jade and other valuable objects, possibly from as far away as the Andean region of South America; hieroglyphic writing; astronomy; and an elaborate calendar.

The Mesoamerican calendar was a combination of a 260-day almanac year and the 365-day solar year. A given day in one of the years would only coincide with that in the other every 52 years, a cycle called the Calendar Round. In order to give the Calendar Round a context within a larger timescale, a starting date for both years was devised; the date chosen by the Classic Maya was equivalent to 3113 BC in Christian time. Dates measured from this point are called Long Count dates. Historians divide Mesoamerican civilizations into three periods, the pre-Classic, which lasted until about AD 300, the Classic, until AD 900, and the post-Classic, from 900 until the Spanish conquest. An alternative delineation is: Olmec, Teotihuacán and Aztec, named after the dominant civilizations within each of those periods.

Olmecs

Who precisely the Olmecs were, where they came from and why they disappeared, is a matter of debate. It is known that they flourished from about 1400-400 BC, that they lived in the Mexican Gulf coast region between Veracruz and Tabasco, and that all later civilizations have their roots ultimately in Olmec culture. They carved colossal heads, stelae (tall, flat monuments), jade figures and altars; they gave great importance to the jaguar and the serpent in their imagery; they built large ceremonial centres such as San Lorenzo and La Venta. Possibly derived from the Olmecs and gaining importance in the first millennium BC was the centre in the Valley of Oaxaca at Monte Albán. This was a major city, with certain changes of influence, right through until the end of the Classic period. Also derived from the Olmecs was the Izapa civilization, on the Pacific border of present-day Mexico and Guatemala. The progression from the Olmec to the Maya civilization seems to have taken place here with obvious connections in artistic style, calendar use, ceremonial architecture and the transformation of the Izapa long-lipped god into the Maya long-nosed god.

Teotihuacán

Almost as much mystery surrounds the origins of Teotihuacán as those of the Olmecs. Teotihuacán, 'the place where men become gods', was a great urban state, holding in its power most of the Central Highlands of Mexico. Its influence can be detected in the Maya area, Oaxaca and the civilizations on the Gulf coast that succeeded the Olmecs. The monuments in the city itself, which still stands beyond the outskirts of Mexico City, are enormous, the planning precise; it is estimated that by the seventh century AD some 125,000 people were living in its immediate vicinity. Early evidence did not suggest Teotihuacán's power was gained by force, but research indicates both human sacrifice and sacred warfare took place. For reasons unknown, Teotihuacán's influence over its neighbours ended around 600 AD. Its glory coincided with that of the Classic Maya, but the latter's decline occurred some 300 years later, at which time a major change affected all Mesoamerica.

Toltecs

The start of the post-Classic period, between the Teotihuacán and Aztec horizons, was marked by an upsurge in militarism. In the semi-deserts to the north of the settled societies of central Mexico and Veracruz lived groups of nomadic hunters. These people, who were given the general name of Chichimecs, began to invade the central region and were quick to adopt the urban characteristics of the groups they overthrew. The Toltecs of Tula were one such invading force, rapidly building up an empire stretching from the Gulf of Mexico to the Pacific in central Mexico. Infighting by factions within the Toltecs split the rulers and probably hastened the empire's demise sometime after 1150. The exiled leader Topíltzin Quetzalcóatl (Feathered Serpent) is possibly the founder of the Maya-Toltec rule in the Yucatán (the Maya spoke of a Mexican invader named Kukulcán – Feathered Serpent). He is certainly the mythical figure the Aztec ruler, Moctezuma II, took Cortés to be, returning by sea from the east.

Zapotecs and Mixtecs

Another important culture to develop in the first millennium AD was the Mixtec, in western Oaxaca. The Mixtecs infiltrated all the territory held by the Zapotecs, who had ruled Monte Albán during the Classic period and had built many other sites in the Valley of Oaxaca, including Mitla. The Mixtecs, in alliance with the Zapotecs, successfully withstood invasion by the Aztecs.

Aztecs

The process of transition from semi-nomadic hunter-gathering to city and empire-building continued with the Aztecs, who bludgeoned their way into the midst of rival city states in the vacuum left by the destruction of Tula around 1150. They rose from practically nothing to a power almost as great as Teotihuacán in about 200 years. From their base at Tenochtitlán in Lake Texcoco in the Valley of Mexico they aggressively extended their sphere of influence from the Tarascan Kingdom in the north to the Maya lands in the south. Not only did the conquered pay heavy tribute to their Aztec overlords, but they also supplied the constant flow of sacrificial victims needed to satisfy the deities, at whose head was Huitzilopochtli, the warrior god of the Sun. The speed with which the Aztecs adapted to a settled existence and fashioned a highly effective political state is remarkable. Their ability in sculpting stone, in pottery, in writing books, and in architecture (what we can gather from what the Spaniards did not destroy) was great. Surrounding all this activity was a strictly ritual existence, with ceremonies and feasts dictated by the two enmeshing calendars. It is impossible to say whether the Aztec Empire would have gone the way of its predecessors had the Spaniards not arrived to precipitate its collapse. Undoubtedly, the Europeans received much assistance from people who had been oppressed by the Aztecs and who wished to be rid of them. Within two years Cortés, with his horses, an array of military equipment and relatively few soldiers, brought to an end an extraordinary culture.

Maya

The best known of the pre-Conquest indigenous civilizations of the present Central American area was the Maya, thought to have evolved in a formative period in the Pacific highlands of Guatemala and El Salvador between 1500 BC and about 100 AD. After 200 years of growth it entered what is known today as its Classic period when the civilization flourished in Guatemala, El Salvador, Belize, Honduras and Mexico (Chiapas, Campeche and Yucatán). The Maya civilization was based on independent and antagonistic city states, including Tikal, Uaxactún, Kaminaljuyú, Iximché, Zaculeu and Quiriguá in Guatemala; Copán in Honduras; Altun Ha, Caracol, Lamanai in Belize; Tazumal and San Andrés in El Salvador; and Palenque, Bonampak (both in Chiapas), Uxmal, Mayapán, Tulum, Cobá and the Puuc hill cities of Sayil, Labná and Kabah (all on the Yucatán Peninsula) in Mexico. Recent research has revealed that these cities, far from being the peaceful ceremonial centres once imagined, were warring adversaries, striving to capture victims for sacrifice. Furthermore, much of the cultural activity, controlled by a theocratic minority of priests and nobles, involved blood-letting, by even the highest members of society. Royal blood was the most precious offering that could be made to the gods. This change in perception of the Maya was the result of the discovery of defended cities and of a greater understanding of the Maya's hieroglyphic writing. Although John Lloyd Stephens's prophecy that "a key surer than that of the Rosetta stone will be discovered" has not yet been fulfilled, the painstaking decipherment of the glyphs has uncovered many secrets of Maya society (see *Breaking the Maya Code* by Michael D Coe, Thames and Hudson).

Alongside the preoccupation with blood was an artistic tradition rich in ceremony, folklore and dance. They achieved paper codices and glyphic writing, which also appears on stone monuments and their fine ceramics; they were skilful weavers and traded over wide areas, though they did not use the wheel and had no beasts of burden. The cities were all meticulously dated. Maya art is a mathematical art: each column, figure, face, animal, frieze, stairway and temple expresses a date or a time relationship. When, for example, an ornament on the ramp of the Hieroglyphic Stairway at Copán was repeated some 15 times, it was to express that number of elapsed 'leap' years. The 75 steps stand for the number of elapsed intercalary days. The Maya calendar was a nearer approximation to sidereal time than either the Julian or the Gregorian calendars of Europe; it was only .000069 of a day out of true in a year. They used the zero centuries in advance of the Old World, plotted the movements of the sun, moon, Venus and other planets, and conceived a cycle of more than 1800 million days.

Their tools and weapons were flint and hard stone, obsidian and fire-hardened wood, and yet with these they hewed out and transported great monoliths over miles of difficult country, and carved them over with intricate glyphs and figures that would be difficult enough with modern chisels. Also with those tools they grew lavish crops. To support urban populations now believed to number tens of thousands, and a population density of 150 per sq km (compared with less than one per sq km today), an agricultural system was developed of raised fields, fertilized by fish and vegetable matter from surrounding canals. The height of the Classic period lasted until AD 900-1000, after which the Maya concentrated into Yucatán after a successful invasion of their other lands by non-Maya people (this is only one theory; another is that they were forced to flee due to drought and a peasant rebellion). They then came under the influence of the Toltecs who invaded Yucatán (Chichén Itzá is seen as an example of a Maya city that displays many Toltec features). From then on their culture declined. The Toltecs gradually spread their empire as far as the southern borders of Guatemala. They in turn were conquered by the Aztecs, who did not penetrate Central America.

Conquest and colonial rule

The remarkable conquest of Mexico began when 34-year-old Hernán Cortés disembarked near the present Veracruz with about 500 men, some horses and cannon, on 21 April 1519. They marched into the interior, arrived at the Aztec capital of Tenochtitlán in November and were admitted into the city as guests of the reigning monarch, Moctezuma. There they remained until June of the next year, when Pedro de Alvarado, in the absence of Cortés, murdered hundreds of natives to quell his own fear of a rising. At this treacherous act they did in fact rise, and it was only by good luck that the Spanish troops, with heavy losses, were able to fight their way out of the city on the Noche Triste (the Night of Sorrows) of 30 June. Next year Cortés came back with reinforcements and besieged the city. It fell on 30 August 1521, and was utterly razed. Cortés then turned to the conquest of the rest of the country. One of the main factors in his success was his alliance with the Tlaxcalans, old rivals of the Aztecs. The fight was ruthless, the Aztecs were soon overcome and 300 years of Spanish rule followed.

On the eve of the Spanish conquest of Guatemala there were a number of dominant Maya groups, but dissent within some of these groups was exploited by the invading Spanish, who conquered the country bit by bit from 1524 through to 1697. Under Pedro de Alvarado the *encomienda* system was introduced whereby the Maya were forced to work land that was previously theirs and pay tribute to the colonialists in the form of crops. In return they received Christian instruction. They were treated like slaves and gradually died in their thousands from western diseases.

Settlement and economy

The groups of Spanish settlers were few and widely scattered, a fundamental point in explaining the political fragmentation of Central America today. Panama was ruled from Bogotá, but the rest of Central America was subordinate to the Viceroyalty at Mexico City, with Antigua, Guatemala, as an Audiencia for the area until 1773, and thereafter Guatemala City. The small number of Spaniards intermarried freely with the locals, accounting for the predominance of *mestizos* in present-day Central America. But the picture has regional variations. In Guatemala, where there was the highest native population density, intermarriage affected fewer of the natives, and over half the population today is still purely *indígena* (indigenous).

In the early years of colonial rule, Spanish grandees stepped into the shoes of dead Aztec lords and inherited their great estates, soon to be integrated into the *hacienda* system with its absolute title to the land and almost feudal way of life. Within the first 50 years, all the *indígenas* in the populous southern valleys of the plateau had been Christianized and harnessed for the economy. By the end of the 16th century, the Spaniards had founded most of the towns that are still important, tapped great wealth in mining, stock raising and sugar-growing, and firmly imposed their way of life and beliefs. Government was by a Spanish-born upper class, based on the subordination of the *indígena* and mestizo populations and there was a strict dependence on Spain for all things. As with the rest of Hispanic America, Spain excluded from government both Spaniards born in Mexico and the small body of educated *mestizos*, a policy which eventually led to rebellion.

Independence and nationhood

In Mexico, the standard of revolt was raised in 1810 by the curate of Dolores, Miguel Hidalgo. The *Grito de Dolores* (*Mueran los gachupines* – Perish the Spaniards), collected 80,000 armed supporters, and had it not been for Hidalgo's loss of nerve and failure to engage the Spaniards, the capital might have been captured in the first month. In the rest of Central America, the independence movement kicked off on 5 November 1811, when José Matías Delgado, a priest and jurist born in San Salvador, organized a revolt with another priest, Manuel José Arce. They proclaimed the independence of El Salvador, but the Audiencia at Guatemala City suppressed the revolt and took Delgado prisoner. For the next decade, fighting across the region ensued, creating bitter differences. It was the revolution of 1820 in Spain itself that finally precipitated independence. On 24 February 1821, a loyalist general turned rebel, Agustín de Iturbide, proclaimed an independent Mexico with his Plan de Iguala. The Central American *criollos* decided to follow his example, and a declaration of Independence, drafted by José Cecilio del Valle, was announced in Guatemala City on 15 September 1821. Iturbide invited the provinces of Central America to join with him and, on 5 January 1822, Central America was declared annexed to Mexico. However, Delgado refused to accept this decree.

Iturbide, who had now assumed the title of Emperor Agustín I, sent an army south under Vicente Filísola to enforce his authority in the regions under Delgado's influence. Filísola had completed his task when he heard of Iturbide's abdication, and at once convened a general congress of the Central American provinces. It met on 24 June 1823, and established the Provincias Unidas del Centro de América. The Mexican Republic acknowledged their Independence on 1 August 1824, and Filísola's soldiers were withdrawn.

The United Provinces of Central America

The new congress, presided over by Delgado, appointed a provisional governing junta, which promulgated a constitution modelled on that of the United States in November 1824. The Province of Chiapas was not included in the Federation, as it had already adhered to Mexico in 1821. Guatemala City, by force of tradition, soon became the seat of government.

The first President under the new constitution was Delgado's brother-in-arms, Manuel José Arce, a liberal. One of his first acts was to abolish slavery. El Salvador, protesting that he had exceeded his powers, rose in December 1826. Honduras, Nicaragua and Costa Rica joined the revolt, and in 1828 General Francisco Morazán, in charge of the army of Honduras, defeated the federal forces, entered San Salvador and marched against Guatemala City. He captured the city on 13 April 1829, and established that contradiction in terms: a liberal dictatorship. Many conservative leaders were expelled and church and monastic properties confiscated. Morazán himself became President of the Federation in 1830. He was a man of considerable ability; he ruled with a strong hand, encouraged education, fostered trade and industry, opened the country to immigrants, and reorganized the administration. In 1835 the capital was moved to San Salvador.

These reforms antagonized the conservatives, however, and there were several uprisings. The most serious revolt was among the *indígenas* of Guatemala, led by Rafael Carrera, an illiterate *mestizo* conservative and a born leader. Years of continuous warfare followed, during the course of which the Federation withered away. As a result, the federal congress passed an act that allowed each province to assume the government it chose, but the idea of a federation was not quite dead. Morazán became President of El Salvador. Carrera, who was by then in control of Guatemala, defeated Morazán in battle and forced him to leave the country. But in 1842, Morazán overthrew Braulio Carrillo, then dictator of Costa Rica, and became president himself. At once he set about rebuilding the Federation, but was defeated by the united forces of the other states and was shot on 15 September 1842. With him perished any practical hope of Central American political union.

Mexico

The nation of Mexico was formally created on 4 October 1824, with General Guadalupe Victoria as president. Conservatives stood for a highly centralized government; Liberals favoured federated sovereign states. The tussle of interests resulted in endemic civil war. In 1836, Texas, whose cotton-growers and cattle-ranchers had been infuriated by the abolition of slavery in 1829, rebelled against the dictator, Santa Ana, and declared its Independence. It was annexed by the United States in 1845. War broke out and US troops occupied Mexico City in 1847. Next year, under the terms of the treaty of Guadalupe Hidalgo, the US acquired half Mexico's territory: all the land from Texas to California and from the Río Grande to Oregon.

Benito Juárez

A period of liberal reform dominated by independent Mexico's great hero, the Zapoteco, Benito Juárez, began in 1857. The church, in alliance with the conservatives, hotly contested his programme and the constant civil strife wrecked the economy. Juárez was forced to suspend payment on the national debt, causing the French to invade and occupy Mexico City in 1863. They imposed the Archduke Maximilian of Austria as Mexican Emperor, but under US pressure, withdrew their troops in 1867. Maximilian was captured by the Juaristas at Querétaro, tried, and shot on 19 June. Juárez resumed control of the country and died in July 1872.

General Porfirio Díaz

Sebastián Lerdo de Tejada, the distinguished scholar who followed Juárez, was soon tricked out of office by General Porfirio Díaz, who ruled Mexico from 1876 to 1910. Díaz's paternal, though often ruthless, central authority introduced a period of 35 years of peace. A superficial prosperity followed, but the main mass of peasants had never been so wretched. It was this open contradiction between dazzling prosperity and hideous distress that led to the start of civil war (known as the Mexican Revolution) in November 1910, and to Porfirio Díaz's self-exile in Paris.

The Mexican Revolution

A new leader, Francisco Madero, championed a programme of political and social reform, which included the restoration of stolen lands. Madero was initially supported by revolutionary leaders such as Emiliano Zapata in Morelos, Pascual Orozco in Chihuahua and Pancho Villa, also in the north. During his presidency (1911-1913), Madero neither satisfied his revolutionary supporters, nor pacified his reactionary enemies. After a coup in February 1913, led by General Victoriano Huerta, Madero was brutally murdered, but the great cry, 'Tierra y Libertad' (Land and Freedom) was not to be quieted until the election of Alvaro Obregón to the Presidency in 1920. Before then, Mexico was in a state of civil war, leading first to the exile of Huerta in 1914, then the dominance of Venustiano Carranza's revolutionary faction over that of Zapata (assassinated in 1919) and Villa.

The PRI

In 1946, the official ruling party assumed the name Partido Revolucionario Institucional (PRI), and held a virtual monopoly over all political activity. In the late 1980s, disaffected PRI members and others formed the breakaway Partido de la Revolución Democrática (PRD), which rapidly gained support. On New Year's Day of the election year, 1994, at the moment when the North American Free Trade Agreement (NAFTA) came into force, a guerrilla group, The Ejército Zapatista de Liberación Nacional (EZLN) briefly took control of several towns in Chiapas. Despite ongoing unrest, PRI candidate Ernesto Zedillo Ponce de León, a US-trained economist and former education minister, won a comfortable majority in the August elections.

Ernesto Zedillo

On 20 December, just after his inauguration, Zedillo devalued the peso, claiming that political unrest was causing capital outflows. On 22 December a precipitate decision to allow the peso to float against the dollar caused an immediate crisis of confidence and investors in Mexico lost billions of dollars as the peso's value plummeted. Mexicans were hard hit by the recession and the ruling position of the PRI was damaged. In Chiapas, Zedillo suspended the controversial PRI governor, but the tension between the EZLN and the army continued as a 72-hour campaign to apprehend the EZLN leader, Subcomandante Marcos, failed. Talks recommenced in April, with the EZLN calling a ceasefire but the first peace accord was not signed until February 1996. Mid-term congressional elections held in July 1997 showed the PRI's grip on power was beginning to fade. They suffered a huge blow at the polls, and for the first time ever it lost control of Congress, winning only 239 seats. The PRD surged to become the second largest party in the lower house, with 125 deputies, while the right-wing PAN won 122.

Vicente Fox

During the 1999 presidential elections, Zedillo relinquished his traditional role in nominating his successor and the PRI had a US-style primary election to select a candidate. The PAN, meanwhile, chose former Coca-Cola executive Vicente Fox to lead their campaign. On 2 July 1999, Mexicans gave power to Fox, former governor of Guanajuato, and the PAN, prising it from the PRI for the first time in 71 years. An admirer of 'third way' politics and of ex-US President Bill Clinton and UK Prime Minister Tony Blair, Fox took office on 1 December 2000 announcing czar-led initiatives that would tackle government corruption, drug-trafficking, crime and poverty, and the economic conditions that drive migration to the US. He proved to be a personable, if ineffectual president. One critic dismissively said Fox was "90% image and 10% ideas".

Felipe Calderón

Elections in July 2006 saw a new president leading Mexico. A close and ill-fought electoral result gave Felipe Calderón, the candidate of the ruling conservative National Action Party (PAN) a narrow win over Andrés Manuel López Obrador of the centre-left Party of the Democratic Revolution (PRD), pushing Roberto Madrazo of the Institutional Revolutionary Party (PRI) into third place. Calderón came to power looking to reduce poverty, violence, tax evasion, corruption and his own salary by 10%. Public infrastructure projects on roads, airports, bridges and dams would also intend to stem outward migration of Mexico's workforce. Ultimately, however, Calderón's term was dominated by his extremely bloody war on drugs, which began on 11 December 2006 with the dispatch of 6500 troops to Michoacán, and rapidly escalated to the involve 45,000 soldiers nationwide, along with state and federal police. Despite the military-led crack-downs against the cartels and high-profile arrests of corrupt political stooges, Calderón's war failed to stem the flow of cocaine over the US border – or the flow of weapons from the opposite direction. The official death toll at the close of Calderón's administration in 2012 was 60,000, but some estimates put the figure twice as high, excluding the 27,000 who have gone missing.

Return of the PRI

Amid civic protests and accusations of electoral fraud, Enrique Peña Nieto, a telegenic PRI candidate and former governor of Mexico state, was elected to office with 38% of the vote. Many feared a return to the old-school corruption and repression that so characterized former PRI administrations, despite Peña Nieto's smooth reassurances that his party, unlike the ineffectual PAN, knows how to govern. To date, his most significant act has been the liberalization of Mexico's energy sector, which is likely to culminate in the privatization of the national oil company, Pemex. Meanwhile, the war on drugs has continued to claim lives. In September 2014, 43 male students from the Teachers' College of Ayotzinapa, Guerrero, who had been commandeering buses to attend a march, were arrested by local police at the behest of the mayor and his wife, handed over to a local drug cartel and, according to subsequent confessions, driven to a remote garbage dump, summarily executed and incinerated. Illustrating the on-going collusion between political and criminal groups in Mexico, the incident has sparked fury and nationwide protests.

Belize

Throughout the country, especially in the forests of the centre and south, there are many ruins of the Classic Maya period, which flourished here and in neighbouring Guatemala from the fourth to the ninth century and then, mysteriously (most probably because of drought), emigrated to Yucatán. It is estimated that the population was then 10 times what it is now.

The first settlers were English, with their black slaves from Jamaica, who came in about 1640 to cut logwood, then the source of textile dyes. The British Government made no claim to the territory but tried to secure the protection of the wood-cutters by treaties with Spain. Even after 1798, when a strong Spanish force was decisively beaten off at St George's Caye, the British Government still failed to claim the territory, though the settlers maintained that it had now become British by conquest.

When they achieved Independence from Spain in 1821, both Guatemala and Mexico laid claim to sovereignty over Belize, but these claims were rejected by Britain. Long before 1821, in defiance of Spain, the British settlers had established themselves as far south as the River Sarstoon, the present southern boundary. Independent Guatemala claimed that these settlers were trespassing and that Belize was a province of the new republic. By the middle of the 19th century Guatemalan fears of an attack by the United States led to a rapprochement with Britain. In 1859, a convention was signed by which Guatemala recognized the boundaries of Belize while, by Article 7, the United Kingdom undertook to contribute to the cost of a road from Guatemala City to the sea "near the settlement of Belize"; an undertaking that was never carried out.

Heartened by what it considered a final solution of the dispute, in 1862 Great Britain declared Belize, still officially a settlement, a colony, and a Crown Colony nine years later. Mexico, by treaty, renounced any claims it had on Belize in 1893, but Guatemala, which never ratified the 1859 agreement, renewed its claims periodically.

Independence and after

Belize became independent on 21 September 1981, following a United Nations declaration to that effect. Guatemala refused to recognize the independent state, but in 1986 President Cerezo of Guatemala announced an intention to drop his country's claim to Belize. A British military force was maintained in Belize from Independence until 1993, when the British government announced that the defence of Belize would be handed over to the government on 1 January 1994, and that it would reduce the 1200-strong garrison to about 100 soldiers who would organize jungle warfare training facilities. The last British troops were withdrawn in 1994 and finance was sought for the expansion of the Belize Defence Force. Belize was admitted into the OAS in 1991 following negotiations with Guatemala and Britain. As part of Guatemala's recognition of Belize as an independent nation (ratified by Congress in 1992), Britain will recompense Guatemala by providing financial and technical assistance to construct road, pipeline and port facilities that will guarantee Guatemala access to the Atlantic.

Border friction is an ongoing issue between Belize and Guatemala, and in early 2000 tensions overflowed when Guatemalans took some members of the Belizean Defence Force hostage for several days, eventually resulting in some Guatemalans being shot. Tensions were stretched to the limit, and periodically continue to rise and fall but now seem to have cooled. Low-key negotiations continue between the two countries and in 2003 both countries agreed a draft settlement at Organization of American States (OAS) brokered talks. Progress was painfully slow, with Belize and Guatemala only signing up to a negotiation framework at the end of 2005. In 2007, the **Organisation of American States (OAS)** recommended that the border dispute be resolved in the **International Court of Justice** (ICJ). In 2008, both countries agreed to submit to the court, contingent on the outcome of referenda. Plans for the referenda were suspended in 2013, but both countries are engaged in OAS confidence-building exercises.

Guatemala

In 1825 Guatemala became the capital of the Central American Federation until its dissolution in 1838. From 1839 to 1842, conservative governments restored Spanish institutions in a hark back to the colonial era. This trend was maintained by fiercely pro-church Rafael Carrera, who became president in 1844. He set about restoring church power and invited the Jesuits back into the country (they had been expelled in 1767). He went into exile in 1848 before returning to power in 1851 where he remained until 1865.

The 1871 Liberal Revolution

On Carrera's death, Conservative General Vicente Cerna ruled Guatemala until 1871, when General Justo Rufino Barrios successfully overthrew his regime and introduced a wave of Liberal leadership. Miguel García Granados (1871-1873) reigned briefly, expelling leading clerics and overturning Carrera's invitation to the Jesuits. Thereafter, Justo Rufino Barrios (1873-1885) himself was elected president. He too was vehemently anticlerical. He expropriated church property, using the proceeds to found a national bank, secularized education and marriage. New ports and railways were constructed and coffee production was reformed, transforming Guatemala into a major producer. This was largely accomplished through the confiscation of indigenous lands. Barrios also tried to restore the federation and when the idea foundered he resorted to dictatorial methods. He invaded El Salvador when they refused to cooperate and died in a battle at Chalachuapa. Manuel Lisandro Barillas (1885-1892) followed in his footsteps and again tried unsuccessfully to re-establish Central American union. The Liberal trend continued with General José María Reina Barrios (1892-1898), who confiscated his enemies' property and spent much time quashing internal rebellion. During his term the price of coffee crashed on the world market, but public works using public money continued to be built, causing widespread outrage and revolts. He was assassinated.

Dictatorship and the rise of the United Fruit Company

When Manuel Estrada Cabrera (1898-1920) came to power, his was the longest one-man rule in Central American history. Cabrera encouraged foreign investment, expansion of the railways and the United Fruit Company's foray into Guatemala, granting it some 800,000 ha for the planting of bananas. The company's privileges included a monopoly on transport and a free rein over their own affairs. American interests in Guatemala grew to the point where 40% of all exports were US controlled. Cabrera was eventually toppled amid widespread discontent. Carlos Herrera followed but the old style military did not like his approach. He was overthrown in a bloodless military coup, bringing José María Orellana to power. Orellana negotiated more concessions for United Fruit and the railway company. However, organized protests over plantation workers' rights grew and periodically met with government crackdowns. Orellana, unlike some of his predecessors, died a natural death in 1926.

Jorge Ubico

Jorge Ubico was an efficient but brutal dictator who came to power in 1931. He tightened political control, introduced a secret police, clamped down on workers' discontent and Communist movements, persecuted writers and intellectuals, promoted forced labour and fixed low wage rates. He also extended privileges to the United Fruit Company. These, and other issues, and the fact that he sought constant re-election, provoked widespread demonstrations calling for his resignation. In June 1944, following the death of a teacher in a protest demanding university autonomy, Ubico resigned and a triumvirate of generals assumed power.

October Revolution

On 20 October 1944 there was an armed uprising of La Guardia de Honor, backed by popular support. The military leaders drew up a democratic constitution, abolished forced labour, and upheld the autonomy of the university. Teacher Juan José Arévalo of the Frente Popular Libertador party was then elected president and drew up a plan of social reform. He separated the powers of state, introduced *comedores* for children of poor workers, set up the Department for Social Security, and accepted the existence of the Communist Party. He survived more than 20 military coups and finished his term of five years (1945-1950).

1954 US-backed military coup

Jacobo Arbenz Guzmán, a member of the 1944 military triumvirate, became the elected president in 1950. His 1952 Agrarian Reform Law saw the expropriation of large, underused estates without adequate compensation awarded to their owners – mainly the United Fruit Company, which for years had been under-declaring the value of its land for tax reasons. According to the company, of its 550,000 acres around the Caribbean, 85% of it was not farmed. It was offered a measly US$2.99 an acre for land (440,000 acres) which it said was worth US$75. The company's connections with high-powered players within the US Government and the CIA, and its constant allegation that Communism was percolating through the Guatemalan corridors of power, eventually persuaded the US to sponsor an overthrow of the Arbenz government. Military strikes were launched on the country in June 1954. At the end of the month Arbenz, under pressure from Guatemalan military and the US ambassador John Peurifoy, resigned.

Military rule

In June 1954 Colonel Carlos Castillo Armas took over the presidency. He persecuted and outlawed Communists. He was assassinated in 1957, which provoked a wave of violence and instability and for the next three decades the army and its right-wing supporters suppressed left-wing efforts, both constitutional and violent, to restore the gains made under Arévalo and Arbenz. Many thousands of people, mostly leftists but also many Maya without political orientation, were killed during this period.

The rise of the guerrilla movement

On 13 November 1960, a military group, inspired by revolution in Cuba, carried out an uprising against the government. It was suppressed but spawned the Movimiento 13 de Noviembre, which then joined forces with the Guatemalan Workers' Party. In 1962, student demonstrations ended in bloodshed, which resulted in the creation of the Movimiento 12 de Abril. These movements then merged to form Fuerzas Armadas Rebeldes (FAR) in 1962.

During this period, Arévalo made a move to re-enter the political fold. A coup d'état followed. Guerrilla and right-wing violence began to increase in the late 1960s. In the early 1970s the guerrillas re-focused. The FAR divided into FAR and the EGP (Ejército Guerrillero de los Pobres, Guerrilla Army of the Poor), which operated in the north of the country. In 1972 the Organización Revolucionaria del Pueblo en Armas (ORPA) was formed. The EGP was led by Rolando Morán, a supporter of the Cuban Revolution. The group's first action took place in the Ixil Triangle in 1975. The ORPA was led by Commandante Gaspar Ilom, also known as Rodrigo Asturias, son of Nobel Prize for Literature winner Miguel Angel Asturias.

The worst of the conflict

Throughout the 1970s and early 1980s the worst atrocities of the war were committed. General Kjell Eugenio Laugerud García's presidency was characterized by escalating violence, which led the US to withdraw its support for the Guatemalan government in 1974. In 1976, a devastating earthquake struck Guatemala killing 23,000 people. This prompted widespread social movements in the country to improve the lives of the poor.

At the same time, guerrilla activity surged. Meanwhile, the US, believing the human rights situation had improved, resumed military sales to Guatemala. But in 1981 the military unleashed a huge offensive against the guerrillas who united to confront it with the formation of the Unidad Revolucionaria Nacional Guatemalteca (URNG). The situation worsened when Ríos Montt came to power in 1982 following a coup d'état. He presided over the bloodiest period of violence with the introduction of the scorched-earth policy, massacring whole villages in an attempt to root out bands of guerrillas. Ríos Montt was ousted by his defence minister, General Oscar Mejías Victores, in a coup in August 1983.

Return of democracy

Mejía Victores permitted a Constituent Assembly to be elected in 1984, which drew up a new constitution and worked out a timetable for a return to democracy. He also created numerous 'model villages' to rehouse the displaced and persecuted Maya, who had fled in their thousands to the forests, the capital, Mexico and the US. Presidential elections in December 1985 were won by civilian Vinicio Cerezo Arévalo of the Christian Democrats (DC), who took office in January 1986. He was the first democratically elected president of Guatemala since 1966. In the 1990 elections Jorge Serrano Elías of the Solidarity Action Movement made Guatemalan history by being the first civilian to succeed a previous civilian president in a change of government.

Civil unrest

By 1993, however, the country was in disarray. The social policies pursued by the government had alienated nearly everybody and violence erupted on the streets. Amid growing civil unrest, President Serrano suspended the constitution, dissolved Congress and the Supreme Court, and imposed press censorship. International and domestic condemnation of his actions was immediate. After only a few days, Serrano was ousted by a combination of military, business and opposition leaders and a return to constitutional rule was promised. Congress approved a successor, Ramiro de León Carpio, previously the human rights ombudsman. He soon proved as capable as his predecessors, however, and the public's distaste of corrupt congressional deputies and ineffectual government did not diminish. The reform of election procedures and political parties had been called for by a referendum in 1994, which obliged Congressional elections to be called. The result gave a majority of seats to the Guatemalan Republican Front (FRG), led by ex-president Ríos Montt, who was elected to the presidency of Congress for 1994-1996. Ríos Montt's candidate in the 1995 presidential election, Alfonso Portillo, lost by a slim margin to Alvaro Arzú of the National Advancement Party. Arzú proposed to increase social spending, curtail tax evasion, combat crime and bring a speedy conclusion to peace negotiations with the URNG guerrillas.

Towards peace

One of the earliest moves made by President Serrano was to speed up the process of talks between the government and the URNG, which began in March 1990. The sides met in Mexico City in April 1991 to discuss such topics as democratization and human rights, a reduced role for the military, the rights of indigenous people, the resettlement of refugees and agrarian reform. Progress, however, was slow. In August 1995 an accord was drawn up with the aid of the UN's Guatemala mission (MINUGUA) and the Norwegian government. The timetable proved over-ambitious, but, on taking office in January 1996, President Arzú committed himself to signing a peace accord. In February 1996 he met the

URNG leadership, who called a ceasefire in March. On 29 December 1996 a peace treaty was signed ending 36 years of armed conflict. An amnesty was agreed which would limit the scope of the Commission for Historical Clarification and prevent it naming names in its investigations of human rights abuses.

Peacetime elections and the Portillo Government

The 1999 elections went to a second round with self-confessed killer Alfonso Portillo of the FRG winning 62% of the vote against his rival Oscar Berger, the candidate of President Arzú's ruling PAN. Portillo subsequently promised to reform the armed forces, solve the killing of Bishop Gerardi and disband the elite presidential guard, so implicated in the human rights abuses. Common crime, as well as more sinister crimes such as lynchings, plagued Portillo's term and seemed to increase.

The new millennium generally brought mixed results for justice. The former interior minister Byron Barrientos resigned in December 2001 and faced accusations of misappropriating US$6 million in state funds. In June 2002, ex-president Jorge Serrano was ordered to be arrested on charges which included embezzlement of state funds. He remains exiled in Panama. In October 2002, a former colonel in the Guatemalan army, Colonel Juan Valencia Osorio, was found guilty of ordering the murder of anthropologist Myrna Mack and sentenced to 30 years' imprisonment. However, the appeal court overturned his conviction in 2003.

Also in October 2002, the four men imprisoned for their role in the 1998 murder of Guatemalan Bishop Gerardi had their convictions overturned. A retrial was ordered. In 2003 Ríos Montt mounted a legal challenge to a rule which prohibits former coup leaders running for president. The constitutional court ruled he could stand in the autumn parliamentary elections. The UN High Commission for Human Rights announced it would open an office in Guatemala City. More details can be found at www.ghrc-usa.org.

Oscar Berger

A new era in Guatemalan politics began with the election of Oscar Berger as president in December 2003. After coming second to Portillo in the 1999 elections as candidate for PAN, Berger led the newly formed Gran Alianza Nacional (GANA) to electoral victory with 54% of the vote over his centre-left rival Alvaro Colom. Berger assumed the presidency promising to improve access to clean water, education and health care for all citizens. He also persuaded indigenous leader and Nobel Prize winner Rigoberta Menchú to join his government to work towards a more just country. Berger's presidency provided slight economic growth and attempts to strengthen the country's institutions, despite low tax revenues, organized crime, discrimination and poverty.

Alvaro Colom

Elections in November 2007 were also a close affair, with second round run-off providing Alvaro Colom with a narrow victory for the Unidad Nacional de la Esperanza (National Unity of Hope) and 53% of the vote. Colom took office vowing to fight poverty with a government that would have a Mayan face, while promising to reduce organized crime. During his tenure, Los Zetas drug gang, former wing of the Mexican Gulf Cartel, moved into Guatemala, with smuggling concentrated in northern regions, particularly Petén. Dozens of murders have since been linked with the ruthless gang, which is thought to include former members of the Kaibiles – the elite Guatemalan army squad, notorious for its brutalities during Guatemala's 1960-1996 civil war.

Otto Pérez Molina

In January 2012, Otto Pérez Molina was elected to office. A controversial figure, he graduated from the School of the Americas to become Guatemala's Director of military intelligence. He was also once a member of Guatemala's notorious Kaibiles, and after becoming president, he was accused of participating in scorched earth policies, torture and genocide, which he denied. Despite his authoritarian background, Pérez Molina took the somewhat liberal stance of proposing the full legalization of drugs during a UN visit. In fact, Guatemala continues to receive considerable military aid for the war on drugs, which critics say is being used to beef up security and crush public dissent against mining, hydroelectric and other foreign-owned projects; indigenous activists and trade unionists continue to be assassinated. In 2013, Efraín Ríos Montt was found guilty of genocide and crimes against humanity. Outrageously, the ruling was subsequently overturned by the constitutional court on a technicality. As of January 2015, his re-trail had been suspended.

Culture

About 9% of the Mexican population are considered white, about 30% *indígena* (indigenous); with about 60% *mestizos*, a mixture in varying proportions of Spanish and *indígena*. Mexico also has infusions of Europeans, Arabs and Chinese. There is a national cultural prejudice in favour of the indigenous rather than the Spanish element, though this does not prevent indígena from being looked down on by the more Hispanic elements. There is hardly a single statue of Cortés in the whole of Mexico, although he does figure, pejoratively, in the frescoes of Diego Rivera and his contemporaries. On the other hand the two last Aztec emperors, Moctezuma and Cuauhtémoc, are national heroes.

Indigenous peoples

Out of the 15 distinct indigenous groups inhabiting Oaxaca, two predominate. The Zapotecs, descended from the builders of Monte Albán, number around 770,000 and occupy the central and eastern parts of the state. Their historical rivals, the Mixtec, whose name means 'cloud people', are around 720,000 and mostly dwell in the western part of Oaxaca, along with the states of Guerrero and Puebla.

The market continues to be the point of meeting and convergence for Oaxaca's indigenous groups. Traditional dances play a vital role in their cultural life, including the famous Zapotec feather dance, where the conquest is re-enacted with enormous headdresses of red, blue and white feathers. Craft traditions, too, are a central pillar of Oaxaqueña culture, especially weaving, a revered art that has been passed between mother and daughter for millennia. Hand-woven without patterns on waist-strap looms, Mixtec textiles often feature colourful geometric shapes or stylised animals, all worked into unique productions that instantly identify their village of origin.

The Maya are not a homogenous group, but a complex family comprised by numerous distinct ethnicities, each with their own language. The Yucatec Maya, occupying the Yucatán Peninsula, number some 2.45 million (with 892,723 Yucatec speakers) and are Mexico's biggest indigenous group after the Nahuas. They speak a single language with many distinct (but mutually intelligible) regional dialects, and lead lives with differing degrees of modernity.

In eastern Chiapas, the Lacandón are a particularly fascinating, though sparsely numbered, lowland Maya group. Known as Hach Winik in their own language, which means 'real people', they are believed to be descended from refugees who fled Guatemala and Yucatán during the Spanish Conquest. In the highlands of Chiapas, the rugged topography provides niches for a network of 13 distinct ethnic groups, each with their own attire. Tzeltal, Tzotzil, Tojolabal and Mam are their main languages. Community life is orientated around the family, a cargo system of civic duties, and religion – for which Alteños, as highlanders are called, are especially famous.

The 2010 National Census put the population of Belize at 321,115. The urban/rural distribution continues to be roughly 50:50. About 25% of the population are predominantly black and of mixed ancestry, the so-called Creoles, a term widely used in the Caribbean. They predominate in Belize City, along the coast and on the navigable rivers. About half of the population are mestizo; 10% are Maya, who predominate in the north between the Hondo and New rivers and in the extreme south and west. About 5% of the population are Garífuna (black Caribs), descendants of those deported from St Vincent in 1797; they have a distinct language, and can be found in the villages and towns along the southern coast. They are good linguists, many speaking Mayan languages as well as Spanish and 'Creole' English. They also brought their culture and customs from the West Indies, including religious practices and ceremonies, for example Yankanu (John Canoe) dancing at Christmas time. The remainder are of unmixed European ancestry (the majority Mennonites, who speak a German dialect, and are friendly and helpful) and a rapidly growing group of North Americans. The Mennonites fall into two groups, generally speaking: the most rigorous, in the Shipyard area on The New River, and the more 'integrated' in the west, Cayo district, who produce much of Belize's poultry, dairy goods and corn. The newest Mennonite settlements are east of Progresso Lagoon in the northeast. There are also East Indian and Chinese immigrants and their descendants.

Language
English is the official language, although for some 180,000 the lingua franca is 'Creole' English. Spanish is the lingua franca for about 130,000 people and is widely spoken in the northern and western areas. In addition, it is estimated that 22,000 people speak Mayan languages, 15,000 Garífuna and 3000 German.

Guatemala

The word *ladino* applies to any person with a 'Latin' culture, speaking Spanish and wearing Western clothes, though they may be pure Amerindian by descent. The opposite of ladino is *indígena*; the definition is cultural, not racial. Guatemala's population in 2013 was estimated to be 15.47 million. The indigenous people of Guatemala are mainly of Maya descent. The largest of the 22 indigenous Maya groups are K'iche', Q'eqchi' and Mam. When the Spaniards arrived from Mexico in 1524 those who stayed settled in the southern highlands around Antigua and Guatemala City and intermarried with the groups of native subsistence farmers living there. This was the basis of the present *mestizo* population living in the cities and towns as well as in all parts of the southern highlands and in the flatlands along the Pacific coast; the indigenous population is still at its most dense in the western highlands and Alta Verapaz. They form two distinct cultures: the almost self-supporting indigenous system in the highlands, and the *ladino* commercial economy in the lowlands. *Mestizo* are mixed Amerindian-Spanish or assimilated Amerindian. About half the total population are classed as Amerindian (Maya) – estimates vary from 40-65%.

Costume and dress
Indigenous dress is particularly attractive, little changed from the time the Spaniards arrived: the colourful head-dresses, *huipiles* (tunics) and skirts of the women, the often richly patterned sashes and kerchiefs, the hatbands and tassels of the men vary greatly, often from village to village. Unfortunately a new outfit is costly, the indigenous people are poor, and jeans are cheap. While men are adopting Western dress in many villages, women have been slower to change.

Land &
environment

Landscape and geography

Mexico

The complex land mass that is Mexico is the result of millions of years of geological moulding, a process that still continues today. The country continues to be regularly ignited by the spectacular eruptions of Popocatépetl, 60 km to the east of the capital, which has been slowly wakening from a 65-year slumber for several years. Likewise to the west of the capital, Colima Volcano is closed to climbers, as activity that has been growing steadily in the last few years looks certain to result in an eruption.

Mexico is roughly a quarter of the US in size, with which it has a frontier of 2400 km. The southern frontier of 885 km is with Guatemala and Belize. There is 2780 km of coast on the Gulf of Mexico and the Caribbean, and 7360 km on the Pacific. The geographical structure of the country is extremely complicated, but may be simplified (with large reservations) as a plateau flanked by ranges of mountains roughly paralleling the coasts. The two Sierra Madre ranges come together in the south, where an east–west line of some 1400 volcanic vents known as the Sierra (or Cordillera) Volcánica cross the country from the state of Veracruz in the east to the state of Jalisco in the west. To the east, the mountains of Oaxaca are still rugged, but a little lower (between 1800 and 2400 m), with much less rainfall. Population is sparse and subsistence crops are sown on incredibly steep slopes.

To the south, the Pacific coast of Oaxaca is forbidding and its few ports of little use, though there is tourism. After some 560 km, the highlands fall away into the low-lying Isthmus of Tehuantepec. Very different are the Gulf coast and Yucatán; half this area is classed as flat, and much of it gets enough rain the year round, leading to its having become one of the most important agricultural and cattle raising areas in the country. The Gulf coast also provides most of Mexico's oil and sulphur. Geographically, North America may be said to come to an end in the Isthmus of Tehuantepec. South of the Isthmus the land rises again into the thinly populated highlands of Chiapas, which extend for about 300 km southeast to the border with Guatemala.

East of Chiapas, the Yucatán is a limestone platform, a feature that rings the Gulf of Mexico all the way to Florida and is recognized as a separate chunk of the North American plate. It is comparatively flat and characterised by natural caverns, wells, sinkholes (cenotes) and white, sandy beaches. The northeast corner of Yucatán is the point nearest to Cuba and where the Caribbean Sea meets the Gulf of Mexico. It is the water passing through this passage that initiates the current known as the Gulf Stream, with its dramatic effect on the climates of Europe, thousands of miles away. It is calculated that at times, driven by strong trade winds, the surface water here is moving at as much as 6 km per hour.

Perhaps the world's most dramatic geological happening ever recorded took place in Yucatán. It is now generally agreed that the cataclysm that almost ended life on the planet 65 million years ago was a small asteroid, weighing perhaps one billion tonnes, colliding with the earth at 160,000 kph. This left a hole many kilometres deep and over 150 km wide in the Yucatán, now known as the Chicxulub Crater. This event destroyed almost everything on earth from the dinosaurs to ammonites, leaving only the most primitive organisms. Fortunately for us, life was able to re-establish itself.

Belize

The coastlands are low and swampy with much mangrove, many salt and fresh water lagoons and some sandy beaches. In the north the land is low and flat, while in the southwest there is a heavily forested mountain massif with a general elevation of between 2000 and 3000 ft. In the east are the Maya Mountains, not yet wholly explored, and the Cockscomb Range which rises to a height of 3675 ft at Victoria Peak. Further west are some 250 square miles of the Mountain Pine Ridge, with large open spaces and some of the best scenery in the country.

From 10 to 40 miles off the coast an almost continuous, 184-mile-long line of reefs and cayes (or cays) provides shelter from the Caribbean, and forms the longest coral reef in the Western Hemisphere (the fifth longest barrier reef in the world). Most of the cayes are quite tiny, but some have been developed into tourist resorts. Many have beautiful sandy beaches with clear, clean water, where swimming and diving are excellent. However, on the windward side of inhabited islands, domestic sewage is washed back on to the beaches, some of which are also affected by tar.

The most fertile areas of the country are in the foothills of the northern section of the Maya Mountains: citrus fruit is grown in the Stann Creek valley, while in the valley of the Mopan, or upper Belize River, cattle raising and mixed farming are successful. The northern area of the country has long proved suitable for sugar cane production. In the south bananas and mangoes are cultivated. The lower valley of the Belize River is a rice-growing area as well as being used for mixed farming and citrus cultivation.

Guatemala

A lowland ribbon, nowhere more than 50 km wide, runs the whole length of the Pacific shore. Cotton, sugar, bananas and maize are the chief crops of this strip. There is some stock raising as well. Summer rain is heavy and the lowland carries scrub forest. From this plain the highlands rise sharply to heights of between 2500 and 4000 m and stretch some 240 km to the north before sinking into the northern lowlands.

A string of volcanoes juts boldly above the southern highlands along the Pacific. There are intermont basins at from 1500 to 2500 m in this volcanic area. Most of the people of Guatemala live in these basins, which are drained by short rivers into the Pacific and by longer ones into the Atlantic. One basin west of the capital, ringed by volcanoes and with no apparent outlet, is Lago de Atitlán.

The southern highlands are covered with lush vegetation over a volcanic subsoil. This clears away in the central highlands, exposing the crystalline rock of the east–west running ranges. This area is lower but more rugged, with sharp-faced ridges and deep ravines modifying into gentle slopes and occasional valley lowlands as it loses height and approaches the Caribbean coastal levels and the flatlands of El Petén. The lower slopes of these highlands, from about 600 to 1500 m, are planted with coffee. Above 1500 m is given over to wheat and the main subsistence crops of maize and beans. Deforestation is becoming a serious problem. Where rainfall is low there are savannas; water for irrigation is now drawn from wells and these areas are being reclaimed for pasture and fruit growing.

Two large rivers flow down to the Caribbean Gulf of Honduras from the highlands: one is the Río Motagua, 400 km long, rising among the southern volcanoes; the other, further north, is the Río Polochic, 298 km long, which drains into Lago de Izabal and the Bahía de Amatique. There are large areas of lowland in the lower reaches of both rivers, which are navigable for considerable distances; this was the great banana zone.

To the northwest, bordering on Belize and Mexico's Yucatán Peninsula, lies the low, undulating tableland of El Petén almost one-third of the nation's territory. In some parts there is natural grassland, with woods and streams, suitable for cattle, but large areas are covered with dense hardwood forest. Since the 1970s large-scale tree felling has reduced this tropical rainforest by some 40%, especially in the south and east. However, in the north, which now forms Guatemala's share of the Maya Biosphere Reserve, the forest is protected, but illegal logging still takes place.

Ecosystems

Central America is the meeting place of two of the world's major biological regions: the Nearctic to the north and the Neotropical to the south. It has a remarkable geological and climatic complexity and consequently an enormous range of habitats: rainforests, dry forests, cloud forests, mangroves and stretches of wetlands.

Lowland rainforests

The region's lowland rainforests are home to an extraordinary cornucopia of biological life. They are densely vegetated and largely inhospitable places, characterized by high temperatures, humidity and rainfall. Life is sustained by an intricate web of relationships, invariably driven by the struggle for survival. Predation, particularly of nests, is intensive and widespread, as is competition for food and light; anyone unfortunate enough to find themselves stranded in a rainforest may find little to sustain them. Symbiotic relationships are very common, with plants often having creative and specialized methods of pollination and seed dispersal. Parasitic relationships are also prolific and often quite gruesome, such as wasps that inject their eggs inside the living bodies of ants. Rainforests incorporate several distinct layers commencing with the forest floor, which is usually clear of vegetation and quite dark due to the multiple canopies above it. The exception is the site of a recent tree fall, which is always worth scrutinizing for its new growth and activity.

Despite the rainforest's profusion of plants, its topsoil is very thin and nutrient-poor, causing many trees to have sprawling, buttressed roots near the surface. When a plant or animal dies, it is rapidly broken down by bacteria and insects, and its nutrients taken up by living vegetation via a network of mycorrhizal fungi; brush away some topsoil to see it. Between the canopy and the forest floor, the understorey is home to numerous small animals. It is still a relatively dark place and most of its plants – typically shrubs and palms – need large leaves to maximize photosynthesis. Rodents are a fairly common sight, as are amphibians. Rivers, streams, ponds and other bodies of water tend to draw larger mammals, but most are nocturnal and rarely seen by humans. The canopy itself is teeming with plant life as vines, orchids and epiphytes compete for every available ray of light. The rainforest's highest canopy – the emergent layer – contains just a few tall trees, the giants of the forest, home to rare bird species.

Tropical dry forests

Low-lying tropical dry forests receive far less precipitation than rainforests. They are home to numerous deciduous trees that must shed their leaves in the dry season in order to conserve water. The loss of leaves opens many gaps in the forest canopy, encouraging the growth of prolific underbrush. Many plants and trees have found strategies to cope with the dry conditions, including some that have evolved chlorophyll in their bark and others with swollen roots and stems that act as reservoirs. Resident animal species are broadly comparable to those of the rainforests, but ultimately less numerous and biodiverse. Some of them, including a few amphibians and reptiles, practise estivation – a state of dormancy where they burrow deep into the mud and sleep out the summer. The coming of the rains is a fascinating time in the tropical dry forest, when numerous creatures emerge, flowers start blooming and the vegetation turns green virtually overnight.

Cloud forests

Highland cloud forests are characterized by persistent mist and cloud cover. They are considerably cooler than rainforests with daytime temperatures of around 10-20°C. Due to the almost constant blanket of fog, sunlight is greatly reduced, but there is an immense amount of precipitation and cloud forests play a crucial role in maintaining highland drainage and watersheds. They are extremely lush places, home to scores of green mosses, lichens, ferns, fungi, orchids and bromeliads. Trees are generally short with dense, compact crowns that cause wind-driven clouds to condense. Cloud forests also boast reasonably high biodiversity and high rates of endemism thanks to their numerous valleys and ridges, which many animals find impassable.

Wetlands and mangrove forests

Wetlands can be found on all three coastlines and are endowed with an abundance of water in different forms: fresh, salty, flowing and stagnant. Wetlands offer a diversity of ecological niches including sedge marshes, swamps, bogs, flood plains, coastal lagoons and mangrove forests. Proliferating in intertidal or estuarine areas, mangroves include a broad family of halophytic (salt-tolerant) trees. They serve a vital function by trapping sediment, protecting the shore from erosion and building land. The forests have a low canopy and a low diversity of trees, usually dominated by red mangroves, which can be recognized by their dark stilted roots that hold them above the surface of the water. Mangroves are important nurseries for fish, birds, amphibians and crustaceans, including numerous crabs and shrimps.

Beaches and shores

The shorelines of southern Mexico, Belize and Guatemala can be rocky, sandy or muddy. Low tide often reveals rock pools filled with clams and mussels, or teeming mud flats strewn with crabs and shrimps, all drawing waders and hungry seabirds. Larger avian species, including pelicans and pterodactyl-like frigate birds, are a common sight on any shore. Some of the region's beaches see impressive migrations of endangered sea turtles, including leatherback, hawksbill, loggerhead and olive ridley.

Wildlife

Around three million years ago, the merging of North and South America into a single landmass sparked a mass migration of animals between both continents. Known as the Great American Faunal Interchange, it was a significant moment in the earth's natural history, heralding bold new patterns of species settlement, adaptation, predation and, in some cases, extinction. The event was accompanied by the Great American Schism, which separated the Pacific and Atlantic oceans and set marine species on their own unique evolutionary paths.

Today, southern Mexico, Belize and Guatemala represent the range limit for numerous North and South American animal species, as well as a land bridge for dozens of types of migratory birds. The majority of tour operators listed in this guide will offer nature-oriented tours and there are several national parks, *biotopes* or protected areas throughout the region, each with its own highlights.

Mammals

Primates are among the most easily sighted mammals in the region. Howler monkeys are noticeable for the huge row they make, especially around dawn or dusk. The spider monkey is more agile and slender and uses its prehensile tail to swing around the canopy. The smaller, white-throated capuchins are also commonly seen, moving around in noisy groups. The most frequently spotted carnivore is the white-nosed coati, a member of the racoon family, with a long snout and ringed tail. Members of the cat family are rarely seen; those in the area include the bobcat (in Mexico only), jaguar, puma, ocelot and margay. The largest land mammal in the region is Baird's tapir, weighing up to 300 kg, but it is a forest species and very secretive. More likely to be seen are peccaries, medium-sized pig-like animals that are active both day and night. The white-tailed deer can often be spotted at dawn or dusk in drier, woodland patches. The smaller red brocket is a rainforest deer and more elusive. Rodent species you might see include the forest-dwelling agouti, which looks rather like a long-legged guinea pig. Considerably larger is the nocturnal paca (gibnut in Belize), another forest species. Many species of bat are found throughout the region.

Birds

Toucans and the smaller toucanets are widespread throughout the tropical areas of the region and easy to spot. Other popular sightings include the hummingbird, frequently drawn to sugar-feeders, and the scarlet macaw. The resplendent quetzal, the national symbol of Guatemala, is brilliant emerald green, with males having a bright scarlet breast and belly and long green tail streamers. The harpy eagle is extremely rare with sightings a possibility in rainforest region of northern Guatemala, Belize and southern Mexico. Other rare birds include the threatened horned guam, found only in high cloud forests. Along the coasts are masses of different seabirds, including pelicans, boobies and the magnificent frigate bird. In the coastal wetlands of the Yucután pink flamingos can be spotted.

Reptiles and amphibians

Mexico has more reptiles than any other country in the world. Snakes are rarely sighted, but if you are lucky you could see a boa constrictor curled up digesting its latest meal. In contrast, lizards are everywhere, from small geckos walking up walls in your hotel room to the large iguanas sunbathing in the tree tops. The American crocodile and spectacled caiman are both found throughout the area, with the latter being seen quite frequently. Morlet's crocodile is found only in Mexico, Belize and Guatemala. You'll certainly hear frogs and toads, even if you do not see them. However, the brightly coloured poison-dart frogs and some of the tree frogs are well worth searching out. Look for them in damp places, under logs and moist leaf litter, in rock crevices and by ponds and streams; many will be more active at night. Turtles have been nesting in the region for thousands of years; females will typically swim ashore at night, dig a nest, lay their eggs and depart. The temperature of the nest will determine the future sex of the hatchling: above 29°C female, below 29°C male. The eggs will hatch simultaneously and the young turtles will inundate the sea in an evolutionary mechanism believed to give them the best chances of survival.

Insects and spiders

There are uncounted different species of insect in the area. Probably most desirable to see are the butterflies, though some of the beetles, such as the jewel scarabs, are also pretty spectacular. If you are fascinated by spiders, look out for tarantulas, there are many different species.

Marine wildlife

The whale shark makes a seasonal migration through the coastal waters of Belize and Honduras between March and May. Less natural shark encounters can be had off Caye Caulker, Belize, and Isla Mujeres, on the Yucatán, Mexico, where hand-feeding brings in sting rays and nurse sharks for close but safe encounters. Marine mammals that can be sighted include whales, dolphins and manatees.

Books

Archaeology

Some of the larger sites, such as Palenque, have museums with bookstores. The Anthropology Museum in Mexico City is also a great place to stock up on archaeological guides.

Coe, MD *The Maya*. Essential recommended reading for the Maya archaeological area.
Coe, MD *Breaking the Maya Code*. An in-depth account of how the hieroglyphics of the Maya were eventually read.
Schele, L and Friedel, D *A Forest of Kings*. Linda Schele's work in deciphering the narratives contained in Classic Mayan monuments has been crucial to our understanding of Mayan history. Highly recommended; there are many other intriguing titles by the same author.

History

Dunkerley, James *Power in the Isthmus: A Political History of Modern Central America (1989)*. A good history of the smaller republics.
Leon-Portilla, Miguel *The Broken Spears*. A fascinating account of the Spanish conquest as narrated by the Aztecs. Recommended.
Prescott, William *History of the Conquest of Mexico (1849)*. Reliable and dated, but an old favourite.
Thomas, Hugh *Conquest: Cortes, Montezuma, and the fall of the Old Mexico (1995)*. A more up-to-date overview.

Literature

Asturias, Miguel Angel *Hombres de maíz*. The key text by Guatemala's Nobel-prize winning poet, diplomat and author. Also try *Mulata de tal* and *El señor president*.

Greene, Graham *The Lawless Roads*. Greene's classic journey through Chiapas and Tabasco during the anticlerical purges of the 1930s. Also see his masterpiece, *The Power and the Glory*.
Huxley, Aldous *Eyeless in Gaza*. The story of an Oxford graduate who takes up arms with Mexican revolutionaries. By the same author, *Beyond the Mexique Bay* is a journey through the Caribbean, Guatemala and Mexico during the 1930s
Lawrence, D H *The Plumed Serpent*. Lawrence's classic is a fictional exploration of Aztec religion and a criticism of Catholicism.
Lowry, Malcolm *Under the Volcano*. Set in Mexico and apparently inspired by the cantinas of Oaxaca City, Lowry's delirious depiction of alcoholic ruin is a masterpiece and vastly underrated.
Menchú, Rigoberta I *Rigoberta Menchú*. The best-selling autobiographical account of life and hardship in rural Guatemala, which won Menchú the Nobel Peace Prize.
Payeras, Mario *Los días de la selva*. A first-hand account of the guerrilla movement in the 1970s.
Wilson, Jason *Traveller's Literary Companion, South and Central America (1993)*. A general guide to the literature of the region with extracts from works by Latin American writers and by non-Latin Americans about the various countries; it also has very useful bibliographies.

Travel

Daniels, Anthony *Sweet Waist of America: Journeys around Guatemala*. A modern-day travelogue, published 1990.
Franz, Carl *The People's Guide to Mexico*. Highly recommended, practical and entertaining. There is also a website: www.peoplesguide.com.

Stephens, John L *Incidents of Travel in Central America, Chiapas, and Yucatán.* This classic and pioneering tome by the 19th-century explorer was the first reliable survey of Mayan ruins in the region. Entertaining and fascinating. Recommended, along with the sequels.

Tree, Isabella *Sliced Iguana – Travels in Mexico (2007).* Gets the real flavour of Mexico and is a great travel companion.

Wildlife

Beletsky, Les *Ecotravellers' Wildlife Guides.* One for Tropical Mexico and one for Belize and Northern Guatemala.

Emmon, Louise *Neotropical Rainforest Mammals: A Field Guide.* This will help with identifying wildlife.

Howell, Steve and Webb, Sophie *A Guide to the Birds of Mexico and Northern Central America.*

Films

On the international big screen Mexico has probably suffered more than most from stereotypical images painting the whole nation as a bunch of lazy, good-for-nothing scoundrels, crooks and corrupt officials. The Western genre relied heavily on the scenic locations around Durango producing classics from the 1950s through the works of Sam Peckinpah up to the all-star *Mask of Zorro*. Many other US productions have used Mexico's tropical locations for films such as *Night of the Iguana*, *Romancing the Stone* and *Medicine Man*, and the blockbuster *Titanic*, which was shot at Rosarito, Baja California, close to Tijuana. But the national film industry has grown in prominence in recent years with international successes including *Como agua para chocolate* (Like Water for Chocolate), *Danzón*, *Amores Perros* (nominated for an Oscar and winner of the 2002 Bafta for best foreign film), *Y tu mamá también*, a road movie about love, sex, friendship, politics and the blind haste to grow up, and *Apocalypto*, filmed in the Yucatán jungle and El Petén and set during the decline of the Mayan civilization (with Yucatec dialogue throughout). Another hit, *Frida*, celebrates the life of the painter Frida Kahlo and her relationship with Diego Rivera, how the couple took the art world by storm and her controversial affair with Leon Trotsky. *Sin dejar huella* (Without a Trace) is a women's road movie following a journey through Mexico and ending in the Yucatán, whilst *Sin Nombre* explores gang culture in Tapachula.

Guatemalan films include *El Norte* (1983), which follows the plight of a Guatemalan brother and sister who seek a new life after experiencing the trials of their village massacre, and *When the Mountains Tremble* (1983), a hard-hitting film demonstrating the desperation of national governments and guerrillas. A more recent release, the award-winning *La Jaula de Oro* (The Golden Cage) (2013) tells the story of three Guatemalan teenagers and their journey to become illegal immigrants in the US.

For films about Belize, you could try tracking down *Three Kings of Belize*, a documentary that follows three musicians, Paul Nabor, Wilfred Peters and Florencio Mess.

Practicalities

Getting there

All countries in Latin America (in fact across the world) officially require travellers entering their territory to have an onward or return ticket and may at times ask to see that ticket. Although rarely enforced at airports, this regulation can create problems at border crossings. In lieu of an onward ticket out of the country you are entering, any ticket out of another Latin American country may sometimes suffice, or proof that you have sufficient funds to buy a ticket (a credit card will do). International air tickets are expensive if purchased in Latin America.

Air

Fares from Europe and North America to Latin American destinations vary. Peak periods and higher prices correspond to holiday season in the northern hemisphere. The very busy seasons are as follows: 7 December to 15 January and July to mid-September. If you intend travelling during those times, book as far ahead as possible. Check with an agency for the best deal for when you wish to travel.

There is a wide range of offers to choose from in a highly competitive environment. An indication of cost is difficult to give due to the large number of variables, not least the current fluctuations in currency and the wide variations in oil prices in recent years. The main factors are frequency of flights and popularity of destination at a particular time of year. As a rough guide a three-month London–Mexico return in August is around US$1200. In November the same flight falls to US$1000. Travellers from Australia and New Zealand are getting an increasingly better deal compared with recent years, with special offers occasionally down to AUS$1900 flying direct to Mexico City. The more regular price is close to AUS$3200.

Fares fall into three groups, and are all on scheduled services: **Excursion** (return) fares: these have restricted validity either seven to 90 days, or seven to 180 days, depending on the airline. They are fixed-date tickets where the dates of travel cannot be changed after issue without incurring a penalty. **Yearly fares**: these may be bought on a one-way or return basis, and usually the returns can be issued with the return date left open. You must, however, fix the route. **Student** (or Under-26) fares: one way and returns available, or 'open jaws' for people intending to travel a linear route and return from a different point from that which they entered.

Flights from Europe

It is worth considering Mexico City as an entry/exit point. Air fares between February and June can be very reasonable (although the same does not apply to Cancún, when high season signals a steep price climb) and European carriers include **Air France**, **British Airways**, **Iberia**, **KLM** and **Lufthansa**. With the promotion of Cancún as a gateway from Europe, there are a large number of scheduled flights from Europe to the Yucatán peninsula. The best deals can be found from November to January and carriers include **Air Berlin**, **Air Europa**, **Air France**, **Blue Panorama Airways**, **British Airways**, **Condor**, **Jet Airfly**, **Lufthansa**, **Nordwind**, **Orbest**, **Virgin Atlantic** and **XL Airways**. There are also some very affordable no-frills seasonal charter flights (for example **Thomas Cook**, **Thomson Airways**, **TUfly Nordic**, **LOT**, **EuroAtlantic Airways** and **Arkefly**). Beyond Mexico, there are few direct flights to the region (one option is **Iberia** to Guatemala) and you will usually have to travel via the US.

Flights from the US and Canada

Flying to Mexico from the US offers a very wide range of options. The main US carriers are **American Airlines**, **US Airways**, **Delta** and **United**. The main departure points are Atlanta, Miami, Dallas/Fort Worth, Los Angeles and San Francisco. For low-cost flights to Mexico, try **Spirit Air** or **Jet Blue**. From Canada, the options are less varied, but regular flights serve the main cities with direct flights from Montreal and Toronto with **Air Canada**. Keep an eye out for special offers, which can produce extremely cheap flights (often at very short notice). From the US to Guatemala, you can fly with **American Airlines**, **Delta**, **Spirit Air** and **United**. Belize is served by **American Airlines**, **Delta** and **United** (many travellers find it cheaper to fly into Cancún and travel overland to Belize, see box, page 511).

Boat

Following the coastal route doesn't have to be done from the land side, as thousands of sailors who follow the good-weather sailing around the coast of Mexico and Central America can confirm. Indeed there seem to be increasing numbers of people travelling this way. Between California, the Panama Canal and Florida dozens of marinas await the sailor looking to explore the region from the sea. A guide to the marinas and sailing ports of the region is *Cruising Ports: the Central American Route*, and *Mexico Boating Guide* by Captain Pat Rains, published by Point Loma Publishing in San Diego. Captain Rain is an experienced navigator of Mexican and Central American waters with over 30 Panama transits under her cap (www.centralamericanboating.com).

Travelling by freighter to the region is possible as a paid passenger, but since fares include room and board for your time at sea, costs are comparable to international flights. Aside from the obvious adventure appeal, it is really only worth considering if you are shipping a vehicle from Europe or the US. Enquiries regarding passages should be made through agencies in your own country. In the UK, **Strand Voyages** have information on occasional one-way services to the Gulf of Mexico from Europe. Details on shipping cars are given in the relevant country sections. For boat travel within the region, see Getting around, opposite.

In Europe
The Cruise People, T020-7723-2450, www.cruise people.co.uk.
Globoship, Switzerland, T31-313 0004, www.globoship.com.
Strand Voyages, T020-7802-2199, www.strandtravel.co.uk.

In the US
Freighter World Cruises, T1-800-531-7774, www.freighterworld.com.
Travltips Cruise and Freighter Travel Association, T1-800-872-8584, www.travltips.com.

Road

Travel from the US

There are a multitude of entry points to Mexico from the US, the main ones being Tijuana, Nogales, Ciudad Juárez, Piedras Negras, Nuevo Laredo and Matamoros. Crossing the border is simple and hassle-free for foot passengers and reasonably straightforward for people travelling with their own vehicle. All border towns have bus terminals that provide long-distance bus services.

Getting around

Bus travel is the most popular style of transport for independent travellers. An excellent network criss-crosses the region varying in quality from luxurious intercity cruisers with air conditioning, videos and fully reclining seats, to beaten-up US-style school buses or 'chicken buses' with busted suspension and holes in the floor.

Travelling under your own steam is also very popular. Driving your own vehicle – car, camper van, motorbike and bicycle – offers wonderful freedom and may not be as expensive or as bureaucratic as you think. From the emails we receive, the ever-greater cooperation between the nations of Central America is producing dramatic benefits at border crossings for those who decide to go it alone. Indeed, since 2006, when Guatemala, El Salvador, Honduras and Nicaragua signed the **Central America-4**, it's been even easier (see box, page 509). With the comprehensive road network it's easy to miss out on other sensible choices. Don't shun the opportunity to take a short flight. While you'll need to enquire about precise costs, the view from above provides a different perspective and the difference in cost may not be as great as you think. Getting around in Central America is rarely a problem whether travelling by bus, car, bike, in fact almost any mode of transport.

There is just one caveat that stands good across all situations: be patient when asking directions. Often Latin Americans will give you the wrong answer rather than admit they do not know. Distances are notoriously inaccurate so ask a few people.

Air

All countries have a domestic flight service and some of the national airlines offer connections throughout Central and Latin America. Prices can be steep due to a lack of competition, but it is definitely worth considering an aerial 'hop' if it covers a lot of difficult terrain and you get the bonus of a good view. From Mexico City and Cancún, the main regional carriers are **Aeroméxico**, **Avianca**, **Copa**, **Interjet** (recommended), **VivaAerobus** and **Volaris**. From Belize City, **Tropic Air** and **Maya Island Air** serve Cancún, Honduras and Guatemala (Flores and Guatemala City). From Guatemala City, the regional carriers are **Aeroméxico**, **Avianca**, **Copa**, **Interjet**, **Transportes Aereos Guatemaltecos** (Flores, Honduras, El Salvador) and **Veca Airlines** (El Salvador). Remote destinations are invariably served by small aircraft with stringent weight restrictions and extra charges for large items such as surf boards; check with the airlines before setting out.

Boat

Keeping all options open, water transport has to be a consideration – although not a very realistic one – in terms of reaching a distant destination. Most water transport consists of small boats with outboard motors. They travel relatively short distances in localized areas, usually along tropical rivers or between off-shore islands, where road transport is otherwise lacking. Due to the high cost of fuel, they are frequently crowded and somewhat expensive compared to buses. If hiring a boat privately, it is best to share costs with other travellers. Overcharging is very possible and when calculating costs you need to consider the weight of cargo (including passengers), distance covered, engine horse-power, fee for the driver, port taxes (if any) and, most importantly, the quantity of fuel used.

You'll find just a few regular ferry schedules that avoid circuitous land routes – the main journey is from the Mexican border town of Chetumal to the northern Cayes of Belize, which skips Belize City; see box, page 511. Crossing the Usumacinta river between Guatemala and Mexico is a well-established (if remote) option that connects Chiapas with the Petén; see box, page 512. There are also ferry connections between Punta Gorda in Belize and Lívingston in Guatemala. See box, page 514.

Road

Bus and colectivo

There is an extensive road system with frequent bus services throughout Mexico and Central America. Costs, quality and levels of comfort vary enormously; see country sections below for an overview. As a general rule, in mountainous country (and after long journeys), do not expect buses to get to their destination anywhere near on time. Avoid turning up for a bus at the last minute; if it is full it may depart early. Try to sit near the front; going round bends and over bumps has less impact on your body near the front axle, making the journey more comfortable and reducing the likelihood of motion sickness (on some long journeys it also means you are further from the progressively smelly toilets, if available, at the back of the bus). Tall travellers are advised to take aisle seats on long journeys as this allows more leg room.

When the journey takes more than three or four hours, meal stops at country inns or bars, good and bad, are the rule. Often no announcement is made on the duration of the stop; ask the driver and follow him, if he eats, eat. See what the locals are eating – and buy likewise, or make sure you're stocked up on food and drink at the start. For drinks, stick to bottled water, soft drinks or coffee (black). The food sold by vendors at bus stops may be all right; watch if locals are buying. Do not leave valuable items on the bus during stops. Importantly, make sure you have a sweater or blanket to hand for long bus journeys, especially at night; even if it's warm outside, the air conditioning is often set to blizzard.

Southern Mexico Mexican buses are generally very efficient and put US **Greyhound** buses to shame. In some cities there is a central bus terminal (in Mexico City there are four, one at each point of the compass), in others there are a couple: one for first-class services, one for second. A third variation is division by companies. The entire network is privatized and highly competitive, although in practise there is often little difference between carriers. In the south of the country, ADO ① www.ado.com.mx, is the main operator and it has several subsidiaries, including OCC and ADO GL. Most intercity routes are served by comfortable first-class buses with reclining seats, air conditioning, Spanish-language movies and toilet. For those seeking extra luxury, **ADO Platino** offers a soft drinks, snacks and almost horizontally aligned seats. It is highly advisable to book your tickets several days in advance when travelling at Christmas, Semana Santa or other national holidays. If your journey is longer than six hours, it is sensible to book 24 hours ahead. First-class fares are usually 10% dearer than second-class ones and the superior classes 30-40% more than first class. On a long journey you can save the price of a hotel room by travelling overnight, but in some areas this is dangerous and not recommended. You can book tickets in advance on the ADO website or with **Boletotal** ① www.boletotal.mx.

Belize Public transport between most towns is by bus and, with the short distances involved, there are few long journeys to encounter. Trucks carry passengers to many

Border cooperation

In June 2006, Guatemala, El Salvador, Honduras, and Nicaragua entered into a 'Central America-4 (CA-4) Border Control Agreement'. Under the terms of the agreement, citizens of the four countries may travel freely across land borders from one of the countries to any of the others without completing entry and exit formalities at immigration checkpoints. US citizens and other eligible foreign nationals, who legally enter any of the four countries, may similarly travel among the four without obtaining additional visas or tourist entry permits for the other three countries. Immigration officials at the first port of entry determine the length of stay, up to a maximum period of 90 days.

isolated destinations. Most buses are ex-US school buses with small seats and limited leg room. There are a few ex-Greyhounds, mostly used for 'express' services and charters. It is recommended to buy tickets for seats in advance at the depot before boarding the bus. To find out about bus schedules go to www.guidetobelize.info (then select travel and then bus). Most buses have no luggage compartments so bags that do not fit on the luggage rack are stacked at the back. Get a seat at the back to keep an eye on your gear, but rough handling is more of a threat than theft.

Guatemala There is an extensive network of bus routes throughout the country. Like Belize, the chicken buses (former US school buses) are mostly in a poor state of repair and overloaded. Faster and more reliable Pullman services operate on some routes. Correct fares should be posted. We receive regular complaints that bus drivers charge tourists more than a local, a practice that is becoming more widespread. One way to avoid being overcharged is to watch for what the locals pay or ask a local, then tender the exact fare on the bus. Many long-distance buses leave very early in the morning. Make sure you can get out of your hotel/*pension*. For international bus journeys make sure you have small denomination local currency or US dollar bills for border taxes. At Easter there are few buses on Good Friday or the Saturday and buses are packed with long queues for tickets for the few days before Good Friday. Many names on bus destination boards are abbreviated; for example, Guate – Guatemala City; Chichi – Chichicastenango; Xela/Xelajú – Quetzaltenango, and so on.

Colectivos (shuttles and taxis) In Mexico and Guatemala, a *colectivo* can refer to an economical shuttle van (also called a combi, especially in Chiapas), or to a shared taxi, where the fare is divided between four or five passengers, or where the driver picks up and drops off passengers between destinations. The distances covered are comparatively short with most journey times under four hours. The advantage of colectivos is that they often travel backdoor routes and supply a speedy alternative to conventional buses (for example, Oaxaca City to Puerto Escondido). They are, however, less comfortable than ADO. For safety and security, it is best to avoid using colectivo taxis in Mexico and Guatemala City.

On many popular routes throughout the region there are tourist shuttle vans that can be booked through hotels and travel agencies. These are pricier than regular *colectivos* but they travel longer distances and can take a lot of the hassle out of journeys that involve several changes or border crossings (for example, San Cristóbal de las Casas to Antigua). They will also pick you up from your hotel. **Belize Shuttles** ① *Belize International*

Airport, Ladyville, T631-1749, in the USA T757-383 8024 and Canada T647-724 2004, www. belizeshuttlesandtransfers.com, offer transfers to and from Belize City, to many other parts of the country, and to Cancún in Mexico and Flores in Guatemala (for the ruins at Tikal).

International buses These link the capital cities providing an effective way of quickly covering a lot of ground. There are several companies but the main operator is **Ticabus** ⓘ *www.ticabus.com*, with headquarters in Costa Rica. However, bear in mind that Panama–Guatemala with **Ticabus** takes almost three days and costs over US$100, plus accommodation in Managua and San Salvador. You may want to consider flying if you need to get through more than one country quickly.

Crossing borders

Travellers who are eligible for tourist cards or their equivalent (including most European, Australian and North American visitors) find that crossing borders in Central America a relatively straightforward process. Those travellers who require visas, however, may not always find them available; approach the relevant consulate (offices in the capital or big cities) before setting out for the border. For Customs and duty free, see page 520; for Visas and immigration, see page 533.

Some crossings levy exit and entrance taxes, along with occasional *alcaldía* fees; the amounts vary. 'Unofficial' taxes are not uncommon and sometimes it can be easier to pay a few extra dollars than enter into drawn-out dispute. Asking for a '*factura*' (receipt) can help. Many immigration officers will ask for evidence of onward travel – either a return flight or a bus ticket – along with funds. Leaving Mexico, there are no exit fees, but you must present a receipt for your FMM tourist card (often included in air fares) to avoid being charged US$22. The overland departure tax for Belize is BZ$37.50 (not US dollars), payable in cash only (Belizean or US). There is no overland departure tax payable when leaving Guatemala.

If you use international buses, expect long queues and tedious custom searches. If you're light on luggage, it is usually quicker to use local buses and cross the border on your own. Some drivers may be subjected to bureaucratic delays. Preparation is the best guarantee of a speedy crossing; check in advance which documents you will require and make several copies before setting out (see car documents below for more on procedures). The busiest borders are often frequented by unpleasant characters. Changing money is OK, but check the rate and carefully count what you're given; rip-offs can occur. For essential information, see Border crossing boxes on pages 511-518.

Car

If driving, an international driving licence is useful, although not always essential. Membership of motoring organizations can also be useful for discounts such as hotel charges, car rentals, maps and towing charges.

The kind of motoring you do will depend on your car. A 4WD is not necessary, although it does give you greater flexibility in mountain and jungle territory. Wherever you travel you should expect from time to time to find roads that are badly maintained, damaged or closed during the wet season, and delays because of floods, landslides and huge potholes.

Be prepared for all manner of mechanical challenges. The electronic ignition and fuel metering systems on modern emission-controlled cars are allergic to humidity, heat and dust, and cannot be repaired by mechanics outside the main centres. Standard European and Japanese cars run on fuel with a higher octane rating than is commonly available in North, Central or South America. Note that in some areas gas stations are few and far between. Fill up when you see one as the next one may be out of fuel.

BORDER CROSSING
Mexico–Belize

Chetumal–Corozal
The main border crossing is Santa Elena for Chetumal/Corozal. Santa Elena is 12 km north of Corozal, from where there are onward connections to Belize City (three to four hours). Chetumal is 11 km north of Santa Elena and has connections to the Yucatán Peninsula and Quintana Roo beaches; see also page 211. There's a modern 24-hour immigration terminal here and formalities are usually swift. If entering Belize, it's not strictly necessary to change dollars as they are accepted everywhere at a fixed rate of 1:2. It is easier to change Mexican pesos at the border than inside Belize.

La Unión–Blue Creek
A less widely used crossing is at La Unión/Blue Creek (not recommended unless you like a challenge). There are immigration facilities here but officials are only used to dealing with Mexicans and Belizeans, so delays are likely. See also page 303.

Documents Land entry procedures for all countries are simple though time-consuming, as the car has to be checked by customs, police and agriculture officials. All you need is the registration document in the name of the driver or, in the case of a car registered in someone else's name, a notarized letter of authorization. In Guatemala, the car's entry is stamped into the passport so you may not leave the country even temporarily without it.

Most countries give a limited period of stay, but allow an extension if requested in advance. Of course, do be very careful to keep **all** the papers you are given when you enter, to produce when you leave. An army of 'helpers' loiters at each border crossing, waiting to guide motorists to each official in the correct order, for a tip. They can be very useful, but don't give them your papers. Bringing a car in by sea or air is much more complicated and expensive; generally you will have to hire an agent to clear it through.

Insurance for the vehicle against accident, damage or theft is best arranged in the country of origin. In Latin American countries it is very expensive to insure against accident and theft, especially as you should take into account the value of the car increased by duties calculated in real (that is non-devaluing) terms. If the car is stolen or written off, you will be required to pay very high duty on its value. A few countries insist on compulsory third-party insurance, to be bought at the border; in other countries it's technically required, but not checked up on (again, see page 514 for details on **Sanborn's** and other insurers, who will insure vehicles for driving in Mexico and Central America). Get the legally required minimum cover – which is not expensive – as soon as you can, because if you should be involved in an accident and are uninsured, your car could be confiscated.

If anyone is hurt, do not pick them up (you become liable). Seek assistance from the nearest police station or hospital if you are able to do so. You may find yourself facing a hostile crowd, even if you are not to blame.

Expect frequent road checks by police, military (especially Honduras, where there is a check point on entering and leaving every town), agricultural and forestry produce inspectors, and any other curious official who wants to know what a foreigner is doing driving around in his domain. Smiling simple-minded patience is the best tactic to avoid harassment.

BORDER CROSSING
Mexico–Guatemala

Tapachula–El Carmen/Ciudad Tecún

The principal border town is Tapachula, with a crossing via the international Talismán Bridge or at Ciudad Hidalgo (see page 120). For onward connections, see also Tapachula Transport, page 122.

The Talismán–El Carmen route rarely sees much heavy traffic. It's better to change money in Tapachula than with money-changers at the border. Both Mexican and Guatemalan immigration (200 m apart) are open 24 hours. Talismán is 16 km from Tapachula, from where ADO buses depart to major destinations in Chiapas and Oaxaca. This crossing also offers easy access to the Soconusco region along the Mexican Pacific coast. Once in Guatemala, there are connections to Malacatán and onwards to Quetzaltenango.

The main Pan-American Highway crossing, which also connects with Tapachula, is Ciudad Hidalgo–Tecún Umán. Both immigration offices are open 24 hours. Tapachula is 40 km from Ciudad Hidalgo, 30 minutes, with connections to the Soconuso and beyond. Once in Guatemala, there are connections to Coatepeque, Mazatenango and Retalhuleu. There are also a few express buses daily to Guatemala, five hours.

Ciudad Cuauhtémoc–La Mesilla

The fastest, easiest and most scenic route between Chiapas and western Guatemala is via Ciudad Cuauhtémoc. Currency exchange rates are not generally favourable at the border. ATMs are in La Mesilla on the Guatemala side.

For a good, first-hand overview of the challenges of travelling overland in your own vehicle, get hold of a copy of *Panama or Bust*, by Jim Jaillet, www.panamaorbust.com, which covers the challenges of preparing for and completing a year-long trip from the US to Panama and back.

Security Spare no ingenuity in making your car secure. Avoid leaving the car unattended except in a locked garage or guarded parking space. Remove all belongings and leave the empty glove compartment open when the car is unattended. Also lock the clutch or accelerator to the steering wheel with a heavy, obvious chain or lock. Street children will generally protect your car in exchange for a tip. Note down key numbers and carry spares of the most important ones, but don't keep all spares inside the vehicle.

Shipping a vehicle to Central America Two recommended shipping lines are **Wallenius Wilhelmsen** ① *head office in Norway, T+47-6758-4100, for other offices visit www.2wglobal. com*, and, in the US, **American Cargo Service Inc** ① *T305-592-8065*. Motorcyclists will find good online recommendations at www.horizonsunlimited.com.

Car hire

While not everyone has the time or inclination to travel with their own car, the freedom that goes with renting for a few days is well worth considering, especially if you can get a group of three or four together to share the cost. The main international car hire companies

Immigration offices on both sides are open 0600-2100. On the Mexican side, there is a cheap hotel, a restaurant and ADO bus station, from where infrequent ADO buses operate to major destinations. Frequent *colectivo* shuttles go to Comitán (with onward connections to San Cristóbal de las Casas). The Guatemalan border is a few kilometres from Ciudad Cuautémoc, but cannot be walked; take a taxi/*colectivo* instead. In Guatemala, buses go to Huehuetenango (two hours) and on to Quetzaltenango (four hours). See also page 142.

Tenosique–El Ceibo

An interesting route is southeast from Palenque via Tenosique and El Ceibo, offering access to the Petén in Guatemala. Try to bring the currency you need, although local shops or restaurants may exchange. Both immigration offices are open 0700-1800. *Colectivos* and taxis travel from El Ceibo to the market at Tenosique and there are onward connections to Palenque (two hours). In Guatemala, there are several daily buses to Flores/Santa Elena (four to five hours). See also page 147.

Frontera Corozal–Bethel/La Técnica

Alternatively, you can cross at Frontera Corozal–Bethel/La Técnica for Santa Elena/Flores, a relatively easy crossing on the Río Usumacinta. From Corozal the boat journey to Bethel is 40 minutes, US$30-60 per boat. The journey to La Técnica is five minutes, US$3.50 per person, from where you must take a bus to Bethel for formalities. Immigration on both sides is open 0900-1800. Note robberies have been reported on the road to La Técnica; check the security situation before setting out. In Guatemala there are just a handful of daily buses to Flores/Santa Elena, so arrive early. See also pages 158 and 159. It is four hours by bus to Palenque from Frontera Corozal, so set out early.

operate in all countries, but tend to be expensive. Hotels and tourist agencies will tell you where to find cheaper rates, but you will need to check that you have such basics as a spare wheel, toolkit, functioning lights, etc. If you plan to do a lot of driving and will have time at the end to dispose of it, investigate the possibility of buying a second-hand car locally; since hiring is so expensive it may work out cheaper and will probably do you just as well.

Car hire insurance Check exactly what the hirer's insurance policy covers. In many cases it will only protect you against minor bumps and scrapes, not major accidents, or 'natural' damage (for example flooding). Ask if extra cover is available. Also find out, if using a credit card, whether the card automatically includes insurance. Beware of being billed for scratches that were on the vehicle before you hired it. When you return the vehicle make sure you check it with someone at the office and get signed evidence that it is returned in good condition and that you will not be charged.

Driving in southern Mexico

Vehicles may be brought into Mexico on a **tourist permit** for 180 days each year. You can enter and leave as often as you like during that time, but you must have a new tourist card or visa on each occasion you enter. The necessary documents are: passport, birth certificate or naturalization papers; tourist card; vehicle registration (if you do not own the car, a notarized letter from the vehicle's owner or the hire company is necessary); and a valid international or national driving licence. Two photocopies are required for each. There are

BORDER CROSSING
Belize–Guatemala

Benque Viejo–Menchor de Mencos
The most commonly used crossing is between Benque Viejo del Carmen and Melchor de Mencos (see page 290), popular with those travelling between Belize and Tikal. Taxi rip-offs are common; bargain hard. For currency exchange, there are good rates on the street; or try Banrural at the border (0700-2000). Both immigration offices are open 0600-2000. There are several buses a day from Melchor de Mencos to Santa Elena (Flores), two to three hours; *colectivo* 1½ hours. In Belize, there are regular buses to Belize City. If you leave Santa Elena, Guatemala, at 0500, you can be in Belize City by 1200. Also direct buses operate from Flores to Chetumal (Mexico) with Línea Dorada.

Punta Gorda–Puerto Barrios/Lívingston
Another crossing is by sea between Punta Gorda and Puerto Barrios. Boat services go from Punta Gorda in Belize to Puerto Barrios and Lívingston in Guatemala; see page 323. They include **Requena Water Taxi**, 12 Front Street, T722-2070, departing from the dock opposite immigration. Schedules change and are irregular; arrive as early as possible or better yet, arrange in advance. It's best to buy quetzals in Guatemala. At Belizean immigration, obtain stamps from the customs house near the pier on Front Street and allow up to two hours for processing. If you arrive in Guatemala by boat, check into immigration immediately. Offices are in Puerto Barrios and Lívingston; both open 24 hours. There are highway connections from Puerto Barrios to Guatemala City and Flores and in Belize, there are connections with southern Belize.

heavy fines for overstaying or failing to surrender your entry documents at the end of your visit. It takes 10 days to extend a permit, so ask for more time than you need. The Sanborn's website (www.sanbornsinsurance.com) is an excellent source of information.

Around US$50 is charged for the permit, payable only by credit card, not a debit card, in the name of the car owner. You also have to buy a bond in cash to the value of the vehicle according to its age (a set scale exists, US$200-400). The payment is divided into two parts, the bond itself and administration costs; the latter is retained by the authorities and only the bond is refunded.

On entry, go to *Migración* for your tourist card, then go to the **Banjército** desk and sign an *Importación Temporal de Vehículos/Promesa de retornar vehículo*, which bears all vehicle and credit card details so that if you sell your car illegally you can be debited for the import duty. Next you purchase the *Solicitud de importación temporal*, which must be displayed on the windscreen. Then go to *Copias* to photocopy all necessary documents.

Insurance Foreign insurance will not be honoured; be sure that the company you insure with will settle accident claims inside Mexico. Entering Mexico from Guatemala presents few local insurance problems now. **Tepeyac** ⓘ *www.mapfretepeyac.com, or through English-speaking agents www.mexadventure.com, T800-485 4075*, has an office in Tapachula; and **Seguros La Provincial** ⓘ *Av General Utrillo 10A, upstairs, San Cristóbal de las Casas, also has* an office in Cuauhtémoc: *Av Cuauhtémoc 1217 ground floor, Sr García Figueroa, T5-604-0500*. Otherwise, try **Segumex** in Tuxtla Gutiérrez. In Mexico City, try **Grupo Nacional Provincial** ⓘ *Río de la Plata 48, T528-67732, www.gnp.com.mx*, which has offices in many towns; or **Sanborn's Mexican Insurance Service** ⓘ *2009 S 10th St, McAllen, TX 78505-0310, T956-686-0711, www.sanbornsinsurance.com*. Policy prices vary greatly between companies.

Petrol/diesel All *gasolina* is now unleaded and all petrol stations are franchised by Petróleos Mexicanos (PEMEX). Fuel costs are likely to be in flux with the floating of Pemex in 2015, approximately: regular, US$1/l; premium, US$1.07/l; diesel US$1.07. Petrol stations are not self-service; it is normal to give the attendant a small tip.

Assistance **Angeles Verdes** (Green Angels) ⓘ *www.av.sectur.gob.mx*, patrol many of Mexico's main roads. Call them toll-free on T078; every state also has an Angeles Verdes hotline. The drivers speak English, are trained to give first aid, make minor auto repairs and deal with flat tyres. Assistance is provided free of charge, you pay for the fuel.

Road tolls A toll is called a *cuota*, as opposed to a non-toll road, which is a *vía libre*. There are many toll charges and the cost works out at around one peso per kilometre. Check out your route, and toll prices, on the **Traza Tu Ruta** section of www.sct.gob.mx.

In case of accident Do not abandon your vehicle. Call your insurance company immediately to inform it. Do not leave Mexico without first filing a claim. Do not sign any contract or agreement without a representative of the insurance company being present. Always carry with you, in the insured vehicle, your policy identification card and the names of the company's adjusters. A helpline for road accidents is available by phoning T02 and asking the operator to connect you to T55-5684 9715 or T55-5684 9761.

Warnings On all roads, if the driver flashes their lights they are claiming right of way and the oncoming traffic must give way. At *Alto* (Halt) signs, all traffic must come to a complete stop. Always avoid driving at night because night-time robberies are on the increase. Sleeping policemen or speed bumps can be hazardous as there are often no warning signs; they are sometimes marked *zona de topes*, or incorrectly marked as *vibradores*.

Car hire Car rental is very expensive in Mexico, from US$35-45 a day for a basic model (plus 15% sales tax). The age limit is normally at least 25 and you'll need to place a deposit, normally against a credit card, for damage. It can be cheaper to arrange hire in the US or Europe. Renting a vehicle is nearly impossible without a credit card. It is twice as expensive to leave a car at a different point from the starting point than it is to make a round trip. Rates will vary from city to city. Make sure you have unlimited mileage.

Driving in Belize

Motorists should carry their own driving licence and certificate of vehicle ownership. Third-party insurance is mandatory and can be purchased at any border: US$12.50 a week, US$25 a month, cars and motorbikes are the same, cover up to US$10,000 from the **Insurance Corporation of Belize** ⓘ *7 Daly St, Belize City, T224-5328, www.icbinsurance.com*. Border offices are open Monday-Friday 0500-1700, Saturday 0600-1600. There are also offices in every district. Valid international driving licences are accepted in place of Belize driving permits. Fuel costs about US$1.50 a litre.

BORDER CROSSING

Belize–Honduras

Placencia–Puerto Cortés
There is a weekly boat service from Placencia, via Mango Creek, to Puerto Cortés (see page 319); in good weather the crossing takes two hours. Obtain all necessary exit stamps and visas before sailing.

Dangriga–Puerto Cortés
A cabin cruiser, *Nesymein Neydy*, travels from Dangriga to Puerto Cortés every Thursday and Saturday at 0900, arriving in Puerto Cortés around 1400, around US$50. The boat leaves the North Riverside dock. Ensure all your paperwork is in order before departure.

Car hire When choosing a car rental company (see page 269) check if it will release registration papers to enable cars to enter Guatemala or Mexico. Without obtaining them at the time of hire it is impossible to take hire cars across national borders. Car hire cost is high in Belize owing to the heavy wear and tear on the vehicles. You can expect to pay between US$65 for a Suzuki Samuri and US$125 for an Isuzu Trooper per day. Drive carefully as road conditions are constantly changing and totally unpredictable, with speed bumps, cyclists and pedestrians appearing around every bend. When driving in the Mountain Pine Ridge area it is prudent to check carefully on road conditions at the entry gate; good maps are essential. Emory King's annually updated *Drivers' Guide to Belize* is helpful when driving to the more remote areas.

Driving in Guatemala

Think carefully before driving a vehicle in Guatemala as it can be hazardous. Of the 14,000 km of roads, the 45% that are paved have improved greatly in recent years and are now of a high standard, making road travel faster and safer. Even cycle tracks (*ciclovías*) are beginning to appear on new roads. However, a new driving hazard in the highlands is the deep gully (for rainwater or falling stones) alongside the road. High clearance is essential on many roads in remoter areas and a 4WD vehicle is useful.

Bringing a vehicle into Guatemala requires the following procedure: presentation of a valid international driving licence; a check by **Cuarantena Agropecuaria** (Ministry of Agriculture quarantine) to check you are not importing fruit or vegetables; at **Aduana** (Customs) you must pay US$4.50 for all forms and a tourist vehicle permit for your vehicle. A motorcycle entry permit costs the same as one for a car. The description of your vehicle on the registration document must match your vehicle's appearance exactly. You must own the car/motorcycle and your name must be on the title papers. When entering the country, ask the officials to add any important accessories you have to the paper. Car insurance can be bought at the borders.

On leaving the country by car or motorcycle, two stamps on a strip of paper are required: surrender the vehicle permit at customs and the **Cuarantena Agropecuaria** (quarantine) inspection, which is not always carried out. It is better not to import and sell foreign cars in Guatemala, as import taxes are very high.

BORDER CROSSING

Guatemala–Honduras

Links with Honduras are possible on the Caribbean near Corinto (see page 435); for the ruins at Copán the best crossing is El Florido (see page 465). The crossing at Agua Caliente is another option.

El Florido

A popular and busy crossing, but straightforward for pedestrians. If entering Honduras just to visit Copán ruins, you can get a temporary 72-hour exit pass, but you must return on time. There are numerous money-changers, but you'll find better rates in Copán. Immigration offices are open 0700-1900. Minibuses run all day until 1700 to Copán ruins and, on the Guatemalan side, there are numerous minibus services to Guatemala City and Antigua.

Entre Ríos–Corinto

This is a Caribbean coast crossing. A road connects Puerto Barrios (Guatemala) and Puerto Cortés (Honduras) with a bridge over the Motagua river. Get your exit stamp in Puerto Barrios or Lívingston if you are leaving by boat to Honduras. If you arrive by boat, go straight to either of these offices. Honduran immigration is at Corinto if crossing from Puerto Barrios in Guatemala. In Honduras, there are connections to the northern coast. Buses leave Corinto for Omoa and Puerto Cortés every hour or so. In Guatemala there is access to Guatemala City and Santa Elena/Flores.

Agua Caliente

A busy crossing, but quicker, cheaper and more efficient than the one at El Florido. There are banks, a tourist office, *comedor* and *hospedaje* on the Honduran side. If leaving Honduras, keep some lempiras for the ride from Agua Caliente to Esquipulas. Immigration on both sides is open 0700-1800. In Honduras there are several buses daily from Agua Caliente to San Pedro Sula, six to seven hours, and frequent services to Nueva Ocotepeque. In Guatemala minibuses go to Esquipulas with connections to Guatemala City, Chiquimula and the highway to Flores.

Petrol/disese 'Normal' costs US$1.07, 'premium' US$1.09, and diesel is US$1.09 per litre, though prices are in flux due to changing oil prices. Unleaded (*sin plomo*) is available in major cities, at Melchor de Mencos and along the Pan-American Highway, but not in the countryside, although it is gradually being introduced across the country.

Car hire Average rates are US$35-100 per day. Credit cards or cash are accepted for rental. Local cars are usually cheaper than those at international companies; if you book ahead from abroad with the latter, take care that they do not offer you a different vehicle claiming your original request is not available. Cars may not always be taken into neighbouring countries (none are allowed into Mexico or Belize); rental companies that do allow their vehicles to cross borders charge for permits and paperwork. If you wish to drive to Copán, you must check this is permissible and you need a letter authorizing you to take the vehicle in to Honduras. **Tabarini** and **Hertz** allow their cars to cross the border.

BORDER CROSSING
Guatemala–El Salvador

El Salvador and Guatemala are covered under the CA-4 border control agreement (see box, page 509) but you must still submit to immigration formalities before proceeding.

Frontera–San Cristóbal

The main Pan-American highway crossing, used by international buses and heavy traffic. Immigration on both sides is open 0600-2200, but it's usually possible to cross outside these hours with extra charges. In El Salvador, there are regular buses to Santa Ana, No 201, with connections to San Salvador, 1½ hours. In Guatemala, there are buses to Guatemala City, two to three hours.

Valle Nuevo–Las Chinamas

The fastest road link from San Salvador to Guatemala City, but it's busy. It's a straightforward crossing though with quick service if your papers are ready. Change currency with the women in front of the ex-ITSU office; there's a good quetzal-dollar rate. Immigration offices on both sides are open 0800-1800. In El Salvador there are frequent buses to Ahuachapán, No 265, 25 minutes, with connecting services to San Salvador, No 202. Alternatively, try to negotiate a seat with an international Pullman bus; most pass between 0800 and 1400. Onwards to Guatemala there are connections to Guatemala City, two hours.

Ciudad Pedro Alvarado–La Hachadura

This border is at the bridge over the Río Paz, with a filling station and a few shops nearby. It's increasingly popular, thanks to improved roads. Private vehicles require a lot of paperwork and can take two hours to process. It gives access to El Salvador's Pacific Coast, and there are services to San Salvador's Terminal Occidente, No 498, three hours, and to Ahuachapán, No 503, one hour. The last bus to Sonsonate is at 1800. In Guatemala, there is access to the Pacific coast and Guatemala City.

Anguiatú

Normally a quiet border crossing, except when there are special events at Esquipulas in Guatemala. Immigration offices are open 0600-1900. Once in El Salvador there are buses to Santa Ana, No 235A, two hours, and to Metapán, 40 minutes, from where a rough but very scenic road runs to El Poy. In Guatemala, there's good access north to Tikal. Head for the Padre Miguel junction, 19 km from the border, from where you can make connections to Chiquimula and Esquipulas.

Cycles and motorbikes

Cycling Unless you are planning a journey almost exclusively on paved roads – when a high-quality touring bike would probably suffice – a mountain bike is recommended. The good-quality ones are incredibly tough and rugged. Although touring bike and to a lesser extent mountain bike spares are available in the larger Mexicana and Central American cities, you'll find that locally manufactured goods are often shoddy and rarely last. In some countries, such as Mexico, imported components can be found but they tend to be very expensive. Buy everything you can before you leave home.

The **Expedition Advisory Centre** ⓘ *T+44-(0)20-7591-3030, www.rgs.org*, has published a booklet on planning a long-distance bike trip titled *Bicycle Expeditions,* by Paul Vickers. Published in March 1990, it is available as a PDF from the website or £5 for a photocopy. In the UK the **Cyclists' Touring Club** ⓘ *T0844-736-8450, www.ctc.org.uk*, has information on touring, technical information and discusses the relative merits of different types of bikes.

Motorbikes People are generally very friendly to motorcyclists and you can make many friends by returning friendship to those who show an interest in you. Buying a bike in the States and driving down works out cheaper than buying one in Europe. In making your choice go for a comfortable bike. The motorcycle should be off-road capable, without necessarily being an off-road bike. A passport, international driving licence and bike registration document are required.

Security This is not a problem in most countries. Try not to leave a fully laden bike on its own. A D-lock or chain will keep the bike secure. An alarm gives you peace of mind if you leave the bike outside a hotel at night. Look for hotels that have a courtyard or more secure parking and never leave luggage on the bike overnight or whilst unattended. Also take a cover for the bike.

Border crossings All borders in Central America seem to work out at about US$20 per vehicle. The exceptions to this are Mexico (see above). All borders are free on exit, or should be on most occasions. Crossing borders on a Sunday or a holiday normally incurs double the standard charges in Central American countries. It is sometimes very difficult to find out exactly what is being paid for. If in doubt, ask to see the boss and/or the rule book.

Hitchhiking

Hitchhiking in Mexico and Central America is reasonably safe and straightforward for males and couples, provided you speak some Spanish. It is a most enjoyable mode of transport: a good way to meet the local people, to improve one's languages and to learn about the country. If trying to hitchhike away from main roads and in sparsely populated areas, however, allow plenty of time, and ask first about the volume of traffic on the road. On long journeys, set out at the crack of dawn, which is when trucks usually leave. They tend to go longer distances than cars. However, it should be said that hitchhiking involves inherent risks and should be approached sensibly and with caution.

Maps

Maps from the **Institutos Geográficos Militares** in capital cities are often the only good maps available in Latin America. It is therefore wise to get as many as possible in your home country before leaving, especially if travelling overland. An excellent series of maps covering the whole region and each country is published by **International Travel Maps** (**ITM**) ⓘ *T604-273-1400, www.itmb.com*, most with historical notes by the late Kevin Healey.

An excellent source of maps is **Stanfords** ⓘ *12-14 Long Acre, Covent Garden, London, WC2E 9LP, T+44-020-7836-1321, www.stanfords.co.uk, also in Bristol and Manchester.*

Essentials A-Z

Children

Travel with children can bring you into closer contact with Latin American families and generally presents no special problems; in fact, the path is often smoother for family groups. Officials tend to be more amenable where children are concerned. Always carry a copy of your child's birth certificate and passport photos. For an overview of travelling with children, visit www.babygoes2.com.

Public transport

Overland travel in Latin America can involve a lot of time spent waiting for public transport. It is easier to take biscuits, drinks, bread, etc with you on longer trips than to rely on meal stops where the food may not be to taste. All airlines charge a reduced price for children under 12 and less for children under 2. Double check the child's baggage allowance though; some are as low as 7 kg. On long-distance buses children generally pay half or reduced fares. For shorter trips it is cheaper, if less comfortable, to seat small children on your knee. Often there are spare seats that children can occupy after tickets have been collected. In city and local buses, small children do not generally pay a fare, but are not entitled to a seat when paying customers are standing. On sightseeing tours you should always bargain for a family rate; often children can go free. Note that a child travelling free on a long excursion is not always covered by the operator's travel insurance.

Hotels

Try to negotiate family rates. If charges are per person, always insist that 2 children will occupy 1 bed only, therefore counting as 1 tariff. If rates are per bed, the same applies. It is quite common for children under 12 to be allowed to stay for no extra charge as long as they are sharing your room.

Customs and duty free

Duty free allowances and export restrictions for each country are listed below. It goes without saying that drugs, firearms and banned products should not be traded or taken across international boundaries.

Mexico

Adults entering Mexico are allowed to bring in up to 6 litres of wine and 3 litres of spirits; 20 packs of cigarettes, or 25 cigars, or 200 g of tobacco and medicines for personal use. Goods imported into Mexico with a value of more than US$500 (with the exception of computer equipment, where the limit is US$4000) have to be handled by an officially appointed agent. If you are carrying more than US$10,000 in cash you should declare it. You may not take archaeological artefacts out of the country. Full details and latest updates are available at www.aduanas.sat.gob.mx.

Belize

Import allowances are: 200 cigarettes, 50 cigars or 250 g of tobacco; 1 litre of alcohol, spirits and/or wine. No fruit or vegetables may be brought into Belize; searches are infrequent, but can be thorough. Pets must have proof of rabies inoculations and a vet's certificate of good health.

Guatemala

You are allowed to take in, free of duty, personal effects and articles for your own use, 5 litres of alcohol, 2 kg of confectionery, and 500 g of tobacco in any form. Temporary visitors can take in any amount in quetzales or foreign currencies. The local equivalent of US$100 per person may be reconverted into US dollars on departure at the airport, provided a ticket for immediate departure is shown. You may not import or export meat, fish, vegetables or fruit.

Disabled travellers

In most Latin American countries, facilities for disabled travellers are severely lacking. Most airports and hotels and restaurants in major resorts have wheelchair ramps and adapted toilets. Pavements are often in such a poor state of repair that walking is precarious.

Some travel companies specialize in exciting holidays, tailor-made for individuals depending on their level of disability. Disabled Travelers, www.disabledtravelers.com, provides travel information for disabled adventurers and includes a number of links, reviews and tips. You might also want to read *Nothing Ventured*, edited by Alison Walsh (Harper Collins), which gives personal accounts of worldwide journeys by disabled travellers, plus advice and listings.

Dress

Casual clothing is adequate for most occasions although men may need a jacket and tie in some restaurants. Dress conservatively in indigenous communities and small churches. Topless bathing is generally unacceptable.

Drugs

Users of drugs without medical prescription should be particularly careful, as some countries impose heavy penalties – up to 10 years' imprisonment – for even the simple possession of such substances. The planting of drugs on travellers, by traffickers or the police, is not unknown. If offered drugs on the street, make no response at all and keep walking. Note that people who roll their own cigarettes are often suspected of carrying drugs and are subjected to close searches.

If you are taking illegal drugs – even ones that are widely and publically used – be aware that authorities do set traps from time to time. Should you get into trouble, your embassy is unlikely to be very sympathetic.

Electricity

127 volts/60 Hz, US-style 2-pin plug.

Embassies and consulates

For a list of Mexican, Belizean and Guatemalan embassies abroad, see http://embassy.goabroad.com.

Gay and lesbian travellers

Most of Mexico and Central America is not particularly liberal in its attitudes to gays and lesbians. Having said that, times are changing and you'll find there is a gay scene with bars and clubs at least in most of the bigger cities and resorts. Helpful websites include www.gayscape.com, www.gaypedia.com and www.iglta.org (International Gay and Lesbian Travel Association).

Health

See your GP or travel clinic at least 6 weeks before departure for general advice on travel risks and vaccinations. Try a specialist travel clinic if your own GP is unfamiliar with health conditions in Mexico and Central America. Make sure you have sufficient medical travel insurance, get a dental check, know your own blood group and if you suffer a long-term condition such as diabetes or epilepsy, obtain a Medic Alert bracelet/ necklace (www.medicalert.co.uk). If you wear glasses, take a copy of your prescription.

Vaccinations

Vaccinations for tetanus, hepatitis A and typhoid are commonly recommended for all countries covered in this book. In addition, yellow fever vaccination is required if entering from an infected area (ie parts of South America). Vaccinations may also be advised against tuberculosis, hepatitis B, rabies and diptheria and, in the case of Guatemala, cholera. The final decision, however, should be based on a consultation with your GP or travel clinic. In all cases you should confirm your primary courses and boosters are up to date.

Health risks

The most common cause of **travellers' diarrhoea** is from eating contaminated food. In Central America, drinking water is rarely the culprit, although it's best to be cautious (see below). Swimming in sea or river water that has been contaminated by sewage can also be a cause; ask locally if it is safe. Diarrhoea may be also caused by viruses, bacteria (such as E-coli), protozoal (such as giardia), salmonella and cholera. It may be accompanied by vomiting or by severe abdominal pain. Any kind of diarrhoea responds well to the replacement of water and salts. Sachets of rehydration salts can be bought in most chemists and can be dissolved in boiled water. If symptoms persist, consult a doctor. Most towns have at least one laboratory where you can test for parasites (eg amoebas) and other nasties, but be aware that depending on the hatching cycle, you may require several days of consecutive testing before pathogens show up. Tap water in the major cities may be safe to drink but it is advisable to err on the side of caution and drink only bottled or boiled water. Avoid ice in drinks unless you trust that it is from a reliable source.

Travelling in high altitudes can bring on **altitude sickness**. On reaching heights above 3000 m, the heart may start pounding and the traveller may experience shortness of breath. Smokers and those with underlying heart or lung disease are often hardest hit. Take it easy for the first few days, rest and drink plenty of water, you will feel better soon. It is essential to get acclimatized before undertaking long treks or arduous activities.

Malaria precautions are essential for some parts of Mexico and Central America, particularly some rural areas. Once again, check with your GP or travel clinic well in advance of departure. Avoid being bitten by mosquitoes as much as possible. Sleep off the ground and use a mosquito net and some kind of insecticide. Mosquito coils release insecticide as they burn and are available in many shops, as are tablets of insecticide, which are placed on a heated mat plugged into a wall socket.

If you get sick

Contact your embassy or consulate for a list of doctors and dentists who speak your language, or at least some English. Good-quality healthcare is available in the larger centres but it can be expensive, especially hospitalization. Make sure you have adequate insurance (see below).

Useful websites

www.btha.org British Travel Health Association.

www.cdc.gov US government site that gives excellent advice on travel health and details of disease outbreaks.

www.fco.gov.uk British Foreign and Commonwealth Office travel site has useful information on each country, people, climate and a list of UK embassies/consulates.

www.fitfortravel.scot.nhs.uk A-Z of vaccine/health advice for each country.

www.numberonehealth.co.uk Travel screening services, vaccine and travel health advice, email/SMS text vaccine reminders and screens returned travellers for tropical diseases.

Insurance

Insurance is strongly recommended and policies are very reasonable. If you have financial restraints, the most important aspect of any insurance policy is medical care and repatriation. Ideally you want to make sure you are covered for personal items too. Read the small print before heading off so you are aware of what is covered and what is not, what is required to submit a claim and what to do in the event of an emergency. Always buy insurance before setting out as your options will be more limited and generally quite costly once you've departed from your home country.

Internet

Public access to the internet is endemic with cybercafés in both large and small towns. Many hotels and cafés also have Wi-Fi. Speeds and connections are often unreliable, particularly with smart phones and data hungry applications that place strain on the bandwidth. When using public Wi-Fi, please be considerate of other users.

Language

Spanish is spoken throughout most of Mexico and Central America and, while you will be able to get by without knowledge of Spanish, you will probably become frustrated and feel helpless in many situations. English, or any other language, is useless off the beaten track (except in Belize). A pocket dictionary and phrase book together with some initial study or a beginner's Spanish course before you leave are strongly recommended. If you have the time, book 1-2 weeks of classes at the beginning of your travels. Some areas have developed a reputation for language classes, including Antigua and Quetzaltenango in Guatemala. The better-known centres normally include a wide range of cultural activities and supporting options for homestay. A less well-known centre is likely to have fewer English speakers around. For details, see Language schools in the What to do sections of individual towns and cities.

Not all the locals speak Spanish, of course; you will find that some indigenous people in the more remote areas – the highlands of Guatemala for example – speak only their indigenous languages, although there will usually be some people in a village who can speak Spanish. Regarding pronunciation in Guatemala, 'X' is pronounced 'sh', as in Xela (shay-la).

Language tuition

Arranging language tuition internationally is increasingly popular.

AmeriSpan, 1334 Walnut St (PO Box 58129), 6th floor, Philadelphia, PA 19107, T1-215-751-1100, T1-800-879-6640, www.amerispan.com (also with offices in Antigua, Guatemala). One of the most comprehensive options, offering Spanish immersion programmes, educational tours, volunteer and internship positions throughout Latin America.

Cactus Language, 4 Clarence House, T0845-130-4775, www.cactuslanguagetraining. com. Spanish language courses from 1 week in duration in Mexico and Central America, with pre-trip classes in the UK. Also has additional options for volunteer work, diving and staying with host families.

Institute for Spanish Language Studies, in the US on T1-866-391-0394, www.isls.com. Has schools in Mexico, offering innovative and flexible programmes.

Spanish Abroad, T1-888-722-7623 (USA and Canada), T1-602-778-6791 (worldwide), www.spanishabroad.com. Intensive Spanish immersion programmes throughout Latin America for those wishing to study abroad.

Media

Latin America has more local and community radio stations than practically anywhere else in the world; a shortwave (world band) radio (or an equivalent phone app) offers a practical means to brush up on the language, sample popular culture and absorb some of the richly varied regional music. International broadcasters also transmit across Central America in both English and Spanish, these include the **BBC World Service**, www.bbc.co.uk/worldservice/index.shtml for schedules and frequencies, the **Voice of America**, www.voa.gov, and Boston (Mass)-based **Monitor Radio International**, operated by Christian Science Monitor, www.csmonitor.com. **Putumayo World Music**, www.putumayo.com specialize in the exotic sounds of Mexican music.

Mexico

The influential daily newspapers are: *Excelsior*, *Novedades*, *El Día*, *Uno Más Uno*, *El Universal*, *El Heraldo*, *La Jornada* (www.jornada. unam.mx, more to the left, with *Tiempo Libre*, listing cultural activities in Mexico City), *La Prensa* (a popular tabloid, with the largest circulation) and *El Nacional* (mouthpiece of the government). There are influential weekly magazines: *Proceso*, *Siempre*, *Epoca* and *Quehacer Político*. The political satirical weekly is *Los Agachados*. *The Miami Herald* is stocked by most newsstands.

Belize

There are no daily newspapers in Belize. News is available in the weeklies, which generally come out on Friday morning, with the forthcoming Sunday's date: *The Belize Times* (PUP supported), *The Guardian* (UDP supported), *The Reporter* and *Amandala*. Good coverage of Ambergris Caye is provided by *The San Pedro Sun*; likewise, *Placencia Breeze* covers Placencia. Small district newspapers are published sporadically. Radio station *Love FM* (95.1FM) is the perfect summary of Belize on the airwaves. Try www.belizeweb.com for Belizean internet radio.

Guatemala

The main newspaper is *Prensa Libre* (www. prensalibre.com). The *Guatemala Post*, www.guatemala post.com, is published in English online. *Siglo Veintiuno*, www. sigloxxi.com, is a good newspaper. One of the most popular papers is *Nuestro Diario*, a tabloid with more gory pics than copy. The *Revue*, www.revuemag.com, produced monthly in Antigua, carries articles, maps, advertisements, lodgings, tours and excursions, covering Antigua, Panajachel, Quetzaltenango, Río Dulce, Monterrico, Cobán, Flores and Guatemala City.

Currency and exchange

For up-to-the-minute exchange rates visit www.xe.com.

While most – but not all – countries in Mexico and Central America have their own currencies, the most useful foreign currency in the region is the US dollar. Banks and *casas de cambio* are increasingly able to change euros but the dollar is still the most readily accepted and changed.

The 3 main ways of keeping in funds while travelling are still US dollars cash, plastic (credit cards) and US dollar TCs.

Mexico

→ *US$1=$15.09 pesos (Apr 2015).*
The monetary unit is the Mexican peso, represented by '$' – the dollar sign – which provides great potential for confusion, especially in popular tourist places where prices are higher and often quoted in US dollars (US$).

Belize

→ *US$1=Bz$2 (stabilized).*
The monetary unit is the Belize dollar. Currency notes issued by the Central Bank are in denominations of 100, 50, 20, 10, 5 and 2 dollars, and coins of 2 dollars and 1 dollar; 50, 25, 10, 5 and 1 cent coins are in use. The American expressions quarter (25c), dime (10c) and nickel (5c) are used, although 25c is sometimes referred to as a shilling. US dollars are accepted everywhere. A common cause for complaint or misunderstanding is uncertainty about which currency you are paying in. The price tends to be given in US$ when the hundred Belizean dollar mark is breached; make sure it is clear from the start whether you are being charged in US or Belizean dollars.

Guatemala

→ *US$1=7.65 quetzales (Apr 2015).*
The unit is the quetzal, divided into 100 centavos. There are coins of 1 quetzal,

50 centavos, 25 centavos, 10 centavos, 5 centavos and 1 centavo. Paper currency is in denominations of 5, 10, 20, 50, 100 and 200 quetzales.

There is often a shortage of small change; ask for small notes when you first change money to pay hotel bills, transport, etc.

Cash

The chief benefit of taking US dollars is that they are accepted almost everywhere. However, in some places they are only accepted if they are in excellent condition – no small tears, rips, nicks, holes or scribbles. When ordering money at home bear this in mind. Take a selection of bills including several low-value US dollar bills (US$5 or US$10) which can be carried for changing into local currency if arriving in a country when banks or *casas de cambio* are closed, and for use in out of the way places when you may run out of local currency. They are also very useful for shopping: shopkeepers and *casas de cambio* tend to give better exchange rates than hotels or banks (but see below).

If your budget is tight it is essential to avoid situations where you are forced to change money regardless of the rate; watch weekends and public holidays carefully and never run out of local currency. Take plenty of local currency, in small denominations, when making trips away from the major towns and resorts.

Whenever possible change your money at a bank or a *casa de cambio*. Black markets and street changers have largely disappeared; avoid them if you can as you are unlikely to get a significantly better rate and you place yourself a greater risk of being ripped off. If you need to change money on the street, do not do so alone. If you are unsure about rates of exchange when you enter a country, check at the border with more than one changer, or ask locals or any traveller who may be leaving that country. Whenever you leave a country, sell any local currency before leaving; the further you get away from a country, the less

the value of a country's money and in some cases you may not be able to change it at all.

Note In Belize, the government has restricted the exchange of foreign currency to government-licensed *casas de cambio*, but these only operate in major towns. You can still find some money changers at the borders, but the exchange rate is not as high as it has been, and there is a risk of both you and the money changer being arrested and fined.

Debit and credit cards

Debit and credit cards are ideal for travelling, providing ready access to funds without carrying large amounts of cash on your person. In an ideal world taking a couple of cards (one Visa and one MasterCard) will make sure you are covered in most options. It is straightforward to obtain a cash advance against a credit card and even easier to withdraw cash from ATMs (Remove your credit card from the machine immediately after the transaction to avoid it being retained; getting it back can be difficult.) You may have to experiment with different ATM networks, especially in Guatemala, as they do work consistently. Keep a backup supply of cash until you figure out which ones support your card. The rates of exchange on ATM withdrawals are the best available for currency exchange but your bank or credit card company imposes a handling charge which is a percentage of the transaction, so try to avoid using your card to withdraw small amounts of cash. If your card is lost or stolen, immediately contact the 24-hr helpline of the issuer in your home country (find out the numbers to call before travelling and keep them in a safe place).

Currency cards

If you don't want to carry lots of cash, prepaid currency cards allow you to preload money from your bank account, fixed at the day's exchange rate. They look like a credit or debit card and are issued by specialist money-changing companies, such as **Travelex** and **Caxton FX**, and the **Post Office**. You can top up and check your balance by phone, online and sometimes by text.

Traveller's cheques

Traveller's cheques (TCs) are almost obsolete, shops and restaurants won't change them, but they do provide peace of mind against theft. Denominations of US$50 and US$100 are preferable, with a few of US$20 to increase your options. American Express or Visa US dollar TCs are recommended, but less commission is often charged on Citibank or Bank of America TCs if they are cashed at Latin American branches of those banks. Several banks charge a high fixed commission for changing TCs because they don't really want the bother. *Casas de cambio* are usually a much better choice for this service. Some establishments may ask to see a passport and the customer's record of purchase before accepting. Keep the original purchase slip in a separate place to the TCs and make a photocopy for security. The better hotels will normally change TCs for their guests (often at a poor rate).

Cost of travelling

Mexico and Belize are roughly 50-100% more expensive than Guatemala and most expensive on the coast and in resort towns. As a very approximate average calculation for all 3 countries, thrifty budget travellers can get by on US$25-40 a day, but that means that you won't be able to afford to take many excursions. A more realistic and sustainable budget is US$40-70. Plenty of travellers manage on smaller budgets but it's probably better to spend a little longer at home saving up, and then have a good time while you're away, rather than find yourself adding up the small change on a Sat night to see if you can afford a weekly beer. **Note** If you intend to do a lot of travelling in Mexico, bus transport can eat up a significant portion of your budget.

Opening hours

Mexico
Banks Mon-Fri 0900-1330 (some stay open later), Sat 0900-1230.
Businesses 0900/1000-1300/1400, then 1400/1500-1900 or later. Business hours vary considerably according to the climate and local custom.

Belize
Businesses 0800-1200, 1300-1600 and Fri 1900-2100, with half day on Wed. Small shops open additionally most late afternoons and evenings, and some on Sun 0800-1000.
Government and commercial offices Mon-Fri 0800-1200 and 1300-1600.

Guatemala
Banks Mon-Fri 0900-1500, Sat 0900-1300. Some city banks are introducing later hours, up to 2000; in the main tourist towns and shopping malls, some banks are open 7 days a week. **Shops** 0900-1300 and 1500-1900, often mornings only on Sat.

Photography

There is a charge of US$3-5 for the use of video cameras at historical sites. For professional camera equipment, including a tripod, the fee is much higher. Never take photos of indigenous people without prior permission.

Police

Probably the best advice with regards the police in Mexico and Central America is to have as little to do with them as possible. An exception to this rule are the tourist police, who operate in some of the big cities and resorts, and provide assistance. In general, law enforcement in Latin America is achieved by periodic campaigns, not systematically.

You may be asked for identification at any time and should therefore always have ID on you. If you cannot produce it, you may be jailed. If you are jailed, you should contact your embassy or consulate and take advice. In the event of a vehicle accident in which anyone is injured, all drivers involved are automatically detained until blame has been established, and this does not usually take less than 2 weeks. If a visitor is jailed his or her friends should provide food every day. This is especially important for people on a special diet, such as diabetics.

The giving and receiving of bribes is not recommended. However, the following advice may prove useful. Never offer a bribe unless you are fully conversant with the customs of the country. Wait until the official makes the suggestion, or offer money in some form that is apparently not bribery, for example 'In our country we have a system of on-the-spot fines (multas de inmediato). Is there a similar system here?' Do not assume that officials who accept a bribe are prepared to do anything else that is illegal. You bribe them to do their job, or not do it, or to do it more quickly, or more slowly. You do not bribe them to do something which is against the law. The mere suggestion would make them very upset. If an official suggests that a bribe must be paid before you can proceed on your way, be patient (assuming you have the time) and they may relent. Bear in mind that by bribing you are participating in a system that may cause you immense frustration.

Post

Postal services vary in efficiency from country to country and prices are quite high; pilfering is frequent. All mail, especially packages, should be registered. Check before leaving home if your embassy will hold mail and if so for how long, in preference to the Poste Restante/General Delivery (Lista de Correos) department of a country's Post Office. Cardholders can use Amex agencies. If you're expecting mail and there seems to be no mail at the Lista under the initial letter of your surname, ask them to look under the initial of your forename or your middle name.

If your name begins with 'W', look for letters under 'V' as well, or ask. For the smallest risk of misunderstanding, use title, initial and surname only.

Public holidays

Mexico
Feb/Mar Carnival/Mardi Gras. Traditionally throughout Latin America, this week is a time for celebration before the hardships of Lent; in Mexico it is particularly popular in Mérida.
15 Sep Cry for Independence. Celebrations which are particularly impressive in Mexico City.
16 Sep Independence Day. Regional festivities and parades.
2 Nov Day of the Dead. The souls of the deceased return to earth and family and friends turn out in costume and to meet them.
12 Dec Pilgrimage of thousands to the Basílica de Guadalupe, in northeast Mexico City, the most venerated shrine in Mexico. Well worth a visit.

Belize
10 Sep St George's Cay Day, with celebrations in Belize City that start with river races in San Ignacio.
19 Nov Settlement Day, celebrating the liberation (or arrival) of the Garífuna from distant shores. Also celebrated in Guatemala.

Guatemala
Mar/Apr Semana Santa, particularly colourful in Antigua with floats carrying Christ over wonderfully coloured and carefully placed carpets of flowers; also spectacular in Santiago Atitlán.
Nov Todos Santos Cuchumatán. All Saints' Day in the small town of Todos Santos, a colourful and drunken horse race with lots of dancing and antics. See box, page 404.

Punctuality

Punctuality is more of a concept than a reality in Latin countries. The mañana culture reigns supreme and any arrangement to meet at, say 1900, will normally rendezvous somewhere between 2000 and 2100. However, the one time you are late to catch a bus, boat or plane, it will leave on time – the rule is hurry up and wait.

Safety

Generally speaking, most places in Latin America are no more dangerous than any major city in Europe or North America and the people, if anything, are friendlier and more open. In provincial towns, main places of interest, on daytime buses and in ordinary restaurants the visitor should be quite safe. Nevertheless, in large cities (particularly in crowded places such as markets and bus stations) crime exists, mostly of the opportunistic kind. If you are aware of the dangers, act confidently and use your common sense, you will lessen many of the risks. The following tips, endorsed by travellers, are meant to forewarn, not alarm.

Keep all documents secure; hide your main cash supply in different places or under your clothes. Extra pockets sewn inside shirts and trousers, pockets closed with a zip or safety pin, money belts, neck or leg pouches, and elasticated support bandages for keeping money and cheques above the elbow or below the knee have been repeatedly recommended. Pouches worn outside the clothes are not safe. Keep cameras in bags (preferably with a chain or wire in the strap, so it can't be slashed) and don't wear fancy wristwatches or jewellery. Carry your small day pack in front of you.

Mexico

In recent years, Mexico's feuding drug cartels have been the cause of much unpleasant violence but, despite the horrific scenes reported by the international media, the problem is largely confined to the US border in sketchy *barrios* you are unlikely to see. Millions of people travel safely to Mexico every year and the Yucatán's homicide rate is actually lower than that in much of rural North America. If you are unfortunate enough to be a victim of crime, it is most likely to be an opportunistic theft, against which you must take the usual sensible precautions. Cars are a prime target; never leave possessions visible inside the car and park in hotel car parks after dark. Avoid travelling at night; if at all possible make journeys in daylight. Avoid lonely beaches, especially if you are a single woman. Speaking Spanish is a great asset for avoiding rip-offs targeting gringos, especially short changing and overcharging (both rife).

Belize

While attacks on foreigners are extremely rare, precautions are still advised, particularly if travelling alone or at night or in deserted areas. Crimes against travellers are harshly punished. Despite the apparent availability of illegal drugs, the authorities are keen to prevent their use. The penalties for possession of marijuana are 6 months in prison or a US$3000 fine, minimum.

Guatemala

In some parts of the country you may be subject to military or police checks. Local people can be reluctant to discuss politics with strangers. Do not necessarily be alarmed by 'gunfire', which is much more likely to be fireworks and bangers, a national pastime, especially early in the morning.

Robberies and serious assaults on tourists are becoming more common. While you can do nothing to counter the bad luck of being in the wrong place at the wrong time, sensible precautions can minimize risks. Single women should be especially careful. Tour groups are not immune and some excursion companies take precautions. Do not travel at night if at all possible and take care on roads that are more prone to vehicle hijacks: the road between Flores and the Belizean border, the highway between Antigua and Panajachel and the principal highway between the capital and El Salvadorean border. Assaults and robberies on the public (former US) buses have increased. There have been a high number of attacks on private vehicles leaving the airport.

Asistur, T1500/2421-2810 is a 24-hr, year-round tourist assistance programme for any problem or question. There is also a national tourist police force, **POLITUR**, T5561-2073, or for emergencies: T120/122/123. Other useful numbers include: **National police** T110; and **tourist police** in Antigua T832-7290.

Safety on public transport

When you have all your luggage with you at a bus station, be especially careful: don't get into arguments with any locals if you can help it and clip, tie or lock all the items together with a chain or cable if you are waiting for some time, or simply sit on top of your backpack. Take a taxi between airport/bus station/railway station and hotel, if you can afford it. Keep your bags with you in the taxi and pay only when you and your luggage are safely out of the vehicle (but keep an eye on it your luggage!). Avoid night buses unless essential or until you are comfortable travelling in the area; avoid arriving at night whenever possible; and watch your belongings whether they are stowed inside or outside the cabin (rooftop luggage racks create extra problems, which are sometimes unavoidable – many bus drivers cover rooftop luggage with plastic sheeting, but a waterproof bag or outer sack can be invaluable for protecting your luggage and for stopping someone rummaging through the top of your bag). Major bus lines often issue a luggage ticket when bags are stored in the hold; this is generally a safe system. When getting on a bus, keep your ticket handy as you will probably have to show it at some point. Finally, be wary of accepting food, drink, sweets or cigarettes from unknown fellow travellers on buses or trains; although extremely rare, they may be drugged, and you could wake up hours later without your belongings. In this connection, never accept a bar drink from an opened bottle (unless you can see that the bottle is in general use); always have it uncapped in front of you. Do not take shared taxis with strangers you have met on the bus, no matter how polite or well-dressed.

Scams

A number of distraction techniques such as mustard smearers and paint or shampoo sprayers and strangers' remarks like 'what's that on your shoulder?' or 'have you seen that dirt on your shoe?' are designed to distract you for a few critical moments in which time your bag may be grabbed. Furthermore, supposedly friendly assistance asking if you have dropped money or other items in the street work on the same premise. If someone follows you when you're in the street, let him catch up with you and give him the 'eye'. While you should take local advice about being out at night, do not assume that daytime is any safer. If walking after dark on quiet streets, walk in the road, not on the pavement.

Be wary of 'plain-clothes policemen'; insist on seeing identification and going to the police station by main roads. Do not hand over your identification (or money – which they should not need to see anyway) until you are at the station. On no account take them directly back to your lodgings. Be even more suspicious if they seek confirmation of their status from a passer-by. If someone implies they are asking for a bribe, insist on a receipt. If attacked, remember your assailants may well be armed, and try not to resist.

It is best, if you can trust your hotel, to leave any valuables you don't need in a safe-deposit. Always keep an inventory of what you have deposited. If you don't trust the hotel, lock everything in your pack and secure that in your room. If you do lose valuables, you will need to report the incident to the police for insurance purposes.

Sexual assault

This is extremely rare, but if you are the victim of a sexual assault, you are advised in the first instance to contact a doctor (this can be your home doctor if you prefer). You will need tests to determine whether you have contracted any sexually transmitted diseases; you may also need advice on post-coital contraception. You should also contact your embassy, where consular staff are very willing to help in cases of assault.

Student and teacher travellers

If you are in full-time education you will be entitled to an **International Student Identity Card (ISIC)**, which is distributed by student travel offices and travel agencies in over 100 countries. ISIC gives you special prices on all forms of transport (air, sea, rail, etc), and a variety of other concessions and services. Contact the **International Student Travel Confederation (ISTC)**, T+31-20-421 2800, www.isic.org. Student cards must carry a photograph if they are to be of any use for discounts in Latin America. The ISIC website provides a list of card-issuing offices around the world. Teachers may want to take an **International Teacher Identity Card (ITIC)** distributed by ISTC (above), as discounts are often extended to teachers.

Tax

Mexico

Currently US$65 on international flights (dollars not always accepted so bring 900 pesos, cash only); always check when purchasing if departure tax is included in ticket price as it usually is.

Impuesto al Valor Agregado (IVA) applies to most goods and services at 16%. Hotel tax is 3-5%.

Belize

Departure tax, usually included in flights, is US$39.25. Hotel Room Tax is 9%; General Sales Tax (GST) is 12.5% on other goods and services.

Guatemala

There is a 17% ticket tax on all international tickets sold in Guatemala. There is also a US$30 or quetzal equivalent international departure tax payable at the airport.

The tourist institute **INGUAT** tax is 10%. Service charge is usually an extra 12%.

Telephone

Many of the telecommunications networks have been privatized and prices have fallen considerably. In some areas, services have even improved. Consequently keeping in touch by phone is no longer prohibitively expensive. International telecom charge cards are useful and available from most countries; obtain details before leaving home. For the US AT&T's **USA Direct**, **Sprint** and **MCI** are all available for calls to the US. It is much cheaper than operator-assisted calls. Internet calls (eg via **Skype**, **Whatsapp** and **Viber**) are also possible if you have access to Wi-Fi.

Using a mobile in most of Mexico and Central America is very expensive. In addition to the hassle of having to charge your phone, research whether it is worth your while. Mobile phone calls will be cheaper if you buy a SIM card for the local network; in-country calls are likely to be considerably cheaper than using your home-based account. The initial cost of the SIM is getting more affordable (as little as US$3 in Honduras), but check the cost of calls. Also bear in mind that the number you use at home will not work. Some networks, eg **O2**, provide an app so you can use the time on your contract if you access the app via Wi-Fi.

Mexico

→ *Country code T+52; operator T020; international operator T090; directory enquiries T040.*

Most destinations have a 7-digit number and 3-digit regional code (Mexico City is an exception). The format of a number, depending on the type of call, should be as follows: **local** 7- or 8-digit phone number;

regional long-distance access code (01) + regional code (2- or 3-digit code) + 7- or 8-digit number; **international** international direct-dialling code + country code + regional code + 7- or 8-digit number. Most public phones take phone cards only (**Ladatel**) costing 30 or 50 pesos from shops and news kiosks everywhere. Reverse-charge (collect) calls can be made from any blue public phone; say you want to *llamar por cobrar*. Pre-paid phone cards are expensive for international calls. Of other pre-paid cards, the best value are **Ekofon**, www.ekofon.com.

Belize

→ *Country code T+501. Information T113. International operator T115.*

If you have many calls to make, a card phone works out much cheaper. There is a direct-dialling system between the major towns and to Mexico and USA. Local calls cost US$0.25 for 3 mins, US$0.12 for each extra min within the city, US$0.15-0.55 depending on zone. **Belize Telemedia Ltd**, 1 Church St, Belize City, Mon-Sat 0800-1800, Sun and holidays 0800-1200, has an international telephone, telex and internet service. The entire country's telephone directory is online at www.belizetelemedia.net.

The much-maligned Belizean telephone system is steadily modernizing. Formed in 2007 out of the old BTL, Belize Telemedia is promising to provide the world down the phone line.

Most people now have a mobile phone and most parts of the country have coverage. All towns have a telephone office and in most villages visitors can use the community phone. Payphones and card phones are fairly commonplace in Belize City and elsewhere.

Guatemala

→ *Country code T+502, Directory enquiries T+154.*

All phone numbers in the country are on an 8-figure basis. There are 2 main

service providers – **Telgua** and **Telefónica**. Telefónica sells cards with access codes, which can be used from any private or public Telefónica phone. Telgua phone booths are ubiquitous and use cards sold in values of 20 and 50 quetzales. From a **Telgua** phone, dial 147 before making an international call.

Most businesses offering a phone-call service charge a minimum of US$0.13 for a local call, making a phone card a cheaper option.

International calls can be made from phone booths; however, unlike the local calls, it is cheaper to phone from an internet café or shop, which tend to offer better rates.

Mobile phone SIM cards are affordable, with good deals costing around US$10-20 for the card, which includes free calls. **Comcel** and **PCS** offer mobile phone services. Rates are around US$0.03 per min for a national call, US$1.20 for international.

Operator calls are more expensive. For international calls via the operator, dial T147-110. For calling card and credit-card call options, you need a fixed line in a hotel or private house. First you dial 9999 plus the following digits: For **Sprint USA**, dial 136; **AT&T Direct**: 190; **Germany**: 049; **Canada**: 198; **UK (BT)**: 044; **Switzerland**: 041; **Spain**: 034, **Italy**: 039.

Collect calls may be made from public Telgua phones by dialling T147-120.

Time

Southern Mexico is in Central Standard Time (CST), 6 hrs behind GMT. Daylight Saving Time runs from the 1st Sun in Apr to the last Sun in Oct (when it is 5 hrs behind GMT). Belize and Guatemala are also - 6 hrs GMT.

Tipping

Normally 10-15%; the equivalent of US$0.25 per bag for porters, the equivalent of US$0.20 for bell boys, and nothing for a taxi driver unless for some kind of exceptional service.

Tourist information

All countries in the region have a tourist board but not all have an international presence. Fortunately the internet makes it possible to get the latest information on developments in a country. **South American Explorers**, USA, T607-277-0488, www.saexplorers.org, is a very useful resource. Despite the name, the whole of Latin America is covered and members receive help with travel planning as well as informed access on books and maps covering the region.

Useful websites

www.latinnews.com Up-to-date site with political comment.

www.planeta.com A phenomenal resource, which is staggering for its detail on everything from ecotourism and language schools to cybercafés.

www.revuemag.com Growing regional guide in print and online, focusing on Guatemala with coverage of Belize.

Mexico

Tourist offices are listed throughout the text. In Europe, information is available in several different languages by calling T00-800-1111-2266. In North America call T1-800-446-3942.

Mexico's web presence is phenomenal, some of the reliable, informative and useful websites that have been round for a while include:

www.mexconnect.com General information.

www.mexperience.com Well-constructed site updated daily, with current affairs, feature articles and advice on travel in Mexico. Look out for the forum where comments from fellow travellers are exchanged.

www.sectur.gob.mx Tourism Secretariat's site, with less glossy links but equally comprehensive information.

www.visitmexico.com Mexico Tourist Board site, a comprehensive multilingual site with information on the entire country.

Belize

Useful websites on Belize include the following:

www.belizenet.com, **www.belize.net** and **www.belize.com** Good search engines with general information.

www.governmentofbelize.gov.bz The government site on the country, packed with information on the official angle.

www.belizeaudubon.org and **www.pfbelize.org** Cover many protected areas and have a strong conservation focus.

www.ambergriscaye.com, **www.gocayecaulker.com**, **www.placencia.com** and **www.southernbelize.com** Useful sites.

www.belizex.com Covers the Cayo area.

www.belizereport.com The online version of the *Belize Report*.

www.belizenews.com Local news and links to the local newspapers (*Amandala*, *The Belize Times*, *The Reporter* and *The Guardian*).

Guatemala

The country's official tourist office is the **Instituto Guatemalteco de Turismo (INGUAT)**, 7 Av, 1-17, Zona 4, Centro Cívico, Guatemala City, T2421-2800, www.visitguatemala.com. Mon-Fri 0800-1600. INGUAT provides bus times, hotel lists and road maps. Staff are helpful. They also have an office at the airport, open daily 0600-2400.

The Guatemalan Maya Centre, 94b Wandsworth Bridge Rd, London SW6 2TF, T020-7371-5291, www.maya.org.uk, has information on Guatemala, the Maya, a library, video archive and a textile collection; visits by prior appointment.

Regional websites covering some of the more popular areas include **www.atitlan.com**, **www.mayaparadise.com** (Río Dulce/Lívingston), **www.cobanav.net** (Cobán) and **www.xelapages.com** (Quetzaltenango). **Posada Belén** in Guatemala City run a very informative site packed with information, www.guatemalaweb.com. Of the several publications with websites, the *Revue*, **www.revuemag.com**, is probably the most useful to the visitor.

Visas and immigration

If you are thinking of travelling from your own country via the USA, or of visiting the USA after Latin America, you are strongly advised to get your visa and find out about any other requirements from a US Consulate in your own country before travelling. If you are eligible for a visa waiver, you are now required to register in advance with the **Electronic System for Travel Authorization (ESTA)**, www.esta.cbp.dhs.gov/esta/. You will need to do this before setting out.

For US nationals, the implications of the **Western Hemisphere Travel Initiative**, which came into force on 1 Jan 2008, should be considered if entering Mexico. You will need a passport to re-enter the US once you have left and visited Mexico.

All international travel requires that you have at least 6 months remaining on a valid passport. Beyond a passport, very little is required of international travellers to Mexico and Central America. However, there are a few little tricks that can make your life a lot easier. Latin Americans, especially officials, are very document-minded. If staying in a country for several weeks, it is worthwhile registering at your embassy or consulate. Then, if your passport is stolen, the process of replacing it is faster and easier. It can also be handy to keep some additional passport-sized photographs together with photocopies of essential documents – including your flight ticket – separately from the originals.

It is your responsibility to ensure that your passport is stamped in and out when you cross borders. The absence of entry and exit stamps can cause serious difficulties; seek out the proper immigration offices if the stamping process is not carried out as you cross. Also, do not lose your entry card; replacing it can cause you a lot of trouble and possibly expense. If planning to study in Mexico or Central America for a long period, make every effort to get a student visa in advance.

Mexico

Virtually all international travellers require a passport to enter Mexico. Upon entry you will be issued a tourist card known as a **Forma Migratoria Múltiple (FMM)**, valid for up to 180 days. The card comes with a fee,

The **Derecho de No Migrante (DNI)** costs approximately US$22, which you must pay upon exit, or if you prefer, upon entry – be sure to get a stamp and keep all receipts. If arriving in Cancún or Mexico City, the DNI is often included in airfares. Nonetheless, when exiting at land borders, you must present evidence of this to avoid being charged a 2nd time (this issue has been frequently reported at the Mexico–Belize border). On your plane ticket, the DNI is indicated by the code 'UK' – print the page and highlight it. Note your FMM must surrendered when leaving the country to avoid problems later. If you are in Mexico for 7 days or less and you return to your country of origin, you are exempt from the DNI.

If your stamp bears less than 180 days, you can extend it up to the limit at any **National Institute of Migration** office; you can find details at www.inm.gob.mx. To renew a tourist card by leaving the country, you must stay outside Mexico for at least 72 hrs.

Take TCs or a credit card as proof of finance. At the border crossings with Belize and Guatemala, you may be refused entry into Mexico if you have less than US$200 (or US$350 for each month of intended stay, up to a maximum of 180 days). Likewise, if you are carrying more than US$10,000 in cash or TCs, you must declare it.

If a person under 18 is travelling alone or with one parent, both parents' consent is required, certified by a notary or authorized by a consulate. A divorced parent must be able to show custody of a child. (These requirements are not always checked by immigration authorities and do not apply to all nationalities.) Further details are available from any Mexican consulate.

Belize

All nationalities need passports, as well as sufficient funds and, officially, an onward ticket, although this is rarely requested for stays of 30 days or less. Visas are not usually required by nationals from countries within the EU, Australia and New Zealand, most Caribbean states, the USA and Canada. Citizens of India, Israel, Austria and Switzerland do need a visa. There is a **Belizean Consulate** in Chetumal, Mexico, at Armada de México 91, T+52-983-21803, US$25. If you need a visa it is best to obtain one in Mexico City or your home country before arriving at the border.

Guatemala

Only a valid passport is required for citizens of all Western European countries; USA, Canada, Mexico, all Central American countries, Australia, Israel, Japan and New Zealand. The majority of visitors get 90 days on arrival.

Visa renewal must be done in Guatemala City after 90 days, or on expiry. Passport stamp renewal on expiry for those citizens only requiring a valid passport to enter Guatemala must also be done at the immigration office at **Dirección General de Migración**, 6 Avenida, 3-11, Zona 4, Guatemala City, T2411-2411, Mon-Fri 0800-1600 (0800-1230 for payments). This office extends visas and passport stamps only once for a further period of time, depending on the original time awarded (maximum 90 days). Since 2006, when Guatemala signed a Central America-4 (CA-4) Border Control Agreement with El Salvador ((see box, page 518), Honduras, and Nicaragua you will have to visit a country outside of these 3 to re-enter and gain 90 days. These rules have been introduced to stop people leaving the country for 72 hrs (which is the legal requirement) every 6 months and returning, effectively making them permanent residents.

Weights and measures

In Mexico and Guatemala, the metric system is used. In Belize, imperial and US standard weights and measures.

Women travellers

Some women experience problems, whether accompanied or not; others encounter no difficulties at all. Unaccompanied Western women will at times be subject to close scrutiny and exceptional curiosity. Don't be unduly scared. Simply be prepared and try not to over-react. When you set out, err on the side of caution until your instincts have adjusted to the new culture. Women travelling alone could consider taking a wedding ring to prevent being hassled. To help minimize unwanted attention, consider your clothing choices. Do not feel bad about showing offence. When accepting an invitation, make sure that someone else knows the address you are going to and the time you left. Ask if you can bring a friend (even if you do not intend to do so). A good rule is always to act with confidence, as though you know where you are going, even if you do not. Someone who looks lost is more likely to attract unwanted attention. Do not disclose to strangers where you are staying.

Working

Two main areas provide opportunities for unskilled volunteers: childcare – often at orphanages or schools – and nature projects. Be warned, spontaneous volunteering is becoming more difficult. Organizations that use volunteers have progressed and plan their personnel needs so you may be required to make contact before you visit. Many organizations now charge volunteers for board and lodging and projects are often for a minimum of 4 weeks. Guatemala in particular has fairly well-developed and organized volunteer programmes.

Many developed countries have nationally organized volunteer programmes. The **US Peace Corps**, T1-800-424-8580, www.peacecorps.gov, is the most prominent in the region, working with countries on development projects with 2-year assignments for US citizens in countries throughout Mexico and Central America.

Variations on the volunteering programme are to enrol on increasingly popular gap-year programmes. These normally incorporate a period of volunteer work with a few months of free time at the end of the programme for travel.

Experiment in International Living, T+44-1684-562577, www.eiluk.org, is the UK element of a US international homestay programme that arranges stays with families in Mexico and Central America with social projects based on the ethos that if you want to live together, you need to work together. It's an excellent way to meet people and learn the language.

Volunteering in Guatemala

Asociación de Rescate y Conservación de Vida Silvestre (ARCAS), T2478-4096, www.arcasguatemala.com. Runs projects involving working with nature and wildlife, returning wild animals to their natural habitat.

Casa Alianza, 13 Av, 0-37, Zona 2 de Mixco, Col la Escuadrilla Mixco, Guatemala City, T2250-4964, www.casa-alianza.org. A project that helps street children.

Casa Guatemala, 14 Calle, 10-63, Zona 1, Guatemala City, T2331-9408, www.casa-guatemala.org. Runs a project for abandoned and malnourished children at Río Dulce.

Comité Campesino del Altiplano, on Lake Atitlán, 10 mins from San Lucas, T5804-9451, www.ccda.galeon.com. This **Campesino Cooperative** now produces Fair Trade organic coffee buying from small farmers in the region; long-term volunteers are welcome but Spanish is required.

Fundación Mario Dary, Diagonal 6, 17-19, Zona 10, Guatemala City, T2333-4957, fundary@intelnet.net.gt. Operates conservation, health and education projects on the Punta de Manabique and welcomes volunteers.

Proyecto Ak' Tenamit, 11 Av 'A', 9-39, Zona 2, Guatemala City, T2254-1560, www.aktenamit.org, based at Clínica Lámpara, 15 mins upriver from Lívingston. This project was set up to help 7000 civil-war-displaced Q'eqchi' Maya who now live in the region in 30 communities.

Proyecto Mosaico Guatemala, 3 Av Norte 3, Antigua. T7832-0955, www.promosaico.org. An information centre and clearing house for volunteers, with access to opportunities all over the country.

Quetzaltrekkers, Casa Argentina, 12 Diagonal, 8-43, Zona 1, Quetzaltenango, T7765-5895, www.quetzaltrekkers.com. Volunteer opportunities for hiking guides and office workers, minimum 3-month commitment.

UPAVIM, Calle Principal, Sector D-1, Col La Esperanza, Zona 12, Guatemala City, T2479-9061, www.upavim.org. This project helps poor families, providing social services and education for the workers using fairtrade principles.

There are also opportunities to work in children's homes in Quetzaltenango (Xela). 2 organizations are **Casa Hogar de Niños** and the **Asociación Hogar Nuevos Horizontes**. Also check out Xela-based volunteering information organization **www.entremundos.org**. Several language schools in Xela fund community development projects and seek volunteers. Make enquiries in town or via www.xelapages.com.

The London-based **Guatemala Solidarity Network**, www.guatemalasolidarity.org.uk, can assist with finding projects that look at human rights issues.

Index → Entries in **bold** refer to maps

FOOTPRINT

Features

Acknowledgements

Claire Boobbyer and Peter Hutchison are the original authors of the *Belize, Guatemala and Southern Mexico Handbook* and thanks to their painstaking work on the book's first two editions, you are today holding the best guide to the region in your hands. Long overdue credit goes to Jane Pelly, a Guatemala insider and human rights activist who contributed significant updates to a previous edition. Travel writer Anna Maria Espsäter worked on earlier versions of the Southern Mexico chapters. This third edition of *Belize Guatemala and Southern Mexico Handbook* represents a significant stylistic departure from previous ones and special thanks goes to Jo Williams for overhauling the book's entire look and feel, and for her usual careful editing. At the Footprint office in Bath, thanks to Felicity Laughton for her patience, and to Patrick Dawson for putting the project on the rails. At home, the author would like to thank Jennifer Kennedy, Terri Wright, Al Peacock-Johns, Jo Arghiris, Dan Roberts, Charlie and Thea for their ongoing moral support. Last but not least, thanks to all the readers who took the time to write to us with their comments, criticisms and recommendations; these are always great to read and gratefully received.

Credits

Footprint credits
Editor: Jo Williams
Production and layout: Emma Bryers
Maps: Kevin Feeney
Colour section: Angus Dawson

Publisher: Patrick Dawson
Managing Editor: Felicity Laughton
Administration: Elizabeth Taylor
Advertising sales and marketing:
John Sadler, Kirsty Holmes

Photography credits
Front cover: ElHielo/Shutterstock.com
Back cover: Top: Roberto Romanin/
Shutterstock.com. Bottom: Wollertz/
Shutterstock.com

Colour section
Inside front cover: shutterstock: Vilainecrevette;
superstock: ElHielo, Robert Harding Picture
Library/Robert Harding Picture Library. **Page 1**:
shutterstock: soft_light. **Page 2**: shutterstock:
The Visual Explorer. **Page 4**: shutterstock: Vadim
Petrakov, javarman. **Page 5**: shutterstock:
Jess Kraft, Wolverine1023; superstock: age
fotostock/age fotostock, age fotostock/age
fotostock. **Page 6**: shutterstock: Brandon
Bourdages, Angelo Giampiccolo, ElHielo;
superstock: Animals Animals/Animals Animals.
Page 7: shutterstock: soft_light, LaiQuocAnh;
superstock: Travel Library Limited/Travel Library
Limited. **Page 10**: shutterstock: DC_Aperture.
Page 11: shutterstock: rui vale sousa. **Page 12**:
shutterstock: f9photos; superstock: Travel
Library Limited/Travel Library Limited. **Page 13**:
shutterstock: holbox; superstock: Luis Davilla/
age fotostock. **Page 14**: shutterstock: Tati Nova
photo Mexico; superstock: Chico Sanchez/
age fotostock. **Page 15**: dreamstime: Wollertz/
Dreamstime.com; shutterstock: loca4motion/
Shutterstock.com; superstock: Frederic Soreau/
age fotostock. **Page 16**: superstock: Mint
Images/Mint Images.

Printed in Spain by GraphyCems

Publishing information
Footprint Belize, Guatemala &
Southern Mexico
3rd edition
© Footprint Handbooks Ltd
May 2015

ISBN: 978 1 919120 08 8
CIP DATA: A catalogue record for this book
is available from the British Library

® Footprint Handbooks and the
Footprint mark are a registered
trademark of Footprint Handbooks Ltd

Published by Footprint
6 Riverside Court
Lower Bristol Road
Bath BA2 3DZ, UK
T +44 (0)1225 469141
F +44 (0)1225 469461
footprinttravelguides.com

Distributed in the USA by
National Book Network, Inc.

Every effort has been made to ensure that
the facts in this guidebook are accurate.
However, travellers should still obtain advice
from consulates, airlines, etc about travel
and visa requirements before travelling.
The authors and publishers cannot
accept responsibility for any loss, injury
or inconvenience however caused.

Map symbols

□	Capital city	▨	Building
○	Other city, town	▣	Sight
≕	International border	♜♜	Cathedral, church
≕	Regional border	🏯	Chinese temple
⊖	Customs	🛕	Hindu temple
⬯	Contours (approx)	⍒	Meru
▲	Mountain, volcano	🕌	Mosque
⇌	Mountain pass	△	Stupa
⊾	Escarpment	✡	Synagogue
⬳	Glacier	⊞	Tourist office
⬚	Salt flat	🏛	Museum
⬚	Rocks	✉	Post office
⩫	Seasonal marshland	Ⓟ	Police
⬚	Beach, sandbank	Ⓢ	Bank
🌊	Waterfall	@	Internet
↝	Reef	♩	Telephone
═══	National highway	🏪	Market
──	Paved road	➕	Medical services
──	Unpaved or ripio (gravel) road	Ⓟ	Parking
╌╌╌	Track	⛽	Petrol
⋮⋮⋮	Footpath	⛳	Golf
──	Railway	⁘	Archaeological site
┅■	Railway with station	♦	National park, wildlife reserve
✈	Airport		
🚌	Bus station	⚘	Viewing point
Ⓜ	Metro station	▲	Campsite
----	Cable car	⌂	Refuge, lodge
╫╫╫	Funicular	🏰	Castle, fort
⛴	Ferry	🐟	Diving
ⅢⅢ	Pedestrianized street	🌴	Deciduous, coniferous, palm trees
Ⅹ Ⅽ	Tunnel		
→	One way-street	🌳	Mangrove
⫼⫼⫼	Steps	⌂	Hide
⤨	Bridge	🍷	Vineyard, winery
⊥⊥⊥	Fortified wall	⚗	Distillery
⌐○⌐	Park, garden, stadium	⌙	Shipwreck
●	Where to stay	✕	Historic battlefield
❷	Restaurants	▷	Related map
❶	Bars & clubs		

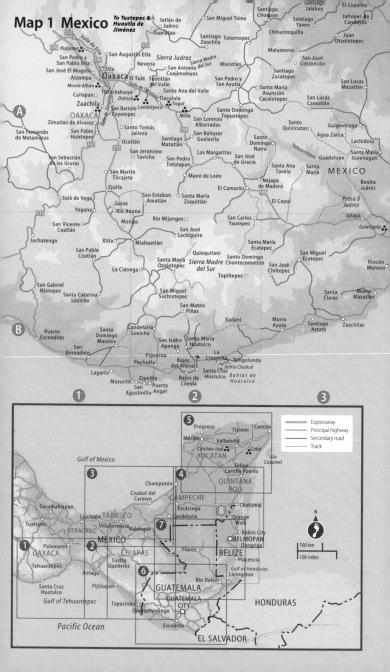

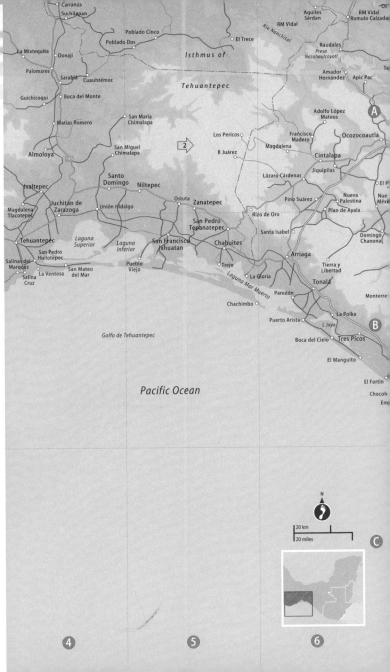

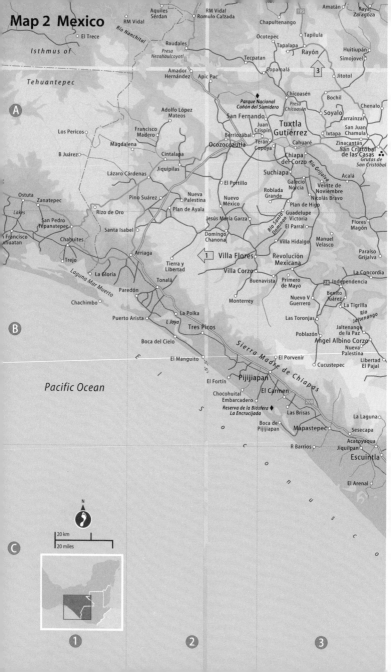

Map 3 Mexico

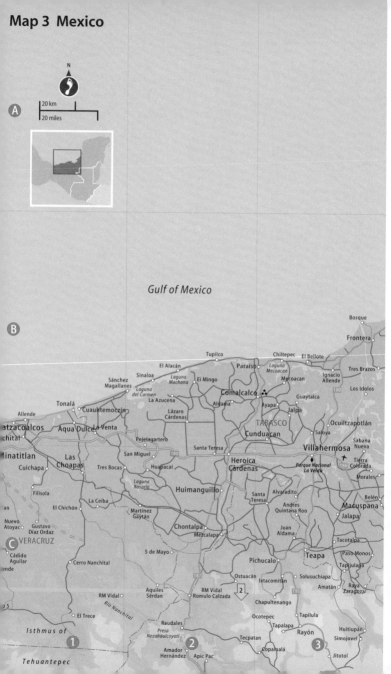

N

20 km
20 miles

Gulf of Mexico

A

B

C

Bosque
Frontera
Tupilco
Chiltepec El Bellote
El Alacán Paraiso Tres Brazos
Sinaloa El Mingo Laguna Ignacio
Sánchez Laguna Mecoacan Mecoacan Allende Los Idolos
Magallanes Machana Comalcalco
Laguna del Carmen La Azucena Aldama Ayapa Guaytalca
Tonalá Cuauhtemoczin Lázaro Jalpa Ocuiltzapotlán
Allende La Venta Cárdenas TABASCO Sabana
Aqua Dulce Pejelagartero Cunduacan Saloya Nueva
atzacoalcos Santa Teresa Villahermosa Tierra
chital San Miguel Heroíca Colorada
inatitlan Las Tres Bocas Huapacal Cárdenas Parque Nacional Morales
Cuichapa Choapas La Venta
Laguna Santa Belén
Filisola Rosario Huimanguillo Teresa Alvaradito Macuspana
La Ceiba Andrés Jalapa
El Chichón Martínez Quintana Roo
Nuevo Gaytán Chontalpa Juan Tacotalpa
Atoyac Gustavo Mezcalapa Aldama Paso Monos
Díaz Ordaz Pichucalo Teapa Tapijulapa
VERACRUZ 5 de Mayo Raya
Cádido Ostuacán Ixtacomitán Solusuchiapa Amatán Zaragoza
Aguilar Cerro Nanchital
nde RM Vidal Aquiles Romulo Calzada Chapultenango
Sérdan RM Vidal Ocotepec Tapilula
El Trece Río Nanchital Tapalapa Rayón Huitiupán
Isthmus of Raudales Tecpatan Copainalá Simojovel
Presa Amador Apic Pac
Tehuantepec Nezahaulcoyotl Hernández Jitotol

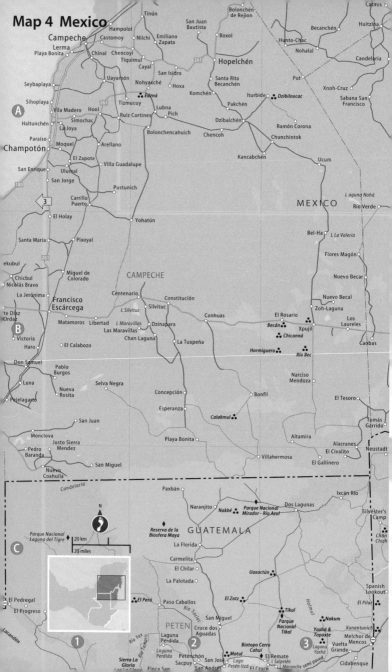

Map 4 Mexico

Catmis

Tinún
Bolonchén
de Rejón

Hampolol
San Juan
Bautista

Becanchén
Huitzina

Campeche
Castomoy
Nilchi
Emiliano
Zapata
Boxol
Hunto-Chac
Nohalal

Lerma
Chinal
Chencoyi
Tiquimuy
Cayal
Candelaria

Playa Bonita
Uayamón
San Isidro
Nohyaxché
Hoxa
Hopelchén
Put
Xnoh-Cruz
Sabana San
Francisco

Seybaplaya
Hool
Tizmucuy
Edzná
Komchén
Santa Rita
Becanchén
Iturbide
Dzibilnocac
Pakchén

Sihoplaya
Lubna
Pich
Dzibalchén

A
Vila Madero
Ruíz Cortines
Ramón Corona

Haitunchén
Simonac
La Joya
Bolonchencahuich
Chencoh
Chunchintok

Paraíso
Moquel
Arellano
Kancabchén
Ucum

Champotón
El Zapote
Villa Guadalupe

San Enrique
Ulumal
MEXICO

San Jorge
Pustunich
Laguna Nohá

3
Carrillo
Puerto
Río Verde

El Holay
Yohatún
Bel-Ha
L La Valería

Santa María
Pixoyal
Flores Magón

ekubul
Miguel de
Colorado
CAMPECHE
Nuevo Becar

Chicbul
Nicolás Bravo
Centenario
Constitución
Nuevo Becal

La Jerónima
L Silvituc
Silvituc
El Rosario
Zoh-Laguna

te Díaz
Ordaz
Francisco
Escárcega
Libertad
L Maravillas
Dzinapara
Conhuas
Becán
Xpujil
Los
Laureles

B
Matamoros
Las Maravillas
Chan Laguna
La Tuxpeña
Chicanná
Caobas

Victoria
Haro
El Calabozo
Hormiguero
Río Bec

Don Samuel
Pablo
Burgos
Narciso
Mendoza

Luna
Nueva
Rosita
Selva Negra
Concepción
Bonfil
El Tesoro

Pejelagarto
Esperanza
Calakmul
Altamira
Tomás
Garrido

San Juan
Playa Bonita
Alacranes
El Civalito
Neustadt

Monclova
Justo Sierra
Mendez
Villahermosa
El Gallinero

Pedro
Baranda
San Miguel

Nuevo
Coahuila
Candelaria
Paxbán
Ixcán Río
Silvester's
Camp

C
Parque Nacional
Laguna del Tigre
Naranjito
Nakbé
Parque Nacional
Mirador - Río Azul
Dos Lagunas
Chan
Chich

20 km
Reserva de la
Biosfera Maya
GUATEMALA
Spanish
Lookout

20 miles
La Florida

El Pedregal
El Perú
Carmelita
Uaxactún
Melchor de
Mencos
El Pilar

El Progreso
Paso Caballos
El Chilar
El Zotz
Tikal
Nakum
Xunantunich
Cidabenque

La Palotada
Parque
Nacional
Tikal
Yaxhá &
Topoxte
Vuelta
Grande

San Miguel
Holmul
Yaxhá
Laguna
Yaxhá

1
Laguna
Perdida
Cruce dos
Aguadas
PETÉN
Biotopo Cerro
Cahuí

2
Laguna
Perdida
Petenchón
Sacpuy
Motul
Lago
Petén Itzá
El Remate
L Salpetén
L Macanché semi paved
3

Lacandón
Sierra La
Gloria
San José
San Andrés
El Cruce

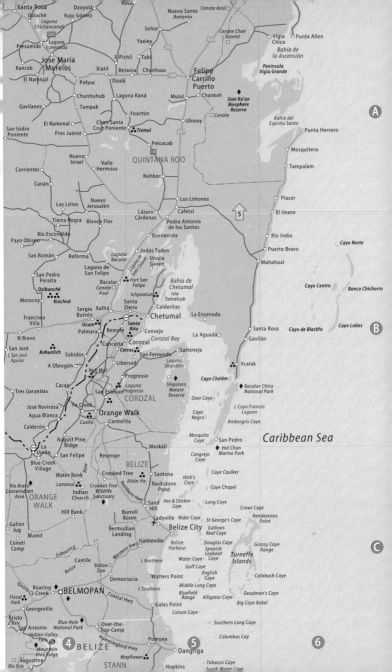

Map 5 Mexico

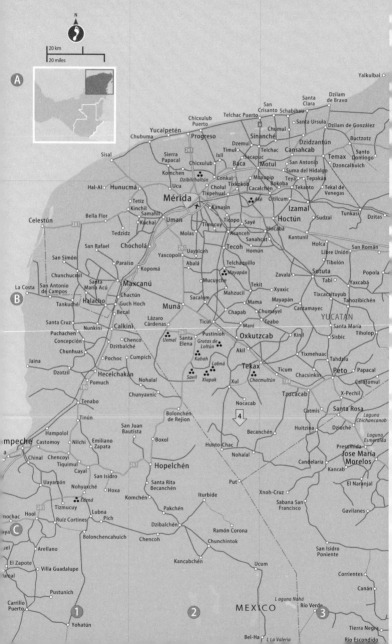

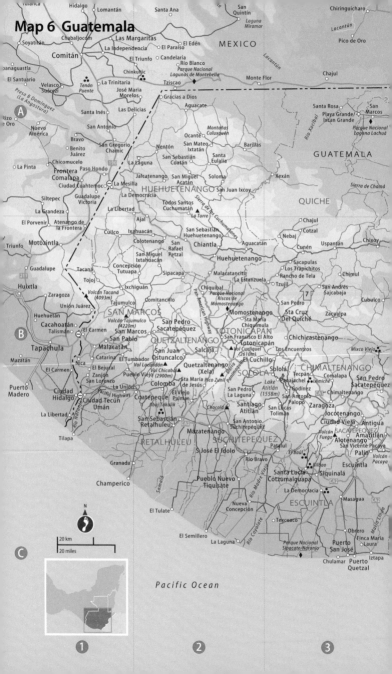

Map 7 Guatemala

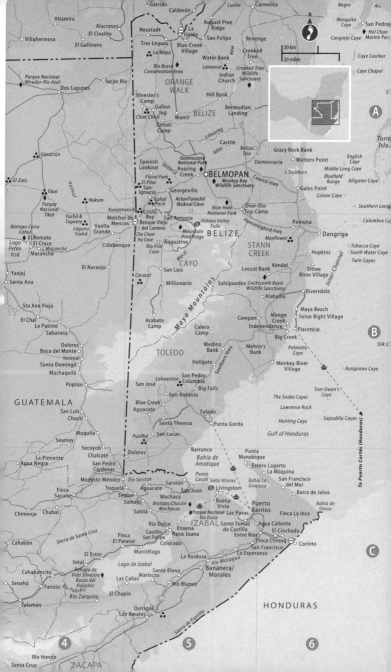

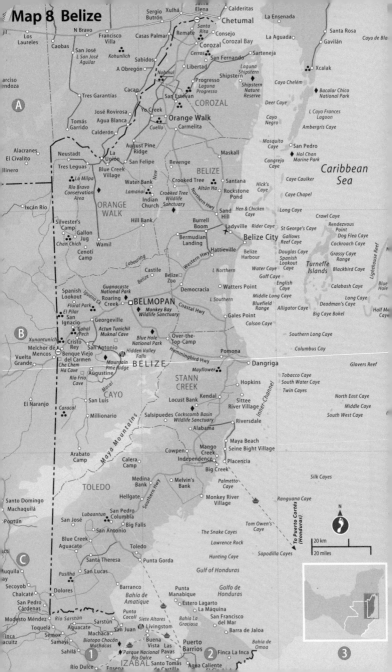